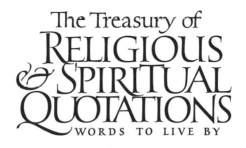

The Treasury of
RELIGIOUS
& SPIRITUAL
QUOTATIONS
WORDS TO LIVE BY

Created by The Stonesong Press, Inc.
Designed by Janet Wertsching Kanca
Cover Illustration and Calligraphy by John Stevens

Copyright © 1994 The Stonesong Press, Inc.
Based in part on *The World Treasury of Religious Quotations.*
    Copyright © 1966 Ralph L. Woods

Library of Congress Cataloging in Publication Data
The Treasury of religious & spiritual quotations : words to live by /
    edited by Rebecca Davison and Susan Mesner.
        p.   cm.
      ISBN 0-89577-549-2
      1. Religion—Quotations, maxims, etc. 2. Spirituality—
Quotations, maxims, etc. I. Davison, Rebecca, 1946–
II. Mesner, Susan. III. Title: Treasury of religious and spiritual
quotations.
PN6084.R3T74 1994
200—dc20   93-28016

Printed in the United States of America

The Treasury of
RELIGIOUS
& SPIRITUAL
QUOTATIONS

WORDS TO LIVE BY

Edited by
Rebecca Davis and Susan Mesner

The Reader's Digest Association, Inc.
Pleasantville, N.Y./Montreal

ONTENTS

Actions		15
Adversity		18
Agape		20
Aggression and Violence		21
Agnosticism		23
Alcohol		24
Ambition		25
Angels		26
Anger		27
Anti-Semitism		28
Anxiety and Fear		29
Apocalypse		32
Art		33
Asceticism		37
Aspiration		38
Atheism		39
Authority		40

Beauty	43
Belief and Believers	44
Bible	49
Body and Soul	56
Brotherhood	58
Buddhism	61

Capital Punishment	63
Cause	64
Celibacy	64
Certainty	65
Chance	65
Change	66
Character	67
Charity	69
Chastity	72
Children	73
Christianity	75
Church	78

Church and State	81
Clergy	82
Coercion	86
Comfort	87
Commandments	88
Commitment	89
Community	89
Compassion	91
Competition	93
Conceit	93
Conduct and Behavior	94
Confession	96
Conformity	98
Consciousness	106
Contemplation	107
Contentment	109
Conversion	110
Conviction	111
Courage	112
Creation	113
Cross	118

Damnation	119
Death	120
Deeds	128
Desire	130
Despair	132
Destiny	133
Detachment	134
Devil	135
Devotion	138
Discipline	139
Discord	140
Divinity	141
Doctrine	142
Doubt	144
Duty	145

E	Ecstacy	149
	Ecumenism	150
	Education	151
	Emotion	156
	Enemy	157
	Enlightenment	158
	Envy and Jealousy	158
	Equality	160
	Error	162
	Eternity	163
	Ethics	164
	Evil	166
	Evolution	170
	Existence	172
F	Failure and Defeat	175
	Faith	176
	Fall	183
	Family	185
	Fellowship	187
	Finding God	188
	Forgiveness	191
	Freedom	193
	Free Will	197
	Friendship	202
G	God	203
	Good and Evil	214
	Grace	215
	Greed	218
	Grief	219
	Guilt	219
H	Happiness	221
	Hatred	223
	Healing	225
	Health	226
	Heaven and Hell	227
	Hell	229
	Holiness	231
	Holy Spirit	232
	Honesty	233

Honor	234
Hope	234
Humanism	237
Humankind	241
Human Spirit	251
Humility	252
Humor	255
Hypocrisy	256

 Ideals | 257 |
Idleness	259
Idolatry	259
Ignorance	260
Immortality	261
Inspiration	267
Intellect	268

Jesus Christ	271
Joy	274
Judaism	276
Judgment	281
Justice	283

| Knowledge | 287 |

Laughter	291
Law	292
Liars and Lies	293
Life and Death	294
Literature	298
Liturgy	299
Loneliness	300
Love	303
Lust	312

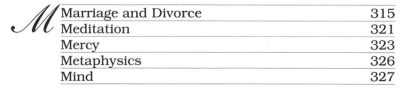 Marriage and Divorce | 315 |
Meditation	321
Mercy	323
Metaphysics	326
Mind	327

Miracles	331
Moderation	334
Money	336
Morality	339
Motherhood	345
Mourning	346
Music	347
Mysteries	350
Mystical Experience	352

Nature	355
Neighbor	360
Nonviolence	362

Obedience	365
Old Age	366
Opinions	367
Oppression	369
Optimism	371
Original Sin	372
Orthodoxy	374

Pain	377
Passion	378
Paths	380
Patience	381
Peace	383
Peace of Mind	385
Penitence	387
Perfection	388
Persecution	390
Pessimism	392
Philosophy	393
Piety	396
Pity	397
Pleasure	398
Poetry	401
Pope	403
Poverty	403
Power	407
Prayer	410
Preaching	422

Predestination	427
Prejudice	429
Pride	430
Progress	432
Prophecy and Prophets	435
Protestantism	438
Providence	439
Psalms	441
Purity	441

Race	444
Racial Injustice	447
Reality	448
Reason	452
Redemption	456
Reform	456
Reincarnation	459
Religion	460
Repentance	477
Responsibility	479
Resurrection	481
Revelation	484
Revenge	487
Reverence	488
Reward and Punishment	489
Right	491
Righteousness	492
Risk and Safety	494
Ritual	495

Sacrifice	497
Saints and Sinners	499
Salvation	502
Sanctity	505
Security	506
Self	507
Serenity	509
Sermons	510
Sexuality	511
Shame	515
Silence	516
Sin	518
Sincerity	523

	Skepticism	524
	Sorrow	525
	Soul	527
	Spirituality	534
	Success	536
	Suffering	538
	Suicide	542
	Supernatural	544
	Superstition	545
	Symbols	546
T	Tao	548
	Technology	549
	Temptation	552
	Theology	554
	Thoughts	559
	Time	561
	Tolerance	564
	Tradition	568
	Trinity	570
	Trust	572
	Truth	573
U	Unity	581
	Universe	584
V	Values	590
	Vanity	591
	Vice	592
	Virtue	593
	Vision	596
W	War	598
	Wealth	606
	Will	612
	Wisdom	615

Wonder		618
Work		618
World		624
Worldliness		632
Worship		634

Y Youth   639

Z Zeal   640

 his collection brings together the wisdom of the ages. It offers you the observations of many of the world's great thinkers—commentary about life and death, good and evil, time and eternity; commentary that is compassionate, trenchant, instructive, consoling, inspirational. But THE TREASURY OF RELIGIOUS & SPIRITUAL QUOTATIONS is first and foremost an essential reference work that will prove to be a valuable resource for the general reader as well as for members of the clergy, researchers, and speechwriters. It includes the familiar and sheds light on the wise and inspired thinking of less-well-known figures too.

In addition, this single volume contains memorable passages from the works of notable philosophers, scientists, and writers concerning religion and spirituality, and a lesser number of important statements by acknowledged agnostics and atheists.

The quotations, gathered from both ancient and modern sources, cover a broad spectrum of religious traditions—Christianity, Judaism, Buddhism, Hinduism, Confucianism, Taoism, Islam, Zoroastrianism, and other-less familiar sects—and many important philosophical works from around the world. The preponderance of quotations, however, are derived from Western culture and religious tradition.

The Revised Standard Version of the Bible is quoted extensively, and numerous excerpts from other sacred texts, such as the Talmud, the Koran, the Upanishads, and the Bahagavad Gita, are included.

The source for each quotation is given as completely as possible along with the earliest date on which it was used. When the date could not be ascertained, the author's birth and death dates are shown. And when even those dates are unknown, the century or an approximation of the century is listed.

Quotations are categorized under more than two hundred subject headings, ranging from the esoteric to the universal. All entries are alphabetized by author under the subject heading.

THE TREASURY OF RELIGIOUS & SPIRITUAL QUOTATIONS is based on The World Treasury of Religious Quotations by Ralph L. Woods. Long out of print, Mr. Woods's monumental work has been reorganized and revised to constitute the framework of this volume. Many of the more obscure and now somewhat dated quotations in the original have been replaced by more than a thousand new quotations. Mr. Woods carefully documented the quotations he found. This volume would not have been possible without his diligent scholarship.

ctions

Thou wilt find rest from vain fancies if thou
dost every act in life as though it were thy last.
—Marcus Aurelius, *Meditations of*, c. 170

Through faith man experiences the meaning of the world;
through action he is to give to it a meaning.
—Leo Baeck, *Essence of Judaism*, 1922

Action is the antidote to despair.
—Joan Baez, in *Rolling Stone*, 1983

To act is to be committed, and to be committed is to be in
danger.
—James Baldwin, *The Fire Next Time*, 1963

Every moral act of love, of mercy, and of sacrifice brings to
pass the end of the world where hatred, cruelty, and
selfishness reign supreme.
—Nicholas Berdyaev, *Dream and Reality*, 1939

Activity is better than inertia. Act, but with self-control. . . .
The world is imprisoned in its own activity, except when
actions are performed as worship of God.
—*Bhagavad-Gita*, between 5th and 2nd centuries B.C.

Let not the fruit of action be your motive to action. Your
business is with action alone, not with the fruit of action.
—*Bhagavad-Gita*, between 5th and 2nd centuries B.C.

Perform all necessary acts, for action is better than inaction;
none can live by sitting still and doing nought; it is by action
only that a man attains immunity from action.
—*Bhagavad-Gita*, between 5th and 2nd centuries B.C.

We have left undone those things which we ought to have
done; and we have done those things which we ought not to
have done.
—*The Book of Common Prayer*, 1662

Only by his action can a man make [himself/his life] whole. . . . You are responsible for what you have done and the people whom you have influenced. IN THE END IT IS ONLY THE WORK THAT COUNTS.
—Margaret Bourke-White, *Notes*, c. 1965,
in Vicki Goldberg, *Margaret Bourke-White: A Biography*, 1986

We have to understand that the world can only be grasped by action, not by contemplation. The hand is more important than the eye. . . . The hand is the cutting edge of the mind.
—Jacob Bronowski, *Ascent of Man*, 1973

Man's action is enclosed in God's action, but it is still real action.
—Martin Buber, *Hasidism*, 1948

Every man is the son of his own works.
—Miguel de Cervantes, *Don Quixote*, 1605

If our conscience tells us that we ought to perform a particular act, it is our moral duty to perform it.
—Frederick Copleston, *Aquinas*, 1955

What you believe matters less than your capacity for belief—and your willingness to translate belief into constructive action.
—Elizabeth Hanford Dole, address, Dartmouth College commencement,
The New York Times, June 6, 1991

Even a child makes himself known by his acts, whether what he does is pure and right.
—*Holy Bible*, Proverbs 20:11

Whatever a man sows, that he will also reap.
—*Holy Bible*, Galatians 6:7

But be doers of the word, and not hearers only, deceiving yourselves.
—*Holy Bible*, James 1:22

Action is the normal completion of the act of will which begins as prayer. That action is not always external, but it is always some kind of effective energy.
—W.R. Inge, *Speculum Animae*, 1911

Every man feels instinctively that all the beautiful senti-
ments in the world weigh less than a single lovely action.
—James Russell Lowell, *Rousseau and the Sentimentalists*, 1870

Religion is full of difficulties, but if we are often puzzled what
to think, we need seldom be in doubt what to do.
—John Lubbock, *Pleasures of Life*, 1887

Men must be decided on what they will not do, and then they
are able to act with vigor in what they ought to do.
—Mencius, *Works of* (c. 300 B.C.)

A human act once set in motion flows on for ever to the great
account.
—George Meredith, *Rhoda Fleming*, 1865

It is in our power to stretch out our arms and, by doing good
in our actions, to seize life and set it in our soul.
—Origen, *On the Soul*, c. 240

The greatest of all the mysteries of life, and the most terrible,
is the corruption of even the sincerest religion, which is not
daily founded on rational, effective, humble, and helpful
action.
—John Ruskin, *Sesame and Lilies*, 1865

Pray to God, but row for the shore.
—Russian proverb

But how can it be *known* that you are in earnest
If the act follows not upon the word?
—J.C.F. von Schiller, *The Piccolomini*, 1799

The question "Are we doing well?" is unrealistic; there are no
measures. The test is: "Are we doing right?" For that, there is
a measure—what Christ has told us to do.
—Frank J. Sheed, *Sheed and Ward Trumpet*, Spring 1964

We know what a person thinks not when he tells us what he
thinks, but by his actions.
—Isaac Bashevis Singer,
in *The New York Times Magazine*, November 26, 1978

It is through a religious act that people set meaning over
against meaninglessness, wholeness over against being
fragmented, courage over against fear.
—Dorothee Sölle, *Death by Bread Alone*, 1978

17

ACTIONS

An act of faith is an act of a finite being who is grasped by and turned to the infinite.

—Paul Tillich, *Dynamics of Faith*, 1957

ADVERSITY

We cannot be guilty of a greater act of uncharitableness, than to interpret the afflictions which befall our neighbors, as *punishment* and *judgments*.

—Joseph Addison, *The Spectator*, 1714

O, do not pray for easy lives. Pray to be stronger men. Do not pray for tasks equal to your powers. Pray for powers equal to your tasks.

—Phillips Brooks, *Going Up to Jerusalem*, 1890

It appears that when life is broken by tragedy God shines through the breach.

—George A. Buttrick, *Prayer*, 1942

Everyone is the artificer of his own misfortune.

—Miguel de Cervantes, *Don Quixote*, 1615

Don't go around the agony. It took me years to find out that trying to avoid it doesn't work. You must simply go through the middle of it. . . . Someday, somewhere, this moment of agony will be useful to you. This horror will be useful. The killer is bitterness—the other killer is drive without real desire.

—Colleen Dewhurst, in *The Christian Science Monitor*, June 18, 1987

Affliction is a *treasure*, and scarce any man hath *enough* of it. No man hath *affliction* enough that is not matured and ripened by it, and made fit for God by that *affliction*.

—John Donne (1573–1631), *Devotions*, XVIII

The first question to be answered by any individual or any social group, facing a hazardous situation, is whether the crisis is to be met as a challenge to strength or as an occasion for despair.

—Harry Emerson Fosdick, *The Challenge of the Present Crisis*, 1917

As the earth is but a point in respect of the heavens, so are earthly troubles compared to heavenly joys.

—George Herbert, Letter to his mother, May 29, 1622

If you faint in the day of adversity, your strength is small.

—*Holy Bible*, Proverbs 24:10

Corn is not separated but by threshing, nor men from worldly impediments but by tribulation.
—St. John Chrysostom, *Hom.* 2 in 3 *Matt.*, c. 388

If you have not clung to a broken piece of your old ship in the dark night of the soul, your faith may not have the sustaining power to carry you through to the end of the journey.
—Rufus M. Jones, *The Radiant Life*, 1944

Ill Fortune never crush't that man whom good Fortune deceived not.
—Ben Jonson, *Discoveries*, 1641

Affliction is able to drown out every earthly voice . . . but the voice of eternity within a man it cannot drown.
—Sören Kierkegaard, *Christian Discourses*, 1847

We live in a world in which the worst looks as if it is going to happen and the worst often does happen, and yet out of the anguish and waste, love and trust come in new forms.
—Robert A.K. Runcie, Archbishop of Canterbury, in *Los Angeles Times*,
March 27, 1989

Calamity is virtue's opportunity.
—Seneca, *De Providentia*, c. 64 A.D.

Heaven-sent calamities you may stand up against, but you cannot survive those brought on by yourself.
—*Shu Ching*, c. 490 B.C.

Man's freedom is never in being saved troubles, but it is the freedom to take trouble for his own good, and to make the trouble an element in his joy.
—Rabindranath Tagore, *Sadhana*, 1913

Why art thou troubled, that all things come not to thee as thou desirest? Who is he that hath all things at his own will?. . . There is no man in this world without some manner of tribulation or anguish, though he be king or pope.
—Thomas à Kempis, *Imitation of Christ*, 1441

Adversity in the things of this world opens the door for spiritual salvation.
—A.J. Toynbee,
in *The New York Times Magazine*, December 26, 1954

19

ADVERSITY

No Christian escapes a taste of the wilderness on the way to the Promised Land.

—Evelyn Underhill, *The Fruits of the Spirit*, 1942

There are not so many lessons in glad times. Adversity is by far the better teacher. Adversity will be a part of almost all our lives. So it is not in escaping adversity, but in answering it, that our character is defined.

—Christopher Warren, in *Los Angeles Times*, September 29, 1987

It is only when we are stricken by calamity that we are able to yield certain sparks, a certain sacred fire. This is the meaning of wars, revolutions, sickness.

—Alexander Yelchaninov (1881–1934), *Fragments of a Diary*

AGAPE

Love is the air that I breathe, like oxygen. When I lack it, I feel atrophied, asphyxiated. When I have it, I feel I am growing. And so this growth is linked to others, or to a collective other. If I realize that I do not love you, my faith diminishes, and I breathe less and less of the oxygen of life. When I feel linked to you, in communion with you, there is a current of love that passes between us, and the intensity can multiply. And the more this love grows, the more the faith becomes luminous, the more I feel linked to the collective other. I am speaking of God.

—Jean-Bertrand Aristide, in *Interview Magazine*, October 1991

Love has been assigned to woman as her supreme vocation, and when she directs it toward a man, she is seeking God in him; but if human love is denied her by circumstance, if she is disappointed or overparticular, she may choose to adore divinity in the person of God Himself.

—Simone de Beauvoir, *The Second Sex*, 1949

History tells us that the pendulum of time is sweeping to extremes of subjectivism, to cults of selfishness and savage irresponsibility. We must bring it back to balance by taking up the burdens of mankind as our own, with an entirely new vision and confidence. And we must do this perhaps as a condition for continued existence itself.

—Philip Berrigan, *No More Strangers*, 1965

Love one another with brotherly affection; outdo one another in showing honor.

—*Holy Bible*, Romans 12:10

So faith, hope, love abide, these three; but the greatest of
these is love.

—*Holy Bible*, I Corinthians 13:13

Whoever does not do right is not of God, nor he who does not
love his brother. For this is the message which you have
heard from the beginning, that we should love one another.

—*Holy Bible*, 1 John 3:10-11

The Greek New Testament word for this overflowing divine
love is *agape* . . . God's own love spontaneously to all
creatures, not by reason of their worth or merit, not moved
by any gain for himself, not caused by any external force or
value, but coming freely from his boundless generosity.

—Paul E. Johnson, *Christian Love*, 1951

Agape translated in the New Testament variously as charity
(and as love) comes to us as a quite new creation of
Christianity. . . . Without it nothing that is Christian would
be Christian. Agape is Christianity's own original basic
conception.

—Anders Nygren, *Agape and Eros*, 1953

The Christian idea of love, called *agape*, I interpret as a kind
of affectionate, perceptive concern for other people.

—Charles P. Taft, in *Ladies' Home Journal*, December 1961

Agape means love for another self not because of any lovable
qualities which he or she may possess, but purely and
entirely because it is a self capable of experiencing happiness
and misery and endowed with the power to choose between
good and evil. The love of man is thus more than a feeling, it
is a state of the will.

—Obert C. Tanner, *One Man's Search*, 1989

AGGRESSION AND VIOLENCE

The only way that we can solve the problem of aggression is
the way that Jesus advocated: "Father, forgive them for they
know not what they do." Again it was said by Buddha: "If one
man conquer in battle a thousand times thousand men, and
if another conquer himself, he is the greatest of conquerors."

—Swami Akhilananda, *Mental Health and Hindu Psychology*, 1951

The only thing that's been a worse flop than the organization
of non-violence has been the organization of violence.

—Joan Baez, *Daybreak*, 1970

There is no social order without violence. There can,
therefore, be no social order which is ratified in the sign of
the cross.
—Peter L. Berger, *The Precarious Vision*, 1962

The blood of man should never be shed but to redeem the
blood of man. It is well shed for our family, for our friends,
for our God, for our country, for our kind. The rest is vanity;
the rest is crime.
—Edmund Burke, *Letters on a Regicide Peace*, 1797

The morality of the violence will depend on its proportion to
the aggression. One will not rout a burglar with an atomic
bomb.
—John R. Conney, in *Theology Digest*, Winter 1957

Where wisdom is called for, force is of little use.
—Herodotus, *Histories*, II, c. 430 B.C.

You have heard that it was said, "An eye for an eye and a
tooth for a tooth." But I say to you, Do not resist one who is
evil. But if anyone strikes you on the right cheek, turn to
him the other also.
—*Holy Bible*, Ezekiel 7:23

Any human society that is established on relations of force
must be regarded as inhuman, inasmuch as the personality
of its members is repressed or restricted.
—Pope John XXIII, *Pacem in Terris*, April 1963

Violence is an admission that one's ideas and goals cannot
prevail on their own merits.
—Edward M. Kennedy, June 10, 1970, in Thomas P. Collins and
Louis M. Savary, eds., *A People of Compassion*, 1972

Fight in the way of Allah against those who fight against you,
but begin not hostilities. Allah loveth not aggressors.
—*Koran*, c. 625

We are effectively destroying ourselves by violence
masquerading as love.
—R.D. Laing, *Politics of Experience*, 1967

It is impossible for the Christian and true church to subsist
without the shedding of blood, for her adversary, the devil, is
a liar and a murderer.
—Martin Luther (1483–1546), *Table-Talk*

In violence, we forget who we are.
—Mary McCarthy, *On the Contrary*, 1961

The theology of violence must not lose sight of the real problem, which is not the individual with a revolver but *death and even genocide as big business.*
—Thomas Merton, *Faith and Violence*, "Toward a Theology Resistance," 1968

Let there be no violence in religion. If they embrace Islam they are surely directed; but if they turn their backs, verily to thee belongs preaching only.
—Mohammed (570–632), in W. Muir, *Life of Mohammed*

The belief that human brutality is a vestigial remnant of man's animal or primitive past . . . [is] one of the dearest illusions of modern culture.
—Reinhold Niebuhr, *Faith and History*, 1949

Abstain from shedding blood . . . for blood that is spilt never sleeps.
—Saladin, *Instruction to His Son*, 1193, quoted in S. Lane-Poole, *Saladin*

Violence can only be concealed by a lie, and the lie can only be maintained by violence. Any man who has once proclaimed violence as his method is inevitably forced to take the lie as his principle.
—Alexander Solzhenitzyn, Nobel Prize lecture, 1973

The resource to force, however unavoidable, is a disclosure of the failure of civilization, either in the general society or in a remnant of individuals.
—Alfred North Whitehead, *Adventures of Ideas*, 1933

Agnosticism

I do not pretend to know where many ignorant men are sure—that is all that agnosticism means.
—Clarence Darrow, at Scopes Trial, July 13, 1925

The mistake of agnosticism, it seems to me, has been that it has said not merely, "I do not know," but "I will not consider."
—G. Lowes Dickinson, *Religion*, 1905

Agnosticism denies to the human mind a power of attaining knowledge which it does possess. . . . Agnosticism, as such, is a theory about knowledge and not about religion.
—Richard Downey, *Critical and Constructive Essays*, 1934

Agnosticism is the everlasting perhaps.
—Francis Thompson, *Paganism Old and New*, 1910

Defensible agnosticism is that of the person who admits that he does not know, and is consequently open to learning.
—D.E. Trueblood, *Philosophy of Religion*, 1957

ALCOHOL

Drunkenness is the ruin of reason. It is premature old age. It is temporary death.
—St. Basil, *Homilies*, c. 375

Toward evening, about supper-time, when the serious studies of the day are over, is the time to take wine.
—St. Clement of Alexandria, *Paedagogus*, c. 220

The man who is master of himself drinks gravely and wisely.
—Confucius, *The Book of Poetry*, c. 500 B.C.

Morally, and in view of our Lord's first recorded miracle, it is not tenable to maintain, as some do, that alcohol is an evil and its consumption innately wrong.
—J. Dominian, *Psychiatry and the Christian*, 1962

It is not permitted to a human being to make himself incapable of acting like a human being. Excessive drinking offends God because it is a mutilation of the mind to a greater or lesser degree.
—John C. Ford, *Sanctity and Success in Marriage*, 1956

Bread is made for laughter, and wine gladdens life.
—*Holy Bible*, Ecclesiastes 10:19

Be sober, as God's athlete. The prize is incorruption and life eternal.
—St. Ignatius of Antioch, *Letter to Polycarp*, c. 109

The drunken man is a living corpse.
—St. John Chrysostom, *Homilies*, c. 388

Wine was given us of God, not that we might be drunken, but that we might be sober; that we might be glad, not that we get ourselves pain.
—St. John Chrysostom, *Homilies*, c. 388

Wine gives great pleasure, and every pleasure is of itself a good.
> —Samuel Johnson, *Boswell's Life of*, April 28, 1778

The blacksmith did ignorantly conduct this burglar into his family's heart. It was the bottle Conjuror. Upon the opening of that fatal cork, forth flew the fiend, and shriveled up his home.
> —Herman Melville, *Moby Dick*, 1851

Intemperance is the pestilence which killeth pleasure; temperance is not the flail of pleasure; it is the seasoning thereof.
> —Michel de Montaigne, *Essays*, III, 1588

Drunkenness spoils health, dismounts the mind, and unmans man. It reveals secrets, is quarrelsome, lascivious, impudent, dangerous, and mad.
> —William Penn, *Fruits of Solitude*, 1693

If God forbade drinking would He have made wine so good?
> —Armand Richelieu, *Mirame*, c. 1625

O thou invisible spirit of wine, if thou hast no name to be known by, let me call thee Devil!
> —William Shakespeare, *Othello*, 1604

When the wine goes in the murder comes out.
> —*Talmud*, c. 200

Temperance is not the absence of passion, but is the transfiguring of passion into wholeness. Without it . . . you will have the senses usurping sovereignty and excluding the spirit; you will have them deciding good and evil and excluding God.
> —Gerald Vann, *The Heart of Man*, 1945

Wine . . . is one of the noblest cordials in nature.
> —John Wesley, *Journal*, September 9, 1771

AMBITION

Children, you must remember something. A man without ambition is dead. A man with ambition but no love is dead. A man with ambition and love for his blessings here on earth is ever so alive.
> —Pearl Bailey, *Talking to Myself*, 1971

Ambition tyrannizes over our souls.
—Robert Burton, *Anatomy of Melancholy*, II, 1621

Ambition, commensurate with the powers which each man can discover in himself, should be frankly recognized as a part of Christian duty.
—Lord Charnwood, *Abraham Lincoln*, 1916

Ambition is to the mind what the cap is to the falcon; it blinds us first, and then compels us to tower by reason of our blindness.
—Charles Caleb Colton, *Lacon*, 1822

And do you seek great things for yourself? Seek them not.
—*Holy Bible*, Jeremiah 45:5

Set your minds on things that are above, not on things that are on the earth.
—*Holy Bible*, Colossians 3:2

There is no guilt greater than to sanction ambition.
—Lao-tzu, *Tao Te Ching*, between 6th and 3rd century B.C.

ANGELS

We should pray to the angels, for they are given to us as guardians.
—St. Ambrose, *On Bereavement*, c. 380

Therefore for Spirits, I am so far from denying their existence that I could easily believe, that not only whole Countries, but particular persons, have their Tutelary and Guardian Angels.
—Thomas Browne, *Religio Medici*, 1635

The angels are the dispensers and administrators of the Divine beneficence toward us; they regard our safety, undertake our defense, direct our ways, and exercise a constant solicitude that no evil befall us.
—John Calvin, *Institutes*, I, 1536

Do not neglect to show hospitality to strangers, for thereby some have entertained angels unawares.
—*Holy Bible*, Hebrews 13:2

Every breath of air and ray of light and heat, every beautiful prospect, is, as it were, the skirts of their garments, the waving of the robes of those whose faces see God.
—John Henry Newman, sermon, Michaelmas Day 1831

We do not realize that, as Chesterton reminded us, the angels fly because they take themselves so lightly.
—Alan Watts, *The Way of Liberation*, 1983

ANGER

He who holds back rising anger like a rolling chariot, him I call a real driver; other people are but holding the reins.
—*Dhammapada*, c. 5th century B.C.

Reason opposes evil the more effectively when anger ministers at her side.
—Pope St. Gregory the Great, *Morals on the Book of Job*, 584

God clearly cannot be angry—at least in the crude sense of being in a rage, and losing his temper and throwing things at people—for to suffer such anger is limitation, and God is unlimited.
—Christopher Hollis, *The Noble Castle*, 1941

A soft answer turns away wrath, but a harsh word stirs up anger.
—*Holy Bible*, Proverbs 15:1

He who is slow to anger has great understanding, but he who has a hasty temper exalts folly.
—*Holy Bible*, Proverbs 14:29

Let not the sun go down on your anger.
—*Holy Bible*, Ephesians 4:26

You have heard that it was said to the men of old, "You shall not kill; and whoever kills shall be liable to judgment." But I say to you that every one who is angry with his brother shall be liable to judgment; whoever insults his brother shall be liable to the council, and whoever says, "You fool!" shall be liable to the hell of fire.
—*Holy Bible*, Matthew 5:21-22

There is a holy anger, excited by zeal, which moves us to reprove with warmth those whom our mildness failed to correct.
—St. Jean Baptiste de la Salle, *Les devoirs du chrétien*, 1703

ANGER

As long as anger lives, she continues to be the fruitful mother of many unhappy children.

—St. John Climacus (525–600), *Climax*

He is a fool who cannot be angry; but he is a wise man who will not.

—Proverb

Anger deprives a sage of his wisdom, a prophet of his vision.

—Simeon, b. Lakish, *Talmud*, c. 500

It is a universal poison of an infinite object; for no man was ever so amorous as to love a toad, none so envious as to repine at a condition of the miserable, no man so timorous as to fear a dead bee; but anger is troubled at every thing, and every man, and every accident.

—Jeremy Taylor, *Holy Living*, 1650

"Black grace." An influx of extraordinary powers, an almost infinite growth of energy, can be observed in angry men.

—Alexander Yelchaninov (1881–1934), *Fragments of a Diary*

ANTI-SEMITISM

Anti-Semitism was always there, but it was dormant. It is like something in a freezer that you opened up. It began to thaw and then, suddenly, it came to life again.

—Shmuel Almog, in *Los Angeles Times*, June 12, 1990

Anti-Semitism in any form is a barbaric insult to our culture and our civilization, which have been moulded by Christianity, and as a breakdown of Christian values, which have become confused and lacking in humanity.

—Karl Barth, *Community, Church and State*, 1946

Perhaps the saddest thing to admit is that those who rejected the Cross have to carry it, while those who welcomed it are so often engaged in crucifying others.

—Nicholas Berdyaev, *Christianity and Anti-Semitism*, 1938

Of all the bigotries that ravage the human temper there is none so stupid as the anti-Semitic. It has no basis in reason, it is not rooted in faith, it aspires to no ideal.

—Lloyd George, in Hearst Newspapers, July 22, 1923

Strange inconsistency! to persecute in the name of religion those who had given the religion.

—Madison C. Peters, *Justice to the Jews*, 1899

Anti-Semitism is . . . a movement in which we, as Christians, cannot have any part whatever.
—Pope Pius XI, to Belgian pilgrims, September 1938

It is not possible for Christians to take part in anti-Semitism. We are Semites spiritually.
—Pope Pius XI, address, September 1938

In large part, anti-Semitism is the direct result of religious indoctrination.
—Milton Steinberg, *The Making of the Modern Jew*, 1934

ANXIETY AND FEAR

Fear is an emotion indispensable for survival.
—Hannah Arendt, in *The New Yorker*, November 21, 1977

Everything on earth gives cause for fear, and the only freedom from fear is to be found in the renunciation of all desire.
—Bhartri-hari (c. 7th century), *Wisdom of the Hindus*

In religion fear and approval to some extent *must* always combine. . . . In religion approval implies devotion, and devotion seems hardly possible, unless there is some fear, if only the fear of estrangement.
—F.H. Bradley, *Appearance and Reality*, 1894

"Fear of God," . . . never means to the Jews that they ought to be afraid of God, but that, trembling, they ought to be aware of his incomprehensibility. . . . Only through the fear of God does man enter so deep into the love of God that he cannot again be cast out of it.
—Martin Buber, *Israel and the World*, 1948

Hope without risk is not hope.
—Dom Helder Camara, 1984

One does not fear God because He is terrible, but because he is literally the soul of goodness and truth, because to do him wrong is to do wrong to some mysterious part of oneself.
—Joyce Cary, *Except the Lord*, 1953

First, my son, fear God; for, to fear God is wisdom, and, being wise, thou canst not err.
—Miguel de Cervantes, *Don Quixote*, 605

The confidence that attends a Christian's belief makes the believer not fear men, to whom he answers, but still he fears his God.
—Samuel Taylor Coleridge, *Aids to Reflection*, 1825

When internal examination discovers nothing wrong, what is there to be anxious about, what is there to fear?
—Confucius (5th century B.C.), *The Chinese Classics*

Fear always springs from ignorance.
—Ralph Waldo Emerson, *The American Scholar*, 1837

Fear is the parent of cruelty.
—James Anthony Froude, *Short Studies in Great Subjects*, 1883

Fear knocked at the door. Faith answered. No one was there.
—Hind's Head Hotel, Bray, England (on the front of the ancient mantel)

Fear of things invisible, is the natural seed of that which every one in himself calleth religion.
—Thomas Hobbes, *Leviathan*, 1651

Have no anxiety about anything, but in everything by prayer and supplication with thanksgiving let your requests be made known to God. And the peace of God, which passes all understanding, will keep your hearts and minds in Christ Jesus.
—*Holy Bible*, Philippians 4:6-7

There is no fear in love; but perfect love casteth out fear: because fear hath torment. He that feareth is not made perfect in love.
—*Holy Bible*, I John 4:18

Therefore I tell you, do not be anxious about your life, what you shall eat or what you shall drink, nor about your body, what you shall put on. Is not life more than food, and the body more than clothing? . . . But seek first his kingdom, and his righteousness, and all these things shall be yours as well.
—*Holy Bible*, Matthew 6:25, 33

Yea, though I walk through the valley of the shadow of death, I will fear no evil: for thou art with me; thy rod and thy staff they comfort me.
—*Holy Bible*, Psalms 23:4

It is fear that first made the gods.
>—David Hume, *Natural History of Religion*, 1755

Why is life sped up so? Why are things so terribly,
unbearably precious that you can't enjoy them but can only
wait breathless in dread of their going?
>—Anne Morrow Lindbergh, *Hour of Gold, Hour of Lead*, 1973

Being anxious people, we want to know exactly what the next
steps will be. But we need to know . . . that people have gone
before us and people will come after us who live in these
same mysteries of God.
>—Camille S. Littleton, *Women of the Word*, 1984

Fear is an uneasiness of the mind, upon the thought of
future evil likely to befall us.
>—John Locke, *Essay Concerning Human Understanding*, 1690

Until love, which is the truth towards God, is able to cast out
fear, it is well that fear should hold.
>—George Macdonald, *Unspoken Sermons*, 1st Series, 1869

It is the fear of punishment either of the king, or of hell, or of
society that keeps people away from sin.
>—*Mahabharata*, c. 800 B.C.

It is folly to fear God. God is good by his own nature, man by
his industry.
>—Michel de Montaigne, *Essays*, Bk. 2, ch. 12, 1580

It is love which makes Christian fear differ from servile
dread, and true faith differ from the faith of devils.
>—John Henry Newman, *The Development of Christian Doctrine*, 1845

Anxiety is love's greatest killer.
>—Anais Nin, *The Diary of Anais Nin*, Vol. V, 1974

Fear can infect us early in life until eventually it cuts a deep
groove of apprehension in all our thinking. To counteract it,
let faith, hope and courage enter your thinking. Fear is
strong, but faith is stronger yet.
>—Norman Vincent Peale, *Have a Great Day—Every Day*, 1985

Pain is the source of compassion, and compassion shifts our
perspective on pain, which frees us from the fear of death.
>—Maggie Ross, in *Creation Spirituality*, September/October 1992

The reason why our public life is so disordered and our
private life so hampered by anxiety is because we will not be
still and know God.
>—A. Maude Royden, in *Federal Council Bulletin*, January 1931

To fear love is to fear life, and those who fear life are already
three parts dead.
>—Bertrand Russell, *Marriage and Morals*, 1929

The only known cure for fear is faith.
>—William S. Sadler, *The Mind at Mischief*, 1929

Most souls are afraid of God precisely because of His
Goodness. . . . Our greatest fear is not that God may not love
us enough but that He may love us too much.
>—Fulton J. Sheen, *Peace of Soul*, 1949

What greater challenge does any of us have than taking on
our own mortality and facing it with strength and peace and
love?
>—Bernie Siegel, in *New Age Journal*, May/June 1989

It is our very fear of the future that distorts the *now* that
could lead to a different future if we dared to be whole in the
present.
>—Marion Woodman, *The Pregnant Virgin,*
>*A Process of Psychological Transformation*, 1985

To live in fear and falsehood is worse than death.
>—*Zend-Avesta*, 6th century B.C.

APOCALYPSE

What until recently seemed to be only the apocalyptic
fantasies of the Christian faith has today entered the sphere
of the soberest scientific calculations; the sudden end of
history.
>—Emil Brunner, *Eternal Hope*, 1954

There is in the world today a degree of dread that we may
have outlived our string on this planet through our own
foolishness, which we don't seem to be able to control. And
the result of it may be the extermination of our species.
>—Roderic Gorney, in *Los Angeles Times*, June 6, 1991

There is . . . an entirely new factor in the modern apocalypse: the end of the world is ushered in, not by divine intervention or the long-range planning of an ultimately benevolent providence, but by human error, stupidity, malevolence, or the lure of oblivion.
—Douglas John Hall, *Imaging God: Dominion and Stewardship*, 1986

We live in an impenitent age; fearing . . . the same sort of world-catastrophe which our ancestors hoped for.
—Ronald A. Knox, *Lightning Meditations*, 1961

All the noonday brightness of human genius [is] destined to extinction in the vast death of the solar system, and that the whole temple of man's achievement must inevitably be buried beneath the debris of a universe in ruins—all these things if not quite beyond dispute, are yet so nearly certain that no philosophy which rejects them can hope to stand.
—Bertrand Russell, *Mysticism and Logic*, 1925

ART

Art is the soul of a people.
—Romare Bearden, interviewed in *Encore*, October 1972

I feel that art has something to do with the achievement of stillness in the midst of chaos. A stillness which characterizes prayer, too, and the eye of the storm. I think that art has something to do with an arrest of attention in the midst of distraction.
—Saul Bellow, in George Plimpton, *Writers at Work*, 1967

Love rests on the preservation of our species; art is our instinctive instrument for the preservation of the individual, of the unique man, woman and child, and the means of evolution of us all into something able and worthy of survival on the living earth.
—Earle Birney, *The Cow Jumped Over the Moon: The Writing and Reading of Poetry*, 1972

So long as the secret of art remains undeciphered, the Christian has only one instrument at his disposal, his conscience; but he has a conscience as a Christian and one as an artist, and these two consciences are not always in agreement.
—Heinrich Böll, *Art and Religion*, 1959

The Churches may still be entitled to decide whether some
one is a Christian (the Recording Angel can confirm or annul
the verdict); but the Churches are not entitled to decide
whether some one is an artist.

—Heinrich Böll, *Art and Religion*, 1959

Nature is not at variance with Art, nor Art with Nature, they
both being servants of His Providence. Art is the perfection of
Nature. . . . Nature is the Art of God.

—Thomas Browne, *Religio Medici*, 1635

Art is the stored honey of the human soul, gathered on wings
of misery and travail.

—Theodore Dreiser, *Seven Arts*, February 1917

Art is revelation. If a painting shows only what is there, it is
not art. Art like fine music or high literature must carry the
beholder beyond this world and all that appears in it,
transport him to the shores of the eternal world and enable
him to see and hear the things not given to the tongue of
man to utter.

—James M. Gillis, *If Not Christianity, What?*, 1935

Architecture paves the way, as it were, for the adequate
realization of the God, toiling and wrestling in his service
with external nature, and seeking to extricate it from the
chaos of finitude, and the abortiveness of chance.

—G.W.F. Hegel (1770–1831), *The Philosophy of Art*, publ. posth.

It is for artists to remind humanity of the unconquerable and
to assert the eternity of ideas.

—John Oliver Hobbes, *The Dream and the Business*, 1906

God creates Art by man, having for a tool the human
intellect. The great Workman has made this tool for himself;
he has no other.

—Victor Hugo, *William Shakespeare*, 1864

As soon as religion becomes prosaic or perfunctory art
appears somewhere else.

—Suzanne K. Langer, *Feeling and Form*, 1953

Art is a fundamental necessity in the human state. "No
man," says St. Thomas following Aristotle, "can live without
pleasure." Therefore a man deprived of the pleasures of the
spirit goes over to the pleasures of the flesh.

—Jacques Maritain, *Art and Scholasticism*, 1946

If a thing uplifts and delights the Soul by the very fact of being granted to its intuition, it is good to lay hold, it is beautiful.

—Jacques Maritain, *The Philosophy of Art*, 1923

Music and art and poetry attune the soul to God because they induce a kind of contact with the Creator and Ruler of the Universe.

—Thomas Merton, *No Man Is an Island*, 1955

The highest experience of the artist penetrates not only the sensible surface of things into their inmost reality, but even beyond that to God himself.

—Thomas Merton, in *The Commonweal Reader*, 1950

Good art is nothing but a replica of the perfection of God and a reflection of His art.

—Michelangelo, *Dialogues*, 1538

The role of art is to express through the body the mystery of a soul. Through the body—that is to say by way of all the signs—visual, audible, mobile.

—Jean Mouroux, *The Meaning of Man*, 1948

Today, in the secular world, it is almost wholly through the arts that we have a living reminder of the terror and nobility of what we are.

—J. Robert Oppenheimer, address, New York City, March 1963

All noble art, with all noble religion, breathes gratitude for life. . . . Great art is a song of praise, an overflowing of life back to its source, a dithyramb of thanksgiving and gratitude.

—A.R. Orage, *Nietzsche in Outline and Aphorism*, 1910

Through art the senses, far from weighing down the soul and nailing it to earth, should serve it as wings on which to rise above transient trifles and paltriness toward that which is eternal, true, beautiful, toward the only real good . . . toward God.

—Pope Pius XII, address, March 9, 1950

What joy to the artist who sees shining forth in every creature the resplendent light of the Creator! How noble the mission of the artist who helps the less gifted, to see to appreciate the natural beauty of the humblest things and through them the beauty of God!

—Pope Pius XII, address, May 19, 1948

Art is an exercise of the whole being of man, not to compete with God but to coincide better with the order of Creation, to love it better, and to reestablish ourselves in it.

—Denis de Rougement, address, May 1950, quoted by S.R. Hooper, *Spiritual Problems in Contemporary Literature*, 1952

All the sacred play of art is only a distant copying of that infinite play of the world, that work of art which is eternally fashioning itself.

—Friedrich Schlegel, *Gespräch über die Poesie*, 1800

If art can reveal the truth, art can also lie. An artist can be not only divinely inspired, but diabolically inspired.

—George Bernard Shaw, in *The Christian Commonwealth*, October 14, 1908

Mankind was never so happily inspired as when it made a cathedral.

—Robert Louis Stevenson, *An Inland Voyage*, 1878

Cathedrals are an unassailable witness to human passion. Using what demented calculation could an animal build such places? I think we know. An animal with a gorgeous genius for hope.

—Lionel Tiger, *Optimism: The Biology of Hope*, 1979

All art requires courage.

—Anne Tucker, *The Woman's Eye*, 1973

Art owes its origin to Nature herself, that this beautiful creation the world supplied the first model, while the original teacher was that divine intelligence which has not only made us superior to the other animals, but like to Himself.

—Giorgio Vasari, *The Lives of the Painters*, 1550

Religion is the everlasting dialogue between humanity and God. Art is its soliloquy.

—Franz Werfel, *Between Heaven and Earth*, 1944

Modern art, modern poetry, at their best say to me: You
must change your life! Such art represents a demand, even a
rebuke. It sees through us.
> —Amos N. Wilder, *Theology and Modern Literature*, 1958

ASCETICISM

The purpose of Calvary was not the death of Christ but the
resurrection, and the purpose of asceticism is not to
annihilate life but to increase it, to further the life of grace
and life of rational nature as well.
> —Louis Cognet, *Christian Asceticism and Modern Man*, 1955

Asceticism prepares the soul for the mystical union, which
then renders the exercise of the virtues and our apostolate
much more supernatural and fruitful.
> —Reginald Garrigou-Lagrange, *Christian Perfection and Contemplation*, 1937

The well-intentioned ascetic may be in some danger of
becoming the sanctified egoist.
> —Alfred Graham, *Christian Thought and Action*, 1951

The holy law imposes not asceticism. It demands that we . . .
grant each mental and physical faculty its due.
> —Judah Halevi, *Seter ha-Kuzari*, c. 1135

The ideal man is the non-attached man. Non-attached to his
bodily sensations and lusts. Non-attached to his cravings for
power and possessions. Non-attached even to science and
speculation and philanthropy.
> —Aldous Huxley, *Ends and Means*, 1937

The "dark night of the Soul," the tragic asceticism that is one
of the phases of dogmatic belief, is not the necessary
accompaniment of the presence of God, though it has often
been a very beautiful one.
> —Wyndham Lewis, *Time and Western Man*, 1927

Asceticism, or the sacrifice of one's personal inclinations, is
unquestionably the heart of the Christian religion and of all
great religions.
> —Henry C. Link, *The Return to Religion*, 1936

The ideal of asceticism represents moral effort as essentially
sacrifice, the sacrifice of one part of human nature to
another, that it may live the more completely in what
survives of it.
> —Walter Pater, *Marius the Epicurean*, 1885

Asceticism is the denial of the will to live.
—Arthur Schopenhauer, "On the Sufferings of the World," *Essays*, 1851

Prayer, fasting, vigils, and all other Christian practices . . . do not constitute the aim of our Christian life: they are but the indispensable means of attaining that aim. *For the true aim of the Christian life is the acquisition of the Holy Spirit of God.*
—St. Seraphim of Sarov (1757–1833), quoted by N. Matilov in *Conversation of Saint Seraphim on the Aim of the Christian Life*

[Jainism is] one of the most emphatic protests the world has ever known against accounting luxury, wealth or comfort as the main things in life.
—M. Stevenson, *The Heart of Jainism*, 1915

Forsake thyself, resign thyself, and thou shalt enjoy great inward peace.
—Thomas à Kempis, *Imitation of Christ*, 1441

ASPIRATION

Dost thou wish to rise? Begin by descending. You plan a tower that shall pierce the clouds? Lay first the foundation on humility.
—St. Augustine (354–430), *Sermon 10 on the Words of God*

A man's reach should exceed his grasp, or what's heaven for?
—Robert Browning (1812–89), "Andrea del Sarto"

If you aspire to the highest place it is no disgrace to stop at the second, or even the third.
—Cicero, *De Oratore*, c. 80 B.C.

Aspirations for the infinite constantly act upon us. They are more deeply rooted than desires on the surface of experience, and nothing in this world can ever satisfy them.
—E. Le Roy, *The Problem of God*, 1929

A certain glorious sorrow must ever mingle with our life; all our actual is transcended by our possible; our visionary faculty is an overmatch for our experience; like the caged bird, we break ourselves against the bars of the finite, with a wing that quivers for the infinite.
—James Martineau, *Hours of Thought on Sacred Things*, 1879

To love the beautiful, to desire the good, to do the best.
—Motto of Moses Mendelssohn (1729–86)

Aspiration shows us the goal and the distance to it;
inspiration encourages with a view to how far we have come.
Aspiration gives us the map of the journey; inspiration
furnishes the music to keep us marching.
—Ralph W. Sockman, *The Highway of God*, 1941

ATHEISM

Often we find atheism both in individual and society a
necessary passage to deeper religious and spiritual truth:
one has sometimes to deny God in order to find Him.
—Sri Aurobindo, *The Human Cycle*, 1950

Atheist: A man who has no invisible means of support.
—John Buchan, *Reader's Digest*, October 1941

No man in a thousand has the strength of mind or goodness
of heart to be an atheist.
—Samuel Taylor Coleridge, *Letters to Thomas Allsop*, c. 1820

We are too ready to assume that we know, better than the
unbeliever, what ails him.
—Thomas Merton, in *The Way*, May 1963

Atheism leads not to badness but only to an incurable
sadness and loncliness.
—W.P. Montague, *Belief Unbound*, 1930

There is no equivalent word in Sanskrit for the word atheism.
In the Gita mention is made of those who do not believe in
God, the intelligent principle, but these are spoken of merely
as of "deluded intellect."
—Swami Prabhavananda, *The Spiritual Heritage of India*, 1963

Atheism is aristocratic.
—M.M.I. Robespierre, speech, Paris, November 1, 1793

I shall always maintain that whoso says in his heart, "There
is no God," while he takes the name of God upon his lips, is
either a liar or a madman.
—Jean Jacques Rousseau, *Émile*, 1762

My atheism, like that of Spinoza, is true piety towards the
universe and denies only gods fashioned by men in their own
image, to be servants of their human interests.
—George Santayana, *Soliloquies in England*, 1922

The energy of atheists, their tireless propaganda, their spirited discourses, testify to a belief in God which puts to shame mere lip worshippers. They are always thinking of God.

—Fulton J. Sheen, *Religion Without God*, 1928

Fervid atheism is usually a screen for repressed religion.

—Wilhelm Stekel, *Autobiography*, 1950

Some are atheists by neglect; others are so by affectation; they that think there is no God at some times do not think so at all times.

—Benjamin Whichcote, *Moral and Religious Aphorisms*, 1753

The unbelief of today is more affirmative than the shallow skepticism of yesterday. The poignant atheism is more pregnant than the dogmatic rationalism of yesterday.

—Amos N. Wilder, *Theology and Modern Literature*, 1958

AUTHORITY

Being head of the Church is like putting together a jigsaw puzzle while riding on a roller coaster.

—John M. Allin, address, Trinity Institute, April 22, 1975

If . . . we follow the general Christian intention of abiding by the person and work of Jesus as central and decisive in directing us toward the realities of our human situation in respect to God and the world, it is shattering to contrast the Biblical notion of dominion with the opportunism of those who interpreted the Genesis mandate to "have dominion . . . over all the earth" as man's license to exploit his natural environment. For the authority of Jesus and the understanding of his dominion grow out of his availability and service to men, expressed in patterns of caring and compassion which eventually qualify his "dominion over all the earth."

—Conrad Bonifazi, "Biblical Roots of an Ecologic Conscience," *This Little Planet*, 1970

In religious matters it is holiness which gives authority.

—Samuel Taylor Coleridge, *Aids to Reflection*, 1825

And Jesus called them to him and said to them, "You know that those who are supposed to rule over the Gentiles lord it over them, and their great men exercise authority over them. But it shall not be so among you; but whoever would be great among you must be your servant, and whoever would be first among you must be slave of all."

—*Holy Bible*, Mark 10:42-44

A basic requirement is that a person not look upon his authority as giving him a right to all kinds of privileges, and, much more, that he not use it to appropriate the community's resources to himself. Similarly, authority is in the service of truth, and not vice versa: something is not true because the authorities say so, but rather, the authorities must speak the truth.

—Bakole wa Ilunga, *Paths of Liberation*, 1984

Like every good teacher, authority should labor to render itself useless.

—Auguste Sabatier, *Religion of Authority and the Religion of the Spirit*, 1904

eauty

Beauty is undoubtedly the signature of the Master to the work in which he has put his soul; it is the divine spirit manifested.
—Honoré de Balzac (1799–1850), *Treasure Bits from*

Beauty, I believe, comes from God; therefore there can be no beauty without goodness.
—Baldassare Castiglione, *Libro del Cortegiano*, 1518

A more secret, sweet and overpowering beauty appears to man when his heart and mind open to the sentiment of virtue. Then he is instructed in what is above him.
—Ralph Waldo Emerson, *Divinity School Address*, July 15, 1838

The beautiful is holiness, visible, holiness seen, heard, touched, holiness tasted.
—Eric Gill, *Last Essays*, 1942

The first of all beautiful things is the continual possession of God.
—St. Gregory Nazianzen (325–390), *Epistolae*, 212

The Divine beauty is not adorned with any shape or endowment of form, or with any beauty of color, but is contemplated as excellence in unspeakable bliss.
—St. Gregory of Nyssa (c. 335–c. 395), *On the Making of Man*

Beauty is merely the Spiritual making itself known sensuously.
—G.W.F. Hegel (1770–1831), *The Philosophy of Religion*, publ. posth.

One thing have I asked of the Lord, that will I seek after; that I may dwell in the house of the Lord all the days of my life, to behold the beauty of the Lord, and to inquire in his temple.
—*Holy Bible*, Psalms 27:4

The beautiful is the symbol of the morally Good.
—Immanuel Kant, *Critique of Judgment*, 1790

I can never feel certain of any truth, but from a clear perception of its beauty.
—John Keats, *Letter to George Keats*, 1818

The natural and primitive relationship of soul to soul is a relationship of beauty. For beauty is the only language of the soul. . . . It has no other life, it can produce nothing else.
—Maurice Maeterlinck, *The Treasure of the Humble*, 1895

In every man's heart there is a secret nerve that answers to the vibrations of beauty.
—Christopher Morley, *Essays*, 1928

He who loves the Beautiful is called a lover because he partakes of that inspiration.
—Plato, *Phaedrus*, c. 370 B.C.

Beauty is a pledge of the possible conformity between soul and nature, and consequently a ground of faith in the supremacy of good.
—George Santayana, *The Sense of Beauty*, 1896

Would you see true beauty? Look at the pious man or woman in whom spirit dominates matter; watch him when he prays, when a ray of the divine beauty glows upon him when his prayer is ended; you will see the beauty of God shining in his face.
—Girolamo Savonarola, *28th Sermon on Ezekiel*, c. 1489

Beloved Pan, and all ye other gods who haunt this place, give me beauty in the inward soul.
—Socrates' prayer, Phaedrus, in Plato, *Dialogues*, c. 399 B.C.

The perception of beauty is a moral test.
—Henry David Thoreau, journal, June 21, 1852

Beauty captivates the flesh in order to obtain permission to pass right through to the soul. . . . When the feeling for beauty happens to be associated with the sight of some human being, the transference of love is made possible, at any rate in an illusory manner. But it is all the beauty of the world, it is universal beauty, for which we yearn.
—Simone Weil, *Gravity and Grace*, 1952

BELIEF AND BELIEVERS
A person can do other things against his will; but belief is possible only in one who is willing.
—St. Augustine, *Tractate XXVI in Joann.*, c. 416

Understanding is the reward of faith. Therefore seek not to understand that thou mayest believe, but believe that thou mayest understand.
—St. Augustine, *On the Gospel of St. John*, XXIX, c. 416

The human understanding is no dry light, but receives an infusion from the will and affections. . . . What a man had rather were true he more readily believes.
—Francis Bacon, *Novum Organum*, 1620

It is always easier to believe than to deny. Our minds are naturally affirmative.
—John Burroughs, *The Light of Day*, 1900

It is not really a question of what a man is made to believe but of what he must believe; what he cannot help believing.
—G.K. Chesterton, *The Catholic Church and Conversion*, 1926

Belief is the natural possession of beings possessing minds.
—Martin C. D'Arcy, *The Nature of Belief*, 1958

The belief in God has often been advanced as . . . the most complete of all distinctions between man and the lower animals. It is, however, impossible . . . to maintain that this belief is innate or instinctive in man.
—Charles Darwin, *The Descent of Man*, 1871

Be sure to choose what you believe and know why you believe it, because if you don't choose your beliefs, you may be certain that some belief, and probably not a very creditable one, will choose you.
—Robertson Davies, *The Manticore*, 1972

Man is being born to believe, and if no church comes forward with all the title deeds of truth . . . he will find altars and idols in his own heart and his own imagination.
—Benjamin Disraeli, speech, Oxford, November 25, 1864

Believe to the end, even if all men went astray and you were left the only one faithful; bring your offering even then and praise God in your loneliness.
—Feodor Dostoevsky, *The Brothers Karamazov*, 1880

There is no enlightenment in questions, but only barbarism in belief.
—Louis Dudek, *Epigrams*, 1975

Men in the nineteenth century were sad that they could no longer believe in God; they are more deeply saddened now by the fact that they can no longer believe in man.

—Irwin Edman, *Candle in the Dark*, 1939

All ages of belief have been great; all of unbelief have been mean.

—Ralph Waldo Emerson, in *North American Review*, May 1878

We are born believing. A man bears beliefs, as a tree bears apples.

—Ralph Waldo Emerson, "Worship," *Conduct of Life*, 1860

They dare not believe because they are afraid that what they most deeply want is not true.

—Nels F.S. Ferré, *Faith and Reason*, 1946

He does not believe that does not live according to his belief.

—Thomas Fuller, *Gnomologia*, 1732

I believe in God—this is a fine, praise-worthy thing to say. But to acknowledge God wherever and however He manifest Himself, that in truth is heavenly bliss on earth.

—J.W. von Goethe (1749–1832), *Maxims and Reflections*

Belief consists not in the nature and order of our ideas, but in the manner of their conception, and in their feeling to the mind . . . something *felt* by the mind, which distinguishes the ideas of the judgment from the fictions of the imagination.

—David Hume, *Of the Understanding*, 1748

We should always be disposed to believe that which appears to us to be white is really black, if the hierarchy of the Church so decides.

—St. Ignatius Loyola, *Spiritual Exercises*, 1541

He is less remote from the truth who believes nothing, than he who believes what is wrong.

—Thomas Jefferson, *Notes on the State of Virginia*, 1781

The Bible never commands us to believe, though it commends belief. Such a command would be useless. Belief cannot be coerced.

—Morris Joseph, *Judaism as Creed and Life*, 1903

Those who believe and do not obscure their faith with wrong,
they are those who shall have security and they are guided.
> —*Koran,* 7th century

Do you think that I should possess the gift of causing you to
believe in God, if the germ of that belief did not exist in the
depths of your heart, if there were not in your soul that
which Tertullian called *a testimony naturally Christian?*
> —Jean Baptiste Lacordaire, *Conferences of,* c. 1850

We believe willingly what we love, and rarely what we love
not. To the question of divine faith is united the question of
divine virtue.
> —Jean Baptiste Lacordaire, *Thoughts and Teachings of,* 1902

What takes place in us when we believe is a phenomenon of
intimate and superhuman light.
> —Jean Baptiste Lacordaire, *Conférences de Notre
> Dame de Paris,* 17th conference, 1850

Amid the greatest difficulties of my Administration, when I
could not see any other resort, I would place my whole
reliance in God, knowing that all would go well, and that He
would decide for the right.
> —Abraham Lincoln, to a group of visitors, 1863

Belief in God is not always beneficial to human life. Falsely
used, it may become an escape from reality or a justification
for a dogmatic arrogance that destroys the very fibre of
human community.
> —Edward LeRoy Long, Jr., *Religious Belief of American Scientists,* 1952

It is simply absurd to say you believe, or even want to
believe, if you do not anything He tells you.
> —George Macdonald, *Unspoken Sermons,* 2nd Series, 1886

To believe in God must mean to live in such a manner that
life could not possibly be lived if God did not exist.
> —Jacques Maritain, in *The Review of Politics,* July 1949

The average man who goes wrong in belief does it when he
forgets that there are other truths besides his favorite one.
> —Cleland B. McAfee, *Near to the Heart of God,* 1954

It really takes a hero to live any kind of spiritual life without
religious belief.
> —Mary McCarthy, in *The Observer,* October 14, 1979

Belief in God is acceptance of the basic principle that the universe makes sense, that there is behind it an ultimate purpose.
—Carl Wallace Miller, *A Scientist's Approach to Religion*, 1947

A man may be a heretic to the truth if he believes things only because his pastor says so, or the assembly so determines, without knowing other reason; though his belief be true, yet the very truth he holds becomes his heresy.
—John Milton, *Aeropagitica*, 1644

We believe nothing so firmly as what we least know.
—Michel de Montaigne, *Essays*, 1580

The belief of a God, so far from having any thing of mystery in it, is of all beliefs the most easy, because it arises to us . . . out of necessity.
—Thomas Paine, *The Age of Reason*, 1795

It is your own assent to yourself, and the constant voice of your own reason, and not of others, that should make you believe.
—Blaise Pascal, *Pensées*, 1670

Belief is thought at rest.
—Charles S. Peirce (1839–1914), *Collected Papers*

Faith is belief, and belief has, over and above its intellectual character, an aspect of firmness, persistence, and subjective certainty.
—Ralph Barton Perry, *Puritanism and Democracy*, 1944

Fewer beliefs, more belief.
—James A. Pike, in *Life*, September 19, 1969

A religious man who says in his heart there is a God receives his life daily by divine appointment as a gift and a task set before him.
—Paul Ramsey, *Nine Modern Moralists*, 1962

My son, keep your spirit always in such a state as to desire that there be a God, and you will never doubt it.
—Jean Jacques Rousseau, *Émile*, 1762

I do not know of any compelling evidence for anthropomorphic patriarchs controlling human destiny from some
hidden celestial vantage point, but it would be madness to
deny the existence of physical laws. Whether we believe in
God depends very much on what we mean by God.
—Carl Sagan, *Broca's Brain*, 1979

Travellers from one religion to another, people who have lost
their spiritual nationality, may often retain a neutral and
confused residuum of belief, which they may egregiously
regard as the essence of all religion.
—George Santayana, *Reason in Religion*, 1905

And this I do believe above all, especially in times of greater
discouragement, that I must BELIEVE—that I must believe
in my fellow men—that I must believe in myself—that I must
believe in God—if life is to have any meaning.
—Margaret Chase Smith, *This I Believe*, 1954

To say a man is bound to believe, is neither truth nor sense.
—Jonathan Swift, *Thoughts on Religion*, 1728

One great gain that the scientific use of the comparative
method in religion has brought us is the duty of genuine
reverence for other men's beliefs. . . . Whatever thoughts any
human soul is seeking to live by, deserve the reverence of
every other human soul.
—William Temple, *The Universality of Christ*, 1921

If there exists a man of faith in God joined to a life of purity
and moral elevation, it is not so much the believing in God
that makes him good, as the being good, thanks to God, that
makes him believe in Him.
—Miguel de Unamuno, *Tragic Sense of Life*, 1921

BIBLE

The Bible . . . is the classical book of noble ethical sentiment.
In it the mortal fear, the overflowing hope, the quivering
longings of the human soul . . . have found their first, their
freshest, their fittest utterance.
—F. Adler, *Creed and Deed*, 1877

Holy Scripture is so exalted that there is no one in the world
. . . wise enough to understand it so fully that his intellect is
not overcome by it. Nevertheless, man can stammer
something about it.
—Blessed Angela of Foligno (1248–1309), *Book of Vision and Instructions*

Other books were given for our information, the Bible was
given for our transformation.

—Anonymous

It is one of the glories of the Bible that it can enshrine
many meanings in a single passage. . . . Each man marvels
to find in the divine Scriptures truths which he has himself
thought out.

—St. Thomas Aquinas, *De Potentia*, 1263

It [the Bible] furnished good Christians an armor for their
warfare, a guide for their conduct, a solace in their sorrows,
food for their souls.

—Gaius Glenn Atkins, *Religion in Our Times*, 1932

If in these books I meet anything which seems contrary to
truth I shall not hesitate to conclude that the text is faulty,
or that the translator has not expressed the meaning of that
passage, or that I myself do not understand.

—St. Augustine (345–430) to St. Jerome, *Ep.* LXXXVII, I

Scripture, which proves the truth of its historical statements
by the accomplishment of its prophecies, gives no false
information.

—St. Augustine, *The City of God*, Book XVI, Ch.9; 426

We must be on guard against giving interpretations of
Scripture that are far-fetched or opposed to science, and so
exposing the word of God to the ridicule of unbelievers.

—St. Augustine, *De Genesi ad litteratum*, c. 415

We ought to listen to the Scriptures with the greatest
caution, for as far as understanding of them goes we are as
but little children.

—St. Augustine, *Tractate* XVIII *in Joann.*, P.L. XXXV, c. 416

Prosperity is the blessing of the Old Testament; adversity is
the blessing of the New.

—Francis Bacon, *Essays*, 1597

I wish to show that there is one wisdom which is perfect, and
that this is contained in the Scriptures.

—Roger Bacon, *Opus Maius*, 1267

Because they [the Scriptures] are only a declaration of the fountain and not the fountain itself, therefore they are not to be esteemed the principal ground of all truth and knowledge nor yet the adequate, primary rule of faith and manners.
—Robert Barclay, *Apology*, 1678

The study of inspired Scripture is the chief way of finding our duty.
—St. Basil (330–379), letter to Gregory of Nazianzen

When read intelligently, the Bible reveals itself as the immortal epic of a people's confused, faltering, but indomitable struggle after a nobler life in a happier world.
—Lewis Browne, *The Graphic Bible*, 1928

Unspeakable mysteries in the Scriptures are often delivered in a vulgar and illustrative way; and being written unto man, are delivered, not as they truly are, but as they may be understood.
—Thomas Browne, *Religio Medici*, 1635

It is only in the scriptures that the Lord hath been pleased to preserve his truth in perpetual remembrance; it obtains the same complete credit and authority with believers, where they are satisfied of its divine origin, as if they heard the very words pronounced by God Himself.
—John Calvin, *Institutes*, I, 1536

Scripture is the school of the Holy Spirit, in which, as nothing is omitted that is both necessary and useful to know, so nothing is taught but what is expedient to know.
—John Calvin, *Institutes*, III, 1536

There is nothing empty and nothing idle in divine literature, but what is said is always said for some useful purpose in order that this purpose may be received in its proper meaning and bring salvation.
—Cassiodorus, *The Divine Letters*, c. 550

We ought, indeed, to expect occasional obscurity in such a book as the Bible . . . but God's wisdom is a pledge that whatever is necessary for *us*, and necessary for salvation, is revealed too plainly to be mistaken.
—William Ellery Channing (1780–1842), *Works*

Intense study of the Bible will keep any writer from being vulgar in point of style.
—Samuel Taylor Coleridge, *Table-Talk*, June 14, 1830

The Bible does not provide a model for family life. Nor does it supply many images of truly emancipated women, though there are a few. Rather, the importance of biblical faith for the freeing of women from the cultural and religious images by which they have been held for so long in bondage lies elsewhere. It lies in the inclusive vision of biblical religion which sees God's ultimate purpose as the liberation and maturation of all human beings, and of all creation, to their full potential in a cosmic feast of love and joy.
—Harvey Cox, *The Seduction of the Spirit*, 1973

You venture to judge the Bible and up to a point it submits to your judgment, and then you may find the roles reversed—you are in the dock and the Bible is the judge pronouncing sentence upon you.
—A.C. Craig, *Preaching in a Scientific Age*, 1954

The great principle dominating the composition of Scripture is that of the ascent towards discovery.
—Henri Daniel-Rops, *What Is the Bible?*, 1958

The whole of the Bible is inspired, but we cannot venture to describe the mode or method of this inspiration, but accept it as a fact of which faith assures us.
—*Declaration of the United Lutheran Church in America*, October 11, 1938

Great consequences have flowed from the fact that the first truly popular literature in England—the first which stirred the hearts of all classes of people . . . was the literature comprised within the Bible.
—John Fiske, *The Beginnings of New England*, 1900

The Bible becomes ever more beautiful the more it is understood.
—J.W. von Goethe, *Wilhelm Meister's Travels*, 1830

One must read the Bible continually to prevent the image of truth being obscured in us.
—Julian Green, *Journal*, 1961

It is, as it were, a kind of river, if I may so liken it, which is
both shallow and deep, wherein both the lamb may find
footing and the elephant float at large.
—Pope St. Gregory the Great, *Magna Moralia,* 584

The Bible is the only literature in the world up to our century
which looks at women as human beings, no better and no
worse than men.
—Edith Hamilton, *Spokesmen for God:
The Great Teachers of the Old Testament,* 1948

Scripture has been, and can be, the most dangerous weapon
in the world unless it is carefully read and understood in full
context.
—Sydney J. Harris, *Pieces of Eight,* 1982

The Bible, the greatest medicine chest of humanity.
—Heinrich Heine, *Ludwig Marcus,* 1844

What a book! great and wide as the world, rooted in the
abysmal depths of creation and rising aloft into the blue
mysteries of heaven. . . . Sunrise and sunset, promise and
fulfillment, birth and death, the whole human drama,
everything is in this book. . . . It is the book of books, *Biblia.*
—Heinrich Heine, *Ludwig Boerne,* 1840

There are no words in the world more knowing, more
disclosing and more indispensable, words both stern and
graceful, heart-rending and healing.
—Abraham Joshua Heschel, *God in Search of Man,* 1955

So far as such equality, liberty and fraternity are included
under the democratic principles which assume the same
names, the Bible is the most democratic book in the world.
—Thomas Henry Huxley, *Science and the Christian Tradition,* 1902

Throughout the history of the Western world the Scriptures
have been the great instigators of revolt against the worst
forms of clerical and political despotism. The Bible has been
the Magna Charta of the poor and of the oppressed.
—Thomas Henry Huxley, *Controverted Questions,* 1892

Everything in the Sacred Book shines and glistens, even in
its outer shell: but the marrow of it is sweeter: if you want
the kernel, you must break the shell.
—St. Jerome (340–420), *Epistula LXIX*

If there is anything in this life which sustains a wise man and induces him to maintain his serenity amidst the tribulations and adversities of the world, it is in the first place, I consider, the meditation and knowledge of the Scriptures.

—St. Jerome, *In Ephesius*, c. 400

When you are really instructed in the Divine Scriptures, and have realized that its laws and testimonies are the bonds of truth, you can contend with adversaries.

—St. Jerome (340–420), *Epistula LXXVIII*

You cannot make your way into the Holy Scriptures without having someone to go before you and show you the road.

—St. Jerome, *Epistula LIII ad Paulinum*, 340

The Bible is not the sole basis of our religion, for in addition to it we have two other bases. One of these is anterior to it: namely, the fountain of reason. The second is posterior to it; namely, the source of tradition. Whatever, therefore, we may not find in the Bible, we can find in the two other sources.

—Saadia ben Joseph (892–942), *The Book of Beliefs and Opinions*

Take all this book upon reason that you can, and the balance on faith, and you will live and die a happier and better man.

—Abraham Lincoln, letter to Speed, 1864

If a theologian does not want to err, he must have all Scripture before his eyes, must compare apparently contradictory passages and, like the two cherubim facing each other from opposite sides, must find agreement of the difference in the middle of the mercy seat.

—Martin Luther (1483–1546), quoted in *What Luther Says*

It teaches us to see, feel, grasp, and comprehend faith, hope, and charity far otherwise than mere human reason can; and when evil oppresses us it teaches how these virtues throw light upon darkness, and how, after this poor, miserable existence of ours on earth, there is another and eternal life.

—Martin Luther (1483–1546), *Table-Talk*

Private interpretation meant that any group of men, however ignorant, need only be able to read the Bible to be in possession of the ultimate, undeniable truth about almost any important question of human life.

—Everett Dean Martin, *Liberty*, 1930

The Bible is by no means the simple and easily understood book which many imagine. If reading it with simple faith has brought consolation to many, it has also brought misunderstanding and dissension. It is easy for men to read their own meanings into it and then proclaim them as the word of God, equally binding on all men.
—Everett Dean Martin, *Liberty*, 1930

When one rereads the Bible as a Jew, Protestant, Orthodox or Roman Catholic, he may read it as a mirror of his preconceptions; when encouraged to read it in the contexts of other traditions, he is apt to find something hitherto overlooked.
—Martin E. Marty, in *The New York Times Book Review*, February 9, 1964

When you eat fish, you don't eat the bones. You eat the flesh. Take the Bible like that.
—Robert R. Moton, in *New York Post*, May 17, 1964

Western civilization is founded upon the Bible; our ideas, our wisdom, our philosophy, our literature, our art, our ideals come more from the Bible than from all other books put together. It is a revelation of divinity and of humanity.
—William Lyon Phelps, *Human Nature in the Bible*, 1922

You can learn more about human nature by reading the Bible than by living in New York.
—William Lyon Phelps, radio speech, 1933

The devil can cite Scripture for his purpose.
—William Shakespeare, *The Merchant of Venice*, c. 1595

Its object is not to convince the reason, but to attract and lay hold of the imagination.
—Baruch Spinoza, *Tractatus Theologico-Politicus*, 1670

How many times one has laid the Bible aside in favor of what seemed more real and compelling . . . only to be driven back to it again by the great hunger to let the measured dignity and beauty of its language stir in him an emotion like that which comes in listening to classical music or in seeing a finely proportioned building.
—Douglas V. Steere, *Prayer and Worship*, 1938

We advise all who feel hemmed in by a closed and stifling world to open the Old and New Testaments. They will there find vistas, which will liberate them, and the excellent food of the only true God.
—Emmanuel Suhard, *The Church Today*, 1953

Men suffer from intellectual dyspepsia when they attempt to swallow the Bible whole, accepting at face value the mathematics and rhetoric of a people who thought in poetry rather than in prose.
—A.M. Sullivan, *The Three-Dimensional Man*, 1965

Sometimes, when I read spiritual treatises . . . my poor little mind grows weary, I close the learned book . . . and I take the Holy Scriptures. Then all seems luminous, a single word opens up infinite horizons to my soul, perfection seems easy.
—St. Thérèse of Lisieux (1873–1897), *Autobiography*, publ. posth.

The trouble with the Bible has been its interpreters, who have scaled down and whittled down that sense of infinitude into finite and limited concepts.
—Alfred North Whitehead, December 1939,
Dialogues of, as recorded by Lucien Price

A man has found himself when he has found his relation to the rest of the universe, and here is the Book in which those relations are set forth.
—Woodrow Wilson, speech, May 7, 1911

The books of the Old Testament, in their entirety, provide the most final and profound literature of human loneliness that the world has known.
—Thomas Wolfe, *The Hills Beyond*, 1941

BODY AND SOUL

Those are right who hold that the soul is neither independent of body nor itself a body; for it is not a body, but something belonging to the body, and therefore is present in a body, and a body of a certain kind.
—Aristotle (384–322 B.C.), *De Anima*

The created soul is gifted with the knowledge which is proper to it; but after it is united to the body, it is withdrawn from receiving those impressions which are proper to it, by reason of the very darkness of the body.
—Avicebrón (Solomon ben Judah ibn-Gabirol) (1021?–58), *Fountain of Life*

You cannot devalue the body and value the soul—or value anything else. The prototypical act issuing from this division was to make a person a slave and then instruct him in religion—a "charity" more damaging to the master than to the slave.
—Wendell Berry, *The Unsettling of America*, 1977

These bodies are perishable; but the dwellers in these bodies are eternal, indestructible, and impenetrable.
—*Bhagavad-Gita*, between 5th and 2nd centuries B.C.

Man has no body distinct from his soul; for that called body is a portion of the soul discern'd by the five senses, the chief inlets of soul in this age.
—William Blake, *The Marriage of Heaven and Hell*, 1790

I must assert in the most unqualified way that it is primarily and mainly for the sake of saving the soul that I seek the salvation of the body.
—William Booth, *In Darkest England and Way Out*, 1980

"If my body," said Shun, "is not my own, pray whose is it?" "It is the bodily form entrusted to you by Heaven and Earth. Your life is not your own. It is a blended harmony, entrusted to you by Heaven and Earth" replied Ch'eng, his tutor.
—Chuang-tzu (4th century B.C.), *Texts of Taoism*

The eye is the lamp of the body. So, if your eye is sound, your whole body will be full of light.
—*Holy Bible*, Matthew 6:22

My great religion is a belief in the blood, the flesh, as being wiser than the intellect. We can go wrong in our minds. But what our blood feels and believes and says, is always true.
—D.H. Lawrence, letter to Ernest Collings, January 17, 1913, *Collected Letters of*, 1962

The soul is born with the body, it grows and decays with the body, therefore it perishes with the body.
—Lucretius, *De Rerum Natura*, Lib. III, c. 60 B.C.

There is nothing the body suffers that the soul may not profit by.
—George Meredith, *Diana of the Crossways*, 1885

The body is a source of endless trouble to us. . . . It fills us full of loves, and lusts, and fears, and fancies of all kinds, and endless foolery, and in fact, as men say, takes away from us the power of thinking at all.

—Plato, "Phaedrus," in *Dialogues*, 399 B.C.

The body of a man is not a home but an inn—and that only briefly.

—Seneca, *Epistulae morales ad Lucilium*, c. A.D. 63

In no creature except man is there any act which involves such an interactivity of matter and spirit, body and soul.

—Fulton J. Sheen, *Peace of Soul*, 1949

The soul organizes the body as an expression of itself, as its instrument, as its intermediary with the world outside.

—John Ternus, *God, Man and Universe*, 1950

The body is immersed in the soul, as a wick is dipped in oil; and its flame of active energy is increased or diminished by the strength or weakness of the fecundizing soul.

—Francis Thompson, *Health and Holiness*, 1905

There is something more menacing than the destruction of men's bodies, of their material environment, their comfort and security; and that is the voiding of the human spirit.

—Gerald Vann, *The Water and the Fire*, 1954

Surely health is an instrumental value. We discipline our bodies and minds *in order that* these bodies may be instrumental to the divine harmony in this discordant world.

—Kenneth Vaux, in *Utne Reader*, August/September 1985

Body and soul are not two substances but one. They are man becoming aware of himself in two different ways.

—C.F. von Weizsächer, *The History of Nature*, 1949

BROTHERHOOD

There is no one in the whole human family to whom kindly affection is not due by reason of the bond of a common humanity, although it may not be due on the ground of reciprocal love.

—St. Augustine, *To Proba*, 412

Brotherhood is Religion!

—William Blake, *Jerusalem*, 1820

Christian brotherhood is not an ideal, but a divine reality . . .
a spiritual and not a psychic reality.
—Dietrich Bonhoeffer, *Life Together*, 1938

The word of him who wishes to speak with God without
speaking with men goes astray.
—Martin Buber, *Between Man and Men*, 1947

The pious man owes to his brethren all that it is in his power
to give.
—John Calvin, *Institutes*, 1536

Each man, simply because he exists, holds a right on other
men or on society for existence.
—Thomas Chalmers (1780–1847), *Selections from*

When you see your brother, you see God.
—St. Clement of Alexandria, *Stromateis*, 150

No man is an *Island*, entire of it self; every man is a piece of
the *Continent*, a part of the *main* . . . any man's *death*
diminishes *me*, because I am involved in *Mankind*; and
therefore never send to know for whom the *bell* tolls; it tolls
for *thee*.
—John Donne (1573–1631), *Devotions Upon Mergent Occasions*

Until you become really, in actual fact, a brother to every
one, brotherhood will not come to pass.
—Feodor Dostoevsky, *The Brothers Karamazov*, 1880

I am hindered of meeting God in my brother, because he has
shut his own temple doors, and recites fables merely of his
brother's or his brother's brother's God.
—Ralph Waldo Emerson, "Self-Reliance," *Essays*, I, 1841

Your brother needs your help, but you meanwhile mumble
your little prayers to God, pretending not to see your
brother's need.
—Desiderius Erasmus, *Enchiridion*, 1501

The dignity of resembling the Almighty is common to all men;
we should then love them all as ourselves, as living images of
the Deity. It is on this title that we belong to God.
—St. Frances de Sales, *Treatise on the Love of God*, 1607

To love our neighbor with a love of charity is to love God in man or man in God and consequently, to love God alone for His own sake and creatures for the love of God.
—St. Frances de Sales, *Treatise on the Love of God*, 1607

The founders of the great world religions, Gautama Buddha, Jesus, Lao-tzu, Mohammed, all seem to have striven for a worldwide brotherhood of man; but none of them could develop institutions which would include the enemy, the unbeliever.
—Geoffrey Gorer, *The New York Times Magazine*, November 27, 1966

He who bears another, is borne by another.
—Pope St. Gregory the Great (540–604), in *Ezech*

It is not by driving away our brother that we can be alone with God.
—George Macdonald, *Alex Forbes*, Vol. 2, 1865

Oh! my dear fellow beings, why should we longer cherish any social acerbities, or know the slightest ill-humor or envy! Come; let us squeeze hands all round; nay, let us squeeze ourselves into each other; let us squeeze ourselves universally into the very milk and sperm of kindness.
—Herman Melville, *Moby Dick*, 1851

Increase, O God, the spirit of neighborliness among us, that in peril we may uphold one another, in calamity serve one another, in suffering tend one another and in homeliness and loneliness in exile befriend one another. Grant us brave and enduring hearts that we may strengthen one another, till the disciplines and testing of these days be ended.
—Prayer used in air-raid shelters, England, World War II, 1939–45

The Fatherhood of God, as revealed by Jesus Christ, should lead us towards a Brotherhood, which knows no restriction of race, sex or social class.
—Society of Friends, Great Britain, 1918

Perhaps the clearest and deepest meaning of brotherhood is the ability to imagine yourself in the other person's position, and then treat that person as if you were him. This form of brotherhood takes a lot of imagination, a great deal of sympathy, and a tremendous amount of understanding.
—Obert C. Tanner, *One Man's Search*, 1989

In proportion as you advance in fraternal charity, you are increasing in your love of God.
—St. Teresa of Ávila, *The Interior Castle*, 1577

You are a part of the Infinite. This is your nature. Hence you are your brother's keeper.
—Swami Vivekananda (1863–1902), *Works of*

Every step toward wider understanding and tolerance and good will is a step in the direction of that universal brotherhood Christ proclaimed.
—H.G. Wells, *Reader's Digest*, May 1935

To consider mankind otherwise than brethren, to think favors are peculiar to one nation and exclude others plainly supposes a darkness in the understanding.
—John Woolman, *Journal*, 1774

BUDDHISM

Moreover, brethren, though robbers, who are highwaymen, would with a two-handed saw carve you in pieces limb by limb, yet if the mind of any one of you should be offended thereat, such an one is no follower of my gospel.
—Buddha (6th century B.C.), *Some Sayings of*, trans. by F.L. Woodward

Why does the Master say that Buddhism is democratic? Because of this one idea—all living beings have the Buddha Nature and all can become Buddhas. Now, if that isn't totally egalitarian, what is?
—Heng Ch'an, "Sila and the Modern Age," *Vajra Bodhi Sea*, April 1992

The teachings of Buddhism are vast and great, not narrow and small, not bounded in any way, limitless and vast, level, equal, free, and comfortable. Such a principle you might say is the smallest, yet it is also the greatest. There is no past and no present, no high and no low, it is both extremely vast and yet also ultimately fine. Buddhism is no bigger than an ant, and a mosquito, and also expansive and boundless.
—Dhyana Master Hua, "Chan Talks," *Vajra Bodhi Sea*, April 1992

The word used for religion in Buddhism is *brahma-cariya* which may be translated as "the ideal life"—any way of life which anyone may consider to be the ideal as a consequence of his holding a certain set of beliefs about the nature and destiny of man in the universe.
—G.P. Malalasekera and K.N. Jayatilleke,
Buddhism and the Race Question, 1958

Buddhism refuses to countenance any self-cultivation or beautification of the soul. It ruthlessly exposes any desire of enlightenment or of salvation that seeks merely the glorification of the ego and the satisfaction of its desires in a transcendent realm. It is not that this is "wrong" or "immoral" but that it is simply impossible.

—Thomas Merton, *Zen and the Birds of Appetite*, 1968

Outside of Christianity, at any rate, there is no other religion which has put so much stress upon love as has Buddhism. Universal pity, sympathy for all suffering beings, good will to every form of sentient life, these things characterized the Tathagata [the Buddha] as they have few others of the sons of men.

—J.B. Pratt, *The Pilgrimage of Buddhism*, 1928

The original Buddhist goal of nirvana (or "salvation," if one wishes to use a Western term) was the realization that life's meaning lay in the here-and-now and not in some remote realm or celestial state far beyond one's present existence.

—Nancy Wilson Ross, *Buddhism: A Way of Life and Thought*, 1980

All the teachings of Buddha can be summed up in one word: dhamma. . . . It means truth, that which really is. It also means law, the law which exists in a man's own heart and mind. It is the principle of righteousness. . . . Dhamma . . . exists not only in a man's heart and mind; it exists in the universe also. All the universe is an embodiment and revelation of dhamma. Dhamma is the true nature of every existing thing.

—Venerable U. Thittila, *The Path of the Buddha*, 1956

The whole approach to Buddhism is to develop transcendental common sense, seeing things as they are, without magnifying what is or dreaming about what we would like to be.

—Chogyam Trungpa, *The Myth of Freedom*, 1976

apital Punishment

Those who by God's commands have waged war, or who, wielding the public power, and in conformity with the divine laws, have put criminals to death, these have by no means violated the commandment *Thou shalt not kill.*
—St. Augustine, *The City of God*, Lib. 1, cap. xxi; 426

It does not please good people in the Catholic Church when an evil man, even a heretic, is put to death.
—St. Augustine, *Contra Cresconium*, c. 406

If by the law of God all Christians are forbidden to kill . . . how can it be compatible for magistrates to shed blood?. . . The magistrate does not act at all from himself, but merely executes the judgments of God. . . . We can find no objection to the infliction of public vengeance, unless the justice of God be restrained from the punishment of crimes.
—John Calvin, *Institutes*, 1536

The verdict of capital punishment destroys the only indisputable human community there is, the community in the face of death.
—Albert Camus, in *Evergreen Review*, 1962

Religious values . . . are the only ones on which the death penalty can be based, since according to their own logic they prevent that penalty from being final and irreparable: it is justified only insofar as it is not supreme.
—Albert Camus, in *Evergreen Review*, 1962

Though every other man who wields a pen should turn himself into a commentator on the Scriptures—not all their united efforts, pursued through our united lives, could ever persuade me that Executions are a Christian law.
—Charles Dickens, letter to *Daily News*, March 16, 1846

Assassination on the scaffold is the worst form of assassination, because there it is invested with the approval of society.
—George Bernard Shaw, *Man and Superman*, 1903

Cause

It is for me easier to suppose that there are causes that elude, and must forever elude, our search, rather than to suppose that there are no causes at all.
—E.N. da C. Andrade, in *The Listener*, July 10, 1947

The potency of a cause is greater, the more remote the effects to which it extends.
—St. Thomas Aquinas, *Summa c. Gent*. III, c. lxxxvii, 1260

It is obvious that there is some First Principle, and that the causes of things are not infinitely many . . . neither can the Final Cause recede to infinity.
—Aristotle, *Metaphysics*, II, 11, 1-2, c. 322 B.C.

The principle of causality, limited exclusively to explaining the interconnection of *phenomena*, and void of any *metaphysical* significance, has become incapable of making the mind pass from the world to God. Man's mind, if not his heart, has become godless, and knowledge, or science, has dethroned wisdom.
—Charles Journet, *The Meaning of Evil*, 1961

As the tiny mountain rivulet as well as the majestic lake and river, after many windings and turnings, all trace their course at last down to the ocean's mighty shore, so all things and all living creatures, all trace their origin and existence back to God, their Creator.
—John A. O'Brien, *The Origin of Man*, 1947

Man is forever climbing up the ladder of secondary causes to the First and Supreme Cause—God Himself.
—John A. O'Brien, *Truths Men Live By*, 1947

Celibacy

It is an unnatural and impious thing to bar men of this Christian liberty, too severe and inhuman an edict.
—Robert Burton, *Anatomy of Melancholy*, III, 1621

Celibacy he [St. Paul] has no doubt is the ideal state, first because the time is short and detachment from the things of this age is required, and secondly because marriage diverts man and woman alike from the service of God.
—C.H. Dodd, *Evolution of Ethics*, 1927

He will possess an eminent degree of chastity so that the
mind which is to consecrate the body of Christ may be pure
and free from all defilement of the flesh.
> —St. Isidore of Seville (560–636), *The Perfection of the Clergy*

In this world men have a liking for women; he who
knows (and renounces) them will easily perform his duties
as a monk.
> —*Jaina Sutras*, between 600 and 200 B.C.

A preacher of the gospel, if he is able with a good conscience,
to remain unmarried, let him so remain; but if he cannot
abstain, living chastely, then let him take a wife; God has
made this plaster for that sore.
> —Martin Luther (1483–1546), *Table-Talk*

CERTAINTY

This restless, obstinate search after an unattainable
certainty is very evidently the work of nature, not of grace.
> —François Fénelon (1651–1715), *Spiritual Letters*

I am certain of nothing but of the holiness of the heart's
affections, and the truth of the Imagination.
> —John Keats, letter, November 22, 1817

Man cannot accept certainties; he must discover them.
> —John Middleton Murry, *The Necessity of Art*, 1919

[Christians] cannot give easy answers, the simplistic
guarantee of heaven, visions of certainty, the security of
escape from the essential, never-ending quest for meaning
that is the mark of those who are in touch with the spirit of
our century. We cannot give what we do not have. Certainty
has never been our possession. It has always been our
illusion.
> —John Shelby Spong, *Into the Whirlwind*, 1983

CHANCE

The doctrine of Chance in the eternal world corresponds to
that of Free Will in the internal.
> —Henry Thomas Buckle, *History of Civilization in England*, Vol. I, 1913

Chance implies an absolute absence of any principle.
> —Chuang-tzu (4th century B.C.), in *Texts of Taoism*, ed. J. Legge

Again I saw that under the sun the race is not to the swift, nor the battle to the strong, nor bread to the wise, nor riches to the intelligent, nor favor to the men of skill; but time and chance happen to them all.
>—*Holy Bible*, Ecclesiastes 9:11

Chance cannot possibly be the origin of things. For it presupposes an encounter of causal series. . . . Chance, that is to say, necessarily implies preordination. To hold that the universe can be explained by a primordial chance is self-contradictory.
>—Jacques Maritain, *Metaphysics*, 1939

The way we face this factor of chance helps to determine the spirit and quality of our lives. When we count on chance in lieu of preparation and prudence we weaken our characters.
>—Ralph W. Sockman, *The Meaning of Suffering*, 1961

His Sacred Majesty, Chance, decides everything.
>—Voltaire, letter, February 26, 1767

CHANGE

In spite of all our hopes, dreams, and efforts, change is real and forever. Accept it fearlessly. Investigate the unknown; neither fear nor worship it.
>—Joseph A. Bauer, "Love Me Tender, Love Me True,"
>*Religious Humanism*, Summer 1991

We must adjust to changing times and still hold to unchanging principles.
>—Jimmy Carter, quoting his high-school teacher Julia Coleman,
>inaugural address, January 20, 1977

God is on the side of the poor, the oppressed, the persecuted. When this faith is proclaimed and lived in a situation of political conflict between the rich and the poor, and when the rich and powerful reject this faith and condemn it as heresy, we can read the signs and discern something more than a crisis. We are faced with a *kairos*, a moment of truth, a time for decision, a time of grace, a God-given opportunity for conversion and hope.
>—Center of Concern, *The Road to Damascus:*
>*A Challenge to the Churches of the World*, 1989

I think that all human systems require continuous renewal. They rigidify. They get stiff in the joints. They forget what they cared about. The forces against it are nostalgia and the enormous appeal of having things the way they have always been, appeals to a supposedly happy past. But we've got to move on.

—John W. Gardner, in *The New York Times*, July 21, 1989

The seen is the changing, the unseen is the unchanging.

—Plato, *Phaedrus, Dialogues*, 399 B.C.

Religion will not regain its old power until it can face change in the same spirit as does science. Its principles may be eternal, but the expression of those principles requires continual development.

—Alfred North Whitehead, *Science and the Modern World*, 1927

He who rejects change is the architect of decay. The only human institution which rejects progress is the cemetery.

—Harold Wilson, in *The New York Times*, January 24, 1967

CHARACTER

The trouble with modern civilization is that we so often mistake respectability for character.

—Anonymous

There is no more important element in the formation of a virtuous character than a rightly directed sense of pleasure and dislike; for pleasure and pain are coextensive with life, and they exercise a powerful influence in promoting virtue and happiness in life.

—Aristotle, *Nicomachean Ethics*, c. 340 B.C.

Grandeur of character lies wholly in force of soul, not in the force of thought, moral principles, and love, and this may be found in the humblest conditions of life.

—William Ellery Channing, *Self-Culture*, 1838

An envious, stingy, dishonest man does not become respectable by means of much talking only, or by the beauty of his complexion.

—*Dhammapada*, c. 5th century B.C.

Although to be driven back upon oneself is an uneasy affair at best, rather like trying to cross a border with borrowed credentials, it seems to me now the one condition necessary to the beginnings of real self-respect. Most of our platitudes notwithstanding, self-deception remains the most difficult deception.

—Joan Didion, *Slouching Towards Bethlehem*, 1968

Whether on the floor of Congress or in the boardrooms of corporate America or in the corridors of a big city hospital, there is no body of professional expertise and no anthology of case studies which can supplant the force of character which provides both a sense of direction and a means of fulfillment. It asks, not what you want to be, but who you want to be.

—Elizabeth Hanford Dole, address, Dartmouth College commencement, *The New York Times*, June 6, 1991

Character isn't inherited. One builds it daily by the way one thinks and acts, thought by thought, action by action. If one lets fear or hate or anger take possession of the mind, they become self-forged chains.

—Helen Gahagan Douglas, speech, Marlboro College, 1975, *A Full Life*, 1982

That which we call character is a reserved force which acts directly by presence, and without means. It is conceived of as a certain undemonstrable force, a familiar or genius, by whose impulses the man is guided, but whose counsels he cannot impart.

—Ralph Waldo Emerson, "Character," *Essays*, 1844

Out of our beliefs are born deeds. Out of our deeds we form habits; out of our habits grow our characters; and on our character we build our destination.

—Henry Hancock, *Alpha Xi Delta Magazine*, 1957

Character is higher than intellect.

—Jean Paul Richter, *Tital*, 1803

The man who could write his name on a piece of paper, whether or not he possessed the spiritual fineness to honor those words in speech, was by some miraculous formula a more highly developed and sensitized person than the one who had never had a pen in hand, but whose spoken word was inviolable and whose sense of honor and truth was paramount. With false reasoning was the quality of human character measured by man's ability to make with an implement a mark upon paper.

—Luther Standing Bear, *Land of the Spotted Eagle*, 1933

While we inherit our temperament, we must build our character.

—William L. Sullivan, *Worry! Fear! Loneliness!*, 1950

Your character is developed according to your faith. This is the primary religious truth from which no one can escape.

—Alfred North Whitehead, *Religion in the Making*, 1927

Do not think about your character. If you will think about what you ought to do for other people, your character will take care of itself. Character is a by-product and any man who devotes himself to its cultivation in his own case will become a selfish prig.

—Woodrow Wilson, address, October 1914

CHARITY

That money will be more profitable to you . . . if you so give it to a poor man that you actually bestow it on Christ.

—St. Ambrose, *Exposit. Evan. Secundum Luc.*, 390

If there is among them *the Christians* a man that is poor and needy, and they have not an abundance of necessaries, they fast two or three days that they may supply the needy with their necessary food.

—Aristeides, *Apology*, c. 150

The chill of charity is the silence of the heart: the flame of charity is the clamor of the heart.

—St. Augustine, *Enarratio in Ps. XXXVII*, c. 415

The bread that you store up belongs to the hungry; the cloak that lies in your chest belongs to the naked; and the gold that you have hidden in the ground belongs to the poor.

—St. Basil, *Homilies*, c. 375

Charity is no substitute for justice, but it cannot be ignored or derided without failing utterly to comprehend its meaning and its potent influence in regulating and sublimating our social relations and responsibilities.

—Bishops of Administrative Board of National Catholic Welfare Council, *The Church and Social Order*, 1940

Let the rich minister aid to the poor; and let the poor give thanks to God, because He hath given him one through whom his wants may be supplied.

—St. Clement of Rome, *Epistle to the Corinthians*, c. 100

A disciple having asked for a definition of charity, the Master said LOVE ONE ANOTHER.
—Confucius (5th century B.C.), *Gems of Chinese Literature*, trans. by Giles.

If we want the perfect host to take us into his eternal home when we come to knock at his door, he has told us himself what we have to do: we must be ready to open our own door to the earthly guests that come our way.
—Jean Danielou, *The Lord of History*, 1958

This only is charity, to do all, all that we can.
—John Donne (1572–1631), *Sermons of*

Whosoever takes up the burden of his neighbor . . . and ministers unto those in need out of the abundance of things he has received and keeps out of God's bounty—this man becomes a god to those who receive from him, and this man is an imitator of God.
—*Epistle to Diognetus*, c. 200

Blessed is he who considers the poor! The Lord delivers him in the day of trouble.
—*Holy Bible*, Psalms 41:1

If there is among you a poor man, one of your brethren, any of your towns within your land which the Lord your God gives you, you shall not harden your heart or shut your hand against your poor brother, but you shall open your hand to him, and lend him sufficient for his need, whatever it may be.
—*Holy Bible*, Deuteronomy 15:7-8

The perfection of the Christian life principally and essentially consists in charity . . . which in some sort unites or joins man to his end.
—Pope John XXII (1316–34), the bull. *Ad Conditorem*

It would be a pious act to share our clothes and food even with the wicked. For it is to the humanity in a man that we give, and not to his moral character.
—Julian the Apostate (332–363), *Letter to a Priest*

If you give alms publicly, it is well; but it is better to give them secretly. Allah knows what you do.
—*Koran*, c. 625

Where has the Scripture made merit the rule or measure
of charity?
—William Law, *A Serious Call to the Devout and Holy Life*, 1728

Charity is an universal benevolence whose fulfillment the
wise carry out conformably to the dictates of reason so as to
obtain the greatest good.
—G.W. von Leibniz, letter to Arnauld, March 23, 1690

Whilst traces of divine power and wisdom appear even in the
wicked man, charity, which, as it were is the special mark of
the Holy Ghost, is shared in only by the just.
—Pope Leo XIII, *The Holy Spirit*, 1904

The term justice may even be used for charity; for charity
renders a man's will conformable to the whole law of God,
and accordingly charity in a way contains within itself the
sum of all the virtues.
—Lessius, *De Justitia et Jure*, Lib. 11, cap. 1, 1605

There are eight rungs in charity. The highest is when you
help a man to help himself.
—Maimonides, *Yad: Matnot Anigim*, 1180

Bread for myself is a material question; bread for my
neighbor is a spiritual question.
—Jacques Maritain, *Freedom in the Modern World*, 1936

The trick of living is to slip on and off the planet with the
least fuss you can muster. I'm not a professional
philanthropist, and I'm not running for sainthood. I just
happen to think that in life we need to be a little like the
farmer who puts back into the soil what he takes out.
—Paul Newman, in *Ladies' Home Journal*, July 1988

Charity is above all a hymn of love. Real, pure love is the gift
of oneself; it is the desire of diffusion and complete donation
that is an essential part of goodness.
—Pope Pius XII, address, April 3, 1940

Charity never humiliated him who profiteth from it, nor ever
bound him by the chains of gratitude, since it was not to him
but to God that the gift was made.
—Antoine de Saint-Exupéry, *Flight to Arras*, 1942

Of all your toil which God gives you, give in simplicity to all who need, not doubting to whom you shall give and to whom not; give to all, for to all God wishes gifts to be made of his own bounties.

—*Shepherd of Hermas*, c. 148

A clergyman wrote to a wealthy and influential businessman requesting a subscription to a worthy charity and soon received a curt refusal which ended, "As far as I can see, this Christian business is just one continuous Give, give, give." Replied the clergyman, "I wish to thank you for the best definition of the Christian life I have yet heard."

—W.F.A. Stride, in *Old Farmer's Almanac*, 1939

Whatever you give to others, give with love and reverence. Gifts must be given in abundance, with joy, humility, and compassion.

—*Taittiriya Upanishad*, prior to 400 B.C.

Charity knows no race no creed.

—*Talmud*, c. 500

He who gives alms in secret is greater than Moses.

—*Talmud*, c. 200

CHASTITY

Chastity takes its name from the fact that reason chastises concupiscence, which like a child, needs curbing.

—St. Thomas Aquinas, *Summa Theologiae*, 1272

Continence is a greater good than marriage.

—St. Augustine, *On the Good of Marriage*, c. 401

Continence is an angelic exercise.

—St. Augustine, *On the Good of Marriage*, c. 401

Chaste women are often proud and forward, as presuming upon the merit of their chastity.

—Francis Bacon, *Essays*, 1625

If you ask a chaste man why he is chaste, he should say, not on account of heaven or hell, and not on account of honour and disgrace, but solely because it would seem good to me and please me well even though it were not commanded.

—Martin Luther (1483–1546), *Works*, Vol. X

Of all forms of continence, the bridling of the tongue is the most difficult.
—Pythagoras (6th century B.C.), *Pythagoras Source Book*, ed. by K.S. Guthrie

Chastity is a wealth that comes from abundance of love.
—Rabindranath Tagore, *Stray Birds*, 1916

Salvation, in the case of men as well as of women, depends chiefly on the observance of chastity.
—Tertullian, *On Female Dress*, c. 220

Chastity is the flowering of man; and what are called Genius, Heroism, Holiness, and the like, are but various fruits which succeed it.
—Henry David Thoreau, *Walden*, 1854

The Counsel of Chastity . . . means the spirit of poverty applied to our emotional life—all the clutch and feverishness of desire, the "I want" and "I must have" taken away and replaced by absolute singlemindedness, purity of heart.
—Evelyn Underhill, *The Fruits of the Spirit*, 1942

CHILDREN

If a child is to keep alive his inborn sense of wonder, he needs the companionship of at least one adult who can share it, rediscovering with him the joy, excitement and mystery of the world we live in
—Rachel Carson, *The Sense of Wonder*, 1965

The spiritual interests of children have a lot to teach us. . . . I have listened to children of eight or nine or 10 getting to the heart of the Bible. I have found in elementary schools a good deal of spiritual curiosity that does not reflect mere indoctrination.
—Robert Coles, in *Time*, January 21, 1991

A child is a man in a small letter, yet the best copy of Adam before he tasted of Eve, or the Apple; . . . He is Nature's fresh picture newly drawn in oil, which time and much handling dims and defaces. His soul is yet a white paper unscribbled with observations of the world, wherewith at length it becomes a blurred notebook. He is purely happy because he knows no evil.
—John Earle, *Micro-Cosmographie*, 1628

Our children are growing up now in an ethically polluted
nation where substance is being sacrificed daily for shadow.
—Marian Wright Edelman, speech, Howard University, May 12, 1990

[A] society that puts the needs of its children dead last is a
society "progressing" rapidly toward moral ruin.
—Jean Bethke Elshtain, "Just War and American Politics,"
The Christian Century, January 15, 1992

The child-soul is an ever-bubbling fountain in the world of
humanity.
—Friedrich Froebel (1782–1852), *Aphorisms*

And they were bringing children to him, that he might touch
them; and the disciples rebuked them. But when Jesus saw
it he was indignant, and said to them, "Let the children come
to me, do not hinder them; for to such belongs the kingdom
of God. Truly, I say to you, whoever does not receive the
kingdom of God like a child shall not enter it.
—*Holy Bible*, Mark 10:13-15

Train up a child in the way he should go, and when he is old
he will not depart from it.
—*Holy Bible*, Proverbs 22:6

The sublimest song to be heard on earth is the lisping of the
human soul on the lips of children.
—Victor Hugo, *Ninety-Three*, 1874

We take care of our possessions for our children. But of the
children themselves we take no care at all. What an
absurdity is this! Form the soul of thy son aright, and all the
rest will be added hereafter.
—St. John Chrysostom (340–407), *Select Library of Nicene
and Post-Nicene Fathers*, Vol. 13, 1st Series

The unwarped child, with his spontaneous faith and
confidence in goodness, is the best illustration of that spirit
which fits the Kingdom of God.
—Rufus M. Jones, *The Testimony of the Soul*, 1936

Build me a son, O Lord, who will be strong enough to know
when he is weak and brave enough to face himself when he
is afraid . . . whose wishes will not take the place of deeds; a
son who will know Thee . . . whose heart will be clear, whose
goal will be high, a son who will master himself before he
seeks to master other men.
—Douglas MacArthur, in *The New York Times*, April 5, 1964

Every child comes with the message that God is not yet
discouraged of man.
—Rabindranath Tagore, *Stray Birds*, 1916

To bring into the world an unwanted human being is as
antisocial an act as murder.
—Gore Vidal, in *Esquire*, October 1968

CHRISTIANITY

My chief reason for choosing Christianity was because the
mysteries were incomprehensible. What's the point of
revelation if we could figure it out ourselves? If it were wholly
comprehensible, then it would be just another philosophy.
—Mortimer Adler, in *Christianity Today*, November 19, 1990

Because they acknowledge the goodness of God towards
them, lo! on account of them there flows forth the beauty
that is in the world.
—Aristeides, *Apology*, c. 150

For truly great and wonderful is their teaching to him that is
willing to examine and understand it. And truly this people is
a new people, and there is something divine mingled with it.
—Aristeides, *Apology*, c. 150

They [Christians] walk in humility and kindness, and
falsehood is not found among them, and they love one
another. They despise not the widow, and grieve not the
orphan. He that hath distributeth liberally to him that
hath not.
—Aristeides, *Apology*, c. 150

To a world stricken with moral enervation Christianity
offered its spectacle of an inspired self-sacrifice; to men who
refused themselves nothing, it showed one who refused
himself everything.
—Matthew Arnold, *Culture and Anarchy*, 1869

We claim to be Christian, but that is a claim never really
verified or completed. It is rather a process of becoming,
since man is by definition one who becomes himself—a
painful but glorious process, as history tells us.
—Daniel Berrigan, "Statement at Sentencing,"
Prison Journals, May 24, 1968

Christianity is an uneasy, a tragic, an impossible faith, in high tension between the real and the ideal, the "is" and the "ought"—that is one of the sources of its strength.
—Crane Brinton, *A History of Western Morals*, 1959

Christianity is a scheme beyond our comprehension.
—Joseph Butler, *Analogy of Religion*, 1736

Christianity, even if it cannot persuade men to rise to the contemplation of the spiritual things, embodies principles which may at least have the effect of bringing the dreamers down to earth. Because it confronts the problem of human sin, it can face our difficulties and dilemmas without evasions.
—Herbert Butterfield, *Christianity, Diplomacy and War*, 1953

Thus, whatever elements of truth, whatever broken and scattered rays of light the old religions contained, Christianity takes up into itself, explaining all, harmonizing all, by a divine alchemy transmuting all, yet immeasurably transcending all.
—John Caird, *An Introduction to the Philosophy of Religion*, 1880

Its truth and greatness come to an end on the cross, at the moment when this man cries out that he has been forsaken. If we tear out these last pages of the New Testament, then what we see set forth is a religion of loneliness and grandeur. Certainly, its bitterness makes it unbearable. But that is its truth.
—Albert Camus, *Notebooks*, 1935–1942

How did Christianity arise and spread abroad among men?
. . . It arose in the mystic deeps of man's soul; and was spread abroad by the "preaching of the word," by simple, altogether natural and individual efforts; and flew, like hallowed fire, from heart to heart, till all were purified and illuminated by it.
—Thomas Carlyle, *Critical and Miscellaneous Essays*, 1857

The more I examine Christianity, the more I am struck with its universality. I see in it a religion made for all regions and all times, for all classes and all stages of society.
—William Ellery Channing (1780–1842), *Works*

Christianity is always out of fashion because it is always sane; and all fashions are mild insanities.
—G.K. Chesterton, *The Ball and the Cross*, 1909

The goal of the Christian life is not to save your soul but to transcend yourself, to vindicate the human struggle of which all of us are a part, to keep hope advancing.
—William Sloane Coffin, *Living the Truth in a World of Illusions*, 1985

To be a Christian is not purely to serve God, but it is also an ethic, a service to mankind; it is not merely a theology but also an anthropology.
—Albert Dondeyne, *Faith and the World*, 1962

Even those who have renounced Christianity and attack it, in their inmost being still follow the Christian ideal, for hitherto neither their subtlety nor the ardor of their hearts has been able to create a higher ideal of man and of virtue than the ideal given by Christ of old.
—Feodor Dostoevsky, *The Brothers Karamazov*, 1880

Men of simple understanding, little inquisitive, and little instructed, make good Christians.
—Michel de Montaigne, *Essays*, 1580

Those whom we see to be Christians without the knowledge of the prophets and evidences, nevertheless judge of their religion as well as those who have that knowledge. They judge it by the heart, as others judge of it by the intellect.
—Blaise Pascal, *Pensées*, 1670

The true Christian, product of a Christian education, is the supernatural man who thinks, judges, and acts consistently in accordance with right reason illumined by the supernatural light of the example and teaching of Christ.
—Pope Pius XI, *Encyclical on Christian Education*, 1931

The true Christian is the true citizen, lofty of purpose, resolute in endeavor, ready for a hero's deeds, but never looking down on his task because it is cast in the day of small things.
—Theodore Roosevelt, speech, December 30, 1900

Before the twelfth century the nations were too savage to be Christian, and after the fifteenth too carnal to be Christian.
—John Ruskin, *Val d'Arno*, 1874

Penetrate a little beneath the diversity of circumstances, and it becomes evident that in Christians of different epochs . . . there is veritably a single fundamental and identical spirit of piety and charity, common to those who have received grace; an inner state which before all things is one of love and humility, of infinite confidence in God, and of severity for one's self, accompanied with tenderness for others.
—C.A. Sainte-Beuve, *Port Royal*, I, 1860

In other religions, one must be purified before he can knock at the door; in Christianity, one knocks on the door as a sinner, and He Who answers to us heals.
—Fulton J. Sheen, *Peace of Soul*, 1949

A man becomes a Christian, he is not born one.
—Tertullian, *Testimony of the Soul*, c. 210

Whatever makes men good Christians makes them good citizens.
—Daniel Webster, speech, December 22, 1820

If you wish your children to be Christians you must really take the trouble to be Christian yourselves. Those are the only terms upon which the home will work the gracious miracle.
—Woodrow Wilson, address, October 1904

No man is a true Christian who does not think constantly of how he can lift his brother, how he can assist his friend, how he can enlighten mankind, how he can make virtue the rule of conduct in the circle in which he lives.
—Woodrow Wilson, address, October 1914

CHURCH

The real Church is the lowliest, the poorest, the meanest, weakest thing that can possibly exist under God's heaven, gathered as it is around a manger and a Cross. . . . And the real Church is also the highest, richest, most radiant and mighty thing under God's heaven.
—Karl Barth, *Community, Church and State*, 1946

A church needs poor men and wicked men as much as it needs pure men and virtuous men and pious men.
—Henry Ward Beecher (1813–87), sermon

We have become a Church of administrations and institutions, expressions of our consuming desire to "belong," to win a secure niche for ourselves, and with our energies engaged in erecting and maintaining our structures we often forget why we raised them at all.
—Philip Berrigan, *No More Strangers*, 1965

Wherever we see the Word of God purely preached and heard, and the sacraments administered according to Christ's institution, there, it is not to be doubted, a church of God exists.
—John Calvin, *Institutes*, IV, 1536

It is a miracle in itself that anything so huge and historic in date and design should be so fresh in the affections. It is as if a man should find his own parlor and fireside in the heart of the Great Pyramid.
—G.K. Chesterton, *Catholic Church and Conversion*, 1926

The great achievement of the Catholic Church lay in harmonizing, civilizing the deepest impulses of ordinary, ignorant people.
—Kenneth Clark, *Civilization*, 1970

It is the peculiar property of the Church that when she is buffeted she is triumphant, when she is assaulted with argument she proves herself in the right, when she is deserted by her supporters she holds the field.
—St. Hilary of Poitiers (c. 315–367), *On the Trinity*

A community of solitude before God.
—Richard Hocking, in *Bulletin of GeneralTheological Seminary*, June 1951

The miracle is that the divine nature of the Church is not altogether obscured by the all too human nature of her members.
—Walter Marshall Horton, *Christian Theology*, 1958

Where the Church is, there is the Spirit of God; and where the Spirit of God is, there is the church and all grace, and the Spirit is truth.
—St. Irenaeus, *Contra Haereses*, III, c. 175

Church in Greek means convocation, or assembly in Latin, because all are called to be members of it.
—St. Isidore, *Etymologies*, c. 634

The Church sometimes forgets that at least part of her divine commission is "to comfort the afflicted and to afflict the comfortable."

—John E. Large, *The Small Needle of Doctor Large*, 1962

The expectation that with integration blacks would rush to join white [church] denominations never materialized. The fact is the black church has remained the institution that consistently reflects the aspirations and hopes and lives of African-Americans. That has given it a certain stability that white denominations can only hope to emulate.

—C. Eric Lincoln, in *Ebony*, August 1991

Church: A place in which gentlemen who have never been to Heaven brag about it to persons who will never get there.

—H.L. Mencken, *A Little Book in C Major*, 1916

The mystery of the Church consists in the very fact that *together* sinners become *something different* from what they are as individuals; this "something different" is the Body of Christ.

—J. Meyendorff, *Ecumenical Review*, 1960

There is a true Church wherever one hand meets another helpfully, and that is the only holy or Mother Church which ever was, or ever shall be.

—John Ruskin, *Sesame and Lilies*, 1865

We look upon this visible church, though black and spotted, as the hospital and guest-house of sick, halt, maimed, and withered, over which Christ is Lord, Physician, and Master.

—Samuel Rutherford (1600–61), *Letters of* (Letter CCCLXIV)

In times of prosperity the church administers; in times of adversity the church shepherds.

—Fulton J. Sheen, *The Priest Is Not His Own*, 1963

The authority of the Church is not the consecrated earthly image of the Heavenly Ruler of the Church, but it is a medium through which the Spiritual substance of our lives is preserved and protected and reborn.

—Paul Tillich, *The New Being*, 1955

Although the Church may actually never yet have expressed Christianity to perfection, there is at least no inherent impediment here to the attainment of a perfect harmony, since the Church has been called into existence for this purpose and no other.
—Arnold J. Toynbee, *A Study of History*, V, 1939

In general the churches, visited by me too often on weekdays . . . bore for me the same relation to God that billboards did to Coca-Cola; they promoted thirst without quenching it.
—John Updike, *A Month of Sundays*, 1975

CHURCH AND STATE

If the Church takes up its share of political responsibility, it must mean that it is taking that human initiative which the State cannot take; it is giving the State the impulse which it cannot give itself.
—Karl Barth, *Community, Church and State*, 1946

The "establishment of religion" clause of the First Amendment means at least this: Neither a State nor the Federal Government can set up a church. Neither can pass laws which aid one religion, aid all religion, or prefer one religion to another.
—Justice Hugo L. Black, U.S. Supreme Court, majority decision, *Everson vs. Board of Education of Township of Ewing, New Jersey*, 1947

We repeat and again reaffirm that neither a state nor the Federal Government can constitutionally force a person "to profess a belief or disbelief in any religion." Neither can constitutionally pass laws or impose requirements which aid all religions as against non-believers, and neither can aid those religions based on a belief in the existence of God as against those religions founded on different beliefs.
—Justice Hugo L. Black, U.S. Supreme Court, *Torcaso vs. Watkins*, 1961

Those whom they are accustomed to call clerics—should once for all be kept absolutely free from all public offices, that they be not withdrawn away by any error or sacrilegious fault from the worship which they owe to the Divinity, but rather without any hindrance serve to the utmost of their own law.
—Emperor Constantine, to Anulinus, quoted in Eusebius, *Ecclesiastical History*, c. 325

Congress shall make no law respecting an establishment of religion, or prohibiting the free exercise thereof.
—*Constitution of the United States*, Amendment I, December 15, 1791

Leave the matter of religion to the family altar, the church and the private school, supported entirely by private contributions. Keep the church and the State forever separate.

—Ulysses S. Grant, speech, Des Moines, Iowa, 1875

When churches succumb to the pressures of secular life and fail to exhibit a distinctive quality of faith and life, the separation of church and state . . . loses its point.

—W.S. Hudson, *The Great Tradition of American Churches*, 1953

I believe in an America where the separation of church and state is absolute, where no Catholic prelate would tell the President (should he be a Catholic) how to act and no Protestant minister would tell his parishioners for whom to vote.

—John F. Kennedy, speech, Houston, Texas, September 12, 1960

With us, separation of church and state was never intended to mean separation of religion from society.

—James A. Pike, in *The New York Times*, July 13, 1962

The dogmas of civil religion ought to be few, simple. . . . The existence of a mighty, intelligent, and beneficent Divinity, possessed of foresight and providence, the life to come, the happiness of the just, the punishment of the wicked, the sanctity of the social contract and the laws; these are its positive dogmas; its negative dogmas I confine to one, intolerance.

—Jean Jacques Rousseau, *The Social Contract*, 1762

Our constitutional policy . . . does not deny the value or necessity for religious training, teaching or observance. Rather it secures their free exercise. But to that end it does deny that the state can undertake or sustain them in any form or degree.

—Justice Wiley Blount Rutledge, dissenting opinion, *Everson v. Board of Education of Township of Ewing, New Jersey*, 1947

God requireth not any uniformity of religion to be enacted and enforced in any civil state.

—Roger Williams, *The Bloudy Tenant of Persecution*, 1644

CLERGY

I don't believe women can be priests any more than they can be fathers or husbands.

—John M. Allin, in *The New York Times*, October 1, 1977

Preacher's silent prayer before speaking:
Lord, fill my mouth with worthwhile stuff,
And nudge me when I've said enough.

—Anonymous

Vainly does the preacher utter the Word of God exteriorly
unless he listens to it interiorly.
—St. Augustine (354–430), *Sermon* CLXXIX

The essence of the priest is that he should believe himself,
however humbly and secretly, to be set in a certain sense
between humanity and God.
—Arthur Christopher Benson, *From a College Window*, 1906

We who are charged with announcing the message of Christ
need to learn the incomparable lesson that he taught us by
his own example. He taught first of all with his life, and only
then did he preach.
—Dom Helder Camara, in Penny Lernoux, *People of God*, 1989

If I had to counsel a young preacher, I should say: When
there is any difference felt between the foot-board of the
pulpit and the floor of the parlor, you have not yet said that
which you should say.
—Ralph Waldo Emerson, address, May 25, 1879

[A rabbi] should not despair if people do not do as much as
they should. Every parent has that with children. God is
merciful.
—Rabbi Louis Finkelstein, in *The New York Times*, September 1, 1985

The test of a preacher is that his congregation goes away
saying, not What a lovely sermon, but I will do something!
—St. Francis de Sales, *Introduction to the Devout Life*, 1609

To a philosophic eye the vices of the clergy are far less
dangerous than their virtues.
—Edward Gibbon, *The Decline and Fall of the Roman Empire*, I, 1776

The pastors are to be fervidly zealous about the inner
wants of their subjects, without neglecting the care of their
outer wants.
—Pope St. Gregory the Great, *Pastoral Care*, 590

The priest is the same as the people, when he does the same
as they do, and has the same aspirations as they.
—Pope St. Gregory the Great, *Pastoral Care*, 590

The Redeemer of mankind in the day-time exhibits His miracles in cities, and spends the night in devotion to prayer upon the mountain, namely, that He may teach all perfect preachers, that they should neither entirely leave the active life, from love of the speculative, nor wholly slight the joys of contemplation.

—Pope St. Gregory the Great, *Morals on the Book of Job*, 584

Many wear God's clothes that know not their Master.

—Joseph Hall, *Meditations and Vows*, 1606

Priests are no more necessary to religion than politicians to patriotism.

—John Haynes Holmes, *Sensible Man's View of Religion*, 1933

And I will give you shepherds after my own heart, who will feed you with knowledge and understanding.

—*Holy Bible*, Jeremiah 3:15

I want them "dunked"—plunged deeply into life, brought up gasping and dripping, and returned to us humble and ready to learn.

—Reul Howe, *Anglican World*, on candidates for the priesthood, 1964

He, beyond all others, should make it his special duty to read the Scriptures, to study the canons, to imitate the examples of the saints, to give himself up to watching, fasting and prayer, to preserve peace with his brethren, to despise no member of the Church, to condemn no one without proof, to excommunicate no one without consideration.

—St. Isidore of Seville (560–636), *The Perfection of the Clergy*

Avoid, as you would the plague, a clergyman who is also a man of business.

—St. Jerome (340–420), *Letter to Nepotian*

Since we are all priests alike no man may put himself forward, or take upon himself, without our consent or election, to do that which we all alike have power to do.

—Martin Luther, *Address to the Christian Nobility of the German Nation*, 1520

One of the men of the French court once said to a famous court preacher, "Sire, your sermons terrify me, but your life reassures me."

—Clarence E. Macartney, *Preaching Without Notes*, 1946

[T]here are women who, with full episcopal authority, are performing all the priestly functions except the sacramental ones: this must call into very serious question the traditional understanding of what priesthood is and indeed what the role of the sacraments is within a Christian community.
—Sara Maitland, *A Map of the New Country Women and Christianity*, 1983

Were I a preacher, I should, above all other things, preach the practice of *the presence of* God.
—Nicholas Herman of Lorraine, Brother Lawrence,
Practice of the Presence of God, c. 1666

The priest is concerned with other people for the sake of God and with God for the sake of other people.
—Robert A.K. Runcie, Archbishop of Canterbury, "The Character of a Priest,"
Seasons of the Spirit, 1983

It is far better to have fewer and good priests than to have many and bad priests, for these last call down the anger of God upon the cities and the peoples.
—Girolamo Savonarola, *Sermon Against Tyrants*, 1497

The minister's task is to lead men from what they want to what they need.
—Ralph W. Sockman, *The Highway of God*, 1941

The task of the preacher is to lift men above the low view of their times, to give them the elevation and outlook which enables them to distinguish currents from eddies.
—Ralph W. Sockman, *The Highway of God*, 1941

The priest should be a man above human weaknesses. He should be a stranger to every diversion. . . . All eyes keep watch upon him to see that he fulfills his mission. He is of little use or none, unless he has made himself austere, unyielding to any form of pleasure.
—Synesius, *To His Brother*, c. 400

There is nothing the clergyman can know which the layman cannot know. Clergymen are not more adept than others at the art of worship and may be less so.
—D.E. Trueblood, *The Logic of Belief*, 1942

There is something uniquely valuable that women and men bring to ordained ministry, and it has been distorted and defective as long as women have been debarred. Somehow men have been less human for this loss.
—Bishop Desmond Tutu, *Crying in the Wilderness*, 1978

The number of good preachers may have decreased. But so
has the number of good listeners.
—Spencer Wilson, in *The Times* (London), August 20, 1968

Whenever any are true ministers of Jesus Christ, it is from
the operation of His Spirit upon their hearts, first purifying
them, and thus giving them a just sense of the conditions
of others.
—John Woolman, *The Journal of*, 1774

COERCION

The lash may force men to physical labor; it cannot force
them to spiritual creativity.
—Sholem Asch, *What I Believe*, 1941

Kings and bishops cannot command the wind, so they
cannot command faith; and as the wind bloweth where it
listeth, so it is [with] every man that is born of the Spirit.
—Leonard Busher, *Religious Peace*, 1614

We need only ask those who force consciences, "Would you
like to have yours forced?" and immediately their own
consciences, which are worth more than a thousand
witnesses, will convict and make them dumb.
—Sebastian Castellio, (1513–63), *Counsel to France in Her Distress*

No human power can force the impenetrable entrenchments
of liberty in the human heart. Force can never persuade
men; it can only make them hypocrites.
—François Fénelon (1651–1715), *Selections from*

Compulsion in religion is distinguished peculiarly from
compulsion in every other thing. I may grow rich by an art I
am compelled to follow; I may recover health by medicines I
am compelled to take against my own judgment; but I
cannot be saved by a worship I disbelieve and abhor.
—Thomas Jefferson, *Notes on Religion*, 1776

Millions of innocent men, women and children, since the
introduction of Christianity, have been burned, tortured,
fined and imprisoned, yet we have not advanced one inch
toward uniformity. What has been the effect of coercion?
To make one half of the world fools and the other half
hypocrites.
—Thomas Jefferson, *Notes on Virginia*, 1782

Since by nature all men are equal in human dignity, it follows that no one may be coerced to perform interior acts. That is in the power of God alone, Who sees and judges the hidden designs of men's hearts.

—Pope John XXIII, *Pacem in Terris*, April 1963

Let there be no compulsion in religion.

—*Koran*, c. 625

The Church is wont to take earnest heed that no one shall be forced to embrace the Catholic faith against his will, for, as St. Augustine wisely reminds us, "Man cannot believe otherwise than of his own free will."

—Pope Leo XIII, *The Christian Constitution of States*, 1885

Since belief or unbelief is a matter of everyone's conscience . . . the secular power should be content to attend to its own affairs, and permit men to believe one thing or another as they are able and willing, and constrain no one by force.

—Martin Luther, *On Secular Authority*, 1522

That Religion, or the duty which we owe to our Creator, and the manner of discharging it, can be directed only by reason and conviction, not by force or violence.

—James Madison, *Journal of the Virginia Convention*, 1776

The man who says to me, "Believe as I do, or God will damn you," will presently say, "Believe as I do, or I shall assassinate you."

—Voltaire, *Treatise on Toleration*, 1766

COMFORT

We cannot go to Heaven on beds of down.

—Richard Braithwaite, *The English Gentlemen*, 1631

God laughs at a man who says to his soul, Take thy ease.

—Abraham Cowley, *Of Myself*, 1665

The lust for comfort, that stealthy thing that enters the house as a guest, and then becomes a host, and then a master.

—Kahlil Gibran, *The Prophet*, 1923

Come to me, all who labor and are heavy laden, and I will give you rest.

—*Holy Bible*, Matthew 11:28

87

COMFORT

Who can for very shame desire to enter into the Kingdom of Christ with ease, when himself entered not into his own without pain?

—Sir Thomas More, *Dialogue of Comfort*, 1535

The Superior Man rests in this—that he will indulge in no luxurious ease.

—*Shu Ching*, 6th century B.C.

Whatsoever I can desire or imagine for my comfort: I look for it not here, but hereafter. For if I might alone have all the comforts of the world and enjoy all its delights: it is certain that they could not long endure.

—St. Thomas à Kempis, *Imitation of Christ*, 1441

COMMANDMENTS

Let not one kill any living being. Let not one take what is not given to him. Let not one speak falsely. Let not one drink intoxicating drinks. Let not one be unchaste.

—Buddha (563–483 B.C.), "Five Moral Rules," quoted in R.C. Dutt,
Civilization of India

You shall love the Lord your God with all your heart, and with all your soul, and with all your mind. This is the great and first commandment. And a second is like it, you shall love your neighbor as yourself. On these two commandments depend all the law and the prophets.

—*Holy Bible*, Matthew 22:37-40

There is no set of laws, not even the Ten Commandments, which came directly from heaven in finished form and to which we must conform. . . . There is also no such thing as sin in the technical sense.

—Walter Donald Kring, sermon, *The New York Times*, December 3, 1962

The old formulas, which we still regard as holy command-ments . . . become empty words because they no longer fit the trend of time.

—Henry Lanz, *In Quest of Morals*, 1941

Without commandments, obliging us to live after a certain fashion, our existence is that of the "unemployed." This is the terrible spiritual situation in which the best youth of the world finds itself today. By dint of feeling itself free, exempt from restrictions, it feels itself empty.

—José Ortega y Gasset, *Revolt of the Masses*, 1930

COMMITMENT

Commitment does not stop with contemplation. It seeks issue in work. For the God discovered thus is a God at work, reconciling the world to Himself.
—Robert L. Calhoun, *God and the Common Life*, 1935

One of the disconcerting facts about the spiritual life is that God takes you at your word.
—Dorothy Day, *The Long Loneliness*, 1952

You shall be careful to perform what has passed your lips, for you have voluntarily vowed to the Lord your God what you have promised with your mouth.
—*Holy Bible*, Deuteronomy 23:23

There can be no true knowledge of ultimate things, that is to say, of God and man, of duty and destiny, that is not born in a concern and perfected in a commitment.
—John Mackay, *A Preface to Christian Theology*, 1941

A life without surrender is a life without commitment.
—Jerry Rubin, *Growing (Up) at 37*, 1976

Commitment means that it is possible for a man to yield the nerve center of his consent to a purpose or cause, a movement or an ideal, which may be more important to him than whether he lives or dies.
—Howard Thurman, *Disciplines of the Spirit*, 1963

COMMUNITY

We were born to unite with our fellowmen, and to join in community with the human race.
—Cicero, *De Finibus*, c. 50 B.C.

Entirely by yourself as an individual you can go to hell, but alone you cannot go to heaven, for to go to heaven we need what one may call the natural grace of the mutual dependence on each other here on earth.
—Francis Devas, *The Law of Love*, 1955

They all knelt together and suddenly—not a barrier of any kind remained, not a sundering distinction in the whole throng; but every life flamed into the other, and all flamed into the one Life and were hushed in ineffable peace.
—Zephrine Humphrey, *The Edge of the Woods and Other Papers*, 1913

Do not try to persuade yourselves that you can do anything good on your own; on the contrary, do all in common; one prayer, one petition, one mind, one hope in the unity of love and in innocent joy—this is Jesus Christ than whom there is nothing higher.
—St. Ignatius of Antioch, *Letter to the Magnesians*, c. 109

Prayers for the community take precedence over those for ourselves . . . and he who sets its claim above his private interests is especially acceptable to God.
—Flavius Josephus, *Against Apion*, c. A.D. 93

The ultimate issue of "community" is, What do we owe other people? In our society, where individualism plays such an important role, we don't have a public ethic about what we owe others.
—Dan Lewis, in *Time*, June 27, 1988

We are not isolated souls, singular, lonely, called and engaged in a solitary effort. We are members of a great Company, and whether we think it or not, we pray in Company.
—John W. Lynch, *Hourglass*, 1952

Community is important because discipleship is costly. It is a formidable task, beyond the scope of any individual, to challenge empires and religious authorities that oppress the poor. Jesus, of course, does not promise his followers an easy life. However, he does promise that in the midst of costly discipleship they will find that many of the things they sacrifice will be experienced more fully in community.
—Jack Nelson-Pallmeyer, *Brave New World Order*, 1992

People are coming to church not simply to partake of the sacred but to partake of sacred community.
—Milton J. Rosenberg, in *Pastoral Psychology*, June 1957

We hunger for a kind of group association in which, through being ourselves, we may get to something greater than ourselves. We long to touch the transcendent, and, furthermore, to do it in the company of others who, by sharing our experiences, verify and confirm them.
—Milton J. Rosenberg, in *Pastoral Psychology*, June 1957

Not through imitating nor yet through loving any mere individual human being can we be saved, but only through loyalty to the "Beloved Community."
—Josiah Royce, *The Problem of Christianity*, I, 1908

The church is a community of Christ, bought with a price, where everyone is welcome. In this new community the presence of the risen Lord continues to break open its traditions so that life in the Spirit is always in the process of being renewed, and worship itself includes the daily practice of hospitality or table fellowship with the stranger.
—Letty M. Russell, "Bought with a Price," *The Christian Century,* January 29, 1992

What the world desperately needs is bridges, individuals and groups who, like Christ himself, put an end to all the distances which divide men and which hinder their access to truth, dignity, and full human development. This is another way of saying that the world needs community; it needs models of community to convince it that the diverse and warring elements in the human family can be reconciled.
—Sisters of the Immaculate Heart, Los Angeles, 1967, quoted in Sarah Bentley Doely, ed., *Women's Liberation and the Church*

The dominant fact of the twentieth century is that the entire population of the earth is now included within a single community. There are no more ocean barriers, no mountain barriers, no barriers of the north and south poles, no barriers of any kind. There is only one race now—it is the human race.
—Obert C. Tanner, *One Man's Search,* 1989

Often communities that are the most cohesive are also hostile and fearful of outsiders. Community spirit says, "Take care of your own." The ethical challenge is to make people see that the world is their community.
—Richard Taub, in *Time,* June 27, 1988

The moving finger of God in human history points ever in the same direction. There must be community.
—Howard Thurman, *Disciplines of the Spirit,* 1963

COMPASSION

Compassion is as natural as respiration.
—Joseph De Maistre, *Les Soirées de Saint-Petersbourg,* 1821

Compassion is the chief law of human existence.
—Feodor Dostoevsky, *The Idiot,* 1869

In the alchemy of man's soul almost all noble attributes—
courage, honor, love, hope, faith, duty, loyalty, and so on—
can be transmuted into ruthlessness. Compassion alone
stands apart from the continuous traffic between good and
evil proceeding within us. Compassion is the antitoxin of the
soul: where there is compassion, even the most poisonous
impulses remain relatively harmless.

—Eric Hoffer, *Between the Devil and the Dragon*, 1982

I sought my soul but my soul I could not see. I sought my
God but my God eluded me. I sought my brother—and I
found all three.

—London Church News Services, May 1986

Jesus was murdered because the Spirit he experienced and
embodied reflected a compassionate God. The society he
confronted, despite religious appearances, could not tolerate
compassion. . . . It is one of the tragedies of the Jesus story
and our own that unjust societies in desperate need of
compassion are often incapable of receiving it precisely
because compassion challenges the privileges and power of
those who benefit from existing inequalities.

—Jack Nelson-Pallmeyer, *Brave New World Order*, 1992

For though our Saviour's Passion is over, his Compassion is
not.

—William Penn, *Some Fruits of Solitude*, 1693

I wept because I had no shoes, then I met a man who had
no feet.

—Sa'di (1193–1292)

All the kindness which a man puts out into the world works
on the heart and thoughts of mankind.

—Albert Schweitzer, *Memoirs of Childhood and Youth*, 1931

God is in every created being or thing: be cruel towards
none, neither abuse any by intemperance.

—Jeremy Taylor, *Holy Living*, 1650

Kindness has converted more people than zeal, science, or
eloquence.

—Mother Teresa, *Contemplative in the Heart of the World*, 1985

The hidden and awful Wisdom which apportions the
destinies of mankind is pleased so to humiliate and cast
down the tender, good and wise; and to set up the selfish,
the foolish, or the wicked. Oh, be humble, my brother, in
your prosperity! Be gentle with those who are less lucky, if
not more deserving.

—William Makepeace Thackeray, *Vanity Fair*, 1848

Our lack of compassion, our ruthlessness towards other
men, is an impenetrable curtain between ourselves and God.

—Alexander Yelchaninov (1881–1934), *Fragments of a Diary*

COMPETITION

Just as the unity of human society cannot be built upon
class warfare, so the proper ordering of economic affairs
cannot be left to free competition alone.

—Pope Pius XI, *Quadragesimo Anno*, 1931

The principle of competition appears to be nothing more than
a partially conventionalized embodiment of primeval
selfishness . . . the supremacy of the motive of self-interest. . . .
The Christian conscience can be satisfied with nothing less
than the complete substitution of motives of mutual
helpfulness and goodwill for the motive of private gain.

—*Social Creed*, Federal Council of Churches of Christ in America, 1932

A competitive society is a society of envy.

—Dorothee Sölle, *The Arms Race Kills*, trans. by Gerhard A. Elston, 1983

CONCEIT

Do not say things. What you are stands over you the while,
and thunders so that I cannot hear what you say to the
contrary.

—Ralph Waldo Emerson, *Letters and Social Aims*, 1876

Only by the supernatural is man strong; nothing is so weak
as an egotist.

—Ralph Waldo Emerson, *The Young American*, 1844

Conceit lies in thinking you want nothing.

—Epictetus, *Moral Discourses*, c. 110

When all else has been subjugated, only the vice of vainglory
lurks in the midst of the virtues.

—Desiderius Erasmus, *Enchiridion*, 1501

I am glad I am guilty of some sins, else I might be guilty of one of the greatest sins of all—conceit.

—M. Hurwitz, *Imre Noam*, 1877

To identify consciousness with that which merely reflects consciousness—this is egoism.

—Patanjali (2nd century B.C.), *Yoga Aphorisms*

No sickness worse than imagining thyself to be perfect can afflict thy soul.

—Jallaludin Rumi (1207–73), *Masnavi*

The wise of all the earth have said in their hearts always, "God is, and there is none beside Him"; and the fools of all the earth have said in their hearts always, "I am, and there is none beside me."

—John Ruskin, *For Clavigera*, 1880

Account not thyself better than others lest peradventure thou be held worse in the sight of God that knoweth what is in man.

—Thomas à Kempis, *Imitation of Christ*, 1441

If you do not see clearly, but are still arrogant about your attainment, then you will totally lose whatever power you have gained. The relationship between your arrogance and your abilities is quite exact.

—Tripitaka Master Hua, "Contemplating the Oneness of Everything," *Vajra Bodhi Sea*, March 1992

CONDUCT AND BEHAVIOR

Christian conduct is the operation of the rational soul in accordance with a correct judgment and aspiration after the truth, which attains its destined end through the body, the soul's consort and ally.

—St. Clement of Alexandria, *The Instructor*, Ch. 13, c. 220

The true guide of our conduct is no outward authority, but the voice of God, who comes down to dwell in our souls, who knows all our thoughts.

—J.E.E. Dalberg-Acton (Lord Acton), address, 1877

The earthly city is never free from the dangers of bloodshed, sedition and war. A human being cannot even be certain of "his own conduct on the morrow," let alone specify and adjudicate that of others in ways he or she foreordains. In this world of discontinuities and profound yearnings, of sometimes terrible necessities, a human being can yet strive to maintain or to create an order that approximates justice; to prevent the worst from happening; and to resist the seductive lure of imperial grandiosity.

—Jean Bethke Elshtain, "Just War and American Politics,"
The Christian Century, January 15, 1992

My generation of radicals and breakersdown never found anything to take the place of the old virtues of work and courage and the old graces of courtesy and politeness.

—F. Scott Fitzgerald (1896–1940), letter to his daughter, in *The Letters of*, 1963

As I have seen, those who plow iniquity and sow trouble reap the same.

—*Holy Bible*, Job 5:8

Give to him who begs from you, and do not refuse him who would borrow from you.

—*Holy Bible*, Matthew 5:42

When you give a dinner or a banquet, do not invite your friends or your brothers or your kinsmen or rich neighbors, lest they also invite you in return, and you be repaid. But when you give a feast, invite the poor, the maimed, the lame, the blind.

—*Holy Bible*, Luke 14:12-13

The human race is tolerated in the universe only on strict condition of good behavior.

—L.P. Jacks, *Constructive Citizenship*, 1928

On Judgment Day, God will not ask to what sect you belonged, but what manner of life you led.

—I.M. Kagan, *Hafetz Hayyim*, 1873

Do the best you can, no matter how insignificant it may seem at the time. While you may be a lowly foot soldier . . . no one knows more about solving a problem than the person at the bottom.

—Sandra Day O'Connor, address, Rockford (Illinois) College commencement,
USA Today, May 24, 1989

Live with men as if God saw you; converse with God as if
men heard you.
—Seneca, *Epistulae Morales ad Lucilium*, c. A.D. 63

The highest conduct is that which conduces to the greatest
length, breadth, and completeness of life.
—Herbert Spencer, *Principles of Ethics*, 1893

√Reward is what you receive, merit is what you do.
—St. Thomas Aquinas, *Disputations Concerning Truth*, 13th century

CONFESSION

In proportion as a man who has done wrong, confesses it,
even so far he is freed from guilt, as a snake from its slough.
—*Code of Manu*, between 1200 and 500 B.C.

The great danger is that in the confession of any collective
sin, one shall confess the sins of others and forget our own.
—Georgia Harkness, *The Resources of Religion*, 1936

The purpose of sacramental Confessions is atonement—at-
one-ment—with God.
—Caryll Houselander, *Guilt*, 1941

Confession heals, confession justifies, confession grants
pardon of sin, all hope consists in confession, in confession
there is a chance for mercy.
—St. Isidore of Seville (560–636), *Dialogue Between Erring Soul and Reason*

For him who confesses, shams are over and realities have
begun; he has exteriorized rottenness . . . he lives at least on
a basis of veracity.
—William James, *Varieties of Religious Experience*, 1902

Not God, but you, the maker of the confession, get to know
something by your act of confession. Much that you are able
to keep hidden in the dark, you first get to know by your
opening it to the knowledge of the all-knowing.
—Sören Kierkegaard, *Purity of Heart*, 1846

They who after they have done a base deed or committed a
wrong against themselves, remember God, and implore
forgiveness of their sins—and not persevere in what they
have wittingly done amiss; as for these! Pardon from the
Lord shall be their recompense.
—*Koran*, 7th century

Our confession has to bring to light the unknown, the unconscious darkness, and the undeveloped creativity of our deeper layers.
—Fritz Kunkel, *In Search of Maturity*, 1943

To confess one's sins is to honor the Holy One.
—Joshua b. Levi, *Talmud: Sanhedrin*, c. 500

Atonement, rather than growth, is the aim of the religious confessional, whereas psychotherapy does not require that you feel sorry for your sins as long as you outgrow them!
—Joshua Loth Liebman, *Peace of Mind*, 1946

Private confession . . . is wholly commendable, useful and indeed necessary. I would not have it cease, but rather I rejoice that it exists in the Church of Christ, for it is the one and only remedy for troubled consciences.
—Martin Luther, *The Babylonian Captivity*, 1520

With regard to the precepts of the Torah . . . if a person transgresses any of them, either wilfully or in error, and repents and turns away from his sin, he is under a duty to confess before God . . . this means confess in *words*.
—Maimonides (1135–1204), *Repentance*

A generous and free-minded confession doth disable a reproach and disarm an injury.
—Michel de Montaigne, *Essays*, 1588

To utter forth our sin, merits the remission of sin.
—Origen (185–254), *Hom, iii on Leviticus*

If we are to climb the heights of spiritual creativity, we must confess our sins and bring forth fruit worthy of repentance.
—Kirby Page, *Living Creatively*, 1932

We confess our little faults only to persuade others that we have no great ones.
—La Rochefoucauld, *Maxims*, 1665

To confess a fault freely is the next thing to being innocent of it.
—Publilius Syrus, *Setentiae*, c. 50 B.C.

CONFESSION

While [confession] abases the man, it raises him; while it covers him with squalor, it renders him more clean; while it accuses, it excuses; while it condemns, it absolves.
—Tertullian, *On Repentance*, c. 200

Jesus obliged us to confess our sins for our own sake rather than for His. . . . Confession is simply a Hospital of Souls, where the Good Samaritan, through the instrumentality of the priest, goes about binding up wounds and pouring in oil and wine; a hospital where the Divine Physician displays His healing art.
—Alfred Wilson, *Pardon and Peace*, 1947

CONFORMITY

For thirty years my ear listened to nothing but my own conscience, but for thirty years since then my state has been such that my conscience has listened to none but God.
—al-Muhasibi (died 857), in Margaret Smith, *An Early Mystic of Bagdad*

Conscience is the perfect interpreter of life.
—Karl Barth, *The Word of God and the Word of Man*, 1957

The most miserable pettifogging in the world is that of a man in the court of his own conscience.
—Henry Ward Beecher, *Life Thoughts*, 1858

Many are the devices and marvelous the elaborations by which men everywhere seek to avoid condemnation before that inner tribunal known as conscience.
—Anton T. Boisen, *The Exploration of the Inner World*, 1936

Whoever acts without conscience, or against conscience, though the very thing he does should be good, sins by doing it.
—Louis Bourdalove (1632–1704), *Sermons*

It is the conscience alone which is a thousand witnesses to accuse us.
—Robert Burton, *Anatomy of Melancholy*, III, 1621

Even Freud assumes that, when Freudian light has dawned upon us by Freudian psychoanalysis, we are under obligation to walk in the light. Thus Freud makes backdoor confession that we are responsible creatures; that is, people of conscience.
—George A. Buttrick, *Christ and Man's Dilemma*, 1946

For conscience, instead of allowing us to stifle our
perceptions, and sleep on without interruption, acts as an
inward witness and monitor, reminds us of what we owe to
God, points out the distinction of good and evil, and thereby
convicts us of departure from duty.

—John Calvin, *Institutes*, II, 1536

Conscience is an oracle of the Divinity.

—William Ellery Channing (1780–1842), *Works*

Conscience is an actuated or reflex knowledge of a superior
power and an equitable law; a law impressed, and a power
above impressing it.

—Stephen Charnock (1628–1680), *Existence and Attributes of God*

If you would have a good conscience, you must by all means
have so much light, so much knowledge of the will of God, as
may regulate you, and show you your way, may teach you
how to do, and to speak, and think, as in His presence.

—Samuel Taylor Coleridge, *Aids to Reflection*, 1825

O clear conscience, and upright! How doth a little failing
wound thee sore.

—Dante, *"Purgatory," Divine Comedy*, c. 1310

A person who holds for the moral authority of conscience will
also hold for the individual's freedom to follow his conscience
without interference from the State.

—Eric D'Arcy, *Conscience and Its Right of Freedom*, 1961

For one man who thanks God that he is not as other men
are, there are a few thousand who offer thanks that they are
as other men, sufficiently as others to escape attention.

—John Dewey, *Human Nature and Conflict*, 1922

He that purchases a Manor, will think to have an exact
Survey of the Land: But who thinks to have so exact a survey
of his Conscience, how that money was got, that purchased
that Manor?

—John Donne, sermon, funeral of Sir William Cockayne,
December 26, 1626

The greatest event in natural history was the birth of
conscience in the human mind. That was the moment when
man put aside his strongest natural instinct, which was self-
interest.

—Lecomte du Noüy, in *Reader's Digest*, June 1948

Whoso would be a man, must be a non-conformist.
—Ralph Waldo Emerson, *Self-Reliance*, 1841

A guilty conscience needs no accuser.
—English proverb

God does not make clones. Each person is different, a tribute to God's creativity. If we are to love our neighbors as ourselves, we must accept people as they are and not demand that they conform to our own image.
—Henry Fehren, in *U.S. Catholic*, March 1991

The voice of conscience, which imposes on each his particular duty, is the light-beam on which we come forth from the bosom of the Infinite, and assume our place as particular individual beings; it fixes the limits of our personality.
—J.G. Fichte (1762–1814), *A Divine Government of the World*

There is nothing real, lasting, imperishable in me, but these two elements: the voice of conscience, and my free obedience.
—J.G. Fichte (1762–1814), *The Vocation of Man*

I have not always known what I wanted, but I have always known what I did not want—for example, conformity. The world would be so unexciting if it were uniform.
—Vigdis Finnbogadottir, in *World Press Review*, September 1990

A quiet conscience sleeps in thunder.
—Thomas Fuller, *Gnomologia*, 1732

Freedom of conscience is a natural right, both antecedent and superior to all human laws and institutions whatever: a right which laws never gave and which laws never take away.
—John Goodwin, *Might and Right Well Met*, 1648

Temptation is the voice of the suppressed evil; conscience is the voice of the repressed good.
—J.A. Hadfield, *Psychology and Morals*, 1923

The moral sense, or conscience, is as much a part of man as his leg or arm.
—Thomas Jefferson, letter to Peter Carr, 1787

God's law enters our mind and draws it to itself by stirring
up conscience, which itself is called the law of our mind.
> —St. John Damascene (700?–754?), *De Fide Orthodoxa*, 4.22

More does God desire of thee the least degree of purity of
conscience than all the works that thou canst perform.
> —St. John of the Cross (1542–91), *Spiritual Sentences and Maxims*

For us one of the saddest days in life is the day we allow the
herd-fear to conquer the highest judgments and instincts of
the soul.
> —E. Stanley Jones, *Victorious Living*, 1936

It is the voice of our ideal self, our complete self, our real self,
laying its call upon the will.
> —Rufus Jones, *The Nature and Authority of Conscience*, 1920

Conscience is an instinct to judge ourselves in the light of
moral laws. It is not a mere faculty; it is an instinct.
> —Immanuel Kant, *Lecture at Königsberg*, 1775

Conformity is the jailer of freedom and the enemy of growth.
> —John F. Kennedy, address to the United Nations, September 25, 1961

Throughout eternity an infinite stillness reigns wherein
the conscience may talk with the individual. . . . It must
be heard.
> —Sören Kierkegaard, *Purity of Heart*, 1846

Success, recognition, and conformity are the bywords of the
modern world where everyone seems to crave the
anesthetizing security of being identified with the majority.
> —Martin Luther King, Jr., *Strength of Love*, 1963

The beautiful idea that every man has with him a Guardian
Angel is true indeed: for Conscience is ever on the watch,
ever ready to warn us of danger.
> —John Lubbock, *The Pleasures of Life*, 1887

This principle of making the individual conscience the
judge of law, and in last resorts the final justification of
disobedience, is psychologically necessary for any
free people.
> —Everett Dean Martin, *Liberty*, 1930

Conscience is the guardian in the individual of the rules which the community has evolved for its own preservation.
—W. Somerset Maugham, *The Moon and Sixpence*, 1919

On close scrutiny, the beast within us looks suspiciously like a sheep.
—Sarah J. McCarthy, "Why Johnny Can't Disobey," *The Humanist*, September/October 1979

When one has too many answers, and when one joins a chorus of others chanting the same slogans, there is, it seems to me, a danger that one is trying to evade the loneliness of a conscience that realizes itself to be in an inescapably evil situation. We are under judgment.
—Thomas Merton, "Events and Pseudo-Events," *Faith and Violence*, 1968

Conscience can become hardened like water becoming ice. . . . It films over gradually, and at last becomes hard; and then it can bear a weight of iniquity.
—Sebastian Miklas, *Sanctify Your Emotions*, 1955

Conscience is a feeling in our own mind, a pain, more or less intense, attendant on violation of duty, which in properly cultivated moral natures rises, in the more serious cases, into shrinking from it as an impossibility.
—John Stuart Mill, *Utilitarianism*, 1863

He who lets the world, or his own portion of it, choose his plan of life for him has no need for any other faculty than the ape-like one of imitations.
—John Stuart Mill, *On Liberty*, 1859

It is not because men's desires are strong that they act ill; it is because their consciences are weak. There is no natural connection between strong impulses and a weak conscience. The natural connection is the other way.
—John Stuart Mill, *On Liberty*, 1859

It is the American vice, the democratic disease which expresses its tyranny by reducing everything unique to the level of the herd.
Henry Miller, *The Wisdom of the Heart*, 1941

I fear yet this iron yoke of outward conformity hath left a
slavish print upon our necks. . . . We do not see that while
we still affect by all means a rigid external formality, we may
as soon fall again into a gross conforming stupidity . . .
which is more to the sudden degeneration of a Church than
many . . . petty schisms.

—John Milton, *Areopagitica*, 1644

The belief in authority is the source of conscience; which is
therefore not the voice of God in the heart of man, but the
voice of some men in man.

—Friedrich Nietzsche, *Human, All Too Human*, 1878

Like an opiate, sin drugs a conscience to drowsiness and
stupor. Prayer stabs it wide awake.

—John A. O'Brien, *The Test of Courage*, 1943

More potent than all the brass-buttoned policemen in the
land is the restraining power of conscience.

—John A. O'Brien, *Truths Men Live By*, 1947

Men never do evil so fully and so happily as when they do it
for conscience's sake.

—Blaise Pascal, *Pensées*, 1670

It is reasonable to concur where Conscience does not forbid
compliance; for Conformity is at least a Civic Virtue . . . it is
a Weakness in Religion and Government where it is carried
to Things of an Indifferent Nature, since . . . Liberty is always
the Price of it.

—William Penn, *Some Fruits of Solitude*, 1693

My prison shall be my grave before I will budge a jot; for I
owe my conscience to no mortal man.

—William Penn, in the Tower of London, 1669, *Passages from Writings of*

There is not witness so terrible, no accuser so potent, as the
conscience that dwells in every man's breast.

—Polybius, *Histories*, c. 125 B.C.

All too often a clear conscience is merely the result of a
bad memory.

—Proverb

The conscience is not automatically infallible; it can easily make mistakes, and it is very difficult to distinguish its voice—the real voice of conscience—from the voice of precipitation, passion, convenience or self-will, or of moral primitiveness.

—Karl Rahner, *Nature and Grace*, 1964

Conscience is the voice of values long and deeply infused into one's sinew and blood.

—Elliot L. Richardson, in *Life*, 1973

The decrees of conscience are not judgments but feelings.

—Jean Jacques Rousseau, *Émile*, 1762

A brave man hazards life, but not his conscience.

—J.C.F. von Schiller, *The Death of Wallenstein*, 1799

The work of conscience keeps the same hours as the owl.

—J.C.F. von Schiller, *Kabale und Liebe*, 1784

A good conscience enlists a multitude of friends; a bad conscience is distressed and anxious, even when alone.

—Seneca (4 B.C.–A.D. 65), *Epistles* 43.5

Our cosmic universe is not outside. Spiritual astronomy does not establish its observatories on mountains in California, but in consciences.

—Antonin Sertillanges, *Recollections*, 1950

A peace above all earthly dignities,
A still and quiet conscience.

—William Shakespeare, *King Henry VIII*, c. 1611

Conscience does make cowards of us all.

—William Shakespeare, *Hamlet*, Act II, sc. 1, c. 1603

My conscience hath a thousand several tongues,
And every tongue brings in a several tale,
And every tale condemns me for a villain.

—William Shakespeare, *King Richard III*, c. 1593

The abundant life . . . is a life wherein we are both sheep and shepherd . . . a life lived heeding the voice of the keeper of the flock . . . (and) finding ourselves shepherds, too.
—Doris Graf Smith, *Women of the Word*, 1984

A person may sometimes have a clear conscience simply because his head is empty.
—Ralph W. Sockman, *How to Believe*, 1953

We are called, irrevocably, to step over the lines we have drawn for ourselves, to do battle with everything that says we and those around us, cannot change, and to step out into the unlimited, abundant life that God has been holding out to us since the world began.
—Barbara Brown Taylor, *Women of the Word*, 1984

Every conscience, whether it be true or faulty, and whether it is concerned with bad acts or indifferent acts, is binding, and therefore anyone who acts against his conscience commits sin.
—St. Thomas Aquinas (1225–74), *Quodibet*, q. e, a. 22

I am not bound to direct my conscience according to the council of one single kingdom against the general council of Christendom.
—St. Thomas More, to his judges after they had condemned
him to death, 1535

The spirit in us is a disturber of the peace. It challenges. It is that random humor that shakes up, discontents the contented, discomforts the comfortable.
—Dan Turner, in *Creation Spirituality*, May/June 1992

Love is the source and substance of our conscience. . . . If it were not for our unquenchable need to love and to be loved there would be no conscience; there would remain only animal fear and animal aggression.
—Gregory Zilboorg, *Psychoanalysis and Religion*, 1962

CONSCIOUSNESS

O what a world of unseen visions and heard silences, this insubstantial country of the mind! What ineffable essences, these touchless rememberings and unshowable reveries! And the privacy of it all! A secret theater of speechless monologue and prevenient counsel, an invisible mansion of all moods, musings, and mysteries, an infinite resort of disappointments and discoveries. A whole kingdom where each of us reigns reclusively alone, questioning what we will, commanding what we can. A hidden hermitage where we may study out the troubled book of what we have done and yet may do. An introcosm that is more myself than anything I can find in a mirror. This consciousness that is myself of selves, that is everything, and yet nothing at all—what is it?

—Julian Jaynes, *The Origin of Consciousness in the Breakdown of the Bicameral Mind*, 1976

I incline to the idealistic theory that consciousness is fundamental, and that the material universe is derivative from consciousness. . . . In general the universe seems to me to be nearer to a great thought than to a great machine.

—James Jeans, to J.W.N. Sullivan, *Contemporary Mind: Some Modern Answers*, 1934

An expansion of the individual consciousness toward a harmony with Infinite Consciousness demands of the individual that he take on, commensurately, other characteristics of his Creator.

—Leonard E. Read, in *The Freeman*, June 1964

When mystical activity is at its height, we find consciousness possessed by a sense of a being at once *excessive and identical* with the self: great enough to be God; interior enough to be me.

—E. Recéjac, *Essay on the Being of the Mystical Knowledge*, 1899

Consciousness is the inner light kindled in the soul . . . a music, strident or sweet, made by the friction of existence.

—George Santayana, *The Realm of Truth*, 1938

We are obliged to regard every phenomenon as a manifestation of some Power by which we are acted upon: though Omnipresence is unthinkable, yet . . . we are unable to think of limits to the presence of this Power. . . . And this consciousness of an Incomprehensible Power . . . is just that consciousness on which Religion dwells.

—Herbert Spencer, *First Principles*, 1862

I hold that it is in the Transcendental Feeling, manifested normally as Faith in the Value of Life, and ecstatically as a sense of timeless Being . . . that Consciousness comes nearest to the object of metaphysics, Ultimate Reality.
—J.A. Stewart, *The Myth of Plato*, 1905

The consciousness of each of us is evolution looking at itself and reflecting.
—Pierre Teilhard de Chardin, *The Phenomenon of Man*, 1955

CONTEMPLATION

One may not be so given up to contemplation as to neglect the good of his neighbor, nor so taken up with the active life as to omit the contemplation of God.
—St. Augustine, *The City of God*, XIX, 426

Contemplation is an inward gaze into the depths of the soul and, for that very reason, beyond the soul to God.
—Hans Urs von Balthasar, *Prayer*, 1961

In the higher part of contemplative life, a man is above himself and under his God.
—*The Cloud of Unknowing*, 14th century

Great becomes the fruit, great the advantage of earnest contemplation, when it is set round with upright conduct. Great becomes the fruit, great the advantage of intellect when it is set round with earnest contemplation.
—*Dialogues of the Buddha* (6th century B.C.), Part II

The life of work is necessary and the life of contemplation is good. In service the man gathers the harvest that has been sown in contemplation.
—Meister Eckhart (1260?–1327?), in R.B. Blakney, *Meister Eckhart*

When thou hast stabilized thine heart in right faith, and steadfast hope, and perfect love, then thou shalt heave up thine heart in high contemplation of thy Creator.
—St. Edmund of Canterbury, *Mirror of St. Edmund*, c. 1230

Because the earthly life of pious folk is nothing but a contemplation and kind of shadowing of that other, they sometimes feel a foretaste and a glow of the reward to come.
—Desiderius Erasmus, *The Praise of Folly*, 1511

Those who wish to hold the fortress of contemplation, must first of all train in the camp of action.
—Pope St. Gregory the Great, *Book of Morals*, 584

Contemplation is that condition of alert passivity, in which the soul lays itself open to the divine Ground within and without, the immanent and transcendent Godhead.
—Aldous Huxley, *The Perennial Philosophy*, 1945

Let it be well understood that God does not lead to perfect contemplation all who give themselves resolutely to the interior life. Why is that? God alone knows.
—St. John of the Cross (1542–91), *The Dark Night of the Soul*

When God leads any one along the highest road of obscure contemplation and aridity, such an [sic] one will think himself lost.
—St. John of the Cross (1542–91), *Ascent of Mount Carmel*

Christian contemplation is not something esoteric and dangerous. It is simply the experience of God that is given to a soul purified by humility and faith.
—Thomas Merton, in *Commonweal*, October 1958

To me it seems that contemplation is joyful song of God's love taken in mind, with sweetness of angels' praise. This is jubilation, this is the end of perfect prayer and high devotion in this life.
—Richard Rolle (c. 1300–49), *The Mending of Life*

Do not defile in contemplation thought that is pure in his own nature.

But abide in the bliss of yourself and cease those torments.
—Saraha, *Saraha's Treasury of Songs*, 10th century

There are many persons who desire the contemplative life, but they will not practice the things which lead to it.
—Thomas à Kempis, *Imitation of Christ*, 1441

If we are to be saved from our futility we must recover the faculty of being still: we must make an enclave of silence within our own souls.
—Gerald Vann, *The High Green Hill*, 1951

CONTENTMENT

Bad will be the day for every man when he becomes absolutely contented with the life that he is living . . . when there is not forever beating at the doors of his soul some great desire to do something larger.
—Phillips Brooks (1835–93), *Perennials from*

True contentment is a real, even an active virtue—not only affirmative but creative. It is the power of getting out of any situation all there is in it.
—G.K. Chesterton, *A Miscellany of Men*, 1912

Be content with your daily bread, and remember that in the desert manna gathered for a future day grew putrid at once.
—François Fénelon (1651–1715), *Spiritual Letters*

Contentment consisteth not in adding more fuel, but in taking away some fire; not in multiplying of wealth, but in subtracting men's desires.
—Thomas Fuller, *The Holy State*, 1642

Not that I complain of want; for I have learned, in whatever state I am, to be content. I know how to be abased, and I know how to abound; in any and all circumstances I have learned the secret of facing plenty and hunger, abundance and want.
—*Holy Bible*, Philippians 4:11-12

Only when we feel that through all our vicissitudes some unfathomable purpose runs, and that by meeting life nobly and courageously we can co-operate in the fulfillment of that purpose, do we find peace.
—Alice Hegan Rice, *Happiness Road*, 1942

The sufficiency of contentment is an enduring and unchanging sufficiency.
—Lao-tzu, *Tao Te Ching*, between 6th and 3rd century B.C.

What though I am not so happy as I desire, 'tis well I am not so wretched as I deserve.
—Arthur Warwick, *Spare Minutes*, 1637

CONVERSION

What man most needs now is to apply his conversion skills to those things that are essential for his survival. He needs to convert facts into logic, free will into purpose, conscience into decision. He needs to convert historical experience into a design for a sane world.

—Norman Cousins, *In Place of Folly,* 1961

Until a man realizes sin as the death of his own higher self and as a rebellion against the law of his true happiness, there is no true conversion of heart towards the higher life.

—Father Cuthbert, *God and the Supernatural,* 1920

I read about an Eskimo hunter who asked the local missionary priest, "If I did not know about God and sin, would I go to hell?" "No," said the priest, "not if you did not know." "Then why," asked the Eskimo earnestly, "did you tell me?"

—Annie Dillard, *Pilgrim at Tinker Creek,* 1974

To be converted is to commit oneself to the process of the poor and oppressed, to commit oneself lucidly, realistically, and concretely. It means to commit oneself not only generously, but also with an analysis of the situation and a strategy of action. To be converted is to know and experience the fact that, contrary to the laws of physics, we can stand straight, according to the Gospel, only when our center of gravity is outside ourselves.

—Gustavo Gutierrez, *A Theology of Liberation,* 1973

Truly, I say to you, unless you turn and become like children, you will never enter the kingdom of heaven.

—*Holy Bible,* Matthew 18:3

There is no man, no "unbeliever," whose supernatural conversion to God is not possible from the dawn of reason onwards.

—Étienne Hugueny, *Le scandale édifiant d'une exposition missionaire,* 1933

Conversion for me was not a Damascus Road experience. I slowly moved into an intellectual acceptance of what my intuition had always known.

—Madeleine L'Engle, "Writer, Wife, Theologian," *Anglican Digest,* Pentecost 1983

We do not try to convert non-Christians by showing them their errors, but by showing how the separate truths they hold ought to develop into the Oneness of truth.

—Bernard Leeming, *Unitas,* XI, No. 2, 1952

There isn't any doubt about it, the human soul cannot go on for ever in sin without some desire to free itself. . . . Conversion simply means turning around.
—Vincent McNabb, *God's Way of Mercy*, 1928

You have not converted a man because you have silenced him.
—John Morley, *On Compromise*, 1874

Where a profound change in philosophy, ideology, or ethics occurs, the hidden but encompassing struggle is particularly significant. Thus conversion cannot be regarded as a sudden or dramatic event.
—Leon Salzman, *Psychiatry*, 1953

Conversion is primarily an unselfing.
—E.T. Starbuck, *The Psychology of Religion*, 1901

CONVICTION

He who holds convictions, respects convictions.
—Leo Baeck, *Essence of Judaism*, 1936

Conviction, were it never so excellent, is worthless till it convert itself into Conduct.
—Thomas Carlyle, *Sartor Resartus*, 1836

Any activity pursued in behalf of an ideal and against obstacles and in spite of threats of personal loss because of conviction of its general and enduring value is religious in quality.
—John Dewey, *A Common Faith*, 1937

One man esteems one day as better than another while another man esteems all days alike. Let every one be fully convinced in his own mind.
—*Holy Bible*, Romans 14:5

Convictions are the mainsprings of action, the driving powers of life. What a man lives are his convictions.
—Francis C. Kelley, address, Oklahoma City, November 28, 1933

He who begins life by stifling his convictions is in a fair way for ending it without any convictions to stifle.
—John Morley, *On Compromise*, 1874

COURAGE

The loving God never forsakes a hero on earth if his courage fail not.
—*Andreas*, prior to 1100

To stand held only by the invisible chains of higher duty, and, so standing, to let the fire creep up to the heart—that is the truer heroism.
—Phillips Brooks (1835–93), *Perennials from*

The hero is he who lives in the inward sphere of things, in the True, Divine, Eternal, which exists always . . . His life is a piece of the everlasting heart of nature itself.
—Thomas Carlyle, *Lectures on Heroes*, 1840

Courage is rightly esteemed the first of human qualities, because . . . it is the quality which guarantees all others.
—Winston S. Churchill, *Great Contemporaries*, 1937

Never can true courage dwell with them, who, playing tricks with conscience, dare not look at their own vices.
—Samuel Taylor Coleridge (1772–1834), *Fears in Solitude*

The Master said: "To see what is right and not do it, is want of courage."
—Confucius, *Analects*, 5th century B.C.

People glorify all sorts of bravery except the bravery they might show on behalf of their nearest neighbors.
—George Eliot, *Middlemarch*, 1872

Courage is a virtue only in so far as it is directed by prudence.
—François Fénelon, *Adventures de Télémaque*, 1699

Be strong and of good courage.
—*Holy Bible*, Deuteronomy 31:23

Life, misfortunes, isolation, abandonment, poverty, are battlefields which have their heroes; obscure heroes, sometimes greater than the illustrious heroes.
—Victor Hugo, *Les Misérables*, 1862

Courage without conscience is a wild beast.
—Robert G. Ingersoll, speech, May 1882

It is from numberless diverse acts of courage and belief that human history is shaped. Each time a man stands up for an ideal or acts to improve the lot of others or strikes out against injustice, he sends forth a tiny ripple of hope, and crossing each other from a million different centers of energy and daring those ripples build a current which can sweep down the mightiest walls of oppression and resistance.
—Robert F. Kennedy, address, "Day of Affirmation," University of Capetown, South Africa, June 6, 1966

Courage is never to let your actions be influenced by your fears.
—Arthur Koestler, *Arrow in the Blue*, 1951

The strangest, most generous, and proudest of all virtues is true courage.
—Michel de Montaigne, *Essays*, 1588

Perfect valor is to do without witness what one would do before all the world.
—La Rochefoucauld, *Maxims*, 1665

It takes a brave man to look into the mirror of his own soul to see written there the disfigurements caused by his own misbehavior.
—Fulton J. Sheen, *Ways to Happiness*, 1953

There is a quiet courage that comes from an inward spring of confidence in the meaning and significance of life. Such courage is an underground river, flowing far beneath the shifting events of one's experience, keeping alive a thousand little springs of action.
—Howard Thurman, *Disciplines of the Spirit*, 1963

CREATION

To suppose that God formed man from the dust with bodily hands is very childish . . . . God neither formed man with bodily hands nor did he breathe upon him with throat and lips.
—St. Augustine, *Commentary on the Book of Genesis*, 415

The Absolute neither creates nor is created—in the current sense of making or being made. We can speak of creation only in the sense of the Being becoming in form and movement what it already is in substance and status.
—Sri Aurobindo, *The Life Divine*, 1949

It is easier to think of the world without a creator than of a
creator loaded with all the contradictions of the world.
—Simone de Beauvoir, in *Time*, April 8, 1966

Creation provides for the orderly parameters within which
human existence is lived. Creation is affirmed as benevolent,
embodying the possibilities of goodness. To be wise, then, is
to recognize and actualize the potential for full life already
inherent in the created order. To know God is to discern the
harmonious order for which we were created: *persons to God;*
person to each other; and persons to the rest of nature,
—Bruce C. Birch, and Larry L. Rassmussen,
The Predicament of the Prosperous, 1978

Creation means the transformation of an otherwise chaotic
world into a thing of order and beauty. It is the shaping of an
indifferent matter into a world of value.
—John Elof Boodin, *God and Creation*, 1934

By spreading out creation in time and space, there is no
reduction in the mystery.
—*The British Journal for the Philosophy of Science*, 1954

When a certain shameless fellow mockingly asked a pious
old man what God had done before the creation of the world,
the latter aptly countered that he had been building hell for
the curious.
—John Calvin, *Institutes*, I, 1536

Man does not bring to God's altar the stuff of nature in itself,
in its initial structure, but something he has made and
molded out of nature for the nourishment and the
inspiration of men.
—Wilford O. Cross, *Prologue to Ethics*, 1963

There is a grandeur in this view of life, with its several
powers, having been originally breathed by the Creator into a
few forms or into one.
—Charles Darwin, *The Origin of Species*, 1859

Christianity has traditionally appeared to place its major
emphasis on creation as a specific event while the Indian
tribal religions could be said to consider creation as an
ecosystem present in a definable place.
—Vine Deloria, Jr., *God Is Red*, 1973

We ought to beware lest, in our presumption, we imagine that the ends which God proposed to Himself in the creation of the world are understood by us.
—René Descartes, *Principles of Philosophy*, 1644

In the Koran, Allah asks, "The heaven and the earth all in between, thinkest thou I made them *in jest?*" It's a good question. What do we think of the created universe, spanning an unthinkable void with an unthinkable profusion of forms? Or what do we think of nothingness, those sickening reaches of time in either direction? If the giant water bug was not made in jest, was it then made in earnest?
—Annie Dillard, *Pilgrim at Tinker Creek*, 1974

Not once in the dim past, but continuously by conscious mind is the miracle of the Creation wrought.
—A.S. Eddington, *The Nature of the Physical World*, 1929

We could enjoy the story of creation if we were sure it were not true. . . . Faced with the fact that the story of creation is true, that God did indeed so call everything from nothingness, we are caught up breathless, almost incapable of protest.
—Walter Farrell, *My Way of Life*, 1952

Creation is the subject of the scientist's search and mystical commitment, and it is the source of all worship and the goal of all morality.
—Matthew Fox, *Creation Spirituality*, 1991

Creation means . . . that He has infused His own being into another thing which thereby has taken an independent existence of its own.
—Erich Frank, *Philosophical Understanding and Religious Truth*, 1945

Creation is simply an overwhelming outpouring, the overflow of infinite goodness.
—Thomas J. Higgins, *Perfection Is for You*, 1953

All of creation is a song of praise to God.
—Hildegard of Bingen (1098–1179), *Illuminations of*, 1985

In the beginning God created the heavens and the earth. The earth was without form and void, and darkness was upon the face of the deep; and the Spirit of God was moving over the face of the waters.

—*Holy Bible*, Genesis 1:1-2

The scientific investigator is wholly incompetent to say anything at all about the first origin of the material universe.

—Thomas Henry Huxley, *Science and Hebrew Tradition*, 1870

The creation, or rather the development of Nature spreads by degrees . . . with a continuous advance to an even greater breadth, in order that, in the process of eternity, the infinity of space may be filled with worlds and systems of worlds.

—Immanuel Kant, *Allegemeine Naturgeschichte*, 1755

It is the presence of God that, without cessation, draws the creation from the abyss of its own nothingness above which His omnipotence holds it suspended, lest of its own weight it should fall back therein.

—La Croix de Jesus Chardon (17th century), in Bremond's
History of Religious Thought in France

In whatever manner God created the world, it would always have been regular and in a certain general order. God, however, has chosen the most perfect, that is to say, the one which is at the same time the simplest in hypothesis and the richest in phenomena.

—G.W. von Leibniz, *Discourse on Metaphysics*, 1685

This universe existed in the shape of Darkness, unperceived. . . . Then the Divine Self-existent, himself indiscernible, but making all this, the great Elements and the rest, discernible, appeared with irresistible creative power, dispelling the darkness.

—*The Manu-Smriti*, c. 200 B.C.

The primeval account of Adam and Eve in the plenitude of created and creative power . . . is a picture of such divine exhilaration in creation as forces us, if we are asked to say summarily why God made the world, to affirm that He made it for fun!

—Alexander Miller, *The Renewal of Man*, 1955

It may be difficult to believe in creation, but it is more difficult to believe that the first thing, even if only an atom, or an electron, was not created.

—J.F. Noll, *Christian Faith Before the Bar of Reason*, 1948

The only part of man that is immediately *created* is the human soul.
—John A. O'Brien, *Truths Men Live By*, 1946

The creation is the bible of the Deist. He there reads in the hand-writing of the Creator himself, the certainty of his existence, and the immutability of his power.
—Thomas Paine, *The Age of Reason*, 1795

The creation speaketh a universal language. . . . It cannot be counterfeited; it cannot be lost; it cannot be suppressed. . . . It preaches to all nations and all worlds; and this Word of God reveals to man all that it is necessary for him to know.
—Thomas Paine, *The Age of Reason*, 1795

Who knows for certain? Who shall declare it? Whence was it born, and whence came this creation? The gods were born after this world's creation. Then who can know from whence it has arisen? . . . He who surveys it in the highest heaven, He only knows, or haply he may know not.
—*Rig-Veda*, between 1000 and 600 B.C.

We were intellectually intoxicated with the idea that the world could make itself without design, purpose, skill, or intelligence; in short, without life.
—George Bernard Shaw, preface, *Back to Methuselah*, 1921

Why did God make the universe?. . . God is Good, and being Good He could not, as it were, contain Himself; consequently, He told the secret of His Goodness to nothingness and that was Creation. The world is the overflow of Divine Goodness. Begotten of the Goodness of God, the Goodness of God is in it.
—Fulton J. Sheen, *The Philosophy of Religion*, 1948

. . . this is the meaning of life—continuously to add something we haven't known so far. That, anyway, is the meaning of all existing things. Existence is built upon the idea of the creative—that there is always something unknown to be discovered, which causes and motivates new perception, new studies, the energy to go on.
—Karlheinz Stockhausen, in *Opera News*, May 16, 1988

The end of creation is that all things may return to the Creator and be united with Him.
—Emmanuel Swedenborg, *The Divine Love and Wisdom*, 1763

According to Augustine, the passage "Let the earth bring forth the green herb" means, not that plants were then actually produced in their proper nature, but that a germinative power was given the earth to produce plants by the work of propagation.

—St. Thomas Aquinas (1226–74), *Quaestiones Disputatae,* 1268

I looked upon the works of God in this visible creation, and an awfulness covered me: my heart was tender and often contrite, and a universal love to my fellow creatures was increased in me.

—John Woolman, *Journal,* 1774

CROSS

What does the apotheosis of the Cross mean, if not the death of death, the defeat of sin, the beatification of martyrdom, the raising to the skies of voluntary sacrifice, the defiance of pain?

—Henri Amiel, *Journal,* 1882

Perhaps the saddest thing to admit is that those who rejected the Cross have to carry it, while those who welcomed it are so often engaged in crucifying others.

—Nicholas Berdyaev, *Christianity and Anti-Semitism,* 1940

By the wood of the Cross the bitterness of the Law is changed into the sweetness of spiritual understanding, and the people of God can quench its thirst.

—Origen (185–254), *In Exod.*

The Cross does not abolish suffering, but transforms it, sanctifies it, makes it fruitful, bearable, even joyful, and finally victorious.

—Joseph Rickaby, *An Old Man's Jottings,* 1925

amnation

All sins tend to be addictive, and the terminal point of addiction is what is called damnation.

—W.H. Auden, *A Certain World*, 1970

Lucifer is as immortal as Michael, and Judas as immortal as St. Peter: But that which we call immortality in the damned, is but a continual dying; howsoever it must be called life, it hath all the qualities of death, saving the ease, and the end, which death hath, and damnation hath not.

—John Donne, sermon, January 29, 1625

It is apparently easier to accept damnation as poetic material than purgation or beatitude; less is involved that is strange to the modern mind.

—T.S. Eliot, "Dante," *Selected Essays*, 1917–32

Those who entertain an extreme and inordinate dread of being damned, show that they have more need of humility and submission than of understanding.

—St. Francis de Sales (1567–1622), *Consoling Thoughts of*

The damned come into fatal collision with God, the infinite Good, in whom their beatitude was to be found: that is the pain of damnation.

—Charles Journet, *The Meaning of Evil*, 1961

Few are saved, infinitely more are damned.

—Martin Luther (1483–1546), *Table-Talk*

No man is condemned for anything he has done; he is condemned for continuing to do wrong.

—George Macdonald, *Unspoken Sermons*, 3rd series, 1887

How anyone can believe in eternal punishment . . . or in any soul which God has made being "lost," and also believe in the love, nay, even in the justice, of God, is a mystery indeed.

—C.G. Montefiore, *Liberal Judaism*, 1903

Deceitfulness and arrogance and pride
Quickness to Anger, harsh and evil speech . . .
These be the signs, my Prince! of him whose birth
Is fated for the region of the vile.

—"The Song Celestial," *Bhagavad-Gita*, 5th to 2nd century B.C.

DEATH

The day of death is when two worlds meet with a kiss: this world going out, the future world coming in.

—Jose b. Abin, *Talmud J: Yebamot*, c. 400

A painting on a canvas of infinite size, worked on eternally, would be without focus, meaning and probably without beauty. A painting, as life, needs limits. While I have an almost insatiable craving for knowledge, I believe death to be the final and perhaps greatest teacher—the one that provides the key to the ultimate questions life has never answered. In my darkest hours I have been consoled by the thought that death at least is a payment for the answer of life's haunting secrets.

—Morris B. Abram, in *The Wall Street Journal*, November 28, 1988

The first sign of love to God is not to be afraid of death, and to be always waiting for it. For death unites the friend to his friend—the seeker to the object which he seeks.

—al-Ghazzali (born 1058), *Alchemy of Happiness*

The meaning of death is not the annihilation of the spirit, but its separation from the body, and that the resurrection and day of assembly do not mean a return to a new existence after annihilation, but the bestowal of a new form or frame to the spirit.

—al-Ghazzali (born 1058), *Alchemy of Happiness*

By the death of One the world was redeemed. . . . We prove by this divine example that death alone found immortality and that death redeemed itself.

—St. Ambrose, *Two Books on the Death of Satyrus*, 375

Death not merely ends life, it also bestows upon it a silent completeness, snatched from the hazardous flux to which all things human are subject.

—Elizabeth Arden, *The Life of the Mind*, 1978

And as for death, if there be any gods, it is no grievous thing to leave the society of men. The gods will do thee no hurt, thou mayest be sure. But if it be so that there be no gods, or that they take no care of the world, why should I desire to live in a world void of gods, and of all divine providence.

—Marcus Aurelius, *Meditations*, c. 170

The act of dying is also one of the acts of life.

—Marcus Aurelius, *Meditations*, c. 170

Deep within life is the need to orient it toward death. The one incontrovertible item of our knowledge about death is that it gives notice of itself as motion, we go toward it, we go through it. It never loses its *goingness*.
—Mary Austin, *Experience Facing Death*, 1931

It is as natural to die as to be born; and to a little infant, perhaps the one is as painful as the other.
—Francis Bacon, *Essays*, 1597

As a man casting off worn-out garments, taketh new ones, so the dweller in the body, casting off worn-out bodies, entereth into others that are new.
—*Bhagavad-Gita*, between 5th and 2nd centuries B.C.

For certain is death for the born, and certain is birth for the dead; therefore over the inevitable thou shouldst not grieve.
—*Bhagavad-Gita*, between 5th and 2nd centuries B.C.

Death is the enlightener. The essential thing concerning it must be that it opens the closed eyes, draws down the veil of blinding mortality, and lets the man see spiritual things.
—Phillips Brooks, *Perennials*, 1898

Death is not something which does not take place until the end of life. Rather, death is the signature of this so-called life.
—Emil Brunner, *Eternal Hope*, 1954

I've always been worried about my damn soul—maybe I worry too much. But you carry in one hand a bundle of darkness that accumulates each day. And when death finally comes, you say, right away, "Hey buddy, glad to see ya!"
—Charles Bukowski, in *Los Angeles Times*, November 3, 1987

Earth to earth, ashes to ashes, dust to dust; in sure and certain hope of the Resurrection.
—Burial service, *The Book of Common Prayer*, 1662

"You should not be discouraged; one does not die of a cold," the priest said to the bishop.
The old man smiled. "I shall not die of a cold, my son. I shall die of having lived."
—Willa Cather, *Death Comes for the Archbishop*, 1927

There is a remedy to all things except Death.
—Miguel de Cervantes, *Don Quixote*, 1615

How do I know that the love of life is not a delusion; and that the dislike of death is not like a child that is lost and does not know the way home?

—Chuang-tzu (4th century B.C.), *Texts of Taoism*

Truly is it said, "For the Wise Man life is conformity to the motions of Heaven, death is but part of the common law of Change."

—Chuang-tzu (4th century B.C.), *Three Ways of Thought in Ancient China*

I look forward to my dissolution as to a secure haven, where I shall at length find a happy repose from the fatigues of a long journey.

—Cicero, *Essays on Old Age*, 44 B.C.

The life of the dead consists in being present in the minds of the living.

—Cicero, *Orationes Phillipiae*, c. 60 B.C.

Death is the liberator of him whom freedom cannot release, the physician of him whom medicine cannot cure, and the comforter of him whom time cannot console.

—Charles Caleb Colton, *Lacon*, 1822

It is God's law, that as things rose so they should fall, as they waxed so should grow old, the strong become weak, and the great become little, and when they have become weak and little, they end.

—Cyprian (200–258), *To Demetrian*

The noble Soul in old age returns to God as to that port whence she set forth on the sea of this life. And as the good mariner, when he approaches port, furls his sails . . . so should we furl the sails of our worldly affairs and turn to God with our whole mind and heart, so that we may arrive at that port with all sweetness and peace.

—Dante, *The Convito*, c. 1310

As a well-spent day brings happy sleep, so life well used brings happy death.

—Leonardo da Vinci (1452–1519), *Notebooks of*

Not in the sky, not in the midst of the sea, not even in the clefts of the mountains is there a spot in the whole world where, if a man abide there, death could not overtake him.

—*Dhammapada*, c. 5th century B.C.

We have a winding sheet in our Mother's womb, which grows with us from our conception, and we come back into the world, wound up in that winding sheet, for we come to seek a grave.
—John Donne, sermon, February 29, 1627

Dying is that breakdown in an organism which throws it out of correspondence with some necessary part of the environment. Death is the result produced, the want of correspondence—failure to adjust internal relations to external relations.
—Henry Drummond, *Natural Law in the Spiritual World*, 1883

Man, tree, and flowers are supposed to die; but the fact remains that God's universe is spiritual and immortal.
—Mary Baker Eddy, *Science and Health*, 1908

Never say about anything, "I have lost it," but only "I have given it back." Is your child dead? It has been given back. Is your wife dead? She has been returned.
—Epictetus, *Discourses*, c. 110

So long as we live death is absent from us; and when it is present, we shall not exist any more. So during our life and after death we have nothing to fear from death.
—Epicurus (340–270 B.C.), *Epistle ad Menoeceum*

Our life is not so pleasant that those who escape from it need to be much lamented.
—St. Francis de Sales (1567–1622), *Consoling Thoughts of*

When the hour comes when life must be lost that you may find it in God, when danger of death is on you, and you see plainly that to obey God you must sacrifice life, then, I know not how, it comes to pass that what before seemed a very clear precept is involved in incredible darkness.
—St. Francis Xavier, letter to the Society of Jesus at Rome, May 1546

In the last analysis, it is our conception of death which decides our answers to all the questions that life puts to us.
—Dag Hammarskjold, *Markings*, 1964

The man of wisdom . . . rejoices at the prospect of death, when the soul is disenthralled from the body.
—Abraham Hasdai, *Sefer Ha Tapuah*, 1230

We sometimes congratulate ourselves at the moment of waking from a troubled dream: it may be so at the moment of death.
—Nathaniel Hawthorne, journal, October 25, 1835

Old men go to death; death comes to young men.
—George Herbert, *Jacula Prudentum*, 1651

If we are, at death, to enter the dream life stripped of its absurdities, I confess for one I rather like the prospect.
—Henry Holt, *On the Cosmic Relations*, 1914

All go to one place; all are from the dust, and all turn to dust again.
—*Holy Bible*, Ecclesiastes 3:20

Truly, truly I say to you, unless a grain of wheat falls into the earth and dies, it remains alone; but if it dies, it bears much fruit.
—*Holy Bible*, John 12:24

Every cradle asks us "Whence," and every coffin, "Whither?" The poor barbarian, weeping above his dead, can answer these questions as intelligently as the robed priest of the most authentic creed.
—Robert Ingersoll (1833–99), *Address at a Child's Grave*

The house of mourning teaches charity and wisdom.
—St. John Chrysostom, *Homilies*, c. 388

What, I pray you, is dying? Just what it is to put off a garment. For the body is about the soul as a garment; and after laying this aside for a short time by means of death, we shall resume it again with the more splendor.
—St. John Chrysostom, *Homilies*, c. 388

What is death at most? It is a journey for a season; a sleep longer than usual. If thou fearest death, thou shouldest also fear sleep.
—St. John Chrysostom, *Homilies*, c. 388

Death is not the cessation of life, but an incident in it. It is but the "narrows," to use the Psalmist's striking expression, through which the soul passes on its fateful voyage.
—Morris Joseph, *Judaism as Creed and Life*, 1903

To think of death and to prepare for death, is not a surrender; it is a victory over fear.
—Paul Wilhelm von Keppler, *More Joy*, 1911

When you touch your mortality, what used to be tragedies are mere inconveniences.
—Jack Klugman, in *The Washington Post*, May 28, 1990

Every soul must taste of death.
—*Koran*, c. 625

It is those who have not really lived—who have left issues unsettled, dreams unfulfilled, hopes shattered, and who have let the real things in life (loving and being loved by others, contributing in a positive way to other people's happiness and welfare, finding out what things are *really you*) pass them by—who are most reluctant to die.
—Elisabeth Kübler-Ross, in Anne Bancroft, *Weavers of Wisdom*, 1989

Let the athletes die young and laurel-crowned. Let the solders earn the Purple Hearts. Let women die old, white-crowned, with human hearts.
—Ursula K. Le Guin, "The Space Crone," 1976, *Dancing at the Edge of the World*

The grave is but a covered bridge leading from light to light, through a brief darkness.
—Henry Wadsworth Longfellow, *A Covered Bridge at Lucerne*, 1851

None but those shadowed by death's approach are suffered to know that death is a blessing; the gods conceal this from those who have life before them, in order that they may go on living.
—Lucan, *De Bello Civili*, c. A.D. 48

If you knew what He knows about death you would clap your listless hands.
—George Macdonald, *Unspoken Sermons*, 3rd series, 1887

Possessed by delusion, a man toils for his wife and child; but whether he fulfills his purpose or not, he must surrender the enjoyment thereof. When one is blessed with children and flocks and his heart is clinging to them, Death carries him away as doth a tiger a sleeping deer.
—*Mahabharata*, XII, c. 800 B.C.

Death is only a launching into the region of the strange Untried; it is but the first salutation to the possibilities of the
immense Remote, the Wild, the Watery, the Unshored.
—Herman Melville, *Moby Dick*, 1851

No one who is fit to live need fear to die. . . . To us here,
death is the most terrible word we know. But when we have
tasted its reality, it will mean to us birth, deliverance, a new
creation of ourselves.
—G.S. Merriam, *A Living Faith*, 1876

It is uncertain where death looks for us; let us expect her
everywhere: the premeditation of death is a forethinking of
liberty.
—Michel de Montaigne, *Essays*, xix, 1580

No man dies before his hour. The time you leave behind was
no more yours, than that which was before your birth, and
concerneth you no more.
—Michel de Montaigne, *Essays*, xix, 1580

Let children walk with Nature, let them see the beautiful
blendings and communions of death and life, their joyous inseparable unity, as taught in woods and meadows . . . and
they will learn that death is stingless indeed, and as beautiful as life.
—John Muir, *A Thousand Mile Walk to the Gulf*, 1867

With regard to death in the obvious sense, all men die; it is
this death which we consider as a dissolution. Of this death
no human soul dies.
—Origen, *On the Soul*, c. 240

For Death is no more than a turning of us over from Time
to Eternity.
—William Penn, *Some Fruits of Solitude*, 1718

The fear of death is indeed the pretense of wisdom, and not
real wisdom, being a pretense of knowing the unknown; and
no one knows whether death, which men in their fear apprehend to be the greatest evil, may not be the greatest good.
—Plato, "Apology," *Dialogues*, 399 B.C.

Your dead cease to love you and the land of their nativity as soon as they pass the portals of the tomb and wander way beyond the stars. They are soon forgotten and never return. Our dead never return. Our dead never forget the beautiful world that gave them being.

—Seattle, 1854, in *The Portable North American Reader*, 1974

That day, which you fear as being the end of all things, is the birthday of your eternity.

—Seneca, *Epistulae ad Lucilium, Epis.* c. 11, c. A.D. 63

When death is spoken of as a tearing asunder, we forget that it tears especially the veil of appearances and of deceptions which conceal from our view the depth of reality and of others and ourselves.

—Antonin Sertillanges, *Recollections*, 1950

Why are happy people not afraid of Death, while the insatiable and the unhappy so abhor that grim feature?

—Logan Pearsall Smith, *Afterthoughts*, 1931

And how, O my judges, I desire to prove to you that the real philosopher has reason to be of good cheer when he is about to die, and that after death he may hope to obtain the greatest good in the other world.

—Socrates, "Phaedo," Plato, *Dialogues*, 399 B.C.

Death is what takes place within us when we look upon others not as gift, blessing, or stimulus but as threat, danger, competition.

—Dorothee Sölle, *Death by Bread Alone*, 1978

It is impossible that anything so natural, so necessary, and so universal as death should ever have been designed by Providence as an evil to mankind.

—Jonathan Swift, *Thoughts on Religion*, 1728

Of all the evils of the world which are reproached with an evil character, death is the most innocent of its accusation.

—Jeremy Taylor, *The Rule and Exercises of Holy Dying*, 1651

That which is the end of any natural thing, cannot be evil in itself; since that which is according to nature, is directed to an end by divine providence.

—St. Thomas Aquinas, *Summa Contra Gentiles*, III, 1260

For nothing is there that may more effectually withdraw the soul from the wretched affections of the body than may the remembrance of death.

—St. Thomas More, *The Four Last Things*, 1522

It is man only who is able to face his death consciously; that belongs to his greatness and dignity. . . . Man's knowledge that he has to die is also man's knowledge that he is above death.

—Paul Tillich, *The Shaking of the Foundations*, 1948

Death is a detail. Death is nothing more than changing gears in the journey of life.

—Hubert van Zeller, *We Die Standing Up*, 1949

Death gives life its fullest reality.

—Anthony Dalla Villa, *Eulogy* for Andy Warhol, St. Patrick's Cathedral, New York City, April 1, 1987

Each night is but the past day's funeral, and the morning his resurrection: why then should our funeral sleep be otherwise than our sleep at night?

—Arthur Warwick, *Spare Minutes*, 1637

DEEDS

Not by the Creed but by the Deed.

—F. Adler, *Motto of the Ethical Culture Society*

We have left undone those things which we ought to have done; and we have done those things which we ought not to have done.

—*The Book of Common Prayer* (American version), 1876

An evil deed, like freshly drawn milk, does not turn sour at once.

—*Dhammapada*, c. 5th century B.C.

No man can become a saint in his sleep.

—Henry Drummond, *The Greatest Thing in the World*, 1890

God plays and laughs in good deeds, whereas all other deeds, which do not make for the glory of God, are like ashes before Him.

—Meister Eckhart (14th century), *Works*

For if any one is a hearer of the word and not a doer, he is like a man who observes his natural face in a mirror; for he observes himself and goes away and at once forgets what he was like. But he who looks into the perfect law, the law of liberty, and perseveres, being no hearer that forgets but a doer that acts, he shall be blessed in his doing.

Holy Bible, James 1:23-25

There is no more contemptible type of human character than that of the nerveless sentimentalist and dreamer who spends his life in a weltering sea of sensibility and emotion, but who never does a manly concrete deed.

—William James, *Principles of Psychology*, 1890

Sick or well, blind or seeing, bond or free, we are here for a purpose and however we are situated, we please God better with useful deeds than with many prayers or pious resignation.

—Helen Keller, *My Religion*, 1927

The good deed drives away the evil deeds.

—*Koran, Sura*, II. 116, c. 625

If we are often puzzled what to think, we need seldom be in doubt what to do.

—John Lubbock, *The Pleasures of Life*, 1887

The Lord of this universe becomes pleased with him who is engaged in doing good to the world, since the Lord is its soul and refuge.

—*Mahanirvana Tantra*, prior to 5th century B.C.

It is not enough to do good; one must do it in the right way.

—John Viscount Morley, *On Compromise*, 1874

Good deeds are the best prayer.

—Serbian proverb

It matters not whether a man does much or little, if only he directs his heart towards Heaven.

—*Talmud*, c. 200-500

Rabbi Eleazar used to say: One whose wisdom exceeds his deeds may be compared to a tree whereof the branches are many and the roots few, so that when the winds come it is uprooted and turned upon its face.

—*Talmud*, c. 200-500

DEEDS

What makes Christ's teachings difficult is that they obligate
us to do something about them.
—John J. Wade, *Conquering with Christ*, 1942

Seek ye for a store of good deeds, men and women! for a
store of good deeds is full of salvation.
—*Zend-Avesta*, c. 6th century B.C.

DESIRE

A contented mind is the greatest blessing a man can enjoy in
this world; and if in the present life his happiness arises
from the subduing of his desires, it will arise in the next from
the gratification of them.
—Joseph Addison (1672–1719), *Selections from the Spectator*

If the comforts of the world are considered as paramount,
then there will be desire for more and more comfort and
pleasure. The result will be apprehension and anxiety.
—Swami Akhilananda, *Mental Health and Hindu Psychology*, 1951

If a man acts from the motive of Desire, he is not under compulsion because Desire is followed by pleasure; and what is
done for the sake of pleasure is not compulsory.
—Aristotle (384–322 B.C.), *Magna Moralia*, I, xii, 3-4

People have a feeling of "Give it to me quick." The contemporary mind feels a kind of relief when it sees things rapidly
consummated.
—Saul Bellow, interview, *People*, March 3, 1989

That man attains peace who, abandoning all desires, moves
about without attachment and longing, without the sense of
"I" and "mine."
—*Bhagavad-Gita*, between 5th and 2nd centuries B.C.

Cut down the whole forest of desire, not just one tree only.
—*Dhammapada*, c. 5th century B.C.

When we start deceiving ourselves into thinking not that we
want something or need something, not that it is a pragmatic
necessity for us to have it, but that it is a *moral imperative*
that we have it, then is when we join the fashionable mad-
men, and then is when the thin whine of hysteria is heard in
the land, and then is when we are in bad trouble.
—Joan Didion, *Slouching Towards Bethlehem*, 1968

When all desires of the heart shall cease, then man becomes immortal; then he attains to union with absolute being.
　　　　　　　　　　　　—*Katha Upanishad*, prior to 400 B.C.

Our visions begin with our desires.
　　　　　　　　　　　—Audre Lorde, in Claudia Tate, *Black Women Writers at Work*, 1983

All moral rules must be tested by examining whether they tend to realize ends that we desire. I say ends that we desire, not ends that we *ought* to desire. . . . Outside human desires there is no moral standard.
　　　　　　　　　　　—Bertrand Russell, *What I Believe*, 1925

It is doubtful that any heavier curse could be imposed on man than the gratification of all his wishes without effort on his part, leaving nothing for his hopes, desires or struggles.
　　　　　　　　　　　—Samuel Smiles, *Self-Help*, 1859

In my experience, there is only one motivation, and that is desire. No reason or principles contain it or stand against it.
　　　　　　　　　　　—Jane Smiley, *Ordinary Love*, 1989

Whensoever a man desireth aught above measure, immediately he becometh restless. The proud and avaricious man is never at rest; while the poor and the lowly of heart abide in the multitude of peace.
　　　　　　　　　　　—Thomas à Kempis, *Imitation of Christ*, c. 1441

With the ceasing of craving, grasping ceases; with the ceasing of grasping, coming into existence ceases.
　　　　　　　　　　　—*Upadana Sutra*, c. 300 B.C.

Craving is the hankering after pleasure, or existence, or success. It is the germ from which springs all human misery.
　　　　　　　　　　　—Vinaya, Mahavagga, between 5th and 1st century B.C.

Conquer desire and you will conquer fear. But as long as you are a slave you must be a coward.
　　　　　　　　　　　—John Wesley, letter to Samuel Furley, February 21, 1756

If all beings are Buddha, why all this striving?
　　　　　　　　　　　—Dogen Zenji, in Robert Aitken, *The Mind of Clover*, 1984

DESPAIR

The shoddy work of despair, the pointless work of pride,
equally betray Creation. They are wastes of life.
—Wendell Berry, "Healing," *What Are People For?*, 1990

'Tis an epitome of hell, an extract, a quintessence, a com-
pound, a mixture of all feral maladies, tyrannical tortures,
plagues, and perplexities.
—Robert Burton, *Anatomy of Melancholy*, III, 1621

Despair is one of Hell's catchpolls.
—Thomas Dekker, *The Honest Whore*, 1630

Despair is the conclusion of fools.
—Benjamin Disraeli, *Alroy*, 1833

We feel like strangers on our own streets. Where we should
feel the safest, we rather feel that no one would help us if we
were in trouble, that what happens to us, whether good or
bad, makes no difference to the world around us—that *we*
make no difference.
—Suzanne Gordon, *Lonely in America*, 1976

My God, my God, why hast thou forsaken me?
—*Holy Bible*, Psalms 22:1

He who despairs of pardon for his sin, damns himself by despair rather than by the crime he has committed.
—St. Isidore of Seville (560–636), *Dialogue between Erring Soul and Reason*

When the sinner despairs of the forgiveness of sin, it is almost as if he were directly picking a quarrel with God.
—Sören Kierkegaard, *Sickness unto Death*, 1849

God is more near in man's despair
Than man has wisdom to beware.
—John Masefield, *The Coming of Christ*, 1928

Modern man's despair is not despair of God at all, but
despair of all that is not God. Beyond that certain despair
lies Christian hope, the certainty that God alone is enough
for man.
—William McNamara, *The Art of Being Human*, 1962

No man has the right to despair, since each was the messenger of a thing greater than himself. Despair was the rejection of God within oneself.

—Antoine de Saint-Exupéry, *Flight of Arras*, 1942

Despair is the sin which cannot find—because it will not look for it—forgiveness.

—Hubert van Zeller, *We Die Standing Up*, 1940

DESTINY

Destiny, n. A tyrant's authority for crime and a fool's excuse for failure.

—Ambrose Bierce, *Devil's Dictionary*, 1906

We are material in the hands of the Genius of the universe for a still larger destiny that we cannot see in the everlasting rhythm of worlds.

—John Elof Boodin, *Cosmic Evolution*, 1925

Life and Death, existence and non-existence, success and non-success, poverty and wealth, virtue and vice, good and evil report, hunger and thirst, warmth and cold—these all revolve upon the changing wheel of Destiny.

—Chuang-tzu, c. 300 B.C.

The highest moral ideal either for a people or for an individual is to be true to its destiny . . . to leave the known for the unknown.

—Christopher Dawson, in *The Sociological Review*, 1925

Destiny waits in the hand of God.

—T.S. Eliot, *Murder in the Cathedral*, 1935

God has for no man a fixed and final destiny in the sense of either an inexorable fate or an assured security. . . . There is nothing in all creation that can separate us from God and his loving care.

—Georgia Harkness, *The Providence of God*, 1960

Men heap together the mistakes of their lives, and create a monster which they call Destiny.

—John Oliver Hobbes, *The Sinner's Comedy*, 1892

DETACHMENT

The man who, casting off all desires, lives free from attachment; who is free from egoism and from the feeling that this or that is mine, obtains tranquillity.

—*Bhagavad-Gita*, c. 5th century B.C.

The prophet and the martyr do not see the hooting throng. Their eyes are fixed on the eternities.

—Benjamin Cardozo, *Law and Literature*, 1931

The virtue of poverty means complete detachment; we are not to depend on things, but they on us. . . . You will get detachment from things and from self by merely giving yourself to God, and accepting yourself as you find yourself to be.

—John Chapman, *Spiritual Letters*, 1935

Detachment, serenity—vague, almost empty words, except in those moments when we would have answered by a smile if we had been told we had only a few minutes left to live.

—E. M. Cioran, *Drawn and Quartered*, 1971

Now that my heart is closed against all desire for earthly things, now that I have no longer any sense for the transitory and perishable, the universe appears before my eyes clothed in a more glorious form.

—J.G. Fichte (1762–1814), *The Vocation of Man*

If thou wilt be a spiritual pilgrim, thou shalt strip thyself naked of all that thou hast.

—Walter Hilton, *Scale of Perfection*, c. 1390

Detachment, the foundation of all mystic techniques, may be compressed into the formula: I will not to will.

—Arthur Koestler, *The Yogi and the Commissar*, 1945

Nothing short of religion will inspire self-detachment. A man will refuse for the sake of himself as a finite human animal to undergo the discipline to which he will gladly submit, once he is brought into conscious relation with God.

—Rom Landau, *Sex, Life and Faith*, 1946

He saw God's foot upon the treadle of the loom, and spoke it;
and therefore his shipmates called him mad. So man's insanity is heaven's sense; and wandering from all mortal reason, man comes at last to that celestial thought, which to
reason is absurd and frantic; and weal or woe, feels then un-
compromised, indifferent as his God.

—Herman Melville, *Moby Dick*, 1851

Fools! give up thy thirst for wealth, banish all desires from
thy heart. Let thy mind be satisfied with what is gained by
the *Karma.*

—*Mohamudgara* (c. 800), sometimes attributed to Shankara,
in F. Max Müller, *Six Systems*

O God! Give to Thine enemies whatever Thou hast assigned
to me of this world's goods, and to Thy friends whatever
Thou hast assigned to me in the life to come; for Thou Thyself art sufficient for me.

—Rabia a-Adawiyya (717–801), in P.K. Hitti, *History of the Arabs*

Detachment is not a denial of life but a denial of death; not a
disintegration but the condition of wholeness; not a refusal
to love but the determination to love truly, deeply and fully.

—Gerald Vann, *Eve and the Gryphon*, 1946

DEVIL

God may use Satan for His own purposes. Elements emerge
from the chaos of evil and are built up into good.

—S. Alexander, *Space, Time and Deity*, 1920

Satan transforms himself as it were into an angel of light,
and often sets a snare for the faithful by means of the divine
Scriptures themselves. Thus does he make heretics, thus
weaken faith, thus attack the requirements of piety.

—St. Ambrose, *Exposito in c.* iv *Lucas, n.* 26, 333

But he who is the Prince
Of darkness, Mara—knowing this was Buddha
Who should deliver men . . .
Gave unto all his evil powers command.
Wherefore there trooped from every deepest pit
The fiends who war with Wisdom and the Light
Nor knoweth one
Not even the wisest, how those fiends of Hell
Battled that night to keep the Truth from Buddha.

—Edwin Arnold, *The Light of Asia* (based largely on a late Buddhist epic), 1850

The Devil often transforms himself into an angel to tempt
men, some for their instruction and some for their ruin.
—St. Augustine, *The City of God*, XV, 426

Satan is too hard a master. He would never command as did
the Other with divine simplicity: "Do likewise." The devil will
have no victim resemble him. He permits only a rough caricature, impotent, abject, which has to serve as food for eternal irony, the mordant irony of the depths.
—Georges Bernanos, *The Dairy of a Country Priest*, 1937

Of the evil spirit [Ahriman] are the law of violence, the religion of sorcery, the weapons of fiendishness, and the perversion of God's [Ahura Mazda's] creations, and his desire is
this: Inquire not concerning me, and do not understand me;
for if ye ask about me and understand me, ye will not thereafter follow me.
—*Bunsahis*, 7th century B.C.

A history of Satanism would be a history of the whole human
race; it would be a history of errors and crimes, of idolatry
and false religions, of hatred and war, of the reign of sin and
death, of the road leading to hell.
—Nicolas Corte, *Who Is the Devil?*, 1958

The devil has power to suggest evil, but he was not given the
power to compel you against your will.
— St. Cyril of Jerusalem, *Catechetical Lectures*, 350

I think if the devil doesn't exist, but man has created him, he
has created him in his own image and likeness.
—Feodor Dostoevsky, *The Brothers Karamazov*, 1880

The Evil Will lures man in this world, then testifies against
him in the world to come.
—Jonathan B. Eleazar, *Talmud*, 200–500

Men should know that the will of Satan is always unrighteous but that his power is never unjust. The iniquities he
proposes to commit, God allows in all justice.
—Pope St. Gregory (540–604), *P.L.* LXXV, 564

Popular devotion is to religious life what the link with people
and family, country and home, is to the natural life.
—Romano Guardini, *Prayer in Practice*, 1957

Resist the devil and he will flee from you.

—*Holy Bible*, James 4:7

At all times, too many Christians have behaved as though the devil were a First Principle, on the same footing as God. They have paid more attention to evil and the problem of its eradication than to good.

—Aldous Huxley, *The Devils of Loudon*, 1952

There is little in Satan's speeches that can give pain to a pious ear.

—Samuel Johnson, *Essay on Milton*, 1781

What we see in Satan is the horrible co-existence of a subtle and incessant intellectual activity with an incapacity to understand anything.

—C.S. Lewis, Preface to John Milton, *Paradise Lost*, 1942

The Devil seduces us at first by all the allurements of sin, in order thereafter to plunge us into despair; he pampers up the flesh, that he may by-and-by prostrate the spirit.

—Martin Luther (1483–1546), *Table-Talk*

That there is a Devil is a thing doubted by none but such as are under the influence of the Devil.

—Cotton Mather, *A Discourse on Wonders of the Invisible World*, 1692

If one believes in the truth of the Bible, it is impossible to doubt the reality of the Devil for a single moment.

—Denis de Rougement, *The Devil's Share*, 1944

Nowhere in the Sacred Scripture do we find warrant for the popular myth of the Devil as a buffoon. . . . Rather is he described as an angel fallen from heaven, and as "the Prince of this world," whose business it is to tell us that there is no other world.

—Fulton J. Sheen, *Communism and the Conscience of the West*, 1948

Belief in the Devil as an adversary playing havoc with God's plans is not a very satisfactory answer to the mystery of iniquity.

—Ralph W. Sockman, *How to Believe*, 1953

It is one of the malicious devices of the devil to fill us with shame at the prospect of being defeated by evil preoccupations, so that we shall be hindered from lifting our eyes to God in contrition and praying to be freed of them.

—St. Nilus Sorsky (1433–1505), *The Monastic Rule*

The Evil One can not act *directly* on our higher faculties, the intellect and the will. God . . . alone can enter there and touch the mainspring of the will without doing violence to it.

—Adolphe Tanqueray, *The Spiritual Life*, 1490

The Devil's cleverest wile is to make men believe that he does not exist.

—Gerald C. Treacy, *The Devil!*, 1952

The devil is free to remain good, but there is no good in him.

—St. Thomas Aquinas, *De Malo*, q. XVI, 1268

DEVOTION

Of all devotions the best devotion is to utter the name of God.

—Arjan (died 1606), in M.A. Macauliffe, *The Sikh Religion*, III

True devotion . . . presupposes love of God; rather, it is nothing else than the true love of God.

—St. Francis de Sales, *Introduction to the Devout Life*, 1609

Adoration is the surge of the spirit of man upward and Godward.

—Georgia Harkness, *Prayer and the Common Life*, 1948

But Ruth said, "Entreat me not to leave you or to return from following you; for where you go I will go, and where you lodge, I will lodge; your people shall be my people, and your God my God . . . "

—*Holy Bible*, Ruth 1:16

But they who wait for the Lord shall renew their strength, they shall mount up with wings like eagles, they shall run and not be weary, they shall walk and not faint.

—*Holy Bible*, Isaiah 40:31

Adoration is the use of intellect, feeling, will and imagination in making acts of devotion directed towards God in his personal aspect or as incarnated in human form.

—Aldous Huxley, *The Perennial Philosophy*, 1944

There is no devotion without virtue.
—*Japji*, attributed to Guru Nanak (1496–1538)

Devotion, which is a derivative of the Latin word for *to vow*, means to yield oneself, to commit oneself, to consecrate oneself to the object of devotion, without regard to the sacrifice or suffering involved.
—Douglas V. Steere, *Door into Life*, 1948

The simple adoration of a God has preceded all the systems in the world.
—Voltaire, *Philosophical Dictionary*, II, 1764

DISCIPLINE

As the saving doctrine of Christ is the soul of the Church, so discipline forms the ligaments by which the members of the body are joined together and kept each in its proper place.
—John Calvin, *Institutes*, IV, 1536

When strict with oneself one rarely fails.
—Confucius, *Sayings of*, 5th century B.C.

Discipline means power at command; mastery of the resources available for carrying through the actions undertaken. To know what one is to do and to move to do it promptly and by the use of the requisite means is to be disciplined, whether we are thinking of an army or the mind. Discipline is positive.
—John Dewey, *Democracy and Education*, 1916

One's own self is the most difficult to subdue.
—*Dhammapada*, c. 5th century B.C.

And you shall remember all the way which the Lord your God has led you these forty years in the wilderness, that he might humble you, testing you to know what was in your heart, whether you would keep his commandments, or not.
—*Holy Bible*, Deuteronomy 8:2

Self-discipline must necessarily be in proportion to the misuse of any sense or power, but it is the true use of it we aim at in every act of self-discipline.
—B. W. Maturin, *Self-Knowledge and Self-Discipline*, 1939

Who is mighty? He who subdues his [evil] inclination. . . . He that ruleth his spirit is better than he that taketh a city.
—Pirke Aboth, *Talmud*, between 2nd and 4th century

DISCIPLINE

Self-discipline never means giving up anything—for giving up
is a loss. Our Lord did not ask us to give up the things of
earth, but to exchange them for better things.
—Fulton J. Sheen, *Lift Up Your Hearts*, 1950

I have indeed no other business in life than to go about per-
suading you all, young and old, to care less for your bodies
and your possessions and to make the protection of your
souls your chief concern.
—Socrates, "Apology," in Plato, *Dialogues*, 399 B.C.

DISCORD

There can be no contradiction or schism where God is. His
truth cannot be otherwise than one truth, one life, one love.
—Karl Adam, *The Spirit of Catholicism*, 1924

The discords of Christendom have drowned the finest strains
of music in the human soul.
—Peter Ainslie, *The Message of the Disciples for the Union of the Church*, 1913

Have we not one God, and one Christ, and one Spirit of grace
poured out upon us? And is there not one calling in Christ?
Why do we divide and tear asunder the members of Christ,
and raise up strife against our own body, and reach such
a pitch of madness as to forget that we are members of one
another?
—St. Clement of Rome, *Letter to the Corinthians*, c. 100

Most of the great schisms and heresies have their roots in
social or national antipathies.
—Christopher Dawson, *Science for a New World*, 1934

If the churches persist in presenting humanity with the
spectacle of a Christendom at logger-heads with itself they
might as well give up.
—Alfred Delp, *Prison Meditations of Father Alfred Delp*, 1963

So long as we cling to any humanly devised definitions,
which we insist upon as articles of faith necessary to salvation, we shall inevitably insure discord for all time.
—R.T. Grenfell, *The Adventure of Life*, 1911

Every kingdom divided against itself is laid waste, and no
city or house divided against itself will stand.
—*Holy Bible*, Matthew 12:25

The causes of division lie deep in the past, and are by no means simple or wholly blameworthy. Yet none can doubt that self-will, ambition, lack of charity among Christians have been principal factors in the mingled process responsible for the breaches of Christendom.
—Lambeth Conference (of Anglican Bishops), 1920

Disown the idea of an abiding God as the Creator and the ultimate end of all men, and you can only have peoples in various times and places, each working for its own ends in terms of their own time and place. Hence place must forever war against place, and time against time.
—Louis J.A. Mercier, address, October 30, 1942

The fact today is not simply that we hold different views but that we have become different types of men, with different styles of interior life. We are therefore uneasy in one another's presence.
—John Courtney Murray, *We Hold These Truths*, 1960

So long as a man quarrels and disputes about doctrines and dogmas, he has not tasted the nectar of true faith; when he has tasted it, he becomes quiet and full of peace.
—Sri Ramakrishna, *Sayings of*, 1903

There are enough targets to aim at without firing at each other.
—Theodore Roosevelt, address, National Federation of Churches, 1902

Let those who call themselves Catholics, or Protestants, or Jews recall that the function of their religion is to intensify the spiritual life of man and not to empty the vials of bitterness into hearts, stirring up one against another.
—Fulton J. Sheen, *Way to Happiness*, 1953

DIVINITY

He who would see the Divinity must see him in his Children.
—William Blake, *Jerusalem*, 1820

What is there of the divine in a load of brick? What . . . in a barber's shop?. . . Much. All.
—Ralph Waldo Emerson, journal, July 18, 1834

Divinity is not something supernatural that ever and again invades the natural order in a crashing miracle. Divinity is not in some remote heaven, seated on a throne. Divinity is love. . . . Wherever goodness, beauty, truth, love, are—there is the divine.
> —Harry Emerson Fosdick, *The Hope of the World*, 1933

Divinity is in its omniscience and omnipotence like a wheel, a circle, a whole, that can neither be understood, nor divided, nor begun nor ended.
> —Hildegard of Bingen (1098–1179), *Illuminations of*, 1985

The divine shall mean for us only such a primal reality as the individual feels impelled to respond to solemnly and gravely, and neither by a curse nor a jest.
> —William James, *Varieties of Religious Experience*, 1902

Divinity finds its image in human and social constructs. The way we think about God ultimately will be the way we think about ourselves and our institutions.
> —M. Douglas Meeks, *God the Economist*, 1989

We may think of the Divine as a fire whose outgoing warmth pervades the Universe.
> —Plotinus (203–262), *Enneads*

Man is to become divine by realizing the divine. Idols or temples, or churches or books are only the supports, the help of his spiritual childhood.
> —Swami Vivekananda, address, Parliament of World Religions, 1893

DOCTRINE

There is no revealed doctrine proclaimed by the Church which is not contained in its exact substance in the sources of revelation, that is, in Scripture and Tradition. But it is not always expressly revealed in its specific content, and is often contained so to say wrapped up in other truths.
> —Karl Adam, *The Spirit of Catholicism*, 1924

Doctrine is nothing but the skin of truth set up and stuffed.
> —Henry Ward Beecher, *Life Thoughts*, 1858

It is clear that religion must have some doctrine, and it is clear again that such doctrine will not be ultimate truth.
> —F.H. Bradley, *Appearance and Reality*, 1894

It is indeed harmful to come under the sway of utterly new and strange doctrines.

—Confucius, *Sayings of*, 5th century B.C.

Religious doctrines were determined not by the logic of a few but by the needs of the many; they were a frame of belief within which the common man, inclined by nature to a hundred unsocial actions, could be formed into a being sufficiently disciplined and self-controlled to make society and civilization possible.

—Will Durant, *The Reformation*, 1957

A false doctrine cannot be refuted; for it rests upon the conviction that the false is true.

—J.W. von Goethe (1749–1832), *Maxims and Reflections*

A purely doctrinal faith has a certain instability in itself, for it often deserts us in consequence of difficulties which meet us in our speculation, though we find ourselves inevitably returning to it again and again.

—Immanuel Kant, *Critique of Pure Reason*, 1781

No doctrine is defined until it is violated.

—John Henry Newman, *On the Development of Christian Doctrine*, 1845

I do not find that Jesus laid down any basic doctrine beyond that of a universal loving God and a universal brotherhood of man.

—Albert Jay Nock, *Memoirs of a Superfluous Man*, 1943

Christian doctrine right now is chaotic. At no time in recent centuries has the Christian tradition as a force been taken as seriously by as broad a constituency as it now is. But the means of formulating what that tradition implies or what specific issues before us mean can't seem, somehow, to come together.

—Jaroslav Pelikan, in *U.S. News & World Report*, June 26, 1989

In-so-far as the rule of truth is prior in time, so far must all later doctrines be judged heresies.

—Tertullian, *Adversus Hermogenes*, I, c. 206

The least one can demand of people who judge doctrine is that they should judge of it in the sense in which the teacher himself understood it.

—Leo Tolstoy, *What I Believe*, 1895

DOCTRINE

It behooves Christian doctrine . . . to be consolidated by
years, enlarged by time, refined by age, and yet, withal, to
continue uncorrupt and unadulterate, complete and perfect
in all the measurements of its parts.

—St. Vincent of Lérins, *A Commonitory*, 434

DOUBT

The first key to wisdom is assiduous and frequent questioning. . . . For by doubting we come to inquiry, and by inquiry
we arrive at truth.

—Peter Abelard, *Yes and No*, c. 1120

In 1890 the "liberal" was debating whether there were two
Isaiahs; in 1930 the extreme "modernist" was debating
whether there was a personal God.

—Gaius Glenn Atkins, *Religion in Our Times*, 1932

Never be afraid to doubt, if only you have the disposition
to believe, and doubt in order that you may end in believing
the truth.

—Samuel Taylor Coleridge, *Aids to Reflection*, 1825

If you would be a real seeker after truth, it is necessary
that at least once in your life you doubt, as far as possible,
all things.

—René Descartes, *Principles of Philosophy*, 1644

Doubt is the trouble of a soul left to itself, which wants to
see what God hides from it, and out of self-love seeks impossible securities.

—François Fénelon (1651–1715), *Spiritual Letters*

But doubt is as crucial to faith as darkness is to light.
Without one, the other has no context and is meaningless.
Faith is, by definition, uncertainty. It is full of doubt, steeped
in risk. It is about matters not of the known, but of the
unknown.

—Carter Heywood, *A Priest Forever*, 1976

To have doubted one's own first principles is the mark of a
civilized man.

—Oliver Wendell Holmes, *Collected Legal Papers*, 1920

And Gideon said to him, "Pray, sir, if the Lord is with us,
why then has all this befallen us? And where are all his wonderful deeds which our fathers recounted to us?"

—*Holy Bible*, Judges 6:13

There may be a measure of truth in the traditional doctrine
that . . . all doubt is at bottom a dishonest rationalization
of sin.
—John Hutchison, *Faith, Reason and Existence*, 1956

Doubt is nothing but a trivial agitation on the surface of the
soul, while deep down there is a calm certainty.
—François Mauriac, *God and Mammon*, 1946

Doubts are more cruel than the worst of truths.
—Molière, *The Misanthrope*, 1666

It is only after doubt has come that intellectual belief arises.
To entertain reasons for believing in the existence of a thing
presupposes the possibility of its non-existence.
—James Bisset Pratt, *The Psychology of Religion and Belief*, 1907

Doubt is good for the human soul, its humility, and con-
sequently its greater potential ultimately to discover its
Creator.
—Emanuel Rackman, *One Man's Judaism*, 1970

Once I heard a man say: "I spent twenty years trying to come
to terms with my doubts. Then one day it dawned on me that
I had better come to terms with my faith. Now I have passed
from the agony of the questions I cannot answer into the
agony of answers I cannot escape. And it's a great relief."
—David E. Roberts, *The Grandeur and Misery of Man*, 1955

Doubt is part of all religion. All the religious thinkers were
doubters.
—Isaac Bashevis Singer, in *The New York Times*, December 3, 1978

Serious doubt is confirmation of faith. It indicates the seri-
ousness of the concern, its unconditional character.
—Paul Tillich, *Dynamics of Faith*, 1957

DUTY

Never to tire, never to grow cold; to be patient, sympathetic,
tender; to look for the budding flower and the opening heart;
to hope always, like God, to love always—this is duty.
—H.F. Amiel, journal, May 27, 1849

A man's own natural duty, even if it seems imperfectly done,
is better than work not naturally his own, even if this is well
performed.
—*Bhagavad-Gita*, between 5th and 2nd centuries B.C.

To do my duty in that state of life unto which it shall please God to call me.

—*The Book of Common Prayer*, 1662

If a man like Hitler gained a position from which he had the power to do magnified harm, it is quite conceivable that he never could have reached it but for the minor sins and small delinquencies and petty lapses from duty on the part of multitudes of men.

—Herbert Butterfield, *Christianity, Diplomacy and War*, 1953

While still unable to do your duty to the living, how can you do your duty to the dead?. . . Not yet understanding life, how can you understand death?

—Confucius, *Analects*, 5th century B.C.

Let no one forget his own duty for the sake of another's, however great; let a man after he has discovered his own duty, be always attentive to his duty.

—*Dhammapada*, c. 5th century B.C.

Service is the rent each of us pays for living—the very purpose of life and not something you do in your spare time or after you have reached your personal goals.

—Marian Wright Edelman, speech, Howard University, May 12, 1990

In duty the individual finds his liberation; liberation from dependence on mere natural impulse.

—G.W.F. Hegel, *The Philosophy of Right*, 1821

We who are strong ought to bear with the failings of the weak, and not to please ourselves.

—*Holy Bible*, Romans 15:1

"Learn what is true in order to do what is right," is the summary of the whole duty of man, for all who are unable to satisfy their mental hunger with the east wind of authority.

—Thomas Henry Huxley, *Lay Sermons*, 1870

Duty is the necessity of acting out of respect for the law. . . . An action from duty must eliminate entirely the influence of inclinations and thus every object of the will.

—Immanuel Kant, *Metaphysics of Ethics*, 1785

Those who gain no experience are those who shirk the King's highway for fear of encountering Duty seated by the roadside.
—George Macdonald, *Thomas Wingfold*, 1876

Right is the faith of the individual. Duty is the common collective faith.
—Joseph Mazzini, *Essays*, 1887

The path of duty lies in what is near, and men seek for it in what is remote. The work of duty lies in what is easy, and men seek for it in what is difficult.
—Mencius, c. 300 B.C.

A sense of duty is moral glue, constantly subject to stress.
—William Safire, in *The New York Times*, May 23, 1986

Duty becomes a disease with us; it drags us ever forward. . . . This duty, this idea of duty is the midday summer sun which scorches the innermost soul of mankind. . . . The only true duty is to be unattached and to work as free beings, to give up all work unto God.
—Swami Vivekananda (1863–1902), *Works of*

A sense of duty pursues us ever. It is omnipresent, like the Deity.
—Daniel Webster, argument at trial of J.F. Knapp, 1830

An act of duty is law in practice.
—Benjamin Whichcote, *Moral and Religious Aphorisms*, 1753

Ecstasy

The beginning of ecstasy is the lifting of the veil and the vision of the Divine Guardian, and the presence of understanding, and the contemplation of the invisible, and the discoursing on secret things and perceiving the non-existent, and it means that you pass away from where you are.

—Ziyad B. al-Arabi (9th century), in Margaret Smith, *Readings From the Mystics of Islam*

For when, through love, the soul goes beyond all work of the intellect and all images in the mind, and is rapt above itself (a favor only God can bestow), utterly leaving itself, it flows into God: then is God its peace and fullness. . . . It sinks down into the abyss of divine love, where, dead to itself, it lives in God.

—Louis de Blois (1506–66), *Works*

The soul is created in a place between Time and Eternity: with its highest powers it touches Eternity, with its lower Time.

—Meister Eckhart (1260–1327), *Sermons*

No writers have insisted more strongly than the mystics themselves on the fact that ecstasy can be counterfeited by diabolic influences, or even by hysteria.

—Ronald A. Knox, *Enthusiasm*, 1950

Ecstasy means living in another. Here, you are living in the being you love; you are living in the race whose history you summarize, whose function you fulfill, whose life you gather in your hands and pass on to the future ages; you are living (if you have eyes to see), in God.

—Gerald Vann, *The Heart of Man*, 1945

Ecstasy is from the contemplation of things vaster than the individual and imperfectly seen perhaps, by all those that still live.

—William Butler Yeats, *Dramatis Personae*, 1935

ECUMENISM

> We need to find out, not a formula, but a temper—not a
> creed, but a Faith—which is common to all, and which un-
> derlies all, and supports all, and inspires all.
> —T.H. Bindley, in *The Modern Churchman*, September 1921

> Until the eschatological moment when we can break bread
> together around the Lord's Table, we must foster a spirit that
> will at least make it possible for us to break bread together
> around a dining room table.
> —Robert McAfee Brown, *An American Dialogue*, 1960

> Underneath all differences of theological expression, there is
> a common gospel which makes the Church, in fact, one.
> —William A. Brown, *A Teacher and His Times*, 1940

> The cause of Christian unity can best be served neither by re-
> ligious controversy nor by political action, but by the theolog-
> ical virtues: faith, hope and charity. And these virtues must
> be applied both in the intellectual and religious spheres.
> —Christopher Dawson, *The Judgment of the Nations*, 1942

> The very problem of Christian reconciliation is not that of a
> *correlation* of parallel traditions, but precisely that of the
> *reintegration* of a distorted tradition.
> —Georges Florovsky, in Ecumenical Review, January 1960

> How the principle of Christian democracy can be repro-
> claimed for the unity of the distorted and disunited Christen-
> dom constitutes one of the gravest problems before us today.
> —Frank Gavin, *Seven Centuries of the Problem of Church and State*, 1938

> The modern Ecumenical Movement thus unites the Catholic
> ideal of Christian unity with the Protestant ideal of Christian
> liberty, and promises to break the tragic deadlock between
> those opposite but equally essential trends in Christian life
> and thought.
> —Walter Marshall Horton, *Christian Theology*, 1958

> I think all Christians, whether papists or Protestants, agree
> in the essential articles, and that their differences are trivial,
> and rather political than religious.
> —Samuel Johnson, *Boswell's Life of*, June 25, 1763

> Our separated brethren are not theological adversaries to be
> refuted, but friends seeking with us a deeper love of Christ.
> —Bernard Leeming, *Unitas*, XI, No. 2, 1952

The road to unity is the road to repentance. It demands resolute turning away from all those loyalties to the lesser values of the self, the denomination, and the nation, which deny the inclusiveness of divine love.

—H. Richard Niebuhr, *Social Sources of Denominationalism*, 1929

Christendom must regain its life and vigor, and form itself once again into one visible Church without regard for national frontiers. It must pour out the old cornucopia of blessings on the people once again.

—Novalis (1772–1801), *Christendom or Europe*, 1826

A clergyman was once asked whether the members of his church were united. He replied that they were perfectly united—frozen together.

—*Old Farmer's Almanac*, 1865

The pope—and we know this well—is without doubt the most serious obstacle on the ecumenical road.

—Pope Paul VI, quote, May 29, 1967

Christian religions mix about as well as holy water and holy oil.

—Barbara Rosewicz, in *The Wall Street Journal*, April 5, 1985

Religions are cut off from one another by barriers of mutual incomprehension . . . the sense of the absolute stands on a different plane in each of them.

—Frithjof Schon, *Gnosis*, 1957

The ecumenical movement . . . is able to heal divisions which have become historically obsolete, to replace confessional fanaticism by interconfessional cooperation, to conquer denominational provincialism, and to produce a new vision of the unity of all churches in their foundation.

—Paul Tillich, *Systematic Theology*, III, 1964

EDUCATION

Nothing in education is so astonishing as the amount of ignorance it accumulates in the form of inert facts.

—Henry Adams, *The Education of Henry Adams*, 1906

The soul and mind and life are powers of living and can grow, but cannot be cut out or made. . . . One can indeed help the being to grow . . . but even so, the growth must still come from within.

—Sri Aurobindo, *The Life Divine*, 1949

Next to the care of our own souls a right education of our children is greatest.
— John Bellers, *Epistles to Friends Concerning Education*, 1697

Education tends to be diagrammatic and categorical, opening up no sluices in the human imagination on the wonder or beauty of their unique estate in the cosmos. Little wonder that it becomes so easy for our young to regard human hurt casually or to be uninspired by the magic of sensitivity.
— Norman Cousins, in *Saturday Review*, 1965

The primary business of school is to train children in co-operative and mutually helpful living; to foster in them the consciousness of mutual interdependence.
— John Dewey, *The School and Society*, 1899

The trouble with some Christian colleges is that they exist as promotional or maintenance institutions of the Church, and are not, in a high and holy sense, educational.
— Nels F.S. Ferré, *Christian Faith and Higher Education*, 1954

Education—the process of driving a set of prejudices down your throat.
— Martin H. Fischer, *Fischerisms*, 1937

Without religious preparation in childhood, no true religion and no union with God is possible for men.
— Friedrich Froebel (1782–1852), *Aphorisms*

Encourage free schools and resolve that not one dollar appropriated for their support shall be appropriated to the support of any sectarian schools.
— Ulysses S. Grant, address, Des Moines, Iowa, 1875

A child that is early taught that he is God's child, that he may live and move and have his being in God, and that he has, therefore, infinite strength at hand for the conquering of any difficulty, will take life more easily, and probably will make more of it.
— Edward Everett Hale (1822–1909), quoted in E.D. Starbuck, *Psychology of Religion*

The first thing education teaches you is to walk alone.
— A.A. Horn, in *Trader Horn*, 1927

Education is the instruction of the intellect in the laws of Nature, under which name I include not merely things and their forces, but men and their ways; and the fashioning of the affections and of the will into an earnest and loving desire to move in harmony with those laws.
—Thomas Henry Huxley, *Lay Sermons*, 1870

The vast population around us are limited to schools of secularism—and in this way secularism is fast becoming the religion of America.
—John Ireland, address, August 11, 1913

Education is typically carried out without specific and continuous reference to the central spiritual values of our culture and without the reverent cultivation of those values which it is the function of religion to maintain.
—F. Ernest Johnson, *The Social Gospel Re-Examined*, 1940

Where Jewish education is neglected, the whole content of Judaism is reduced to merely an awareness of anti-Semitism. Judaism ceases then to be a civilization, and becomes a complex.
—M.M. Kaplan, *Future of the American Jew*, 1948

A good many people will obviously agree with it, others will disagree. . . . We have in this a very easy remedy, and that is to pray ourselves. And I would think it would be a welcome reminder to every American family that we can pray a good deal more at home. We can attend our churches with a good deal more fidelity. And I would hope that all of us would support the Constitution and the responsibility in interpreting it.
—John F. Kennedy, commenting on the U.S. Supreme Court decision banning prayers in the public schools, June 1963

It is essential for the moral development of the child to start with some form of belief in a divine order, whose framework he will at first take for Gospel truth until the spiritual content matures into symbolic interpretation.
—Arthur Koestler, *The Trail of the Dinosaur and Other Essays*, 1955

Religious education is . . . a God-centered business which so infuses the child's entire life that it must move from the baptismal font and on to the altar, but with the core of its spirit in the continuing atmosphere of a Christian home.
—John E. Large, *The Small Needle of Doctor Large*, 1962

No church can sincerely subscribe to the theory that questions of faith do not enter into the education of children.
—Walter Lippmann, *A Preface to Morals*, 1929

And neither mind nor character can be made without a spiritual element. This is just the element that has grown weak, where it has not perished, in our education, and therefore in our civilization, with disastrous results.
—Richard Livingstone, *On Education*, Part II, 1945

As for the parochial school of Christian and Jew, let us regard it as an element of American democracy and as an expression of the freedom of American culture. It is a means of preserving the diversity of cultures within our land.
—Joseph H. Lookstein, *Jewish Education*, XXI, 1949

Reflection is easy and commitment is easy; but the two together—that is an educational task demanding the highest powers.
—Howard Lowry, *The Mind's Adventure: Religion and the Higher Education*, 1950

There is only one sound method of moral education. It is in teaching people to think.
—Everett Dean Martin, *The Meaning of a Liberal Education*, 1926

The danger of education, I have found, is that it so easily confuses means with ends. Worse than that, it quite easily forgets both and devotes itself merely to the mass production of uneducated graduates—people literally unfit for anything except to take part in an elaborate and completely artificial charade which they and their contemporaries have conspired to call "life."
—Thomas Merton, *Love and Living*, 1980

We fervently believe that prayers, Bible readings and sectarian practices should be fostered in the home, church and synagogue, that public institutions such as the public school should be free of such practices.
—Uri Miller (for the Synagogue Council of America), *The New York Times*, June 18, 1963

Functionally viewed, American public education emancipated from sectarianism is indirectly the only universal teacher of religious values in the United States.
—Conrad Henry Moehlman, *School and Church: The American Way*, 1944

Twentieth century public school education is avowedly dealing with values and loyalties, that is to say, with theology
and ethics.
—James Hastings Nicholas, Religion in America, 1958

Education is nothing more than the polishing of each single
link in the great chain that binds humanity together and
gives it unity.
—Johann Heinrich Pestalozzi (1746–1827), The Education of Man: Aphorisms

When we look at the troubled state of the present world . . .
one thing becomes manifest. This is the failure of recent educational practice to prepare men in terms of heart and will to
prevent the strife, misunderstanding, and willfulness that
now arise.
—Nathan M. Pusey, Religion and Freedom of Thought, 1954

Education is the leading of human souls to what is best, and
making what is best out of them; and these two objects are
always attainable together, and by the same means.
—John Ruskin, Stones of Venice, 1853

And what is the education of mankind if not the passage
from faith in authority to personal conviction, and to the
sustained practice of the intellectual duty to consent to no
idea except by virtue of its recognized truth, to accept no fact
until its reality has been, in one way or another, established.
—Auguste Sabatier, The Religions of Authority and Religions of the Spirit, 1904

Religious education is the directed process of helping growing persons progressively to achieve the experience defined
as religious. . . . It is not anything added to education nor
something apart from it. It is a certain quality of education.
—Theodore G. Soares, Religious Education, 1928

Religious exercises are not constitutionally invalid if they
simply reflect differences which exist in the society from
which the school draws its pupils. They become constitutionally invalid only if their administration places the sanction of
secular authority behind one or more particular religious or
irreligious beliefs.
—Justice Potter Stewart, U.S. Supreme Court, dissenting opinion on prayer and
Bible reading in the public schools, June 17, 1963

The principle of learning [higher education] consists in preserving man's clear character, in giving new life to the people, and in dwelling in perfection, or the ultimate good.
—Ta Hsueh (Great Learning), attributed to Confucius, 5th century B.C.

Parents have a prior right to choose the kind of education that shall be given to their children.
—*United Nations Universal Declaration of Human Rights*, Article 26, 1948

The greatest and most urgent task of educators today is to instill ineradicably into the young precisely the utility of the useless, the value of the things that produce no cash returns but that make the "soul worth saving."
—Gerald Vann, *The Water and the Fire*, 1954

EMOTION

The emotion felt by a man in the presence of nature certainly counts for something in the origin of religions.
—Henri Bergson, *The Two Sources of Morality and Religion*, 1935

No religion that ministers only to the intellect and not also to the emotions can meet the needs of men, and this accounts in large measure for the failure of all essentially intellectual religions to gain popular favor.
—Edwin Grant Conklin, *Man, Real and Ideal*, 1940

Emotionalism never finds depths of truth, but depth of truth cannot be had apart from a full and free emotional response.
—Nels F.S. Ferré, *Faith and Reason*, 1946

He who is slow to anger is better than the mighty, and he who rules his spirit than he who takes a city.
—*Holy Bible*, Proverbs 16:32

The spiritual life is not a thing without emotions. The saints weep at the thought of their own sins and the goodness of God; their hearts beat to the bursting point within them, they shout and dance for joy; they die to see God.
—Jean Mouroux, *Christian Experience*, 1954

Religion is never devoid of emotion, any more than love is. It is not a defect of religion, but rather its glory, that it speaks always the language of feeling.
—D.E. Trueblood, *The Logic of Belief*, 1942

Fine emotions can be cheapened, and cheap emotions can be refined, but no emotions can be, with safety, wallowed in.
—Hubert van Zeller, *We Die Standing Up*, 1949

ENEMY

He who loves his enemies betrays his friends; this surely is
not what Jesus meant.
—William Blake, *The Everlasting Gospel*, 1810

But I say to you, Love your enemies and pray for those who
persecute you, so that you may be sons of your Father who
is in heaven; for he makes his sun rise on the evil and on the
good, and sends rain on the just and on the unjust.
—*Holy Bible*, Matthew 5:44-45

Do not rejoice when your enemy falls, and let not your heart
be glad when he stumbles.
—*Holy Bible*, Proverbs 24:17

If your enemy is hungry, feed him; if he is thirsty, give
him drink; for by so doing you will heap burning coals upon
his head.
—*Holy Bible*, Romans 12:20

We have met the enemy and he is us.
—Walt Kelly, "Pogo" (cartoon), Earth Day 1971

If we could read the secret history of our enemies, we should
find in each man's life sorrow and suffering enough to disarm all hostility.
—Henry Wadsworth Longfellow, *Driftwood*, 1861

I need my enemy in my community. He keeps me alert, vital.
. . . But beyond what we specifically learn from our enemies,
we need them emotionally; our psychic economy cannot get
along well without them. . . . [O]ur enemy is as necessary for
us as is our friend. Both together are part of authentic
community.
—Rollo May, *Power and Innocence*, 1972

To be an enemy is a sin; to have one is a temptation.
—Benjamin Whichcote, *Moral and Religious Aphorisms*, 1753

The greatest concerns of men are these, to make him who is
an enemy a friend, to make him who is wicked righteous,
and to make him who is ignorant learned.
—*Zend-Avesta*, 6th century B.C.

ENLIGHTENMENT

In this world, aspirants may find enlightenment by two different paths. For the contemplative is the path of knowledge; for the active is the path of selfless action.
> —*Bhagavad-Gita*, between 500 and 200 B.C.

There is no enlightenment outside of daily life.
> —Thich Nhat Hanh, *Zen Keys*, 1974

Going back to the origin is called peace; it means reversion to destiny. Reversion to destiny is called eternity. He who knows eternity is called enlightened.
> —Lao-tzu, *Tao Te Ching*, c. 500 B.C.

The ultimate aim of man [in Hinduism] is liberation; liberation not only from the bondage of the flesh, but also from the limitation of a finite being. In other words, *moksha* means becoming a perfect spirit like the Supreme Spirit. . . . But the law of *Karma* postulates that every individual has to pass through a series of lives either on earth or somewhere else before he attains *moksha* or liberation.
> —D.S. Sarma, *The Religion of the Hindus*, 1953

ENVY AND JEALOUSY

When I look upon the tombs of the great, every emotion of envy dies in me. . . . When I see kings lying by those who deposed them, when I consider rival wits placed side by side, or the holy men that divided the world with their contests and disputes, I reflect with sorrow and astonishment on the little competitions, factions, and debates of mankind.
> —Joseph Addison (1672–1719), *Meditations in Westminster Abbey*

If a vain man meets a holy man, he will envy only the respect that others show him.
> —Hari Dass Baba, 1969

Envy is a coal come hissing hot from hell.
> —Philip James Bailey, *Festus*, V, 1846

Perhaps the most dangerous aspect of envy is not envy itself, but the denial of it.
> —Joseph H. Berke, *The Tyranny of Malice*, 1988

Selfishness is the deepest root of all unhappiness. . . . It feeds an insatiable hunger that first eats up everything belonging to others and then causes a creature to devour itself.
> —Dom Helder Camara, 1984

To attune your spirit to your own special place in the world is never to know envy, or malice, or despair.

—Carlos Castaneda, 1979

It is not love that is blind, but jealousy.

—Lawrence Durrell, *Justine*, 1957

For all the unkind things said about envy, it would only be fair to acknowledge that not all envy is destructive. If envy leads us to work hard and to improve our skills, it becomes a stimulant to self-improvement. God has given us no quality that cannot be used for good.

—Sidney Greenberg, *Say Yes to Life*, 1982

Jealousy is said to be the offspring of love. Yet unless the parent makes haste to strangle the child, the child will not rest till it has poisoned the parent.

—J.C. Hare, *Guesses at Truth*, 1827

Envy's special aversion is successful covetousness.

—Henry S. Haskins, *Meditations in Wall Street*, 1940

There is but one man who can believe himself free from envy, and it is he who has never examined his own heart.

—C.A. Helvetius, *De l'esprit*, 1758

You shall not covet your neighbor's house; you shall not covet your neighbor's wife, or his manservant, or his maid-servant, or his ox, or his ass, or anything that is your neighbor's.

—*Holy Bible*, Exodus 20:17

An envious heart makes a treacherous ear.

—Zora Neale Hurston, *Their Eyes Were Watching God*, 1937

In a consumer society there are inevitably two kinds of slaves: the prisoners of addiction and the prisoners of envy.

—Ivan Illich, *Tools for Conviviality*, 1973

Anguish and heartbreak may not be distributed very evenly around the world, but they are distributed very widely. If we knew the facts, we would very rarely find someone whose life was to be envied.

—Harold Kushner, *When Bad Things Happen to Good People*

ENVY AND JEALOUSY

Envy is uneasiness of the mind, caused by the consideration of a good we desire, obtained by one we think should not have it before us.
—John Locke, *Essay Concerning Human Understanding*, 1690

Spite is never lonely; envy always tags long.
—Mignon McLaughlin, *The Neurotic's Notebook*, 1963

Jealousy is the most dreadfully involuntary of all sins.
—Iris Murdoch, *The Black Prince*, 1973

Envy, the meanest of vices, creeps on the ground like a serpent.
—Ovid, *Epistulae ex Ponto*, c. A.D. 5

He that envies is possessed of self-made hurts.
—Shaikh Saadi, *Gulistan*, c. 1265

Moral indignation is in most cases 2 percent moral, 48 percent indignation and 50 percent envy.
—Vittorio de Sica, *The Observer*, 1961

A jealous person is doubly unhappy—over what he has, which is judged inferior, and over what he has not, which is judged superior. Such a person is doubly removed from knowing the true blessings of creation.
—Desmond Tutu, 1988

EQUALITY

Under the Guru's instruction regard all men as equal, since God's light is contained in the heart of each.
—Arjan (died 1606), in M.A. Macauliffe, *The Sikh Religion*

I believe that the more we think, the more we become convinced that the instinct which asks for equality is a low one, and that equality, if it were completely brought out, would furnish play for the lower instincts and impulses of man.
—Phillips Brooks, *New Starts in Life and Other Sermons*, 1897

The Christian view of man knows no graded scale of essential and fundamental worth; there is no divine right of whites which differ from the divine rights of Negroes.
—Kyle Haselden, *The Racial Problem in Christian Perspective*, 1959

Have we not all one father? Has not one God created us?
Why then are we faithless to one another, profaning the
covenant of our fathers?

—*Holy Bible*, Malachi 2:10

It is not true that some human beings are by nature superior
and others inferior. All men are equal in their natural dignity. Consequently there are no political communities which
are superior by nature and none which are inferior by
nature.

—Pope John XXIII, *Pacem in Terris*, April 1963

Since women are becoming ever more conscious of their
human dignity, they will not tolerate being treated as mere
material instruments, but demand rights befitting a human
person both in domestic and in public life.

—Pope John XXIII, *Pacem in Terris*, April 1963

An earthly kingdom cannot exist without inequality of persons. Some must be free, others serf, some rulers, other
subjects.

—Martin Luther, *Works*, XVIII, 1525

Lamentably, it is an historical fact that privileged groups seldom give up their privileges voluntarily. Individuals may see
the light and give up their unjust posture; but as Reinhold
Niebuhr has reminded us (*Moral Men—Immoral Society*),
groups tend to be more immoral than individuals.

—Martin Luther King, Jr., *Why We Can't Wait*, 1964

Religion consisteth not in mere words; he who looketh on all
men as equal is religious.

—Guru Nanak (1496–1538), in M.A. Macauliffe, *The Sikh Religion*

Human society, as established by God, is composed of un-
equal elements, just as parts of the human body are un-
equal; to make them all equal is impossible, and would mean
the destruction of human society itself.

—Pope Pius X, *Apostolic Letter on Catholic Action*, December 1903

Open the tombs and see the bones there mixed in mockery!
Which dust was servant, which was lord's?—open the tomb
and see!

—Shaikh Saadi, *Gulistan*, c. 1265

It was the contemplation of God that created men who were equal, for it was in God that they were equal. . . . As the manifestation of God, they were equal in rights. As the servants of God, they were also equal in their duties.
—Antoine de Saint-Exupéry, *Flight to Arras*, 1942

There is in Christ and in the Church no inequality on the basis of race or nationality, social condition or sex.
—Second Vatican Council, *Constitution on the Church*, November 1964

No reasonable man will think more highly of himself because he has office or power in this world; he is no more than a prisoner whom the chief gaoler has set over his fellow-prisoners, until the executioner's cart comes for him, too.
—St. Thomas More, *The Four Last Things*, 1522

ERROR

Error, falsehood, evil are cosmic powers, but relative in their nature, not absolute, since they depend for existence upon the perversion or contradiction of their opposites, and are not like truth and good, self-existing absolutes, inherent aspects of the Supreme Self-Existent.
—Sri Aurobindo, *The Life Divine*, 1949

There is no error in religion, of whatever nature, which is a sin when it is involuntary. . . . We have an inalienable right to profess those doctrines which we believe comformable to the pure truth.
—Pierre Bayle (1647–1706), *Critique Generale, Works*, II

There is nothing final about a mistake, except its being taken as final.
—Phyllis Bottome, *Strange Fruit*, 1928

Error makes the circuit of the globe while Truth is pulling on her boots, and no error ever is or ever can be harmless.
—Orestes Brownson, in *Brownson's Quarterly*, July 1864

Free expression of error should be tolerated, not as an approval of error itself, but because we love our neighbor so much that we do not want him to be a man who talks *as if* he knew the truth, but to be a man who knows it.
—Étienne Gilson, *Dogmatism and Tolerance*, 1952

As long as we honestly wish to arrive at truth we need not fear that we shall be punished for unintentional error.
—John Lubbock, *The Pleasures of Life*, 1887

It is a great gain when error becomes manifest, for it then ceases to deceive the simple.
—Roger J. McHugh, *Christianity and the Sceptic*, 1950

Error struggling on towards the living truth is more fruitful than dead truth.
—Romaine Rolland, *Jean Christophe*, 1912

All men are liable to err; but when an error hath been made, that man is no longer witless or unblest who heals the ill into which he hath fallen, and remains not stubborn.
—Sophocles (495–406 B.C.), *Antigone*

If you shut your door to all errors truth will be shut out.
—Rabindranath Tagore, *Stray Buds*, 1916

ETERNITY

Our whole eternity is to take its color from those hours which we here employ in virtue or in vice.
—Joseph Addison, *The Spectator*, 1712

The eternal life is not the future life; it is life in harmony with the true order of things—life in God.
—Henri Amiel, journal, 1882

Eternity is the lifetime of the Almighty.
—Anonymous

In the eternal nothing passeth but the whole is present; whereas no time is all at once present.
—St. Augustine, *Confessions*, XI, 33, 397

Whatever that which feels, which has knowledge, which wills, which has the power of growth, it is celestial and divine, and for that reason must of necessity be eternal.
—Cicero, *Tusculanae Disputationes*, Bk. 1, ch. 27, 44 B.C.

All the sophistry of the Predestinarians rests on the false notion of eternity as a sort of time antecedent to time. It is timeless, present with and in all times.
—Samuel Taylor Coleridge, *Aids to Reflections*, 1825

It is from the very element of the eternal and the unlimited, which the materialist seeks to deny, that the true progress of the human race has sprung.
—Christopher Dawson, *God and the Supernatural*, 1920

Eternal life is not a life for the future. By charity we start eternity right here below.

—Henri de Lubac, *Paradoxes*, 1948

Today, eternity enters into time, and time, sanctified, is caught up into eternity.

—Thomas Merton, *A Thomas Merton Reader*, 1963

The idea of life after death is clearly an embarrassment to modern thinking—most major philosophers have ridiculed it—but it is just as clearly the touchstone of all religion. Religion says that being human has eternal meaning. If religion announces that life is over at the grave, then it is not talking about what people expect religion to discuss.

—Jacob Neusner, in *Newsweek*, March 27, 1989

Peace, Rest and Bliss dwell only where there is no where and no when.

—Arthur Schopenhauer, *Parega und Paralipomena*, II, 1862

It is not possible that we should remember that we existed before our body, for our body can bear no trace of such existence, neither can eternity be defined in terms of time or have any relation to time. But notwithstanding, we feel and know that we are eternal.

—Baruch Spinoza, *Ethics*, 1677

All things are eternal by their very nature.

—*Sutra-Krit-Anga*, between 600 and 200 B.C.

To Zen, time and eternity are one.

—D.T. Suzuki, *Zen Buddhism*, 1956

Since the moral law can rightfully command us to live as aspirants to eternity, eternity must really be our destination.

—A.E. Taylor, *Faith of a Moralist*, 1930

It is difficult to imagine a temporary Heaven, for if the souls in Heaven knew that their bliss would end, this knowledge alone would prevent their happiness from being perfect.

—Gerald C. Treacy, *After Death—What?*, 1927

ETHICS

In the atomic age, each individual, each party, each state, must feel itself responsible to humanity in its entirety and not merely to its own group or ideal.

—R. Raymond Aron, in *The Ethics of Power*, 1962

The distinctive element in Christian ethics is the primacy of love, the self-giving love that is known fully to Christian faith in the cross of Christ.

—John Bennett, *Goals of Economic Life*, 1943

There is no individual Christian ethic . . . God's command places us in relation to our neighbor, not to ourselves.

—Emil Brunner, *The Divine Imperative*, 1937

The ethics of the Gospel find their sanction upon no lower level than the eternal purpose of God.

—F.C. Grant, *The Practice of Religion*, 1946

Jewish ethics is rooted in the doctrine of human responsibility, that is, freedom of the will.

—Joseph H. Hertz, *The Pentateuch and Haftorahs*, 1936

The ethical progress of society depends, not on imitating the cosmic process, still less in running away from it, but in combating it.

—Thomas Henry Huxley, *Evolution and Ethics*, 1893

I am not sure whether what the philosophers call ethical absolutes exist, but I am sure that we have to act as if they existed. Ethics must be freed from its utilitarian chains.

—Arthur Koestler, *The Trail of the Dinosaur and Other Essays*, 1955

Our very lives depend on the ethics of strangers, and most of us are always strangers to other people.

—Bill Moyers, address, University of Texas at Austin commencement, *The Christian Science Monitor*, July 27, 1988

The domination of class and self-preservative church ethics over the ethics of the gospel must be held responsible for much of the moral ineffectiveness of Christianity in the West.

—H. Richard Niebuhr, *Social Sources of Denominationalism*, 1929

You are wrong, my friends, if you think a man with a spark of decency in him ought to calculate life or death; the only thing he ought to consider is whether he does right or wrong.

—Plato, *Apology*, 399 B.C.

It is only an ethical movement which can rescue us from the slough of barbarism, and the ethical comes into existence only in individuals.

—Albert Schweitzer, *The Decay and Restoration of Civilization*, 1923

The next step in the development of an ethical theology must be the translation of the categories of divinity into terms compatible with democratic ethics. We must learn to think of God as the immanent co-worker, always toiling with His children rather than as a sovereign to whom they are subject.

—Gerald Binney Smith, *Social Idealism and the Changing Theology*, 1913

EVIL

For as a picture is often more beautiful and worthy of commendation if some colors in themselves are included in it, than it would be if it were uniform and of a single color, so from an admixture of evil the universe is rendered more beautiful and worthy of commendation.

—Pierre Abelard, *Epitome Theologiae Christianae*, c. 1135

Nothing can be evil on the part of God. For a thing is evil on our part only because we transgress the limit and bound set for us and do what we have no right to do. But the Creator is subject to no one and bound by no command.

—Al-Ash'ari (died 935), *Kitáb al-Luma*

The sad truth is that most evil is done by people who never make up their minds to be either good or evil.

—Hannah Arendt, in *The New Yorker*, December 5, 1977

No evil could exist where no good exists.

—St. Augustine, *Enchiridion*, 421

Evil is the footstool of good, and there is no absolute evil.

—Rabbi Israel Baal Shem-Tov (1700–60), in *Judaism*, 1961

There is no need to go searching for a remedy for the evils of the time. The remedy already exists—it is the gift of one's self to those who have fallen so low that even hope fails them. Open wide your heart.

—René Bazin, *Redemption*, 1908

The very absence of evil would constitute a problem since there would, then, be nothing to jar us out of an attitude of self-sufficiency.

—John Bennett, *Christian Realism*, 1941

The gates have been opened to evil in part because of a terrible discrepancy between the human ideals and actual possibilities—terrible heresies concerning the nature of man and the structure of the historical universe.

—Herbert Butterfield, *Christianity, Diplomacy and War*, 1953

There neither were formerly, nor are there now, nor will there be again, more or fewer evils in the world. For the nature of all things is one and the same, and the generation of evils is always the same.
—Celsus, quoted by Origen, *Against Celsus*, Bk. 4, ch. 62, 246

The belief in a supernatural source of evil is not necessary; men alone are quite capable of every wickedness.
—Joseph Conrad, *Under Western Eyes*, 1911

Do you know that oftentimes a root has split a rock, when suffered to remain in it? Give no lodgment to the seed of evil, seeing that it will break up your faith.
—St. Cyril of Jerusalem, *Catechetical Lectures*, 350

Even if the water falls drop by drop, it will fill the pot; and the fool will become full of evil, even though he gather it little by little.
—*Dhammapada*, c. 5th century B.C.

If we could see the amount of wretchedness, moral as well as physical, which each minute produces . . . our minds would not stand the shock. If evil were not hidden like impure germs disseminated in our system, there would not be a single sane person on earth.
—Ernest Dimnet, *What We Live By*, 1932

If evil is due to ignorance, then all professors should be saints.
—Richard S. Emrich, in *Detroit News*, June 25, 1961

Non-cooperation with evil is as much a duty as is cooperation with good.
—Mohandas K. Gandhi (1869–1948), quoted in Louis Fischer, *The Life of Mahatma Gandhi*, 1950

Reflect frequently on death and impermanence. If you are conscious of the certainty of death, it will not be difficult for you to avoid evil and it will not be difficult for you to practice virtue.
—Ge-She-Pu-to-pa, *Mirror of Kun-Zang-Le-Ma*, 1850

What is evil but good tortured by its own hunger and thirst?
—Kahlil Gibran, *The Prophet*, 1923

Woe to those who call evil good and good evil, who put darkness for light and light for darkness, who put bitter for sweet and sweet for bitter!
—*Holy Bible*, Isaiah 5:20

Lo you now, how vainly mortal men do blame the gods! For of us they say comes evil, whereas they even of themselves, through the blindness of their own hearts, have sorrows beyond that which is ordained.
—Homer, *Odyssey*, between 12th and 9th centuries B.C.

It is not more strange that there should be evil spirits than evil men—evil unembodied spirits than evil embodied spirits.
—Samuel Johnson, *Boswell's Tour of the Hebrirides*, August 16, 1773

There is nothing beside a spiritual world; what we call the world of the senses is Evil in the spiritual world, and what we call Evil is only the necessity of a moment in our eternal evolution.
—Franz Kafka (1883–1924), *Reflections*

God uses evil to educate His children for a place in His kingdom.
—Kaufman Kohler, *Jewish Theology*, 1918

Repay evil with good and, lo, between whom and you there was enmity will become your warm friend.
—*Koran*, c. 625

What is thus the power of evil? It is the very power of the good that evil wounds and preys upon. The more powerful this good is, the more powerful evil will be—not by virtue of itself, but by virtue of this good.
—Jacques Maritain, *St. Thomas and the Problem of Evil*, 1942

The ancientest evil, if it be known to us, bears always lighter upon us than a new one of which we know but little.
—Michel de Montaigne, *Essays*, 1580

The real problem of evil, the problem that justifies every assault upon war and poverty and disease, is to reduce it to amounts that can be spiritually assimilated.
—Lewis Mumford, *Living Philosophies*, 1931

We use evil in every moment of our existence to hold evil in check.
—Reinhold Niebuhr, *Radical Religion*, Winter 1936

The challenge of aggressive evil can be met only by the power
of aggressive good.
—Swami Nikhilanandar, *Perspectives on a Troubled Decade*, 1950

When we deny the evil in ourselves, we dehumanize ourselves, and we deprive ourselves not only of our own destiny
but of any possibility of dealing with the evil of others.
—J. Robert Oppenheimer, address, New York, March 1963

Unwittingly, evil serves as a beacon to warn others away
from its own shoals.
—M. Scott Peck, *The Road Less Traveled*, 1978

The exit of evil works the entrance of virtue.
—Philo (20 B.C.?–20 A.D.?), *Sacrifices of Abel and Cain*

It will never be possible to get rid of evil altogether, for there
must always be something opposite to good.
—Plato, *Theaetetus*, c. 360 B.C.

We are not the principle of our evils and that evil does not
come from ourselves, but that evil exists prior to ourselves;
evil possesses man, and he possesses it in spite of himself.
—Plotinus (203–262), *First Ennead*

There are wicked people who would be much less dangerous
if they were wholly without goodness.
—La Rochefoucauld, *Maxims*, 1665

God makes all things good; man meddles with them and they
become evil.
—Jean Jacques Rousseau, *Émile*, 1762

Deal firmly, yet tenderly, with evil, as if it were a disease in
your own person, and the people will entirely put away their
faults.
—*Shu-Ching*, 6th century B.C.

The difficult thing is not to escape death but to escape
wickedness.
—Socrates, in Plato, *Apology*, 399 B.C.

By evil I understand that which we certainly know hinders
us from possessing anything that is good.
—Baruch Spinoza, *Ethics*, 1677

169

Every prudent man tolerates a lesser evil for fear of preventing a greater good.

—St. Thomas Aquinas, *De Veritate*, q. 5, a.4, ad 4, 1259

There are a thousand hacking at the branches of evil to one who is striking at the root.

—Henry David Thoreau, *Walden*, 1854

Do what you can, some evil will inhere in it; but do all without regard to personal result, give up all results to the Lord, then neither good nor evil will affect you.

—Swami Vivekenananda (1863–1902), *Complete Works of*, VII

Judaism teaches that those who commit terrible deeds are not monsters. They are human beings who have done monstrous things. If they truly were beasts, they would be blameless. They are human and responsible because they have betrayed their humanness.

—David J. Wolpe, *In Speech and in Silence: The Jewish Quest for God*, 1992

Wicked is he who is good to the wicked.

—Yasna (Zoroastrian), 6th century B.C.

EVOLUTION

If the notion of a gradual rise in Beings from the meanest to the most High be not a vain imagination, it is not improbable that an Angel looks down upon a Man, as Man doeth upon a Creature which approaches the nearest to the rational Nature.

—Joseph Addison, *The Spectator*, November 17, 1714

Evolution seems to close the heart to some of the plainest spiritual truths while it opens the mind to the wildest guesses advanced in the name of science.

—William Jennings Bryan, letter to *The New York Times*, February 22, 1922

Although the creationist . . . must of necessity hold that there was a "first man," it is of no consequence whether he looked like a Pithecanthropoid or a Caucasoid.

—James D. Buswell III, *Evolution and Christian Thought*, 1959

The whole of evolution is, in reality, a process of self-realizing a moral purpose; the correlation of mind and brain is just the phenomenal aspect of the real correlation of our mind with the divine power which sustains us.

—George A. Coe, *Education in Religion and Morals*, 1904

Evolution, the story of man, traced for us by the scientist, is seen as the travail of God's energy, creating man in His own image.
—C.A. Coulson, *Science and Christian Belief*, 1955

In itself the theory of evolution, which asserts the variability of species of animals and plants, is by no means opposed to religious truths. It neither includes a necessity of assuming the origin of the human soul from the essentially lower animal soul, nor is it an atheistic theory.
—J. Donat, *The Freedom of Science*, 1914

Evolution is comprehensible only if we admit that it is demanded by finality.
Lecomte du Noüy, *Human Destiny*, 1947

Not only is natural selection not the instrument of a god's sublime purpose, it is not even the best mechanism for achieving evolutionary progress.
—Julian Huxley, *Evolution, the Modern Synthesis*, 1942

Evolution as a method of creation fits a divine and spiritual interpretation as completely as creation by fiat does.
—Rufus M. Jones, *A Call to What Is Vital*, 1949

One of the interesting and little-remarked-on side products of Darwin's theory of evolution is that, if it's really true that human beings evolved from creatures that were not human, anything present to human beings, however complicated, can't be simply and totally absent from animal life. And that means that whatever we may have lost in dignity as a result of this theory of evolution, the animals and the living world as such have gained.
—Leon R. Kass, in conversation with Bill Moyers, *A World of Ideas*, 1989

Evolution is not just the history of a species, but the whole evolution of life. To understand that, you have to find the road maps—the way in which species are related in evolutionary terms.
—Michael Novacek, in *The New York Times*, December 10, 1991

Instead of lessening the dignity of man's origin, evolution actually exalts it, by placing it far above the moistened dust or mud of the earth to living creatures endowed by God with sentiency and a form of intelligence.
—John A. O'Brien, *The Origin of Man*, 1947

171

Evolution begins and ends with the purposes of God.
—Henry Fairfield Osborn, *Evolution and Religion in Education*, 1926

The teaching authority of the Church does not forbid that, in conformity with the present state of science and theology, the doctrine of evolution should be examined and discussed by experts in both fields, in so far as it deals with research on the origin of the human body, which it states to come from pre-existent organic matter.
—Pope Pius XII, *Humani generis*, August 1950

We are at a crossroads in human history. Never before has there been a moment so simultaneously perilous and promising. We are the first species to have taken our evolution into our own hands.
—Carl Sagan, *Broca's Brain*, 1969

Though frightened for a moment by evolution, the Christian now perceives that what it offers him is nothing but a magnificent means of feeling more at one with God and of giving himself more to him.
—Pierre Teilhard de Chardin, *The Phenomenon of Man*, 1955

EXISTENCE

Being is as it were a torrent, in and out of which bodies pass, coalescing and cooperating with the whole, as the various parts in us so with one another.
—Marcus Aurelius, *Meditations*, c. 170

It remains a fact and the fixed and necessary constitution of being, that all of its constituents are misery.
—Buddha, *Anguttara-Nikaya*, 6th century B.C.

The Portal of God is Non-Existence. All things sprang from Non-Existence. Existence could not make existence existence. It must have proceeded from Non-Existence. And Non-Existence and Nothing are one.
—*Chuang-tzu*, c. 300 B.C.

The utility of the house depends on the empty spaces. Thus, while the existence of things may be good, it is the nonexistent in them which makes them serviceable.
—Lao-tzu, *Tao Te Ching*, between 6th and 3rd centuries B.C.

Human existence is girt round with mystery: the narrow region of our experience is a small island in the midst of a boundless sea.

—J.S. Mill, *Three Essays on Religion*, 1874

It is the stupidity of our minds that prevents us from seeing existence as a mystery wilder than the dreams of Devil or God.

—Llewelyn Powys, *Earth Memories*, 1938

This thing we call existence—is it not a something which has its roots far down below in the dark, and its branches stretching out into the immensity above. . . . Not a chance jumble; a living thing, a One?

—Oliver Schreiner, *The Story of an African Farm*, 1883

As long as we look at our own existence as meaningless, there is no point whatever in desiring to effect anything in the world.

—Albert Schweitzer, *The Anatomy of Frustration*, 1936

If nothing existed except receivers of existence, where would the existence come from?

—Frank J. Sheed, *The Advocate*, January 1960

We are separated from the mystery, the depth, and the greatness of our existence. We hear the voice of that depth; but our ears are closed.

—Paul Tillich, *The Shaking of the Foundations*, 1949

ailure and Defeat

To be human is to be challenged to be more divine. Not even to try to meet such a challenge is the biggest defeat imaginable.

—Maya Angelou, 1993

Defeat is a school in which Truth always grows strong.

—Henry Ward Beecher, *Life Thoughts*, 1858

We are co-creators with God, not puppets on a string waiting for something to happen.

—Leo Booth, in *Creation Spirituality*, July/August 1992

The important thing is to begin again, humbly and courageously, after every fall.

—Dom Helder Camara, 1984

As always, victory finds a hundred fathers, but defeat is an orphan.

—Count Galeazzo Ciano, diary, September 9, 1942

Out of defeat can come the best in human nature. As Christians face storms of adversity, they may rise with more beauty. They are like trees that grow on mountain ridges— battered by winds, yet trees in which we find the strongest wood.

—Billy Graham, 1991

In some circumstances, the refusal to be defeated is a refusal to be educated.

—Margaret Halsey, *No Laughing Matter*, 1977

It is often much more difficult to learn from victory than from defeat. In defeat, questions are asked about what went wrong, so that those mistakes will not be made in the future. But victory seldom creates the need to inquire as to its sources.

—Gary Hart, in *The Washington Post*, May 5, 1991

When all our efforts have come to nothing, we naturally tend to doubt not just ourselves, but also whether God is just. At those moments, our only hope is to seek every evidence that God *is* just, by communing with the people we know who are strongest in their faith.

—Bill Moyers, 1986

We have some strange thought that God has predestined
everything, that God has willed everything like it is. God's
will is in process, and you're in the process with God. God
works with us, and God works for us.

—Michael Pfleger, *U.S. Catholic*, July 1992

We are never defeated unless we give up on God.

—Ronald Reagan, 1984

A series of failures may culminate in the best possible result.

—Gisela Richter, in *My Memoirs; Recollection of an Archaeologist's Life*, 1972

We no longer want masses of people like those who have
been trifled with for so long. We want persons like fruitful
fig trees who can say yes to justice and no to injustice and
can make use of the precious gift of life, regardless of the
circumstances.

—Archbishop Oscar Romero, 1989

If you don't want bad things to happen to you, be dead or be
in another species. If you are alive, things happen. So the
question then is, Why *not* me?

—Bernie Siegel, *New Age Journal* May/June 1989

If everything is coming your way, you are probably in the
wrong lane. Adversity and defeat are more conducive to spiritual growth than prosperity and victory.

—John Steinbeck, 1967

When the hot word of God is poured over a cold, cold world,
things break, and it is into this brokenness that we are
called . . . with fire in our bones, to show a frightened world
that it is not the heat of the fire that we fear, but the chill
that lies ahead if the fire goes out.

—Barbara Brown Taylor, *Women of the Word*, 1984

FAITH

Religious faith, on which sacred theology rests, is itself a supernatural act of the human intellect and is thus a divine
gift.

—Mortimer Adler, *Vital Speeches*, December 1949

In Judaism faith is . . . the capacity to perceive the abiding . . .
in the transitory, the invisible in the visible.

—Leo Baeck, *Essence of Judaism*, 1936

Faith is not a thing which one "loses," we merely cease to shape our lives by it.
—Georges Bernanos, *Diary of a Country Priest*, 1937

You can keep a faith only as you can keep a plant, by rooting it into your life and making it grow there.
—Phillips Brooks, *Perennials*, 1898

A belief may be larger than a fact. A faith that is overdefined is the very faith most likely to prove inadequate to the great moments of life.
—Vannevar Bush, *Science Is Not Enough*, 1967

It is faith and not logic which is the supreme arbiter.
—Samuel Butler, *The Way of All Flesh*, 1884

You can do very little with faith, but you can do nothing without it.
—Samuel Butler, *Notebooks of*, 1912

Faith consists, not in ignorance, but in knowledge; and that, not only of God, but also of the divine will.
—John Calvin, *Institutes*, I, 1536

Religious faith is not a storm cellar to which men and women can flee for refuge from the storms of life. It is, instead, an inner spiritual strength which enables them to face those storms with hope and serenity. Religious faith has the miraculous power to lift ordinary human beings to greatness in seasons of stress.
—Sam Ervin, *Humor of a Country Lawyer*, 1983

Faith *is* obscure. By faith a man moves through darkness; but he moves securely, his hand in the hand of God. He is literally seeing through the eyes of God.
—Walter Farrell, *The Looking Glass*, 1951

Of all mad faiths maddest is the faith that we can get rid of faith.
—Harry Emerson Fosdick, *On Being a Real Person*, 1943

Without faith man becomes sterile, hopeless, and afraid to the very core of his being.
—Erich Fromm, *Man for Himself*, 1947

We cannot live on probabilities. The faith in which we can live bravely and die in peace must be a certainty, so far as it professes to be a faith at all, or it is nothing.
—J.A. Froude, *A Plea for Free Discussion of Theological Difficulties*, 1863

Not to have faith is not a personal fault, it is a misfortune.
—Étienne Gilson, *The Philosopher and Theology*, 1962

Faith in God may be an elective in our university of daily living. In the presence of death it assumes crucial significance.
—Sidney Greenberg, *Treasury of Comfort*, 1954

God does not die on the day when we cease to believe in a personal deity, but we die on the day when our lives cease to be illumined by the steady radiance, renewed daily, of a wonder, the source of which is beyond all reason.
—Dag Hammarskjöld, *Markings*, 1964

More necessary than faith in the gods is faith that man can give justice, brotherhood, peace and all his beloved moral values embodiment in human relations.
—A. Eustace Haydon, *This Is My Faith*, 1956

Faith is not an easy virtue but in the broad world of man's total voyage through time to eternity, faith is not only a gracious companion, but an essential guide.
—Theodore M. Hesburgh, in *The Way*, June 1963

Faith is an awareness of divine mutuality and companionship, a form of communion between God and man.
—Abraham Joshua Heschel, *Man Is Not Alone*, 1951

Faith is a gift of God which man can neither give or take away by promise of rewards or menaces of torture.
—Thomas Hobbes, *Leviathan*, 1651

For we walk by faith, not by sight.
—*Holy Bible*, II Corinthians 5:7

If you have faith as a grain of mustard seed, you will say to this mountain, "Move hence to yonder place," and it will move; and nothing will be impossible to you.
—*Holy Bible*, Matthew 17:20

Faith is like the little night-light that burns in a sickroom; as long as it is there, the obscurity is not complete, we turn toward it and await the daylight.
—Abbe Huvelin, *English Church Review*, 1911

Faith is not a momentary feeling, but a struggle against the discouragement that threatens us every time we meet with resistance.
—Bakole wa Ilunga, *Paths of Liberation*, 1984

Faith always contains an element of risk, of venture; and we are impelled to make the venture by the affinity and attraction which we feel in ourselves.
—W.R. Inge, *Faith and Its Psychology*, 1910

Faith means belief in something concerning which doubt is still theoretically possible; and as the test of belief is willingness to act, one may say that faith is the readiness to act in a cause the prosperous issue of which is not certified to us in advance.
—William James, in *Princeton Review*, July 1882

Faith furnishes prayer with wings, without which it cannot soar to Heaven.
—St. John Climacus (525–600), *Climax*

We do not speak of faith unless the reality which we are to reach surpasses our own powers of discovery.
—Eugène Joly, *What Is Faith?*, 1958

A little boy playing on the deck of a ship in a mighty storm was asked by a passenger if he wasn't afraid. "No, I'm not afraid. My father is the captain of the ship."
—Rufus M. Jones, *The Radiant Life*, 1944

It is a free belief, not in that for which dogmatical proofs for the theoretically determinant Judgment are to be found, or in that to which we hold ourselves bound, but in that which we assume on behalf of a design in accordance with laws of freedom.
—Immanuel Kant, *Critique of Judgment*, 1790

The contemporary divorce between faith and reason is not the result of a contest for power or for intellectual monopoly, but of a progressive estrangement without hostility or drama, and therefore all the more deadly.
—Arthur Koestler, *The Sleepwalkers*, 1959

Like a tree, it shades the evil as well as the good. The crucial question is this: in what soil are you rooting your faith?
—John E. Large, *The Small Needle of Doctor Large*, 1962

The integral and true Faith is a great bulwark to which nothing can be added or taken from by anyone; if the Faith is not single, it does not exist at all.
—Pope St. Leo the Great (440–461), quoted by Pope John XXIII, November 11, 1961

Faith is trust, and it is therefore primarily volitional and emotional. Belief, on the other hand, is primarily intellectual: it is the assent of the mind. But while belief is not itself faith, faith where there is no belief in something quite impossible.
—Edwin Lewis, *A Philosophy of the Christian Revelation*, 1940

Faith is the assent to any proposition not thus made out by the deductions of reasons; but upon the credit of the proposer, as coming from God, in some extraordinary way of communication.
—John Locke, *Essay Concerning Human Understanding*, 1690

Nothing that is contrary to, and inconsistent with, the clear and self-evident dictates of reason, has a right to be urged or assented to as a matter of faith, wherein reason hath nothing to do.
—John Locke, *Essay Concerning Human Understanding*, 1690

God our Father has made all things depend on faith so that whoever has faith will have everything, and whoever does not have faith will have nothing.
—Martin Luther, *Freedom of a Christian*, 1520

Reason is the greatest enemy that faith has: it never comes to the aid of spiritual things, but—more frequently than not—struggles against the divine Word, treating with contempt all that emanates from God.
—Martin Luther (1483–1546), *Table-Talk*

The fundamental error commonly made lies in considering faith as a kind of knowledge. . . . Faith, however, is not a kind of knowledge, but rather a practical attitude of the will.
—John Macmurray, *Adventure*, 1928

He that hath faith hath wisdom; he that hath wisdom hath peace. He that hath no wisdom and no faith, whose soul is one of doubt, is destroyed.

—*Mahabharata*, c. 800 B.C.

Faith must not be slow to reason, nor reason to adore.

—Lakdasa J. de Mel, sermon, 10th Lambeth Conference, St. Paul's Cathedral, August 25, 1968

Faith is the soul's consciousness of its Divine relationship and exalted destiny.

—G.S. Merriam, *A Living Faith*, 1876

Faith faces everything that makes the world uncomfortable—pain, fear, loneliness, shame, death—and acts with a compassion by which these things are transformed, even exalted.

—Samuel H. Miller, in *Look*, December 19, 1961

The light of faith confers upon us undreamed-of enhancement of our vision, an extension of our understanding, an enrichment of our natural powers beyond the powers of words to convey.

—Rosalind Murray, *The Forsaken Fountain*, 1948

Faith must make a venture and is rewarded by sight.

—John Henry Newman, *Loss and Gain*, 1848

Why should we be willing to go by faith? We do all things in this world by faith in the word of others. By faith only we know our position in the world, our circumstances, our rights and privileges, our fortunes, our parents, our brothers and sisters, our age, our mortality. Why should Religion be an exception?

—John Henry Newman, *Essays and Sketches*, Vol. 1, 1838

Faith is not a dam which prevents the flow of the river of reason and thought; it is a levee which prevents unreason from flooding the countryside.

—Fulton J. Sheen, *Preface to Religion*, 1946

It is always right that a man should be able to render a reason for the faith that is within him.

—Sydney Smith, *Lady Holland's Memoirs*, I, 1855

The beginning of faith is practically empty of content. It is pure trust.

—Brother David Steindl-Rast, *Gratefulness, The Heart of Prayer*, 1984

Faith is verification by the heart; confession by the tongue;
action by the limbs.

—Sufi proverb

Faith is the foretaste of that knowledge which hereafter will
make us happy.

—St. Thomas Aquinas (1225–74), *Opusc.* xiii, *Compendium Theologiae*

Faith means being grasped by a power that is greater than
we are, a power that shakes us and turns us, and transforms and heals us. Surrender to this power of faith.

—Paul Tillich, *The New Being*, 1955

Faith is the sense of life, that sense by virtue of which man
does not destroy himself, but continues to live on. It is the
force whereby we live.

—Leo Tolstoy, *My Confession*, 1879

Without faith a prayer has only form. Without faith a prayer
has no heart or flame.

—Guy Everton Tremaine, *The Prayer Life of Jesus*, 1954

Nothing in this world is so marvelous as the transformation
that a soul undergoes when the light of faith descends upon
the light of reason.

—W. Bernard Ullathorne, *Endowments of Man*, 1889

Faith consists in believing not what seems true, but what
seems false to our understanding. . . . Divine faith . . . is evidently nothing more than incredulity brought under subjec-
tion, for we certainly have no other faculty than the
understanding by which we can believe; and the objects of
faith are not those of the understanding.

—Voltaire, *Philosophical Dictionary*, I, 1764

Faith will not be restored in the West because people believe it
to be useful. It will return only when they find that it is true.

—Barbara Ward, *Faith and Freedom*, 1954

You know that if you get in the water and have nothing to
hold on to, but try to behave as you would on dry land, you
will drown. But if, on the other hand, you trust yourself to
the water and let go, you will float. And this is exactly the situation of faith.

—Alan Watts, *The Way of Liberation*, 1983

Authentic tidings of invisible things, of ebb and flow, and ever'during power, and central peace. Subsisting at the heart of endless agitation.

—William Wordsworth, *The Prelude*, 1800

Mencius said: If a scholar have not faith, how shall he take a firm hold of things.

—*Works of Mencius* (371–288 B.C.)

Faith is a free choice; wherever there is a desire of proof . . . there is no faith.

—Alexander Yelchaninov (1881–1934), *Fragments of a Diary*

FALL

By the fall the divine witness in man was extinguished as a candle is blown out and from our corrupt human nature no saving light proceeds.

—Robert Barclay (1648–90), *Works*, Vol. 1

The Fall could not take place in the natural world, because this world is itself the result of the Fall. The Fall is an event in the spiritual world, and in this sense it is anterior to the world, for it took place before time and, in fact, produced time as we know it.

—Nicholas Berdyaev, *Freedom and the Spirit*, 1935

The "Fall" did not happen once and for all and become an inevitable fate, but it continually happens here and now in all its reality.

—Martin Buber, *Israel and the World*, 1949

God not only foresaw the fall of the first man, and in him the ruin of his posterity, but also at his own pleasure arranged it.

—John Calvin, *Institutes*, 1536

A Fall of some sort or other . . . is the fundamental postulate of the moral history of man. Without this hypothesis, man is unintelligible; with it, every phenomenon is explicable. The mystery is too profound for human insight.

—Samuel Taylor Coleridge, *Table-Talk*, May 1, 1830

The old conceptions of the fall of man and of the total depravity of the race were good foundations for the *regime* of a beneficient despot, but not for the *regime* of self-governing freemen.

—Charles W. Eliot, *Why the Republic May Endure*, 1894

The Fall is the eternal Mythus of Man . . . in fact, the very transition by which he becomes man.
—G.W.F. Hegel (1770–1831), *The Philosophy of History*, publ. posth.

The fall is not historical. It does not take place in any concrete human act. It is the presupposition of such acts.
—Reinhold Niebuhr, *Beyond Tragedy*, 1937

To fall into the truth and rise a just man—a transfiguring fall—that is sublime.
—Victor Hugo, *William Shakespeare*, 1864

I interpret [the] hypothetical fall of man to be the groping of newly conscious men to narratize what has happened to them, the loss of divine voices and assurances in a chaos of human directive and selfish privacies.
—Julian Jaynes, *The Origin of Consciousness of the Breakdown of the Bicameral Mind*, 1976

The Fall is not from some superior grade of civilization or even from a better-developed body. It is wholly from a supernatural way of being, and no imaginable "natural" science can ever discover anything about it.
—C.C. Martindale, *The Catholic Bedside Book*, 1953

Unless this fact of the "Fall of Man"—or, if you will, the dogma of original sin—be admitted, Christianity simply collapses like a pricked balloon. . . . For without the Fall, there would be no need of the Incarnation and Redemption, the two cardinal points of Christian belief.
—William J. McGucken, *The Philosophy of Catholic Education*, 1951

Since Adam's fall, all men begotten after the common course of nature are born with sin, that is, without the fear of God, without trust in Him, and with fleshly appetites.
—Philip Melanchthon, *Augsburg Confession*, 1530

While the legend of the Fall passes away, the doctrine of the Fall remains.
—William N. Rice, *Christian Faith in an Age of Science*, 1903

The fall of man is the very foundation of revealed religion. If this be taken away, the Christian system is subverted, nor will it deserve so honorable an appellation as that of a cunningly devised fable.
—John Wesley (1703–91), *Works*, Vol. I, p. 176

FAMILY

The joys of parents are secret; and so are their griefs and fears; they cannot utter the one; nor they will not utter the other. Children sweeten labors; but they make misfortunes more bitter.

—Francis Bacon, *Essays*, 1597

Parents belong to the world of the past; children belong to the world of the future. Both share the world of the present, but neither can enter or fully understand the other's world and time. It is easier to communicate across miles than across years. We meet and laugh awhile; we separate and grieve awhile. And then we remember.

—Joseph A. Bauer, "Love Me Tender, Love Me True," *Religious Humanism*, Summer 1991

The men and women who, for good reasons and bad, revolt against the family are, for good reasons and bad, simply revolting against mankind.

—G.K. Chesterton, *Heretics*, 1905

To found a family. I think it would have been easier for me to found an empire.

—E. M. Cioran, *Drawn and Quartered*, 1971

Like any other human institution the nuclear family is neither sacred nor eternal. It is one way, among many others, of organizing human life. Furthermore, it seems now to be one which has outlived most of the usefulness it ever had and is in need of remolding.

—Harvey Cox, *The Seduction of the Spirit*, 1973

From the loving example of one family a whole state becomes loving.

—*The Great Learning*, c. 500 B.C.

Whoever does the will of God is my brother, and sister, and mother.

—*Holy Bible*, Mark 3:35

Fathers, do not provoke your children, lest they become discouraged.

—*Holy Bible*, Colossians 3:21

Honor your father and your mother that your days may be long in the land which the Lord your God gives you.

—*Holy Bible*, Exodus 20:12

Call it a clan, call it a network, call it a tribe, call it a family. Whatever you call it, whoever you are, you need one.
—Jane Howard, *Families*, 1978

The family you come from isn't as important as the family you're going to have.
—Ring Lardner (1855–1933)

Parents hold from nature their right of training the children to whom they have given birth, with the obligation super-added of shaping and training the education of their littles on to the end for which God vouchsafed the privilege of transmitting life.
—Pope Leo XIII, *Sapientiae Christianae*, 1890

Families will not be broken. Curse and expel them, send their children wandering, drown them in floods and fires, and old women will make songs out of all these sorrows and sit in the porches and sing them on mild evenings.
—Marilynne Robinson, *Housekeeping*, 1980

Every noble youth looks back, as to the chiefest joy which this world's honor ever gave him, to the moment when first he saw his father's eyes flash with pride, and his mother turn away her head, lest he should take her tears for tears of sorrow.
—John Ruskin, *A Joy Forever*, 1857

We don't have choices about who our parents are and how they treated us, but we have a choice about whether we for-give our parents and heal ourselves.
—Bernie Siegel, in *New Age Journal*, May/June 1989

An ounce of parent is worth a pound of the clergy.
—Spanish proverb

The family's survival depends on the shared sensibility of its members.
—Elizabeth Stone, *Black Sheep and Kissing Cousins*, 1988

All happy families resemble one another; every unhappy fam-ily is unhappy in its own way.
—Leo Tolstoy, opening line of *Anna Karenina*, 1876

FELLOWSHIP

A branch cut off from its neighbor branch cannot but be cut off from the whole plant. In the very same way a man severed from one man has fallen away from the fellowship of all men.
—Marcus Aurelius, *Meditations*, c. 170

In the Christian church we cannot interpret human nature except as fellowship.
—Karl Barth, *Church Dogmatics*, III:2, 1951

Coffee hour does not force any political point of view on anyone; thus, in a time of radicalization of the pulpit, the social hall has become the sanctuary of the church. Radicals and Reaganites can carry on about anything from Kierkegaard to croquet as they sip coffee after church.
—Jim Burklo, "Coffee Hour: America's True Religion," *Co-Evolution Quarterly*, Spring 1984

Dost thou love and fear God? It is enough! I give thee the right hand of fellowship.
—Common greeting of John Wesley (1703–91)

After justice has rendered impartial decision it is charity that brings men back to fellowship.
—James Gibbons, pastoral letter, 1919

The all-important question is not whether human life will survive upon this planet. Rather, it is whether the souls of men will be fit to use God's gift of personal survival in an eternal fellowship.
—Georgia Harkness, *The Modern Rival of Christian Faith*, 1953

And all who believed were together and had all things in common; and they sold their possessions and goods and distributed them to all, as any had need.
—*Holy Bible*, Acts 2:44-45

God has created mankind for fellowship, and not for solitariness, which is clearly proved by this strong argument: God, in the creation of the world, created man and woman, to the end that the man in the woman should have a fellow.
—Martin Luther (1483–1546), *Table-Talk*

The distinctive thing about fellowship is its lesson of self-subordination.
—Gregory Vlastos, *The Religious Way*, 1934

We who have been created for fellowship with God repudiate it continually; and the whole of mankind does this along with us. Every man is his own Adam and all men are solidarily Adam.

—John Whale, *Christian Doctrine*, 1941

FINDING GOD

Know that all that is other than God veils you from Him. . . . If it were not for your alienation, you would look upon Him face to face.

—al-Ghazali (fl. A.D. 1100), in Margaret Smith, *Al-Ghazali*

If ye do not recognize God, at least recognize His signs.

—Al-Hallaj (10th century), in A.J. Arberry, *Sufism*

We cannot go where God is not, and where God is, all is well.

—Anonymous

We do not walk to God with the feet of our body, nor would wings, if we had them, carry us to Him, but we go to Him by the affections of our soul.

—St. Augustine (354–430), *Sermon XXXLIV*

The quest of man for God, which becomes in the end the most ardent and enthralling of all his quests, begins with the first vague questioning of nature and a sense of something unseen both in himself and her.

—Sri Aurobindo, *The Life Divine*, 1949

He alone is God who can never be sought in vain: not even when He cannot be found.

—St. Bernard of Clairvaux, *De Consideratione*, c. 1150

The man who does not need God will not find God.

—George Brantl, *Catholicism*, 1962

Every day people are straying away from the church and going back to God. Really.

—Lenny Bruce, "Religions Inc.," in John Cohen, ed.,
The Essential Lenny Bruce, 1967

The truth of God is so concealed in us and above us, that we need a special intuition, a supernatural light, light infused in our hearts by God Himself.

—R.L. Bruckberger, *Toward the Summit*, 1956

Not only has God planted in our minds this seed of religion, but has also manifested Himself in the whole fabric of His creation, so placing Himself before our view that we cannot open our eyes without being constrained to behold Him.

—John Calvin, *Institutes*, I, VI, i, 1536

The search for God is, indeed, an entirely personal undertaking. By the exercise of the normal activities of his consciousness, man may endeavor to reach an invisible reality both immanent in and transcending the material world. Thus, he throws himself into the most audacious adventure that one can dare.

—Alexis Carrel, *Man, the Unknown*, 1935

For silence is not God, not speaking is not God, fasting is not God, nor eating is not God; loneliness is not God, nor company is not God; nor yet any of all the other two such contraries. He is hid between them, and may not be found by any work of thy soul, but all only by love of thine heart.

—*The Cloud of Unknowing*, 14th century

Nobody hath found God by walking his own way.

—Ram Das (c. 1580), in M.A. Macauliffe, *The Sikh Religion*

To come to God there is a straight line for every man everywhere.

—John Donne, *Sermons*, no. 67, 1640

Suppose a man is hiding and he stirs, he shows his whereabouts thereby; and God does the same. No one could ever have found God; he gives himself away.

—Meister Eckhart (1260?–1327?), *Meister Eckhart*

God Himself does not speak prose, but communicates with us by hints, omens, inferences and dark resemblances in objects lying all around us.

—Ralph Waldo Emerson, *Poetry and Imagination*, 1876

The place where man vitally finds God . . . is within his own experience of goodness, truth, and beauty, and the truest images of God are therefore to be found in man's spiritual life.

—Harry Emerson Fosdick, *Adventurous Religion*, 1926

There are innumerable definitions of God because his manifestations are innumerable. They overwhelm me with wonder
and awe and for a moment stun me. But I worship God as
Truth only. I have not found him, but I am seeking after
Him. I am prepared to sacrifice the things dearest to me in
pursuit of this quest.

—Mohandas K. Gandhi, *My Experiment with Truth*, 1927

The other is infinitely distant from me, more distant than the
farthest stars. I can wander through all the ways of space
that are geometrically possible, traverse land and sea and fly
in the upper air, without coming one pace nearer to where
the other dwells. Nevertheless the other is infinitely near me.

—Karl Heim, *The Certitude of Faith*, 1923

I didn't know what she was saying when she moved her lips
in a Baptist church or a Catholic cathedral or, less often, in
a synagogue, but it was obvious that God could be found
anywhere.

—Lillian Hellman, *An Unfinished Woman*, 1969

The Lord is good to those who wait for him, to the soul that
seeks him.

—*Holy Bible*, Lamentations 3:25

Ye will seek me and find me; when you seek me with all
your heart.

—*Holy Bible*, Jeremiah 29:13

My greatest desire is that I may perceive the God whom I find
everywhere in the external world, in like manner also within
and inside myself.

—Johannes Kepler (1571–1630), in J.W. von Goethe, *Maxims and Reflections*

When one finds one's Self, one has found God; and finding
God one has found one's Self.

—Anandamayi Ma, *As the Flower Sheds Its Fragrance*, 1983

Man is close to God when he is close to the people. If we
think of God as something in favor of the betterment of
man, both materially and spiritually, and if we act in a way
that brings about that betterment—if we do not cling to
riches, selfishness or greed—then I believe we are getting
closer to God.

—Daniel Ortega *World Press Review*, April 1987

He who in truth seeketh after God with all his heart will remove his mind far away from every earthly thing and he will direct the gaze of his understanding towards God.
—Palladius of Egypt, *Paradise of the Fathers*, c. 300

Ever since the days of Adam, man has been hiding from God and saying, "God is hard to find."
—Fulton J. Sheen, *Peace of Soul*, 1949

All things, by desiring their own perfection, desire God Himself; inasmuch as the perfection of all things are so many similitudes of the divine essence.
—St. Thomas Aquinas, *Summa Theologiae*, 1272

When men shout that "God is dead," this can only mean that He is not in the place where they are looking for Him.
—W.A. Visser 't Hooft, in *The New York Times*, December 20, 1965

God only comes to those who ask him to come; and he cannot refuse to come to those who implore him long, often and ardently.
—Simone Weil, *Waiting for God*, 1951

We think we must climb to a certain height of goodness before we can reach God. But . . . if we are in a hole the Way begins in the hole. The moment we set our face in the same direction as His, we are walking with God.
—Helen Wodehouse, *Inner Light*, I, 1931

Our God, the God of our fathers, is a hidden God; and not until we are bathed in sorrow are we enabled to discern him.
—Stefan Zweig, *Jeremiah*, 1917

FORGIVENESS

The remission of sins. For it is by this that the Church on earth stands: it is through this that what has been lost, and was found, is saved from being lost again.
—St. Augustine, *Enchiridion*, 421

Forgiveness is the fragrance the violet sheds on the heel that has crushed it.
—Anonymous

"I can forgive, but I cannot forget," is only another way of saying, "I will not forgive." A forgiveness ought to be like a cancelled note, torn in two and burned up, so that it can never be shown against the man.
—Henry Ward Beecher, *Life Thoughts*, 1858

Disconsolate soul, dejected spirit, bruised and broke, ground and trodden, attenuated, evaporated, annihilated heart come back; hear thy reprieve and sue for thy pardon; God will not take thee away in thy sins; thou shalt have time to repent.
—John Donne, sermon, February 11, 1627

Where is the foolish person who would think it in his power to commit more than God could forgive.
—St. Francis de Sales (1567–1622), *Consoling Thoughts of*

And forgive us our debts, / As we also have forgiven our debtors. . . . For if you forgive men their trespasses, your heavenly Father also will forgive you.
—*Holy Bible*, Matthew 6:12, 14

A wise man will make haste to forgive, because he knows the true value of time, and will not suffer it to pass away in unnecessary pain.
—Samuel Johnson, *The Rambler*, December 24, 1751

No sin is too big for God to pardon, and none to small for habit to magnify.
—Bahya ben Joseph ibn Pakuda, *Hobot HaLebabot*, 1040

In the absolution . . . a distressed sinner is pardoned. By what authority is he pardoned? Not by human command, but by God's command.
—Martin Luther, sermon, 1528

Allah, Most High, says: He who approaches near to me one span, I will approach to him one cubit; and he who approaches near to me one cubit, I will approach near to him one fathom; and whoever approaches me walking, I will come to him running, and he who meets me with sins equivalent to the whole world, I will greet him with forgiveness equal to it.
—*Mishkat-ul-Masabih*, 7th century

Forgiving love is a possibility only for those who know they are not good, who feel themselves in need of divine mercy.
—Reinhold Niebuhr, *An Interpretation of Christian Ethics*, 1935

Force may subdue, but Love gains; and he that forgives first, wins the laurel.

—William Penn, *Some Fruits of Solitude*, 1693

To err is human, to forgive divine.

—Alexander Pope, *An Essay on Criticism*, 1711

We pardon in the degree that we love.

—La Rochefoucauld, *Maxims*, 1665

I must practice unlimited forgiveness because, if I did not, I should be wanting in veracity to myself, for it would be acting as if I myself were not guilty in the same way as the other has been guilty towards me.

—Albert Schweitzer, *Civilization and Ethics*, 1923

We witness . . . by being a community of reconciliation, a forgiving community of the forgiven.

—Bishop Desmond Tutu, *Crying in the Wilderness*, 1982

Freedom

Man's freedom is his inner worth. . . . His guilt alone can rob him of it.

—Michael Beer, *Clytemnestra*, 1823

The essence of religious liberty is that men should feel that there is nothing whatever that stands between themselves and God.

—Arthur Christopher Benson, *From a College Window*, 1906

To be free from everything is to be—nothing. Only nothing is quite free, and freedom is abstract nothingness.

—F.H. Bradley, *Ethical Studies*, 1927

The more man trusts in and affirms his freedom the more likely he is to misuse the freedom which he confuses with absolute, i.e., divine, freedom.

—Emil Brunner, *Eternal Hope*, 1954

Leave every church Independent; not Independent from brotherly Counsel, God forbid it that we should refuse that; but when it comes to power, that one Church shall have the power over the rest, then look for a Beast.

—John Cotton, *An Exposition of the Thirteenth Chapter of the Revelation*, 1656

Freedom (or this principle of freedom) is the greatest gift conferred by God on human nature; for through it we have our felicity here as men, through it we have our felicity elsewhere as deities.
—Dante, *De Monarchia*, c. 1300

He whose body is chained, and his soul unbound, is free.
—Epictetus (60–140), *Moral Discourses of*

Man is that animal in which appetites, passions, and rationality must learn to work together for the joyful fulfillment of meaning, and man is "free" in the human sense of that word, to the extent that he understands his own actions and the influence on them of all that he is and all that impinges upon him, and to the extent that he consequently *chooses* his path amid a variety of options.
—Douglas A. Fox, *Buddhism, Christianity, and the Future of Man*, 1972

It is dangerous to take human freedom for granted, to regard it as a prerogative rather than as an obligation, as an ultimate fact rather than as an ultimate goal. It is the beginning of wisdom to be amazed at the fact of our being free.
—Abraham Joshua Heschel, *The Insecurity of Freedom*, 1966

When we have reached the point of measuring the stature of our freedom by the height of the pile of our discarded inhibitions, is anyone minded to die for this eviscerated ghost of that modern liberty which once was sacred because it was important?
—William Ernest Hocking, *What Man Can Make of Man*, 1942

Too much liberty is as life-destroying as too much restraint.
—Aldous Huxley, *Do What You Will*, 1929

A man's worst difficulties begin when he is able to do as he likes.
—Thomas Henry Huxley, "Address on University Education," *Collected Essays*, 1902

Christianity promises to make men free; it never promises to make them independent.
—W.R. Inge, *The Philosophy of Plotinus*, 1918

The legitimate powers of government extend to such acts only as are injurious to others. But it does me no injury for my neighbor to say there are twenty Gods, or no God.
—Thomas Jefferson, *Notes on Virginia*, 1779

Virtue cannot be fully attained without liberty and the absence of liberty proves that virtue in its full protection is wanting. Therefore a man is free in proportion to the measure of his virtues, and the extent to which he is free determines what his virtues can accomplish.

> —John of Salisbury, *Policraticus*, 1159

When freedom does not have a purpose, when it does not wish to know anything about the rule of law engraved in the hearts of men and women, when it does not listen to the voice of conscience, it turns against humanity and society.

> —Pope John Paul III, in *The New York Times*, May 12, 1985

Every human being has the right to honor God according to the dictates of an upright conscience, and therefore the right to worship God privately and publicly.

> —Pope John XXIII, *Pacem in Terris*, April 1963

Let your cry be for free souls rather than for freedom. Moral liberty is the only really important liberty.

> —Joseph Joubert, *Pensées*, 1842

Liberty, rightly understood, is an inestimable blessing, but liberty without wisdom, and without justice, is no better than wild and savage licentiousness.

> —Chancellor Kent, debate in the New York Constitutional Convention, 1821

No citizen enjoys genuine freedom of religious conviction until the state is indifferent to every form of religious outlook from Atheism to Zoroastrianism.

> —Harold Laski, *Grammar of Politics*, 1925

For no man can, if he would, conform his faith to the dictates of another. All the life and power of true religion consists in the outward and full persuasion of the mind; and faith is not faith without believing.

> —John Locke, *A Letter Concerning Toleration*, 1685

I believe in a religion that believes in freedom. Any time I have to accept a religion that won't let me fight a battle for my people, I say to hell with that religion.

> —Malcolm X, *By Any Means Necessary*, 1970

A man is said to act freely when he acts according to the ultimate ideal of his nature.

> —J.M.C. McTaggart, *Some Dogmas of Religion*, 1906

A superficial freedom to wander aimlessly here or there, to taste this or that, to make a choice of distractions (in Pascal's sense) is simply a sham. It claims to be a freedom of "choice" when it has evaded the basic task of discovering who it is that chooses.

—Thomas Merton, *Love and Living*, 1979

The sense of sharing a common fate, which is the basis of enduring comradeship and love, is also the firmest foundation for a free society.

—Henry Alonzo Myers, *Are Men Equal?*, 1945

The good man always acts sensibly, and therefore, he alone is free.

—Philo, *Every Good Man Is Free*, c. A.D. 10

A religious body which denies legitimate freedom is in danger of becoming a demonic institution which blasphemously claims to be an absolute.

—W. Norman Pittenger, *The Churchman*, September 1958

Man is condemned to be free. Condemned, because he did not create himself, yet is nevertheless at liberty, and from the moment that he is thrown into this world he is responsible for everything he does.

—Jean Paul Sartre, *Existentialism and Humanism*, 1948

Freedom does not mean that right to do whatever we please, but rather to do whatever we ought. . . . The right to do whatever we *please* reduces freedom to a physical power and forgets that freedom is a moral power.

—Fulton J. Sheen, *The Wit and Wisdom of Bishop Fulton J. Sheen*, 1968

Christian freedom is neither the lonely rebellion of an atheistic existentialist nor the self-will of the rugged individualist. It is freedom-in-community.

—Roger L. Shinn, *Religious Education*, April 1958

Every man is free to do what he will, provided he infringes not upon the equal freedom of any other man.

—Herbert Spencer, *The Principles of Ethics*, IV, 1898

Not only is freedom of thought and speech compatible with piety and the peace of the State, but it cannot be withheld without destroying at the same time both the peace of the State and piety itself.

—Baruch Spinoza, *Theological-Political Treatise*, 1670

What our constitution indispensably protects is the freedom
of each of us, be he Jew or agnostic, Christian or atheist,
Buddhist or free thinker, to believe or disbelieve, to worship
or not to worship, to pray or keep silent, according to his
own conscience, uncoerced and unrestrained by government.
— Justice Potter Stewart, U.S. Supreme Court, dissenting opinion, June 17, 1963

All who allow themselves a wrong liberty make themselves
their own aim and object.
—Henry Suso (1300–66), *Life of Blessed Henry Suso by Himself*

Everyone has the right to freedom of thought, conscience
and religion; this right includes freedom to change his religion or belief, and freedom, either alone or in community
with others, and in public or in private, to manifest his religion or belief in teaching, practice, worship and observance.
—*United Nations Universal Declaration of Human Rights*, Article 18, 1948

Vedanta [Hindu] says there is nothing that is not God. . . .
The living God is within you. . . . The only God to worship is
the human soul in the human body.
—Swami Vivekananda, speech, 1896, in *Yoga and Other Works*

God grants liberty to those who love it, are always ready to
guard and defend it.
—Daniel Webster, address, January 26, 1830

What do you suppose will satisfy the soul, except to walk free
and own no superior?
—Walt Whitman, "Laws for Creation," *Leaves of Grass*, 1892

Religious liberty includes freedom to change one's religion
or belief without consequent social, economic and political
disabilities. Implicit in this right is the right freely to maintain one's belief or disbelief without external coercion or
disability.
—World Council of Churches, 1961

FREE WILL

All is foreseen, yet man is endowed with free will.
—Akiba (50–132), *Mishna: Abot*

God . . . created man; He has also created the circumstances under which he lives and acts; but still He has endowed man with discretion to choose how to act. . . . And as he can exercise his discretion or his will in doing a thing or not doing it, he is responsible for his own deeds, and made to suffer the consequences.

—Muhammad Ali, *The Religion of Islam*, 1936

Where we are free to act, we are also free to refrain from acting, and where we are able to say No, we are also able to say Yes.

—Aristotle, *Nicomachean Ethics*, Bk. III, ch. 5, 340 B.C.

Free will is of itself sufficient for evil but, so far as good is concerned, it does nothing unless aided by all-powerful goodness.

—St. Augustine, *De correptione et gratia*, ch. 11, 427

Take away free will and there remaineth nothing to be saved. . . . Salvation is given by God alone, and it is given only to the free-will; even as it cannot be wrought without the consent of the receiver it cannot be wrought without the grace of the giver.

—St. Bernard, *Treatise Concerning Grace and Free Will*, c. 1128

He produces not only our choice, but also the very freedom that is in our choice. . . . In order to understand that God creates our free will in us, we must understand only that He wills us to be free. But He wills not only that we should be free in power, but that we should be free in its exercise.

—Jacques Benique Bossuet (1627–1704), *Treatise on Free Will*

You may fetter my leg, but my will not even Zeus can overpower.

—Epictetus, *Discourses*, c. 110

God commands us to pray without ceasing, to watch, to struggle, and to contend for the reward of eternal life. Why does He wish to be prayed to endlessly for that which He has already decreed to grant or not to grant, since being immutable He cannot change His decrees?

—Desiderius Erasmus, *Of Free Will*, 1524

To deny the freedom of the will is to make morality impossible.

—James A. Froude, *Short Studies: Calvinism*, 1871

All choice, when one comes to think of it, is terrifying; liberty where there is no duty to guide it, terrifying.
—André Gide, *The Fruits of the Earth*, 1949

There would be no sense in arguing about determinism or indeterminism if all our arguments were rigidly determined in advance.
—Morris Ginsberg, *On the Diversity of Morals*, 1957

The more the will submits itself to grace, the more it does all that in it lies to make itself absolutely, fully, and constantly dependent, so much the more will it be free.
—J.N. Grou, *Maximes Spirituelles*, 1872

The human will has no more freedom than that of the higher animals, from which it differs only in degree, not in kind.
—Ernest Haeckel, *The Riddle of the Universe*, 1899

Freedom is a fundamental character of the will, as weight is of matter. . . . That which is free is the will. Will without freedom is an empty word.
—G.W.F. Hegel, *Grundlinien der Philosophie des Rechts*, 1821

The price we pay for liberty is that so far as a man is free to do right he is also free to do wrong.
—L.T. Hobhouse, *Elements of Social Justice*, 1949

The greatest power God gave us is the power to choose. We have the opportunity to choose whether we're going to act or procrastinate, believe or doubt, pray or curse, help or heal. We also choose whether we're going to be happy or whether we're going to be sad.
—Lou Holtz, address, Gonzaga University commencement,
The Christian Science Monitor, June 12, 1989

Free Will does not say that everything that is physically conceivable is also morally possible. It merely says that of alternatives that really *tempt* our will more than one is really possible.
—William James, *Unitarian Review*, September 1884

All theory is against the freedom of the will; all experience for it.
—Samuel Johnson, *Boswell's Life of*, April 15, 1778

What else can the freedom of the will be but autonomy, that is, the property of the will to be a law unto itself?
—Immanuel Kant, *Critique of Practical Reason*, 1788

Free will, though it makes evil possible, is also the only thing that makes possible any love of goodness or joy worth having.
—C.S. Lewis, *The Case for Christianity*, 1943

God foresees, foreordains, and accomplishes all things by an unchanging, eternal, and efficacious will. By this thunderbolt freewill sinks shattered in the dust.
—Martin Luther, *De servo arbitrio*, 1525

The falsity of determinism lies simply in the dogma that the future is already determinate. But if this were so there would be no future; the future would be already past.
—John Macmurray, *The Self as Agent*, 1958

The theory of man's perfectly free will is one of the fundamental principles of the law of our teacher Moses, and of those who follow the Law.
—Maimonides, *Guide for the Perplexed*, 1190

Either free-will is a fact, or moral judgment a delusion.
—James Martineau, *Types of Ethical Theory*, 1886

To deny free will is to make mankind nothing but driftwood on the inexorable river of fate, and how we jostle one another is beyond our power to help.
—J.A. McWilliams, *Philosophy for the Millions*, 1942

There is not one among you whose sitting-place is not written by God whether in the fire or in Paradise.
—Mohammed, *Speeches and Table-Talk of*, 7th century

Behind all faith . . . lies the plain fact that man, as a creature of free will, cannot shirk the ultimate responsibility for his own fate.
—Paul Elmer More, *The Catholic Faith*, 1931

When the cards are dealt and you pick up your hand, that is determinism; there's nothing you can do except to play it out for whatever it may be worth. And the way you play your hand is free will.
—Jawaharlal Nehru, in Norman Cousins, *Who Speaks for Man?*, 1953

How can a man be morally responsible, if his choices, like all other events in the universe, could not have been otherwise than they in fact were?

—P.H. Nowell-Smith, in *Mind*, October 1951

The fact that man is physically free to worship God or not, should never be construed to mean that he is morally free to ignore his Creator

—John A. O'Brien, *Religion—Does It Matter?*, 1944

According to the Buddha the will is free, effort is worth while, man makes his own fate, deeds have consequences, knowledge is possible, the body is not the real self, and death is not its end.

—J.B. Pratt, *The Pilgrimage of Buddhism*, 1928

If choice is real, if there really are alternatives, it follows that in choosing between them we are exhibiting our power as real agents, real causes and initiators of new departures in the flow of cosmic change, we thereby prove the existence of free causes.

—F.C.S. von Schiller, *Riddle of the Sphinx*, 1910

No amount of libido, or passion, no external force, and no inner prompting to sin can make the human action of man anything but free. We are never tempted beyond our strength. Every moral failure is ours alone, because our choices are our own.

—Fulton J. Sheen, *Lift Up Your Hearts*, 1950

Against the formidable array of cumulative evidence for Determinism, there is but one argument of real force: the immediate affirmation of consciousness in the moment of deliberate action.

—Henry Sidgwick, *Method of Ethics*, 1906

There is no free will in the human mind: it is moved to this or that volition by some cause, and that cause has been determined by some other cause, and so on infinitely.

—Baruch Spinoza, *Ethics*, 1677

Determinism, if taken seriously, would involve the further notion that all intellectual judgment is itself determined, but this would have to apply even to the judgment that determinism is true.

—D.E. Trueblood, *Philosophy of Religion*, 1957

201

FREE WILL

We are neither free from all conditioning nor inexorably bound. We have neither too much nor too little freedom. We have just enough to be responsible.

—Paul Weiss, *Man's Freedom*, 1950

FRIENDSHIP

Friendship being incompatible with truth, only the mute dialogue with our enemies is fruitful.

—E. M. Cioran, *Drawn and Quartered*, 1971

I awoke this morning with devout thanksgiving for my friends, the old and the new. Shall I not call God, the Beautiful, who daily showeth himself so to me in his gifts.

—Ralph Waldo Emerson, "Friendship," *Essays*, 1844

To become Love, Friendship needs what Morality needs to become Religion—the fire of emotion.

—Richard Garnett, Preface, *Der Flagello Myrteo*, 1897

No longer do I call you servants, for the servant does not know what his master is doing; but I have called you friends, for all that I have heard from my Father I have made known to you.

—*Holy Bible*, John 15:15

The very possibility of friendship with God transfigures life. The religious convictions, thus, tend inevitably to deepen every human friendship, to make it vastly more significant.

—Henry Churchill King, *The Laws of Friendship*, 1909

Friendship with a man is friendship with his virtue, and does not admit of assumptions of superiority.

—Mencius, c. 300 B.C.

Friendship . . . is an Union of Spirits, a Marriage of Hearts, and the Bond thereto Virtue.

—William Penn, *Fruits of Solitude*, 1693

Holy Friendship that has medicine for all the wretchedness is not to be despised. From God it truly is, that amid the wretchedness of this exile, we be comforted with the counsel of friends until we come to Him.

—Richard Rolle (c. 1300–49), *The Fire of Love*, Bk. 2

**od**

The individual man is partly the animal from which he has come, and partly the God who is coming into him; but God is steadily displacing the animal.

—Lyman Abbott, *Evolution of Christianity*, 1892

If men wish to draw near to God, they must seek Him in the hearts of men.

—Abu Said ibn Abi Khayr (died 1049), in Margaret Smith, *Readings from the Mystics of Islam*

Man thinks, God directs.

—Alcuin, *Epistles*, c. 800

We must recognize that the death of God is a historical event: God has died in our time, in our history, in our existence.

—Thomas J. Altizer, in *Time*, October 22, 1965

No one who understands the reality that God is can think that God does not exist.

—St. Anselm of Canterbury, *The Proslogion*, 1100

The way God has been thought of for thousands of years is no longer convincing; if anything is dead, it can only be the traditional *thought* of God.

—Hannah Arendt, in *The New Yorker*, November 21, 1970

God is in thy heart, yet thou searchest for Him in the wilderness.

—Arjan (died 1606), in M.A. Macauliffe, *The Sikh Religion*

"God" is a convenient way of expressing our wonder in the vast splendor of the universe, and our humility over the modesty of man's achievements.

—Brooks Atkinson, in *The New York Times*, April 23, 1963

The divine Nature, free and perfect and blissful, must be manifested in the individual in order that it may manifest in the world.

—Sri Aurobindo, *Synthesis of Yoga*, 1950

Now as God is infinite and omnipresent in all places, he consequently is within the bodies of men, as well as without them. . . . He penetrates all beings and spirits more thoroughly than the visible light at noonday doth the air.
—John Bellers, *Essays*, 1699

God is designated One to suit our comprehension, not to describe his character. *His character is capable of division, He Himself is not.* The words are different, the paths are many, but one thing is signified: the paths lead to one Person.
—St. Bernard of Clairvaux, *De Consideratione*,
Bk. v, Cap. viii, c. 1150

This shining, immortal Person who is in the heart, and, with reference to oneself, this shining, immortal Person—who is in the body—he, indeed, is just this Soul, this Immortal, this Brahma, this All.
—*Brhadaranyaka Upanishad*, prior to 400 B.C.

The God of the "other religions" is always an idol.
—Emil Brunner, *Revelation and Reason*, 1946

There is an unborn, an unoriginated, an unmade, an uncompounded; were there not, O mendicants, there would be no escape from the world of the born, the originated, the made, and the compounded.
—Buddha (6th century B.C.), *Udana*, VIII

Upon supposition that God exercises a moral government over the world, the analogy of His natural government suggests and makes it creditable that His moral government must be a scheme quite beyond our comprehension.
—Joseph Butler, *Analogy of Religion*, pt. I, ch. 7, 1736

The concept of God has become virtually synonymous with a goodness and a power that transcends us, an elusive, often static spirit beyond our reach, ontologically uninvolved with us.
—Katie G. Cannon et al., *God's Fierce Whimsy*, 1985

Brahman is supreme; he is self-luminous, he is beyond all thought. Subtler than the subtlest is he, farther than the farthest, nearer than the nearest. He resides in the heart of every being.
—*Chandogya Upanishad*, prior to 400 B.C.

Within the city of Brahman, which is the body, there is the heart, and within the heart there is a little house. This house has the shape of a lotus, and within it dwells that which is to be sought after; inquired about, and realized.

—*Chandogya Upanishad*, prior to 400 B.C.

God is another name for human intelligence raised above all error and imperfection, and extended to all possible truth.

—William Ellery Channing (1780–1842), *Works*

The only God whom our thoughts can rest on, our hearts cling to, and our conscience can recognize, is the God whose image dwells in our own souls.

—William Ellery Channing (1780–1842), *Works*

There is no race so wild and untamed as to be ignorant of the existence of God.

—Cicero, *De Natura Deorum*, 44 B.C.

When you say law, I say God.
When you say peace, justice, love, I say God.
When you say God, I say liberty, justice, peace.

—Dom Pedro Casaldaliga, in Penny Lernoux, *People of God*, 1989

Why indeed must "God" be a noun? Why not a verb—the most active and dynamic of all?. . . The anthropomorphic symbols for God may be intended to convey personality, but they fail to convey that God is Be-ing.

—Mary Daly, *Beyond God the Father: Toward a Philosophy of Women's Liberation*, 1973

In my most extreme fluctuations I have never been an atheist in the sense of denying the existence of God.

—Charles Darwin, *Life and Letters*, I, 1887

When man substituted God for the Great Goddess he at the same time substituted authoritarian for humanistic values.

—Elizabeth Gould Davis, *The First Sex*, 1971

The white man has lost his soul. But he is so small-minded that he has confused his soul with God.

—Vine Deloria, Jr., in Stan Steiner, *The New Indians*, 1968

Of faith I have nothing, only of truth: that this one God is a brute and traitor, abandoning us to time, to necessity and the engines of matter unhinged. This is no leap; this is evidence of things seen.

—Annie Dillard, *Holy the Firm*, 1977

And we must dare affirm that the Creator, by reason of love, is drawn from his transcendent throne above all things to dwell within the heart of all things, while he yet stays within himself.

—Dionysius the Areopagite, *The Divine Names*, c. 500

I find in the universe so many forms of order, organization, system, law, and adjustment of means to ends, that I believe in a cosmic intelligence and I conceive God as the life, mind, order, and law of the world.

—Will Durant, *This I Believe*, 1954

A conviction, akin to religious feeling, of the rationality or intelligibility of the world lies behind all scientific work of a higher order. This firm belief, a belief bound up with deep feeling, in a superior mind that reveals itself in the world of experience, represents my conception of God.

—Albert Einstein, in *The American Weekly*, 1948

God who creates and is nature, is very difficult to understand, but He is not arbitrary or malicious.

—Albert Einstein (1879–1955), words carved above the fireplace in a room at Fine Hall, Princeton, New Jersey

All Spiritual being is in man. A wise old proverb says, "God comes to see us without bell": that is, as there is no screen or ceiling between our heads and the infinite heavens, so is there no bar or wall in the soul where man, the effect, ceases, and God, the cause, begins.

—Ralph Waldo Emerson, "The Over-Soul," *Essays*, 1841

When you have shut your doors and darkened your room, remember never to say that you are alone, for you are not alone, but God is within, and your genius is within.

—Epictetus, *Discourses of*, c. 110

If a drop of water, thrown into an ocean of some priceless essence, were alive, and could speak and declare its condition, would it not cry out with great joy: O mortals! I live indeed, but I live not myself, but this ocean lives in me, and my life is hidden in this abyss?

—St. Francis de Sales, *Treatise on the Love of God*, 1607

We say to ourselves, it would be very nice if there were a God, who was both creator of the world and a benevolent providence, if there were a moral world order and a future life, but at the same time it is very odd that this is all just as we should wish it ourselves.

—Sigmund Freud, *The Future of an Illusion*, 1928

I believe in the absolute oneness of God and therefore of humanity. What though we have many bodies? We have but one soul. . . . I know God is neither in heaven nor down below, but in everyone.

—Mohandas K. Gandhi (1869–1948), *The Essential Gandhi*

Good God or bad god, true God or false god, kind God or cruel god, man will have some god. The God-idea is indestructible.

—James M. Gillis, *If Not Christianity, What?*, 1935

The modern philosophical atheist who asks man to free himself from God doesn't understand that God is man's element. To ask him to rid himself of God is like asking the fish to free itself from the sea, the bird from the air.

—James M. Gillis, *This Mysterious Human Nature*, 1956

I don't know about God. . . . The only things I know are what I see, hear, feel and smell.

—Günther Grass, in the Paris *Herald-Tribune*, March 23, 1970

The more one is drawn into the maelstrom of human doing, the more one's days and nights are preoccupied by the sheer busyness of living, the more distant becomes the "still small voice": that is all a discreet and self-effacing God permits himself in dealing with his creatures.

—Timothy S. Healy, address, Boston College commencement, in *The New York Times*, May 21, 1991

God is of no importance unless He is of supreme importance.

—Abraham Joshua Heschel, *Man Is Not Alone*, 1951

The marvels of God are not brought forth from one's self. Rather, it is more like a chord, a sound that is played. The tone does not come out of the chord itself, but rather, through the touch of the musician. I am, of course, the lyre and harp of God's kindness.

—Hildegard of Bingen (1098–1179), *Illuminations of*, 1985

The name of God is Truth.

—Hindu proverb

By denying the existence, or providence of God, men may shake off their ease, but not their yoke.

—Thomas Hobbes, *Leviathan*, 1651

God is the Eternal Substance, and is known as such; God is also the Eternal Order of things; but God is That Which does whatever Substance is found to do.

—William E. Hocking,
The Meaning of God in Human Experience, 1912

But the word of God grew and multiplied.

—*Holy Bible*, Acts 12:24

For the word of God is living and active, and sharper than any two-edged sword, piercing to the division of soul and spirit, of joints and marrow, and discerning the thoughts and intentions of the heart.

—*Holy Bible*, Hebrews 4:12

God is spirit, and those who worship him must worship in spirit and truth.

—*Holy Bible*, John 4:24

I am the Alpha and the Omega, the first and the last, the beginning and the end.

—*Holy Bible*, Revelations 22:13

The Lord is my shepherd, I shall not want; he makes me lie down in green pastures. He leads me beside still waters; he restores my soul. He leads me in paths of righteousness for his name's sake.

—*Holy Bible*, Psalms 23:1-3

Then Moses stretched out his hand over the sea; and the Lord drove the sea back by a strong east wind all night, and made the sea dry land, and the waters were divided. And the people of Israel went into the midst of the sea on dry ground, the waters being a wall to them on their right hand and on their left.

—*Holy Bible*, Exodus 14:21-22

With God all things are possible.

—*Holy Bible*, Matthew 19:26

God . . . is not a transcendent being living in a distant heaven whence from time to time he intervenes in the affairs of the earth. He is an ever-present spirit guiding all that happens to a wise and holy end.

—David Hume, *Dialogues Concerning Natural Religion*, 1779

The God whom science recognizes must be a God of universal laws exclusively, a God who does a wholesale, not a retail business. He cannot accommodate his processes to the convenience of individuals.

—William James, *Varieties of Religious Experience*, 1902

The prince of darkness may be a gentleman, as we are told he is, but whatever the God of earth and heaven is, He can surely be no gentleman. His menial services are needed in the dust of our human trials, even more than his dignity is needed in the empyrean.

—William James, *Pragmatism*, 1907

The traits often assigned to Deity, the qualities of personality, of love, of truth, properly belong only to poetry and symbolism.

—David Starr Jordan, *The Higher Foolishness*, 1927

It is necessary that one should be convinced of God's existence, but not so necessary that one should prove it.

—Immanuel Kant, *The Only Possible Ground of Proof for a Demonstration of the Existence of God*, 1763

God's Word is not simply a communication or an objective statement, but a positive command which does not permit man to assume the attitude of a spectator or to enjoy mere disinterested research.

—Adolph Keller, *Religion and the European Mind*, 1934

God is the East and the West, and wherever ye turn, there is God's face.

—*Koran*, 7th century

The will of God prevails. In great contests, each party claims to act in accordance with the will of God. Both may be, and one must be, wrong. God cannot be for and against the same things at the same time.

—Abraham Lincoln, *A meditation* written in 1862, copied and preserved by John Hay

An eternal, most powerful, and most knowing being; which whether any one will please to call God, it matters not.
—John Locke, *Essay Concerning Human Understanding*, 1690

Search yourself and you will find God.
—Kurdish proverb

He, the eternal, dwells concealed in the heart of all beings. Though himself devoid of all senses, he is the illuminator of all the senses, the source of their powers.
—*Mahanirvana Tantra*, prior to 6th century B.C.

How is it, then, that the voice of God is not more distinctly heard by men? The answer to this question is: To be heard it must be listened for.
—Désiré Joseph Mercier, *Conferences of*, 1907

Man creates God just as he creates himself, and he creates God in his own image, often as he aspires to be, often as he in reality is.
—M.F. Ashley Montagu, *This Is My Faith*, 1956

To wish there should be no God is to wish that things which we love and strive to realize and make permanent, should be only temporary and doomed to frustration and destruction.
—W.P. Montague, *Belief Unbound*, 1930

The existence and essence of God are one and the same.
—C.G. Montefiore, *Liberal Judaism*, 1903

Delight is keener, suffering is richer, thought is more exciting, love and friendship are deeper, steadier in the long perspective of God.
—Barbara Spofford Morgan, *Skeptics' Search for God*, 1947

A knower of Brahman becomes Brahman.
—*Mundaka Upanishad*, prior to 400 B.C.

The existence of a Being endowed with intelligence and wisdom is a necessary inference from a study of celestial mechanics.
—Isaac Newton, *Principia*, 1687

God must not be thought of as a physical being, or as having any kind of body. He is pure mind. He moves and acts without needing any corporeal space, or size, or form, or color, or any other property of matter.

—Origen, *De principiis*, c. 254

God is ourselves.

—Harry A. Overstreet, *Hibbert Journal*, Vol. XI, 1913

There is a God within us, and we glow when He stirs us.

—Ovid, *Fasti*, c. A.D. 5

If you bring forth what is within you, what you bring forth will save you. If you do not bring forth what is within you, what you do not bring forth will destroy you.

—Elaine Pagels, "Gnostic Gospel of Thomas," *The Gnostic Gospels*, 1979

The metaphysical proofs of God are so remote from the reasoning of men and so complicated, that they make but little impression.

—Blaise Pascal, *Pensées*, 1670

The legs of those who require proofs of God's existence are made of wood.

—Persian proverb

God, surrounding all things, is Himself not surrounded.

—Philo (20 B.C.?–A.D. 40?), *Fugitives*, 14, *Allegories*

God is not external to anyone, but is present with all things, though they are ignorant that He is so.

—Plotinus (205–270), *Ennead*, vi, 9

You see many stars at night in the sky but find them not when the sun rises. . . . Because you behold not God in the days of your ignorance, say not there is no god.

—Sri Ramakrishna, *His Life and Sayings*

I seemed alone with immensity, and there came at last that melting of the divine darkness into the life within me for which I prayed. Yes, I still belonged, however humbly, to the heavenly household.

—George W. Russell, *The Candle of Visions*, 1918

There can, of course, be no disproof of the existence of God—
particularly a sufficiently subtle God. But it is a kindness
neither to science nor religion to leave unchallenged inadequate arguments for the existence of God.

—Carl Sagan, *Broca's Brain*, 1969

God to me is a mystery, but is the explanation for the miracle of existence—why there is something instead of nothing.

—Allan R. Sandage, in *The New York Times*, March 12, 1991

Everything is permissible if God does not exist, and as a result man is forlorn, because neither within him nor without
does he find anything to cling to.

—Jean Paul Sartre, *Existentialism*, 1947

God be prais'd, that to believing souls
Gives light in darkness, comfort in despair!

—William Shakespeare, *King Henry VI*, 1592

Brahman resembles not the world, and (yet) apart from
Brahman there is naught; all that which seems to exist outside of It (Brahman) cannot exist save in an illusory manner,
like the semblance of water in the desert.

—Shankara (788–820), quoted by René Guénon,
Man and His Becoming

I am sustained by a sense of the worthwhileness of what I
am doing; a trust in the good faith of the process which created and sustains me. That process I call God.

—Upton Sinclair, *What God Means to Me*, 1935

Whatever we conceived to be in the power of God necessarily
exists.

—Baruch Spinoza, *Ethics*, Prop. 35, 1677

The best proof of God's existence is what follows when we
deny it.

—William L. Sullivan, *Epigrams and Criticisms in Miniature*, 1936

While the ideas about God may appear to change, the experience of God appears to abide with men in all ages.

—Obert C. Tanner, *One Man's Search*, 1989

Without the slightest doubt *there is something* through which material and spiritual energy hold together and are complementary. In last analysis, *somehow or other*, there must be a single energy operating in the world.

—Pierre Teilhard de Chardin, *The Phenomenon of Man*, 1955

To see God as male is idolatry. It is like the worship of images in man's own shape. God as male, as the father, is only a metaphor, but . . . the church has forgotten this and has taken it literally.

—Barbara Thiering, in *World Press Review*, January 1988

To know that God exists in a general and confused way is implanted in us by nature, inasmuch as God is man's beatitude. For man naturally desires happiness, and what is naturally desired by man is naturally known by him.

—St. Thomas Aquinas, *Summa Theologica*, 1272

Everything we say about God is symbolic. Such a statement is an assertion about God which itself is not symbolic.

—Paul Tillich, *Systematic Theology*, II, 1957

God is always with us, why should we not always be with God?

—W.B. Ullathorne, *Humility and Patience*, 1909

If God did not exist it would be necessary to invent Him.

—Voltaire, letter to M. Saurin, November 10, 1770

It is the experience of myriads of trustful souls, that this sense of God's unfailing presence with them in their going out and in their coming in, and by night and day, is a source of absolute repose and confident calmness.

—Charles Voysey, *The Mystery and Pain of Death*, 1892

One thing I have no worry about is whether God exists. But it has occurred to me that God has Alzheimer's and has forgotten we exist.

—Jane Wagner, *The Search for Intelligent Life in the Universe*, performed by Lily Tomlin, 1986

Where there is no God, there would be no personal identity, no persistent past and no realization of what is really possible.

—Paul Weiss, *Religious Experience and Truth*, 1962

Once you accept the existence of God—however you define him, however you explain your relationship to him—then you are caught forever with his presence in the center of all things.

—Morris West, *The Clowns of God*, 1981

GOOD AND EVIL

If therapy for minds in distress requires a reorientation of perspective, it may well turn out that the historic religious conceptions of good and evil have a special merit for modern minds caught in the web of psychological terminology.

—Gordon W. Allport, *The Individual and His Religion*, 1950

There no doubt is good in all the bitter woes that come upon us, because evil cannot proceed from God.

—Rabbi Israel Baal Shem-Tov (1700–60), quoted in *Judaism*

Pleasure is in itself a good; nay, even setting aside immunity to pain, the only good; pain is in itself an evil; and, indeed, without exception, the only evil; or else the words good and evil have no meaning.

—Jeremy Bentham, *Principles of Morals and Legislation*, 1789

Good and evil are so set, differing from each other just as reward and punishment are in opposition to each other: hence the rewards, which we see fall to the good, must correspond precisely to the punishment of the evil on the other side.

—Boethius, *Consolations of Philosophy*, c. 524

Nothing gives such force in getting rid of evil as this belief that the good is the only reality.

—Bernard Bosanquet, address, Ethical Society, 1886

It has always been my own belief that what can perpetuate itself is good and what is evil destroys itself, and that this is the principle on which all rational religious thought must be based.

—Lyman Bryson, *Perspectives on a Troubled Decade*, 1950

If a man foolishly does me wrong, I will return to him the protection of my ungrudging love; the more evil comes from him, the more good shall go from me; the fragrance of goodness always comes to me, and the harmful air of evil goes to him.

—Buddha, *Sermon on "Abuse," Sutra of Forty-two Sections*, c. 5th century B.C.

Good and evil coexist and are blended. Each modifies the other.

—William Newton Clarke, *The Christian Idea of God*, 1909

Is it not Satan's sophism for all time when he says to Eve: "You will be like God, knowing good and evil!" To possess all the light, you must also possess all the darkness! To "know life," you must have abused it. To attain truth, you must have experienced error.

—Nicolas Corte, *Who Is the Devil?*, 1958

The perception of Good and Evil—whatever choice we may make—is the first requisite of spiritual life.

—T.S. Eliot, *After Strange Gods*, 1934

When good befalls a man he calls it Providence, when evil Fate.

—Knut Hamsun, *Vagabonds*, 1909

We all measure good and evil by the pleasure and pain we feel at present, or expect hereafter.

—Thomas Hobbes, *Philosophical Rudiments Concerning Government and Society*, 1651

Where there is good there must be evil, [the transition from one to the other] is truly [like] the turning over of one's hand. Goodness, however, is so from the very beginning, whereas evil comes into existence only as a result of such a turning over.

—Lu Wang (Lu Hsian-Shan) (1139–92), from *Lu Hsian-shan, a Twelfth Century Chinese Idealist Philosopher*, 1944

If ever there was an apocalyptic era, in which the forces of good and evil, in the soul of every man as well as in the soul of every nation, were locked in a combat truly mortal, that era is ours.

—John Julian Ryan, in *America*, January 30, 1960

It is precisely the conflict between the good or divine principle, on the one hand, and the evil or adverse principle on the other, which constitutes the meaning of human life and human history, from the beginning to the end of time.

—Friedrich Schlegel, *Philosophy of History*, 1829

GRACE

It is not in virtue of its liberty that the human will attains to grace, it is much rather by grace that it attains to liberty.

—St. Augustine, *De Corrupt. et Gracia*, VIII, 427

The world of sin confronts the world of grace like the reflected picture of a landscape in the blackness of very still, deep waters.
—Georges Bernanos, *The Diary of a Country Priest*, 1937

Grace is necessary to salvation, free will is equally so; but grace in order to give salvation, free will in order to receive it.
—St. Bernard, *De gratia et libero arbitrio*, c. 1150

To feel in ourselves the want of grace, and to be grieved for it, is grace itself.
—Robert Burton, *Anatomy of Melancholy*, III, 1621

Usually grace begins by illuminating the soul with a deep awareness, with its own light.
—Diodicus, *Spiritual Perfection*, 5th century

Grace only works effectively in us in proportion to our unremitting correspondence to it.
—François Fénelon (1651–1715), *Spiritual Letters*

Allah guideth whomsoever he pleaseth, by grace, and he leadeth astray whomsoever he pleaseth, by justice.
—*Fiqh Akbar*, c. 10th century

The chains of grace are so powerful, and yet so sweet, that though they attract our heart, they do not shackle our freedom.
—St. Francis de Sales, *Treatise on the Love of God*, 1607

Grace does not destroy our liberty by its certain efficacy; rather by that very efficacy divine grace moves the free will without doing violence to it.
—Reginald Garrigou-Lagrange,
Christian Perfection and Contemplation, 1937

For by grace you have been saved through faith; and this is not your own doing, it is the gift of God—not because of works, lest any man should boast.
—*Holy Bible*, Ephesians 2:8-9

But for the grace of God, what sinner would have returned to God? For it is the nature of sin to darken our souls, to bind us hand and foot.
—St. John Sergieff of Cronstadt (1829–1908), *My Life in Christ*

Grace is not something that comes in from the outside and says "No, you are doing it wrong, let me show you how to do it." Grace is not a kind of auxiliary steam, supplementing our feeble powers with a force not of the same character. Grace does not replace nature, it perfects nature, transmutes something that belongs to earth and makes it glow with the radiance of heaven.

—Ronald A. Knox, *Bridegroom and Bride*, 1957

Grace is sufficient to enable us to be accounted entirely and completely righteous in God's sight.

—Martin Luther, *Preface to Romans*, 1522

If grace takes hold of us and remakes us in the depths of our being, it is so that all our actions should feel its effects and be illuminated by it.

—Jacques Maritain, *True Humanism*, 1936

Grace is nothing else than the forgiveness or remission of sins.

—Philip Melanchthon, *Loci Communes*, 1521

The holy man hath made God's grace germinate; the perverse have lost their capital.

—Guru Nanak (1496–1538), in M.A. Macauliffe, *The Sikh Religion*

Grace is nothing if not the final power; and power is force if it is not grace.

—John Oman, *Honest Religion*, 1941

Sanctity or sanctifying grace is a divine gift, an inexpressible copy of the highest divinity and the highest goodness, by means of which we enter a divine rank through a heavenly generation.

—Pseudo-Dionysius, *Ep. 2 ad. Caim.*, c. 500 A.D.

To receive grace we need only to love its Donor.

—Mathias Scheeben, *The Glories of Divine Grace*, 1886

It is painfully clear that modern consciousness has taken a detour off the primordial pathways to grace. Day by day people die as victims of this route. The road is getting rougher. At the end lies a cliff. Around us our leaders, good lemmings all, exhort us to stay the course.

—Charlene Spretnak, *States of Grace*, 1991

GRACE

The grace given us is the grace for struggle and not the grace for peace.
—Adolphe Tanqueray, *The Spiritual Life*, 1490

Grace is nothing else but a certain beginning of glory in us.
—St. Thomas Aquinas, *Summa Theologica*, 1272

Divine graces works for an infinite and eternal good, which cannot fall under the dominion of the senses, and in consequence the mind moves the senses to deeds of virtue.
—Giovanni Vico, *The New Science*, 1725

GREED

From love comes grief, from greed comes fear; he who is free from greed knows neither grief nor fear.
—*Dhammapada*, c. 5th century B.C.

Wherever the body is, there the eagles will be gathered together.
—*Holy Bible*, Matthew 24:28

Covetousness is the greatest of monsters, as well as the root of all evil.
—William Penn, *Some Fruits of Solitude*, 1693

Money is the standard now. It's the new religion. We have two religions in this country, fundamentalism and money, and I don't know which is worse. I don't see the death of greed. I see people worried that they may have come along a couple of years too late.
—Felix G. Rohatyn, in *Esquire*, June 1988

Covetousness makes a man miserable, because riches are not means to make a man happy.
—Jeremy Taylor, *Holy Living*, 1650

Avaricious men do not reach heaven, so they are fools, who give no regard to charity.
—*Udanavarga*, 300 B.C.

I lose God, I lose the world, I lose myself, if I want only to clutch at things and use them only for my own pleasure or profit.
—Gerald Vann, *The Divine Pity*, 1946

GRIEF

Only when grief finds its work done can God dispense us from it.
—Henri Amiel, journal, 1882

Out of the depths I cry to thee, O Lord! Lord, hear my voice! Let thy ears be attentive to the voice of my supplications! If thou, O Lord, should mark iniquities, Lord, who could stand?
—*Holy Bible*, Psalms 130:1-3

Great grief is a divine and terrible radiance which transfigures the wretched.
—Victor Hugo, *Les Misérables*, 1862

Love remembered and consecrated by grief belongs, more clearly than the happy intercourse of friends, to the eternal world; it has proved itself stronger than death.
—W.R. Inge, *Personal Religion and the Life of Devotion*, 1924

Grief and death were born of sin, and devour sin.
—St. John Chrysostom, *Homilies*, c. 388

Grief is a species of idleness.
—Samuel Johnson, letter to Mrs. Thrale, March 17, 1773

Both the ancestry and posterity of Grief go further than the ancestry and posterity of Joy.
—Herman Melville, *Moby Dick*, 1851

Grief is more evil than all the spirits, and is most terrible to the servants of God, and corrupts man beyond all the spirits and wears out the Holy Spirit.
—Shepherd of Hermas, c. 148

Those griefs smart most which are seen to be of our own choice.
—Sophocles (495–406 B.C.), *Oedipus the King*

GUILT

Guilt: the gift that keeps on giving.
—Erma Bombeck, quoted by John Skow, in *Time*, July 2, 1984

By confession, repentance, by austerity, and by reciting the Veda a sinner is freed from guilt.
—*The Code of Manu*, between 1200 and 500 B.C.

The sense of guilt implies in some vague outline the ideas of a broken moral order and an offended God.
—William Cunningham, *Essays on Theological Questions*, 1905

The experience of guilt feelings is of crucial interest both to psychiatry and religion.
—J. Dominian, *Psychiatry and the Christian*, 1962

My child can be no more guilty or deserving of punishment for my sin than he can see with my eyes and feel with my nerves.
—Washington Gladden, *How Much Is Left of the Old Doctrines*, 1900

I am suspicious of guilt in myself and in other people; it is usually a way of not thinking, or of announcing one's own fine sensibilities the better to be rid of them fast.
—Lillian Hellman, *Scoundrel Time*, 1976

Wash me thoroughly from my iniquity, and cleanse me from my sin! For I know my transgressions, and my sin is ever before me.
—*Holy Bible*, Psalms 51:2-3

The present crisis with all its cruelty, brutality and callousness is ample proof of the ineffectiveness of years and years of Christian "moralising" about the need for love. The problem that we are dealing with here in South Africa is not merely a problem of personal guilt, it is a problem of injustice.
—*The Kairos Document*, rev. 2nd ed., 1986

In law a man is guilty when he violates the rights of another. In ethics he is guilty if he only thinks of doing so.
—Immanuel Kant, *Lecture at Königsberg*, 1775

It is not a gain that guilt should be wholly forgotten. On the contrary, it is loss and perdition. But it is a gain to win an inner intensity of heart through a deeper and deeper inner sorrowing over guilt.
—Sören Kierkegaard, *Purity of Heart*, 1846

Either guilt has to be incurred deliberately or it has not. Sin cannot be in part the choice of the individual, in part the result of the fall or the "sin of man."
—H.D. Lewis, *Morals and the New Theology*, 1947

Happiness

No one truly knows happiness who has not suffered, and the redeemed are happier than the elect.
—Henri Amiel, journal, 1882

True happiness flows from the possession of wisdom and virtue and not from the possession of external goods.
—Aristotle (384–322 B.C.), *Politics* (Book VII of the Analysis)

He is truly happy who has all that he wishes to have, and wishes to have nothing which he ought not to wish.
—St. Augustine, *To Proba*, 412

Happiness is, literally, god within, or good.
—Marcus Aurelius, *Meditations*, c. 170

It is that highest of all good things, and it embraces in itself all good things. . . . Wherefore happiness is a state which is made perfect by the union of all good things.
—Boethius, *The Consolations of Philosophy*, c. 525

Since happiness is nothing else but the enjoyment of the Supreme good, and the Supreme good is above us, no one can be happy who does not rise above himself.
—St. Bonaventure, *The Journey of the Mind to God*, 1259

There may be Peace without Joy, and Joy without Peace, but the two combined make Happiness.
—John Buchan, *Pilgrim's Way*, 1940

By *happiness* we are to understand the internal satisfaction of the soul, arising from the possession of good; and by good, whatever is suitable or agreeable to man for his preservation, perfection, convenience, or pleasure.
—Jean Jacques Burlamaqui, *Works of*, I, ch. 2, 1763

Perfect happiness is the absence of happiness.
—Chuang-tzu, c. 300 B.C.

We cannot be happy until we can love ourselves without egotism and our friends without tyranny.
—Cyril Connolly, *The Condemned Playground: Essays*, 1927–44

It is good to tame the mind, which is difficult to hold in and flighty, rushing wherever it listeth; a tamed mind brings happiness.

—*Dhammapada*, c. 5th century B.C.

The first and indispensable requisite of happiness is a clear conscience, unsullied by the reproach or remembrance of an unworthy action.

—Edward Gibbon, *Autobiography*, 1789

I believe in God—this is a fine, praise-worthy thing to say. But to acknowledge God wherever and however he manifests himself, that in truth is heavenly bliss on earth.

—J.W. von Goethe, *Maxims and Reflections*, 1829

A cheerful heart is a good medicine.

—*Holy Bible*, Proverbs 17:22

The supreme happiness of life is the conviction that we are loved.

—Victor Hugo, *Les Misérables*, 1862

Happiness is to "become portion of that around me.". . . We are happy only when the self achieves union with the not-self. Now both self and not-self are states of our consciousness.

—Aldous Huxley, *Texts and Pretexts*, 1932

It would be a great thing if people could be brought to realize that they can never add to the sum of their happiness by doing wrong.

—John Lubbock, *The Pleasures of Life*, 1887

He is the happiest man who best understands his happiness; for he is of all men most fully aware that it is only the lofty ideal that separates gladness from sorrows.

—Maurice Maeterlinck, *Thoughts from Maeterlinck*, 1903

He who never sacrificed a present to a future good, or a personal to a general one, can speak of happiness only as the blind do of colors.

—Horace Mann, *Thoughts*, 1867

The first requisite for the happiness of the people is the abolition of religion.

—Karl Marx, *A Criticism of the Hegelian Philosophy of Right*, 1844

What is happiness? The feeling that power increases, that resistance is overcome.

—Friedrich Nietzsche, *Anti-Christ*, 1889

Our Savior has nowhere promised to make us infallibly happy in this world.

—Pope Pius XII, address, July 2, 1941

Happiness is gained by a use, and right use, of the things of
life, and the right use of them, and good-fortune in the use of
them is given by knowledge.

—Plato, "Euthydemus," *Dialogues*, c. 370 B.C.

When we try to reach real happiness on cheap terms, what
we get is bound to be cheap.

—David Roberts, *The Grandeur and Misery of Man*, 1955

The happiness which we receive from ourselves is greater
than that which we obtain from our surroundings. . . . The
world in which a man lives shapes itself chiefly by the way in
which he looks at it.

—Arthur Schopenhauer, *Essays*, 1841

Happiness is essentially a state of going somewhere, whole-
heartedly, one-directionally, without regret or reservation.

—William H. Sheldon, *Psychology and the Promethean Will*, 1936

Of no mortal say "That man is happy," till vexed by no grievous ill he pass Life's goal.

—Sophocles, *Oedipus Tyrannis*, 4th century B.C.

HATRED

An hour spent in hate is an eternity withdrawn from love.

—Ludwig Boerne (1786–1837), *Fragmente and Aphorismen*, no. 191

There would be no place for hatred among wise men. For
who but the foolish would hate good men? And there is no
cause to hate bad men. Vice is as a disease of the mind, just
as feebleness shows ill-health to the body.

—Boethius, *Consolations of Philosophy*, c. 524

Let a man overcome anger by kindness, evil by good. . . .
Victory breeds hatred, for the conquered is unhappy. . . .
Never in the world does hatred cease by hatred; hatred
ceases by love.

—Buddha (563–483 B.C.),
quoted by Radakrishnan in *Indian Philosophy*

Malice drinketh up the greater part of its own poison.
—Thomas Fuller, *Gnomologia*, 1732

My neighbor despises me, he is wrong, because he is of no more importance than I am, and God has forbidden him to despise me.
—Jean Grou, *Meditations in the Form of a Retreat*, c. 1795

He who conceals hatred has lying lips, and he who utters slander is a fool.
—*Holy Bible*, Proverbs 10:18

The malicious have a dark happiness.
—Victor Hugo, *Les Misérables*, 1862

God . . . is only father in the sense of father of all. . . . When I hate some one or deny that God is his father—it is not he who loses, but me; for then I have no father.
—Sören Kierkegaard (1813–55), *Journals of*

We may fight against what is wrong, but if we allow ourselves to hate, that is to insure our spiritual defeat and our likeness to what we hate.
—George William Russell (Æ), *The Living Torch*, 1937

Hatred is entrenched in human nature. It is as old as man, as old as man's desire to expunge it. It slumbers in all of us. It can awaken at any time. I am not sure if we can eradicate hate from our hearts, but of this I am certain: It must always be our goal.
—Anatoly Rybakov, in *USA Today*, August 28, 1990

The most malicious kind of hatred is that which is built upon a theological foundation.
—George Sarton, *History of Science*, 1927

Man can be the most affectionate and altruistic of creatures, yet he's potentially more vicious than any other. He is the only one who can be persuaded to hate millions of his own kind whom he has never seen and to kill as many as he can lay his hands on in the name of his tribe or his God.
—Benjamin Spock, *Decent and Indecent*, 1970

Hate is still the main enemy of the human race, the fuel that heats the furnaces of genocide.
—I.F. Stone, "When a Two-Party System Becomes a One-Party Rubber Stamp," in *I.F. Stone's Weekly*, September 9, 1968

Hatred, I consider, is just a standing reproach to the hated person, and owes all its meaning to a demand for love.
—Ian Suttie, *The Origins of Love and Hate*, 1935

Unprovoked hatred is worse than the three cardinal sins.
—*Talmud: Yoma*, 9b., c. 500

Christianity has been almost sentimental in its effort to deal with hatred in human life. It has sought to get rid of hatred by preachments, by moralizing, by platitudinous judgments. It has hesitated to analyze the basis of hatred and to evaluate it in terms of its possible significance in the lives of the people possessed by it. This reluctance to examine hatred has taken on the character of a superstition.
—Howard Thurman, *Jesus and the Disinherited*, 1949

HEALING

Now I am beginning to live a little, and feel less like a sick oyster at low tide.
—Louisa May Alcott, in Edna Dow Cheney,
Louisa May Alcott, Her Life, Letters, and Journals, 1890

The work of healing is in peeling away the barriers of fear and past conditioning that keep us unaware of our true nature of wholeness and love.
—Joan Borysenko, *Mind the Body, Mending the Mind*, 1987

For millennia, shamans and witch doctors . . . made no distinction between physical, emotional, and spiritual healing. To them, all symptoms were signs of something awry in the individual's relationship with the larger universe of spirits and animal powers.
—Katy Butler, in *Family Therapy Networker*,
September/October 1990

Miraculous cures seldom occur. Despite their small number, they prove the existence of organic and mental processes that we do not know. They show that certain mystic states, such as that of prayer, have definite effects.
—Alexis Carrel, *Man, the Unknown*, 1935

To impute our recovery to medicine, and to carry our view no further, is to rob God of His honor, and is saying in effect that He has parted with the keys of life and death, and, by giving to a drug the power to heal us, has placed our lives out of His own reach.
—William Cowper, *Letter to Lady Hesketh*, 1765

It is more necessary for the soul to be healed than the body;
for it is better to die than to live ill.

—Epictetus (1st century), *Enchiridion*

He heals the brokenhearted, and binds up their wounds.

—*Holy Bible*, Psalms 147:3

The religious man, I take it, not only feels the spirit of worship welling up within him in the presence of healing by
prayer, but feels the same spirit when he witnesses a recovery after a skilled surgeon's difficult operation.

—Gerald Kennedy, *A Reader's Notebook*, 1953

All the power of the occult healer lies in his conscious will
and all his art consists in producing faith in the patient.

—Eliphas Levi, *Dogma et Rituel de la Haute Magie*, 1861

The goal is to live a full, productive life even with all that am-
biguity. No matter what happens, whether the cancer never
flares up again or whether you die, the important thing is
that the days that you have had you will have lived.

—Gilda Radner, *It's Always Something*, 1989

The inner voice—the human compulsion when deeply distressed to seek healing counsel within ourselves, and the capacity within ourselves both to create this counsel and to
receive it.

—Alice Walker, *You Can't Keep a Good Woman Down*, 1981

Healing depends on listening with the inner ear—stopping
the incessant blather, and *listening*.

—Marion Woodman, *The Pregnant Virgin,
A Process of Psychological Transformation*, 1985

One may heal with holiness, one may heal with the law, one
may heal with the knife, one may heal with herbs, one may
heal with the Holy Word; amongst all remedies this one is
the healing one that heals with the Holy Word; this one is
that will best drive away sickness from the body of the
faithful.

—*Zend-Avesta*, 6th century B.C.

HEALTH

To be born and in a mortal body is to begin to be sick.

—St. Augustine, *Ennart*, in Ps., c. 415

To keep the body in good health is a duty, for otherwise we shall not be able to trim the lamp of wisdom, and keep our mind strong and clear. Water surrounds the lotus flower, but does not wet its petals.

—Buddha, "Sermon at Benares," in Asvaghosha, *The Fo-Sho-Hing-Tsan-King*, c. 5th century B.C.

Both sin and sickness are error, and Truth is their remedy.

—Mary Baker Eddy, *Science and Health*, 1908

No longer drink only water, but use a little wine for the sake of your stomach and your frequent ailments.

—*Holy Bible*, I Timothy 5:23

Illness is often a blessing. By ravaging the body it frees the soul and purifies it. . . . No man who has never been ill can have a thorough knowledge of himself.

—Romain Rolland, *Jean Christophe*, 1912

It has been increasingly evident, as pointed out by doctors everywhere, that physical health is closely associated with, and often dependent upon, spiritual health.

—Dr. Loring T. Swaim, presidential address, 1942, before the American Rheumatism Association

"But of course your health must come first." Must it? Certainly not if there is anything better to put before it.

—Hubert van Zeller, *We Die Standing Up*, 1949

HEAVEN AND HELL

Where the Soul hath the full measure and complement of happiness; where the boundless appetite of that spirit remains completely satisfied, that it can neither desire addition not alteration; that, I think, is truly Heaven.

—Thomas Browne, *Religio Medici*, 1643

He who knows the joy of Heaven has no grievance against Heaven and no grudge against men; he is unembarrassed by things, and unrebuked by the spirits of the departed.

—Chuang-tzu (4th century B.C.), *Texts of Taoism*

The secret of heaven is kept from age to age. No imprudent, no sociable angel ever dropped an early syllable to answer the longings of saints, the fears of mortals.

—Ralph Waldo Emerson, essay on Swedenborg in *Representative Men*, 1850

Heaven, to those who truly love all, can be heaven only when it has emptied hell.
—Nels F.S. Ferré, *The Christian Understanding of God,* 1951

In my Father's house are many rooms; if it were not so, would I have told you that I go to prepare a place for you?
—*Holy Bible,* John 14:2

To rest in God eternally is the supreme joy of Heaven. Indeed, Heaven has no meaning but that.
—Bede Jarrett, *Meditations for Layfolk,* 1915

In the heaven-world there is no fear; thou art not there, O Death, and no one is afraid on account of old age. Leaving behind both hunger and thirst, and out of the reach of sorrow, all rejoice in the world of heaven.
—*Katha Upanishad,* prior to 400 B.C.

But announce to those who believe and do the things that are right, that for them are gardens 'neath which the rivers flow! So oft as they are fed therefrom with fruit for sustenance, they shall say, "This same was for our sustenance of old." And they shall have its like given to them. Therein shall they have wives of perfect purity, and therein shall they abide for ever.
—*Koran, Sura,* II.23, c. 625

Heaven is not thrown open exclusively to men of heroic calibre.
—Edward Leen, *In the Likeness of Christ,* 1936

What I am interested in is a heaven for humanity—sweating, swearing, toiling, loving, lusting, hating, worshipping, wonderful humanity—unregenerate yet lovable.
—Benjamin Lindsey, *The Companionate Marriage,* 1927

The way to Heaven out of all places is of like length and distance.
—Thomas More, *Utopia,* 1516

Heaven at present is out of sight, but in due time, as snow melts and discovers what it lay upon, so will this visible creation fade away before those greater splendors which are behind it.
—John Henry Newman, *Parochial and Plain Sermons,* 4, 1843

Christianity, faced with the paradox of life leading to death, creates the third alternative of "another world." The attributes of this "other world" are necessarily not of this world: this is a world of time, Heaven is timeless; this is a world of change, Heaven is changeless; since this is a fertile world, then Heaven must be barren and infertile. So Heaven is defined not in opposition to Hades, but in opposition to life, and in most important ways is identical to Hades.

—Carol Ochs, *Behind the Sex of God*, 1977

Heaven is the presence of God.

—Christina Rossetti, *Seek and Find*, 1879

Heaven is above all yet; there sits a judge
That no king can corrupt.

—William Shakespeare, *King Henry VIII*, c. 1611

HELL

There shall not abide eternally in the Fire a single believer, but whoever has in his heart the weight of a single grain of faith shall be brought forth therefrom.

—al-Ghazali (died 1111), *Ihya*

The damned can love no more and therefore they are damned. Hell is the home of incurables. The disease that is beyond cure is their egoism.

—J.P. Arendzen, *Eternal Punishment*, 1928

Hell as a place of retribution for the wicked, which is a comfort to the good, is a fairy tale; there is not a shadow of reality about it; it is borrowed from our everyday world existence with its rewards and punishments. . . . From the point of view of God, there cannot be any hell. To admit hell would be to deny Good.

—Nicholas Berdyaev, *The Destiny of Man*, 1937

Hell has three doors: lust, rage, and greed.

—*Bhagavad-Gita*, between 500 and 200 B.C.

Hell-fire . . . is not literally physical fire. It is present pain of mind, spiritual torment which neither sleep nor time nor any distraction can alleviate.

—R.V.C. Bodley, *In Search of Serenity*, 1955

Heaven has a road, but no one travels it; Hell has no gate but men will bore through to get there.

—Chinese proverb

There is such a thing as hell on earth. For the most part, it is populated by people who fear so deeply that they cannot love.

—F. Forrester Church, *Entertaining Angels*, 1988

Through me one enters the sorrowful city; through me one enters into eternal pain; through me one enters among the lost race. Justice moved my high Maker; divine power made me . . . I endure eternally. All hope abandon, ye who enter here.

—Dante, *Inferno*, c. 1310, inscription over the gate of Hell

Hell is oneself. Hell is alone, and the other figures in it merely projections. There is nothing to escape from and nothing to escape to. One is always alone . . . the final desolation of solitude in the phantasmal world of imagination, shuffling memories, and desires.

—T.S. Eliot, *The Cocktail Party*, 1950

And if your hand causes you to sin, cut it off; it is better for you to enter life maimed than with two hands to go to hell, to the unquenchable fire.

—*Holy Bible*, Mark 9:43

The hell to be endured hereafter, of which theology tells, is no worse than the hell we make for ourselves in this world by habitually fashioning our characters in the wrong way.

—William James, *Psychology*, 1892

Hell begins on the day when God grants us a clear vision of all that we might have achieved, of all the gifts which we have wasted, of all that we might have done which we did not do. . . . For me, the conception of hell lies in two words: "too late."

—Gian-Carlo Menotti, in *Saturday Review of Literature*, April 22, 1950

To deny hell in principle would be to deny man's freedom; to confine it to anything short of eternity would be to limit that freedom.

—J.A. Pike, and W.N. Pittenger, *The Faith of the Church*, 1951

Hell is other people.

—Jean Paul Sartre, *Huis Clos*, 1945

In Hell there is no hope, and consequently no duty, no work, nothing to be gained by praying, nothing to be lost by doing what you like. Hell, in short, being a place where you have nothing to do but amuse yourself, is the paradise of the worthless.
—George Bernard Shaw, *Socialism of,* ed. by J. Fuchs, 1926

Hell is the ego, sated with its own satisfied wishes, having to consume itself forever with no hope of release.
—Fulton J. Sheen, *Way to Happiness,* 1953

There would be no hell for modern man if our men of letters were not calling attention to it.
—Allen Tate, *The Forlorn Demon: Didactic and Critical Essays,* 1953

The damned is no less an inmate of hell because he does not believe in it.
—Franz Werfel, *Between Heaven and Earth,* 1944

I don't believe any man was ever drawn into heaven for fear he would go to hell.
—Woodrow Wilson, address, October 1904

HOLINESS

When a man is made holy, it is from a mere and arbitrary grace: God may for ever deny holiness to the fallen creature as he pleases.
—Jonathan Edwards, sermon, Boston, 1731

In our era, the road to holiness necessarily passes through the world of action.
—Dag Hammarskjöld, *Markings,* 1964

Not holiness alone, but the beauty of holiness, is required to bind our hearts, our whole souls to God.
—Bede Jarrett, *Meditations for Layfolk,* 1915

Now the perfect accordance of the will to the moral law is *holiness,* a perfection of which no rational being of sensible world is capable at any moment of his existence.
—Immanuel Kant, *Critique of Practical Reason,* 1788

The holy is above all aesthetic as well as moral and logical classifications—it is the "wholly other" transcending all worldly values.
—I. Maybaum, *Synagogue and Society,* 1944

A holy person is one who is sanctified by the presence and action of God within him.

—Thomas Merton, *Life and Holiness*, 1963

A being who can create a race of men devoid of real freedom and inevitably doomed to be sinners, and then punish them for being what he has made them, may be omnipotent and various other things, but he is not what the English language has always intended by the adjective holy.

—John Stuart Mill, *Examination of Sir William Hamilton's Philosophy*, 1865

Holiness comes by holy deeds,
Not starving flesh of daily needs.

—Shaikh Saadi, *Gulistan*, c. 1265

At the sight of beauty love always awakes; at the appeal of holiness the divine witness within us at once responds.

—Paul Sabatier, *The Life of St. Francis of Assisi*, 1920

The beauty of holiness has only rarely been exhibited by the principal artists of our period.

—Nathan A. Scott, *Modern Literature and the Religious Frontier*, 1958

"Holy" has the same root as "wholly"; it means complete. A man is not complete in spiritual stature if all his mind, heart, soul, strength are not given to God.

—R.J.H. Stewart, *Spiritual Conferences of*, 1952

The remedy for modern lassitude of body, for modern weakness of will, is Holiness. There alone is the energizing principle from which the modern world persists in divorcing itself.

—Francis Thompson, *Health and Holiness*, 1905

There is such a thing as the danger of a selfish pursuit of holiness.

—Gerald Vann, *Eve and the Gryphon*, 1946

Holiness is the best of all good. Happy the man who is holy with perfect holiness.

—*Zend-Avesta*, 6th century B.C.

HOLY SPIRIT

Just as transparent substances, when subjected to light, themselves glitter and give off light, so does the soul, illuminated by the Holy Spirit, give light to others and itself become spiritual.

—St. Basil, *De Spir. Sancto*, IX, c.375

What is the Divine Spirit? Is the Holy Ghost any other than an Intellectual fountain?
—William Blake, *Jerusalem*, 1820

Because it calculates not, Spirit shines in lonely glory in what is beyond the world. . . . Though Spirit lies beyond the world, it stays ever within them.
—Seng-Chao (388–414), *Book of Chaos*

The Holy Spirit only gives its testimony in favor of works . . . and is in itself nothing but the mental acquiescene which follows a good action in our souls.
—Baruch Spinoza, *Tractatus Theologico-Politicus*, 1670

The Holy Spirit rests on him only who has a joyous heart.
—*Talmud*, 5.1, c. 200–500

HONESTY

It is easy to be honest enough not to be hanged. To be really honest means to subdue one's prepossessions, ideals—stating things fairly, not humoring your argument—doing justice to your enemies . . . making confession whether you can afford it or not; refusing unmerited praise; looking painful truths in the face.
—Aubrey De Vere, *Recollections*, 1897

It is the lying at the top levels of our society that concerns me the most because morality, like water and unlike money, really does trickle down. I am concerned that some at the top have adopted a concept that lying for the higher good is all right—that dishonesty in the name of righteousness is just fine.
—Jim Lehrer, address, Southern Methodist University commencement, in *The Christian Science Monitor*, June 12, 1989

The life of an honest man must be an apostasy and a perpetual desertion. . . . For the man who wishes to remain faithful to truth must make himself continually unfaithful to all the continual, successive, indefatigable renascent errors.
—Charles Péguy, *Basic Verities*, 1943

An honest man's the noblest work of God.
—Alexander Pope, *An Essay on Man*, 1734

Divine Providence has granted this gift to man, that those things which are honest are also the most advantageous.
—Quintilian, *Institutio Oratoria*, c. 90 A.D.

On honesty God's favor is bestowed, I never saw one lost in a straight road.
—Shaikh Saadi, *Gulistan*, c. 1265

"Honesty is the best policy," but he who acts on that principle is not an honest man.
—Richard Whately, *Easy Lessons on Morals*, 1854

To be employed in things connected with virtue is most agreeable with the character and inclinations of an honest man.
—John Woolman, *Serious Considerations on Various Subjects*, 1773

HONOR

Every noble crown is, and on earth forever will be, a crown of thorns.
—Thomas Carlyle, *Past and Present*, 1843

To those whose god is honor, disgrace alone is sin.
—J.C. and A.W. Hare, *Guesses at Truth*, 1827

A man's pride will bring him low, but he who is lowly in spirit will obtain honor.
—*Holy Bible*, Proverbs 29:23

When one has to seek the honor that comes from God only, he will take the withholding of the honor that comes from men very quietly indeed.
—George MacDonald (1824–1905), *Selections from*, ed. by Dewey

For my own part, I believe that honor and money nearly always go together, and that he who desires honor never hates money, while he who hates money cares little for honor.
—St. Teresa of Ávila, *Way of Perfection*, 1565

HOPE

Hope is the parent of faith.
—C.A. Bartol, *Radical Problems*, 1872

Hope, n. Desire and expectation rolled into one.
—Ambrose Bierce, *Devil's Dictionary*, 1906

Give humanity hope and it will dare and suffer joyfully, not counting the cost—hope with laughter on her banner and on her face the fresh beauty of morning.
—John Elof Boodin, *God: A Cosmic Philosophy of Religion*, 1934

Hope requires a very careful symbolization. It must not be expressed too fully in the present tense because hope one can touch and handle is not likely to retain its promissory call to a new future. Hope expressed only in the present tense will no doubt be co-opted by the managers of this age.
—Walter Brueggemann, *The Prophetic Imagination*, 1978

Hope . . . is one of the ways in which what is merely future and potential is made vividly present and actual to us. Hope is the positive, as anxiety is the negative, mode of awaiting the future.
—Emil Brunner, *Eternal Hope*, 1954

Whether in science or in politics, whether in theory or in social policy, every accepted fact was once only a fond hope. Virtually everything now true was once simply someone's dream.
—Richard Celeste, in *Los Angeles Times*, January 13, 1987

One is and remains a slave as long as one is not *cured* of hoping.
—E.M. Cioran, *Drawn and Quartered*, 1971

If you do not hope, you will not find what is beyond your hopes.
—St. Clement of Alexandria, *Stromateis*, c. 193

Hope arouses, as nothing else can arouse, a passion for the possible.
—William Sloane Coffin, Jr., *Once to Every Man*, 1977

Hope is the thing with feathers/That perches in the soul/And sings the tune without the words,/And never stops at all/And sweetest in the gale is heard.
—Emily Dickenson (1830–86), *Poems*

A true Christian should have but one fear—lest he should not hope enough.
—Walter Elliot, *The Spiritual Life*, 1914

Reality has but one shape; hope is many shaped.
—J.W. von Goethe, *Goethe's Opinions*, ed. by Otto Wencksterns, 1853

Hope is the poor man's bread.
—George Herbert, *Jacula Prudentum*, 1651

My days are swifter than a weaver's shuttle, and come to their end without hope.

—*Holy Bible*, Job 7:6

The word which God has written on the brow of every man is Hope.

—Victor Hugo (1802–85), *Treasure Bits from*, ed. by Rose

Prayer breathes hope, and a prayer without hope is a sinful prayer.

—John Sergieff of Cronstadt (1829–1908), *My Life in Christ*

Hope itself is a species of happiness, and, perhaps, the chief happiness which this world affords; but, like all other pleasures immoderately enjoyed, the excesses of hope must be expiated by pain.

—Samuel Johnson, June 8, 1762, *Letters of*

The future has become uninhabitable. Such hopelessness can arise, I think, only from an inability to face the present, to live in the present, to live as a responsible being among other beings in this sacred world here and now, which is all we have, and all we need to found our hope upon.

—Ursula K. Le Guin, "Facing It," *Dancing at the Edge of the World* 1982,

If in the hour of death the conscience is at peace, the mind need not be troubled. The future is full of doubt, indeed, but fuller still of hope.

—John Lubbock, *The Pleasures of Life*, 1887

Everything that is done in the world is done by hope.

—Martin Luther (1483–1546), *Table-Talk*

Hope is some extraordinary spiritual grace that God gives us to control our fears, not to oust them.

—Vincent McNabb, *Joy in Believing*, 1939

What enthusiasm is to the youth and ambition to the apprentice and peace of mind to the invalid, such is hope to the Christians.

—Joseph McSorley, *Be of Good Heart*, 1924

In this vale of Death, God girds us round; and over our gloom, the sun of Righteousness still shines a beacon and a hope. If we bend down our eyes, the dark vale shows her mouldy soil; but if we lift them, the bright sun meets our glance half way, to cheer.
—Herman Melville, *Moby Dick*, 1851

The miserable have no other medicine,/But only hope.
—William Shakespeare, *Measure for Measure*, c. 1604

True to the heart of Jewish religious belief, above both faith and reason, hope reigns supreme.
—Milton Steinberg, *Anatomy of Faith*, 1960

Hope, like faith, is nothing if it is not courageous; it is nothing if it is not ridiculous.
—Thornton Wilder, *The Eighth Day*, 1967

HUMANISM

One would not go far wrong if one defined humanism as Puritanism with a sense of humor.
—J.C.F. Auer and Julian Hartt, *Humanism vs. Theism*, 1951

The Humanist is reconciled to reality and makes his home there, and has a horror of the black-and-white fantasy of heaven and hell.
—H.J. Blackham, *The Humanist Frame*, 1961

Both Buddhism and Jainism threw over wholly the ancient systems of gods. Both repudiated pantheism. Indeed both repudiated any means of achieving life's goal that was not to be formed within oneself.
—Charles S. Braden, *The World's Religions*, 1954

To the question, What is man, whence comes and whither goes he? humanism by its own lights is powerless to reply.
—Henri Bremond, *A Literary History of Religious Thought in France*, I, 1937

Humanism needs Christianity to supplement it just as little as the Christian faith needs humanism. It may even feel that Christianity is an uncomfortable *disturbance to the self-assurance of the mind.*
—Rudolf Bultmann, *Essays*, 1951

No age has more proudly asserted man's supremacy over nature, and yet the "humanism" which proclaimed man's self-sufficiency was accompanied by a sense of powerlessness and frustration.

—Sydney Cave, *The Christian Way*, 1949

Agnosticism and materialism . . . are the fruits of that spiritual heresy of Humanism by which man came to see himself as a whole, instead of a spiritual-social-biological organism in living relation to the real world of spirit, of other men and things.

—V.A. Demant, *Christian Polity*, 1936

The highest and best thing that man can conceive is a human life nobly and beautifully lived—therefore his loyalties and energies should be devoted to the arrangement of conditions which make this possible. The sole issue is how to make this world a place conducive to the living of a noble human life, and then to help people in every possible way to live such lives.

—John H. Dietrich, *Varieties of American Religion*,
ed. by Charles S. Braden, 1936

If you find examples of humanism which are antireligious, or at least in opposition to the religious faith of the place and time, then such humanism is purely destructive, for it has never found anything to replace what it has destroyed.

—T.S. Eliot, "Humanism of Irving Babbit," 1927,
in *Selected Essays*, 1917–32

A humanist, as I understand the term, says, "This world is good enough for me, if only I can be good enough for it."

—William Empson, *Milton's God*, 1961

It is more philosophical to put our relations with things and men on such a footing as to treat the world as the common country of us all.

—Desiderius Erasmus (1466–1536), *Epistles*, II

The failure of the Christian people to effect a real humanism was followed by the rise of what were practically new religions, or substitutes for religion.

—Sir Robert Falconer, *Christianity and Culture*, 1961

Humanism sucks the egg of personality's value and then tries to hatch a higher religion out of it.

—Harry Emerson Fosdick, *As I See Religion*, 1932

It rejects supernaturalism and moral absolutism, and argues that the best possibilities of human beings can be achieved only by a combination of informed intelligence and the candid recognition that man must bear the responsibility for whatever standards he adopts.

—Charles Frankel, in *The New York Times Book Review*, January 14, 1962

On issues of the greatest moral and practical importance Humanism is a fertile and liberating point of view, and one that is thoroughly compatible with a fervent devotion to the highest spiritual interests of mankind.

—Charles Frankel, in *The New York Times Book Review*, January 14, 1962

Human existence has no such simple and direct meaning or goodness as the humanistic American dream. . . . A comfortable chair, a hi-fi set, a powerful car, the protection of a deodorant, a college romance and a paying job, cannot even in combination provide meaning for our life.

—Langdon Gilkey, *Maker of Heaven and Earth*, 1959

The greatest challenge to Christianity today is a popular, bland, respectable faith termed secular humanism. It is often called "The American Way of Life." It is not godless, but it keeps God in His place—the pulpit. It equates the Christian moral code with such terms as decency, brotherhood, the Golden Rule. It is the orthodoxy of the nonbeliever, but it is a ready refuge for the half-believer too. . . . It simply says: "Take up your credit card and follow me."

—Paul J. Hallinan, speech, in *Life*, September 15, 1961

Scientism and anthropocentric humanism are the attractive blooms that adorn a nearly rootless society.

—Georgia Harkness, *The Modern Rival of Christian Faith*, 1953

The humanist stands in a mediating position—he has the ear of the general public and speaks directly to their comprehension as neither the theologian nor the scientist can do.

—Walter M. Horton, *Approach to National Unity*, 1945

The lineaments of the new religion that we can be sure will arise to serve the needs of the coming era. . . . Instead of worshipping supernatural rulers, it will sanctify the higher manifestations of human nature, in art and love, in intellectual comprehension and aspiring adoration, and will emphasize the fuller realization of life's possibilities as a sacred trust.

—Julian S. Huxley, *The Humanist Frame*, 1961

There is no institution in his [the humanist's] private life for regularly bringing his thoughts back to a centre from which he can derive sustenance and power, no routine for enforcing his flagging aspirations and resolutions. He has no means of symbolizing the unity of all in the One in terms of physical association.

—Laurence Hyde, *The Prospects of Humanism*, 1931

Humanism . . . is not a single hypothesis or theorem, and it dwells on no new facts. It is rather a slow shifting in the philosophic perspective, making things appear as from a new centre of interest or point of sight.

—William James, *The Meaning of Truth*, 1909

Will not the humanist, unless he adds to his creed the faith and hope of religion, find himself at last, despite his protests, dragged back into the camp of the naturalist?

—Paul Elmer More, *On Being Human*, 1928

Duty to Man has replaced Duty to God. It is the central point of Humanism.

—Rosalind Murray, in *Columbia*, April 1951

A humanism which is sustained only by the obvious marks of common humanity breaks down when the hysteria of conflict destroys or obscures those obvious human ties.

—Reinhold Niebuhr, *An Interpretation of Christian Ethics*, 1935

A scientific humanism frequently offends the dignity of man, which it ostensibly extols, by regarding human beings as subject to manipulation and as mere instruments of some "socially approved" ends.

—Reinhold Niebuhr, *Christian Realism and Political Problems*, 1953

There are still a few old-fashioned rationalists, free-thinkers, or professional atheists, who mourn the failures of humanitarianism as a universal religion, and who are therefore willing to call themselves religious humanists.

—Herbert Wallace Schneider, *Religion in the 20th Century*, 1952

The Humanist's religion, is the religion of one who says yea to the life here and now, of one who is self-reliant, fearless, intelligent and creative. . . . Its Goal is the mastery of things that they may become servants and instrumentalities to man's spiritual comradeship.

—R.W. Sellars, *The Next Step in Religion*, 1918

Christian humanism is an attempt to get the natural and the supernatural back together in a well-balanced synthesis.
—Paul B. Steinmetz, *The Catholic Bookman's Guide*, 1962

It will perhaps be the great honor of our time to have undertaken what others will bring to a good issue, a humanism embracing the dimensions of the world and adequate to the designs of God.
—Emmanuel Suhard, *The Church Today*, 1953

HUMANKIND

The Good of man is the active exercise of his soul's faculties in conformity with excellence or virtue, or, if there be several human excellences or virtues, in conformity with the best and most perfect of them.
—Aristotle, *Nicomachean Ethics*, I, c. 340 B.C.

Under all the false, overloaded and glittering masquerade, there is in every man a noble nature beneath.
—B. Auerbach, *On the Heights*, 1865

The whole clay of humanity is a condemned clay.
—St. Augustine, *The City of God*, xxi, 42b

Man . . . is destined to realize his potentialities in eternity, in conditions far more real than those which have so far hemmed his efforts.
—Nicholas Berdyaev, *The Meaning of History*, 1936

Man, n. An animal so lost in rapturous contemplation of what he thinks he is as to overlook what he indubitably ought to be.
—Ambrose Bierce, *Devil's Dictionary*, 1906

Only man helps man; only man pities; only man tries to save.
—Robert Blatchford, *God and My Neighbor*, 1903

Man is ever a contingent being in search of necessity.
—George Brantl, *Catholicism*, 1962

There is nothing in religion, there is nothing in Christianity, which has not its roots in human nature and in the fundamental affections of mankind.
—Phillips Brooks, *National Needs and Remedies*, 1890

For every civilization or every period in history it is true today: Show me what kind of God you have and I will tell you
what kind of humanity you possess.
—Emil Brunner, *Man in Revolt*, 1939

Uniqueness is the essential property of man, and it is given
to him in order that he may unfold it.
—Martin Buber, *Jewish Mysticism and the Legends of Baalshem*, 1916

Half dust, half duty, unfit alike to sink or soar.
—Lord Byron, *Manfred*, Act I, sc. 2, 1820

Man is a digestive tube.
—Pierre Cabanis, *Rapports du physique et du moral de l'homme*, 1796

To the eye of Pure Reason what is he? A Soul, a Spirit, and
divine Apparition. Round his mysterious Me, there lies under
all those wool-rags, a Garment of Flesh (or of Senses) contex-
tured in the Loom of Heaven.
—Thomas Carlyle, *Sartor Resartus*, 1836

Yes, truly, if Nature is one, and a living indivisible whole,
much more is Mankind, the Image that reflects and creates
Nature, without which Nature were not.
—Thomas Carlyle, *Sartor Resartus*, 1836

Every man is as Heaven made him, and sometimes a great
deal worse.
—Miguel de Cervantes, *Don Quixote*, 1605

Those thinkers who cannot believe in any gods often assert
that the love of humanity would be in itself sufficient for
them; and so, perhaps, it would, if they had it.
—G.K. Chesterton, *Tremendous Trifles*, 1915

Man is made for the contemplation of heaven, and is in truth
a heavenly plant, to come to the knowledge of God.
—St. Clement of Alexandria, *Exhortation to the Greeks*, c. 200

If man is not rising upwards to be an angel, depend upon
it, he is sinking downwards to be a devil. He cannot stop at
the beast.
—Samuel Taylor Coleridge, *Table-Talk*, August 30, 1833

Man is an embodied paradox, a bundle of contradictions.
—Charles Caleb Colton, *Lacon*, 1822

To love Humanity constitutes all healthy morality.
—Auguste Comte, *Positive Polity*, 1820

Only man is capable of separating himself alike from God
and from nature, and making himself his last end and living
a purely self-regarding and irreligious existence.
—Christopher Dawson, *Christianity and the New Age*, 1931

The destiny of Man is not limited to his existence on earth
and he must never forget that fact. He exists less by the actions performed during his life than by the wake he leaves
behind him like a shooting star.
—Lecomte du Noüy, *Human Destiny*, 1947

If you remove from the word "human" all that belief in the
supernatural has given to man, you can view him finally as
no more than an extremely clever, adaptable and mischie-
vous little animal.
—T.S. Eliot, *Selected Essays*, 1932

Man is a god in ruins.
—Ralph Waldo Emerson, *Nature*, 1836

Our real danger is our sentimental belief that human nature
is naturally good. If human nature is good, we don't need either the wisdom of the Constitution or the Grace of God.
—Ricard S. Emrich, in *Detroit News*, June 25, 1961

I believe that man will not merely endure: he will prevail. He
is immortal, not because he alone among creatures has an
inexhaustible voice, but because he has a soul, a spirit capable of compassion and sacrifice and endurance.
—William Faulkner, speech accepting Nobel Prize, January 1951

Every soul develops itself only by means of other souls, and
there are no longer individual men, but only one humanity.
—J.G. Fichte (1762–1814), *The Vocation of Man*

Humanity's sinful nature . . . is an inherited mortgage and
handicap on the whole human family.
—Harry Emerson Fosdick, *Christianity and Progress*, 1922

Man is trampled by the same forces he has created.
—Juana Frances, *Contemporary Artists*, 1977

Man is not a being different from the animals, or superior to them.
— Sigmund Freud, *Introductory Lectures on Psychoanalysis*, 1917

It is the emancipation from the security of Paradise which is the basis for man's truly human development.
— Erich Fromm, *Psychoanalysis and Religion*, 1950

Theologians and philosophers have been saying for a century that God is dead, but what we confront is the possibility that man is dead, transformed into a thing, a producer, a consumer, an idolator. . . .
— Erich Fromm, address to American Orthopsychiatric Association, San Francisco, April 16, 1966

The only thing we have as human beings that is distinctive is rational thought. But it's so fragile. It's so easy to let any kind of emotionalism overwhelm it. You can undo in a microsecond what it took years to build up.
— Stephen Jay Gould, in *U.S. News & World Report*, February 8, 1988

Man himself is but a tiny grain of protoplasm in the perishable framework of organic nature.
— Ernest Haeckel, *The Riddle of the Universe*, 1899

The time has come for men to turn into gods or perish.
— Alan Harrington, *The Immoralist*, 1969

We cannot acclaim the sacredness of any man until we acknowledge the sacredness of all men.
— Kyle Haselden, *The Racial Problem in Christian Perspective*, 1959

Man is the only animal that laughs and weeps; for he is the only animal that is struck with the difference between what things are, and what they ought to be.
— William Hazlitt, *Lectures on the English Comic Writers*, 1819

The woman was made out of a rib out of the side of Adam; not of his feet to be trampled on by him, but out of his side to be equal with him, under his arms to be protected and, near his heart to be loved.
— Matthew Henry, *Exposition of Genesis*, 1725

God created humankind so that humankind might cultivate the earthly and thereby create the heavenly.
— Hildegard of Bingen (1098–1179), *Illuminations of,* 1985

Man is the only creature in the animal kingdom that sits in judgment on the work of the Creator and finds it bad—including himself and Nature.
—Elbert Hubbard (1859–1915), *Notebook*

The true division of humanity is this: the luminous and the dark.
—Victor Hugo, *Les Misérables*, 1862

Man, physical, intellectual, and moral, is as much a part of nature, as purely a product of the cosmic process, as the humblest weed.
—Thomas Henry Huxley, *Evolution and Ethics*, 1893

Man passes away; his name perishes from record and recollection; his history is as a tale that is told, and his very monument becomes a ruin.
—Washington Irving, *The Sketch-Book*, 1820

In every concrete individual, there is a uniqueness that defies formulation. We can feel the touch of it and recognize its taste, so to speak, relishing or disliking, as the case may be, but we can give no ultimate account of it, and we have in the end simply to admire the Creator.
—William James, *Memories and Studies*, 1911

I sincerely believe . . . in the general existence of a moral instinct. I think it the brightest gem with which human character is studded, and the want of it as more degrading than the most hideous of the bodily deformities.
—Thomas Jefferson, letter to Thomas Law, June 13, 1814

A human life is like a single letter in the alphabet. It can be meaningless. Or it can be part of a great meaning.
—Jewish Theological Seminary of America,
advertisement in New York *Herald-Tribune*, September 5, 1956

Man is a gentle animal.
—St. John Chrysostom, *Homilies*, c. 388

The essential truth . . . is that man is under absolute mandate to express divinity in his own life and his whole nature.
—F. Ernest Johnson, *The Social Gospel Re-examined*, 1940

Of all the treasures which the universe has in its store there is none more sacred and godlike than man, the glorious cast of a glorious image.
—Philo Judaeus, *De Specialibus Legibus*, c. 12

Hitherto man had to live with the idea of his death as an individual; from now onward mankind will have to live with the idea of its death as a species.
—Arthur Koestler, in *The New York Times Magazine*, March 20, 1960

The devil is an optimist if he thinks he can make people worse than they are.
—Karl Kraus, in *Inquiry*, January 23, 1978

We can define man as the being that is aware of the world as a whole. Man is therefore a metaphysical or a religious being. He is religious not accidentally but essentially.
—Richard Kroner, *The Religious Function of Imagination*, 1941

Man is a fallen god who remembers the heavens.
—Alphonse de Lamartine, *Nouvelles méditations poétiques*, 1823

When we women offer our experience as our truth, as human truth, all the maps change. There are new mountains.
—Ursula K. Le Guin, address, Bryn Mawr College commencement, 1986, in *Dancing at the Edge of the World*

Man is not alone and neither his mind nor his conscience nor his creative powers can be truly understood if they are regarded as orphans without some universal Parent.
—Joshua Loth Liebman, *How Can I Believe in God Now?*, 1943

Man is not the creature of a drawing room or the Stock Exchange, but a lonely soul confronted by the Source of all souls.
—Arthur Machen, *Hieroglyphics*, 1923

What happens to a man is less significant than what happens *within* him.
—Thomas Mann, *In Quest of the Bluebird*, 1938

The human being who denies his nature as a created being, ends up by claiming for himself attributes which are a sort of caricature of those that belong to the Uncreated.
—Gabriel Marcel, *Man Against Mass Society*, 1952

To say that a man is a person is to say that in the depths of his being he is more a whole than a part and more independent than servile. It is this mystery of our nature which religious thought designates when it says that the person is the image of God.

—Jacques Maritain, *Education at the Crossroads*, 1943

By . . . acting on the external world and changing it, [man] at the same time changes his own nature.

—Karl Marx, *Das Kapital*, 1867

Of God! that man should be a thing for immortal souls to sieve through!

—Herman Melville, *Moby Dick*, 1851

We see in every member of the human race something that looks like a glimmering at least of heavenly light. . . . The Divine Spirit is as wide in its workings as the Divine Providence.

—G.S. Merriam, *A Living Faith*, 1876

The terrible crisis we face may be nothing less than God's call to us to reach a new level of humanity.

—Samuel H. Miller, in *Look*, December 19, 1961

Everything originates with man himself and that includes all thoughts and feelings concerning God.

—Peter Moen, *Diary*, 1951

To worship mankind as it is would be to deprive it of what alone makes it akin to the divine—its aspirations. For this human dust lives; this misery and crime are dark in contrast to an imagined excellence, they are lighted up by a prospect of good.

—Henry More, in R. Ward, *The Life of*, 1710

To say that a man is made up of certain chemical elements is a satisfactory description only for those who intend to use him as a fertilizer.

—Herbert J. Muller, *Science and Criticism*, 1943

Man, a being endued with reason, cannot on that very account live altogether at random; he is obliged in some sense to live on principle, to live by rule, to profess a view of life, to have an aim, to set up a standard.

—John Henry Newman, *Discourses to Mixed Congregations*, 1849

The central conception of Man in the Gospels is that he is an unfinished creation capable of reaching a higher level by a definite evolution which must begin by his own efforts.
—Maurice Nicoll, *The New Man*, 1950

The proper study of mankind is God and man-before-God in their interrelation.
—H. Richard Niebuhr, *The Purpose of the Church and Its Ministry*, 1956

Post-modern man is more profoundly perplexed about the nature of man than his ancestors were. He is on the verge of spiritual and moral insanity. He does not know who he is.
—F.S.C. Northrop, *Man, Nature and God*, 1962

Man is . . . a walking argument of God's existence, a moving advertisement of God's power, an articulate herald of God's intelligence. As man is the crowning work of God, so we affirm man is the supreme argument and the blinding evidence of God's existence.
—John A. O'Brien, *God: Can We Find Him?*, 1942

The man who was made in God's image is the inner man, the incorporeal, incorruptible, immortal one.
—Origen (185–254), *Homily on Genesis*

We are like men who, knowing little of painting, blame the artist because the colors in his picture are not all beautiful—not seeing that he has given to each part what was appropriate to it.
—Plotinus (205–270), *Enneads*, III, 2, 11

The essence of man lies in this, in his marvelous faculty for seeking truth, seeing it, loving it, and sacrificing himself to it.
—Giuseppe Prezzolini, in *La Voce*, April 13, 1911

It is easier to know mankind than any man.
—La Rochefoucauld, *Maxims*, 1665

Just an aggregate of trillions of cells, each of them a collection of diverse molecules.
—Jean Rostand, *Pensées d'un biologiste*, 1939

Man is the medium between spirit and matter; he is between the visible and the invisible world. He sums them up in his person, as in a universal center.

—Adrien-Emanuel Roquette, *Chata-Ima*
(Life of Roquette), D.R. Lebreton, 1947

Man is strong when he contents himself with being what he is: he is weak when he desires to raise himself above humanity.

—Jean Jacques Rousseau, *Émile*, 1762

In all things it is well to exalt the dignity of Man, by freeing him as far as possible from the tyranny of the non-human Power.

—Bertrand Russell, *Mysticism and Logic*, 1925

Man is the revelation of the Infinite, and it does not become finite in him. It remains the Infinite.

—Mark Rutherford, *More Pages from a Journal*, 1910

It is man who must be restored to his place among men. It is man that is the essence of our culture. Man, the keystone in the arch of the community. Man, the seed from whence springs our victory.

—Antoine de Saint-Exupéry, *Flight to Arras*, 1942

Man is like a precious stone: cut and polished by morals, adorned by wisdom.

—Isaac F. Satanov, *Mishle Asaf*, 1789

What a piece of work is a man! how noble in reason! how infinite in faculty! in form and moving how express and admirable! in action how like an angel! in apprehension how like a god! the beauty of the world!

—William Shakespeare, *Hamlet*, c. 1601

We are like God inasmuch as we have an intellect; we are like beasts inasmuch as we have flesh.

—Fulton J. Sheen, *God and Intelligence*, 1925

We human beings are capable of greater nobility than other species, but we are also potentially much more vicious. No other animal can be persuaded to fear and to hate multitudes of its own kind whom he has never seen.

—Benjamin P. Spock, *Fellowship*, November 1965

To touch the heart of his mystery, we find in him one
thought, strange to the point of lunacy; the thought of duty;
the thought of something owing to himself, to his neighbour,
to his God.

—Robert Louis Stevenson, *Across the Plains*, 1880

"There is nothing new under the sun," says the despairing.
But what about you, O thinking man? Unless you repudiate
reflection, you must admit that you have climbed a step
higher than the animals.

—Pierre Teilhard de Chardin, *The Phenomenon of Man*, 1959

Man, of himself and his own, is nothing, has nothing, can do
and is capable of nothing, but only infirmity, evil, and
wickedness.

—*Theologica Germanica*, 14th century

To speak of the love for humanity is meaningless. There is
no such thing as humanity. What we call humanity has a
name, was born, lives on a street, gets hungry, needs all the
particular things we need. As an abstract, it has no reality
whatsoever.

—Howard Thurman, *Mysticism and the Experience of Love*, 1961

The most intimate motions within the depths of our souls are
not completely our own. For they belong also to our friends,
to mankind, to the universe, and to the Ground of all being,
the aim of our life.

—Paul Tillich, *The Shaking of the Foundations*, 1949

A religious man is guided in his activity not by the consequences of his action, but by the consciousness of the destination of his life.

—Leo Tolstoy, *Confessions*, 1879

Man is the only animal that blushes. Or needs to.

—Mark Twain, *Following the Equator*, 1897

Man is the only significant link between the physical order
and the spiritual one. Without man the universe is a howling
wasteland contemplated by an unseen Deity.

—Morris West, *The Shoes of the Fisherman*, 1963

The still sad music of humanity.

—William Wordsworth, *Tintern Abbey*, 1798

HUMAN SPIRIT

The spirit of man is an inward flame; a lamp the world blows upon but never puts out.

—Margot Asquith, *Autobiography*, Vol. 2, 1922

Although the universe dwarfs man by its size and power, yet he can rest secure in the unique gift of spirit wherewith he can observe and discuss it all.

—John A. Cass, *Quest for Certainty*, 1950

As we grow older, in fact, we discover that the lives of most human beings are worthless except in so far as they contribute to the enrichment and emancipation of the spirit.

—Cyril Connolly, *The Unquiet Grave*, 1944

The revolution of the individual can never become the status quo, because the human spirit, as revealed in Palestine by the founder of Christianity, is limitless.

—Russell W. Davenport and editors of *Fortune U.S.A.:*
The Permanent Revolution, 1951

Our spirit is a being of a nature quite indestructible and its activity continues from eternity to eternity. It is like the sun, which seems to set only to our earthly eyes, but which, in reality, never sets, but shines on unceasingly.

—J.W. von Goethe, *Conversations with Eckermann*, 1, 1848

If I try to think of the "spirit" which a man . . . carries about under his hat, as something devoid of relation to space, and as something indivisible, even in thought, while it is, at the same time, supposed to be in that place and to be possessed of half a dozen different faculties, I confess I get quite lost.

—Thomas Henry Huxley, *Science and Morals*, 1886

Man cannot live without a permanent trust in something indestructible in himself, though both the indestructible element and the trust may remain permanently hidden from him.

—Franz Kafka (1883–1924), *Reflections*

Spirit is at first a new force, a new impetus in man. By its increasing activity it develops into a perfected faculty of the human being.

—Erich Kahler, *Man the Measure*, 1943

The present world crisis . . . is a crisis of man's spirit. It is a great religious and moral upheaval of the human race, and we do not really know half the causes of this upheaval.
—Thomas Merton, in *The Way*, June 1963

We blanch cotton, and strengthen steel, and refine sugar, and shape pottery; but to brighten, to strengthen, to refine, or to form a single living spirit, never enters into our estimate of advantages.
—John Ruskin, *Stones of Venice*, 1853

The spirit can for the time pervade and control every member and function of the body, and transmute what in form is the grossest sensuality into purity and devotion.
—Henry David Thoreau, *Walden*, 1854

In direct proportion as a man recognizes himself as spirit, and lives accordingly, is he able to transcend in power the man who recognizes himself merely as material.
—Ralph Waldo Trine, *In Tune with the Infinite*, 1897

Humility

There is something in humility which strangely exalts the heart.
—St. Augustine, *The City of God*, xiv, 42b

Nothing is more scandalous than a man who is proud of his humility.
—Marcus Aurelius, *Meditations of*, c. 170

For boredom speaks the language of time, and it is to teach you the most valuable lesson of your life—the lesson of your utter insignificance.
—Joseph Brodsky, at Dartmouth College commencement, in *The New York Times*, June 12, 1989

A country possessed of the might of the United States might do better to go into its closet and pray to its Father in secret rather than standing on thc strect corners parading its piety before men.
—A. Roy Eckardt, in *Christian Century*, November 17, 1954

A Christian prefers humility to hope, a moral virtue but not a divine one, favoring pious timidity at the expense of trustfulness towards God.
—Walter Elliot, *The Spiritual Life*, 1914

Be humble, that you may not be humbled.
—Derek Eretz, *Talmud:*, 1.27, c. 500

Blessed are the meek, for they shall inherit the earth.
—*Holy Bible*, Matthew 5:5

Humility is a Divine veil which covers our good deeds, and hides them from our eyes.
—St. John Climacus (525–600), *Climax*

The feelings of my smallness and my nothingness always kept me good company.
—Pope John XXIII, from his will, made public June 6, 1963

Humility provides everyone, even him who despairs in solitude, with the strongest relationship to his fellow man.
—Franz Kafka (1883–1924), *Reflections*

The necessity of getting reconciled with the idea of his possible extinction may breed a new humility and may rid man of that biological jingoism which made him regard himself as the crown of creation.
—Arthur Koestler, in *The New York Times Magazine*, March 20, 1960

Be humble and you will remain entire. The sage does not display himself, therefore he shines. He does not approve himself therefore he is noted. He does not praise himself, therefore he has merit. He does not glory in himself, therefore he excels.
—Lao-tzu, *Tao Te Ching*, variously dated to 3rd century B.C.

Humility is nothing else but a right judgment of ourselves.
—William Law, *Christian Perfection*, 1726

The humility of hypocrites is, of all pride, the greatest and most haughty.
—Martin Luther (1483–1546), *Table-Talk*

In humility alone lies true greatness, and that knowledge and wisdom are profitable only in so far as our lives are governed by them.
—Nicholas of Cusa, *Dialogue on Peace*, 1452

Humility. I have to admit it was the compass who taught me
this virtue. . . . We priests are not humble, not humble at all.
We are tremendous individualists. We always think we are
important because everyone makes us feel important.
—Rogelio Poncelee, *Death and Life in Morazan,* 1989

The sufficiency of merit is to know that my merit is not
sufficient.
—Francis Quarles, *Emblems,* 1635

As it obliged him to respect the presence of God in others,
so it obliged him to respect the presence of God in himself,
to make himself the messenger of God, or the path taken
by God.
—Antoine de Saint-Exupéry, *Flight to Arras,* 1942

The modern man is humble, not with the old humility which
made a man doubt his power, but with the new humility that
makes a man doubt his humanity.
—Fulton J. Sheen, *Old Errors and New Labels,* 1931

Why art thou angry? Be not angry, Tusa,/Meekness is best
for thee, and to restrain/Anger, conceit, hypocrisy is best./It
is for this we live the righteous life.
—*Sutta Nipata* (attributed to Buddha), 6th century B.C.

Let us, like [Mary], touch the dying, the poor, the lonely and
the unwanted according to the graces we have received and
let us not be ashamed or slow to do the humble work.
—Mother Teresa of Calcutta, *Life in the Spirit,* 1983

The more meek that a man is and the more subject to God
the more wise shall he be in all things, and the more patient.
—Thomas à Kempis, *Imitation of Christ,* 1441

Humility like darkness reveals the heavenly lights.
—Henry David Thoreau, *Walden,* 1854

Humility is the modesty of the soul. It is the antidote to
pride.
—Voltaire, *Philosophical Dictionary,* II, 1764

HUMOR

A case might be made for the potentially superior humor of the religious person who has settled once and for all what things are of ultimate value, sacred and untouchable. For then nothing else in the world need be taken seriously.
—Gordon W. Allport, *Personality*, 1937

A sense of humor keen enough to show a man his own absurdities, as well as those of other people, will keep him from the commission of all sins, or nearly all, save those that are worth committing.
—Samuel Butler, *Notebooks of*, 1912

A profound book on laughter might be almost a final theology.
—George A. Buttrick, *God, Pan, and Evil*, 1966

While the [Christian] faith takes care of the ultimate incongruities of life, humor does nicely with the intermediate ones.
—William Sloane Coffin, *Living the Truth in a World of Illusions*, 1985

Humor is one of God's most marvelous gifts. Humor gives us smiles, laughter, and gaiety. Humor reveals the roses and hides the thorns. Humor makes our heavy burden light and smooths the rough spots in our pathways. Humor endows us with the capacity to clarify the obscure, to simplify the complex, to deflate the pompous, to chastise the arrogant, to point a moral, and to adorn a tale.
—Sam Ervin, *Humor of a Country Lawyer*, 1983

Whatever else the creator may be, he/she is not dull or drab or ponderous: Consider the hippo, the orchid, the volcano, the purple-bottomed baboon, the shooting star, and the duck-billed platypus. Noah's ark alone is a comic opera of incredible inventiveness.
—Sydney J. Harris, *Pieces of Eight*, 1982

I have never understood why it should be considered derogatory to the Creator to suppose that He has a sense of humor.
—Dean Inge, *A Rustic Moralist*, 1937

If you don't count some of Jehovah's injunctions, there are no humorists I can recall in the Bible.
—Mordecai Richler, *The Best of Modern Humor*, 1983

HYPOCRISY

Hypocrisy itself does great honor, or rather justice, to religion, and tacitly acknowledges it to be an ornament to human nature.
—Joseph Addison, *The Spectator*, December 8, 1711

The characteristic modern malady is not plain and unvarnished materialism but sham spirituality.
—Irving Babbitt, *Living Philosophies*, 1931

Hypocrite, n. One who, professing virtues that he does not respect, secures the advantage of seeming to be what he despises.
—Ambrose Bierce, *Devil's Dictionary*, 1906

When the Devil goes to mass he hides his tail.
—Creole proverb

You know how to interpret the appearance of the sky, but you cannot interpret the signs of the times.
—*Holy Bible*, Matthew 16:3

Hateful to me even as the gates of Hades is he that hideth one thing in his heart and uttereth another.
—Homer, *Iliad*, c. 10th century B.C.

The idolater worships one object, but there is no limit to the number of mcn thc hypocrite worships.
—Bahya ben Joseph ibn Pakuda, *Hobot HaLebabot*, 1040

Hypocrisy is the homage which vice renders to virtue.
—La Rochefoucauld, *Maxims*, 1665

All is pure hypocrisy, which does not come from the heart, and so accustom the people to cultivate love to God and to their neighbors and to act from it as a motive.
—P.J. Spener, *Pia Desideria*, 1841

Ideals

The ideal life is in our blood, and never will be
still. We feel the thing we ought to be beating
through the thing we are.

—Phillips Brooks, *Perennials*, 1898

The submergence of self in the pursuit of an ideal, the readiness to spend oneself without measure, prodigally, almost
ecstatically, for something intuitively apprehended as great
and noble, spend oneself one knows not why—some of us
like to believe that this is what religion means.

—Benjamin Cardozo, *Values*, 1931

The Christian ideal has not been tried and found wanting. It
has been found difficult; and left untried.

—G.K. Chesterton, *What's Wrong with the World*, 1910

It is the besetting sin of the idealist to sacrifice reality for his
ideals; to reject life because it fails to come up to his ideal;
and this vice is just as prevalent among religious idealists as
secular ones.

—Christopher Dawson, *The Judgment of the Nations*, 1942

Every man possessed of an ideal which engrosses his whole
being, is inevitably and continuously inclined to link its presence in his soul with the presence of the Spirit in the world.

—Ernest Dimnet, *What We Live By*, 1932

If we hang beautiful pictures on the walls of our souls, mental images that establish us in the habitual companionship
of the highest that we know, and live with them long enough,
we cannot will evil.

—Harry Emerson Fosdick, *The Hope of the World*, 1933

Idealism tends to absorb all of objective reality into a system
made up solely of experience . . . Sooner or later the idealist
has to admit that his experience touches something beyond
its own content.

—Langdon Gilkey, *Maker of Heaven and Earth*, 1959

The human soul has still greater need of the ideal than of
the real. It is by the real that we exist; it is by the ideal that
we live.

—Victor Hugo, *William Shakespeare*, 1864

The highest flights of charity, devotion, trust, patience, bravery, to which the wings of human nature have spread themselves have been flown for religious ideals.
—William James, *Varieties of Religious Experience*, 1902

Beautiful ideals, which are creeds, not deeds, are religious window dressing and are meaningless. The test of faith is life.
—George N. Marshall, *Challenge of a Liberal Faith*, 1970

Idealist: one who, on noticing that a rose smells better than a cabbage, concludes that it is also more nourishing.
—H.L. Mencken, *A Little Book in C Major*, 1916

Devotion to an ideal is worship; the higher the ideal, the nobler the worship.
—F.W. Newman, *Theism*, 1858

Ideals are ideas or beliefs when these are objects not only of contemplation or affirmation but also of hope, desire, endeavor, admiration, and resolve.
—Ralph Barton Perry, *Puritanism and Democracy*, 1944

Ideals are like stars; you will not succeed in touching them with your hands. But like the seafaring man on the desert waters, you choose them as your guides, and following them you will reach your destiny.
—Carl Schurz, address, Boston, April 18, 1859

Ideals are thoughts. So long as they exist merely as thoughts, the power latent in them remains ineffective.
—Albert Schweitzer, *Memories of Childhood and Youth*, 1931

When they come downstairs from their Ivory Towers, idealists are apt to walk straight into the gutter.
—Logan Pearsall Smith, *Afterthoughts*, 1931

I am an idealist, I have to admit it. I think human nature is self-interested. But there is such a thing as enlightened self-interest. The trick is to engage self-interest at the point where it touches other people's self-interest. . . . I maintain that my idealism, which is based on some fairly rough experience, is a great deal more realistic than the totally defeatist notion that human beings are born to suffer and kill each other. If one believes that, one should go dig a deep hole and jump into it.
—Brian Urquhart, in *Time*, December 5, 1988

The ideal can lead to killing men for the glory of the Good in the expectation that the Good will be served and will appropriately bless the killer with a crown of glory.
—F.J.E. Woodbridge, *An Essay on Nature*, 1940

IDLENESS

Idleness is the enemy of the soul.
—St. Benedict of Nursia (c. 480–c. 533), *Rule of*

If thou hast nothing to do, thou shalt be haled in pieces with envy, lust, some passion or other.
—Robert Burton, *Anatomy of Melancholy, III*, 1621

When we do ill the Devil tempteth us; when we do nothing, we tempt him.
—Thomas Fuller, *Gnomologia*, 1732

If the Devil finds a man idle he'll set him to work.
—James Kelly, *Complete Collections of Scottish Proverbs*, 1721

There are but few men who have character enough to lead lives of idleness.
—Henry Wheeler Shaw, *Proverbial Philosophy*, 1877

The nurse of sin.
—Edmund Spenser, *The Fairie Queene*, c. 1589

IDOLATRY

Not only is idolatry condemned in its gross form, which takes it for granted that an idol can cause benefit or do harm, but the idea is also controverted that there is any meaning underlying this gross form of worship.
—Muhammad Ali, *The Religion of Islam*, 1936

Idolatry is the *denial of all hope for the future.* The idols of the past were worshipped by people who were afraid of change, who wanted things to remain the same, who did not want a future that was different, who found their security in the status quo. The same is true today.
—Center of Concern, *The Road to Damascus: A Challenge to the Churches of the World*, 1989

All men are idolaters, some of fame, others of self-interest, most of pleasure.
—Baltasar Gracián, *The Art of Worldly Wisdom*, 1647

Ultimately all idolatry is worship of the self projected and objectified: all idolization is self-idolization.

—Will Herberg, *Judaism and Modern Man*, 1951

The idols of the nation are silver and gold, the work of men's hands.

—*Holy Bible*, Psalms 135:15

Not only the adoration of images is idolatry, but also trust in one's own righteousness, works and merits, and putting confidence in riches and power. As the latter is the commonest, so it also is the most noxious.

—Martin Luther (1483–1546)

The mystery of idolatry is that persons reflect what they possess. Idolatry is being possessed by a possession and thereby refusing God's claim on oneself and shirking one's responsibility toward others in the community.

—M. Douglas Meeks, *God the Economist*, 1989

Our idols are by no means dumb and powerless. The sardonic diatribes of the prophets against images of wood and stone do not apply to our images that live, and speak, and smile, and dance, and allure us and lead us off to kill.

—Thomas Merton, "Events and Pseudo-Events," in *Faith and Violence*, 1968

Oh senseless man, who cannot possibly make a worm, and yet will make gods by dozens.

—Michel de Montaigne, *Essays*, Bk. 2, ch. 12, 1580

IGNORANCE

For after all, man knows mighty little, and may some day learn enough of his own ignorance to fall down again and pray.

—Henry Adams, *Letter to Brooks Adams*, 1895

Ignorance is no more the mother of devotion, than the lying harlot, which pleaded before Solomon, was the mother of the living child.

—Thomas Fuller, *Worthies of England*, 1662

While all complain of our ignorance and error, everyone exempts himself.

—Joseph Glanville, *The Vanity of Dogmatizing*, 1661

Neither God nor Allah will save us as long as we worship at the altar of smug ignorance, suffering from the fatal fallacy that what we don't know can't hurt us.
—Sydney J. Harris, *Pieces of Eight*, 1982

I know no disease of the Soul, but Ignorance; not of the Arts and Sciences, but of itself . . . Knowledge is the activity of the soul.
—Ben Jonson, *Discoveries*, 1641

Fools dwelling in darkness, wise in their own conceit, and puffed up with vain knowledge, go round and round, staggering to and fro like men led by the blind.
—*Katha Upanishad, Adhyaya*, 6th century B.C.

The greatest ignorance is when a man hates that which he nevertheless thinks to be good and noble, and loves and embraces that which he knows to be unrighteous and evil.
—Plato, *Laws*, 360 B.C.

Ignorance is the curse of God.
—William Shakespeare, *Henry VI, Part II*, c. 1592

As imprisoned birds do not get out of their cage, so those ignorant of right or wrong do not get out of their misery.
—*Sutra-Krit-Anga*, 600 and 200 B.C.

IMMORTALITY

If I did not believe in a future state, I should believe in no God.
—John Adams, letter to Thomas Jefferson, December 8, 1818

There cannot be a stronger argument that God has designed us for a state of future happiness . . . than that he has thus naturally qualified the soul for it, and made it a being capable of receiving so much bliss.
—Joseph Addison, *The Spectator*, 1714

We could probably prove that throughout history those Christians who have accomplished the most practical benefit in this world are those who have believed most fervently in the next.
—Gordon W. Allport, *The Individual and His Religion*, 1950

We know that it [the soul] survives the body and that being set free from the bars of the body, it sees with clear gaze those things which before, dwelling in the body, it could not see.

—St. Ambrose (340?–397), *Two Books on the Death of Satyrus*

So far as in us lies, we must play the immortal and do all in our power to live by the best element in our nature.

—Aristotle, *Nicomachean Ethics*, c. 340 B.C.

As I draw near the borderland . . . the wonderful light of the other life seems often to shine so joyfully into this one, that I almost forget the past and present, in an eager anticipation of the approaching awakening.

—Elizabeth Blackwell, January 2, 1887,
in *Pioneer Work for Women*, 1895

The word "death" never occurs in the Pyramid Texts except in the negative or applied to a foe. Over and over again we hear the indomitable assurance that the dead lives.

—James H. Breasted, *Development of Religion and Thought in Ancient Egypt*, 1912

It is the sense of boundless possibilities in man which justifies faith in personal immortality.

—William Adams Brown, *The Life of Prayer in a World of Science*, 1927

The more materialistic science becomes, the more angels shall I paint: their wings are my protest in favor of the immortality of the soul.

—E.C. Burne-Jones, *To Oscar Wilde*, c. 1880

Only faith in a life after death in a brighter world where dear ones will meet again—only that and the measured tramp of time can give consolation.

—Winston S. Churchill, *Maxims and Reflections*, 1947

If I err in my belief that the souls of men are immortal, I err gladly, and I do not wish to lose so delightful an error.

—Cicero, *De Senectute*, c. 78 B.C.

Science cannot supply a definite answer to this question. Immortality relates to an aspect of life which is not physical, that is which cannot be detected and measured by any instrument, and to which the application of the laws of science can at best be only a well-considered guess.

—Arthur H. Compton, *The Freedom of Man*, 1935

The supreme desire of everything, and that first given by Nature, is to return to its source; and since God is the source of our souls and Maker of them . . . to him this soul desires above all to return.
—Dante, *Il Convito*, c. 1310

The body dies but the spirit is not entombed.
—*Dhammapada*, c. 5th century B.C.

Our deepest mature conviction is that finite and infinite interpenetrate, as time and eternity interpenetrate, and our problems must be solved in the light of that conviction.
—Lily Douglas, *Immortality*, ed. by B.H. Streeter, 1917

The soul is not composed of parts, and therefore cannot perish by being resolved into constituents.
—Richard Downey, *Critical and Constructive Essays*, 1934

The blazing evidence of immortality is our dissatisfaction with any other solution.
—Ralph Waldo Emerson, *Journal*, July 1855

I believe in the immortality of the soul, not in the sense in which I accept the demonstrable truths of science, but as a supreme act of faith in the reasonableness of God's work.
—John Fiske, *Destiny of Man*, 1884

Neither experience nor science has given man the idea of immortality. . . . The idea of immortality rises from the very depths of his soul—he feels, he sees, he knows that he is immortal.
—François Guizot, *Méditations et Études Morales*, 1883

This concern with the immortality of the soul of man, with its survival in a place no one has ever seen, is part of the wasted energy of the mind.
—Ben Hecht, *A Child of the Century*, 1954

Like many others before me, I have experienced "intimations of immortality." I can no more explain these than the brown seed can explain the flowering tree.
—Robert Hillyer, *This I Believe*, 1952

O death, where is thy victory? O death, where is thy sting?
—*Holy Bible*, I Corinthians 15:55

I neither deny nor affirm the immortality of man. I see no reason for believing in it, but, on the other hand, I have no means of disproving it.
—Thomas Henry Huxley, letter to Charles Kingsley,
September 23, 1860

Though thou sleepest, thou wakest again; though thou diest, thou livest again.
—Inscription on royal Egyptian tomb, c. 2500 B.C.

The man who refuses firmly to entertain the hope of immortality . . . is no more brave and realistic than a man who refuses to open the door of his dark room and come out into the sunshine.
—D.G.M. Jackson, in the *Advocate* (Melbourne, Australia),
November 3, 1949

Immortality is but a way of saying that the determination of expectancy is the essential factor of rationality.
—William James, in *Princeton Review*, July 1883

The doctrine of the immortality of the Soul is an integral part of the Jewish creed. It is more; it is a necessary ingredient of every consistent religious creed.
—Morris Joseph, *Judaism as Creed and Life*, 1903

Above the senses is the mind. Above the mind is the intellect. Above the intellect is the ego. Above the ego is the unmanifested seed, the Primal Cause. And verily beyond the unmanifested seed is the self, the unconditioned Knowing whom one attains to freedom and achieves immortality.
—*Katha Upanishad*, prior to 400 B.C.

Socrates proved the immortality of the soul from the fact that sickness of the soul (sin) does not consume it as bodily sickness consumes the body.
—Sören Kierkegaard (1813–55), *Meditations From*, 1955

Those for whom the belief in immortality is most vivid are the most likely to practice the virtues which have a survival value and the least likely to deviate into either those virtues or those vices which are exclusively human.
—Joseph Wood Krutch, *The Modern Temper*, 1929

Life implies its own continuation. The more intensely one lives, the more difficult it is to think of destruction.
—J.H. Leuba, *The Belief in God and Immortality*, 1921

If I find in myself a desire which no experience in this world can satisfy, the most probable explanation is that I was made for another world.

—C.S. Lewis, *Christian Behavior*, 1943

All the philosophers, ancient and modern, who have attempted without the help of revelation to prove the immortality of man, from Plato down to Franklin, appear to us to have failed deplorably.

—Thomas Babington Macaulay,
Essay on Ranke's "History of the Popes," 1839

The listless, uninterested and unoccupied life is the most dangerous of all. It is better to be interested in frivolities than to be interested in nothing at all. Life is too strong merely to be held in check.

—B.W. Maturin, *The Laws of the Spiritual Life*, 1907

Men's views of immortality become a framework within which earthly ways of life are judged and changed, lived and abandoned.

—Margaret Mead, Garvin Free Lecture, December 3, 1956

Buddhism . . . is so persuaded of survival after death as being the rule, that it grants only to rare and elect souls the privilege of at length laying down the burden of continuous life.

—I.I. Metchnikoff, *The Nature of Man*, 1916

However desperate the chance for survival may be, the chance for collective survival in the sense of an endless material continuance of its race and its culture is more desperate by far.

—W.P. Montague, *The Way of Things*, 1940

As rivers flow into the sea and in so doing lose name and form, even so the wise man, freed from name and form, attains the Supreme Being, the Self-luminous, the Infinite.

—*Mundaka Upanishad*, prior to 400 B.C.

If we have but once seen any child of Adam, we have seen an immortal soul. It has not passed away, as a breeze or sunshine, but it lives; it lives at this moment in one of those many places, whether in bliss or misery, in which all souls are reserved until the end.

—John Henry Newman, *Parochial and Plain Sermons*, 1843

The great lie about immortality destroys every kind of reason, every kind of naturalness in the instincts.
—Friedrich Nietzsche, *The Anti-Christians*, 1887

The root cause of a man's grief and delusion is the identification of the Soul with the body. Fear of death paralyzes him because he is ignorant of the Soul's true nature. The wise perform their duties in the world, cherishing always the knowledge of the Soul's deathlessness.
—Swami Nikhilananda, *Perspectives on a Troubled Decade*, ed. by Bryson, Finklestein, and MacIver, 1950

The survival of personality is neither conceivable nor desirable.
—Max Nordau, *What Happens After Death?*, 1916

I trouble not myself about the manner of future existence. I content myself with believing, even to positive conviction, that the power that gave me existence is able to continue it, in any form and manner he pleases, either with or without this body; and it appears more probable to me that I shall continue to exist hereafter than that I should have had existence, as I now have, before that existence began.
—Thomas Paine, *The Age of Reason*, 1794

When the soul returns into itself and reflects, it passes into . . . the region of that which is pure and everlasting, immortal and unchangeable.
—Plato, "Phaedo," *Dialogues*, 399 B.C.

Mortal man thinks of himself as immortal because his race is immortal: he confuses the drop in the stream with the stream itself.
—Jean Paul Richter, *Hesperus*, 1795

When Judaism speaks of immortality . . . its primary meaning is that man contains something independent of the flesh and surviving it; his consciousness and moral capacity; his essential personality; a soul.
—Milton Steinberg, *Basic Judaism*, 1947

In sickness the soul begins to dress herself for immortality.
—Jeremy Taylor, *Holy Dying*, 1651

Death cannot kill what never dies.
—Thomas Traherne (1636–74), *Centuries of Meditation*

Without wanting to deceive men, it can be said we have as much reason to believe in as to deny the immortality of the being that thinks.

—Voltaire, *Homélie sur l'athéisme*, 1763

Everything science has taught me—and continues to teach me—strengthens my belief in the continuity of our spiritual existence after death.

—Werner Von Braun, in *This Week*, January 24, 1960

I swear I think there is nothing but immortality.

—Walt Whitman, "To Think of Time," *Leaves of Grass*, 1892

INSPIRATION

By inspiration I mean all the affection, attraction, inward reproaches and regrets, perceptions and illuminations with which God moves, working in our hearts through His fatherly love and care, in order to awaken, to kindle, lead, and draw us to heavenly love and holy desires.

—St. Francis de Sales (1567–1622), *A Diary of Meditations*

It usually happens that the more faithfully a person follows the inspirations he receives, the more does he experience new inspirations which ask increasingly more of him.

—Joseph de Guibert, *Theology of the Spiritual Life*, 1953

And in the last days it shall be, God declares, that I will pour out my Spirit upon all flesh, and your sons and your daughters shall prophesy, and your young men shall see visions, and your old men shall dream dreams.

—*Holy Bible*, Acts 2:17

If there were such a thing as inspiration from a higher realm, it might well be that the neurotic temperament would furnish the chief condition of the requisite receptivity.

—William James, *Varieties of Religious Experience*, 1902

High art, high morals, high faith, are impossible among those who do not believe their own inspirations, but only court them for pleasure or profit.

—James Martineau, *Hours of Thought on Sacred Things*, 1879

Inspiration presupposes revelation. Inspiration may be called the guardian of revelation.

—Vincent McNabb, *Frontiers of Faith and Reason*, 1936

The notion that inspiration is something that happened thousands of years ago, and was then finished and done with . . . the theory that God retired from business at that period and has not been heard from since, is as silly as it is blasphemous.

—George Bernard Shaw, *The Quintessence of Ibsenism,* 1890

Demonic inspiration . . . reveals the divine, but as a reality which it fears, which it cannot love, with which it cannot unite.

—Paul Tillich, *Interpretation of History,* 1936

INTELLECT

The Buddha and all his successors warn us against intellectual structures that confine us to an artificial environment, and against concepts that smear over the living fact of things in themselves. Even the idea of the Buddha must be forgotten.

—Robert Aitken, *The Mind of Clover,* 1984

It is the duty of the intellectual to express the right to doubt. Absolutely free utterance exists only in writing. That is the principal message of the intellectual. . . . Intellectuals must be able to speak their lofty words, but . . . they must also descend to reality.

—Yehuda Amichai, in *World Press Review,* February 1987

The more you extend intelligence, unless you extend the moral restraints and influences of the gospel at the same time, the more you sharpen the intellect for evil.

—Orestes Brownson, *Brownson's Views,* 1893

An intellectual is someone whose mind watches itself.

—Albert Camus, *Notebooks,* 1935–42

Intellectuals are the most indoctrinated part of the population. In fact, there are good reasons for this. First, as the literate part of the population, they are the ones most susceptible to propaganda. Second, they are the ideological managers, so they have to internalize the propaganda. They have to believe it.

—Noam Chomsky, in *Mother Jones,* October 1988

Intelligence alone is dangerous if it is not subjected to the intuitive or rational perception of moral values. It has led, not only to materialism, but to monstrosities.

—Lecomte du Noüy, *Human Destiny,* 1947

Religion is the last subject that the intellect begins to understand.
> —Will Durant, *The Reformation*, 1957

How well people manage their emotions determines how effectively they can use their intellectual ability. For example, if someone is facile at solving problems in the quiet of her office, but falls apart in a group, then she will be ineffective in a great many situations.
> —Seymour Epstein, in *The New York Times*, April 5, 1988

In the realm of the spiritual or intellectual . . . the fuller the "vessel," the more one can add to it. The daily, systematic indulgence of the intellect's hunger of knowledge is man's most effective defense against the ever-present onslaughts of boredom. As such it constitutes one of the great pillars of the good life.
> —Simon Greenberg, *A Jewish Philosophy and Pattern of Life*, 1981

When the intellect seeks to understand beyond its powers, it loses even that which it understood.
> —Pope St. Gregory the Great, *Magna Moralia*, 584

The tragedy of our time is "the treason of the clerks," that is, the failure of our best minds to give themselves to contemplation of truth, and their undue preoccupation with immediate problems to the neglect of the deeper problems.
> —Bernard Leeming, in *America*, November 3, 1962

The intellectual is constantly betrayed by his own vanity. Godlike, he blandly assumes that he can express everything in words.
> —Anne Morrow Lindbergh, *The Wave of the Future*, 1940

The intellect is the link that joins us to God.
> —Maimonides, *The Guide for the Perplexed* III, 1190

It too often happens that the religiously disposed are in the same degree intellectually deficient.
> —John Henry Newman, *The Idea of a University*, 1852

We have not so much the privilege of intelligence, viewed as something above and against nonhuman nature, but the responsibility and necessity to convert our intelligence to the earth. We need to learn how to use intelligence to mend the distortions we have created and how to convert intelligence into an instrument that can cultivate the harmonies and balances of the ecological community and bring these to a refinement.

—Rosemary Radford Ruether, *Sexism and God-Talk*, 1983

My deeply held belief is that if a god of anything like the traditional sort exists, our curiosity and intelligence are provided by such a god. We would be unappreciative of those gifts (as well as unable to take such a course of action) if we suppressed our passion to explore the universe and ourselves. On the other hand, if such a traditional god does not exist, our curiosity and our intelligence are the essential tools for managing our survival.

—Carl Sagan, *Broca's Brain*, 1979

Faith in the intellect . . . is the only faith yet sanctioned by its fruits.

—George Santayana, *Reason in Science*, 1906

Modern philosophers have a message for the age, and that is the declaration of independence from the claims of the intellect.

—Fulton J. Sheen, *God and Intelligence*, 1925

[The yarmulke] is an indication that one recognizes that there is something above you. It says, "Above my intellect is a sign of godliness."

—Rabbi Pinchas Stolper, in *The New York Times*, March 26, 1986

Not one word is said in the whole of the New Testament about our Lord's intellect; only always about His Heart.

—Alexander Whyte, *Walk, Conversation and Character of Jesus Christ*, 1905

esus Christ

There was in Him no world-weariness, no strengthless melancholy, no timid shrinking from the fray.

—Karl Adam, *Christ Our Brother*, 1931

We are persecuted because we say that the Son had a beginning but that God was without beginning . . . He is neither part of God, nor of any subjacent matter. For this we are persecuted.

—Arius, *Letter to Eusebius* c. 325

With all its fidelity to the spirit and style of the Jewish scholars of his time, the teaching of Jesus did nevertheless pass beyond the boundary, to stand in a place of its own. Had it not done so it most probably would not have created a world religion.

—Sholem Asch, *What I Believe*, 1941

To see the revelation of God in Christ is a gracious privilege of faith, of the believer and not of the historian.

—Emil Brunner, *The Theology of Crisis*, 1929

The Son, according to his Divinity, is coequal and consubstantial with the Father; true God.

—Henry Bullinger, *The Helvetic Confession*, 1536

What holds true, in all our experience of men, is inverted in him. He grows sacred, peculiar, wonderful, divine, as acquaintance reveals him. At first he is only a man, as the sense reports him to be; knowledge, observation, familiarity, raise him into the God-man.

—Horace Bushnell, *The Character of Jesus*, 1886

[Jesus'] ministry was clearly defined, and the alternatives to the illusion and temptations of the desert were spelled out. A choice was made—life abundant, full, and free for all. Make no mistake about it, the day that choice was made, Jesus became suspect. That day in the temple he sealed the fate already prepared for him. How was the world to understand one who rejected an offer of power and control?

—Joan B. Campbell, in *Sojourners*, August-September 1991

He was exactly what the man with a delusion never is; he
was wise; he was a good judge.
—G.K. Chesterton, *The Everlasting Man*, 1925

Christ is God or He is the world's greatest liar and impostor.
—Dorothy Day, *From Union Square to Rome*, 1938

Caesar hoped to reform men by changing institutions and
laws; Christ wished to remake institutions, and lessen laws,
by changing men.
—Will Durant, *Caesar and Christ*, 1944

Jesus Christ belonged to the true race of prophets. He saw
with open eye the mystery of the soul. Drawn by its severe
harmony, ravished with its beauty, he lived in it, and had
his being there. Alone in all history he estimated the greatness of man.
—Ralph Waldo Emerson, Divinity School address, July 15, 1838

Nothing accords better with the nature of man than the philosophy of Christ, of which the sole end is to give back to
fallen nature its innocence and integrity.
—Desiderius Erasmus, *Notes on Greek Testament*, 1516

Jesus remains the very heart and soul of the Christian
movement, still controlling men, still capturing men—against
their wills very often—changing men's lives and using them
for ends they never dreamed of.
—T.R. Glover, *The Jesus of History*, 1925

Either Jesus was and knew that He was, what He proclaimed
Himself to be, or else He was a pitiable visionary.
—Leonce de Grandmaison, *Jesus Christ*, 1930

He proclaimed that to gain the whole world was nothing if
the soul were injured, and yet he remained kind and sympathetic to every living thing. That is the most astonishing and
the greatest fact about him!
—Adolf von Harnack, *What Is Christianity?*, 1901

Most men find in Jesus a reflection of their own ideals.
—Granville Hicks, *Eight Ways of Looking at Christianity*, 1926

Do not think that I have come to bring peace on earth; I have
not come to bring peace, but a sword.
—*Holy Bible*, Matthew 10:34

His *life*, his spirit, his personality, is incomparably greater
than anything he said, or did, or taught.
—Rufus M. Jones, *The Eternal Gospel*, 1938

What Christ brought to light in the unfolding of the Eternal
Gospel is the Face, the personal aspect, the revelation of the
Heart, the Love, the Grace, the Character-Nature of God. We
see Him at last.
—Rufus M. Jones, *The Eternal Gospel*, 1938

He is an abyss filled with light. One must close one's eyes if
one is not to fall into it.
—Franz Kafka, "Conversations with Kafka," in *Partisan Review*, March-April 1953

For the Christian, Jesus is the Way. All things are measured
by his Way: by his healing grace, his call to forgiveness and
purity of heart, nonviolence and a concern for justice; by his
relinquishment of earthly power and dominance; affirmation
of *agape* (friendship and self-giving Love) as a new basis for
kinship, of change of heart as the requirement for righteousness, and of the transcendent power of suffering.
—Madonna Kolbenschlag, *Lost in the Land of Oz*, 1988

Many, as has been well said, ran after Christ, not for the
miracles, but for the loaves.
—John Lubbock, *The Pleasures of Life*, 1887

The way of Christ is not possible without Christ.
—William Russell Maltby, *Obiter Scripta*, 1952

Jesus would have asserted his freedom and critically examined the status quo from the principle of love, and in so doing he would meet the same fate in the sixteenth century or
even in the twentieth century as he did in his own.
—Mason Olds, "A Developmental Interpretation of Jesus,"
Religious Humanism, Summer 1991

Christ did not find heroism in everyone; whoever showed but
a trace of good will, to him He tendered His hand and inspired him with courage.
—Pope Pius XII, *Allocution*, February 23, 1944

In an evolutionary world, the idea of one man from the past who has already had everything a man could have seems to place a false ceiling on the human potential. It presents a static ideal on which no advance is possible. Indeed, the claim that Jesus was "perfect" needs so much explanation and qualification that perhaps it would better be dropped.
—John A.T. Robinson, *The Human Face of God*, 1973

The truth is, it is not Jesus as historically known, but Jesus as spiritually arisen within men, that is significant for our time, and can help it.
—Albert Schweitzer, *The Quest of the Historical Jesus*, 1906

The whole teaching of Jesus is grounded in what may be termed an ethical mysticism. He is possessed with the thought of love and goodness as so inherent in divine nature that by attaining to them we apprehend God.
—Ernest F. Scott, *The Ethical Teaching of Jesus*, 1924

Just as we find the real meaning of our personality in Christ, so in Christ we find the real meaning and character of our relationship with other persons.
—Aelred Watkin, *The Heart of the World*, 1954

In every decade we instruct Christ as to what He was and is, instead of allowing ourselves to be instructed by Him.
—Amos N. Wilder, *Theology and Modern Literature*, 1958

JOY

To bring joy to a single heart is better than to build many shrines for worship.
—Abu Sa'id Ibn Abi Khayr, in M. Smith, *Readings from the Mystics of Islam*

The contemplation of the divine Being, and the exercise of virtue, are in their own nature so far from excluding all gladness of heart, that they are perpetual sources of it.
—Joseph Addison, *The Spectator*, 1714

The true joy of man is in doing that which is most proper to his nature; and the first property of man is to be kindly affected towards them that are of one kind with himself.
—Marcus Aurelius, *Meditations*, c. 170

God cannot endure that unfestive, mirthless attitude of ours in which we eat our bread in sorrow, with pretentious, busy haste, or even with shame. Through our daily meals He is calling us to rejoice, to keep holiday in the midst of our working day.
—Dietrich Bonhoeffer, *Life Together*, 1938

There is, above all, the laughter that comes from the eternal joy of creation, the joy of making the world new, the joy of expressing the inner riches of the soul—laughter from triumphs over pain and hardship in the passion for an enduring ideal, the joy of bringing the light of happiness, of truth and beauty into a dark world. This is divine laughter par excellence.
—John Elof Boodin, *God: A Cosmic Philosophy of Religion*, 1934

A positive thing; in Joy one does not only feel secure, but something goes out from one's self to the universe, a warm, possessive effluence of love.
—John Buchan, *Pilgrim's Way*, 1940

God send you joy, for sorrow will come fast enough.
—John Clarke, *Pareomiologia Anglo-Latina*, 1639

Cana of Galilee . . . Ah, that sweet miracle! It was not men's grief, but their joy Christ visited, He worked his first miracle to help men's gladness.
—Feodor Dostoevsky, *The Brothers Karamazov*, 1880

You shall have joy, or you shall have power, said God; you shall not have both.
—Ralph Waldo Emerson, *Journal*, October 1842

Life is one long joy, because the will of God is always being done in it, and the glory of God always being got from it.
—F.W. Faber, *The Spirit of Father Faber*, 1914

When I think of God, my heart is so filled with joy that the notes fly off as from a spindle.
—Joseph Haydn, in H.T. Henry, *Catholic Customs and Symbols*, 1925

For his anger is but for a moment, and his favor is for a lifetime.
—*Holy Bible*, Psalms 30:5

Joy is a constituent of life, a necessity of life; it is an element of life's value and life's power. As every man has need of joy, so too, every man has a right to joy. . . . It is a condition of religious living.

—Paul Wilhelm von Keppler, *More Joy*, 1911

I think we all sin by needlessly disobeying the apostolic injunction to "rejoice" as much as by anything else.

—C.S. Lewis, *The Problem of Pain*, 1944

The trouble with many men is that they have got just enough religion to make them miserable. If there is not joy in religion, you have got a leak in your religion.

—William A. (Billy) Sunday, sermon, New York, 1914

Joy is the realization of the truth of one-ness, the oneness of our soul with the world and of the world-soul with the supreme love.

—Rabindranath Tagore, *Gitanjali*, 1913

The joy of a good man is the witness of a good conscience; have a good conscience and thou shalt ever have gladness.

—Thomas à Kempis, *Imitation of Christ*, 1441

No man truly has joy unless he lives in love.

—St. Thomas Aquinas (1225–74), *Opusc.xxxv, de Duobus Pracceptsis*

JUDAISM

Judaism . . . taught the possibility of transmuting pain into spiritual greatness.

—J.B. Agus, in *Judaism*, Fall 1955

A people is not chosen because of any racial superiority; there is no such thing. . . . A people is chosen when it has the will to live in a way which would express God's spirit on earth.

—David Aronson, *The Jewish Way of Life*, 1944

In a way, an American Jew may have nothing more to look forward to than being a critic whose subject is the Torah; if spiritual life in the modern world must be vicarious, then better to struggle along with the children of Israel at Sinai than to dance even with the pioneers at Degania.

—Bernard Avishai, *The Tragedy of Zionism*, 1985

As long as Judaism continues, nobody will be able to say that the soul of man has allowed itself to be subjugated.
—Leo Baeck, *The Essence of Judaism*, 1936

To be a Jew . . . is to be strong with the strength that has outlived persecutions.
—Phyllis Bottome, *The Mortal Storm*, 1937

The Jews gave to the world its three greatest religions, reverence for law, and the highest conceptions of morality.
—Louis D. Brandeis, *The Jewish Problem*, 1919

Becoming a people of God means rather that the attributes of God revealed to it, justice and love, are to be made effective in its own life, in the lives of its members with one another.
—Martin Buber, *At the Turning*, 1952

The Jews were the only people who, from the very beginning knew God, the Creator of the heavens and the earth; the only people, consequently, that could be the custodian of the divine secrets, and it preserved them in a religion that is without equal.
—Samuel Taylor Coleridge (1772–1834), *Table-Talk*

We reject as ideas not rooted in Judaism, the beliefs both in bodily resurrection and in Gehenna and Eden.
—Central Conference of American Rabbis, 1885

The center and soul of all religion, the belief in a personal God, is the pillar of the religion of Israel.
—C.H. Cornill, *Culture of Ancient Israel*, 1914

Judaism is the only religion that has never entered into conflict, and never can, with either science or social progress, and that has witnessed, and still witnesses, all their conquests without a sense of fear.
—James Darmesteter, *Selected Essays*, 1895

Jewry, being a spiritual entity, cannot suffer annihilation: the body, the mould, may be destroyed, the spirit is immortal.
—S.M. Dubnow, *Jewish History*, 1903

If it is true that on the secular side our intellectual life is rooted in Greece and Rome, on the religious side it is rooted in Israel. So long as men recognize the abiding value of religion as the answer to their deepest needs, they will turn with inexhaustible interest to the story of the first beginnings and the gradual development of the people whose faith conquered the civilized world.

—J.R. Dummelow, *One Volume Commentary on the Bible*, 1909

It is to the Jewish nation that humanity owes the deepest debt of gratitude, and it is on that nation that humanity has inflicted the deepest wrongs.

—F.W. Farrar, speech, London, February 1, 1882

Judaism is a way of life which endeavors to transform virtually every human action into a means of communion with God.

—Louis Finkelstein, *Religions of Democracy*, 1941

Hatred for Judaism is at bottom hatred for Christianity.

—Sigmund Freud, *Moses and Monotheism*, 1939

Judaism has a central, unique and tremendous idea that is utterly original—the idea that God and man are partners in the world and that, for the realization of His plan and the complete articulation of this glory upon earth, God needs a committed, dedicated group of men and women.

—T.H. Gaster, at American Council for Judaism, April 20, 1954

Judaism is rooted forever in the soul, blood, life-experience and memory of a particular folk—the Jewish people.

—Solomon Goldman, *Crisis and Decision*, 1938

Judaism, which is throughout rationalistic, is the sole stronghold of free thought in the religious sphere.

—Heinrich Graetz, in *Jewish Quarterly Review*, 1888

Judaism, the religion of the Bible, is the classical paradigm of a God-made religion. It is the assertion—not the philosophical proof—that God exists and that He has spoken and speaks to man, giving him clues to the road that he must follow.

—Arthur Hertzberg, *Judaism*, 1961

Judaism is a *religion of time* aiming at the *sanctification of time*.

—Abraham Joshua Heschel, *The Sabbath*, 1951

The Jew assumes for himself the historic post of a sentinel and soldier of righteousness.

—E.G. Hirsch, *Reform Advocate*, I, 1891

You shall be blessed above all peoples.

—*Holy Bible*, Deuteronomy 7:14

The Jews, through living under Christian princes, are in worse plight than were their ancestors under the Pharaohs. They are driven to leave in despair the land in which their fathers have dwelt since the memory of man. . . . Whenever any unjust attacks upon them come under your notice, redress their injuries, and do not suffer them to be visited in the future by similar tribulations.

—Pope Innocent IV, 1247, in H. Graetz, *History of the Jews*, III

If it be true, as it obviously is, that the Bible is a creation of the Jews, it is also true, though not so obvious, that the Jews are a creation of the Bible.

—Joseph Jacobs, *Jewish Contributions to Civilization*, 1919

To the question "Why does the Jew always answer a question with a question?" the traditional answer is: "Why not?"

—Louis Jacobs, *What Does Judaism Say About. . . ?*, 1973

The Jewish religion is not "extrinsic" to us, but in a certain way is "intrinsic" to our religion. With Judaism, therefore, we have a relationship which we do not have with any other religion. . . . In a certain way it could be said that you [the Jewish people] are our elder brothers.

—Pope John Paul II, in *Los Angeles Times*, June 25, 1987

Judaism is the funded cultural activity which the Jewish people has transmitted from generation to generation.

—Mordecai Kaplan, in *Menorah Journal*, XIII, 1927

Judaism is not only religion and it is not only ethics: it is the sum total of all the needs of a nation, placed on a religious basis.

—Joseph Klausner, *Jesus of Nazareth*, 1926

Every house a temple, every heart an altar, every human being a priest.

—M. Lazarus, *Ethics of Judaism*, 1900

In order to understand the Christian faith, one must understand the Jewish faith. . . .
—Patricia McClurg, in *The Christian Science Monitor*, December 23, 1987

The plainest historical evidence for the effectiveness of religion as a positive social form lies in the history of the Jews.
—John Macmurray, *Creative Society*, 1935

Judaism is the belief that all life should be sanctified and transfigured by religion. . . . Man is to humanize himself by . . . conscious adherence to . . . the moral law.
—C.G. Montefiore, *Liberal Judaism*, 1903

The preservation of the Jews is really one of the most signal and illustrious acts of divine Providence.
—Thomas Newton, *Dissertations on the Prophecies*, 1766

If Jewish thought had never existed the world would have been without Christianity and Islam.
—Leon Roth, *Jewish Thought as a Factor in Civilization*, 1954

The Jewish God is no philosopher and his path is tangled with logical contradictions.
—Leon Roth, *Jewish Thought as a Factor in Civilization*, 1954

If I think of my religion I think of it in terms of my people's religion. I share the faith-life of my group. I like to pray as my fathers prayed.
—Abba Hillel Silver, *Religion in a Changing World*, 1930

The Jewish people have been in exile for 2,000 years; they have lived in hundreds of countries, spoken hundreds of languages and still they kept their old language, Hebrew. They kept their Aramaic, later their Yiddish; they kept their books; they kept their faith.
—Isaac Bashevis Singer, in *The New York Times*, November 26, 1978

The attempt to reduce Judaism to a religion is a betrayal of its true nature.
—Milton Steinberg, *The Making of the Modern Jew*, 1933

Israelites are dearer to the Holy One than angels.
—*Talmud*, 91b., c. 200–500

The particular genius of Judaism is to combine our celebrations of nature—an aspect we share with other religious traditions—with a simultaneous affirmation of the need to transform the human world by freeing it of oppression.
—*Tikkun*, January/February 1988

Eternal faith and eternal people, a living dialogue between God and the Jew, between the Jew and God, and among the Jew, his fellow Jew, and the world.
—Leo Trepp, *Eternal Faith, Eternal People*, 1962

It blends religion, national devotion, cultural aspirations, and the hope for a better future into an inseparable union of purposeful holiness.
—Trude Weiss-Rosmarin, *Jewish Survival*, 1949

The tragedy of modern Jewish life is not anti-Semitism, but the loss of the sense of the worthwhileness of being a Jew.
—Trude Weiss-Rosmarin, *Jewish Survival*, 1949

Ultimately Judaism judges life by action, by deed; it is a system that stresses the importance of proper conduct. Yet it never relinquishes a sense that language can reach to the center of our souls.
—David J. Wolpe, *In Speech and in Silence: The Jewish Quest for God*, 1992

We are proud and happy in that the dread Unknown God of the infinite Universe has chosen our race as the medium by which to reveal His will to the world.
—Israel Zangwill, *Children of the Ghetto*, 1892

JUDGMENT

Indifferent acts are judged by their ends; sins are judged by themselves.
—St. Augustine, *To Consentius, Against Lying*, c. 400

No man can justly censure or condemn another, because indeed no man truly knows another. . . . No man can judge another, because no man knows himself.
—Thomas Browne, *Religio Medici*, 1642

It is rashness to go about to make our shallow reason judge of the works of God, and to call vain and superfluous whatever thing in the Universe is not of use to us.
—Galileo, *Dialogue on the Great World Systems*, 1632

If it be maintained that a man's judgments are themselves completely determined, that he cannot help making the judgments he makes, the answer is that this makes nonsense of all knowledge.
—Morris Ginsberg, *On the Diversity of Morals*, 1957

To judge means to pronounce the verdict in regard to a person, to anticipate, as it were, the punishment that the sinner deserves from God. This is precisely what the self-righteous man does, and what the true Christian always avoids doing.
—Dietrich von Hildebrand, *True Morality and Its Counterfeits*, 1955

Judge not, that you be not judged. For with the judgment you pronounce you will be judged and the measure you give will be the measure you get.
—*Holy Bible*, Matthew 7:1

What else, indeed, is the judgment, as far as we can grasp it, but the naked setting of our soul as it is now at this moment in the sight of God?
—Bede Jarrett, *Meditations for Layfolk*, 1915

The world is judged according to the preponderance of good or evil, and the individual is judged in the same way.
—*Kiddushin, Mishna*, c. 400

Human beings judge one another by their external actions. God judges them by their moral choices.
—C.S. Lewis, *Christian Behavior*, 1943

While it is true that it is a terrible thing to fall into the hands of the living God in judgment, it is a much more terrible thing to fall out of his hand.
—Albert T. Mollegen, *Christianity and Modern Man*, 1961

All universal judgments are treacherous and dangerous.
—Michel de Montaigne, *Essays*, 1580

If it be an evil to judge rashly or untruly any single man, how much a greater sin it is to condemn a whole people.
—William Penn, *A Key Opening the Way*, 1693

Why, for us every day is a day of judgment—every day is a *Dies Irae*, and writes its irrevocable verdict in the flame of its West. Think you that judgment waits till the doors of the graves are opened? It waits at the doors of your houses—it waits at the corners of your streets; we are in the midst of judgment.

—John Ruskin, *Sesame and Lilies*, 1865

Forbear to judge, for we are sinners all.

—William Shakespeare, *Henry VI*, Part II, c. 1591

The *forgiveness* of the world can only be accomplished by the *judgment* of the world.

—Ralph W. Sockman, *The Highway of God*, 1941

Man's advocates are repentance and good deeds.

—*Talmud: Sabbath*, 32a, c. 500

At the day of judgment it shall not be asked of us what we have read, but what we have done; not how well we have said, but how religiously we have lived.

—Thomas à Kempis, *Imitation of Christ*, 1441

JUSTICE

Since all justice is rightness, the justice, which brings praise to the one who preserves it, is in nowise in any except rational beings. . . . This justice is not rightness of knowledge, or rightness of action, but rightness of will.

—St. Anselm, *Dialogue on Truth*, c. 1080

The instinct for justice, when equipped with all the resources of technology, is capable of laying waste to the earth itself.

—Georges Bernanos, *Last Essays of*, 1955

If justice prevails, good faith is found in treaties, truth in transaction, order in government, the earth is at peace, and heaven itself sheds over us its beneficent light and radiates down to us its blessed influence.

—Jacques Benique Bossuet (1627–1704), *Sermon on Justice*

To "justify" means nothing else than to acquit of guilt him who was accused as if his own innocence were confirmed.

—John Calvin, *Institutes*, III, 1536

Let the tears of the poor find more compassion, but not more
justice, from thee than the applications of the wealthy.
—Miguel de Cervantes, *Don Quixote*, 1605

It is necessary to cease to be a man in order to do justice to a
microbe; it is not necessary to cease to be a man in order to
do justice to men.
—G.K. Chesterton, *Heretics*, 1905

The origin of justice is to be sought in the divine law of eternal and immutable morality.
—Cicero, *The Laws*, 52 B.C.

We were never promised a life free from fear and struggle.
We were offered the hope that by committing ourselves to
the struggle for a righteous society in solidarity with the
wretched of the earth we would discover the secret of life.
—Sheila Collins, "Theology in the Politics of Appalachian Women,"
Womanspirit Rising, 1979

A man is not just if he carries a matter by violence; no, he
who distinguishes both right and wrong and guides others,
not by violence, but by the same law, being a guardian of the
law, he is called just.
—*Dhammapada*, c. 5th century B.C.

Justice is truth in action.
—Benjamin Disraeli, speech, February 11, 1851

If a man is at heart just, then in so far is he God; the safety
of God, the immortality of God, the majesty of God, do enter
in that man with justice.
—Ralph Waldo Emerson, Divinity School address, July 15,1838

That amid our highest civilization men faint and die with
want is not due to the niggardliness of nature, but to the injustice of man.
—Henry George, *Progress and Poverty*, 1879

Justice is the sum of all moral duty.
—William Godwin, *An Enquiry Concerning Political Justice*, 1793

It is cheap and easy to decry the injustice of others, but desperately costly to confront our own.
—Richard B. Hayes, "On Hearing Bad News,"
in *Christian Century*, February 26, 1992

Whereas in Greek the idea of justice was akin to harmony, in Hebrew it is akin to holiness.
—Joseph H. Hertz, *The Pentateuch and Haftorahs*, 1936

It is justice which, when sprinkled by the dew of the Holy Spirit, ought to germinate good works through holiness.
—Hildegard of Bingen (1098–1179), *Illuminations of*, 1985

But let justice roll down like waters, and righteousness like an ever-flowing stream.
—*Holy Bible*, Amos 5:24

He shall not judge by what his eyes see, or decide by what his ears hear; but with righteousness he shall judge the poor, and decide with equity for the meek of the earth.
—*Holy Bible*, Isaiah 11:3-4

Our duty is to put an end to evil, to injustice, to oppression and to sin; not to come to an agreement with them. We must not reconcile good with evil, life with death. All Christian reconciliation implies a radical option for justice and for the poor.
—*Kairos Central America*, 1988

O you Moslems, stand fast to Justice, when you bear witness, though it is against yourself, or your parents, or your kin, rich or poor. God is nearer to you than any. Therefore follow not passion, lest you swerve from the Truth.
—*Koran*, c. 625

If God's justice could be recognized as just by human comprehension, it would not be divine.
—Martin Luther, *On the Slave Will*, 1525

Justice is a name for certain classes of moral rules, which concern the essentials of human well-being more nearly, and are therefore of more absolute obligation, than any other rules for the guidance of life.
—John Stuart Mill, *Utilitarianism*, 1863

Holiness toward God and justice toward men usually go together.
—Philo, *Abraham*, A.D. 37

In God's Kingdom the corrupting principles of domination and subjugation will be overcome. People will no longer model social or religious relationships, or even relationships to God after the sort of power that reduces others to servility. Rather they will discover a new kind of power, a power exercised through service, which empowers the disinherited and brings all to a new relationship of mutual enhancement.
—Rosemary Radford Ruether, *Sexism and God-Talk*, 1983

No human actions ever were intended by the Maker of men to be guided by balances of expediency, but by balances of justice.
—John Ruskin, *Sesame and Lilies*, 1865

Justice—Truth is its handmaid, freedom is its child, peace is its companion, safety walks in its steps, victory follows in its train; it is the brightest emanation from the gospel; it is the attribute of God.
—Sydney Smith, *Lady Holland: Memoir*, 1855

To do . . . injustice to another is a far greater evil for the doer of the injustice than it is for the victim.
—Socrates, in Plato, *Dialogues*, 399 B.C.

Justice is that side of love which affirms the independent right of persons within the love relation.
—Paul Tillich, *Systematic Theology*, 1951

I do, it is true, expect more justice from one who believes in a God than from one who has no such belief.
—Voltaire, "Atheist," in *Philosophical Dictionary*, 1764

Whoever tramples on the plea for justice temperately made in the name of peace only outrages peace and kills something fine in the heart of man which God put there when we got our manhood.
—William Allen White, in *Emporia Gazette*, July 26, 1922

The yuppie generation are very good gameplayers, but morally, ethically, they have no idea what they're about. To them, justice is efficiency, not fairness.
—Art Wolfe, in *U.S. News & World Report*, February 23, 1987

Knowledge

The fact that people have religious experiences is interesting from the psychological point of view, but it does not in any way imply that there is such a thing as religious knowledge . . . . Unless he can formulate his "knowledge" in propositions that are empirically verifiable, we may be sure that he is deceiving himself.

—A.J. Ayer, *Language, Truth and Logic*, 1936

The desire of power in excess caused the angels to fall; the desire of knowledge in excess caused man to fall.

—Francis Bacon, *Essays*, 1597

It is a prejudice to believe that knowledge is always rational, that there is no such thing as irrational knowledge. Actually, we apprehend a great deal more through feeling than by intellection.

—Nicholas Berdyaev, *Solitude and Society*, 1947

There is "true" Knowledge. Learn thou it is this:
To see one changeless Life in all the Lives
And in the Separate, One Inseparable.

—*Bhagavad-Gita*, 5th to 2nd century B.C.

For we can only know that we know nothing, and a little knowledge is a dangerous thing.

—Chuang-tzu, c. 300 B.C.

Wicked men grow the worse for their knowledge, but the good improve extremely.

—Phillipe de Comines, *Memoirs*, 1491

If a man's faith is unstable and his peace of mind troubled, his knowledge will not be perfect.

—*Dhammapada*, c. 5th century B.C.

Knowledge is the key that first opens the hard heart, enlarges the affections, and opens the way for men into the kingdom of heaven.

—Jonathan Edwards (1703–58), *Works*, V, 151

Knowledge provides more of a help toward godliness than does beauty, or strength of the body, or wealth.

—Desiderius Erasmus, *Enchiridion*, 1501

It hath been the common disease of Christians from the beginning . . . out of a vain desire to know more than is revealed.
—John Hales, *A Treatise Concerning Schism and Schismatics*, 1641

The fear of the Lord is the beginning of knowledge: but fools despise wisdom and instruction.
—*Holy Bible*, Proverbs 1:7

While it is the summit of human wisdom to learn the limit of our faculties, it may be wise to recollect that we have no more right to make denials than to put forth affirmatives about what lies beyond that limit.
—Thomas Henry Huxley, *Hume*, 1878

Knowledge is the one thing, virtue another; good sense is not conscience, refinement is not humility, nor is largeness and justness of view faith.
—John Henry Newman, *Present Position of Catholics in England*, 1851

We know too much for one man to know much.
—J. Robert Oppenheimer, address, 1954

In God knowledge is infinite; in others it is only a germ.
—Patanjali, *Yoga Aphorisms*, I, 2nd century B.C.

He that has more knowledge than judgment, is made for another man's use more than his own.
—William Penn, *Some Fruits of Solitude*, 1693

All knowledge must be built on our intuitive beliefs; if they are rejected, nothing is left.
—Bertrand Russell, *The Problems of Philosophy*, 1912

There is a lurking fear that some things are not meant "to be known," that some inquiries are too dangerous for human beings to make.
—Carl Sagan, *Broca's Brain*, 1979

God is mysterious, and so (for that matter) is the universe and one's fellow-man and one's self and the snail on the garden path; but none of these is so mysterious as to correspond to nothing within human knowledge.
—Dorothy L. Sayers, *The Mind of the Maker*, 1941

Knowledge is the wing whereby we fly to Heaven.
—William Shakespeare, *Henry VI*, Part II, c. 1591

If we compare our knowledge with that of the ancients, we appear very wise. But we are not nearer to solving the riddle of eternal justice than Cain was.
—Lev Shestov, *All Things Are Possible*, 1977

Knowledge is the food of the soul.
—Socrates, "Protagoras," in Plato, *Dialogues*, 399 B.C.

In every man there are latent faculties by means of which he can acquire for himself knowledge of the higher worlds.
—Rudolf Steiner, *The Way of Initiation*, 1910

Knowledge is nothing but the continually burning up of error to set free the light of truth.
—Rabindranath Tagore, *Sadhana*, 1913

Philosophy seeks knowledge for the sake of understanding, while religion seeks knowledge for the sake of worship.
—William Temple, *Nature, Man and God*, 1934

It does not seem as if knowledge has done the best thing for humanity. In the time of wisdom, I respected my brother's dream and he respected mine.
—John Truedell, in Kay Boyle, "A Day on Alcatraz with the Indians," *Words That Must Somehow Be Said*, 1969

To know a little less and to understand a little more: that, it seems to me, is our greatest need.
—James Ramsey Ullman, *The White Tower*, 1945

Laughter

Jesus pities not all those who laugh, but those who do nothing else but laugh.
—Lyman Abbott, *Christ's Secret of Happiness*, 1907

Laughter is satanic, and, therefore, profoundly human. It is born of Man's conception of his own superiority. . . . It is at once a sign of infinite grandeur and of infinite wretchedness; of infinite wretchedness by comparison with the absolute Being who exists as an idea in Man's mind; of an infinite grandeur by comparison with the animals.
—Charles Baudelaire, *The Essence of Laughter*, 1855

There is a kind of smiling and joyful laughter, for anything I know, which may stand with sober gravity, and with the best man's piety.
—Richard Bernard, *The Isle of Man*, 1626

He who laughs at everything is as big a fool as he who weeps at everything.
—Baltasar Gracián, *The Art of Worldly Wisdom*, 1647

Laughter does not seem to be a sin, but it leads to sin.
—St. John Chrysostom, *Homilies*, c. 388

It is the heart that is not yet sure of its God that is afraid to laugh in His presence.
—George Macdonald, *Sir Gibbie*, 1879

If any laughter of ours does make us incapable of weeping, incapable of entering into the sorrow of the world in which we are dwelling, we ought to feel that there is misery and death in that laughter.
—Frederick D. Maurice (1805–70), *Sermons*

God is the creator of laughter that is good.
—Philo, *The Worse Attacks the Better*, A.D. 33

Weep before God—laugh before people.
—Proverb

Laughter is the hiccup of a fool.
—John Ray, *English Proverbs*, 1670

LAW

If justice is the end of the law, the law the work of the prince, and the prince the image of God, it follows of necessity that the law of the prince should be modelled on the law of God.
—Jean Bodin, *The Six Books of the Republic*, 1579

True law is right reason in agreement with nature; it is of universal application, unchanging and everlasting.
—Cicero, *De Republica*, c. 50 B.C.

It seems to me that religion is part of life. To strike down laws because they are partially religiously motivated would be to strike down most laws.
—Ronald Garet, in *The New York Times*, March 16, 1987

All human laws are fed by the one Divine law; it prevaileth as far as it listeth, and sufficeth for all, and surviveth all.
—Heraclitus (535–475 B.C.), *Fragments*

Now we know that the law is good, if any one uses it lawfully.
—*Holy Bible*, I Timothy 1:8

You shall have one law for the sojourner and for the native; for I am the Lord your God.
—*Holy Bible*, Leviticus 24:22

Where a law is enacted contrary to reason, or to the eternal law, or to some ordinance of God, obedience is unlawful, lest, while obeying man, we become disobedient to God.
—Pope Leo XIII, *Libertas Humana*, 1888

Our legal system would be rendered useless and void if men refused to obey the laws, and the axiom "You can't legislate morality" were accepted.
—Joseph T. Leonard, *Theology and Race Relations*, 1963

There never was any remarkable lawgiver amongst any people who did not resort to divine authority, as otherwise his laws would not have been accepted by the people.
—Niccolò Machiavelli, *The Prince*, 1513

Law cannot restrain evil; for the freedom of man is such that he can make the keeping of the law the instrument of evil.
—Reinhold Niebuhr, *The Nature and Destiny of Man*, II, 1943

Since Christian beliefs are those of but a minority of the people in the world, it follows that we must root our international law in the living beliefs of *all* the religions of the world.
—F.S.C. Northrop, *Man, Nature and God*, 1962

The obligation of repressing moral and religious offenses cannot be an ultimate norm of action. It must be subordinated to higher and more generous norms which, in certain circumstances, allow and even perhaps make it obvious that it is better not to prevent error in order to bring about a greater good.
—Pope Pius XII, address, December 1953

Human law has the true nature of law only in so far as it corresponds to right reason, and therefore is derived from the eternal law. In so far as it falls short of right reason, a law is said to be a wicked law; and so, lacking the true nature of law, it is rather a kind of violence.
—St. Thomas Aquinas, *Summa Theologiae*, 1272

The function of civil law is not to teach theology or even the moral views of the legislator. . . . The morality of divorce, birth control, liquor traffic and the like are one thing. Civil legislation about them is quite another.
—Gustave Weigel, *Catholic Theology in Dialogue*, 1960

The law that will work is merely the summing up in legislative form of the moral judgment that the community has already reached.
—Woodrow Wilson, address, December 1915

LIARS AND LIES

Lying is wrong even to save chastity.
—St. Augustine, *On Lying*, c. 395

It is not the lie that passeth through the mind, but the lie that sinketh in, and settleth in it, that doth the hurt.
—Francis Bacon, *Essays*, 1597

The gravest sins are forbidden in Scripture once, but falsehood is forbidden many times.
—M. Cohen, *Sefer Hasidim Zuta*, 1573

If a man has transgressed one law, and speaks lies, and scoffs at another world, there is no evil he will not do.
—*Dhammapada*, c. 5th century B.C.

> Every violation of truth is not only a sort of suicide in the liar, but is a stab at the health of human society.
> —Ralph Waldo Emerson, *Prudence*, 1841

> The most mischievous liars are those who keep sliding on the verge of truth.
> —J.C. and A.W. Hare, *Guesses at Truth*, 1827

> Sin has many tools, but a lie is the handle which fits them all.
> —Oliver Wendell Holmes, *The Autocrat of the Breakfast Table*, 1858

> His speech was smoother than butter, yet war was in his heart; his words were softer than oil, yet were they drawn swords.
> —*Holy Bible*, Psalms 55:21

> You shall not bear false witness against your neighbor.
> —*Holy Bible*, Exodus 20:16

> Sweeter than truth which aims at ill
> Is falsehood from a well-meant will.
> —Shaikh Saadi, *Gulistan*, c. 1265

> They who lie set the Lord at nought, and become defrauders of the Lord. . . . For they received from him a spirit free of lies.
> —*Shepherd of Hermas*, c. 148

> False words are not only evil in themselves, but they infect the soul with evil.
> —Socrates, in "Apology," Plato, *Dialogues*, 399 B.C.

> Let none of you attend the liar's words and demands. He leads house, clan, district and country into misery and destruction. Resist them, then, with weapons.
> —*Zend-Avesta*, 6th century B.C.

LIFE AND DEATH

> Nothing seems so tragic to one who is old as the death of one who is young, and this alone proves that life is a good thing.
> —Zoe Akins, *The Portrait of Tiero*, 1920

Life is indeed a flower which a morning withers and the beat of a passing wing breaks down; it is the widow's lamp, which the slightest blast of air extinguishes.

—Henri Amiel, *Journal*, 1860

Dying is easy work compared with living. Dying is a moment's transition; living a transaction of years.

—Maltbie D. Babcock, *Thoughts for Everyday Living*, 1901

We get to think of life as an inexhaustible well. Yet everything happens only a certain number of times, and a very small number, really. . . . How many more times will you watch the full moon rise? Perhaps twenty. And yet it all seems limitless.

—Jacqueline Bisset, in *Lear's*, February 1991

In the midst of life we are in death.

—*Book of Common Prayer*, 1662

People say that what we're all seeking is a meaning for life. I don't think that's what we're really seeking. I think that what we're seeking is an experience of being alive, so that our life experiences on the purely physical plane will have resonances within our own innermost being and reality, so that we actually feel the rapture of being alive.

—Joseph Campbell, *The Power of Myth*, with Bill Moyers, 1988

A little gleam of time between two eternities; no second chance to us forever more!

—Thomas Carlyle, *Heroes and Hero Worship*, 1841

What is life but the flower or the fruit which falls, when ripe, but yet which ever fears the untimely frost?

—*Dhammapada*, c. 5th century B.C.

Life is given to us on the definite understanding that we boldly defend it to the last.

—Charles Dickens, *The Chimes*, 1844

Our critical day is not the very day of our death; but the whole course of our life.

—John Donne, sermon, February 29, 1627

Though our natural life were no life, but rather a continual dying, yet we have two lives besides that, an eternal life reserved for heaven, but yet a heavenly life too, a spiritual life, even in this world.

—John Donne, sermon, January 29, 1625

The man who regards life . . . as meaningless is not merely unfortunate but almost disqualified for life.

—Albert Einstein, *The World As I See It*, 1934

The fate of the poor shepherd, who, blinded and lost in the snowstorm, perishes in a drift within a few feet of the cottage door, is an emblem of the state of man. On the brink of the waters of life and truth, we are miserably dying.

—Ralph Waldo Emerson, *The Poet*, 1844

For we brought nothing into the world, and we cannot take anything out of the world.

—*Holy Bible*, I Timothy 6:7-8

I call heaven and earth to witness against you this day, that I have set before you life and death, blessing and curse; therefore choose life, that both you and your descendants may live.

—*Holy Bible*, Deuteronomy 30:19

Life is a narrow vale between the cold and barren peaks of two eternities. We strive in vain to look beyond the heights. We cry aloud, and the only answer is the echo of our wailing cry.

—Robert G. Ingersoll, at his brother's grave, 1879

Be not afraid of life. Believe that life *is* worth living and your belief will help create the fact.

—William James, *The Will to Believe and Other Essays*, 1896

The wise man looks at death with honesty, dignity and calm, recognizing that the tragedy it brings is inherent in the great gift of life.

—Corliss Lamont, in *Journal of Philosophy*, January 1965

The common thread in all great religions is the spiritual quest and realization of the hero-founder that enables him to confront and transcend death and to provide a model for generations of believers to do the same. Thus the lives of Buddha, Moses, Christ, and Mohammed came to encompass various combinations of spirituality, revelation, and ultimate ethical principles that could, for themselves and their followers, divest death of its "sting" of annihilation.
—Robert Jay Lifton, *The Broken Connection*, 1979

Human life, regarded from a merely individual point of view, is deeply sad. Glory, power, grandeur, all perish,—playthings of a day, broken at night.
—Joseph Mazzini, *Essays*, 1887

Only if we suppose that the present life of human beings has an end which lies in part beyond the limits of the present natural order . . . can we find a rational meaning and explanation for human life as we see it.
—Hastings Rashdall, *The Theory of Good and Evil*, II, 1907

Rejoice in this dark hour that thy life dwells in the midst of a wider and larger life.
—Jean Paul Richter, *Reminiscences of the Best Hours of Life*, 1841

What is this world? A dream within a dream—as we grow older each step is an awakening. The Grave the last sleep?—no; it is the last and final awakening.
—Walter Scott (1771–1832), *Journal*

Life is nothing but a journey to death.
—Seneca, *Ad Polybium de consolatione*, c. A.D. 44

Life, like a dome of many-coloured glass,
Stains the white radiance of Eternity,
Until Death tramples it to fragments.
—Percy Bysshe Shelley, *Adonais*, 1820

To be what we are, and to become what we are capable of becoming, is the only end of life.
—Robert Louis Stevenson, *Familiar Studies of Men and Books*, 1881

When all is done, human life is, at the greatest and the best, but like a forward child that must be played with and humored a little to keep it quiet till it falls asleep, and then the care is over.
—William Temple, *Essays: Of Poetry*, c. 1690

To live a good life; to die a holy death—that is everything.
—St. Theresa of Lisieux (1873–97), *Autobiography*

Let us so live that when we come to die even the undertaker will be sorry.
—Mark Twain (1835–1910), *Notebook*, 1935

LITERATURE

The Lord created Heaven and Earth and, as an immediate afterthought, writers.
—Fred de Cordova, *Johnny Came Lately*, 1988

Novelists seldom write for a believing public; they take for granted that their readers will be as themselves, that is, human beings without a definite standard of morals, without preconceived conceptions of truth.
—Martin C. D'Arcy, *The Nature of Belief*, 1958

If we ask what literature is about, we have to answer that it is about the mystery of the human heart and its passage through time.
—Hugh Dinwiddy, *The Springs of Morality*, 1956

The whole of modern literature is corrupted by what I call Secularism . . . it is simply unaware of, simply cannot understand the meaning of, the primacy of the supernatural over the natural life.
—T.S. Eliot, "Religion and Literature," in *Selected Prose*, 1935

There are leaders of the Church who regard literature as a means to one end, edification. That end may be of the highest value, of far higher value than literature, but it belongs to a different world. Literature has nothing to do with edification.
—Graham Greene, *The Lost Childhood and Other Essays*, 1951

Literature, in the meantime—real, great literature—is an instrument of the battle over the fate of man, it is a cry of protest and a voice of hope; it is responsibility.
—Ryszard Kapuscinski, in *New Perspectives Quarterly*, Spring 1989

Literature is the memory of humanity.
—Isaac Bashevis Singer, in *U.S. News & World Report*, November 6, 1978

The subject of the imaginative writer is necessarily men as they are behaving, not as they ought to behave.
—Allen Tate, in *The New Republic*, January 5, 1953

LITURGY

A liturgical movement unaccompanied by a contemplative movement is a kind of romanticism, an escape from time.
—Hans Urs von Balthasar, *Prayer*, 1962

Christianity is a liturgical religion. The Church is first of all a worshipping community. Worship comes first, doctrine and discipline second.
—Georges Florovsky, *One Church*, 1959

Without the worship of the heart liturgical prayer becomes a matter of formal routine; its technically finished performance may give aesthetic pleasure, but the spirit has gone out from it.
—Aelred Graham, *Catholicism and the World Today*, 1952

The liturgy does not say "I" but "We," . . . The liturgy is not celebrated by the individual, but by the body of the faithful.
—Romano Guardini, *The Spirit of the Liturgy*, 1935

The prayers of the liturgy alone can be uttered with impunity by any man, for it is the peculiarity of these inspirations that they adapt themselves in all ages to every state of the mind and every phase of life.
—J.K. Huysmans, *The Cathedral*, 1898

The great danger is that liturgy creates a world of things over against the secular, instead of a vision of the sacredness of the secular.
—Eric James, *The Roots of the Liturgy*, 1962

The liturgical art of the services of the church, like the architectural art of the cathedrals, rouses a response in me which cannot be awakened by any modern service or by any modern building.
—Kirsopp Lake, *The Religion of Yesterday and Tomorrow*, 1925

Great liturgies cannot be manufactured; they grow.
—Arnold Lunn, *Within That City*, 1936

"Liturgy" turns into "contemplation" as soon as our prayer ceases to be a search for God and turns into a celebration, by interior experience, of the fact that we have found Him.
—Thomas Merton, *Bread in the Wilderness*, 1953

Liturgy is . . . not merely something which the individual man or men united in the Church give to God. Liturgy is also the instrument or organ, through which God gives His grace to men.
—Pius Parsch, *Orate Frates*, XXI, 1946–47

The people are better instructed in the truths of the Faith by the annual celebration of our sacred mysteries than by even the weightiest pronouncements of the teachings of the Church.
—Pope Pius XI, December 11, 1925

The liturgy cannot simply be restored, as Williamsburg was restored. The liturgy must be re-inserted into the center of Christian life in the twentieth century. It is not a question of making that life relevant to liturgy; the liturgy must be made relevant to that life.
—Philip Scharper, in *The Critic*, August-September 1962

LONELINESS

The human spirit has fashioned its prayers out of its loneliness, its persuasion of being something other than earth-dust or star-dust.
—Gaius Glenn Atkins, *Religion in Our Times*, 1932

The natural world is the larger sacred community to which we belong. To be alienated from this community is to become destitute in all that makes us human.
—Thomas Berry, in *Creation Spirituality*, September/October 1990

No soul is desolate as long as there is a human being for whom it can feel trust and reverence.
—George Eliot, *Romola*, 1863

Loneliness is a game of pretense, for the essential loneliness is an escape from an inescapable God.
—Walter Farrell, *The Looking Glass*, 1951

The tight boundaries of rural, neighborhood, family-centered America have burst, breaking the bonds of exclusiveness and duty, freeing people for alternatives that seem to have no end, so much do they promise. And yet—the problem of loneliness. When it is mentioned, even the eyes of those who tend to deny its existence flicker inward for a moment.

—Suzanne Gordon, *Lonely in America*, 1976

The secret to overcoming a feeling of loneliness is not going *outside* to meet people. That will only keep you from being alone. The secret is going *inside* yourself, to realize your true kinship with God and with all the human beings that he created.

—Amy Grant, 1992

Loneliness is never more cruel than when it is felt in close propinquity with someone who has ceased to communicate.

—Germaine Greer, *The Female Eunuch*, 1971

Pray that your loneliness may spur you into finding something to live for, great enough to die for.

—Dag Hammarskjold, *Diaries*, 1951

Thou hast caused lover and friend to shun me; my companions are in darkness.

—*Holy Bible*, Psalms 88:18

Our present economic, social and international arrangements are based, in large measure, upon organized lovelessness.

—Aldous Huxley, *The Perennial Philosophy*, 1944

My life is spent in a perpetual alternation between two rhythms, the rhythm of attracting people for fear I may be lonely and the rhythm of trying to get rid of them because I know that I am bored.

—C.E.M. Joad, in *The Observer*, December 12, 1948

The vast loneliness is awe-inspiring—the earth from here is a vast ovation to the big vastness of space.

—Jim Lovell, 1970

All religion, all life, all expression comes down to this: to the effort of the human soul to break through its barrier of loneliness, of intolerable loneliness, and make some contact with another seeking soul, or with what all souls seek, which is (by any name) God.

—Don Marquis, *Chapters for the Orthodox*, 1934

People who like themselves and realize that they are God's creation, are never really lonely. It is only when we lose track of our own value, and our personal connection with the divine, that we are desperate for others to distract us from our loss.

—Richard Nelson, *Island Within*, 1989

Loneliness is dangerous. It's bad for you to be alone, to be lonely, because if aloneness does not lead to God, it leads to the devil. It leads to self.

—Joyce Carole Oates, "Shame," in *The Wheel of Love and Other Stories*, 1970

We are never alone. We are all aspects of one great being. No matter how far apart we are, the air links us.

—Yoko Ono, 1967

We will recognize that each person needs to nourish and be nourished by many persons. . . . It is right, even necessary, to make yourselves available to one another in new loving, caring, and fulfilling ways—without the spectres of old guilts.

—Quaker newsletter, in *Aquarian Conspiracy*, 1980

Loneliness is the poverty of self; solitude is the richness of self.

—May Sarton, *Mrs. Stevens Hears the Mermaids Singing*, 1965

Loneliness is a terrible blindness.

—Christina Stead, *Dark Places of the Heart*, 1966

Loneliness and the feeling of being unwanted is the most terrible poverty.

—Mother Teresa, in *Time*, 1975

Often we know the lonely and fail to reach out in love. We may be shy or find it hard to show love. We may feel that we are being insincere if we try. Then let us accept ourselves as we are—God's imperfect instruments—and pray that he will use us despite our shortcomings.

—Mother Teresa, 1980

Loneliness is the stuff of hell; it is a big price to pay for power and glory.
—Gerald Vann, *The Heart of Man*, 1945

The soul hardly ever realizes it, but whether he is a believer or not, his loneliness is really a homesickness for God.
—Hubert van Zeller, *We Die Standing Up*, 1949

LOVE

Love is the expansion of two natures in such fashion that each includes the other, each is enriched by the other.
—Felix Adler, *Life and Destiny*, 1913

Love at its highest point—love, sublime, unique, invincible—leads us straight to the brink of the great abyss, for it speaks to us directly of the infinite and of eternity. It is eminently religious.
—Henri Amiel, *Journal*, September 2, 1862

In order that we might receive that love whereby we should love, we were ourselves loved, while as yet we had it not.
—St. Augustine, *De gratia Christi*, 426

Let us have *love* and more love; a love that melts all opposition, a love that conquers all foes, a love that sweeps away all barriers, a love that aboundeth in charity, a large-heartedness, tolerance, forgiveness and noble striving, a love that triumphs over all obstacles.
—Abdul Baha (1844–1921), *I Heard Him Say*

The happy man is he who lives the life of love, not for the honors it may bring, but for the life itself.
—R.J. Baughan, *Undiscovered Country*, 1946

Medical science has seen love for quite a while as having an evolutionary cause: It's for the procreation of the species. The view of the body as a machine has had a rather widespread effect. One machine falls in love with another—is that the story?
—Saul Bellow, in *U.S. News & World Report*, September 7, 1987

It is only the souls that do not love that go empty in this world.
—Robert Hugh Benson, *The History of Richard Raynal Solitary*, 1906

303

Love or perish; it is not a new commandment but its full impact was hidden from us, because we had not known, up to
the recent past, that we were capable of mass murder and
even of cosmic murder.

—Philip Berrigan, *No More Strangers*, 1965

Love is never abstract. It does not adhere to the universe of
the planet or the nation or the institution or the profession,
but to the singular sparrows of the street, the lilies of the
field, "the least of these my brethren." Love is not, by its
own desire, heroic. It is heroic only when compelled to be. It
exists by its willingness to be anonymous, humble, and
unrewarded.

—Wendell Berry, "Word and Flesh," *What Are People For?*, 1990

Love, being the highest principle, is the virtue of all virtues,
from whence they flow forth. Love, being the greatest
majesty, is the power of all powers, from whence they sever-
ally operate.

—Jakob Boehme (1575–1624), *A Dialogue between a Scholar and His Master*

Love is the most freely willed of any activity of which we are
able to think.

—Emil Brunner, *The Divine-Human Encounter*, 1944

He who loves brings God and the world together.

—Martin Buber, *At the Turning*, 1952

Let the burden be never so heavy, love makes it light.

—Robert Burton, *Anatomy of Melancholy*, III, 1621

The attraction of one creature for another, even when condemned by reason for its passionate origin, is always worthy
of respect, because it reveals to us something of the order of
creation.

—A. Carré, *Companions for Eternity*, 1947

Love is too strong to be overcome by anything except flight,
nor ought mortal creature to be so presumptuous as to
stand the encounter, since there is need of something more
than human, and indeed heavenly, powers to vanquish human passion.

—Miguel de Cervantes, *Don Quixote*, 1615

Love is a desire of the whole being to be united to some thing, or some being, felt necessary to its completeness, by the most perfect means that nature permits, and reason dictates.

—Samuel Taylor Coleridge, *Lectures on Shakespeare and Milton*, 1808

The Master said: "Love of daring, inflamed by poverty, leads to crime: a man without love, if deeply ill-treated, will turn to crime."

—Confucius, *Sayings of*, 5th century B.C.

As the artist creates patterns in a vain effort to catch a beauty which escapes him, because it is behind his thought and never realized in what he sees, so the love of God beckons and draws the soul of man, though he has never heard the sacred Name.

—Martin C. D'Arcy, *The Nature of Belief*, 1958

If you have a particular faith or religion, that is good. But you can survive without it if you have love, compassion, and tolerance. The clear proof of a person's love of God is if that person genuinely shows love to fellow human beings.

—Dalai Lama, *For the Love of God*, 1990

God's love for us is a mystery and a joy, balanced by the mystery and sorrow of our coldness toward Him.

—James J. Daly, *The Road to Peace*, 1936

The theologian is right. Why not admit it? More than anything else the world needs love.

—Sebastian De Grazia, *The Political Community*, 1948

Let, therefore, no man love anything; loss of the beloved is evil. Those who love nothing, and hate nothing, have no fetters.

—*Dhammapada*, ch. XVI, c. 5th century B.C.

If the higher companionship which love should be does not make men and women nobler, more generous, more ready to sacrifice even their beautiful life for a lofty purpose, there is a suspicion that their love is not love but a combination of egoisms.

—Ernest Dimnet, *What We Live By*, 1932

Love all God's creation, both the whole and every grain of sand. Love every leaf, every ray of light. Love the animals, love the plants, love each separate thing. If thou love each thing thou wilt perceive the mystery of God in all.
—Feodor Dostoevsky, *The Brothers Karamazov*, 1880

True love—the kind we ordinarily attribute to God—is foolish, risky and absolutely necessary. It brings to a standstill the ordinary games of distrust.
—Gail McGrew Eifnig, "Love and Distrust in the Novels of John Le Carré," *The Christian Century*, February 26, 1992

And let no men's sins dishearten thee: love a man even in his sin, Love is our highest word, and the synonym of God.
—Ralph Waldo Emerson, "Love," *Essays*, 1841

No one who is a lover of money, a lover of pleasure, or a lover of glory, is likewise a lover of mankind; but only he who is a lover of virtue.
—Epictetus (1st century), *Enchiridion*

The divine love hovers over the life of man with the vivacious persistence of April calling earth to life.
—Walter Farrell, *The Looking Glass*, 1951

Love is the abridgment of all theology.
—St. Francis de Sales, *Treatise on the Love of God*, 1607

Love is union under the condition of preserving one's integrity.
—Erich Fromm, *The Art of Loving*, 1956

There is no other God than Truth. . . . To see the universal and all-pervading Spirit of Truth face to face one must be able to love the meanest of creation as oneself.
—Mohandas K. Gandhi, *Autobiography*, 1927

Keep Hatred from you; let nothing tempt Your mind to violence;—hold on to love.
—*Gatha Spenta*, Yesna, 7th century B.C.

Love is man's natural endowment, but he doesn't know how to use it. He refuses to recognize the power of love because of his love of power.
—Dick Gregory, *The Shadow That Scares Me*, 1968

A Zaddick once cried from the depth of his heart: "Would I could love the best of men as tenderly as God loves the worst."
—*The Hasidic Anthology*, 1963

It is to the credit of human nature, that, except where its selfishness is brought into play, it loves more readily than it hates.
—Nathaniel Hawthorne, *The Scarlet Letter*, 1850

Love of men leads to the love of God.
—Hindustani proverb

Greater love has no man than this, that a man lay down his life for his friends.
—*Holy Bible*, John 15:13

Love never ends; as for prophecies, they will pass away; as for tongues, they will cease; as for knowledge, it will pass away.
—*Holy Bible*, I Corinthians 13:8

Many waters cannot quench love, neither can floods drown it.
—*Holy Bible*, Song of Solomon 8:7

The love we give away is the only love we keep.
—Elbert Hubbard (1859–1915), *Notebook*

Love has no middle term; either it destroys or it saves.
—Victor Hugo, *Les Misérables*, 1862

Of all the worn, smudged, dog-eared words in our vocabulary, "love" is surely the grubbiest, smelliest, slimiest. . . . And yet it has to be pronounced, for, after all, Love is the last word.
—Aldous Huxley, *Tomorrow and Tomorrow and Tomorrow*, 1952

Were there left but one rock with two loving souls upon it, that rock would have as thoroughly moral a constitution as any possible world which the eternities and immensities could harbor.
—William James, *The Will To Believe*, 1896

Human love and the delights of friendship, out of which are
built the memories that endure, are also to be treasured up
as hints of what shall be hereafter.
—Bede Jarrett, *Meditations for Layfolk*, 1915

Creative love flowing freely among all persons and organizing
their common life—this I take to be the meaning of God in
history.
—F. Ernest Johnson, *The Social Gospel Re-examined*, 1940

The most prevalent failure of Christian love is the failure to
express it.
—Paul E. Johnson, *Christian Love*, 1951

Love means that the attributes of the lover are changed into
those of the Beloved.
—Junayd of Bagdad (died 910), in Al Marghināni, *al-Hidāya*

If love has come to be less often a sin, it has come also to be
less often a supreme privilege.
—Joseph Wood Krutch, in *The Atlantic*, August 1928

When you lay dying, what it's about is the intimacy you've
known, the touch of another human being. Ultimately, what
makes your life worthwhile are the other people you've cared
about.
—Sherry Lansing, in *Cosmopolitan*, August 1989

He who defends with love will be secure; Heaven will save
him, and protect him with love.
—Lao-tzu, *Tao Te Ching*, 6th century B.C.

Not many men may be willing to die for love these days. But
you can't escape the fact that millions are dying daily for the
very *lack* of it.
—John E. Large, *The Small Needle of Doctor Large*, 1962

Love doesn't just sit there, like a stone, it has to be made,
like bread; re-made all the time, made new.
—Ursula K. Le Guin, *The Lathe of Heaven*, 1971

The only place outside Heaven where you can be perfectly
safe from all the dangers and perturbations of love is Hell.
—C.S. Lewis, *The Four Loves*, 1960

God's love is primarily not a response to man's love, but an appeal to it.

—Edwin Lewis, *A Philosophy of the Christian Revelation*, 1940

Love is a force. . . . It is not a result; it is a cause. It is not a product. It is a power, like money, or steam or electricity. It is valueless unless you can give something else by means of it.

—Anne Morrow Lindbergh, *Locked Rooms and Open Doors*, 1974

If you love a person you love him or her in their stark reality, and refuse to shut your eyes to their defects and errors.

—John Macmurray, *Reason and Emotion*, 1936

Love is the high nobility of heaven, the peaceful home of man. To lack love, when nothing hinders us, is to lack wisdom.

—*Mencius*, c. 300 B.C.

"Love" is unfortunately a much misused word. It trips easily off Christian tongue—so easily that one gets the impression it means others ought to love us for standing on their necks.

—Thomas Merton, "Toward a Theology of Resistance," *Faith and Violence*, 1968

He who is not loving to God's creatures and to his own children, God will not be loving to him.

—Mohammed, *Speeches and Table-Talk of*, 7th century

Love is immortality struggling within a mortal frame, and all the mortal pains that flesh is heir to become golden with immortal life as they are touched by love.

—A. Victor Murray, *Personal Experience and the Historic Faith*, 1939

When it is said that God loves man this is not a judgment on what man is like, but on what God is like.

—Anders Nygren, *Agape and Eros*, 1953

Love is sure to be something less than human if it is not something more.

—Coventry Patmore, *The Rod, the Root, and the Flower*, 1895

Nuptial loves bears the clearest marks of being nothing other than the rehearsal of a communion of a higher nature.

—Coventry Patmore, *Principles in Art*, 1889

God loves these three: the person who does not get angry;
the one who does not get drunk, and the one who does not
insist upon his privileges.

—*Pesahim, Talmud*, c. 500

Every creature, being a more or less remote derivation of infinite love, is therefore the fruit of love and does not move except through love.

—Pope Pius XII, address, October 23, 1940

In all conflict with evil, the method to be used is love and
not force. When we use evil methods to defeat evil, it is evil
that wins.

—Sarvepalli Radhakrishnan, *East and West*, 1955

Mysterious is the fusion of two loving spirits: each takes the
best from the other, but only to give it back again enriched
with love.

—Romain Rolland, *Jean Christophe*, 1912

Love is a brilliant illustration of a principle everywhere dis-
coverable: namely, that human reason lives by turning the
friction of material forces into the light of ideal goods.

—George Santayana, *Reason in Society*, 1906

Christ utterly believed and proved with His life that love is
more potent than any possible array of mere physical force.

—Francis B. Sayre, in *Reader's Digest*, July 1948

Love is a mutual self-giving which ends in self-recovery.

—Fulton J. Sheen, *Three to Get Married*, 1951

If matter and energy and chance are all there is, it takes a
man of most unusual courage to build an unselfish love for
humanity on such foundations.

—Edmund W. Sinnott, *Two Roads to Truth*, 1953

Love is the supreme value around which all moral values can
be integrated into one ethical system valid for the whole of
humanity.

—Pitirim A. Sorokin, *The Ways and Power of Love*, 1954

It is impossible to repent of love. The sin of love does not
exist.

—Muriel Spark, in *The New Yorker*, July 10, 1965

So long as we love we serve; so long as we are loved by others, I would almost say we are indispensable; and no man is useless while he has a friend.
—Robert Louis Stevenson, *Lay Morals and Other Papers*, 1898

In love we find a joy which is ultimate because it is the ultimate truth.
—Rabindranath Tagore, *Creative Unity*, 1922

The well of life is love, and he who dwelleth not in love is dead.
—John Tauler (1300–61), sermon for Thursday in Easter Week

Love is the greatest thing that God can give us; for Himself is love; and it is the greatest thing we can give to God.
—Jeremy Taylor, *Holy Living*, 1650

Love in all its subtleties is nothing more and nothing less, than the more or less direct trace marked on the heart of the elements by the psychical convergence of the universe upon itself.
—Pierre Teilhard de Chardin, *The Phenomenon of Man*, 1955

Love has a hem to her garment that reaches to the very dust. It sweeps the stains from the streets and lanes, and because it can, it must.
—Mother Teresa, *Contemplative in the Heart of the World*, 1985

Love is the result of an identification—the identifying of our wills with the will of God, and our fate with that of all men, however obscure, fallen and needy.
—Rose Terlin, *Christian Faith and Social Action*, 1940

If divine love is the author of all existence, it follows that nothing can exist wherein love cannot find expression.
—A.C. Turner, *Concerning Prayer*, 1916

How terrible when people are led to believe, or left to believe, that once they are in love they have nothing to do but live happily ever after, they have nothing further to learn.
—Gerald Vann, *The Heart of Man*, 1945

Nobody is worthy to be loved. The fact that God loves man shows us that in the divine order of ideal things it is written that eternal love is to be given to what is eternally unworthy.
—Oscar Wilde, *De Profundis*, 1905

LOVE

There is a land of the living and a land of the dead and the bridge is love, the only survival, the only meaning.
—Thornton Wilder, *The Bridge of San Luis Rey*, 1927

You must act in your friend's interest whether it pleases him or not; the object of love is to serve, not to win.
—Woodrow Wilson, address, Princeton, May 9, 1907

LUST

Lust is an appetite by which temporal goods are preferred to eternal goods.
—St. Augustine, *On Lying*, c. 395

When a man is enjoying the gratification of sexual passion or the pleasure of eating he ought to feel the presence of poison and be reminded of original sin. That is the nature of every enjoyment connected with lust.
—Nicholas Berdyaev, *The Destiny of Man*, 1937

Lust is a mysterious wound in the side of humanity; or rather at the very source of its life! To confound this lust in man with that desire which unites the sexes is like confusing a tumor with the very organ which it devours.
—Georges Bernanos, *The Diary of a Country Priest*, 1937

Too often the saint has agreed with the debauchee that the only difference between married love and lust is that one is allowcd and the other is not.
—Sydney Cave, *The Christian Way*, 1949

As rain breaks through an ill-thatched roof, so lust breaks through an ill-trained mind.
—*Dhammapada*, c. 5th century B.C.

Lust . . . is both prevalent and reprehensible; but it may be doubted whether it does as much harm in the world day by day as the less socially disreputable misdemeanors of anger and envy.
—Aelred Graham, *Christian Thought and Action*, 1951

What causes wars, and what causes fightings among you? Is it not your passions that are at war in your members? You desire and do not have; so you kill. And you covet and cannot obtain; so you fight and wage war. You do not have, because you do not ask. You ask and do not receive, because you ask wrongly, to spend it on your passions.
—*Holy Bible*, James 4:1-3

In all enjoyment there is a choice between enjoying the other and enjoying yourself through the instrumentality of the other. The first is the enjoyment of love, the second is the enjoyment of lust. When people enjoy themselves through each other, that is merely mutual lust.

—John Macmurray, *Reason and Emotion*, 1936

Love grows, Lust wastes by Enjoyment, and the Reason is, that one springs from an Union of Souls, and the other from an Union of Sense.

—William Penn, *Some Fruits of Solitude*, 1718

What is essentially wrong with lust is not that the body is used carnally but that the situation is such, the human relations are such, that this particular use of the body is the implementation of a wrong spirit.

—James A. Pike, *Beyond Anxiety*, 1952

Marriage and Divorce

People wouldn't get divorced for such trivial reasons, if they didn't get married for such trivial reasons.

—Anonymous

Marriage is that relation between man and woman in which the independence is equal, the dependence mutual, and the obligation reciprocal.

—Louis K. Anspacher, address, December 30, 1934

A divorce is like an amputation; you survive, but there's less of you.

—Margaret Atwood, *Time*, 1973

The union of man and wife is from God, so divorce is from the devil.

—St. Augustine, *On the Gospel of St. John, Trac.* VIII, c. 416

The great thing about marriage is that it enables one to be alone without feeling loneliness.

—Gerald Brenan, *Thoughts in a Dry Season*, 1978

It may be bad, it may be good, as it is a cross and calamity on the one side, so 'tis a sweet delight, an incomparable happiness, a blessed estate, a most unspeakable benefit, a sole content, on the other, 'tis all in the proof.

—Robert Burton, *Anatomy of Melancholy*, III, 1621

Success in marriage requires continence as well as potency. In other words, character is indispensable in well-ordered sexual life.

—Alexis Carrel, in *Reader's Digest*, July 1939

Each marriage in a divorcing society is a monogamous one so long as it lasts, but, since all marriages in such a society are permanent by accident rather than permanent in principle, what a divorcing society tends to produce is a kind of serialized polygamy and polyandry.

—J.V.L. Casserley, *The Bent World*, 1955

The Christian ideal of marriage is that of indissoluble unity. . . . It is difficult to see on what ground failure in marriage should be treated as if it was the one failure for which the penitent cannot be forgiven.

—Sydney Cave, *The Christian Way*, 1949

315

Where both parties to marriage are Christians, divorce is not thought of even as a possibility, for they have resources of spiritual power sufficient to keep their vow.

—Sydney Cave, *The Christian Way*, 1949

If Americans can be divorced for "incompatibility of temper" I cannot conceive why they are not all divorced. I have known many happy marriages, but never a compatible one.

—G.K. Chesterton, *What Is Wrong with the World*, 1910

What makes a marriage is the consent of the partners, their serious intention to live together in some sense, however dimly perceived, as "one flesh," a union of their two separate existences into still a third existence, the marriage itself. . . . The question of external status is entirely and altogether unnecessary.

—William G. Cole, *Sex in Christianity and Psychoanalysis*, 1955

If anyone should say that on account of heresy or the hardships of co-habitation or a deliberate abuse of one party by the other the marriage tie may be loosened, let him be anathema.

—Council of Trent, Sess. XXIV, cap. 5, 1563

The goal in marriage is not to think alike, but to think together.

—Robert C. Dodds, *Two Together*, 1959

To contract before that they will have no children, makes it no marriage, but an adultery; to deny themselves to one another, is as much against marriage as to give themselves to another.

—John Donne, sermon, May 30, 1621

Any concept of marriage which from the first contemplates divorce is incompatible with the Christian ideal and the clearest lessons of human experience.

—Federal Council of Churches of Christ in America, *Report*, 1932

If the emotional and spiritual welfare of both parents and children in a particular family can be served best by divorce, wrong and cheapjack as divorce commonly is, then love requires it.

—Joseph Fletcher, *Harvard Divinity Bulletin*, October 1959

The holy liberty of marriage has a particular force to extinguish the fire of concupiscence; but the frailty of them that enjoy this liberty passes easily from permission to dissolution.

—St. Francis de Sales, *Introduction to the Devout Life*, 1608

Marriage was not instituted for their happiness, nor sexual instinct implanted for its own sake alone. Rather Nature baits the trap with a romantic allurement to induce men and women to fulfil the purpose it has in view—the continuation of life on earth, the preservation of the species.

—P.J. Gannon, *Holy Matrimony*, 1923

Marriage is the most inviolable and irrevocable of all contracts that were ever formed. Every human compact may be lawfully dissolved but this.

—James Gibbons, *Faith of Our Fathers*, 1876

Being united in one flesh means being united in one life. . . . This community of life is human; while it is primarily of the spirit and must not play the part of the beast, neither must it try impossibly to be angelic.

—Henri Gibert, *Love in Marriage*, 1964

Only a marriage with partners strong enough to risk divorce is strong enough to avoid it.

—Carolyn Heilbrun, "Marriage Is the Message," *Ms.*, August 1974

The married are those who have taken the terrible risk of intimacy and, having taken it, know life without intimacy to be impossible.

—Carolyn Heilbrun, "Marriage Is the Message," *Ms.*, August 1974

The great leveler nowadays is divorce; almost everybody thinks about it, whether because we expect to be happy all the time—daily, weekly—or because we want the smell of brimstone in lives made too affluent and easy.

—Edward Hoagland, "Other Lives," *Harper's Magazine*, July 1973

That there is something intrinsically sacred in the marriage contract is evidenced by the fact that all religions, even the most corrupt, always have regarded it as such and surrounded it with religious rites and ceremonies.

—K.J.I. Hochban, *Canadian Messenger of the Sacred Heart*,
August 1950

Marriage itself is not solely an institution for the propagation of children, but is also for the fruition of that richer fellowship God intended when he saw that it was not good for man to live alone.

—George G. Hockman, *Religion in Modern Life*, 1957

For it is better to marry than to be aflame with passion.

—*Holy Bible*, I Corinthians 7:9

Much marriage difficulty and unhappiness are due to the failure of the partners to accept the fact of their finiteness and its meaning. Instead, they hold themselves up to ideals of performance possible only to God.

—Reul Howe, *Sex and Religion Today*, ed. by S. Doniger, 1953

It is fitting for those who marry—both the men and the women—to accomplish their union with the consent of the Bishop, that their marriage may be according to God, and not according to lust.

—St. Ignatius of Antioch, *Ad Polycarp*, c. 109

It is not strange at all that the spread of divorce in a society is accompanied by a diminishing of public morality in all sectors. . . . True love does not exist if it is not faithful. And it cannot exist if it is not honest. Neither can it be in the concrete vocation of matrimony if there is no full promise that lasts until death. Only indissoluble matrimony will be firm and lasting support for the familial community.

—Pope John Paul II, in *Los Angeles Times*, April 9, 1987

To wed is to bring not only our worldly goods but every potential capacity to create more values in living together. . . . In becoming one these two create a new world that had never existed before.

—Paul E. Johnson, *Christian Love*, 1951

Marriage is the best state for man in general; and every man is a worse man in proportion as he is unfit for the married state.

—Samuel Johnson, *Boswell's Life of*, March 1776

And marry not idolatresses until they believe; for assuredly a slave who believeth is better than an idolatress, though she please you more.

—*Koran*, c. 625

Ye may divorce your wives twice; keep them honorably, or put them away with kindness.
—*Koran*, 7th century

To love means to decide independently to live with an equal partner, and to subordinate oneself to the formation of a new subject, a "we."
—Fritz Kunkel, *Let's Be Normal*, 1929

Sacred union of souls beneath the immortal yoke of love freely promised, pleasures and duties for ever in common, misfortunes borne together, joys of paternity tempered by the anxieties of the future, indescribable mingling of good and evil, virtue ever present to sustain the feebleness of the heart against the chafings and trials of life.
—Jean Baptiste Lacordaire (1802–61), *Thoughts and Teachings of*

Marriage is the only sacrament which transforms a human action into an instrument of the divine action, using a human act which up to then had been used for a natural end.
—Jacques Leclercq, *Marriage a Great Sacrament*, 1951

Divorce is born of perverted morals, and leads, as experience shows, to vicious habits in public and private life.
—Pope Leo XIII, *Arcanum divinae sapientae*, February 10, 1880

In Christian marriage the contract is inseparable from the sacrament, and . . . for this reason the contract cannot be true without being a sacrament as well. . . . Hence it is clear that among Christians every marriage is, in itself and by itself, a sacrament.
—Pope Leo XIII, *Arcanum*, February 1880

The system of law and custom which upheld the old theological conception of marriage is today a crumbling, moth-eaten, dangerously toppling ruin which has served its purpose and now needs to be junked.
—Benjamin Lindsey, *The Companionate Marriage*, 1927

Adam could not be happy even in Paradise without Eve.
—John Lubbock, *Peace and Happiness*, 1909

Christ permitted divorce in case of fornication, and compelled no one to remain single; and Paul preferred us to marry rather than to burn, and seemed quite prepared to grant that a man may marry another women in place of the one he has repudiated.

—Martin Luther, *The Babylonian Captivity*, 1520

We are all made for marriage, as our bodies show and as the Scriptures state.

—Martin Luther, letter, March 27, 1525

It is a fusion of two hearts—the union of two lives—the coming together of two tributaries, which after being joined in marriage, will flow in the same channel in the same direction . . . carrying the same burdens of responsibility and obligation.

—Peter Marshall, in Catherine Marshall, *A Man Called Peter*, 1951

It is God who arrangeth marriages. . . . Those whom he hath once joined he joineth for ever.

—Guru Nanak (1496–1538), in M.A. Macauliffe, *The Sikh Religion*

Between a man and his wife nothing ought to rule but love.

—William Penn, *Some Fruits of Solitude*, 1693

The true meaning of marriage is a sublimation of physical passion, in which the intensity and warmth of natural appetite is retained on the higher level of domestic life, and there enriched with the values of parentage, companionship, and fidelity.

—Ralph Barton Perry, *Puritanism and Democracy*, 1944

Marriage, before being a union of bodies, is first and more intimately a union and harmony of minds, brought about not by any passing affection of sense or heart but by a deliberate and resolute decision of the will; and from this cementing of minds, by God's decree, there arises a sacred and inviolable bond.

—Pope Pius XI, *Casti Connubi*, December 31, 1930

State and the law should take no notice of sexual relations apart from children. . . . No marriage ceremony should be valid unless accompanied by a medical certificate of the woman's pregnancy.

—Bertrand Russell, *Letter to Judge B.J. Lindsey*,
in Benjamin Lindsey, *The Companionate Marriage*, 1927

In marriage reverence is more important even than love. . . .
A steady awareness in each that the other has a kinship with
the eternal.

—F.J. Sheed, *Society and Sanity*, 1953

The greatest illusion of lovers is to believe that the intensity
of their sexual attraction is the guarantee of the perpetuity of
their love. It is because of this failure to distinguish between
the glandular and the spiritual . . . that marriages are so full
of deception.

—Fulton J. Sheen, *Three to Get Married*, 1951

If a man and wife prove deserving, the *Shekhinah* dwells
among them. If not, a fire consumes them.

—*Sotah, Mishnah*, c. 400

When a divorced man marries a divorced woman, there are
four minds in the bed.

—*Talmud: Pesahim*, c. 500

Where the flesh is one, one also is the spirit. Together husband and wife pray, together perform their fasts, mutually
teaching, exhorting, sustaining. Equally they are found in
the church of God, equally at the banquet of God, equally in
persecutions and in refreshments.

—Tertullian, *To His Wife*, c. 206

The essential nature of marriage consists in a certain indivisible union of minds by which each one of the consorts is
bound to keep inviolably his faith with the other.

—St. Thomas Aquinas, *Summa Theologicae* III, q. 29, art. 2, 1272

Before marriage man hovers above life, observes it from without; only in marriage does he plunge into it, entering it
through the personality of another.

—Alexander Yelchaninov (1881–1934), *Fragments of a Diary*

The man who has a wife is far above him who lives in continence; he who keeps a house is far above him who has none:
he who has children is far above him who has none.

—*Zend-Avesta*, 6th century B.C.

MEDITATION

Meditation is like a needle after which comes a thread of
gold, composed of affections, prayers and resolutions.

—St. Alphonsus (1696–1787), *Veritable Épouse de J.C.*

But a saint, whether Buddhist or Christian, who knows his business as a saint is rightly meditative and in proportion to the rightness of his meditations is the depth of his peace.
—Irving Babbitt, *Dhammapada*, 1936

If our Faith is to be made vivid, it must be by meditation.
—John Chapman, *Spiritual Letters of*, 1935

It is meditation that leads us in spirit into the hallowed solitudes wherein we find God alone—in peace, in calm, in silence, in recollection.
—J. Crasset, *A Key to Meditation*, 1907

Without knowledge there is no meditation, without meditation there is no knowledge. He who has knowledge and meditation is near to *Nirvana.*
—*Dhammapada*, c. 5th century B.C.

Meditation is no other thing than the attentive thought, voluntarily reiterated and entertained in the mind, to excite the will to holy and salutary affections and resolutions.
—St. Francis of Sales, *Treatise on the Love of God*, 1607

Whatever is true, whatever is honorable, whatever is just, whatever is pure, whatever is lovely, whatever is gracious, if there is any excellence, if there is anything worthy of praise, think about these things.
—*Holy Bible*, Philippians 4:8

Sleep is the best meditation.
—Dalai Lama, in *People*, September 10, 1979

That happiness which belongs to a mind which by deep meditation has been washed clear of all impurity and has entered within the Self, cannot be described by words; it can be felt by the inward power only.
—*Maitranyana Brahmana Upanishad*, c. 1000 B.C.

It is of primary importance that a certain space of time be allotted daily to meditation on eternal things. No priest can omit this without a serious manifestation of negligence and without a grave loss to his soul.
—Pope Pius X, *Haerent animo*, August 4, 1908

Meditation, because it is free of dogma, of historical commitments and narrow prejudices, because it is practiced for the most part silently and therefore secretly, and because it is practiced by some members of all religions—meditation is a channel for seekers of all faiths or no faith, a river into which many streams can freely flow.

—Bradford Smith, *Meditation: The Inward Art*, 1963

A free man thinks of death least of all things, and his wisdom is a meditation not of death but of life.

—Baruch Spinoza, *Ethics*, 1670

Thou art Divine, I know, O Lord Supreme,
Since God found entrance to my heart through Love.
This taught me that for steady inner growth
Quick and silent meditation's best.

—*Zend-Avesta*, 6th century B.C.

MERCY

Mercy is not ordinarily held to consist in pronouncing judgment on another man's deserts, but in relieving his necessities; in giving aid to the poor, not in inquiring how good they are.

—St. Ambrose, *De Nabuthe*, VIII, 40, 395

Mercy to human beings is more acceptable than bathing at the sixty-eight places of pilgrimage, and than all alms offered there.

—Arjan (died 1606), in M.A. Macauliffe, *The Sikh Religion*

And what is more unworthy of mercy than the unhappy man who is proud—too proud to accept mercy.

—St. Augustine, *De Libero Arbitri*, c. 400

If mercy were a sin, I believe I could not keep from committing it.

—St. Bernard of Clairvaux, (1091–1153), *Life and Works of*, ed. by J. Mabillson

When I survey the occurrences of my life, and call into accounting the Finger of God, I can perceive nothing but an abyss and mass of mercies, either in general to mankind, or in particular to myself.

—Thomas Browne, *Religio Medici*, 1635

The essential and unbounded mercy of my Creator is the foundation of my hope, and a broader and surer the universe cannot give me.

—William Ellery Channing (1780–1842), *Works*

When we live at each other's mercy, we had better learn to be merciful.

—William Sloan Coffin, *Living the Truth in a World of Illusions,* 1985

His mercy hath no relation to time, no limitation in time, it is not first, nor last, but eternal, everlasting.

—John Donne, sermon, St. Paul's Cathedral, London, 1621

The French scholar and Christian, Frederick Ozanam, once said that if God has, as of course He has, some mysteries yet unrevealed to us, no doubt they are secrets of mercy.

—Susan L. Emery, *The Inner Life of the Soul,* 1903

God tempers the wind to the shorn lamb.

—English proverb

There is but one sin which makes us unworthy of that Mercy, and that is if we harden ourselves against it and refuse to hope for it.

—François Fénelon (1651–1715), *Spiritual Letters*

We should feel exceeding joy when we observe how God disperses His mercy with a beneficent hand among men and angels, in heaven and upon earth.

—St. Francis de Sales, *Treatise on the Love of God,* 1607

Ultimately, this is what you go before God for: You've had bad luck and good luck and all you really want in the end is mercy.

—Robert Frost, in *Collier's,* April 27, 1956

Blessed are the merciful, for they shall obtain mercy.

—*Holy Bible,* Matthew 5:7

Mercy imitates God, and disappoints Satan.

—St. John Chrysostom, *Homilies,* c. 388

The simple expression of the publican, "God be merciful to me a sinner," was sufficient to open the floodgates of the Divine compassion.

—St. John Climacus (525–600), *Climax*

The mercy which God shall freely bestow on mankind, *there is* none who can withhold; and what he shall withhold, *there is* none who can bestow, besides him.

—*Koran*, c. 625

God seeth different abilities and frailties of men, which may move His goodness to be merciful to their different improvements in virtue.

—William Law, *Christian Perfection*, 1726

God has decreed that those who show no mercy should also perish without mercy.

—Martin Luther, letter, July 21, 1535

If we can see reasons for mercy that are true reasons and not unjust excuses, God sees many more.

—C.C. Martindale, *God and the Supernatural*, 1920

Unless we learn the meaning of mercy by exercising it towards others, we will never have any real knowledge of what it means to love Christ.

—Thomas Merton, *Life and Holiness*, 1963

The good news of the gospel is that there is a resource of divine mercy which is able to overcome a contradiction within our own souls, which we cannot overcome ourselves.

—Reinhold Niebuhr, *Christianity and Power Politics*, 1940

The more merciful Acts thou dost, the more Mercy thou wilt receive.

—William Penn, *Some Fruits of Solitude*, 1718

Once we recognize we are under Divine Wrath, we become eligible for Divine Mercy.

—Fulton J. Sheen, *Communism and the Conscience of the West*, 1948

Pray to God for mercy until the last shovelful of earth is cast upon thy grave.

—*Talmud*, c. 200–500

The work of divine justice always presupposes the work of mercy; and is founded thereon.

—St. Thomas Aquinas, *Summa Theologiae*, 1272

METAPHYSICS

Metaphysics is valid knowledge of both sensible and suprasensible being. Metaphysics is able to demonstrate the existence of suprasensible being, for it can demonstrate the existence of God, by appealing to the evidence of the senses and the principles of reason, and without any reliance upon articles of religious faith.

—Mortimer Adler, *Vital Speeches*, December 1949

Metaphysics is merely our human attempt to decipher the meaning of things.

—John Elof Boodin, *God and Creation*, 1934

A metaphysician is a man who goes into a dark cellar at midnight without a light looking for a black cat that is not there.

—Ascribed to Baron Bowen of Colwood (1835–94)

I will call metaphysical all those propositions which claim to represent knowledge about something which is over or beyond all experience.

—Rudolf Carnap, *Philosophy and Logical Syntax*, 1935

The principles of knowledge, among which is the explication of the principal attributes of God, of the immateriality of the soul, and of all the clear and simple notions that are in us.

—René Descartes, *Principles of Philosophy*, 1644

Metaphysics begins and ends with God.

—Johannes Scotus Erigena, *The Division of Nature*, 1681

It is in reality nothing but an inventory of all our possessions acquired through Pure Reason, systematically arranged.

—Immanuel Kant, *Critique of Pure Reason*, 1781

Metaphysics has for the real object of its investigation three ideas only: *God, Freedom,* and *Immortality.*

—Immanuel Kant, *Critique of Pure Reason*, 1781

An attempt to learn matters of fact by means of logical or moral or rhetorical constructions.

—George Santayana, *Scepticism and Animal Faith*, 1923

He has spent all his life in letting down empty buckets into empty wells, and he is frittering away his age in trying to draw them up again.

—Sydney Smith, in Lady Holland, *A Memoir of Rev. Sydney Smith*, 1855

Metaphysician: A man who excels in writing with black ink on a black ground.

—Talleyrand (1754–1838), in H.S. Leigh, *Jeux d'Esprit*

Metaphysics consists of two parts, first, that which all men of sense already know, and second, that which they can never know.

—Voltaire, *Letter to Frederick the Great*, April 17, 1737

The culmination and fruit of literary artistic expression, and its final fields of pleasure for the human soul, are in metaphysics, including the mysteries of the spiritual world, the soul itself, and the question of immortal continuation of our identity.

—Walt Whitman, footnote, *Democratic Vistas*, 1871

MIND

Mind seems to be an independent substance implanted within the soul and to be incapable of being destroyed.

—Aristotle (384–322 B.C.), *De Anima*, I, 4, 408b

It is in the mind that God has made man to His image and likeness. . . . If the mind is not to be fathomed even by itself that is because it is the image of God.

—St. Augustine, *De Symboli*, I, 2, c. 395

All the choir of Heaven and furniture of earth . . . have not any substance without a mind.

—George Berkeley, *The Principles of Human Knowledge*, 1710

There is one Mind. It is absolutely omnipresent, giving mentality to all things.

—Giordano Bruno, *De monade numero et figura*, 1591

It is good to tame the mind, which is difficult to hold in and flighty, rushing wherever it listeth; a tamed mind brings happiness.

—*Dhammapada*, c. 5th century B.C.

The moral cause of the world lies behind all else in the mind.

—Ralph Waldo Emerson, in *North American Review*, April 1866

If a person had delivered up your body to some passer-by, you would certainly be angry. And do you feel no shame in delivering up your own mind to any reviler, to be disconcerted and confounded?

—Epictetus (1st century), *Echiridion*

When I consider how many and how great mysteries men have understood, discovered, and contrived, I very plainly know and understand the mind of man to be one of the works of God, yea, one of the most excellent.
—Galileo, *Dialogue on the Great World Systems*, 1632

On earth there is nothing great but man; in man there is nothing great but mind.
—William Hamilton, *Lectures on Metaphysics*, c. 1850

The mind is like a sheet of white paper in this: that the impressions it receives the oftenest, and retains the longest, are black ones.
—J.C. and A.W. Hare, *Guesses at Truth*, 1827

There is an unseemly exposure of the mind as well as of the body.
—William Hazlitt, *Sketches and Essays*, 1839

There is no such thing as your mind, my mind, and God's Mind. There's only Mind, in which we all "live and move and have our being."
—Ernest Holmes, *The Science of Mind*, 1938

Mind no longer appears as an accidental intruder into the realm of matter; we are beginning to suspect that we ought rather to hail it as the creator and governor of the realm of matter—not of course our individual minds, but the mind in which the atoms out of which our individual minds have grown exist as thought.
—James Jeans, *The Mysterious Universe*, 1930

The only way to truth that lies open to us at all is the way through our own minds. If we cannot find a clue here in our own human reason, we can find it nowhere.
—Rufus M. Jones, *Pathways to the Reality of God*, 1931

Space and time, and with them all phenomena, are not things by themselves, but representations, and cannot exist outside the mind.
—Immanuel Kant, *The Critique of Pure Reason*, 1781

The mind coupled to religion, is a stronger mind for it, a mind not so readily swayed by the passions that parade as reason under an enlarged vocabulary.
—Henry C. Link, *The Return to Religion*, 1936

It is a shallow mind which can see to the bottom of its own beliefs, and is conscious of nothing but what it can measure in evidence and state in words.
　　　　　　　　　—James Martineau, *Hours of Thought on Sacred Things*, 1879

To know and to think, to see the truth with the eye of the mind, is always a joy. . . . As love is the life of the heart, so is the endeavor after knowledge and truth the life of the mind.
　　　　　　　　　—Nicholas of Cusa, *Dialogue on Peace*, 1452

When we reach the mind of man, we reach the pinnacle of all creation. It is the apex in the pyramid of values to be found in the universe. It is this which constitutes the dignity of man as a moral personality, and makes him a being of surpassing worth.
　　　　　　　　　—John A. O'Brien, *God: Can We Find Him?*, 1942

Only the mind cannot be sent into exile.
　　　　　　　　　—Ovid, *Epistulae ex Ponto*, c. 5

My own mind is my own church.
　　　　　　　　　—Thomas Paine, *The Age of Reason*, 1795

All the bodies that exist, the firmament, the stars, the earth and its kingdoms, are of less value than the least of minds; for it is aware of them, and of itself—while they are aware of nothing.
　　　　　　　　　—Blaise Pascal, *Pensées*, 1670

Man's mind belongs to a category of being essentially different from matter and superior to it, however limitless the dimensions of matter may be.
　　　　　　　　　—Pope Pius XII, *Allocution*, September 7, 1952

An open mind should be more than a catch-all receptacle. It should have a screening mechanism to keep out the trivial, a sorting capacity to organize ideas and reconcile contradictions, and a critical tool to help us decide what we believe. That's the difference between a mind that receives information and a mind that thinks.
　　　　　　　　　—Letty Cottin Pogrebin, in *The New York Times*, January 16, 1989

The human mind must be subject to the general law. . . . Its destiny can be nothing other than to exercise imagination, to invent, and to perfect. No; Men were not made to wander in the forests after the manner of bears and tigers.
　　　　　　　　　—J.B.R. Robinet, *De la Nature*, III, 1766

Physical theory in its present stage strongly suggests the indestructibility of Mind in Time.

—Erwin Schrodinger, *Mind and Matter*, 1958

The man who does not lift his mind above himself does not deserve to be a man.

—Angelus Silesius (1624–77), *Cherubic Pilgrim*

The mind is that place where reflection upon meaning and action hitherto achieved merge and make meaning apparent anew.

—Dorothee Sölle, *Death by Bread Alone*, 1978

Minds are conquered not by arms but by greatness of soul.

—Baruch Spinoza, *Ethics*, IV, 1677

The eternal wisdom of God . . . has shown itself forth in all things, but chiefly in the mind of man, and most of all in Jesus Christ.

—Baruch Spinoza, *Tractatus Theologico-Politicus*, 1670

The human mind cannot be absolutely destroyed with the human body, but there is some part of it which remains eternal.

—Baruch Spinoza, *Ethics*, V, 1677

The mind's highest good is the knowledge of God, and the mind's highest virtue is to know God.

—Baruch Spinoza, *Ethics*, IV, 1677

The final joy of man consists in the superlative activity of his supreme power, namely the activity of mind engaged with incomparable truth.

—St. Thomas Aquinas (1225–74), *Opusc. X, de Causis*, Lect. 1

The *mind* of man has to be accounted for, as well as his body; and if the unforeseen actions of atoms could not have produced a human body, with its wonderful marks of design, still less could they have produced a human mind able to know and argue about them.

—W.H. Turton, *The Truth of Christianity*, 1905

Human beings live—literally live, as if life is equated with the mind—by symbols, particularly words, because the brain is constructed to process information almost exclusively in their terms.

—Edward O. Wilson, *Biophilia*, 1984

MIRACLES

The capacity to reveal Himself through miracles, i.e., by interfering with his own order, is an inherent attribute of God, and all miracles were foreseen by Him.

—Zsolt Aradi, *The Book of Miracles*, 1956

God acts against the wonted course of nature, but by no means does He act against the supreme law; because He does not act against Himself.

—St. Augustine, *Contra Faust*, XXVI, c. 400

That miracles have been, I do believe; that they may yet be wrought by the living, I do not deny; but I have no confidence on those which are fathered on the dead.

—Thomas Browne, *Religio Medici*, 1642

The Miracles of the Church seem to me to rest not so much upon faces or voices or healing power coming suddenly near to us from afar off, but upon our perceptions being made finer, so that for a moment our eyes can see and our ears can hear what is there about us always.

—Willa S. Cather, *Death Comes for the Archbishop*, 1927

Christianity is not only confirmed by miracles, but is in itself, in its very essence, a miraculous religion.

—William Ellery Channing, (1780–1842), *Works*

Miracles are not the proofs, but the necessary results, of revelation.

—Samuel Taylor Coleridge, *Omniana*, 1812

The more we know of the fixed laws of nature the more incredible do miracles become.

—Charles Darwin (1809–82), *Autobiography of*

The idea of a Being who interferes with the sequence of events in the world is absolutely impossible.

—Albert Einstein, *Has Science Discovered God?*, 1931

The word miracle, as pronounced by Christian churches, gives a false impression; it is a monster. It is not one with the blowing clover and the falling rain.

—Ralph Waldo Emerson, *Divinity School Address*, July 15, 1838

No kind of miracle is related in Scripture the counterpart of which cannot be found and found repeatedly in the records of other religions.
—Harry Emerson Fosdick, *The Modern Use of the Bible*, 1934

You think it more difficult to turn air into wine than to turn wine into blood?
—Graham Greene, *Monsignor Quixote*, PBS TV, February 13, 1987

All men wondered to see the water turned into wine. Every day the earth's moisture being drawn into the root of a vine, is turned by the grape into wine, and no man wonders. Full of wonder then are all the things, which men never think to wonder at.
—Pope St. Gregory the Great, *Morals on the Book of Job*, 584

The gospel story is full of miracle and miracles; yet not one bit of that "evidence" would have been visible to a newsreel camera or the observation of a scientifically trained reporter. A miracle is visible only to the heart it touches.
—M. Holmes Hartshorne,
The Promise of Science and the Power of Faith, 1958

I don't believe in miracles because it's been a long time since we've had any.
—Joseph Heller, in conversation with Bill Moyers, *A World of Ideas*, 1989

And he sighed deeply in his spirit, and said, "Why does this generation seek a sign? Truly, I say to you, no sign shall be given to this generation."
—*Holy Bible*, Mark 8:12

No testimony is sufficient to establish a miracle. Unless the testimony be of such a kind, that its falsehood would be more miraculous, than the fact, which it endeavors to establish. . . . A miracle can never be proved, so as to be the foundation of a system of religion.
—David Hume, *On Miracles*, 1748

The miracles are a particular case of the immanence of the divine in matter and we have, therefore, no right to *expect* them to be intelligible.
—C.E.M. Joad, *Recovery of Belief*, 1952

Miracles are God's signature, appended to His masterpiece of creation; not because they ought to be needed, but because they are needed.
—Ronald A. Knox, *Miracles*, 1928

Many a man who is now willing to be shot down for the sake of his belief in a miracle would have doubted, if he had been present, the miracle itself.
—G.C. Lichtenberg, *Reflections*, 1799

A miracle cannot prove what is impossible; it is useful only to confirm what is possible.
—Maimonides, *Guide for the Perplexed*, 1190

What seems the greatest miracle of all, namely, the lack of interruption of the natural order.
—Henry Margenau, *Science Ponders Religion*, 1960

Depend upon it, it is not the want of greater miracles but of the soul to perceive such as are allowed us still, that makes us push all the sanctities into the far spaces we cannot reach. The devout feel that wherever God's hand is, *there* is miracle.
—James Martineau, *Endeavours After a Christian Life*, 1847

Miracles—whether prophetical or of other sorts—always occur in connection with some message from heaven, and are intended by God as a seal, or endorsement of the messenger and his words.
—Aloysius McDonough, *Jesus Christ—The Divine Bridge-Builder*, 1937

To the reverent scientist . . . the simplest features of the world about us are in themselves so awe-inspiring that there seems no need to seek new and greater miracles as evidences of God's care.
—Carl Wallace Miller, *A Scientist's Approach to Religion*, 1947

In what way can a revelation be made but by miracles? In none which we are able to conceive.
—William Paley, *Evidences of Christianity*, 1794

A miracle is an effect which exceeds the natural force of the means employed for it.
—Blaise Pascal, *Pensées*, 1670

No miracle has ever taken place under conditions which science can accept.
—Ernest Renan, *Life of Jesus*, 1863

Miracles are propitious accidents, the natural causes of which are too complicated to be readily understood.
—George Santayana, *Introduction to the Ethics of Spinoza*, 1910

Belief is not dependent on evidence and reason. There is as much evidence that the miracles occurred as that the Battle of Waterloo occurred.
—George Bernard Shaw, Preface, *Androcles and the Lion*, 1914

Miracles were performed for our ancestors, because they sacrificed their lives for the sanctification of the Name.
—*Talmud*, c. 200–500

If the world is really the medium of God's personal action, miracle is wholly normal.
—D.E. Trueblood, *The Logic of Belief*, 1942

All is miracle. The stupendous order of nature, the revolution of a hundred millions of worlds around a million of suns, the activity of light, the life of animals, all are grand and perpetual miracles.
—Voltaire, *Philosophical Dictionary*, II, 1764

A miracle is a law-abiding event by which God accomplishes His redemptive purposes through the release of energies which belong to a plane of being higher than any with which we are normally familiar.
—Leslie D. Weatherhead, *Psychology, Religion and Healing*, 1951

To me every hour of the light and dark is a miracle,
Every cubic inch of space is a miracle.
—Walt Whitman, "Miracles," *Leaves of Grass*, 1856

MODERATION

The Godliest form of self-expression is self-control—maintaining an even keel through the turbulent sea of human life.
—Paul Crouch, "Praise the Lord" (television program), 1992

The opportunity offered by a shrinking economy to experience simple pleasures might be one of God's better gifts to this generation.
—Dolores Curran, in *U.S. Catholic*, June 1991

I believe the purpose of life is happiness. In today's world, being happy is inseparable from being responsible. We need to temper the extremes of our personal nature so that we can realize oneness with the universe. We must keep our destructive qualities from outweighing our constructive qualities.
—Dalai Lama (Tenzin Gyatso), speech, Cornell University, March 26, 1991

I finally awakened to the distinction between getting "high" and becoming "free." Highs are part of the world of polarities: What goes up must come down. The deeper requirement would be to pursue the middle course and be at peace, free from whatever may happen, whether high or low.
—Ram Dass, *Compassion in Action*, 1992

Temptation succeeds best in corrupting the over-zealous Christian or the underachieving Christian. It has far less success with the Christian who maintains a simple, practical, and even-tempered faith.
—Harvey F. Egan, in *Commonweal*, October 1991

Disciplining one's appetite may be the biggest spiritual challenge many of us will face this side of dying. In a world where the future of the planet depends on how many of us will agree to say no to excessive lifestyles, fasting can teach us that physical satisfaction is not the purpose of life.
—Nancy Forest-Flier, in *U.S. Catholic*, March 1992

Of eight things a little is good and much is evil: travel, mating, wealth, work, wine, sleep, spiced drinks, medicine.
—*Gittin, Talmud*, c. 500

The credo "everything in moderation" is only moderately true. As it says in the mezuzah [traditional container with scripture inside, that Jews affix to door frames], "You must love the Lord your God with *all* your heart and with *all* your soul and with *all* your might.
—Sidney Greenberg, *Say Yes to Life*, 1982

Man always travels along precipices. His truest obligation is to keep his balance.
—Pope John Paul II, 1986

The only way we can brush against the hem of the Lord, or hope to be a part of the creative process, is to have the courage, the faith, to exceed—to abandon the middle road and aim for the heights.
—Madeleine L'Engle, 1988

If a person measures his spiritual fulfillment in terms of cosmic visions, surpassing peace of mind, or ecstasy, then he is not likely to know much spiritual fulfillment. If, however, he measures it in terms of enjoying a sunrise, being warmed by a child's smile, or being able to help someone have a better day, then he is likely to know much spiritual fulfillment.
—Arthur Miller, 1975

We also must be willing to do whatever the life force from within suggests. Often it is only a small thing.
—Fran Peavey, in *Creation Spirituality*, March/April 1989

Temperance in all things, including our hopes as well as our fears, is a worthy goal, but it is hardly human to be always temperate. It is far wiser to know how to balance a great sorrow with a great happiness, or a recurrence of dread with a renewal of faith.
—Gail Sheehy, *Passages*, 1976

Intuition is your link to the divine. And to stay in touch with your intuition, you must know, and respect, the limits of your mental energy. Life happens too fast for you ever to think about it all. If people could just be persuaded of this, but they insist on amassing information.
—Kurt Vonnegut, Jr., 1970

MONEY

If you want to know what God thinks of money, look at the people he gives it to.
—American proverb

Money, material though it be, does lie at the base of the most useful work you do. In itself nothing, it is the basis of much of the best effort which can be made for spiritual purposes.
—A.J. Balfour, *The Mind of*, 1918

Money is a dream. It is a piece of paper on which is imprinted in invisible ink the dream of all the things it will buy, all the trinkets and all the power over others. A kind of institutionalized dream which, along with its companion dream-institution of Success, constitutes the main fantasy on which our way of life has been built.
—David T. Bazelon, *The Paper Economy*, 1963

Money, n. A blessing that is of no advantage to us excepting when we part with it.
—Ambrose Bierce, *Devil's Dictionary*, 1906

The wealth he bade his questioner renounce must be taken in a spiritual sense; it was a wealth of passions, a brood of sins in the soul, not money itself, but the love of money.
—St. Clement of Alexandria, (died c. 215), *The Rich Man's Salvation*

The great curse of our modern society is not so much the lack of money as the fact that the lack of money condemns a man to a squalid and incomplete existence.
—Christopher Dawson, *The Modern Dilemma*, 1932

The only money of God is God. He pays never with anything less or anything else.
—Ralph Waldo Emerson, "Friendship," *Essays*, 1844

Those who seek money as a great thing, with immense solicitude, and upon it establish the especial defense of life . . . have fashioned for themselves too many gods.
—Desiderius Erasmus, *Enchiridion*, 1501

He that is of opinion money will do everything may well be suspected of doing everything for money.
—Benjamin Franklin, *Poor Richard's Almanac*, 1753

Money is life to us wretched mortals.
—Hesiod, *Work and Days*, c. 700 B.C.

Every man according as he purposeth in his heart, so let him give; not grudgingly, or of necessity: for God loveth a cheerful giver.
—*Holy Bible*, II Corinthians

If you lend money to any of my people with you who is poor, you shall not be to him as a creditor, and you shall not exact interest from him.
—*Holy Bible*, Exodus 22:25

We ought to change the legend on our money from "In God We Trust" to "In Money We Trust." Because, as a nation, we've got far more faith in money these days than we do in God.
—Arthur Hoppe, in *The Way*, June 1963

The love of money has been in all ages, one of the passions that have given great disturbances to the tranquillity of the world.
—Samuel Johnson, *Rambler*, October 6, 1750

He that serves God for money will serve the Devil for better wages.
—Roger L'Estrange, 1692

Love of money is the disease which makes men most grovel-
ing and pitiful.
—Longinus, *On the Sublime*, c. 250

But it is not the rich man only who is under the domination
of things; they too are slaves who, having no money, are unhappy from the lack of it.
—George Macdonald, *Unspoken Sermons* (1st series), 1869

An American journalist in China watched a Sister cleaning
the gangrenous sores of wounded soldiers. "I wouldn't do
that for a million dollars!" the visitor remarked.
Without pause in her work, the Sister replied, "Neither
would I."
—*Maryknoll, the Field Afar*, 1947

Money is a good servant but a bad master.
—Proverb

When money speaks the truth is silent.
—Russian proverb

The crying need of the nation is not for better morals, cheap-
er bread, temperance, liberty, culture, redemption of fallen
sisters and brothers, nor the grace, love and fellowship of the
Trinity, but simply for enough money.
—George Bernard Shaw, Preface, *Major Barbara*, 1905

You cannot love money and your brethren at the same time.
—Emmanuel Suhard, *The Church Today*, 1953

The image of Caesar is money, the image of God is man. Give
money to Caesar, and give thyself to God.
—Tertullian, *De Idol*, 15, c. A.D. 211

Silly people think that money commands the bodily goods
most worth having.
—St. Thomas Aquinas, *Summa Theologiae*, 1272

Superfluous wealth can buy superfluities only. Money is not
required to buy one necessary of the soul.
—Henry David Thoreau, *Walden*, 1854

MORALITY

In a world in which "God is dead," there is only room for a "morality without sin."
—Paul Aciaux, *The Sacrament of Penance*, 1962

A person may be qualified to do greater good to mankind, and become more beneficial to the world, by morality without faith than by faith without morality.
—Joseph Addison, in *The Spectator*, August 12, 1712

If ignorance and passions are foes of popular morality, it must be confessed that moral indifference is the malady of the cultivated classes.
—Henri Amiel, *Journal*, 1882

It is in God that morality has its foundation and guarantee.
—Leo Baeck, *Essence of Judaism*, 1836

The morality of modern civilized man has turned out to be a terribly thin covering of ice over a sea of primitive barbarity.
—Karl Barth, *Community, Church and State*, 1946

Morality is character and conduct such as is required by the circle or community in which the man's life happens to be passed. It shows how much good men require of us.
—Henry Ward Beecher, *Life Thoughts*, 1858

Well, no human being takes another human being all that seriously any more, and when you have that happening at the very core of a society, then you're looking at a lot of trouble, a great deal of wretchedness, because something in human nature demands a constancy of connection, emotional constancy. There's a secret voice in us which says, "No, this bad; this wrong. I'm alone again, once more cast into outer darkness."
—Saul Bellow, in *The New York Times*, June 3, 1987

It is . . . by the superiority of its morality that a religion wins over souls and reveals to them a certain conception of things.
—Henri Bergson, *The Two Sources of Morality and Religion*, 1935

I think what we are seeing is what you might call trickle-down morality. The elites of the country changed their behavior, at least outward manifestations, in the 1950s. Everyone else is following.
—Douglas Besharov, in *The Washington Post*, September 5, 1989

In reference to our moral conduct, there is not a single principle now known to the most cultivated Europeans which was not likewise known to the ancients.
—H.T. Buckle, *History of Civilization in England*, 1861

If I had to write a book on morality, it would have a hundred pages and ninety-nine would be blank. On the last page I should write: "I recognize only one duty, and that is to love." And, as far as everything else is concerned, I say *no*.
—Albert Camus, *Notebooks*, 1935–1942

If the moral and physical fiber of its manhood and its womanhood is not a state concern, the question is, what is?
—Benjamin Cardozo, *Adler vs. Deegan*, 1929, 251 *N.Y. Reports*, 467

Morality, concerned with bringing human activity into conformity with God's will, has a bearing on everything that touches human rights and duties.
—Catholic Bishops of the U.S., November 1951

To enjoy and give enjoyment, without injury to yourself or others: this is true morality.
—Nicholas Chamfort, *Maxims et pensées*, 1785

Moral force is, unhappily, no substitute for armed force, but it is a very great reinforcement.
—Winston S. Churchill, speech, House of Commons, December 21, 1937

The first principle of Positive morality is the preponderance of social sympathy.
—Auguste Comte, *Positive Polity*, 1820

Man . . . derives his moral sense from the social feelings which are instinctive or innate in the lower animals.
—Charles Darwin, *The Descent of Man*, 1871

Morality is not static but a set of experiments, being gradually worked out by mankind, a dynamic, progressive instrument which we can help ourselves to forge.
—Durant Drake, *Problems of Conduct*, 1935

We need to recognize that both the society and the individual are essential to a morality which we can use in the next century. If we could enter the next century with a wider recognition of that balance—and get away from either collectivistic excesses or the celebration of radical individualism—I think we'd be better for it.
—Amitai Etzioni, in *The Christian Science Monitor*, July 25, 1988

It is not doubtful, but the most certain of all certainties—nay, the foundation of all certainties—the one absolutely valid objective truth—that there is a moral order in the world.
—J.G. Fichte (1762–1814), *A Divine Government in the World*

We now know that anything which is economically right is also morally right; there can be no conflict between good economics and good morals.
—Henry Ford (1863–1937), quoted by C.E. Hudson, *Christian Morals*

The old view that the principles of right and wrong are immutable and eternal is no longer tenable. The moral world is as little exempt as the physical world from the law of ceaseless change, of perpetual flux.
—James Frazer, *The Golden Bough*, Vol. 11, p. vi, 1915

We are at ease with a moral judgment made against someone's private sin—lust or greed. We are much less comfortable judging someone's public ethic—those decisions that can lead to such outcomes as aggression, the abuse of the environment, the neglect of the needy.
—Ellen Goodman, "A Price Tag on Ethics," *The Washington Post*, April 1989

There are two classes of moralists: those who seek to improve the quality of other people's lives, and those who are content to improve their own.
—Paul Gruchow, *Our Sustainable Table*, 1990

The possibility of morality thus depends on the possibility of liberty; for if man be not a free agent, he is not the author of his actions, and has, therefore, no responsibility—no moral personality at all.
—William Hamilton, *Lectures on Metaphysics*, II, 1870

Moral perfection in death is a luxury most men can do without.
—Garret Hardin, *Exploring New Ethics for Survival*, 1972

The splendor and metaphysical reality of morality flashes forth only when the absolute *goodness* is seen not merely as the platonic idea, but as the living God.
—Dietrich Hildebrand, *True Morality and Its Counterfeits*, 1955

Morals is its own religion, exercises its own authority, and reveals its own necessity.
—John Haynes Holmes, in *Religion Today*, 1933

Repay no one evil for evil, but take thought for what is noble in the sight of all.
—*Holy Bible*, Romans 12:17

One of the greatest triumphs of the nineteenth century was to limit the connotation of the word "immoral" in such a way that, for practical purposes, only those were immoral who drank too much or made too copious love. Those who indulged in any or all of the other deadly sins could look down in righteous indignation on the lascivious and the gluttons.
—Aldous Huxley, *Those Barren Leaves*, 1925

The safety of morality lies neither in the adoption of this or that philosophical speculation, or this or that theological creed, but in a real and living belief in that fixed order of nature which sends social disorganization upon the track of immorality, as surely as it sends physical disease after physical trespasses.
—Thomas Henry Huxley, *Science and Morals*, 1886

I never . . . believed there was one code of morality for a public, and another for a private man.
—Thomas Jefferson, letter to Don Valentine de Feronda, 1809

Something does not become moral and just simply because the State has declared it to be a law, and the organization of a society is not a just and right order simply because it has been instituted by the State.
—*The Kairos Document*, rev. 2nd ed., 1986

Morality is not properly the doctrine how we make ourselves happy, but how we make ourselves worthy of happiness.
—Immanuel Kant, *Critique of Practical Reason*, 1788

Mankind has lost its morality because it has lost its God.
—Joseph Klausner, in *Judaism*, January 1953

A moral obligation is no less compelling because it may end in failure.
—Harold J. Laski, *The State in Theory and Practice*, 1935

Religions, considered as moral teachers, are realized and effective only when their moral teaching is in conformity with the teaching of their age.
—W.E.H. Lecky, *History of European Morals*, I, 1869

If no set of moral ideas were truer or better than any other there would be no sense in preferring civilized morality to savage morality, or Christian morality to Nazi morality.
—C.S. Lewis, *The Case for Christianity*, 1943

Morality, if it is not fixed by custom and authority, becomes a mere matter of taste determined by the idiosyncrasies of the moralist.
—Walter Lippmann, *A Preface to Morals*, 1929

Morality is not an imposition removed from life and reason; it is a compendium of the minimum of sacrifices necessary for man to live in company with other men, without suffering too much or causing others to suffer.
—Gina Lombroso, *The Tragedies of Progress*, 1931

Morality without religion is only a kind of dead reckoning— an endeavor to find our place on a cloudy sea by measuring the distance we have run, but without any observation of the heavenly bodies.
—Henry Wadsworth Longfellow, *Kavanagh*, 1849

Most of our so-called "Christian" morality, particularly in the field of sex, has little fundamental relationship to the outlook and spirit of the founder of Christianity.
—John Macmurray, *Reason and Emotion*, 1935

Morality cannot exist one minute without freedom. . . . Only a free man can possibly be moral. Unless a good deed is voluntary, it has no moral significance.
—Everett Dean Martin, *Liberty*, 1930

We don't bring to a consideration of public-policy issues a moral foundation. My experience in public-policy debates has been that you are thought to be rather naive if you introduce the moral dimension.
—Robert S. McNamara, in *The Christian Science Monitor*, July 25, 1988

The moral feelings are not innate, but acquired.
—John Stuart Mill, *Utilitarianism*, 1863

Whereas the old morality saw things as so simple that moral judgment was always easy, the new morality sees things as so complicated that moral judgment becomes practically impossible.
—John Courtney Murray, *We Hold These Truths*, 1960

The order of human existence is too imperiled by chaos, the goodness of man too corrupted by sin, and the possibilities of man too obscured by natural handicaps, to make human order and human possibilities solid bases of the moral imperative.
—Reinhold Niebuhr, *An Interpretation of Christian Ethics*, 1935

Morality is primarily a means of preserving the community and saving it from destruction. Next it is a means of maintaining the community on a certain plane and in a certain degree of benevolence.
—Friedrich Nietzsche, *Human, All Too Human*, 1878

Universal tradition makes it plain that without a higher aid the moral life neither endures nor uplifts itself.
—Martin J. O'Malley, *The Peace of Christ*, 1939

When people talk of the "new morality" they are merely committing a new immorality and looking for a way of introducing contraband goods.
—José Ortega y Gasset, *Revolt of the Masses*, 1930

Morality is a means for the satisfaction of human wants. In other words, morality must justify itself at the bar of life, not life at the bar of morality.
—Max C. Otto, *Things and Ideals*, 1924

Where there is no free agency, there can be no morality.
—William H. Prescott, *The Conquest of Peru*, 1847

Morality is eternal and immutable.
—Richard Price, *The Principal Questions in Morals*, 1758

The fundamental principle of all morality is that man is a being naturally good, loving justice and order; that there is not any original perversity in the human heart, and that the first movements of nature are always right.
—Jean Jacques Rousseau, Reply to Archbishop de Beaumont's Condemnation (of Rousseau's Émile), 1763

There are many religions, but there is only one morality.
—John Ruskin, *Lectures on Art*, 1884

We do not need the laws of Church and State, nor the findings of science and psychiatry, to tell us the simple rules of ethics and morality.
—William Seifriz, *Perspectives on a Troubled Decade*, 1950

Generally speaking, all great societies have come into being and have been maintained through the people's acceptance of certain objective moral standards. Such standards aren't created; they exist and cannot be displaced. They are stronger, indeed, than we are.
—Adlai Stevenson, in *Ladies' Home Journal*, December 1961

The morality code that remains after the religion that produced it is rejected is like the perfume that lingers in an empty bottle.
—Sigrid Undset, *Stages on the Road*, 1934

There is no morality in superstition, it exists not in ceremonies, and has nothing to do with dogmas. . . . Morality is the same among all men who make use of their reason. Morality proceeds from God, like light; our superstitions are only darkness.
—Voltaire, *Philosophical Dictionary*, II, 1764

MOTHERHOOD

The mother's heart is the child's schoolroom.
—Henry Ward Beecher, *Life Thoughts*, 1858

The mother's face and voice are the first conscious objects as the infant soul unfolds, and she soon comes to stand in the very place of God to her child.
—G. Stanley Hall, *Pedagogical Seminary*, June 1891

Motherhood is the keystone of the arch of matrimonial happiness.
—Thomas Jefferson, letter to Martha Jefferson Randolph, 1791

To the mother alone it has been given, that her soul during the nine months should touch the soul of the child, and impose upon it predispositions to truth, gentleness, goodness, the culture of which precious germs she should complete in the light of day, after having sown them in the mysterious mysteries of her maternity.
—Jean Baptiste Lacordaire, *Conferences of*, 1850

345

The mother is indeed a gardener of God doing a veritable priestly work in the Christian care of her children.
—Virgil Michel, in *Catholic Mind*, Vol. 37, 1940

Maternity, with its care, its sufferings, and its risks, calls for and exacts courage; the wife, in the field of honor and of conjugal duty, must be no less heroic than her husband in the field of honor of civil duty, where he makes the gift of his life to his country.
—Pope Pius XII, address, October 21, 1942

The working class mother with a large family is the real heroine . . . of our civilization.
—William Temple, speech, House of Lords, 1942

Mother is the name of God in the lips and hearts of little children.
—William Makepeace Thackeray, *Vanity Fair*, 1848

MOURNING

A family which allows one of its members to die without being wept for shows by that very fact that it lacks moral unity and cohesion; it abdicates, it renounces its existence.
—Émile Durkheim, *The Elementary Forms of the Religious Life*, 1915

Blessed are those who mourn, for they shall be comforted.
—*Holy Bible*, Matthew 5:4

Rejoice with those who rejoice, weep with those who weep.
—*Holy Bible*, Romans 12:15

Bereavement is the deepest initiation into the mysteries of human life, an initiation more searching and profound than even happy love. . . . Bereavement is the sharpest challenge to our trust in God; if faith can overcome this, there is no mountain which it cannot remove.
—W.R. Inge, *Survival and Immortality*, 1919

The sorrow for the dead is the only sorrow from which we refuse to be divorced. . . . The love which survives the tomb is one of the noblest attributes of the soul.
—Washington Irving, *The Sketch Book*, 1819

Since we hope he is gone to God and to rest, it is an ill expression of our love to them that we weep for their good fortune.
—Jeremy Taylor, *Holy Living*, 1650

Music

In its purest form music is not a representational but
rather a nonobjective, nonverbal world, it is a world of it
own, almost a creatio ex nihilo, an occasion for immediacy
of experience, a nonreducible mode of beauty, of contrast
and resolution, of order and of ecstasy flowing through and
beyond the order. Order, and ecstasy rooted in order:
that sounds like the relation between law and love, law
and gospel.

—James Luther Adams, in *Crane Review*, Fall 1967

Music is the greatest good that mortals know,
And all of heaven we have below.

—Joseph Addison (1672–1719), *Song for St. Cecilia's Day*

Each man does his utmost in singing what will be a blessing
to all. Psalms are sung in the home and rehearsed on the
streets. A psalm is learnt without labor and remembered
with delight. Psalmody unites those who disagree, makes
friends of those at odds, brings together those who are out of
charity with one another.

—St. Ambrose (333–397), *Commentary on Psalm I*

I wept at the beauty of your hymns and canticles, and was
powerfully moved at the sweet sound of your Church singing.
These sounds flowed into my ears, and the truth streamed
into my heart.

—St. Augustine, *Confessions*, IX. 397

What is to reach the heart must come from above, if it does
not come thence, it will be nothing but notes—body without
spirit.

—Beethoven, to J.A. Stumpff, 1824, in Marion Scott, *Beethoven*

Let the chant be full of gravity; let it be neither worldly, nor
too rude and poor. . . . Let it be sweet, yet without levity,
and, while it pleases the ear, let it move the heart.

—St. Bernard of Clairvaux (1091–1153), in Alex Robertson, *Christian Music*, 1961

Music being the universal expression of the mysterious and
supernatural, the best that man has ever attained to, is capable of uniting in common devotion minds that are only
separated by creeds, and it comforts our hope with a brighter
promise of unity than any logic offers.

—Robert Bridges, *Collected Essays*, 1935

If the lack of singing is an index of exile, then we are in it, for we are a people who scarcely can sing.
—Walter Brueggemann, *The Prophetic Imagination*, 1978

Music is a tonic for the saddened soul, a Roaring Meg [cannon] against melancholy, to rear and revive the languishing soul.
—Robert Burton, *The Anatomy of Melancholy*, 1621

Music is well said to be the speech of angels.
—Thomas Carlyle, *Essays: The Opera*, 1857

Music doth extenuate fears, furies, appeaseth cruelty, abateth heaviness, and to such as are wakeful it causeth quiet rest; it cures all irksomeness and heaviness of soul.
—Cassiodorus, *The Divine Letters*, c. 550

The musician who would follow religion in all her relations is obliged to learn the art of imitating the harmonies of solitude. He ought to be acquainted with the melancholy notes of the waters and the trees; he ought to study the sound of the winds in the cloister and those murmurs that pervade the Gothic temple, the grass of the cemetery and the vaults of death.
—François René de Chateaubriand, Vicomte de, *The Genius of Christianity*, 1856

It is possible to "have church," as the people would say, without outstanding preaching, but not without good singing.
—James H. Cone, *Speaking the Truth*, 1986

Song is the daughter of prayer, and prayer is the companion of religion.
—François René de Chateaubriand, Vicomte de, *The Genius of Christianity*, 1856

Music and religion are as intimately related as poetry and love; the deepest emotions require for their civilized expression the most emotional of arts.
—Will Durant, *The Age of Faith*, 1950

Music was as vital as the church edifice itself, more deeply stirring than all the glory of glass or stone. Many a stoic soul, doubtful of the creed, was melted by the music, and fell on his knees before the mystery that no words could speak.
—Will Durant, *The Age of Faith*, 1950

The fineness which a hymn or psalm affords
Is, when the soul unto the lines accords.
—George Herbert (1593–1633), *A True Hymn*

The word stands for the body, but the symphony stands for the spirit.
—Hildegard of Bingen (1098–1179), *Illuminations of*, 1985

Praise the Lord with the lyre, make melody to him with the harp of ten strings! Sing to him a new song.
—*Holy Bible*, Psalms 33:2-3

Music is love in search of a word.
—Sidney Lanier, *The Symphony*, 1875

Sacred music, being a complementary part of the solemn liturgy, participates in the general scope of liturgy, which is the glory of God and the sanctification and edification of the faithful.
—Pope Pius X, *Motu Proprio* (on Sacred Music), November 22, 1903

True devotion produces as of itself a song; song, in turn excites devotion, and this reciprocal action augments the value of both, like two mirrors, which, facing each other, multiply the same image even to the profondity, so to speak, of the infinite.
—Joseph Pothier, *Les Mélodies Grégoriennes*, 1880

Our fathers have broken even the strong fortresses by their hymns, the rock by their shouting. They have opened to us the path of the great heaven.
—*Rig-Veda*, c. 1000 B.C.

Though the Church went singing into the world from her foundation, music is to her not an absolute necessity but a most beautiful and desirable embellishment.
—Alec Robertson, *Christian Music*, 1961

Music is the Lost Chord that has strayed hither from heaven.
—P.A. Sheehan, *Under the Cedars and the Stars*, 1903

For changing peoples' manners and altering their customs there is nothing better than music.
—*Shu Ching*, 6th century B.C.

It [music] is the only cheap and unpunished rapture upon earth.
—Sydney Smith, letter to Countess of Carlisle, August 1844

The organ, the master instrument, is the voice of the Christian Church, "the seraph haunted queen of harmony," sounding like an echo from a mystic and hidden world.
—John Lancaster Spalding, *Essays and Reviews*, 1877

Music is as well or better able to praise [God] than the building of the church and all its decorations: it is the Church's greatest ornament . . . religious music without religion is almost always vulgar.
—Igor Stravinsky, in R. Craft, *Conversations with Igor Stravinsky*, 1959

Let my song go forth like the path of the sun!
May all the sons of the Immoral listen—
They who have reached their heavenly homes!
—*Svetasvatara Upanishad*, c. 1000 B.C.

MYSTERIES

The joy of all mysteries is the certainty which comes from their contemplation, that there are many doors yet for the soul to open on her upward and inward way.
—Arthur Christopher Benson, *From a College Window*, 1906

Real faith . . . means holding ourselves open to the unconditional mystery which we encounter in every sphere of our life and which cannot be comprised in any formula. . . .
Real faith means the ability to endure life in the face of this mystery.
—Martin Buber, *Israel and the World*, 1948

What is mysterious, secret, unknown, cannot at the same time be known as an object of faith.
—William Ellery Channing (1780–1842), *Works*

There is nothing beautiful or sweet or great in life that is not mysterious.
—François René de Chateaubriand, *Beauties of the Christian Religion*, 1802

The simple, absolute, and unchangeable mysteries of heavenly Truth lie hidden in the dazzling obscurity of the secret Silence, outshining all brilliance with the intensity of their darkness.
—Dionysius the Areopagite, *On the Divine Names*, c. 500

The most beautiful thing we can experience is the mysterious. It is the source of all true art and science. He to whom this emotion is a stranger, who can no longer pause to wonder and stand rapt in awe, is as good as dead; his eyes are closed.
—Albert Einstein, *The Forum*, October 1930

Willingly I too say, Hail! to the unknown awful powers which transcend the ken of the understanding.
—Ralph Waldo Emerson, "Demonology," *Lectures*, 1839

Perhaps some day, the modern man will learn that mystery is not the prison of the mind of man, it is his home.
—Walter Farrell, *A Companion to the Summa*, 1941

The deepest and strangest mysteries, the weirdest and most wonderful, the most shocking and most sublime, are those that even after all these aeons lie concealed in the dark and tortuous depths of the mind of man.
—James M. Gillis, *The Church and Modern Thought*, 1935

One does not need to fast for days and meditate for hours at a time to experience the sense of sublime mystery which constantly envelops us. All one need do is to notice intelligently, if even for a brief moment, a blossoming tree, a forest flooded with autumn colors, an infant smiling.
—Simon Greenberg, *A Jewish Philosophy and Pattern of Life*, 1981

But we impart a secret and hidden wisdom of God, which God decreed before the ages for our glorification.
—*Holy Bible*, I Corinthians 2:7

The huge concentric waves of universal life are shoreless. The starry sky that we study is but a partial appearance. We grasp but a few meshes of the vast network of existence.
—Victor Hugo, *William Shakespeare*, 1864

Those who concede that we are literally surrounded by mysteries in the natural order are most inconsistent in their refusal to admit mysteries in the supernatural order.
—J.F. Noll, *The Christian Faith Before the Bar of Reason*, 1948

Both the man of science and the man of action live always at the edge of mystery, surrounded by it.
—J. Robert Oppenheimer, address, 1954

The standard device for getting around a logical contradiction by elevating it to the status of a truth beyond logic.
—Max C. Otto, *Religious Liberals Reply*, 1947

There are many theological questions which can be asked—even interesting ones, for which the truest answer this side of the grave is, "I don't know."
—James A. Pike, *Beyond Anxiety*, 1953

When the park-keeper, mistaking Schopenhauer for a tramp, asked him in the Tiergarten at Frankfurt, "Who are you?" Schopenhauer replied bitterly: "I wish to God I knew."
—W.E. Sangster, *The Pure in Heart*, 1954

Mystery is in reality only a theological term for religious allegory. All religions have their mysteries. Properly speaking, a mystery is a dogma which is plainly absurd, but which, nevertheless conceals in itself a lofty truth.
—Arthur Schopenhauer, "A Dialogue," *Essays*, 1851

The heavenly powers are to be reverenced, and not searched into; and their mercies rather by prayers to be sought, than their hidden counsels by curiosity.
—Philip Sidney, *Arcadia*, 1590

If you know the love that can lead you near to heartbreak, if you know not only the heights of ecstasy but the depths of pain, then you will know you stand before a mystery and you will be silenced.
—Gerald Vann, *The Heart of Man*, 1945

MYSTICAL EXPERIENCE

All great mystics declare that they have the impression of a current passing from their soul to God, and flowing back again from God to mankind.
—Henri Bergson, *The Two Sources of Morality and Religion*, 1935

The mystic vision of God, or ecstasy of felt union with Him, is, to those who attain it, an affair of ravishing emotional intensity, of vivid intellectual illumination, and on both of these counts of supreme value.
—Edwin A. Burtt, *Types of Christian Philosophy*, 1957

Each mystic brings back confirmation of his own creed. . . . The mystic brings his theological beliefs to the mystical experience; he does not derive them from it.
—George A. Coe, *The Hibbert Journal*, Vol. VI (1907–08)

Much on earth is hidden from us, but to make up for that we have been given a precious mystic sense of our living bond with the other world, and with the higher heavenly world.
—Feodor Dostoyevski, *The Brothers Karamazov*, 1880

The most beautiful and most profound emotion we can experience is the sensation of the mystical. It is the dower of all true science. . . . To know what is impenetrable to us really exists, manifesting itself as the highest wisdom and the most radiant beauty which our dull faculties can comprehend only in their most primitive forms—this knowledge, this feeling is at the centre of true religiousness.
—Albert Einstein, *Out of My Later Years*, 1950

Mystical experience appears to be no less a product of the nervous system than is the reflex action to a pinprick or the appreciation of a Beethoven symphony.
—Hudson Hoagland, in H. Shapley, *Science Ponders Religion*, 1960

A mystic is not one who sees God in nature, but one for whom God and nature fit into one plane.
—Bede Jarrett, *Meditations for Layfolk*, 1915

By mysticism we mean, not the extravagance of erring fancy, but the concentration of reason in feeling, the enthusiastic love of the good, the true, the one, the sense of the infinity of knowledge and of the marvel of the human faculties.
—Benjamin Jowett, Introduction to his translation of Plato's *Phaedrus*, 1871

One of the marks of the true mystic is the tenacious and heroic energy with which he pursues a definite moral idea.
—J.H. Leuba, *Revue Philosophique*, July 1902

Christian mysticism, whether of the quasi or the mixed type, is connected with a craving for intensity of experience at the cost of clarity and sanity.
—Paul Elmer More, *The Catholic Faith*, 1931

What the world, which truly knows *nothing*, calls "mysticism" is the science of ultimates . . . the science of self-evident Reality, which cannot be "reasoned about," because it is the object of pure reason or perception.
—Coventry Patmore, *The Rod, the Root, and the Flower*, 1907

The visions of the mystics are determined in content by their belief, and are due to the dream imagination working upon the mass of theological material which fills the mind.

—J.B. Pratt, *The Religious Consciousness*, 1921

Mysticism is the art of union with Reality.

—Evelyn Underhill, *Practical Mysticism*, 1914

A religious wakening which does not awaken the sleeper to love has roused him in vain.

—Jessamyn West, *The Quaker Reader*, 1962

Nature

God made the beauties of nature like a child playing in the sand.

—Ascribed to Appolonius of Tyana, c. 50 B.C.

Material nature is the principle of becoming and is so evil that it fills with evil any being which is not yet in it and which does no more than look at it.

—St. Augustine, *Of Continence*, c. 425

Nature is the nature of all things that are; things that are have a union with all things from the beginning.

—Marcus Aurelius, *Meditations*, c. 170

Man is the servant and interpreter of Nature.

—Francis Bacon, *Aphorisms*, 1620

The visible series of effects or sensations imprinted on our minds according to certain fixed and general laws.

—George Berkeley, *Principles of Human Knowledge*, 1710

Believe one who has tried, you shall find a fuller satisfaction in the woods than in books. The trees and the rocks will teach you that which you cannot hear from masters.

—St. Bernard of Clairvaux (1091–1153), *Life and Works of*

The Bible's aim, as I read it, is not the freeing of the spirit from the world. It is the handbook of their interaction. It says that they cannot be divided; that their mutuality, their unity, is inescapable; that they are not reconciled in division, but in harmony.

—Wendell Berry, *The Unsettling of America*, 1977

There exists in that Eternal World the permanent realities of every thing, which we see reflected in this vegetable glass of nature.

—William Blake, *Vision of the Last Judgment*, 1790

If there be any man who is not enlightened by this sublime magnificence of created things, he is blind. If there be any man who is not aroused by the clamor of nature, he is deaf. If there be any one who, seeing all these works of God, does not praise him, he is dumb; if there be any one who, from so many signs, cannot perceive the First Principle, that man is foolish.

—St. Bonaventure, *Intinerarium Mentis in Deum*, 1259

The book of nature is a fine and large piece of tapestry rolled up, which we are not able to see at once, but must be content to wait for the discovery of its beauty and symmetry little by little, as it gradually comes to be more unfolded.

—Robert Boyle, *The Christian Virtuoso*, 1690

Nature, as a whole and in all its elements, enunciates something that may be regarded as an indirect self-communication of God to all those ready to receive it.

—Martin Buber, *At the Turning*, 1952

Art, glory, freedom fail, but nature still is fair.

—Lord Byron, *Childe Harolde*, 1919

We have today to learn to get back into accord with the wisdom of nature and realize again our brotherhood with the animals and with the water and the sea. To say that the divinity informs all things is condemned as pantheism. But pan*theism* is a misleading word. It suggests that a personal god is supposed to inhabit the world, but that is not the idea at all. The idea is . . . of an undefinable, inconceivable mystery, thought of as a power, that is the source and end and supporting ground of all life and being.

—Joseph Campbell, *The Power of Myth*, with Bill Moyers, 1988

Nature . . . is a Volume written in celestial hieroglyphs, in a true Sacred-writing; of which even Prophets are happy that they can read here a line and there a line.

—Thomas Carlyle, *Sartor Resartus*, 1836

Among all the strange things that men have forgotten, the most universal and catastrophic lapse of memory is that by which they have forgotten that they are living on a star.

—G.K. Chesterton, *Defendant*, 1901

Nature is the term in which we comprehend all things that are representable in the forms of Time and Space.

—Samuel Taylor Coleridge, *Aids to Reflection*, 1825

[H]uman beings, as one spin-off of the irrepressibly creative workings of nature, should not be regarded as religiously ultimate themselves but rather as evidencing, along with other forms of emergent life, the ultimacy of an all-encompassing nature.
—Donald A. Crosby, "From God to Nature: A Personal Odyssey,"
Religious Humanism, Summer 1991

The more men know about nature, and the more they rely upon nature, the more agnostic and hopeless they become.
—O.A. Curtis, *The Christian Faith*, 1905

Everything in nature invites us constantly to be what we are.
—Gretel Ehrlich, *The Solace of Open Spaces*, 1985

Man has always frustrated nature, from the time he invented the first tool, and will continue to do so until on his last day on earth he lays down his latest invention.
—Frederick E. Flynn, address to Catholic Physicians'
Guild of Southern California, 1960

Wolves may lose their Teeth, but not their Nature.
—Thomas Fuller, *Gnomologia*, 1732

If one starts out to dominate the natural world, one cannot stop short at that reputedly "rational animal" who, however rational, is also animal—and by all accounts creation's most problematical animal. "Man against nature" becomes "man against humanity" in this sense too, that it contains the obvious directive that what is "natural" within the human species must be brought under control.
—Douglas John Hall, *Imaging God: Dominion and Stewardship*, 1986

Nature is not his [man's] home; it is the sphere of his deciding. He lives in it, but his spirit is not of it. The meaning of his life can never consist in any relationship with nature.
—M. Holmes Hartshorne, *The Promise of Science and the Power of Faith*, 1958

Seen from within, nature is a war of living powers of will.
—Karl Heim, *Transformation of the Scientific World View*, 1953

With nature's help, humankind can set into creation all that is necessary and life sustaining. Everything in nature, the sum total of heaven and of earth, becomes a temple and an altar for the service of God.
—Hildegard of Bingen (1098–1179), *Illuminations of*, 1985

Do not harm the earth, or the sea or the trees.

—*Holy Bible*, Revelation 7:3

While the earth remains, seedtime and harvest, cold and heat, summer and winter, day and night, shall not cease.

—*Holy Bible*, Genesis 8:22

All things in nature work silently. They come into being and possess nothing. They fulfill their function and make no claim. All things alike do their work, and then we see them subside. When they have reached their bloom, each returns to its origin. . . . This reversion is an eternal law. To know that law is wisdom.

—Lao-tzu (6th century B.C.), *Sayings of*

Everything in temporal nature is descended out of that which is eternal, and stands as a palpable visible outbirth of it.

—William Law, *An Appeal to All Who Doubt*, 1740

Nature resolves everything into its component elements, but annihilates nothing.

—Lucretius, *De Rerum Natura*, 57 B.C.

The scheme of Nature regarded in its whole extent, cannot have had, for its sole or even principal object, the good of human or other sentient beings. What good it brings them, is mostly the result of their own exertions.

—John Stuart Mill (1806–73), *Nature*, publ. posth.

We are shown that our life exists with the tree life, that our well-being depends on the well-being of the vegetable life, that we are close relatives of the four-legged beings. In our ways, spiritual consciousness is the highest form of politics. . . . We believe that all living things are spiritual beings. Spirits can be expressed as energy forms manifested in matter. A blade of grass is an energy form manifested in matter—grass matter. The spirit of the grass is that unseen force which produces the species of grass, and it is manifest to us in the form of real grass.

—Mohawk Nation, *Basic Call to Consciousness*, Akwesasne Notes, 1978

Follow the order of nature, for God's sake! Follow it! It will lead who follows; and those who will not, it will drag along anyway.

—Michel de Montaigne, *Essays*, 1588

The mastery of nature is vainly believed to be an adequate substitute for self-mastery.
—Reinhold Niebuhr, in *The Christian Century*, April 22, 1926

Advance in understanding of nature or even in control of nature does not diminish God. God is not the sum total of what man does not know about nature or what man cannot control in nature.
—Walter J. Ong, letter to *The New York Times*, March 8, 1962

I have a hundred times wished that if a God maintains nature, she should testify to Him unequivocally, and that, if the signs she gives are deceptive, she should suppress them altogether.
—Blaise Pascal, *Pensées*, 1670

All are but parts of one stupendous whole,
Whose body nature is, and God the soul.
—Alexander Pope, *An Essay on Man*, 1732

I do account it, not the meanest, but an impiety monstrous to confound God and nature, be it but in terms.
—Walter Raleigh, *History of the World*, 1614

The wild goats that leap along those rocks have as much passion of joy in all that fair work of God as the men that toil among them.
—John Ruskin, *Modern Painters*, IV, 1856

Nature is perfect, wherever we look, but man always deforms it.
—J.C.F. von Schiller, *Die Braut von Messina*, 1803

Nature does nothing for the sake of an end, for that eternal and infinite Being whom we call God or Nature acts by the same necessity by which He exists.
—Baruch Spinoza, *Ethics*, 1677

God does not interfere directly with the natural order, where secondary causes suffice to produce the intended effect.
—Francis Suarez (1548–1617), *De Opere Sex Dierum*

In Nature we best see God under a disguise so heavy that it allows us to discern little more than that someone is there; within our own moral life we see Him with the mask, so to say, half fallen off.
—A.E. Taylor, *Essays Catholic and Critical*, 1938

NATURE

Nature is school-mistress, the soul the pupil; and whatever one has taught or the other learned has come from God—the Teacher of the teacher.

—Tertullian, *De Testimonio Animae*, c. 199

Everything in nature is in continual motion . . . but it will be asked, from whence did she receive her motion? Our reply is, from herself, since she is the great whole, out of which consequently, nothing can exist.

—Paul Henri Thiry, Baron d'Holbach, *The System of Nature*, 1770

Nature has no heart. . . . Absolute nature lives not in our life, nor yet is lifeless, but lives in the life of God: and in so far, and so far merely, as man himself lives in that life, does he come into sympathy with Nature.

—Francis Thompson, *Nature's Immortality*, 1910

A structure of evolving processes. The reality is the process.

—Alfred North Whitehead, *Science and the Modern World*, 1925

After you have exhausted what there is in business, politics, conviviality, love, and so on—what remains? Nature remains.

—Walt Whitman, *Specimen Days*, 1877

NEIGHBOR

The love of our neighbor hath its bounds in each man's love of himself.

—St. Augustine, *On Lying*, c. 395

"Thou shalt love thy neighbor as thyself." Why? Because every human being has a root in the Unity, and to reject the minutest particle of the Unity is to reject it all.

—Rabbi Israel Baal Shem-Tov (1700–60), *Baal-Shem*

In order that to love one's neighbor may be a matter of perfect justice, it is imperative that it be referred to God as its cause. Otherwise how can he love his neighbor without alloy?

—St. Bernard of Clairvaux, *On the Necessity of Loving God*, 1126

It is discouraging to try to be a good neighbor in a bad neighborhood.

—William R. Castle, *Dragon's Teeth in South America*, 1939

I have but one word to say to you concerning love for your neighbor, namely, that nothing save humility can mould you to it; nothing but the consciousness of your own weakness can make you indulgent and pitiful to that of others.
—François Fénelon (1651–1715), *Spiritual Letters of*

These are the things that you shall do: Speak the truth to one another, render in your gates judgments that are true and make for peace, do not devise evil in your hearts against one another.
—*Holy Bible*, Zechariah 8:16–17

As the prudent vintager eats only ripe grapes, and gathers not those which are green, so the eyes of a wise man rests only upon the virtue in others; whereas the eyes of the fool seeks only to discover in his neighbor vices and defects.
—St. John Climacus (525–600), *Climax*

Everything that is unconscious in ourselves we discover in our neighbor, and treat him accordingly. . . . What we combat in him is usually our inferior side.
—C.G. Jung, *Modern Man in Search of a Soul*, 1932

No one may forsake his neighbor when he is in trouble. Everybody is under obligation to help and support his neighbor as he would himself like to be helped.
—Martin Luther, letter, November 1527

A man must not choose his neighbour; he must take the neighbour that God sends him. The neighbour is just the man who is next to you at the moment, the man with whom any business has brought you into contact.
—George Macdonald, *Unspoken Sermons* (1st series), 1869

The love of our neighbour is the only door out of the dungeon of self.
—George Macdonald, *Unspoken Sermons* (1st series), 1869

You are asked to love your neighbor as yourself. You are not called upon to share his opinions. He may be a Pharisee.
—Aubrey Menen, *Dead Man in the Silver Market*, 1953

There is an idea abroad among moral people that they should make their neighbors good. One person I have to make good: myself. But my duty to my neighbor is much more nearly expressed by saying that I have to make him happy—if I may.
—Robert Louis Stevenson, *Across the Plains and Other Essays*, 1880

We are made for one another, and each is to be a supply to his neighbor.
—Benjamin Whichcote, *Moral and Religious Aphorisms*, 1753

No one can love his neighbor on an empty stomach.
—Woodrow Wilson, speech, New York, May 23, 1912

NONVIOLENCE

Non-violence is for the strong, not the weak. But in itself non-violence is a human imperative to be strong.
—James W. Douglass, *The Non-Violent Cross*, 1966

I object to violence because when it appears to do good, the good is only temporary; the evil it does is permanent.
—Mohandas K. Gandhi, *Selections from Gandhi*, 1945

Non-violence is the greatest force at the disposal of mankind. It is mightier than the mightiest weapon of destruction devised by the ingenuity of man.
—Mohandas K. Gandhi, *My Experiment with Truth*, 1927

Let us therefore blush when we ourselves perversely become wolves to our foes. While we remain sheep we have the victory. . . . As soon as we become wolves we are beaten. The Shepherd leaves us. He feeds sheep, not wolves.
—St. John Chrysostom, *Homilies* 33, c. 388

At the center of nonviolence stands the principle of love.
—Martin Luther King, Jr., *Stride Toward Freedom*, 1958

Nonviolence means that we will match your capacity to inflict pain with our capacity to endure it. . . . We have the choice in this world today between nonviolence and nonexistence.
—Martin Luther King, Jr., address, Drew University, February 1964

The disciples of the Prince of Peace . . . have rather consistently held, in practice, that the way to prove the sincerity of faith was not so much nonviolence as the generous use of lethal weapons.

—Thomas Merton, "Toward a Theology of Resistance,"
Faith and Violence, 1968

The essence of right conduct is not to injure anyone; one should know only this, that non-injury is religion.

—*Naladiyar,* c. 500 B.C.

Without nonviolence—mind states of loving kindness and compassion—at the core of our societal constructs, however, even the desire to protect and preserve can be manipulated in service to barbarism masquerading as idealism.

—Charlene Spretnak, *States of Grace,* 1991

Non-violence is not a biblical term but a Western ideal which has evolved in large measure because of the misuse of Christianity by Western powers to justify imperial wars, class injustice and racial prejudice.

—Philip Wheaton and Duane Shank, *Empire & the Word,* 1988

bedience

Duty and genuine goodness are mutually exclusive. . . . The sense of "ought" shows me the Good at an infinite impassable distance from my will. Willing obedience is never the fruit of an "ought" but only of love.
—Emil Brunner, *The Divine Imperative*, 1937

All citizens owe reverence and obedience to the magistrate as the minister of God in all righteous commands, and even their lives when the public safety and welfare require it.
—Henry Bullinger, *The Helvetic Confession*, 1536

The basis of society, of any society, is a certain *pride in obedience*. When this pride no longer exists, the society collapses.
—E.M. Cioran, *Drawn and Quartered*, 1971

Wise people, after they have listened to the laws, become serene, like a deep, smooth, and still lake. . . . Those who, when the Law has been well preached to them, follow the Law, will pass across the dominion of death, however difficult to overcome.
—*Dhammapada*, c. 5th century B.C.

I am the vessel. The draft is God's. And God is the thirsty one.
—Dag Hammarskjold, *Markings*, 1964

Obedience is the "virtue-making virtue."
—George J. Haye, *Obedience*, 1944

It is only as free obedience that obedience is a moral act, not as the purely external fulfillment of some external order.
—H. Hirschmann, *Stimmen der Zeit*, Vol. 161, 1957–58

For as by one man's disobedience many were made sinners, so by one man's obedience many will be made righteous.
—*Holy Bible*, Romans 5:19

The one only reason which men have for not obeying is when anything is demanded of them which is openly repugnant to the natural or divine law.
—Pope Leo XIII, *On Civil Government*, 1881

Christians must necessarily obey their magistrates and laws, save only when they command any sin; for then they must rather obey God than men.

—Philip Melanchthon, *Augsburg Confession*, 1530

All the things that God would have us do are hard for us to do—remember that—and hence, He oftener commands us than endeavors to persuade. And if we obey God, we must disobey ourselves, wherein the hardness of obeying God consists.

—Herman Melville, *Moby Dick*, 1851

Obedience to the spirit of God, rather than to the fair seeming pretense of men, is the best and most dutiful order that a Christian can observe.

—John Milton, *An Apology Against a Pamphlet*, 1642

Simple minds, less curious, less well instructed, are made good Christians, and through reverence and obedience hold their simple belief and abide by the laws.

—Michel de Montaigne, *Essays*, I, 1580

Whenever it be clearly seen that the commands of superiors are contrary to God's commandments, and especially when contrary to the precepts of charity, no one is in such case bound to obedience.

—Girolamo Savonarola, "Sermon," 1496, in *Cambridge Modern History*

If ye love me ye will keep my commandments. (John XIV, 15) If we don't, we shan't. Let no one deceive himself about that. There is no possibility of meeting His claim upon us, unless we truly love Him. So devotion is prior to obedience itself.

—William Temple, *Readings in St. John's Gospel*, 1939

He that strives to draw himself from obedience, withdraws himself from grace.

—Thomas à Kempis, *Imitation of Christ*, 1441

OLD AGE

Grow old along with me!
The best is yet to be,
The last of life for which the first was made.
Our times are in His hand
Who saith: "A whole I planned,
Youth shows but half; trust God: see all nor be afraid."

—Robert Browning (1812–89), "Rabbi Ben Ezra," in *Poems*

He who greets and constantly reveres the aged, four things will increase to him, namely life, beauty, happiness and power.

—*Dhammapada*, c. 5th century B.C.

To walk with God takes courage, and in old age God asks us to walk with Him.

—John La Farge, *Reflections on Growing Old*, 1963

Wisdom is with the aged, and understanding in length of days.

—*Holy Bible*, Job 12:12

Piety is the only proper and adequate relief of decaying man. He that grows old without religious hopes, as he declines into imbecility, and feels pains and sorrows incessantly crowding upon him, falls into a gulf of bottomless misery, in which every reflection must plunge him deeper, and where he finds only new gradations of anguish and precipices of horror.

—Samuel Johnson, in *Rambler*, November 13, 1750

The heart of the old is always young in two things, in love for the world and length of hope.

—Mohammed, *Speeches and Table-Talk of*, 7th century

Never forget . . . that the individuality of man lasts out the greatest suffering and the most entrancing joy alike unscathed, while the body crumbles away in the pains and pleasures of the flesh.

—Jean Paul Richter, *Reminiscences of the Best Hours of Life*, 1841

Old age consoles itself by giving good precepts for being unable to give bad examples.

—La Rochefoucauld, *Maxims*, 1665

OPINIONS

The only sin which we never forgive in each other is a difference of opinion.

—Ralph Waldo Emerson, *Clubs*, 1877

Men are disturbed not by events which happen, but by the opinion they have of these events. Thus death is nothing terrible . . . but the opinion we have about death is that it is terrible, this is the terrifying thing.

—Epictetus, *Enchiridion*, V, c. 110

Error of opinion may be tolerated where reason is left free to combat it.

—Thomas Jefferson, inaugural address, March 4, 1801

If thinking men would have the courage to think for themselves, and to speak what they think, it would be found they do not differ in religious opinions as much as is supposed.

—Thomas Jefferson, letter to John Adams, 1813

Men are never so good or so bad as their opinions.

—James Mackintosh, *Progress of Ethical Philosophy*, 1830

Reward and punish no doctrine; hold out no allurement or bribe for the adoption of theological opinions. . . . Suffer no one to be a searcher of hearts and a judge of opinions . . . to assume the right which the Omniscient has reserved to Himself.

—Moses Mendelssohn, *Jerusalem*, 1783

We can never be sure that the opinion we are endeavoring to stifle is a false opinion; and even if we were sure, it would be an evil still.

—John Stuart Mill, *On Liberty*, 1859

Men are tormented by the opinions they have of things, not by the things themselves.

—Michel de Montaigne, *Essays*, I, 1580

Now we do not care to ascertain whether an opinion is true or false, but only whether it is life-furthering, life-preserving. We start with a certain view of life, think of a few things as necessary to it, and conclude that they are true and objective.

—Sarvepalli Radhakrishnan, *The Reign of Religion in Contemporary Philosophy*, 1922

Wide differences of opinion in matters of religious, political and social belief must exist if conscience and intellect alike are not to be stunted.

—Theodore Roosevelt, speech, April 23, 1910

As the thoughts of man are altogether unfettered, reasoning which disregards the holy texts and rests on individual opinion only has no proper foundation.

—Sankara (c. 750), *Sacred Books of the East*, XXXIV

Truth generally lies in the coordination of antagonistic opinions.
—Herbert Spencer, *Autobiography*, 1904

The notion that one opinion is as good as another will not work in any other area of human experience, why should it work in the area of faith?
—David E. Trueblood, *Philosophy of Religion*, 1957

OPPRESSION

It is too common a sort of oppression for the rich in all places to domineer too insolently over the poor, and force them to follow their wills and to serve their interests, be it right or wrong. . . . An oppressor is an Anti-Christ and an Anti-God . . . not only an agent of the Devil, but his image.
—Richard Baxter, *The Christian Directory*, 1673

Religion sanctions woman's self-love; it gives her the guide, father, lover, divine guardian she longs for nostalgically; it feeds her day-dreams; it fills her empty hours. But, above all, it confirms the social order, it justifies her resignation, by giving her the hope of a better future in a sexless heaven. This is why women today are still a powerful trump in the hand of the Church; it is why the Church is notably hostile to all measures liable to help in women's emancipation. There must be religion for women; and there must be women, "true women," to perpetuate religion.
—Simone de Beauvoir, *The Second Sex*, 1949

As Christians, blacks have been expected to demonstrate a patience, a love, and a tolerance they rarely saw in their teachers and oppressors; but they have, nevertheless, made this Gospel their own. Steeped in the despondency of power-lessness, cursed by the ever-present insufficiency of the means of livelihood, relegated to racist institutions, con-demned by injustice, and propagandized by notions of white supremacy and black degeneracy, blacks have taken the Gospel given to them by those who would use it as an instru-ment of their pacification and have transformed it into a means of liberation.
—John M. Burgess, Introduction, *Black Gospel/White Church*, 1982

The biblical and popular image of God as a great patriarch in heaven, rewarding and punishing according to his mysterious and seemingly arbitrary will, has dominated the imagination of millions over thousands of years. The symbol of the Father God, spawned in the human imagination and sustained as plausible by patriarchy, has in turn rendered service to this type of society by making its mechanisms for the oppression of women appear right and fitting. If God in "his" heaven is a father ruling "his" people, then it is in the "nature" of things and according to divine plan and the order of the universe that society be male-dominated.

—Mary Daly, *Beyond God the Father: Toward a Philosophy of Women's Liberation*, 1973

If we claim that oppressive patriarchal texts are the Word of God then we proclaim God as a God of oppression and dehumanization.

—Elisabeth Schussler Fiorenza, *Bread Not Stone*, 1984

The true reality of the oppressor can only be seen from the point of view of the oppressed.

—Eduardo Galeano, *We Say No Chronicles, 1963 to 1991*, 1992

God does not always punish a nation by sending it adversity. More often He gives the oppressors their hearts' desire, and sends leanness withal into their soul.

—W.R. Inge, *Personal Religion and the Life of Devotion*, 1924

Economic oppression cannot exist without its religious justifications.

—M. Douglas Meeks, *God the Economist*, 1989

God shows mercy by welcoming the oppressed, those excluded from the benefits of the dominant society. God shows mercy for oppressors by welcoming them as participants in the continuing process of putting things right.

—Letty M. Russell, "Bought with a Price," *The Christian Century*, January 29, 1992

Why does suffering single out black people so conspicuously, suffering not at the hands of pagans or other unbelievers, but at the hands of white fellow Christians who claim allegiance to the same Lord and Master?

—Bishop Desmond Tutu, *Crying in the Wilderness*, 1982

The eternal message of the Exodus is not to glory in the defeat of the oppressors or wait until they become the losers and we the victors. . . . The main message is that whichever way you turn in a relationship of exploitation or objectification, you lose.
—Sheila Peltz Weinberg, "Judaism, Feminism, and Peace in the Nuclear Age," *Women of Faith in Dialogue*, 1987

OPTIMISM

All sunshine makes a desert.
—Arab proverb

Nine times out of ten, optimism is a sly form of selfishness, a method of isolating oneself from the unhappiness of others.
—Georges Bernanos, *Last Essays of*, 1955

Optimism, n. The doctrine, or belief that everything is beautiful, including what is ugly, everything good, especially the bad, and everything right that is wrong. . . . An intellectual disorder, yielding to no treatment but death.
—Ambrose Bierce, *Devil's Dictionary*, 1906

An optimist is a believer in the best, and any man who believes that anything less than the best is the ultimate purpose of God, and so the ultimate possibility of God's children, has no business to live upon the earth.
—Phillips Brooks, *National Needs and Remedies*, 1890

The scientific optimism of which Huxley may be taken as a typical exponent was merely a new variety of faith, resting upon certain premises which are no more unassailable than those which have supported other vanished religions in the past.
—Joseph Wood Krutch, *The Modern Temper*, 1929

Nothing is too great or too good to be true. Do not believe that we can imagine things better than they are. In the long run, in the ultimate outlook, in the eye of the Creator, the possibilities of existence, the possibilities open to us, are beyond our imagination.
—Oliver Lodge, *Science and Human Progress*, 1926

Christianity did not come into the world with a fixed, silly grin on its face and vapid Cheerio on its lips. At its center was a cross. That heritage must be saved from being perverted by the Bright-side boys, whether in the pulpit or out of it.
—Halford E. Luccock, *Living Without Gloves*, 1957

All the slippery optimism which has so devitalized the democratic peoples has sprung not from accidental misjudgments about particular events; it has sprung from an essential defect, which is best seen in its intellectual nakedness, in the philosophy of pragmatic liberalism.

—Lewis Mumford, *Faith for Living*, 1940

Optimism believes that the indefinite progress of the universe by technical achievement due to an inherent law of dialectics will result in absolute happiness for humanity. The first duty is thus to believe in the future, to advance, to dedicate oneself unreservedly to the possession of the world.

—Emmanuel Suhard, *The Church Today*, 1953

We are not to take hold of the worse, but rather to be glad we may find hope that mankind has not grown monstrous. Optimism is the madness of maintaining that everything is right when it is wrong.

—Voltaire, *Candide*, 1739

The fact of the religious vision, and its history of persistent expansion, is our one ground for optimism. Apart from it, human life is a flash of occasional enjoyments lighting up a mass of pain and misery, a bagatelle of transient experience.

—Alfred North Whitehead, *Science and the Modern World*, 1925

ORIGINAL SIN

Wherever the Science of Ethics is acknowledged and taught, there the Article of Original Sin will be an Axiom of Faith in all classes . . . a fact acknowledged in all ages, and recognized, but not originating, in the Christian Scriptures.

—Samuel Taylor Coleridge, *Aids to Reflections*, 1825

By which transgression, commonly called Original Sin, was the image of God utterly defiled in man; and he and his posterity of nature become enemies to God, slaves to Satan, and servants to sin.

—*Confession of Faith*, Presbyterian Church of Scotland, August 1, 1560

Original sin . . . has so totally corrupted human nature that man is incapable of any spiritual good and inclined to all evil.

—W.H.T. Dau, *What Is Lutheranism?*, 1930

The guilt of man has upon his soul at first existence, is one and simple, viz., the guilt of the original apostasy, the guilt by which the species first rebelled against God.
—Jonathan Edwards, *The Great Christian Doctrine of Original Sin Defended*, 1758

Each soul as it enters on existence, receives its nature from Him; and to affirm that this "nature is *itself* sinful," and that every cause partakes of the character of its effect, is not only to make God the author of sin, but to make Him *sinful* to boot!
—Chauncey Goodrich, *Quarterly Christian Spectator*, June 1829

Every human being who is conceived by the coition of a man with a woman is born with original sin, subject to impiety and death, and therefore a child of wrath.
—Gratian, *Decretum*, c. 1150

Judaism does not attribute man's constant backsliding to original sin. Every child is born completely untainted.
—Simon Greenberg, *Patterns of Faith in America Today*, 1957

Sin is original in the sense of a permanent human tendency, and the Fall of man happened not once but is perpetual falling away from the life of loving obedience which God requires of us.
—Georgia Harkness, *The Providence of God*, 1960

Original Sin . . . is no positive taint or corruption inherent in our nature, but a negative fact, the deprivation of an un-owed super-human gift intended by God for us—namely, *Ultimate Redemption.*
—C.C. Martindale, *God and the Supernatural*, 1920

Original sin is at work everywhere.
—Karl Marx, *Das Kapital*, I, 649, 1867

We are all . . . tainted from birth with a tendency towards what we know as evil. But the dogma of original sin so extended as to embrace inherited guilt is a pure fabrication of occidental theology.
—Paul Elmer More, *The Catholic Faith*, 1931

Original sin is not an inherited corruption, but it is an inevitable fact of human existence, the inevitability of which is given by the nature of man's spirituality.
—Reinhold Niebuhr, *An Interpretation of Christian Ethics*, 1935

Nothing good and nothing evil, on account of which we are deemed either laudable or blameworthy, is born with us, but is done by us; for we are born not fully developed, but with a capacity for either conduct; we are formed without either vice or virtue.
—Pelagius (c. 370–c. 440), in *The Anti-Pelagin Works of St. Augustine*

A concept of original sin is typical of a view of life which makes the past an authority over the present.
—David Riesman, in *Psychiatry*, Vol. 13, No. 2, 1950

What is the dogma of original sin but a means of making the things of the flesh enter a spiritual system?
—Jacques Rivière, *Études*, 1924

The doctrine of original sin (assertion of the will) and of salvation (denial of the will) is the great truth which constitutes the essence of Christianity.
—Arthur Schopenhauer, "Religion," *Essays*, 1841

If we come into the World infected and depraved with sinful Disposition, then Sin must be natural to us; and if natural, then necessary; and if necessary, then no Sin.
—John Taylor, *The Scripture—Doctrine of Original Sin*, 1746

Each of us takes his place in the center of his own world. But I am not the center of the world, or the standard of reference as between good and bad; I am not, and God is. In other words, from the beginning I put myself in God's place. This is my original sin.
—William Temple, *Christianity and the Social Order*, 1942

Death and all bodily miseries are among the pains of original sin.
—St. Thomas Aquinas, *Summa Theologiae* Ia, IIae, q. 85, 1272

ORTHODOXY

We may observe the behavior of some of the most zealous for orthodoxy, who have often great friendships and intimacies with vicious immoral men, provided they do but agree with them in the same scheme of belief.
—Joseph Addison, *The Spectator*, 1714

Orthodox, n. An ox wearing the popular religious yoke.
—Ambrose Bierce, *Devil's Dictionary*, 1906

And prove their doctrine orthodox,
By apostolic blows and knocks.
—Samuel Butler, *Hudibras*, 1663

Orthodoxy is characterized by a spirit, and a very proper
one, of reverent agnosticism towards the central mysteries of
the faith.
—J.V.L. Casserley, *Retreat from Christianity in the Modern World*, 1952

In Protestantism no system of orthodoxy can determine a
man's faith. The faith is organically related to man's free
spirit and thus is forever being forced to test the creeds and
confessions which are worked out.
—J. Leslie Dunstan, *Protestantism*, 1962

If we were all before the gates of Heaven and the question
were put, "Which of you is orthodox?," the Jew, the Turk and
the Christian would answer in unison, "I am."
—Immanuel Kant, *Lecture at Königsberg*, 1775

Every church is orthodox to itself; to others, erroneous or
heretical.
—John Locke, *A Letter Concerning Toleration*, 1685

It was heresy that made orthodoxy necessary.
—James A. Martin, Jr., *Fact, Fiction and Faith*, 1960

Jesus would find the orthodox doctrinal formulations about
him today as confining as he did those in his own culture.
—Mason Olds, "A Developmental Interpretation of Jesus,"
Religious Humanism, Summer 1991

ain

Man has ever risen near to God by the altar stairs of pain and sorrow.
　　　　　　—S.A. Adler, *The Discipline of Sorrow*, 1906

Certain pains are bad in an absolute manner, others are bad only in so far as they deprive us of some good.
　　　　　　—Aristotle, *Nicomachean Ethics*, c. 340 B.C.

Pain is either an evil for the body—and if so, let the body state its case—or for the soul; but the soul can maintain its own unclouded calm, and refuse to view it as an evil.
　　　　　　Marcus Aurelius, *Meditations*, c. 170

Pain in the human world is the birth of personality, its fight for its own nature.
　　　　　　—Nicholas Berdyaev, *Slavery and Freedom*, 1944

For after all, evil and pain are identical; it is those unable to see pain as the natural result of doing evil that continue to do evil.
　　　　　　—*Dhammapada*, c. 5th century B.C.

Considered in themselves, painful things can never be loved, but considered in the light of their source—as ordained by Providence and the will of God—they are infinitely delightful.
　　　　　　—St. Francis de Sales, *Treatise on the Love of God*, 1607

If I am part of God, if the Self at its core is God, then I cannot deny Him, nor He deny me, and there is no relationship, for He is constrained by His being as I, and He is not the only necessary being, for I am necessary too, and He exists by my will as much as I do by His.
　　　　　　—Anne Freemantle, *The Age of Belief*, 1955

Pain and death always have the last word in this world of ours. . . . There is enough pain in one alley of a big city slum or in one hospital ward to convince even the dreamiest optimist that life is not naturally good.
　　　　　　—Oswald C.J. Hoffmann, *Life Crucified*, 1959

The problems that vex us here will be fully solved hereafter; eternity will explain this brief life. This is the wondrous music which we wring from the jarring notes of the world's pain and sin.

—Morris Joseph, *Judaism as Creed and Life*, 1903

The pearl of great price always begins as a pain in the oyster's stomach!

—John E. Large, *The Small Needle of Doctor Large*, 1962

No pain, no palm; no thorns, no throne; no gall, no glory; no cross, no crown.

—William Penn, *No Cross, No Crown*, 1669

In the garden of humanity, ever since it ceased to be called the earthly paradise, there has ripened, and will always ripen one of the bitter fruits of original sin: pain.

—Pope Pius XII, address, July 14, 1950

Pain and death have become the means of redemption and sanctification for every man who does not deny Christ.

—Pope Pius XII, address, November 12, 1943

There is a kind and quality of pain that is creative, curative, redemptive, and . . . this is a kind of pain which man is privileged to share with God.

—B.H. Streeter, *Reality*, 1926

PASSION

Today—psychologists write with the frankness of Freud or Kinsey on the sexual passions of mankind, but blush and grow silent when the religious passions come in view.

—Gordon W. Allport, *The Individual and His Religion*, 1951

There is no passion in the mind of man so weak but it mates and masters the fear of death.

—Francis Bacon, *Essays*, 1625

If men's passions are deep, their divinity is shallow.

—Chuang-tzu, c. 300 B.C.

Truth needs not the service of passion; yea, nothing so disserves it, as passion when set to serve it. The *Spirit of Truth* is the *Spirit of Meekness*.

—Samuel Taylor Coleridge, *Aids to Reflection*, 1825

We are ne'er like angels till our passion dies.
—Thomas Dekker, *The Honest Whore*, 1630

As rain does not break through a well-thatched house, passion will not break through a well-reflecting mind.
—*Dhammapada*, c. 5th century B.C.

We are not indebted to the Reason of man for any of the great achievements which are the landmarks of human action and human progress. . . . Man is only truly great when he acts from the passions; never irresistible but when he appeals to the imagination.
—Benjamin Disraeli, *Coningsby*, 1844

Theologians have always recognized that passions may overwhelm the person suddenly and completely to the point where freedom of choice does not exist and responsibility is not present.
—J. Dominian, *Psychiatry and the Christian*, 1962

Chastise your passions, that they may not chastise you.
—Epictetus, *Enchiridion*, c. 110

There are some passions so close to virtues that there is danger lest we be deceived by the doubtful distinction between them.
—Desiderius Erasmus, *Enchiridion*, 1501

A man in a passion rides a wild horse.
—Benjamin Franklin, *Poor Richard's Almanac*, 1749

Passion, joined with power, produceth thunder and ruin.
—Thomas Fuller, *Gnomologia*, 1732

The pious man . . . subdues his passions, keeping them in bonds, but giving them their share in order to satisfy them as regards food, drink, cleanliness, etc.
—Judah Halevi, *Cuzari*, II, c. 1135

Nothing great in the world has been accomplished without passion.
—G.W.F. Hegel (1770–1831), *Philosophy of History*, publ. posth.

Passions are spiritual Rebels, and raise sedition against the understanding.
—Ben Jonson, *Discoveries*, 1641

Even he who is lost through passion has not lost so much as
he who has lost passion, for the former had the possibility.
—Sören Kierkegaard, *Postscript*, 1846

It is by their passions that men know they belong to the
same race. They all slip in the same direction; they roll down
the same slope.
—François Mauriac, *Holy Thursday*, 1944

Passion is an unnatural movement of the soul that is the result of a love without reason, or of an irrational aversion for
some concrete object.
—St. Maximus the Confessor, *Centuries of Charity*, c. 626

No passion or affection, with which we are born, can be in itself sinful; it becomes so, only by wilful or careless indulgence.
—Jonathan Mayhew, *Sermons*, 1755

Praised be St. John, the glorified of God! Lord, grant me the
prayers of St. John, disciple and friend whom thou lovest,
apostle of love. Thy love, forever, eternal, that my faith may
become as complete, as flaming and tranquil, as his, and
pierce as deep and speak as simply in the spirit.
—Eric Milner-White, *My God, My Glory*, 1954

The power of the soul for good is in proportion to the
strength of its passion.
—Coventry Patmore, *The Rod, the Root, and the Flower*, 1895

Three passions, simple but overwhelmingly strong, have governed my life: the longing for love, the search for knowledge,
and unbearable pity for the suffering of mankind.
—Bertrand Russell, *Autobiography*, 1967

PATHS

Any path is only a path, and there is no affront, to oneself or
to others, in dropping it if that is what your heart tells
you.. . . . Look at every path closely and deliberately. Try it as
many times as you think necessary. Then ask yourself, and
yourself alone, one question. . . . Does this path have a
heart? If it does, the path is good; if it doesn't it is of no use.
—Carlos Castaneda, *The Teachings of Don Juan*, 1968

As different streams have different sources and with wanderings crooked or straight, all reach the sea, so Lord, the different paths which men take, guided by their different tendencies, all lead to Thee.
—Hindu prayer, in J. James, *The Way of Mysticism*, 1950

Let us not be uneasy that the different roads we may pursue, as believing them the shortest, to that of our last abode; but, following the guidance of the good conscience, let us be happy in the hope that by these different paths we shall all meet in the end.
—Thomas Jefferson, letter to Miles King, September 26, 1814

This middle path . . . is the noble path, namely: right views, right intent, right speech, right conduct, right means of livelihood, right endeavor, right mindfulness, right meditation. . . .Which leads to insights, leads to wisdom, which conduces to calm, to knowledge, to perfect enlightenment, to Nirvana.
—*The Mahavagga of the Vinya Texts*, between 5th and 1st centuries B.C.

Let a Christian follow the precepts of his own faith, let a Hindu and a Jew follow theirs. If they strive long enough, they will ultimately discover God, who runs like a seam under the crusts of rituals and forms.
—Swami Nikhilananda, *Perspectives on a Troubled Decade*, 1950

As one can ascend to the top of a house by means of a ladder or a bamboo or a staircase or a rope, so divers are the ways and means to approach God, and every religion in the world shows one of these ways.
—Sri Ramakrishna, *His Life and Sayings*, 1899

Go Godward: thou wilt find a road.
—Russian proverb

How often do we hear it said: "It doesn't matter what we believe. By different roads we are all heading for the same goal." What assurance have we that all the different roads, mapped out by mere human beings, lead to the same goal?
—John J. Wade, *Conquering with Christ*, 1942

PATIENCE

Patience is the companion of wisdom.
—St. Augustine, *On Patience*, c. 425

Patience, n. A minor form of despair, disguised as a virtue.
—Ambrose Bierce, *Devil's Dictionary*, 1906

It is an easy thing to talk of patience to the afflicted.
—William Blake, *The Four Zoas*, 1797

Patience is sorrow's salve.
—Charles Churchill, *The Prophecy of Famine*, 1763

Be patient with everyone, but above all with thyself. I mean, do not be disheartened by your imperfections, but always rise up with fresh courage.
—St. Francis de Sales (1567–1622), in *The Spirit of*

Faith, Love, and Hope once felt, in a peaceful, sociable hour, a plastic impulse in their nature; together they set to work and created a lovely image, a Pandora in the higher sense, namely Patience.
—J.W. von Goethe (1749–1832), *Maxims and Reflections*

Better is the end of a thing than its beginning; and the patient in spirit is better than the proud in spirit.
—*Holy Bible*, Ecclesiastes 7:8

By your endurance you will gain your lives.
—*Holy Bible*, Luke 21:19

Let us run with perseverance the race that is set before us.
—*Holy Bible*, Hebrews 12:1

If God has taken away all means of seeking remedy, there is nothing left but patience.
—John Locke, *Treatise on Government*, 1690

Patience, the beggar's virtue.
—Philip Massinger, *A New Way to Pay Old Debts*, 1633

They also serve who only stand and wait.
—John Milton, *Sonnet on His Blindness*, c. 1650

Rail not at fickle Fortune! Those who eat
The fruit of bitter Patience find it sweet.
—Shaikh Saadi, *Gulistan*, c. 1265

All men commend patience, although few be willing to practice it.
—Thomas à Kempis, *Imitation of Christ*, 1441

Peace

Let human prudence say what it likes and reason as it pleases, it is impossible to produce true temporal peace and tranquillity by things repugnant or opposed to the peace and happiness of eternity.
—Silvio Antoniano (1540–1603), *The Christian Education of Youth*

It is one thing to see the land of peace from a wooded ridge . . . and another to tread the road that leads to it.
—St. Augustine, *Confessions*, vii, XXI, 397

Peace is that state in which fear of any kind is unknown.
—John Buchan, *Pilgrim's Way*, 1940

Peacemaking is not an optional commitment. It is a requirement of our faith.
—*The Challenge of Peace:, God's Promise and our Response*, Bishops' Pastoral Letter, 1983

Either for God or against God. . . . Upon that choice hangs the fate of the world. In every department of life, in politics and economics, in the sciences and arts, in the State and in domestic life we follow God's laws to peace or bypass them into chaos.
—Richard J. Cushing, *Permanent Industrial Peace*, 1946

Amidst the calm and tranquillity of peace the human race accomplishes most freely and easily its given work. . . . Whence it is manifest that universal peace is the best of those things that are ordained for our beatitude.
—Dante, *De Monarchia*, bk. 1, ch. 4, c. 1300

The world will believe in peace only when the Churches will demonstrate that it can exist.
—J.J.A. Lecomte du Noüy, *Human Destiny*, 1947

Ask not that events should happen as you will, but let your will be that events should happen as they do, and you shall have peace.
—Epictetus, *Manual of*, c. 110

The most disadvantageous peace is better than the most
just war.
—Desiderius Erasmus, *Adagia*, 1508

Peace at any price can be the abnegation of morality entirely,
the refusal of even a negative contribution to righteousness.
—P.T. Forsyth, *The Christian Ethic of War*, 1916

Pax: peace, but what a strange peace, made of unremitting
toil and effort, seldom with a seen result; subject to constant
interruptions, unexpected demands, short sleep at night, little comfort, sometimes scant food; beset with disappointments and usually misunderstood; yet peace all the same,
undeviating, filled with joy and gratitude and love.
—Rumer Godden, *In This House of Brede*, 1969

Blessed are the peacemakers, for they shall be called sons
of God.
—*Holy Bible*, Matthew 5:9

He shall judge between the nations, and shall decide for
many people; and they shall beat their swords into plowshares, and their spears into pruning hooks; nation shall not
lift up sword against nation, neither shall they learn war any
more.
—*Holy Bible*, Isaiah 2:4

Let us then pursue what makes for peace and for mutual
understanding.
—*Holy Bible*, Romans 14:19

Peace is not just the absence of war. It involves mutual respect and confidence between peoples and nations. It involves collaboration and binding agreements. Like a
cathedral, peace must be constructed patiently and with un-
shakable faith.
—Pope John Paul II, homily at Coventry Cathedral, in *Origins*, 1982

If history teaches anything it is that there can be no peace
without equilibrium and no justice without restraint.
—Henry Kissinger, *White House Years*, 1979

There is no way to peace. Peace is the way.
—A.J. Muste, in *The New York Times*, November 16, 1967

Without repentance those who have created peace through their power imagine that they have created pure peace: and suffer from the delusion that the enemies of their peace are God's enemies.

—Reinhold Niebuhr, *Beyond Tragedy*, 1937

It is absurd to seek peace while rejecting God. For where God is left out, justice is left out, and where justice is lacking there can be no hope of peace.

—Pius X, *Supremi apostolatus*, October 4, 1903

Peace is essentially a moral fact, and only subordinately a political fact as a means to the end; peace is above all an act of reconciliation.

—Luigi Sturzo, address to Liturgical Conference, Chicago, 1943

Humanity is in a precarious balance between the forces of violence and the forces of peace. It is by no means clear at this time which of these forces will prevail. We do ask, however, whether religion will now become an aid to the forces of peace or cooperation.

—Obert C. Tanner, *One Man's Search*, 1989

All men desire peace, but few desire the things that make for peace.

—Thomas a Kempis, *Imitation of Christ*, 1441

Peace is self-control at its widest—at the width where the "self" has been lost, and interest has been transferred to coordinations wider than personality.

—Alfred North Whitehead, *Adventures of Ideas*, 1933

The most solid and satisfying peace is that which comes from this constant spiritual warfare.

—Woodrow Wilson, address, May 1911

PEACE OF MIND

As for our proper peace, we have it double with God; here below by faith, and hereafter above by sight. But all peace we have here, be it public or peculiar, is rather a solace to our misery, than any assurance of our felicity.

—St. Augustine, *The City of God*, 426

For nowhere can a mind find a retreat more full of peace or more free from care than his own soul.

—Marcus Aurelius, *Meditations*, c. 170

Let no temporal things be the cause of thy peace; for then wilt thou be as worthless and fragile as they. You would have such a peace in common with the brutes; let thine be that of the angels, which proceeds from truth.

—Guiges du Chastel (1084–1137), *Meditations*

Giving oneself to God, even in the contemplative life, is no way to get peace of mind, but rather to get into the thick of the fighting.

—Jean Danielou, *The Lord of History*, 1958

Lasting peace of mind is impossible apart from peace with God; yet enduring peace with God comes only when a man is ready to surrender his own peace of mind.

—A. Roy Eckardt, in *The Christian Century*, November 17, 1954

Nothing can bring you peace but yourself.

—Ralph Waldo Emerson, "Self-Reliance," *Essays*, 1844

No one can get inner peace by pouncing on it, by vigorously willing to have it. Peace is a margin of power around our daily need. Peace is a consciousness of springs too deep for earthly droughts to dry up. Peace is the gift not of volitional struggle but of spiritual hospitality.

—Harry Emerson Fosdick, radio address, January 6, 1946

Get but that "peace of God which passeth understanding," and the questions of the understanding will cease from puzzling and pedantic scruples be at rest.

—William James, *The Will to Believe and Other Essays*, 1896

The Christian has a deep, silent, hidden peace, which the world sees not, like some well in a retired and shady place. . . . What he is when left to himself and to his God, that is his true life.

—John Henry Newman, *Parochial and Plain Sermons*, Vol. 5, 1843

The Bible nowhere calls upon men to go out in search of peace of mind. It does call upon men to go out in search of God and the things of God.

—Abba Hillel Silver, *Where Judaism Differed*, 1957

The ultimate standpoint of Zen, therefore, is that we have
been led astray through ignorance to find a split in our own
being, that there was from the very beginning no need for a
struggle between the finite and the infinite, that the peace we
are seeking so eagerly after has been there all the time.
    —D.T. Suzuki, *Zen Buddhism*, 1956

PENITENCE

When someone asks for forgiveness and we withhold it, we
think we're binding up the other person. In reality the other
person is unbound because he or she has sought forgiveness. We bind ourselves in unforgiveness when we do not
have a compassionate heart.
    —Michael Crosby, in *U.S. Catholic*, August 1991

We seek sensible consolations impatiently, out of fear of
lacking penitence. Why not let our penitence take the shape
of renouncing the consolation we so eagerly seek?
    —François Fénelon (1651–1715), *Spiritual Letters*

There is no virtue in penance and fasting, which waste the
body; they are only fanatical and monkish.
    —Immanuel Kant, *Lecture at Königsberg*, 1775

Always there remains this need to explain to each other that
we are good. We all have a constant need to be reaffirmed.
    —Sister Corita Kent, *Footnotes and Headlines*, 1967

Concerning penitence or penance we teach that it consists in
the acknowledgment of sins and genuine trust in God, who
forgives them all for Christ's sake.
    —Martin Luther, sermon, 1528

The notion of the need of penance and expiation is lost in
proportion as belief in God is weakened, and the idea of an
original sin and of a first rebellion of man against God becomes confused and disappears.
    —Pope Pius XI, *Caritate Christi Compulsi*, 1932

The time will come when thou wilt wish for one day or hour
to amend, and I know not whither thou shalt obtain it.
    —Thomas à Kempis, *Imitation of Christ*, 1441

If penance is being practiced as it should be, it is an act of
prayer—positively uniting us with the Passion, positively expressing love, positively surrendering self.
    —Hubert van Zeller, *We Die Standing Up*, 1949

Before God created the world, he created Penitence and said
to him: "I am going to create a man in the world, on condition that every time he turns to you you are ready to forgive
him his sins."

—*Zohar*, c. 1290

PERFECTION

The pursuit of perfection, then, is the pursuit of sweetness
and light. He who works for sweetness and light, works to
make reason and the will of God prevail.

—Matthew Arnold, *Culture and Anarchy*, 1869

Man reacheth perfection by each being intent on his own
duty.

—*Bhagavad-Gita*, between 5th and 2nd centuries B.C.

If we knew everything and could feel everything we should
see and feel what finiteness, pain and evil mean, and how
they play a part in perfection itself.

—B. Bosanquet, *The Principle of Individuality and Value*, 1912

There is no one in the world who cannot arrive without difficulty at the most eminent perfection by fulfilling with love
obscure and common duties.

—J.P. de Cassaude, *Abandonment*, 1887

I know of no man perfect in all things at once but still human . . . except Him alone who for us clothed Himself with
humanity.

—St. Clement of Alexandria, *The Miscellanies*, c. 200

The moral goodness of man, the necessary consequence of
his constitution, is capable of indefinite perfection like all his
other faculties, and nature has linked together in an un-
breakable chain truth, happiness and virtue.

—A.N. de Condorcet, *Progress of the Human Mind*, 1794

The love of God never looks for perfection in created beings.
It knows that it dwells with Him alonc. As it never expects
perfection, it is never disappointed.

—François Fénelon, (1651–1715), *Selections from*

I am not a perfect servant. I am a public servant doing my
best against the odds. As I develop and serve, be patient.
God is not finished with me yet.

—Jesse L. Jackson, speech to the Democratic National Convention, July 17, 1984

The law of duty demands moral perfection or holiness. But this is impossible in our present life, therefore it can only be attained by an indefinite progress, and this progress is only possible under the hypothesis of an existence and a personality that are indefinitely prolonged.
—P.A.R. Janet and G. Séailles, *A History of the Problems of Philosophy*, II, 1902

God's perfections are marvelous but not lovable.
—Immanuel Kant, *Lecture at Königsberg*, 1775

Perfection does not consist in any singular state or condition of life, or in any particular set of duties, but in holy and religious conduct of ourselves in every state of Life.
—William Law, *Christian Perfection*, 1726

To love truth for truth's sake is the principal part of human perfection in this world, and the seed-plot of all other virtues.
—John Locke, letter to Anthony Collins, October 1703

The service of God is not intended for God's perfection; it is intended for our perfection.
—Maimonides, *Guide for the Perplexed*, 1190

For frail mortals, perfection is achieved not by never falling, but by rising every time we fall.
—John A. O'Brien, *Religion, Does It Matter?*, 1944

When the soul has passed through all the virtues and reached the summit of perfection, it leaves the world and goes away.
—Origen (185–254), *In Numeros Homilies.*, XXVII

The idea is to have contempt for crime, not for people. . . . It's more useful to think of every other person as another *you*—to think of every individual as a representative of the universe.
—Rolling Thunder, 1974

Repentance . . . is about being restored to ourselves.
—Maggie Ross, in *Creation Spirituality*, September/October 1992

The pain that gives us self-knowledge, willingly sought and moved through, is at the heart of repentance of any kind. Pain is . . . the open space—one meaning of the ancient Hebrew word for salvation—the point of intersection and integration of our selves with one another and all the Creation.
—Maggie Ross, in *Creation Spirituality*, September/October 1992

Perfection is being, not doing; it is not to effect an act but to achieve a character.
—Fulton J. Sheen, *Way to Happiness*, 1953

The ultimate development of the ideal man is logically certain—as certain as any conclusion in which we place the most implicit faith; for instance, that all men will die.
—Herbert Spencer, *Social Statics*, 1851

Perfection and imperfection are really only modes of thought; that is to say, notions which we are in the habit of forming from the comparison with one another of individuals of the same species or genus.
—Baruch Spinoza, *Ethics*, 1677

Many, mistaking *devotions* for *devotion*, imagine perfection to consist in reciting a great number of prayers, in joining sundry religious societies.
—Adolphe Tanqueray, *The Spiritual Life*, 1490

What is Christian perfection? The loving God with all our heart, mind, soul, and strength. This implies that no wrong temper, none contrary to love, remains in the soul; and that all the thoughts, words, and actions are governed by pure love.
—John Wesley (1703–91), *Plain Account of Christian Perfection*

PERSECUTION

Those even who persecuted Christ or His followers, whom they considered it their duty to persecute, are said to have sinned in action; but they would have committed a graver fault if, contrary to their conscience, they had spared them.
—Peter Abelard, *Scito te Ipsum*, c. 1138

A man who is possessed by fear always begins to persecute.
—Nicholas Berdyaev, *Slavery and Freedom*, 1941

It is an undoubted fact that an overwhelming majority of religious persecutors have been men of the purest intentions, of the most admirable and unsullied morals. . . . Such men as these are not bad, they are only ignorant; ignorant of the nature of truth, ignorant of the consequences of their own acts.
—Henry Thomas Buckle, *History of Civilization in England*, 1861

The actual point in question, throughout the centuries of Christian persecution, has never been faith in God, but faith in the Bible as the word of God, and in the Church (this Church or that) as the interpreter of that word.
—Joseph Campbell, *The Masks of God*, 1968

Cruel persecution and intolerance are not accidents, but grow out of the very essence of religion, namely, its absolute claims.
—Morris R. Cohen, *Religion Today*, ed. by A.L. Swift, 1933

Opposition may become sweet to a man when he has christened it persecution.
—George Eliot, *Janet's Repentance*, 1877

Persecution always acts as a jell for members of cults; it proves to them, in the absence of history, liturgy, tradition, and doctrine, that they are God's chosen.
—Barbara Grizzuti Harrison, "Island Pond," *The Astonishing World*, 1992

Blessed are you when men revile you and persecute you and utter all kinds of evil against you falsely on my account. Rejoice and be glad, for your reward is great in heaven, for so men persecuted the prophets who were before you.
—*Holy Bible*, Matthew 5:11-12

It is God, in silence and wisdom, who uses the Church's enemies to perfect His saints and purify His religion.
—Thomas Merton, *The Waters of Siloe*, 1949

The instances cannot be found in the history of mankind, in which an anti-Christian power could long abstain from persecution.
—John Henry Newman, *Oxford University Sermons*, 1843

This is the course I have taken with those who were accused before me as Christians. I asked them whether they were Christians, and if they confessed, I asked them a second and third time with threats and punishment. If they kept to it, I ordered them for execution.

—Pliny the Younger, writing to Trajan from Bithynia, Epp. X, c.112

It is not worldly ecclesiastics that kindle the fires of persecution, but mystics who think they hear the voice of God.

—George Santayana, in *The New Republic*, January 15, 1916

So long as a church is proscribed, it can build up a new society at its own peril without being implicated in the old society's weaknesses and sins.

—A.J. Toynbee, *An Historian's Approach to Religion*, 1956

PESSIMISM

As a philosophy, Pessimism is self-destructive. The mind which conceives the good and the ideal is made in the same breath to deny their value.

—Martin C. D'Arcy, *The Problem of Evil*, 1928

Christianity has never shut its eyes to the reality of the burden of inherited evils that weigh down human history, and for that reason it has been condemned as pessimistic.

—Christopher Dawson, in *The Listener*, August 1933

Some people like to describe the Christian attitude as one of active pessimism. This is indeed our philosophy for the evil days. But I think it is better defined as a tragic optimism.

—Emmanuel Mounier, *Be Not Afraid: A Denunciation of Despair*, 1963

The romantic pessimism which culminates in Freud may be regarded as symbolic of the despair which modern man faces when his optimistic illusions are dispelled; for under the perpetual smile of modernity, there is a grimace of disillusion and cynicism.

—Reinhold Niebuhr, *Nature and Destiny of Man*, I, 1941

The modern pessimist is a Buddhist who has strayed from the Orient, and who in his exodus has left behind him all his fantastic shackles, and has brought with him, together with ethical laws, only the cardinal tenet, "Life is evil."

—Edgar E. Saltus, *Philosophy of Disenchantment*, 1885

The power by virtue of which Christianity was able to overcome first Judaism, and then the heathenism of Greece and Rome, lies solely on its pessimism, in the confession that our state is both exceedingly wretched and sinful, while Judaism and heathenism were both optimistic.
—Arthur Schopenhauer, *Essays*, II, 1841

PHILOSOPHY

A philosopher is a fool who torments himself while he is alive, to be talked about after he is dead.
—Jean Le Rond d'Alembert, *Elements of Philosophy*, 1759

Religion is the search for a value underlying *all* things, and as such is the most comprehensive of all the possible philosophies of life.
—Gordon W. Allport, *Personality*, 1937

A little philosophy inclineth man's mind to atheism, but depth in philosophy bringeth men's minds about to religion.
—Francis Bacon, *Essays*, 1597

Nothing else but the study of Wisdom and Truth.
—George Berkeley, *Principles of Human Knowledge*, 1710

All genuine philosophy is, in the end if not consciously in the beginning, a quest of God.
—André Bremond, *Philosophy in the Making*, 1930

We think for a landlady considering a lodger it is important to know his income, but still more important to know his philosophy.
—G.K. Chesterton, *Heretics*, 1905

Philosophy has the task and the opportunity of helping banish the concept that human destiny here and now is of slight importance in comparison with some supernatural destiny.
—John Dewey, in *Fortune*, August 1944

Unified knowledge unifying life.
—Will Durant, address, Harvard University, 1926

Philosophy is the account which the human mind gives to itself of the constitution of the world.
—Ralph Waldo Emerson, *Representative Men*, 1850

Nature laughs uproariously at them all the time. The fact that they can never explain why they constantly disagree with each other is sufficient proof that they do not know the truth about anything.

—Desiderius Erasmus, *Praise of Folly*, 1509

In earnestly investigating and attempting to discover the reason of all things, every means of attaining to a pious and perfect doctrine lies in that science and discipline which the Greeks call philosophy.

—Johannes Scotus Erigena, *De Divina Praedestinatione*, c. 851

Many talk like philosophers and live like fools.

—Thomas Fuller, *Gnomologia*, 1732

Philosophy is written in that vast book which stands forever open before our eyes. I mean the universe.

—Galileo, *Il Saggiatore*, 1622

Why should those who profess the Christian faith and its doctrines see themselves excluded from philosophy simply because they prefer to philosophize about what they believe?

—Étienne Gilson, *The Philosopher and Theology*, 1962

The wisdom to discern what is essentially and actually right and reasonable in the real world.

—G.W.F. Hegel, *The Philosophy of Mind*, c. 1818

Philosophy loses its influence when it turns revivalist.

—Henry S. Hoskins, *Meditations in Wall Street*, 1940

Philosophy is only a matter of passionate vision rather than of logic—logic only finding reasons for the vision afterwards.

—William James, *Pluralistic Universe*, 1909

In theology the weight of Authority, but in philosophy the weight of Reason is valid.

—Johannes Kepler, *The New Astronomy*, 1608

O philosophers, proud rulers of the human mind, where are your flocks, where are the souls you love with a filial love. . . . Where are the tears dried up, the confessions heard, the amelioration of existence, the consolations which have gone forth from you?

—Jean Baptiste Lacordaire, *Thoughts and Teachings of*, c. 1850

If writers on physics travel outside the boundaries of their own branch, and carry their erroneous teaching into the domain of philosophy, let them be handed over to philosophers for refutation.
—Pope Leo XIII, *Holy Scripture*, 1893

As we well know, the imbecility of "profound" philosophers is so immense that it is exceeded only by the infinite mercy of God.
—Giovanni Papini, *The Devil*, 1955

To ridicule philosophy, that is to be a real philosopher.
—Blaise Pascal, *Pensées*, 1670

No one has taken the name of the Lord his God in vain so frequently and so unconcernedly as the philosopher.
—Ralph Barton Perry, *Present Philosophical Tendencies*, 1912

The acquisition of knowledge . . . knowledge which will do us good.
—Plato, "Euthydemus," *Dialogues*, 4th century B.C.

Men are suffering from the fever of violent emotion, and so they make a philosophy of it.
—Sarvepalli Radhakrishnan, *The Reign of Religion in Contemporary Philosophy*, 1922

Philosophy triumphs easily over past evils and future evils; but present evils triumph over it.
—La Rochefoucauld, *Maxims*, 1665

Philosophy . . . is not a presumptuous effort to explain the mysteries of the world by means of any superhuman insight or extraordinary cunning, but has its origin and value in an attempt to give a reasonable account of our own personal attitude toward the more serious business of life.
—Josiah Royce, *The Spirit of Modern Philosophy*, 1892

Philosophy is a steady contemplation of all things in their order and worth.
—George Santayana, *Three Philosophical Poets*, 1910

Philosophy has become either the errand boy of the natural sciences or the playboy of linguistic shell-games whose name at present is logical positivism.
—Allen Tate, in *The New York Times Book Review*, March 1952

For philosophy it is which is the material of the world's wisdom, the rash interpreter of the nature and dispensation of God. Indeed heresies are themselves instigated by philosophy.

—Tertullian, *On Prescription Against Heretics*, c. 206

A natural interpretation of the universe, a general view of things taken from the point of view of reason.

—St. Thomas Aquinas (1225–74), *The Philosophy of St. Thomas Aquinas*

A philosopher is a sort of intellectual yokel who gawks at things that sensible people take for granted.

—Alan Watts, *The Way of Liberation*, 1983

PIETY

We should no longer be ashamed of feelings, of piety. It is not true that they degrade reason and science. Piety is no less than the intelligence of the soul and we need heart and brains to recover the world in our hands, for the values we cherish.

—Oscar Arias, address, Harvard University commencement, *The Christian Science Monitor*, July 27, 1988

Piety, n. Reverence for the Supreme Being, based on His supposed resemblance to man.

—Ambrose Bierce, *Devil's Dictionary*, 1906

Visible worship is not condemned, but God is pleased only by invisible piety.

—Desiderius Erasmus, *Enchiridion*, 1501

Piety is not an end, but a means: a means of attaining the highest culture through the purest tranquillity of soul.

—J.W. von Goethe (1749–1832), *Maxims and Reflections*

There is no trusting to . . . crazy piety.

—Samuel Johnson, in *Boswell's Life of*, March 25, 1776

Piety requires us to renounce no ways of life where we can act reasonably, and offers what we do to the glory of God.

—William Law, *A Serious Call to the Devout and Holy Life*, 1728

Christian piety all too often has seemed to be the withdrawal from the world and from men, a sort of transcendent egoism, the unwillingness to share the suffering of the world and man.

—Jacques Maritain, *Freedom in the Modern World*, 1936

To carry piety as far as superstition is to destroy it.
—Blaise Pascal, *Pensées*, 1670

Piety in its nobler and Roman sense, may be said to mean man's reverent attachment to the sources of his being and the steadying of his life by that attachment. . . . Piety is the spirit's acknowledgment of its incarnation.
—George Santayana, *Reason in Religion*, 1905

The common element in all howsoever diverse expressions of piety . . . is this: the consciousness of being absolutely dependent, or, which is the same thing, of being in relation with God.
—Friedrich Schleiermacher, *The Christian Faith*, 1822

Volumes might be written upon the impiety of the pious.
—Herbert Spencer, *First Principles*, 1862

PITY

Now when a man suffers himself, it is called misery; when he suffers in the suffering of another, it is called pity.
—St. Augustine, *Confessions*, 397

If, perchance, the scales of justice be not correctly balanced, let the error be imputable to pity, not to gold.
—Miguel de Cervantes, *Don Quixote*, 1605

Pity is sworn servant unto love.
—Samuel Daniel (1562–1619), "The Queen's Arcadia," *Poems*

More helpful than all wisdom is one draught of simple human pity that will not forsake us.
—George Eliot, *The Mill on the Floss*, 1860

He that pities another remembers himself.
—George Herbert, *Outlandish Proverbs*, 1640

To pity the unhappy is not contrary to selfish desire; on the other hand, we are glad of the occasion to thus testify friendship and attract to ourselves the reputation of tenderness, without giving anything.
—Blaise Pascal, *Pensées*, 1670

We pity in others only those evils that we have ourselves experienced.
—Jean Jacques Rousseau, *Émile*, 1762

Pity is a mental illness induced by the spectacle of other people's miseries. . . . The sage does not succumb to mental diseases of that sort.

—Seneca (4 B.C.–A.D. 65), *De Clementia*, II

PLEASURE

The ridiculous chase after imaginary pleasures cannot be sufficiently exposed, as it is the greatest source of those evils which generally undo a nation.

—Joseph Addison (1672–1719), *The Spectator, Selections from*

The man of this world, whenever he feels secure in any pleasure thereof, the world drives over into some unpleasantness, and whenever he attains any part of it and squats him down on it, the world turns him upside down.

—al-Hasan al-Basri (died 728), in *Sūfism*

No pleasure is comparable to the standing upon the vantage-ground of truth.

—Francis Bacon, *Essays*, 1597

Purification of the soul . . . consists in scorning the pleasures that arise through the senses, in not feasting the eyes on the silly exhibitions of jugglers or on the sight of bodies which give the spur to sensual pleasures, in not permitting licentious songs to enter through the ears and drench the soul.

—St. Basil the Great, *Address to Young Men*, c. 370

Pleasure is in itself a good; nay, even setting aside immunity from pain the only good.

—Jeremy Bentham, *The Principles of Morals and Legislation*, 1789

We have never been forbidden to laugh, or to be filled, or to join new possessions to old or ancestral ones, or to delight in musical harmony, or to drink wine.

—John Calvin, *Institutes*, III, 1536

Remorse is the fatal egg by pleasure laid.

—William Cowper (1731–1800), *Progress of Error*

All amusements become a metaphysical trick to deceive our anguish; amusements disengage that fearful, devouring complex of gears which bind us to God's love and to our neighbor's love.

—Jean C. De Menasce, in *The Commonweal Reader*, ed. by E.S. Skillin, 1950

From pleasure comes grief, from pleasure comes fear; he who is free from pleasure knows neither grief nor fear.
—*Dhammapada*, c. 5th century B.C.

A man is to give account in the hereafter for permissible pleasures from which he abstained.
—Isidore Epstein, *Judaism*, 1939

There is wisdom in knowing how to play, to touch lightly, uninvolved and uncommitted, on what is pleasurable.
—Aelred Graham, *Christian Thought and Action*, 1951

There are only three pleasures in life pure and lasting, and all derived from inanimate things—books, pictures, and the face of nature.
—William Hazlitt, *Criticisms of Art*, 1843

Only the prig and the fool refuse their affection to the happy paganism of Theleme, to "laughter and the love of friends"; yet such things are a recreation, not a philosophy. Man cannot rest content with them for a faith.
—Christopher Hollis, *The Noble Castle*, 1941

He who loves pleasure will be a poor man; he who loves wine and oil will not be rich.
—*Holy Bible*, Proverbs 21:17

That thou mayest have pleasure in everything, seek pleasure in nothing.
—St. John of the Cross, *The Ascent of Mount Carmel*, c. 1584

The liberty of using harmless pleasure will not be disputed but it is still to be examined what pleasures are harmless.
—Samuel Johnson, *Rasselas*, 1759

Death spoke, and said: " . . . There is no future for the fool who seeks pleasure, who is befooled by love of wealth. 'This is the world, there is no other.' If one thinks thus, he comes again and again into my power."
—*Katha Upanishad*, prior to 400 B.C.

I do not think the glory of God best promoted by a rigid abstinence from amusements.
—John Keble, *Letters of Spiritual Counsel and Guidance*, XII, 1881

Love of pleasure is the disease which makes men most despicable.
—Longinus, *On the Sublime*, c. 250

Our loving God wills that we eat, drink, and be merry.
—Martin Luther (1483–1546), *Table-Talk*

Is not the modern world seeking in its despair, distractions from inevitable evil? Most of its pleasures are distractions from inevitable death.
—Vincent McNabb, *God's Way of Mercy*, 1928

Pleasure and freedom from pain are the only things desirable as ends.
—John Stuart Mill, *Utilitarianism*, 1863

God might grant us riches, honors, long life and health, but many times to our own hurt: for whatsoever is pleasing to us, is not always healthful for us.
—Michel de Montaigne, *Essays*, bk. 2, ch. 12, 1580

There is pleasure in gold, pleasure in silver and in women, pleasure in the perfume of sandal; there is pleasure in horses, pleasure in couches and in palaces, pleasure in sweets, and pleasure in meats. When such are the pleasures of the body, how shall God's name obtain a dwelling therein?
—Guru Nanak (1496–1538), in M.A. Macauliffe, *The Sikh Religion*

In youth the absence of pleasure is pain; in old age the absence of pain is pleasure.
—*Old Farmer's Almanac*, 1892

Pleasure is the death and failure of desire.
—Jean Paul Sartre, *Being and Nothingness*, 1956

The pleasure of sin is of short duration. . . . It operates on a law of diminishing returns. The more often it is repeated, the more familiar with its face, the less pleasure sin gives.
—Ignatius Smith, *Christ Today*, 1932

No school can avoid taking for the ultimate moral aim a desirable state of feeling called by whatever name, gratification, pleasure, happiness.
—Herbert Spencer, *The Data of Ethics*, 1898

There is nothing pleasurable save what is uniform with the most inmost depths of the divine nature.
—Henry Suso (1300–66), *Life of Blessed Henry Suso by Himself*

The individual soul, forgetful of the Lord, attaches itself to pleasure and thus is bound. When it comes to the Lord, it is freed from all its fetters.
—*Svetasvatara Upanishad*, prior to 400 B.C.

A longing after sensual pleasures is a dissolution of the spirit of a man.
—Jeremy Taylor, *Holy Living*, 1650

I took pleasure where it pleased me, and passed on. I forgot that every little action of the common day makes or unmakes character. . . . I allowed pleasure to dominate me. I ended in horrible disgrace.
—Oscar Wilde, *De Profundis*, 1896

POETRY

More and more mankind will discover that we have to turn to poetry to interpret life for us, to console us, to sustain us. Without poetry, our science will appear incomplete and most of what now passes with us for religion and philosophy will be replaced by poetry.
—Matthew Arnold, *The Study of Poetry*, 1865

We shall not praise the poets when they revile or mock, or when they depict men engaged in amours or drunken, or when they define happiness in terms of an overabundant table or dissolute songs.
—St. Basil the Great, *Address to Young Men*, c. 370

The poet in the last resort is but an evanescent mystic whose mysticism breaks down.
—Henri Bremond, *Prayer and Poetry*, 1927

The psychological mechanism used by grace to raise us to prayer is the same that puts in movement the poetic experience.
—Henri Bremond, *Prayer and Poetry*, 1927

To ask poetry to save us is to impose a burden upon poetry that it cannot sustain. The danger is that we shall merely get an ersatz religion and an ersatz poetry.
—Cleanth Brooks, in *Sewanee Review*, Winter 1953

The expression of the hunger for elsewhere.
—Benjamin De Casseres, *The Muse of Lies*, 1936

The capacity for writing poetry is rare; the capacity for religious emotion of the first intensity is rare; and it is to be expected that the existence of both capacities in the same individual should be rarer still.
—T.S. Eliot, *After Strange Gods*, 1934

Poetry transcends logic as the spiritual transcends the physical and the intellectual. It reveals life eternally and the instruments of time are too mean to record its mystery.
—Hugh l'Anson Fausset, *Studies in Idealism*, 1923

Poetry even at its purest is not prayer; but it rises from the same depths as the need to pray.
—Étienne Gilson, *Choir of Muses*, 1954

Poetry will not save the world. But poetry can force the soul into the precincts of its last evasion.
—Stanley Hopper, *The Crisis of Faith*, 1944

The greater poetry is a flowing in of light from the source of all light, from that King from whom comes our knowledge of the kingly, in whose wisdom we advance, under whose majesty we move, and in whose beauty, if we have cared for beauty, we may come to dwell.
—John Masefield, address, London, 1931

A poem is the very image of life expressed in its eternal truth.
—Percy Bysshe Shelley, *Defense of Poetry*, 1821

A poet participates in the eternal, the infinite, and the one . . . defeats the curse which binds us . . . redeems from decay the visitations of the divinity in man.
—Percy Bysshe Shelley, *Defense of Poetry*, 1821

A man who keeps no secrets from God in his heart, and who, in singing his griefs, his fears, his hopes, and his memories, purifies and purges them all from falsehood. . . . The poet is he whose flesh emerges from the shell, whose soul oozes forth.
—Miguel de Unamuno, *Essays and Soliloquies*, 1925

Poetry and mysticism have . . . this in common, that both alike belong to the field of contemplation rather than of action.
—Helen C. White, *The Metaphysical Poets*, 1936

There is a certain sense in which religion is the only theme of important poetry.
—William K. Wimsatt, Jr., in *New Scholasticism*, January 1958

POPE

We commit to thee, as the chief ruler of the universal Church standing on the firm rock of the Faith, what is to be done.
—*Council of Constantinople to Pope Agatho*, 680

The successor of the Apostles was commissioned to lead the Lord's sheep to pasture, not to fleece them.
—Edward III of England, to Pope Clement VI, c. 1350, in L. Pastor, *History of the Popes*, I

Without the Pope the Catholic Church would no longer be catholic . . . the unity of the Church would utterly collapse.
—Pope Paul VI, *Ecclesiam Suam*, August 1964

The power of jurisdiction of the Roman Pontiff claims the obedience of the faithful in matters not only of *faith and morals* but also of discipline.
—*The Vatican Council*, 1870

The Orthodox Church does not accept the doctrine of Papal authority . . . but at the same time Orthodoxy does not deny to the Holy and Apostolic See of Rome a *primacy of honour*, together with the right (under certain conditions) to hear appeals from all parts of Christendom. . . . [The] Orthodox regard the Pope as the bishop "who presides in love."
—Timothy Ware, *The Orthodox Church*, 1963

POVERTY

Take heed, O poor man, that if your flesh is mortal, your soul is precious and everlasting. If you lack money, you do not lack grace;and if you have no spacious house nor wide acres, the heavens spread above you, the earth is free.
—St. Ambrose, *Hexameron*, c. 389

Although moral conditions are not the sole causes, they are principal causes, of the poverty of the working class throughout the world.
—Henry Ward Beecher (1813–87), *Sermon*

Why, damn it all, after twenty centuries of Christianity, to be
poor ought not still to be a disgrace. Or else you have gone
and betrayed that Christ of yours!
—Georges Bernanos, *The Diary of a Country Priest*, 1937

At the roots of the theology of liberation we find a spirituality, a mysticism: the encounter of the poor with the Lord.
—Leonardo and Clodovis Boff, *Salvation and Liberation*, 1984

Those who have some means think that the most important
thing in the world is love. The poor know that it is money.
—Gerald Brenan, *Thoughts in a Dry Season*, 1978

We see this poverty every day on television. It is another
matter, however, to see it on the spot—to allow it to penetrate all five senses, to let ourselves be touched by the suffering of the poor, to feel their anguish, to experience the filth of
the slums sticking to our skin.
—Cardinal Daneels, in *Liberation Theology: From Dialogue to Confrontation*, 1986

The obligation to provide justice for all means that the poor
have the single most urgent economic claim on the conscience of the nation.
—*Economic Justice for All, Catholic Social Teaching and the
U.S. Economy*, Bishops' Pastoral Letter, 1986

The poor in Jewish thought have a claim to support from the
more fortunate as a matter of right, the "haves" being regarded as mere trustees appointed by Providence on behalf of the
"have-nots."
—Isidore Epstein, *Judaism*, 1939

Poverty often deprives a man of all spirit and virtue.
—Benjamin Franklin, *Poor Richard's Almanac*, 1757

Poverty is not a shame, but the being ashamed of it.
—Thomas Fuller, *Gnomologia*, 1732

Poverty is the open-mouthed, relentless hell which yawns beneath civilized society. And it is hell enough.
—Henry George, *Progress and Poverty*, 1879

The poor know that history is theirs and that if today they must cry, tomorrow they will laugh. That laughter turns out to be an expression of profound confidence in the Lord—a confidence which the poor live in the midst of a history they seek to transform. It is a joy which is subversive of the world of oppression, and therefore it disturbs the dominator; it denounces the fear of those who tremble and reveals the love of the God of hope.
—Gustavo Gutierrez, *La Fuerza Historico de los Pobres*, 1978

Blessed are the poor in spirit, for theirs is the kingdom of heaven.
—*Holy Bible*, Matthew 5:3

For the poor will never cease out of the land; therefore I command you, you shall open wide your hand to your brother, to the needy and to the poor, in the land.
—*Holy Bible*, Deuteronomy 15:11

Happier were the victims of the sword than the victims of hunger, who pined away, stricken by want of the fruits of the field.
—*Holy Bible*, Lamentations 4:9

Poverty urges us to do and suffer anything that we may escape from it, and so leads us away from virtue.
—Horace, *Carmina*, c. 20 B.C.

A decent provision for the poor is the true test of civilization.
—Samuel Johnson, *Boswell's Life of*, 1772

All the arguments which are brought to represent poverty as no evil show it to be evidently a great evil. You never find people laboring to convince you that you may live very happily with a plentiful fortune.
—Samuel Johnson, in *Boswell's Life of*, July 20, 1763

We have used the Bible as if it were the special constable's books—an opium dose for keeping beasts of burden patient while they were being overloaded, a mere book to keep the poor in order.
—Charles Kingsley, *Letter to Chartists*, 1848

The poor man hath title to the rich man's goods; so that the rich man ought to let the poor man have part of his riches to help and comfort him withal.
—Hugh Latimer (1485–1555), *Fifth Sermon on the Lord's Prayer*

No house worth living in has for its cornerstone the hunger
of those who built it.
—Ursula K. Le Guin, "Hunger," 1981, *Dancing at the Edge of the World*

Acts of begging are scratches and wounds by which a man
woundeth his own face; then he who wisheth to guard his
face from scratches and wounds must not beg, unless that a
man asketh from his prince, or in an affair in which there is
no remedy.
—Mohammed, *Speeches and Table-Talk of*, 7th century

Voluntary poverty turns us toward poverty in spirit, just as
does enforced poverty.
—Pie-Raymond Régamy, *Poverty*, 1949

Quit thine oppressions of earth's feeble poor,
That to the sky their curses mount no more.
—Shaikh Saadi, *Gulistan*, c. 1265

The poor don't know that their function in life is to exercise
our generosity.
—Jean Paul Sartre, *Les Mots* (The Words), 1964, "Lire"

It is not the man who has little, but he who desires more,
that is poor.
—Seneca, *Epistulae Morales ad Lucilium*, c. 63

Spiritual poverty consists in esteeming oneself as though not
existing, and God alone as existing . . . in considering God's
will in everything, both for ourselves and others, entirely renouncing our own will.
—John Sergieff of Cronstadt (1829–1908), *My Life in Christ*

As for idle beggards, happy for them if fewer people spent
their foolish pity upon their bodies, and if more shewed some
wise compassion upon their souls.
—Richard Steele, *The Tradesman's Calling*, 1684

Poverty seduces and withdraws men from Heaven as much
as wealth.
—Emmanuel Swedenborg, *Heaven and Hell*, 1758

No man is poor who does not think himself so; but if, in a
full fortune, with impatience he desires more, he proclaims
his wants and his beggarly condition.
—Jeremy Taylor, *Holy Living*, 1650

The hunger for love is much more difficult to remove than
the hunger for bread.
—Mother Teresa of Calcutta, in *Time*, December 4, 1989

First bread, and then religion. We stuff them too much with
religion, when the poor fellows have been starving. No dogmas will satisfy the cravings of hunger.
—Vivekananda (1863–1902), *Works of*

Their more lowly paths have been allotted to them by the
hand of God . . . it is their part faithfully to discharge its duties, and contentedly to bear its inconveniences.
—William Wilberforce, *Practical View of the System of Christianity*, 1797

Every one but an idiot knows that the lower classes must be
kept poor, or they would never be industrious.
—Arthur Young, *Eastern Tour*, 1771

Poverty which is through honesty is better than opulence
which is from the treasure of others.
—*Zend-Avesta*, 6th century B.C.

POWER

You have to turn might into duty and right into obligation. In
effect, societies are ruled either by coercion or manipulation,
by deceit, cheating, ideology, or by power. How do you get to
normative order that avoids the excesses of these things?
That is the basic problem.
—Daniel Bell, in *The New York Times*, February 7, 1989

Absolute power only implies freedom in relation to positive
laws, and not in relation to the law of God.
—Jean Bodin, *The Six Books of the Republic*, 1579

Royal power . . . controls the kingdom as God controls
the world.
—Jacques Benique Bossuet, *La Politique Tirée*, 1679

There is no power of which man has ever dreamed that can
regenerate human character except religion.
—Phillips Brooks, *Essays and Addresses*, 1894

Let all the world learn to give mortal men no greater power
than they are content they shall use, for use it they will. . . .
It is necessary . . . that all power that is on earth be limited,
church-power or other.
—John Cotton, *An Exposition of the Thirteenth Chapter of the Revelation*, 1656

The power of man has grown so great that it has denied
and shut out the power of the Spirit and consequently it is
destroying the world.
—Christopher Dawson, in *Dublin Review*, July 1942

Such power as I possess for working in the political field
derived from my experiments in the spiritual field.
—Mohandas K. Gandhi, *Autobiography*, 1948

The love of power is oppressive in every sphere, but in the religious most of all.
—Romano Guardini, *The Church and the Catholic*, 1953

Pentecost, the healing miracles of the Apostolic Age, the triumphant progress of the religion through the Roman Empire, the heroic deeds of saints and martyrs—all these point
to the sense of a power newly discovered.
—J.A. Hadfield, *The Spirit*, 1919

A power over a man's subsistence amounts to a power over
his will.
—Alexander Hamilton, *The Federalist*, 1788

To suppose that man has a power independent of God, is to
suppose that God's power does not extend to all things, i.e.,
is not infinite.
—David Hartley, *Observations on Men*, 1834

For all power is from the Lord God, and has been with Him
always, and is from everlasting. The power which the prince
has is therefore from God, for the power of God is never lost,
nor severed from Him.
—John of Salisbury, *Policraticus*, 1159

Power at its best is love implementing the demands of justice. Justice at its best is love correcting everything that
stands against love.
—Martin Luther King, Jr., *Where Do We Go from Here: Chaos or Community?*, 1967

I am very doubtful whether history shows us one example of a man who, having stepped outside traditional morality and attained power, has used that power benevolently.

—C.S. Lewis, *The Abolition of Man*, 1947

The highest proof of virtue is to possess boundless power without abusing it.

—T.B. Macaulay, in *Edinburgh Review*, July 1843

To have what we want is riches; but to be able to do without is power.

—George Macdonald (1824–1905), *Selections from*

All power wherever found is power for evil as well as for good; and the greater the power, the greater the evil.

—Vincent McNabb, *From a Friar's Cell*, 1923

Power always protects the good of some at the expense of all the others.

—Thomas Merton, *Faith and Violence*, "Blessed Are the Meek," 1968

Power can be invested with a sense of direction only by moral principles. It is the function of morality to command the use of power, to forbid it, to limit it.

—John Courtney Murray, *We Hold These Truths*, 1960

Unbridled ambition for domination has succeeded the desire for gain; the whole economic life has become hard, cruel and relentless in a ghastly measure.

—Pope Pius XI, *Quadragesimo Anno*, 1931

If Power is bad, as it seems to be, let us reject it, from our hearts. In this lies man's freedom: in determination to worship only the God created by our own love of the good, to respect only the heaven which inspires the insight of our last moments.

—Bertrand Russell, *Mysticism and Logic*, 1918

Power is a dangerous thing to handle, even in religion.

—Joseph R. Sizoo, *Preaching Unashamed*, 1949

One of the paradoxes of our time is that we have more power at our disposal than ever before, and yet we seem more powerless than ever.

—Ralph W. Sockman, *How to Believe*, 1953

PRAYER

Prayer is the drowning and unconsciousness of the soul.
—Jala al-Din Rumini (died 1273), in *Rumi: Poet and Mystic*

The only prayer which a well-meaning man can pray is, O ye gods, give me whate'er is fitting unto me!
—Apollonius of Tyana, c. 50 B.C.

All good and beneficial prayer is . . . at bottom nothing else than an energy of aspiration towards the eternal *not ourselves* that makes for righteousness, of aspiration towards it, and of cooperation with it.
—Matthew Arnold, *Literature and Dogma*, 1873

Do you wish to pray in the temple? Pray in your own heart. But begin by being God's temple, for He will listen to those who invoke Him in His temple.
—St. Augustine, *In Johann. Evang.*, tract XV.6, c. 416

Each prayer has its own proper meaning and it is therefore the specific key to a door in the Divine Palace, but a broken heart is an axe which opens all the gates.
—Rabbi Israel Baal Shem-Tov (1700–60), in *Judaism*

Pray only for the suppression of evil, and never for one's material well-being, for a separating veil arises if one admit the material into the spiritual.
—Rabbi Israel Baal Shem-Tov (1700–60), *Baal-Shem*

The purpose of prayer is to leave us alone with God.
—Leo Baeck, *Essence of Judaism*, 1936

Prayer is the most perfect and most divine action that a rational soul is capable of. It is of all actions and duties the most indispensably necessary.
—Augustine Baker, *Holy Wisdom*, 1876

It is not well for a man to pray cream, and live skim milk.
—Henry Ward Beecher, *Life Thoughts*, 1858

Our prayer ought to be short and pure, unless it happens to be prolonged by inspiration of divine grace. In community, however, let prayer be very short.
—St. Benedict, *Rule of*, c. 530

The wish to pray is a prayer in itself.
—Georges Bernanos, *The Diary of a Country Priest*, 1937

It is a direct approach to the throbbing heart of the universe.
—Israel Bettan, *Post-Biblical Judaism: Its Spiritual Note*, 1930

Do not pray for easy lives; pray to be stronger men. Do not pray for tasks equal to your powers; pray for power equal to your tasks.
—Phillips Brooks, *Perennials*, 1898

Prayer for many is like a foreign land. When we go there, we go as tourists. Like most tourists, we feel uncomfortable and out of place. Like most tourists, we therefore move on before too long and go somewhere else.
—Robert McAfee Brown, in Introduction, in John B. Coburn, *Prayer and Personal Religion*, 1967

To pray alone, and reject ordinary means, is to do like him in Aesop, that when his cart was stalled, lay flat on his back and cried aloud, help Hercules!
—Robert Burton, *Anatomy of Melancholy*, II, 1621

For a man to argue, "I do not go to church; I pray alone," is no wiser than if he should say, "I have no use for symphonies; I believe only in solo music."
—George A. Buttrick, *Prayer*, 1942

No one can find out except by trying whether he needs prayer once an hour, once a week, or less often.
—Richard C. Cabot, *What Men Live By*, 1915

Prayer is and remains always a native and deepest impulse of the soul of man.
—Thomas Carlyle, letter to G.A. Duncan, June 9, 1870

Prayer should be understood, not as a mere mechanical recitation of formulas, but as a mystical elevation, an absorption of consciousness in the contemplation of a principle both permeating and transcending our world.
—Alexis Carrel, *Man, the Unknown*, 1935

When we pray, we link ourselves with the inexhaustible power that spins the universe. We ask that a part of this power be apportioned to our needs. Even in asking, our human deficiencies are filled and we arise strengthened and repaired.
—Alexis Carrel, in *Reader's Digest*, March 1941

We should pray frequently, it is true, but our prayer should be brief lest, while we linger, the deceitful enemy find an opportunity of invading our hearts.

—John Cassian, *Conferences*, IX, 36, c. 420

One should wish for no prayer, except precisely that prayer that God gives us—the only way to pray is to pray, and the way to pray well is to pray well.

—John Chapman, *Spiritual Letters*, 1935

The Christian who prays, recollects himself, that is to say he discovers himself, gathers himself together, frees himself from all useless masters, from all unknown hands, from all fast-holding desires which tear him to pieces and so prevent him from being himself.

—Pierre Charles, *Prayer for All Times*, 1925

Greater than prayer is the spirit in which it is uttered.

—Glenn Clark, *The Soul's Sincere Desire*, 1925

Praying is identifying oneself with the divine Will by the studied renunciation of one's own, not by curbing one's desire but by acquiescing in a stronger Will.

—Paul Claudel, *Lord, Teach Us to Pray*, 1948

And why pierceth it heaven, this little short prayer of one syllable [God]? for it is prayed with a full spirit, in the height and in the depth, in the length and in the breadth of his spirit that prayeth it.

—*The Cloud of Unknowing*, 14th century

When we pray for another, it is not an attempt to alter God's mind toward him. In prayer we add our wills to God's good will . . . that in fellowship with Him He and we may minister to those whom both He and we love.

—Henry Sloane Coffin, *Joy in Believing*, 1956

He who offends against heaven has none to whom he can pray.

—Confucius, *Analects of*, c. 5th century B.C.

In his moments of prayer, when he and God tried to commune with each other, it wasn't his own shortcomings that were brought on the carpet, but God's.

—Clarence Day, *God and My Father*, 1932

A man does a lot of prayer in an enemy prison. Prayer, even more than sheer thought, is the firmest anchor.
—Jeremiah A. Denton, Jr., in George Esper, *The Eyewitness History of the Vietnam War 1961–75,* 1983

And to make a Prayer a right Prayer, there go so many essential circumstances, as that the best man may justly suspect his best Prayer; for, since Prayer must be of faith, Prayer can be but so perfect, as the faith is perfect.
—John Donne, sermon, funeral of Sir William Cockayne, December 26, 1626

Be not forgetful of prayer. Every time you pray, if your prayer is sincere, there will be new feeling and new meaning in it, which will give you fresh courage, and you will understand that prayer is an education.
—Feodor Dostoevsky, *The Brothers Karamazov,* 1880

The quieter it is the more powerful, the worthier, the deeper, the more telling and more perfect the prayer is.
—Meister Eckhart (1260?–1327?), *Meister Eckhart*

The prayer that reforms the sinner and heals the sick is an absolute faith that all things are possible to God—a spiritual understanding of Him, an unselfed love.
—Mary Baker Eddy, *Science and Health,* 1908

We can prove the reality of prayer only by praying.
—Sherwood Eddy, *We Believe in Prayer,* 1930

No man ever prayed heartily without learning something.
—Ralph Waldo Emerson, *Nature,* 1836

The whole function is expressed in a word, it is simply this— the child at his father's knee, his words stumbling over each other from very earnestness, and his wistful face pleading better than his hardly intelligible prayer.
—Frederick W. Faber, *The Spirit of,* 1914

If prayer were a cringing, whining, coaxing of a whimsical God, it would debase a man; where, in fact, it is the shouldering of the burden of his own destiny, a doing of his part in winning heaven.
—Walter Farrell, *My Way of Life,* 1952

Prayer should be the key of the morning and the lock of the night.
—Owen Felltham, *Resolves,* c. 1620

Only a theoretical deity is left to any man who has ceased to commune with God, and a theoretical deity saves no man from sin and disheartenment.
—Harry Emerson Fosdick, *The Meaning of Prayer*, 1915

Prayer is essentially about making the heart strong so that fear cannot penetrate there.
—Matthew Fox, *Creation Spirituality*, 1991

He who prays fervently knows not whether he prays or not, for he is not thinking of the prayer which he makes, but of God, to whom he makes it.
—St. Francis de Sales, *Treatise on the Love of God*, 1607

Work as if you were to live 100 years. Pray as if you were to die tomorrow.
—Benjamin Franklin, *Poor Richard's Almanac*, 1758

A good prayer, though often used, is still fresh and fair in the eyes and ears of Heaven.
—Thomas Fuller, *Good Thoughts in Bad Times*, 1645

Our prayer for others ought never to be: "God, give them the light Thou hast given to me!" but: "God! Give to them all the light and truth they need for their highest development!"
—Mohandas K. Gandhi (1869–1948), in J. Nehru, *The Discovery of India*

It seems to us that the will of God bends when our prayer is heard and granted; yet it is our will alone that ascends. We begin to in time what God has willed us from all eternity.
—Reginald Garrigou-Lagrange, *Christian Perfection and Contemplation*, 1937

When in prayer you clasp your hands, God opens his.
—German proverb

You pray in your distress and in your need; would that you might pray also in the fullness of your joy and in your days of abundance.
—Kahlil Gibran, *The Prophet*, 1923

As a coal is revived by incense, prayer revives the hope of the heart.
—G.W. von Goethe (1749–1832), *Maxims and Reflections of*

It is prayer that brings home to a man the right and claims of God, and the duty of man towards Him.
—Alban Goodier, *Ascetical and Mystical Theology*, 1938

How can one explain such frequent prayer, not only among those who believe in God and life after death but especially among those who do not believe in God or survival? Do they address their prayers "To whom it may concern?"
—Andrew M. Greeley, in *The New York Times*, June 29, 1991

The act of praying centers attention on the higher emotion, unifies the spirit, crystallizes emotions, clarifies the judgments, releases latent powers, reinforces confidence that what needs to be done can be done.
—Georgia Harkness, *Prayer and the Common Life*, 1948

Sometimes I think that just not thinking of oneself is a form of prayer. . . .
—Barbara Grizzuti Harrison, "Prayer (1989)," in *The Astonishing World*, 1992

We have never made a better prayer than when, after having made it, we do not know how it was made, since that is a sure sign that our soul was so attached to God as not to have had enough attention left to reflect upon itself.
—Père Hayneuve (1588–1663), *Solid Virtue*

Prayer . . . is . . . a technique for contacting and learning to know Reality . . . the exploration of Reality by exploring the Beyond, which is within.
—Gerald Heard, *A Preface to Prayer*, 1944

The passionate yearning which is poured forth in prayer does not spring from man's narrow heart, but from God's eternal love to allure and draw man upward toward Himself.
—Friedrich Heiler, *Prayer*, 1932

Each stage of a progressive prayer-life is a stage in the putting to death of the self that God may work and reign.
—E. Herman, *Creative Prayer*, 1925

In prayer we shift the center of living from self-consciousness to self-surrender.
—Abraham Joshua Heschel, *Man's Quest for God*, 1954

Prayer is our humble answer to the inconceivable surprise of living.
—Abraham Joshua Heschel, *Man's Quest for God*, 1954

He who has no prayer free from his thoughts has no weapon for battle. By prayer I mean the prayer which is constantly active in the innermost secret places of the soul.
—Hesychius of Jerusalem, *On Sobriety*, c. 425

Our Lord's first public act was prayer. "As he prayed the heavens were opened." The last act of the Crucified before giving up His life in atonement for the world's sin was prayer.
—Oswald C.J. Hoffmann, *Life Crucified*, 1959

Let the words of my mouth and the meditation of my heart be acceptable in thy sight, O Lord, my rock and my redeemer.
—*Holy Bible*, Psalms 19:14

Pray constantly, give thanks in all circumstances.
—*Holy Bible*, I Thessalonians 5:17

Pray, for all men need the aid of the gods.
—Homer, *Odyssey*, c. 800 B.C.

Now there is no doubt that the prayer of quiet, that a certain formless recollection and loving feeding upon the sense and presence of God, as here and now, is a most legitimate prayer.
—Friedrich von Hügel, *Life of Prayer*, 1929

The actual technique of prayer—the kneeling, the hiding of the face in the hands, the uttering of words in an audible voice, the words being addressed into empty space—helps by its mere dissimilarity from ordinary actions of everyday life to put one into a devout frame of mind.
—Aldous Huxley, *Those Barren Leaves*, 1925

Prayer is nought but a rising desire of the heart into God by withdrawing of the heart from all earthly thoughts.
—Walter Hylton, *The Scale of Perfection*, 1494

Eloquent prayers are apt to be addressed, not to God, but to the congregation.
—L.P. Jacks, *Confession of an Octogenarian*, 1942

The very movement itself of the soul, putting itself into a personal relation of contact with the mysterious power—of which it feels the presence.
—William James, *Varieties of Religious Experience*, 1902

I must get my faith quite clear, or at least as clear as I can, before I settle down to pray. . . . If I leave faith aside, no wonder my prayers are dull, monotonous, a bore to me.
—Bede Jarrett, *Meditations for Layfolk*, 1915

Prayer is not bending to my will, but it is a bringing of my will into conformity with God's will, so that His works may work in and through me.
—E. Stanley Jones, *How to Pray*, 1943

The wish to talk to God is absurd. We cannot talk to one we cannot comprehend—and we cannot comprehend God; we can only believe in Him. The uses of prayer are thus only subjective.
—Immanuel Kant, *Lecture at Königsberg*, 1775

To pray means to relieve one's heart, to bid care begone, to breathe out misery and distress, to breathe in the pure mountain air and the energy of another world.
—Paul Wilhelm von Keppler, *More Joy*, 1911

The shorter our alloted time is, the easier it perhaps is to decide to pray for one's enemies.
—Sören Kierkegaard (1813–55), *Meditations from*

The real tragedy of our prayers is not that God so often refuses to grant them. The tragedy is we so often ask for the wrong thing.
—R.A. Knox, *Retreat for Priests*, 1946

The earth is a mosque for thee; therefore wherever the time of prayer reaches thee, there pray.
—*Koran*, c. 625

Prayer is the queen of the world. Clothed in humble garments, with bowed head, with outstretched hands, it protects the universe by its supplicant majesty.
—Jean Baptiste Lacordaire (1802–61), *Thoughts and Teaching of*

He who has learned to pray has learned the greatest secret of a holy and happy life.
—William Law, *Christian Perfection*, 1726

A single grateful thought toward Heaven is the most perfect prayer.
—G.E. Lessing, *Minna von Barnhelm*, 1767

The efficacy of prayer is not to be judged by whether it fulfills a specific request, but by the power of God which it brings to the person who commits himself to its method.
—E. LeRoy Long, Sr., *Science and Christian Faith*, 1950

Prayer is the one human activity where any inner suggestion of triumph, any shy satisfaction is most likely to be false.
—John W. Lynch, *Hourglass*, 1952

Anything large enough for a wish to light upon, is large enough to hang a prayer upon.
—George Macdonald, *Unspoken Sermons* (1st series), 1869

What debilitates our prayer life . . . is our presupposition that the pressures of life are on one side while God is on some other side.
—George Macleod, *Only One Way Left*, 1956

Our real work is prayer. What good is the cold iron of our frantic little efforts unless first we heat it in the furnace of our prayer? Only heat will diffuse heat.
—Mother Maribel CSMV, in Sister Janet CSMV, *Mother Maribel of Wantage*, 1973

'Tis by our quarrels that we spoil our prayers.
—Cotton Mather, *The Wonders of the Invisible World*, 1693

The highest state of prayer, they say, is when the spirit leaves the body and the world, and, in the act of prayer, loses all matter and all form.
—St. Maximum the Confessor, *Centuries of Charity*, c. 626

There is no going out of sin into Grace without prayer, some sort of desire for Almighty God; some sort of Hope.
—Vincent McNabb, *God's Way of Mercy*, 1928

An angel collects all the prayers offered in the synagogues, weaves them into garlands, and puts them on God's head.
—Meir, *Exod. R.*, 21.4, *Zohar, Gen.*, c. 150

He . . . folded his large brown hands across his chest, uplifted his closed eyes, and offered a prayer so deeply devout that he seemed kneeling and praying at the bottom of the sea.
—Herman Melville, *Moby Dick*, 1851

Prayer, rightly understood, prepares the soul for action, sustains her on life's road when weary and worn, and arms her for the right when the foe assails her.

—Désiré Joseph Mercier, *Conferences of*, 1907

What is the use of praying if at the very moment of prayer we have so little confidence in God that we are busy planning our own kind of answer to our prayer?

—Thomas Merton, *Thoughts in Solitude*, 1958

There is not in the world a kind of life more sweet and delightful than that of a continual conversation with God.

—Nicholas Herman of Lorraine (Brother Lawrence), *Practice of the Presence of God*, c. 1666

You have to have darkness to find a picture on the sensitive plate, and you have to have prayer to bring out the invisible presence of God.

—Fulton Oursler, *Why I Know There Is a God*, 1949

Believe that you are receiving answers to your prayers. Belief tends to create that which is held in the mind by faith.

—Norman Vincent Peale, *Try Prayer Power*, 1959

What a spectacle for heaven and earth is not the Church in prayer! For centuries without interruption, from midnight to midnight, is repeated on earth the divine psalmody of the inspired canticles; there is no hour of the day that is not hallowed by its special liturgy.

—Pope Pius XI, *Caritate Christi Compulsi*, 1932

When we dispute over dogmas we are divided. But when we take to the religious life of prayer and contemplation, we are brought together. The deeper the prayers, the more is the individual lost in the apprehension of the Supreme.

—Sarvepalli Radhakrishnan, *Religion and Society*, 1948

Prayer is religion in act; that is, prayer is real religion. It is prayer that distinguishes the religious phenomenon from such similar or neighboring phenomena as purely moral or aesthetic sentiment.

—Auguste Sabatier, *Esquisse d'une Philosophie de la Religion*, 1891

Prayer is not a substitute for work; it is a desperate effort to work further and to be efficient beyond the range of one's powers.

—George Santayana, *Reason in Religion*, 1905

Our motive for prayer must be the divine will, not our own.
—D. Laurence Scupoli, *The Spiritual Combat*, 1843

Prayer is the constant feeling (the recognition) of our infirmity or spiritual poverty, the sanctification of the soul, the foretaste of future blessedness, the angelic bliss, the heavenly rain, refreshing, watering, and fertilizing the ground of the soul, the power and strength of the soul and body, the purifying and freshening of the mental air, the enlightenment of the countenance, the joy of the spirit, the golden link, uniting the creature to the Creator.
—John Sergieff of Cronstadt, *My Life in Christ*, 1897

All the saints have loved the night prayer. There is no hour so dear to them as the matin-hour, which is in deepest darkness, as it precedes the dawn.
—P.A. Sheehan, *Under the Cedars and the Stars*, 1903

There is no prayer so blessed as the prayer which asks for nothing.
—O.J. Simon, *Faith and Experience*, 1895

Prayer is God's own psychotherapy for His sinful children. It is His method of uncovering unconscious motivations and of recalling to consciousness those things which have been excluded as painful and humiliating.
—Raphael Simon, *Hammer and Fire*, 1959

On all my expeditions, prayer made me stronger, morally and mentally, than any of my non-praying companions.
—Henry M. Stanley, *Autobiography of*, 1909

Prayer enables us to disregard self, and it allows us to become disentangled from the trammels of egotism. In prayer as in nothing else we can find refuge from the degradation of self-love.
—William L. Sullivan, *Worry! Fear! Loneliness!*, 1950

Prayer is the service of the heart.
—*Talmud*, c. 500

He that would pray with effect must live with care and piety.
—Jeremy Taylor, *Holy Living*, 1650

I have not the courage to search through books for beautiful prayers. . . . Unable either to say them all or choose between them, I do as a child would do who cannot read—I say just what I want to say to God, quite simply, and He never fails to understand.

—St. Thérèse of Lisieux (1873–97), *Autobiography*,

Let him never cease from prayer who has once begun it, be his life ever so wicked; for prayer is the way to amend it, and without prayer such amendment will be much more difficult.

—St. Teresa of Avila, *Autobiography*, 1565

Mental prayer is nothing else . . . but being on terms of friendship with God, frequently conversing in secret with Him.

—St. Teresa of Avila, *Life of St. Teresa*, 1565

The only thing which binds God is prayer.

—Tertullian, *De Oratione*, c. 200

It is God Himself who prays through us, when we pray to Him. . . . We cannot bridge the gap between God and ourselves even through the most intensive and frequent prayers; the gap between God and ourselves can only be bridged by God.

—Paul Tillich, *The New Being*, 1955

Systematized prayer is a sort of mental crutch—something to lean upon when the limbs have not sufficient strength to propel the body on their own.

—Hubert van Zeller, *We Die Standing Up*, 1949

A lot of the trouble about prayer would disappear if we only realized—*really* realized, and not just supposed that it was so—that we go to pray not because we love prayer but because we love God.

—Hubert van Zeller, *We Die Standing Up*, 1949

Prayer is the world in tune.

—Henry Vaughan (1622–95), *The Morning Watch*

There is nothing in the world more dreary than a prayer that attempts to inform God of anything at all.

—Edward N. West, address, New York School of Theology, October 2, 1983

He who prays must commit himself and his wants to the transforming power of God. He must seek what is genuinely the greatest good and not merely the specific things which will satisfy his present wants.
—Henry N. Wieman, *Normative Psychology of Religion*, 1935

When the gods wish to punish us they answer our prayers.
—Oscar Wilde, *An Ideal Husband*, 1895

Prayer is not a monologue. It speaks to God and to the community. In the last analysis, religion is not what goes on inside a soul. It is what goes on in the world, between people, between us and God. To trap faith in a monologue, and pretend that it resides solely inside the self, undermines the true interchange of all belief.
—David J. Wolpe, *In Speech and in Silence: The Jewish Quest for God*, 1992

Men have been urged to pray, when they would have done better to think, observe and act.
—H.G. Woods, *Christianity and Civilization*, 1943

Prayer is the greatest of spells, the best healing of all spells. . . . Amongst all remedies this one is the healing one that heals with the Holy Word.
—*Zend-Avesta*, 6th century B.C.

PREACHING

There is no such thing as preaching patience into people, unless the sermon is so long that they have to practice it while they hear.
—Henry Ward Beecher, *Life Thoughts*, 1858

The freedom of the pulpit is freedom to be responsible to the revelation of God in Christ and not to any national or socially dominant ideas concerning what is good.
—John C. Bennett, in *Christian Century*, January 6, 1954

The best preaching is always the natural overflow of a ripe mind.
—James Black, *The Mystery of Preaching*, 1924

But what is the use of preaching the Gospel to men whose whole attention is concentrated upon a mad, desperate struggle to keep themselves alive?
—William Booth, *In Darkest England and the Way Out*, 1890

For the sake, as he sees it, of the ones he preaches to, the preacher is apt to preach the Gospel with the high magic taken out, the deep mystery reduced to a manageable size. . . . The wild and joyful promise of the Gospel is reduced to promises more easily kept. The peace that passeth all understanding is reduced to peace that anybody can understand. The faith that can move mountains and raise the dead becomes faith that can help make life bearable until death ends it. Eternal life becomes a metaphor for the way the good a man does lives after him.

—Frederick Buechner, *Telling the Truth*, 1977

True Christian preaching is . . . a proclamation which claims to be the call of God through the mouth of man and, as the word of authority, demands belief.

—Rudolf Bultmann, *Religion and Culture*, 1959

People are driven from the church not so much by stern truth that makes them uneasy, as by weak nothings that make them contemptuous.

—George A. Buttrick, *Jesus Came Preaching*, 1931

A congregation except in the rarest instances, does not dismiss its minister because of what he preaches, but because of what he does not preach.

— Raymond Calkins, *The Eloquence of the Christian Experience*, 1927

Dust thumped out of the pulpit-cushion is more likely to hide the Gospel from our contemporaries than commend it to them.

—A.C. Craig, *Preaching in a Scientific Age*, 1954

If the beard were all, goats could preach.

—Danish proverb

Condense some daily experience into a glowing symbol, and an audience is electrified.

—Ralph Waldo Emerson, address, May 1877

When we preach unworthily it is not always in vain. There is poetic truth concealed in all the commonplaces of prayer and of sermons, and though foolishly spoken, they may be wisely heard.

—Ralph Waldo Emerson, *Divinity School Address*, July 15, 1838

If what is delivered from the pulpit be a grave, solid, rational discourse, all the congregation grow weary, and fall asleep . . . whereas if the preacher be zealous, in his thumps of the cushion, antic gestures, and spend his glass in telling of pleasant stories, his beloved shall then stand up, tuck their hair behind their ears, and be very devoutly attentive.
—Desiderius Erasmus, *In Praise of Folly*, 1511

My preaching at its best has itself been personal counseling on a group scale.
—Harry Emerson Fosdick, *The Living of These Days*, 1956

Good preaching sounds reveille, not taps.
—James M. Gillis, *This Mysterious Human Nature*, 1956

Preaching is effective as long as the preacher expects something to happen—not because of the sermon, not even because of the preacher, but because of God.
—John E. Hines, *Witness*, July 1977

Preaching is an art, and in this, as in all other arts, the bad performers far outnumber the good.
—Aldous Huxley, *The Devils of Loudon*, 1952

Often read the divine Scriptures; yea, let holy reading be always in thy hand; study that which thou thyself must preach.
—St. Jerome (340–420), *Epistle to Nepotian*

Sir, a woman preaching is like a dog's walking on his hind legs. It is not done well; but you are surprised to find it done at all.
—Samuel Johnson, *Boswell's Life of*, 1772

The Word of God in the Book is a dead letter. . . . In the preacher that Word becomes again as it was when first spoken by prophet, priest, or apostle. It springs up in him as if it were first kindled in his heart.
—Edgar De Witt Jones, *The Royalty of the Pulpit*, 1951

Popular preaching today is sluggish, its popularity based on words which are familiar and images that had content in the agrarian society but are irrelevant to the complex society of industrial civilization.
—Franklin H. Littell, *From State Church to Pluralism*, 1962

Pictorial preaching is the most effective because it is easier to get at the average mind by a picture than by an idea.
—Peter Marshall, in Catherine Marshall, *A Man Called Peter*, 1951

Whenever we hear the Word of God in the human word, the message of the Bible becomes no longer a message out of the past, but an event in the present.
—Alan Richardson and W. Schweitzer, *Biblical Authority for Today*, 1951

The preacher, who naturally uses eloquence, the first of the arts, should make his audience tremble by depicting the miserable state of the man, who, in this life, deserves the condemnation of the people.
—C.H. Saint-Simon, *The New Christianity*, 1825

The priest who has not kept near the fires of the tabernacle can strike no sparks from the pulpit.
—Fulton J. Sheen, *The Priest Is Not His Own*, 1963

Most preachers handle sin as they would handle snakes, at arm's length and with no greater intimacy and for no longer time than is absolutely necessary.
—S.M. Shoemaker, *Realizing Religion*, 1921

That we should practice what we preach is generally admitted; but anyone who preaches what he and his hearers practice must incur the gravest moral disapprobation.
—Logan Pearsall Smith, *Afterthoughts*, 1931

It is no part of the duty of a clergyman to preach upon subjects purely political, but it is not therefore his duty to avoid religious subjects which have been distorted into political subjects.
—Sydney Smith, *Lady Holland's Memoirs*, 1855

The pulpit is in more danger of selling its freedom through catering to the public than of losing its liberty through government pressure.
—Ralph W. Sockman, *The Highway of God*, 1941

Let any preacher honestly probe into the great causes of human misfortune and misery, and nothing will keep people from his church.
—Frederick K. Stamm, *Country Home Magazine*, December 1939

The preaching of divines helps to preserve well-inclined men in the course of virtue, but seldom or never reclaims the vicious.
—Jonathan Swift, *Thoughts on Various Subjects*, 1706

When a debater's point is not impressive, he brings forth many arguments.
—*Talmud Jerushalmi Birakot*, c. 400

God preaches to us in the Scripture, and by his secret assistances and by spiritual thoughts and holy motions.
—Jeremy Taylor, *Holy Living*, 1650

The second thing to be performed by him that preacheth, is a reverent gravity; this is considered first in the style, phrase, and manner of speech, that it be spiritual, pure, proper, simple, and applied to the capacity of the people.
—Walter Travers, *A Directory of Church Government*, 1585

Preach faith till you have it; and then, because you have it, you will preach faith.
—John Wesley (1703–91), *The Heart of Wesley's Journal*

Such preaching of others hath most commanded my heart which hath most illuminated my head.
—Benjamin Whichcote, *Aphorisms*, 1753

The Gospel as the Word of God is properly spoken to the ear and not written for the eye.
—Amos N. Wilder, *Theology and Modern Literature*, 1958

Preaching is the word of the Bible addressed to people who live in the concrete decisions and difficulties of the world.
—Gustave Wingren, *Theology in Conflict*, 1958

The modern pulpit is so often simply the platform for the subjective feelings of the preacher, or of his world view, or of his most recent reading.
—William J. Wolf, *Man's Knowledge of God*, 1955

Preaching the Word of God is as great as hearing it.
—John Wyclif, *The Pastoral Office*, 1378

Black preachers start out not intending to make sense. They create a kind of psychological connection. You end up crying. You end up feeling good. You end up thinking about your mama, and you go away fulfilled. But you're not a bit better off.

—Andrew Young, in *Newsweek*, February 29, 1988

PREDESTINATION

In his eternity and co-eternal word, He has predeterminated what was in time to be manifested.

—St. Augustine, *City of God*, XI, 16, 426

God hath, before the foundation of the world, foreordained some men to eternal life through Jesus Christ, to the praise and glory of His grace; leaving the rest in their sin, to their just condemnation, to the praise of His justice.

—*Baptist Confession of Faith*, 1646

If everything happens according to the eternal foreknowledge and act of the Creator, the responsibility for evil recoils upon God.

—John Elof Boodin, *God and Creation*, 1934

God has from eternity predestinated or freely chosen, of his mere grace, without any respect of men, the saints and whom he will save in Christ.

—Henry Bullinger, *The Helvetic Confession*, 1536

By an eternal and immutable counsel God has once for all determined both whom He would admit to salvation, and whom He would condemn to destruction. . . . To those whom He devotes to condemnation, the gate of life is closed by a just and irreprehensible, but incomprehensible, judgment.

—John Calvin, *Institutes*, III, 1536

Nothing has ever happened which has not been predestinated, and nothing will ever occur.

—Cicero, *De Divinatione*, c. 78 B.C.

That God has foreordained everything is self-evident.

—René Descartes, *Principles of Philosophy*, 1644

It has hitherto seemed that physics comes down heavily on the side of predestination. The quantum theory has entirely removed this bias. Whatever view we may take of free will on philosophical grounds we cannot appeal to physics against it.

—A.S. Eddington, in *Nature*, February 26, 1927

By divine predestination the elect are chosen for eternal happiness, the rest are left graceless and damned to everlasting hell.

—Martin Luther, *De Servo Arbitrio*, 1525

Enveloped in darkness, creatures are not masters of their own weal or woe. They go to heaven or hell urged by God Himself.

—*Mahabharata*, c. 800 B.C.

If Providence is omnipotent, Providence intends whatever happens, and the fact of its happening proves that Providence intended it. If so, everything which a human being can do, is predestined by Providence and is a fulfillment of its design.

—John Stuart Mill (1806–73), *Nature*

The idea of personal predestination could hardly survive amidst the evangelists' earnest entreaties to "come to Jesus."

—Timothy L. Smith, *Revivalism and Social Reform in Mid-19th Century America*, 1957

Whatever comes about, since it is made by God, must therefore be necessarily predetermined by him, because otherwise he would be changing, which in him would be a great imperfection. . . . We therefore deny that God can omit to do what he actually does.

—Baruch Spinoza, *Short Treatise*, 1665

All those whom God hath predestinated unto life . . . and those only—He is pleased, in His appointed and accepted time, effectually to call by His Word and Spirit.

—*Westminster Confession of Faith*, Formulary of the Presbyterian Church of Scotland, 1643

PREJUDICE

Anything that has any remote resemblance to discrimination
is not only anti-American, but anti-Christian as well. Jesus
Christ, the Son of God, declared that second only to the
supreme law binding us to love our God is the law binding
us to love our neighbor.
—Francis J. Haas, *Catholics, Race and Law*, 1947

If we press toward the exact center of the concentric circles
of inclusion and exclusion, we find there the lone individual
in proud and splendid isolation from the rest of mankind.
—Kyle Haselden, *The Racial Problem in Christian Perspective*, 1959

Prejudice, put theologically, is one of man's several neurotic
and perverted expressions of his will to be God.
—Kyle Haselden, *The Racial Problem in Christian Perspective*, 1959

[Prejudice is] our method of transferring our own sickness to
others. It is our ruse for disliking others rather than ourselves.
—Ben Hecht, *A Guide for the Bedeviled*, 1944

Prejudice does not mean false ideas, but only . . . opinions
adopted before examination.
—Joseph de Maistre (1753–1821), *Étude sur la Souveraineté*

Any prejudice whatever will be insurmountable if those who
do not share it themselves, truckle to it, and flatter it, and
accept it as a law of nature.
—John Stuart Mill, *Representative Government*, 1861

The male leaders of the exodus have set themselves up as a
new ruling class of priests, ministers, and magistrates, politicians or party apparatchiks. In the laws of the new community of redemption, women have again been defined as
subordinate or, at best, auxiliary to a male-defined social
order.
—Rosemary Radford Ruether, *Women-Church*, 1985

Every type of discrimination whether social or cultural,
whether based on sex, race, color, social condition, language
or religion, is to be overcome and eradicated as contrary to
God's intent.
—Second Vatican Council, *The Church in the Modern World*, December 1965

An opinion without judgment.
—Voltaire, *Philosophical Dictionary*, II, 1764

Women do not want to be treated as stereotypes of sexual inferiority, but want to be seen as necessary to the full life of a Church that teaches and shows by example the co-discipleship of the sexes as instruments of God's love. They seek a Church where the gifts of women are equally accepted and appreciated.
>   —Rembert G. Weakland, in *Los Angeles Times*, September 17, 1987

Eleven o'clock Sunday morning is still the most segregated hour of the week, and I don't know that anybody can be selfrighteous about church integration.
>   —Andrew Young, in *Issues and Answers*, November 14, 1976

PRIDE

The prouder a man is, the more he thinks he deserves; and the more he thinks he deserves, the less he really does deserve.
>   —Henry Ward Beecher, *Royal Truths*, 1862

I thank God, amongst those millions of Vices I do inherit and hold from Adam, I have escaped one, and that a mortal enemy to Charity, the first and father-sin, not only of man, but of the devil, Pride.
>   —Thomas Browne, *Religio Medici*, 1635

Pride is the sin that sticks close to nature, and is one of the final follies wherein it shows itself to be polluted.
>   —John Bunyan, *The Life and Death of Mr. Badman*, 1680

This acceptable disease, which so sweetly sets upon us, ravishing our senses, lulls our souls asleep, puffs up our hearts as so many bladders.
>   —Robert Burton, *The Anatomy of Melancholy*, I, 1621

Every generous person [will] agree that the one kind of pride which is wholly damnable is the pride of a man who has something to be proud of. . . . And it does him most harm of all to value himself for the most valuable thing on earth—goodness.
>   —G.K. Chesterton, *Heretics*, 1905

What we now call the lust for power, and tend to regard as a fairly modern phenomenon, is in fact almost identical with what our ancestors called the sin of pride, the first of the Seven Deadly Sins.
>   —Colin Clark, *The Springs of Morality*, 1956

Of all the marvellous works of the Deity perhaps there is nothing that the angels behold with such supreme astonishment as a proud man.
—Charles Caleb Colton, *Lacon*, 1820

The first peer and president of Hell.
—Daniel Defoe, *The True-Born Englishman*, 1701

There is perhaps no one of the natural passions so hard to subdue as *pride*. Disguise it, struggle with it, beat it down, stifle it, mortify it as much as one pleases, it is still alive, and will every now and then peep out and show itself.
—Benjamin Franklin, *Autobiography*, 1790

To be proud of virtue is to poison yourself with the antidote.
—Benjamin Franklin, *Poor Richard's Almanac*, 1756

The principal cause of our troubles when we do fall is a secret pride which makes us vexed and irritated at being obliged to acknowledge our fall even to ourselves.
—Jean Grou, *Meditations in the Form of a Retreat*, c. 1795

When man remembers that he is *dust raised up by God* and made tremendously important, then he has Lawful Pride. He knows then that he is "sanctified dust."
—George J. Haye, *Obedience*, 1944

Pride goeth before destruction, and a haughty spirit before a fall.
—*Holy Bible*, Proverbs 16:18

There was one who thought he was above me, and he was above me until he had that thought.
—Elbert Hubbard, *Dictionary and Book of Epigrams*, 1923

Pride thinks its own happiness shines the brighter, by comparing it with the misfortunes of other persons. . . . This is that infernal serpent that creeps into the breasts of mortals.
—St. Thomas More, *Utopia*, 1516

Man falls into pride when he seeks to raise his contingent existence to unconditional significance.
—Reinhold Niebuhr, *The Nature and Destiny of Men*, I, 1941

There is a certain noble pride through which merits shine brighter than through modesty.

—Jean Paul Richter, *Titan*, 1803

People are rarely grateful for a demonstration of their credulity.

—Carl Sagan, *Broca's Brain*, 1979

Pride and self-opinion kindled the flaming sword which waves us off from Paradise.

—Walter Scott, *The Abbot*, 1820

Pride may be allowed to this or that degree, else a man cannot keep up his dignity.

—John Selden, *Table-Talk*, 1689

Holding himself good, one loses his goodness.

—*Shu Ching*, c. 490 B.C.

Pride is a kind of pleasure produced by a man thinking too well of himself.

—Baruch Spinoza, *Ethics*, 1677

God deliver us from anybody who wishes to serve Him and thinks about her own dignity, and fears to be disgraced.

—St. Teresa of Avila, *The Interior Castle*, 1577

If ever a man becomes proud, let him remember that a mosquito preceded him in the divine order of creation!

—*Tosefta: Sanhedrin*, prior to 3rd century

PROGRESS

Like an ox-cart driving in monsoon season or the skipper of a grounded ship, one must sometimes go forward by going back.

—John Barth, in *The New York Times*, September 16, 1984

We can exist only in progress toward another world; we are not fixed in a permanent position within a crude and self-sufficient universe; we dwell in the midst of mystery.

—Nicholas Berdyaev, *Dream and Reality*, 1939

If there were good cause for believing that the earth would be uninhabitable in A.D. 2000 or 2100 the doctrine of Progress would lose its meaning and would automatically disappear.

—J.B. Bury, *The Idea of Progress*, 1932

The vice of the modern notion of mental progress is that it is always something concerned with the breaking of bonds, the effacing of boundaries, the casting away of dogmas.
—G.K. Chesterton, *Heretics*, 1905

In the later nineteenth century the idea of progress became almost an article of faith. This conception was a piece of sheer metaphysics derived from evolutionary naturalism and foisted upon history by the temper of the age.
—R.G. Collingwood, *The Idea of History*, 1946

We cannot leave behind what has once been true, for progress is an advance into truth, a deeper appreciation and love of what is familiar, be it a birthright, or a gift such as Revelation.
—Martin C. D'Arcy, *God and the Supernatural*, 1920

Moral progress in history lies not so much in the improvement of the moral code as in the enlargement of the area within which it is applied.
—Will Durant, *Our Oriental Heritage*, 1935

Man's disease is loneliness; God's is progress.
—Charles Dyer, *Contemporary Dramatists*, 1977

Real human progress depends upon a good conscience.
—Albert Einstein, in *Avukah Journal*, 1932

The real religious problem of our society is to secure the general acceptance of a religion adapted to the requirements of continuous progress towards an ideal, consisting of all humanity.
—Charles A. Ellwood, *The Reconstruction of Religion*, 1922

This generation's deepest need is not these dithyrambic songs about inevitable progress, but a fresh sense of personal and social sin.
—Harry Emerson Fosdick, *Christianity and Progress*, 1922

Life must progress in part by the imprudence of those who undertake the impossible, not knowing what they do.
—William E. Hocking, *The Meaning of Immortality*, 1957

What has been is what will be, and what has been done is what will be done; and there is nothing new under the sun. Is there a thing of which it may be said, "See, this is new"? It has been already in the ages before us.

—*Holy Bible*, Ecclesiastes 1:9-10

The belief in progress, not as an ideal but as an indisputable fact, not as a task for humanity but as a law of Nature, has been the working faith of the West for about a hundred and fifty years.

—W.R. Inge, *The Idea of Progress*, 1920

When a nation makes progress in science, technology, economic life, and the prosperity of its citizens, a great contribution is made to civilization. But all should realize that these things are not the highest good, but only instruments for pursuing such goods.

—Pope John XXIII, *Mater et Magistra*, May 15, 1961

Is it progress if a cannibal uses a fork?

—Stanislaw J. Lec, *Unkempt Thoughts*, 1962

Practically all the progress that man has made is due to the fact that he is mortal. . . . If there were no death, life would become a thing stagnant, monotonous, and unspeakably burdensome.

—Robert W. Mackenna, *The Adventure of Death*, 1917

It is clearly untrue that we are automatically progressing and that the Churches and religion ought to hasten to adjust themselves to all the novelties of our age.

—Karl Mannheim, *Diagnosis of Our Time*, 1944

The idea of progress is the underlying presupposition of what may be broadly defined as "liberal" culture. If that assumption is challenged the whole structure of meaning in the liberal world is imperiled.

—Reinhold Niebuhr, *The Nature and Destiny of Man*, II, 1943

Perhaps . . . the main effect of progress in history is to heighten the possibilities both for achievement and for disaster.

—R.L. Shinn, *Christianity and the Problem of History*, 1953

Progress is not . . . a thing within human control, but a beneficent necessary.

—Herbert Spencer, *First Principles*, 1880

Progress is what happens when inevitability yields to necessity. And it is an article of the democratic faith that progress is a basic law of life.
—Adlai Stevenson, radio address, October 2, 1952

The aim, and test, of progress under a truly Christian dispensation on Earth would not lie in the field of mundane social life; the field would be the spiritual life of individual souls in their passage through this earthly life from birth into this world to death out of it.
—A.J. Toynbee, *Civilization on Trial*, 1948

Progress requires that the subject be enlarged in itself, alteration, that it be transformed into something else.
—St. Vincent of Lerins, *A Commonitory*, 434

If a man has lived in a tradition which tells him that nothing can be done about his human condition, to believe that progress is possible may be the greatest revolution of all.
—Barbara Ward, *The Unity of the Free World*, 1961

A historian without any theological bias whatever . . . cannot portray the progress of humanity honestly without giving a foremost place to a penniless teacher from Nazareth.
—H.G. Wells, in *Reader's Digest*, May 1935

PROPHECY AND PROPHETS

The prophets are the physicians of the diseases of the soul.
—Al-Ghazali (1058–1111), *The Religious Life and Attitude in Islam*

To believe in the prophet is to admit that there is above reason a sphere in which there are revealed to the inner visions truths beyond the grasp of reason.
—Al-Ghazali (1058–1111), *The Religious Life and Attitude in Islam*

Prophets . . . lifted in ecstasy above the natural operation of their minds by the impulses of the Divine Spirit, were inspired to utterance, the Spirit making use of them as a flute-player breathes into his flute.
—Athenagoras, *Apology*, c. 177

The ancient prophets walk through the world of Judaism, like living geniuses reawaking from generation to generation.
—Leo Baeck, *Essence of Judaism*, 1936

No prophet ever sees things under the aspect of eternity. It is always partisan theology, always for the moment, always for the concrete community, satisfied to see only a piece of it all and to speak out of that at the risk of contradicting the rest of it.

—Walter Brueggemann, *The Prophetic Imagination*, 1978

The task of prophecy has been to "discern the signs of the times," to see what God is bringing to pass as the history of peoples and societies unfolds, to point to the judgment he brings upon all institutions.

—John B. Coburn, *Minister*, 1963

Through prophecy Israel became the prophet of mankind.

—Carl Heinrich Cornill, *Prophets of Israel*, 1894

And every prophet that teaches the truth if he does not what he teaches is a false prophet. . . . But whosoever shall say in the spirit: Give me money, or any other thing, ye shall not listen to him: but, if he bid you give for others that are in need, let no man judge him.

—*Didache, The Doctrine of the Twelve Apostles*, c. 2nd century

They [Old Testament prophets] offered to the unfortunate of the earth a vision of brotherhood that became the precious and unforgotten heritage of many generations.

—Will Durant, *Our Oriental Heritage*, 1935

Theologically, contemporary religious radicals employ the metaphor of God as both Liberator and Judge. They understand themselves to be God's spokespersons to the society, not unlike the eighth-century B.C. Hebrew prophets.

—Robert Michael Franklin, *The Journal of Religious Thought*, Winter-Spring 1990–91

In biblical days prophets were astir while the world was asleep; today the world is astir while church and synagogue are busy with trivialities.

—Abraham Joshua Heschel, *The Insecurity of Freedom*, 1966

A prophet is not without honor except in his own country and in his own house.

—*Holy Bible*, Matthew 13:57

Beware of false prophets, who come to you in sheep's clothing but inwardly are ravening wolves. You will know them by
their fruits. Are grapes gathered from thorns, or figs from
thistles?
                                        —*Holy Bible*, Matthew 7:15-16

Thus says the Lord of hosts: "Do not listen to the words of
the prophets who prophesy to you, filling you with vain
hopes; they speak visions of their own minds, not from the
mouth of the Lord."
                                        —*Holy Bible*, Jeremiah 23:16

There is no liberation without prophets. The story of the exodus makes it quite clear that a people does not spontaneously struggle out of a state of wretched dependence.
                                —Bakole wa Ilunga, *Paths of Liberation*, 1984

There were long ago men more ancient than any of the
philosophers now in repute, men who were happy, upright,
and beloved of God, who spoke by the divine Spirit and gave
oracles of the future which are now coming to pass. These
men are called prophets.
                            —St. Justin Martyr, *Dialogue with Trypho*, c. 135

The noble characters in each generation are the prophets
of God.
                        —Hamilton Wright Mabie, *The Life of the Spirit*, 1898

Prophecy consists in the most perfect development of the
imaginative faculty . . . an emanation from the Divine Being.
                            —Maimonides, *Guide for the Perplexed*, 1190

The prophet who dares to speak out against public opinion is
indispensable to the church.
                                —Francis J. McConnell, *Religion Today*, 1933

The prophets . . . are the beating hearts of the Old Testament.
                —Walter Rauschenbusch, *Christianity and the Social Crisis*, 1907

The true prophet is a social worker who is absolutely independent, and neither fears nor submits to, anything
external.
                                —V. Soloviev, *Justification of the Good*, 1918

Prophecy implies a certain obscurity and remoteness from intelligible truth; hence they are more strictly termed "prophets" who see through some vision in the imagination.
—St. Thomas Aquinas, *Summa Theologiae*, 1272

PROTESTANTISM

Protestantism belonged to the same genus of thought as medieval Catholicisim.
—Franklin Le V. Baumer, *Main Currents of Western Thoughts*, 1956

The temptation of Protestantism has always been to magnify freedom at the expense of unity. The temptation of Roman Catholicism, on the other hand, has been to magnify unity at the expense of freedom.
—Samuel McCrea Cavert, *Protestantism: A Symposium*, 1944

Protestantism stiffened into its classical forms under intellectual influences long antedating our modern world, and the chaos and turmoil in Christian thought today are the consequences.
—Harry Emerson Fosdick, *Adventurous Religion*, 1926

A real Protestant is a person who has examined the evidences of religion for himself, and who accepts them because, after examination, he is satisfied of their genuineness and sufficiency.
—P.G. Hamerton, *French and English*, 1889

Far from being the fulfillment of the Reformers' aims, modern Protestantism is in a state of anarchy exceeding even the anarchy that made possible . . . the movements in the sixteenth century to which the name Reformation is commonly given.
—Geddes MacGregor, *The Hemlock and the Cross*, 1963

Protestant philosophers of religion have been concerned above all with the "meaning of God in human experience," "religious values," and "the source of human good." Their thinking has been value-centered rather than God-centered.
—Arnold S. Nash, *Protestant Thought in the Twentieth Century*, 1951

The Protestantism which stems from Luther has continued to concentrate its energies upon maintaining the freedom of the Word and has been inclined to yield to political and economic forces in what seem to be purely temporal matters.
—H. Richard Niebuhr, *The Kingdom of God in America*, 1937

Today we realize better than ever before that, while rejecting many Catholic notions, Protestantism has still kept many authentic Christian values.
—Gerard Philips, *The Role of the Laity in the Church*, 1956

PROVIDENCE

Providence embraces all things equally, however different they may be, even however infinite; when they are assigned to their own places, forms and times, Fate sets them in an orderly motion; so that this development of the temporal order, unified in the intelligence of the mind of God, is Providence.
—Boethius, *Consolations of Philosophy*, c. 525

Man learns to see providence in the great universal forces of nature, in the wind and the rain, in the soil underfoot and in the cloud overhead.
—John Burroughs, *The Divine Soil*, 1908

A firm persuasion of the superintendence of Providence over all our concerns is absolutely necessary to our happiness.
—William Cowper, *Letter to Lady Hesketh*, 1765

Any one thing in the creation is sufficient to demonstrate a Providence to an humble and grateful mind.
—Epictetus, *Discourses of*, c. 110

We ought to repose on Divine Providence, not only for what concerns temporal things, but much more for what relates to our spiritual life and perfection.
—St. Francis de Sales (1567–1622), *Consoling Thoughts of*

If you leap into a Well, Providence is not bound to fetch you out.
—Thomas Fuller, *Gnomologia*, 1732

Nothing is omitted by Divine Providence of what concerns the government of human affairs; but that there may not be other things in the Universe that depend upon the same infinite wisdom, I cannot . . . bring myself to believe.
—Galileo, *Dialogue on the Great World Systems*, 1632

Divine Providence is God's will from which all existing things receive fitting ends.
—St. Gregory of Nyssa (c. 335–c. 395), *Memesius, De. Nat.*, Homilies XLIII

It means that there is significance in everything that happens in the world, and a heart, a concern, and a power stronger than all the powers of the world which is able to fulfill the purpose of its care for man.
—Romano Guardini, *The Loving God*, 1947

Belief in Providence in the most general sense, implies the goodness as well as the power of God in the creation, ordering, and maintaining of this world, embracing the entire world of physical nature, biological life, and human persons.
—Georgia Harkness, *The Providence of God*, 1960

The Lord is a stronghold for the oppressed, a stronghold in times of trouble.
—*Holy Bible*, Psalms 9:9

The Lord is good to all, and his compassion is over all that he has made.
—*Holy Bible*, Psalms 145:9

The belief in free-will is not in the least incompatible with the belief in Providence, provided you do not restrict the Providence to fulminating nothing but fatal decrees.
—William James, *The Will to Believe and Other Essays*, 1896

Events depend principally on Divine Providence which is superior to nature and alone knows the predetermined times of events.
—Louis LeRoy, *On the Vicissitudes or Variety of the Things in the Universe*, 1577

If, as is the more religious theory, Providence intends not all which happens, but only what is good, then indeed man has it in his power, by his voluntary actions, to aid the intentions of Providence.
—John Stuart Mill (1806–73), *Nature*

As there is a particular Providence, so of necessity that Providence is secretly concurring and co-operating with that system which meets the eye, and which is commonly recognized among men as existing.
—John Henry Newman, *Difficulties of Anglicans*, 1850

Faith in providence is faith altogether. It is the courage to say yes to one's own life and life in general, in spite of the driving forces of fate, in spite of the catastrophes of existence and the breakdown of meaning.
—Paul Tillich, *The New Being*, 1955

There are many scapegoats for our blunders, but the most popular one is Providence.
—Mark Twain (1835–1910), *Notebook*

I believe in a general Providence, dear sister, which has laid down from all eternity the law which governs all things, like light from the sun; but I believe not that a particular Providence changes the economy of the world for your sparrow or cat.
—Voltaire, "Providence," in *Philosophical Dictionary*, 1764

PSALMS

Psalmody is the rewarding work of the night, the grateful relaxation of the busy day, the good beginning and the fortifying conclusion of all work. It is the ministry of angels, the strength of the heavenly host, the spiritual sacrifice.
—St. Ambrose (c. 333–397), *Commentary on Psalm I*

Sing psalms and hymns and spiritual songs with thankfulness in your hearts to the Lord.
—*Holy Bible*, Colossians 3:16

It could well be called a "little Bible" since it contains, set out in the briefest and most beautiful form, all that is to be found in the whole Bible.
—Martin Luther, *Preface to the Psalms*, 1528

The Psalms are our Bread of Heaven in the wilderness of our Exodus.
Thomas Merton, *Bread in the Wilderness*, 1953

The Book of Psalms contains the whole music of the heart of man, swept by the hand of his Maker . . . a mirror in which each man sees the motions of his own soul. They express in exquisite words the kinship which every thoughtful human heart craves to find with a supreme, unchanging, loving God.
—Rowland E. Prothero, *The Psalms in Human Life*, 1904

PURITY

Purity of soul cannot be lost without consent.
—St. Augustine, *On Lying*, c. 395

Fortunate indeed is that man who was able to maintain control of his carnal senses in the time of his youth.
—*Bhartrihari: The Springa, Sataka*, c. 625

It is not an inactive virtue; it does not merely consist in not committing certain sins. It means using your life in the way God wants, exercising constant restraint.
—Francis Devas, *The Law of Love*, 1954

The pure and impure stand and fall by their own deeds; no one can purify another.
—*Dhammapada*, c. 5th century B.C.

The Sun is never the worse for shining on a Dunghill.
—Thomas Fuller, *Gnomologia*, 1732

Blessed are the pure in heart: for they shall see God.
—*Holy Bible*, Matthew 5:8

When a man reproached Diogenes for going into unclean places he said, "The sun too penetrates into privies, but it is not polluted by them."
—Diogenes Laertius, 2nd or 3rd century

Purity and stillness are the correct principles for mankind.
—Lao-tzu (6th century B.C.), *Sayings of*

Purity. Of this word itself an impure use has been made. It has become an equivocal word, dragged about everywhere.
—Jacques Maritain, *Art and Poetry*, 1943

Purity is the condition for a higher love—for a possession superior to all possessions: that of God.
—François Mauriac, *What I Believe*, 1962

Abide pure amidst impurities of the world; thus shalt thou find the way of religion.
—Guru Nanak (1496–1538), in M.A. Macauliffe, *The Sikh Religion*

Purity is the sum of all loveliness, as whiteness is the sum of all colors.
—Francis Thompson (1859–1907), *Works*, III

Who knows what sort of life would result if we had attained to purity? If I knew so wise a man as could teach me purity I would go seek him forthwith.
—Henry David Thoreau, *Walden*, 1854

To the virtuous all is pure.
—*Tripitaka*, 80 B.C.

Purity is for man, next to life, the greatest good, that purity
that is procured by the law of Mazda to him who cleanses his
own self with good thoughts, words, and deeds.

—Vendidad, *Zend-Avesta*, c. 700 B.C.

*R*ace

God will not ask man of what race he is. He will ask what he has done.

—*Adi Gronath*, c. 1600

An honorable race is what? The race of men! The race that fears God. A despicable race is what? The race of men! The race that transgresses the commandments.

—*Apochrypha: Ben Sira*, 10.19, c. 300–190 B.C.

It is not just negative inertia and caution which lie behind racial discrimination, but the positive counterfaiths which produce them. The "conflicting valuations" turn out to be a warfare of the gods in the soul of man. Ultimately the racial problem is not one of hypocrisy but idolatry.

—Waldo Beach, *Faith and Ethics: The Theology of H.R. Niebuhr*, 1957

Segregation is the sin. Both in principle and practical procedure it is the sin. . . . We are lost if racial segregation continues. The important issue is not whether you or I may like it.

—A.K. Chalmers, *High Wind at Noon*, 1948

Race prejudice, in its gravest and most typical form, is the passing judgment of criminality or of essential inferiority upon all the members of a racial or ethnic group, with no sufficient intellectual motive for such a judgment.

—John La Farge, *Interracial Justice*, 1937

How can a Christian be at ease in Zion when he sees a man's racial background leads his fellow countrymen to treat him as a second class citizen?

—Harry Emerson Fosdick, *The Meaning of Being a Christian*, 1964

The familiar unbalanced hatred of the Negro race and its individual members is sinful. The failure to repress or attempt to control prejudice and antipathy against the Negro is just as wrong as the neglect to attempt the repression of the passion of anger or of sloth.

—Francis J. Gilligan, *The Morality of the Color Line*, 1929

The decisive weapon in the civil rights struggle was the very complex that the white Southerner most insistently pressed upon the Negro slave—Christianity and the Bible.

—Harry Golden, *Mr. Kennedy and the Negroes*, 1964

The plague of racial injustice is not contained within geographical limits. It is not a regional issue. It is a national issue and a national disgrace.

—Paul J. Hallinan, address, Chicago, January 1963

Not the extremists but the great, white midstream America—i.e. Christian America—produces and preserves the racial chasm in American society.

—Kyle Haselden, in *The New York Times Magazine*, August 2, 1964

By negligence and silence we have all become accessory before the God of mercy to the injustice committed against the Negroes by men of our nation.

—Abraham Joshua Heschel, address, Chicago, January 1963

Few of us realize that racism is man's gravest threat to man, the maximum of hatred for a minimum of reason, the maximum of cruelty for a minimum of thinking.

—Abraham Joshua Heschel, address, Chicago, January 1963

Even though human beings differ from one another by virtue of their ethnic peculiarities, they all possess certain common elements and are inclined by nature to meet each other in the world of spiritual values.

—Pope John XXIII, *Pacem in Terris*, April 1963

The only form of segregation that might conceivably be morally justifiable is segregation by mutual agreement and with equal rights. Even this, it seems to me, is *per se* contrary to the bond of union that should exist between peoples of the same nation and contrary to the common good of the nation itself.

—Gerald Kelley, *Theological Studies*, XIII, 1952

No man has a moral right to use his property, a creature of God, against the children of God. Racial discrimination even in the use of purely private property, is immoral at least as transgressing the supreme law of charity.

—William J. Kenealy, *The New Negro*, 1961

This is not a legal or legislative issue alone. . . . We are confronted primarily with a moral issue. It is as old as the Scriptures and is as clear as the American Constitution. The heart of the question is whether all Americans are to be afforded equal rights and equal opportunities. . . . We face, therefore, a moral crisis as a country and as a people.

—John F. Kennedy, June 1963

One day we shall win freedom, but not for ourselves. We shall so appeal to your heart and conscience that we shall win you in the process, and our victory will be a double victory.
> —Martin Luther King, Jr., *Strength to Love*, 1963

Our present suffering and our nonviolent struggle to be free may well offer to Western civilization the kind of spiritual dynamic so desperately needed for survival.
> —Martin Luther King, Jr., *Strength to Love*, 1963

Deprivation of the right of association with his fellow-men is the basic and fundamental reason for the immorality of racial segregation.
> —Joseph T. Leonard, *Theology and Race Relations*, 1963

Segregation in the church violates something that is basic in the nature of the church. How can a church exclude from "the church of God" those who are children of God? How can it, as "the body of Christ," withhold the privilege of worship from those who have been brought into union with Christ?
> —T.B. Maston, *Segregation and Desegregation: A Christian Approach*, 1959

The chief sin of segregation is the distortion of human personality. It damages the soul of both the segregator and the segregated.
> —Benjamin E. Mays, *The Segregation Decisions*, 1956

Legal segregation or any form of compulsory segregation, in itself and by its very nature imposes a stigma upon the segregated people. . . . We cannot reconcile such a judgment with the Christian view of man's nature and rights.
> —Eugene McManus, *Studies in Race Relations*, 1961

Charity is friendship of men for God, and for fellowmen on account of God. . . . The divine life through charity is the common ground on which all men meet. . . . Such teaching leaves no room for race conflicts or class warfare.
> —A.J. Muench, "Social Charity," *Summa of St. Thomas Aquinas*, III, 1948

Unless we make haste rapidly, by word but especially by example, in bringing complete justice to the American Negro . . . we shall be facing up to the totalitarians with one arm tied behind our back and . . . we shall be risking the vengeance of Almighty God.
> —James E. Murray, address, March 31, 1948

The color line has been drawn so incisively by the church it-self that its proclamation of the gospel of brotherhood has sometimes the sad sound of irony, and sometimes falls upon the ear as unconscious hypocrisy—but sometimes there is in it the bitter cry of repentance.
—H. Richard Niebuhr, *Social Sources of Denominationalism*, 1928

One thing we can be grateful for—it is getting very hard in-deed for a Christian to think that God likes his race better than other races.
—Alan Paton, in *The Christian Century*, March 31, 1954

It is disgraceful that people are being barred from neighbor-hoods and clubs on a basis that would have barred Jesus Himself.
—James A. Pike, in *Look*, March 14, 1961

Whoever exalts race, or the people, or the State, or a particu-lar form of State . . . whoever raises these notions above their standard value and divinizes them to an idolatrous level, dis-torts and perverts an order of the world planned and created by God.
—Pope Pius XI, *Mit Brennender Sorge*, March 1937

The "racial" rejection of the Jew was unknown in the Middle Ages. It was all a matter of belief. The Churchmen were eager to win souls; the conversion of the Jews was an ideal.
—Maurice Samuel, *The Professor and the Fossil*, 1956

The issue is not whether the Negroes want to come; it is whether they are welcomed.
—James Sellers, *The South and Christian Ethics*, 1962

When we are given Christian insight the whole pattern of racial discrimination is seen as an unutterable offense against God, to be endured no longer, so that the very stones cry out.
—World Council of Churches, statement, 1954

RACIAL INJUSTICE

The white man makes himself the agent of God's will and the interpreter of His providence in assigning the range and de-termining the bounds of non-white development. One trem-bles at the blasphemy of this attributing to God the offenses against charity and justice that are apartheid's necessary accompaniment.
—Catholic Bishops of South Africa, statement, July 1957

Racism is so universal in this country, so widespread and deep-seated, that it is invisible because it is so normal.
—Shirley Chisholm, *Unbought and Unbossed*, 1970

Racism is a way of thinking that has dogmatized the notion that one ethnic group is condemned by the laws of nature to hereditary inferiority and another group is marked off as hereditarily superior.
—Joseph F. Doherty, *Moral Problems of Interracial Marriage*, 1949

When a white man in Africa by accident looks into the eyes of a native and sees the human being (which it is chief preoccupation to avoid), his sense of guilt, which he denies, fumes up in resentment and he brings down the whip.
—Doris Lessing, *The Grass Is Singing*, 1950

"Civil Rights" is a term that did not evolve out of black culture, but, rather, out of American law. As such, it is a term of limitation. It speaks only to physical possibilities— necessary and treasured, of course—but not of the spirit.
—Alice Walker, "Silver Writes," 1982, *In Search of Our Mothers' Gardens*, 1983

Racism is so extreme and so pervasive in our American society that no black individual lives in an atmosphere of freedom.
—Margaret Walker, in Janet Sternburg, *The Writer on Her Work*, vol. 1, 1980

One had better die fighting against injustice than to die like a dog or rat in a trap.
—Ida B. Wells (1892), in Alfreda M. Duster,
The Autobiography of Ida B. Wells, 1970

REALITY

That alone is truly real which abides unchanged.
—St. Augustine, *Confessions*, 397

Reality is what I "come up against," what takes me by surprise, the other-than-myself which pulls me up and obliges me to reckon with it and adjust myself to it because it will not consent simply to adjust itself to me.
—John Baillie, *The Sense of the Presence of God*, 1962

Since in ultimate Reality all existence, and all thought and feeling, become one, we may even say that every feature in the universe is the absolutely good.
—F.H. Bradley, *Appearance and Reality*, 1894

I think it more likely than not that in religious and mystical experience man comes into contact with some Reality or aspect of Reality which they do not come into contact with in any other way.

—C.D. Broad, *Hibbert Journal*, 1926

That finest essence which you do not perceive—verily from that finest essence this great tree thus arises. . . . That which is the finest essence—this whole world has that as its soul. That is Reality. That is *Atman.*

—*Chandogya Upanishad*, 700–400 B.C.

God or Spirit is the only independent reality, and any other being or event is but a dependent "phase" or "state" or "product" of this activity.

—Charles E. Garman, *Letters, Lectures, Addresses*, 1909

The Church is always confronting man with the Reality which creates in him the right attitude of mind; namely, the Absolute.

—Romano Guardini, *The Church and the Catholic*, 1935

Were the whole human race to be blotted out, God would still, as from all eternity, be the only reality, and in His existence what is real in us would continue to live.

—J.B.S. Haldane, *Science and Religion*, 1931

Spirit is the only Reality. It is the inner being of the world, that which essentially is, and is *per se.*

—G.W.F. Hegel, *Phenomenology of Mind*, 1807

Thou hast made thy people suffer hard things; thou hast given us wine to drink that made us real.

—*Holy Bible*, Psalms 60:3

Certainly for most of the Bible . . . God is simply not the kind of reality concerning which doubt can be seriously entertained.

—John Hutchinson, *Faith, Reason and Existence*, 1956

Ultimate Reality is not clearly and immediately apprehended except by those who have made themselves loving, pure in heart and poor in spirit.

—Aldous Huxley, *The Perennial Philosophy*, 1945

There is in the human consciousness a sense of reality, a feeling of objective presence, a perception of what we may call "something there," more deep and more general than any of the special and particular senses, by which the current psychology supposes existent realities to be originally revealed.
—William James, *The Varieties of Religious Experience*, 1902

Reality is the pure concept of the understanding, that which corresponds to a sensation in general.
—Immanuel Kant, *Critique of Pure Reason*, 1781

If man's quest for some satisfying reality be baffled by the bleak stretches of interstellar space and the aimless whirling of blazing suns it is but natural that he should turn his gaze inward to find such reality within his own mind.
—Clifford Kilpatrick, *Religion in Human Affairs*, 1929

Under many names, names which are not that of God, in ways known only to God, the interior act of a soul's thought can be directed towards a reality which in fact truly may be God.
—Jacques Maritain, *True Humanism*, 1936

Spiritual reality is a matter of perception, not of proof.
—Peter Marshall, in Catherine Marshall, *A Man Called Peter*, 1951

It may well be possible that it is in our periods of spiritual activity that we come as close as we ever can to reality, that unmovable something which lies, we are sure, behind the changing show of facts on which our minds feed.
—Joseph S. Needham, *The Skeptical Biologist*, 1930

With the authority to name reality returned to our own human hands we become at once free and at the same time suddenly responsible.
—Maureen O'Hara, speech, Association for Humanistic Psychology Conference, August 1, 1992

The supreme reality is incomprehensible in the sense that it cannot be expressed in logical propositions but it is increasingly apprehensible by the purified mind.
—Sarvepalli Radhakrishnan, *Eastern Religion and Western Thought*, 1939

God is, by definition, ultimate reality. And one cannot argue whether ultimate reality really exists. One can only ask what ultimate reality is like.

—J.A.T. Robinson, *Honest to God*, 1963

The nature of one Reality must be known by one's own clear spiritual perception; it cannot be known through a pandit [learned man].

—Shankara (9th century), *Viveka-Chudamani*

On watching our thoughts we see how impossible it is to get rid of the consciousness of an Actuality lying behind Appearances, and how from this impossibility results our indestructible belief in that Actuality.

Herbert Spencer, *First Principles*, 1862

Given the one concept, God, and the whole of reality bursts into lucidity, the rationality of the universe, its uniformity, the emergence of life, of consciousness, and conscience, all become intelligible.

—Milton Steinberg, *Anatomy of Faith*, 1960

If we make the assumption . . . that the fundamental element in Reality is of the nature of Life, it follows that Reality can only be partially understood by the methods of pure science.

—B.H. Streeter, *Reality*, 1926

Reality is in general what truths have to take account of.

—A.E. Taylor, *Elements of Metaphysics*, 1912

God himself culminates in the present moment, and will never be more divine in the lapse of all the ages. And we are able to apprehend at all what is sublime and noble only by the perpetual instilling and drenching of the reality that surrounds us.

—Henry David Thoreau, *Walden*, 1854

Knowledge of reality has never the certainty of complete evidence. . . . Every knowledge of reality by the human mind has the character of higher or lower probability.

—Paul Tillich, *Dynamics of Faith*, 1957

Man is confronted by something spiritually greater than himself which, in contrast to Human Nature and to all other
phenomena, is Absolute Reality. And this Absolute Reality
of which Man is aware is also an Absolute Good for which
he is athirst.

—A.J. Toynbee, *An Historian's Approach to Religion*, 1956

That the religious life is ultimately rooted in the phenomenal
world and that it is to be celebrated accordingly appears in a
saying popular in East Asian Buddhism: "Even a single color
or a single fragrance is nothing other than the Middle Path."
What we call ultimate reality is evident in a single color or
single fragrance disclosed to us in the nondualistic awakening to the world as it is. Walking the Middle keeps our feet on
solid earth and our eyes focused squarely on the ever changing problems that face us.

—Taitetsu Unno, "The Middle Path of Buddhism,"
in *Religious Humanism*, Winter 1992

Reality is just itself, and it is nonsense to ask whether it be
true or false.

—Alfred North Whitehead, *Adventures in India*, 1933

It's not death I fear, it's reality—which means for me that I
will never accomplish or learn or *be* all that I wish I could be
before the final curtain. . . . Having it all is just not possible.

—Joanne Woodward, in *Lear's*, September 1989

REASON

What the good man ought to do he does; for reason in each
of its possessors chooses what is best for itself, and the good
man obeys his reason.

—Aristotle (384–322 B.C.), *Politics*

The Almighty does nothing without reason, though the frail
mind of man cannot explain the reason.

—St. Augustine, *City of God*, 426

We must hold that reason and the works of reason have their
source in God: that from Him they draw their inspiration:
and that if they repudiate their origins by this very act they
proclaim their own insufficiency.

—A.J. Balfour, *Theism and Humanism*, 1915

Our Reason is capable of nothing but the creation of a universal confusion and universal doubt.

—Pierre Bayle, *Dictionary*, 1697

. . . there is the notion that reason can't provide values. So there is a turn to religion. I'm not suggesting religion is unnecessary, but there is a widespread belief that religion can decide values and reason can't.
—Allan Bloom, in *U.S. News & World Report*, May 11, 1987

Reason will find God, but reason will find, too, the need to transcend reason, the promise of more than reason can offer.
—George Brantl, *Catholicism*, 1962

No man serves God with a good conscience, who serves him against his reason.
—Samuel Taylor Coleridge, *Aids to Reflection*, 1825

We should rather marvel greatly if at any time the process by which the eternal counsels are fulfilled is so manifest as to be discerned by our reason.
—Dante, *Conivivio*, c. 1310

The revolters against reason have asserted that . . . when human reason conceives of the deity to be worshipped and rules that the evidence is favorable to the worshipping of such a deity, man is creating his own God.
—L. Harold De Wolf, *Religious Revolt Against Reason*, 1949

Those whom God wishes to destroy, he first deprives of their senses.
—Euripides, *Fragment*, 5th century B.C.

I am immortal, imperishable, eternal, as soon as I form the resolution to obey the laws of reason.
—J.G. Fichte (1762–1814), *The Vocation of Man*

I do not feel obliged to believe that the same God who has endowed us with sense, reason, and intellect has intended us to forgo their use.
—Galileo, *Letter to Grand Duchess of Tuscany*, 1615

Reason inspired by love of truth is the only eye with which man can see the spiritual heavens above us.
—Charles E. Garman, *Letters, Lectures, Addresses*, 1909

I do not believe man possesses an avenue to truth which is superior to his reason.
—Roland B. Gittelsohn, *Man's Best Hope*, 1961

A free activity of the mind, reaching conclusions under no compulsion save that of evidence.
—C.E.M. Joad, *Return to Philosophy*, 1936

Reason cannot injure true Religion, for true Religion is reason.
—M. Joseph, *The Ideal in Judaism*, 1893

My question is, what can we hope to achieve with reason, when all the material and assistance of experience are taken away?
—Immanuel Kant, *Critique of Pure Reason*, 1781

Is it really too much to ask and hope for a religion whose content is perennial but not archaic, which provides ethical guidance, teaches the lost art of contemplation, and restores contact with the supernatural without requiring reason to abdicate?
—Arthur Koestler, *The Trial of the Dinosaur and Other Essays*, 1951

Reason retains its dignity only if it does not yield to the temptation of competing with religious imagination—if it does not transgress its own limitations.
—Richard Kroner, *Perspectives on a Troubled Decade*, 1950

Reason is a faculty far larger than mere objective thought. When either the political or the scientific discourse announces itself as the voice of reason, it is playing God, and should be spanked and stood in the corner.
—Ursula K. Le Guin, address, Bryn Mawr commencement, 1986,
Dancing at the Edge of the World

The existence of one God is according to reason; the existence of more than one God, contrary to reason; the resurrection of the dead, above reason.
—John Locke, *Essay Concerning Human Understanding*, 1690

If each man relies on his individual reason for his religious beliefs, the result will be anarchy of belief or the annihilation of religious sovereignty.
—Joseph de Maistre (1753–1821), *Étude sur la Souveraineté*

We light the chalice of intuition with the flame of reason.
—Robert Upton Nelson, letter to the editor, *Religious Humanism*, Winter 1992

The only true revolt is creation—the revolt against nothingness. Lucifer is the patron saint of mere negativistic revolt.
—Jose Ortega y Gasset, *Mission of the University*, 1930

If we submit everything to reason, our religion will have nothing in it mysterious or supernatural. If we violate the principles of reason, our religion will be absurd and ridiculous.

—Blaise Pascal, *Pensées*, 1670

The fact that religions can be so shamelessly dishonest, so contemptuous of the intelligence of their adherents, and still flourish does not speak very well for the tough-mindedness of the believers. But it does indicate, if a demonstration were needed, that near the core of the religious experience is something remarkably resistant to rational inquiry.

—Carl Sagan, *Broca's Brain*, 1979

The life of reason is no fair reproduction of the universe, but the expression of man alone.

—George Santayana, *The Life of Reason*, 1905

It is doubtful if a truly good world, a better and a fuller life for man, can ever be established through reason alone.

—Edmund W. Sinnott, *Two Roads to Truth*, 1953

If the determinist is right, reasoning can prove nothing: it is merely an ingenious method for providing us with apparently rational excuses for believing what in any case we cannot help believing.

—Burnett H. Streeter, *Reality*, 1926

Human reason is the norm of the human will, according to which its goodness is measured, because reason derives from the eternal law which is the divine reason itself.

—St. Thomas Aquinas, *Summa Theologica*, 1272

If there is no higher reason—and there is not—then my own reason must be the supreme judge of my life.

—Leo Tolstoy, *My Confession*, 1879

The enthronement of reason means the enthronement of man who becomes his own lawgiver.

—W.A. Visser 't Hooft, *The Kingship of Christ*, 1948

Passion and prejudice govern the world; only under the name of reason.

—John Wesley, letter, October 5, 1770

In life as in art the mood of rebellion closes up the channels
of the soul, and shuts out the airs of heaven.
—Oscar Wilde, *De Profundis*, 1909

REDEMPTION

The spiritual history of man, as seen by God, is not one of
progress but of recovery, or redemption.
—Aelred Graham, *Christian Thought and Action*, 1951

Then Jesus told his disciples, "If any man would come after
me, let him deny himself and take up his cross and follow
me. For whoever would save his life will lose it, and whoever
loses his life for my sake will find it.
—*Holy Bible*, Matthew 16:24-25

It was necessary that Adam should be summed up in Christ
that mortality might be swallowed up and overwhelmed by
immortality, and Eve summed up in Mary, that a virgin
should be a virgin's intercessor, and by a virgin's obedience
undo and put away that disobedience of a virgin.
—St. Irenaeus (130–c. 200), *The Demonstration of the Apostolic Preaching*

Redemption is continuous. . . . The spirit of Israel is attuned
to the hum of the redemptive process, to the sound of the
waves of its labors which will end only with the coming of the
days of the Messiah.
—A.I. Kook (1864–1936), *The Zionist Idea*

The sole key to the Bible is the Redemption by Christ and
applied to all subsequent generations by the Church which,
as the Bible clearly teaches, Christ instituted for that purpose.
—Hugh Pope, *The Catholic Church and the Bible*, 1929

Israel does not need to be redeemed by an atoning sacrifice,
because it has already been elected by God.
—Hans Joachim Schoeps, *The Jewish-Christian Argument*, 1961

Perhaps the deepest mystery of redemption and divine love is
precisely that we can be redeemed not only *from* our
squalors but in a sense *in* our squalors.
—Gerald Vann, *The Water and the Fire*, 1954

REFORM

A man who reforms himself has contributed his full share toward the reformation of his neighborhood.
—Anonymous

We may say that the successful reformers are those who are seeking not so much to "make people good" as to share an enthusiasm.

—Charles A. Bennett, *Philosophical Study of Mysticism*, 1923

It is a perversion of the Reformers' intent . . . to charge them with trying to invent a new religion, or to do away with the need for authority, or to inaugurate an "era of private judgment." Their concern . . . was to purify and revitalize an "old" religion, the old but ever living and ever new gospel which they discovered at the heart of the New Testament.

—Robert McAfee Brown, *Patterns of Faith in America Today*, 1957

Someone has said that though the aisles of any church are dirty, only a man on his knees can clean them.

—George A. Buttrick, *Sermons Preached in a University Church*, 1959

The period of the Reformation was a judgment day for Europe, when all the nations were presented with an open Bible and all the emancipation of heart and intellect which an open Bible involves.

—Thomas Carlyle (1795–1881) in Ernest Sutherland Bates, *The Bible Designed to Be Used as Living Literature*

The Reformation . . . by shifting its emphasis from the universal Church . . . to the local churches so apparently smaller than the nations that contain them, prepared the way for a new application of Hebrew messianic ideas to the nations themselves.

—J.V.L. Casserley, *The Dent World*, 1955

One of the besetting fallacies of reformers is the delusion that their plans will be carried out by people who think precisely as they do.

—John Maurice Clark, *Guideposts in a Time of Change*, 1949

Every reform, however necessary, will by weak minds be carried to an excess which will itself need reforming.

—Samuel Taylor Coleridge, *Biographia Literaria*, 1817

The important thing to remember with regard to reform is that it is done within the Church, within the framework of ecclesiastical authority, within the visible Body—it is the work of the Spirit sanctifying the Body. When it takes place outside this framework, it is not reform but a wounding action on the Body of Christ.

—Richard Cushing, Lenten pastoral letter, 1962

The great moral reformers have usually found the greatest opposition not in the "immoral" and impulsive individual, but in the regularly constituted organs of social authority and law.

—Christopher Dawson, *Sociological Review*, July 1925

Reform must come from within, not from without. You cannot legislate for virtue.

—James Gibbons, address, Baltimore, September 13, 1909

If there exists an actual necessity for a great reform amongst a people, God is with it, and it prospers.

—J.W. von Goethe, *Conversations with Eckermann*, 1824

Reformers are those who educate people to appreciate the things they need.

—Elbert Hubbard (1859–1915), *Notebook*

Catholic reform is *not revolution*: it does not aim at the violent overthrow either of values or of authority. . . . Catholic reform is intent upon preserving the continuity of historical development, and hence is not innovation but *renewal.*

—Hans Küng, *The Council, Reform and Reunion*, 1962

One of the marks of a certain type of bad man is that he can't give up a thing without wanting everyone else to give it up. That isn't the Christian way.

—C.S. Lewis, *Christian Behavior*, 1944

Reform and renewal come into institutional structures from the margins of power, policy and status.

—Jon Magnuson, "Spiritual Violence Yet Unhealed," *Christian Century*, February 26, 1992

Such negative terms as "Protestant" and "Reformation" are unhappy designations for a movement that in essence was not protest but affirmation, not reform but conservation, not reaction, but propulsion. Its best name is "evangelical."

—A.R. Mentz, *Protestantism: a Symposium*, 1944

Self-reform is the answer to world-reform.

—Sebastian Miklas, *Sanctify Your Emotions*, 1955

The Reformation, as the religious phase of the Renaissance, invited man to become just independent enough to take the step from one orthodoxy into another.

—H.A. Overstreet, *The Mature Mind*, 1949

The Reformation was . . . a time when prophetic voices spoke but to reaffirm for their own time those great and original Christian convictions which are the well-spring of our Christian life.
—James A. Pike, in *Advance*, October 19, 1953

In efforts to soar above our nature we invariably fall below it. Your reformist demigods are merely devils turned inside out.
—Edgar Allan Poe, *Marginalia*, 1849

The Reformation in England was a parliamentary transaction. All the important changes were made under statutes, and the actions of the King as supreme head of the Church were done under a title and in virtue of powers given him by statute.
—Maurice Powicke, *The Reformation in England*, 1936

If it is true that the Reformation released forces which were to act as a solvent of the traditional attitude of religious thought to social and economic issues, it did so without design, and against the intention of most reformers.
—R.H. Tawney, *Religion and the Rise of Capitalism*, 1926

Be not angry that you cannot make others as you wish them to be, since you cannot make yourself as you wish to be.
—Thomas à Kempis, *Imitation of Christ*, 1441

Contemporary theology must consider the fact that the Reformation was not only a religious gain but also a religious loss.
—Paul Tillich, *Systematic Theology*, III, 1964

A reformer is a guy who rides through a sewer in a glass-bottomed boat.
—James J. Walker, speech, 1928

REINCARNATION

The spiritual perfection which opens before man is the crown of long patient, millennial outflowering of the Spirit in life and nature. This belief in a gradual spiritual progress and evolution is the secret of the almost universal Indian acceptance of the truth of reincarnation.
—Sri Aurobindo, *Silver Jubilee Commemorative Volume of the Indian Philosophical Congress*, 1950

Krishna the god speaking:
Manifold the renewal of my birth. . . .
I come, and go, and come. When righteousness
Declines, O Bhavata! When wickedness
Is strong, I rise, from age to age, and take
Visible shape, and move, a man with men
Succoring the good, thrusting the evil back,
And setting Virtue on her seat again.
>—*Bhagavad-Gita, The Song Celestial,* 5th to 2nd centuries B.C.

Vishnu is not worshipped directly as much as in his reincarnations, of which there are ten, according to tradition. . . [including] Rama, Krishna, Buddha and one to come. Some Vishnuites are inclined to consider Christ as the tenth, thus incorporating Christianity, as they have Buddhism, into Hinduism.
>—Charles S. Braden, *The World's Religions,* 1954

Belief in rebirth is common to several ancient religions of the world, and the distinctive contribution of Hinduism to the doctrine of transmigration is that it has attempted to give a metaphysical and ethical interpretation of that belief.
>—Kenneth W. Morgan, *The Religion of the Hindus,* 1953

All things return eternally, and ourselves with them: We have already existed in times without number, and all things with us.
>—Friedrich Nietzsche, *Thus Spake Zarathustra,* 1885

If survival occurs, then reincarnation may be one form it could take, for all, for many, or only for some human beings. Survival could occur without reincarnation. On the other hand, reincarnation by definition, cannot occur without some preceding survival of a physical death.
>—Ian Stevenson, *The Evidence for Survival from Claimed Memories,* 1961

I, brethren, when I so desire it can call to mind my various states of birth . . . one birth, two—a hundred thousand births . . . in all their specific details . . . my previous states of existence.
>—*Sutta Nipata,* attributed to Buddha (6th century B.C.)

RELIGION
Religion is the life of God in the soul of man.
>—Lyman Abbott, *An Evolutionist's Theology,* 1897

A man is quickly convinced of the truth of religion, who finds it not against his interests that it should be true.
—Joseph Addison, in *The Spectator*, August 23, 1712

If religion be other than Personal and one with the purest friendship, I must affirm that it is yet a stranger in my breast and I am without a God to love, reverence and experience.
—Bronson Alcott (1799–1888), *The Journal of*

A man's religion is the audacious bid he makes to bind himself to creation and to the Creator.
—Gordon W. Allport, *The Individual and His Religion*, 1950

At last religion has come to reckon with the fact that its highest quest is not for a supernatural order but just for natural goodness in the largest and fullest measure.
—E.S. Ames, *The New Orthodoxy*, 1925

The true meaning of religion is this, not simply morality, but *morality touched by emotion.*
—Matthew Arnold, *Literature and Dogma*, 1873

Wherein does religion consist? It consists in doing as little harm as possible, in doing good in abundance, in the practice of love, of compassion, of truthfulness and purity, in all the walks of life.
—Asoka's Edicts, c. 260 B.C.

Religion is a journey, not a destination.
—Anonymous

All religion is an attempt to express . . . what is essentially inexpressible. Every new religion has to create its own language.
—Leo Baeck, *Essence of Judaism*, 1936

Religion is the divinity within us reaching up to the divinity above.
—Bahai saying

No interpretation of religion can be worthy of its great object . . . which does not exhibit it as a thing born of, and nourished by, the fullest daylight of human intelligence.
—John Baillie, *The Roots of Religion in the Human Soul*, 1926

The decline of religion in modern times means simply that religion is no longer the uncontested center and ruler of man's life, and that the church is no longer the final and un-questioned home and asylum of his being.
—William Barrett, *Irrational Man*, 1958

There is a universal religion, made for the alchemists of thought, a religion that emerges from man himself, man re-garded as a divine memento.
—Charles Baudelaire (1821–67), *Journals and Notebook*

Religion is a response, and sometimes a very coherent re-sponse, to the existential predicaments faced by all men in all times.
—Daniel Bell, in *The New York Times*, February 7, 1989

Through religion all men get a little of what a few privileged souls possessed in full.
—Henri Bergson, *The Two Sources of Morality and Religion*, 1935

Religion, n. A daughter of Hope and Fear, explaining to Igno-rance the nature of the Unknowable.
—Ambrose Bierce, *Devil's Dictionary*, 1906

Religion is devoted and loyal commitment to the best that reason and insight can discover. The liberal understands what loyalty to the best means as the authoritarian never can.
—Julius S. Bixler, *Conversations with an Unrepentant Liberal*, 1946

Religions are not revealed; they are evolved. If a religion were revealed by God, that religion would be perfect in whole and in part, and would be as perfect as the first moment of its revelation as after ten thousand years of practice.
—Robert Blatchford, *God and My Neighbor*, 1903

A man's religion is what he thinks about his relation to the universe, or rather, is what he feels about this relation; or better, it is what he *does* about this relation; or best it is *how* he acts.
—R.H. Blyth, *Zen in English Literature*, 1948

No religion in the world is without some elements of truth. No religion is without its profound error.
—Emil Brunner, *The Mediator*, 1934

Religion is born when we accept the ultimate frustration of mere human effort, and at the same time realize the strength which comes from union with superhuman reality.
—John Buchan, *Pilgrim's Way*, 1940

Religion points to that area of human experience where in one way or another man comes upon mystery as a summons to pilgrimage.
—Frederick Buechner, *Summons to Prigrimage*, 1984

You must also own religion in rags, as well as when in silver slippers; and stand by him, too, when bound in irons, as well as when he walketh the streets with applause.
—John Bunyan, *Pilgrim's Progress*, 1678

Religion is the basis of civil society, and the source of all good and of all comfort.
—Edmund Burke, *Reflections on the Revolution in France*, 1790

For where there is no certain knowledge of God, there is no religion.
—John Calvin (1509–64), *Opera*, in *Corpus Reformatorum*

A man must put his mind into his religion if he will keep his heart in it.
—Thomas A. Carney, *The "Lost" Radiance of the Religion of Jesus*, 1937

If morality be regarded as a mere convention, and God as the projection of men's hopes and fears, then the way is open for the false religions which relieve the maimed will of the many from the burden of decision.
—Sydney Cave, *The Christian Way*, 1949

The starting point of the religious experience is wonder.
—Seymour Cohen, *Affirming Life*, 1987

Men will wrangle for religion; fight for it; die for it, anything but—live for it.
—Charles Caleb Colton, *Lacon*, 1820

All human beings have an innate need to hear and tell stories and to have a story to live by . . . religion, whatever else it has done, has provided one of the main ways of meeting this abiding need.
—Harvey Cox, *The Seduction of the Spirit*, 1973

Religion has its origin in the depths of the soul and it can be understood only by those who are prepared to take the plunge.
—Christopher Dawson, *Religion and Culture*, 1947

Religion has shifted to take in every change of the winds, so that its obedience to American culture and political trends is apparent. As life styles have changed, so has the theology of the churches. Manifest destiny became social gospel with barely a backward glance.
—Vine Deloria, Jr., *We Talk, You Listen*, 1970

By dipping us children in the Bible so often, they hoped, I think, to give our lives a serious tint, and to provide us with quaintly magnificent snatches of prayer to produce as charms while, say, being mugged for our cash or jewels.
—Annie Dillard, *An American Childhood*, 1987

Religion is a private matter. Religious thought, to have any kind of integrity at all, must be the most private, tremblingly sacred kind of awareness we have. When religious terminology is bandied about, it loses its religious character and becomes entirely political and coercive.
—E.L. Doctorow, in conversation with Bill Moyers, *A World of Ideas*, 1989

Religion is not mere conformity to moral law, it is an espousal of moral ideals, a dedication of the heart, a loyal devotion, the perpetual renewal of a right spirit within us.
—Durant Drake, *Journal of Religion*, March 1927

Religion has its origin and its support in *dissatisfaction* with life, resulting from reflection on the failure of life to satisfy the primary desires of man.
—K. Dunlap, *Social Pyschology*, 1925

In many respects religion is the most interesting of man's ways, for it is his ultimate commentary on life and his only defense against death.
—Will Durant, *The Age of Faith*, 1950

There is nothing in the Bible to support the view that religion is necessarily a good thing. . . . On the contrary, it is highly suspicious of much that passes for religion.
—A. Roy Eckardt, in *Christian Century*, November 17, 1954

True religion, in great part, consists in holy affections . . . the more vigorous and sensible exercises of the inclination and will of the soul.
—Jonathan Edwards, *Religious Affections*, 1746

The first and last lesson of religion is, "The things that are seen are temporal; the things that are unseen are eternal."
—Ralph Waldo Emerson, *Nature*, 1836

Little by little the barrier grows, and "religion" becomes a *rule* of life, not life itself.
—Michael Fairless, *The Roadmender*, 1895

Religion is the way we react to what we cannot evade.
—Nels F.S. Ferré, *Faith and Reason*, 1946

Religion is something that only secondarily can be taught. It must primarily be absorbed.
—Harry Emerson Fosdick, *World's Work*, February 1929

If men are so wicked as we now see them with religion, what would they be if without it?
—Benjamin Franklin, letter, c. 1786

Religion: What at one time was a dynamic structure, mediating between man and his destiny and interpersonal responsibilities, has become mere mechanical ritual that dwarfs men rather than strengthens them.
—Erich Fromm, in *Look*, May 5, 1964

Religion is the best Armour in the World, but the worst Cloak.
—Thomas Fuller, *Gnomologia*, 1732

A literalistic religion may not reveal so much faith as it does disrespect, for it makes God into a "great big being up there," and turns religion into a space-travel agency, with the sole task of getting people from this low place to that high place.
—Langdon Gilkey, *Maker of Heaven and Earth*, 1959

Without philosophy man cannot know what he makes; without religion he cannot know why.
—Eric Gill, in *The Christian Science Monitor*, August 14, 1980

Religion consists not in knowing many things but in practicing the few plain things we know.
—Joseph Glanvill, *An Essay Concerning Preaching*, 1678

Every man who has interest enough to hire a conventicle may set up for himself and sell off a new religion.
—Oliver Goldsmith, *Citizen of the World*, 1762

In religion, as in human learning, we need a gradual introduction, beginning by the more easily learned matters and the first elements. The Creator comes to our aid so that our eyes, accustomed to darkness, may be gradually opened to the full light of truth.
—St. Gregory of Nyssa (c. 335–395), *On the Holy Spirit*

There is somethig odd about the weakness which irreligious men feel for religion. Almost invariably it becomes their favorite topic.
—Philip Guedella, *A Gallery*, 1924

Whatever else religion may be, it is also anthropology—in the sense that it fosters conceptions of human authenticity on whose basis moral codes can be drawn up and the actual behavior of individuals and societies assessed, challenged, and altered. Religion speaks not only of the divine but of the divine intention for the human.
—Douglas John Hall, *Imaging God: Dominion and Stewardship*, 1986

The perpetual danger which besets religion is that it may substitute gentility and aestheticism for prophetic insight and power.
—Georgia Harkness, *The Resources of Religion*, 1936

Religion is the glorious challenge of human life for the mastery of the planet; the loyal pursuit of the vision of the complete life through the ages.
—A.E. Haydon, in *Journal of Religion*, March 1927

Religion is moral life rising to think, i.e. becoming aware of the free universality of its concrete essence . . . the consciousness of "absolute" truth.
—G.W.F. Hegel, *Philosophy of Mind*, c. 1818

Religion has become an impersonal affair, an institutional loyalty. It survives on the level of activities rather than in the stillness of commitment.
—Abraham Joshua Heschel, *Religion in America*, 1958

The Indian . . . sees his music as indistinct from his dancing and his dancing as indistinct from his worship and his worship as indistinct from his living.
—Jamake Highwater, *Fodor's Indian America*, 1975

Religion that is pure and undefiled before God and the Father is this: to visit orphans and widows in their affliction, and to keep oneself unstained from the world.
—*Holy Bible*, James 1:27

Religion is not an intelligence test, but a faith.
—E.W. Howe, *Sinner Sermons*, 1926

Primitive societies without religion have never been found.
—William Howells, *The Heathens*, 1948

The essence of religion is belief in a relation to God involving duties superior to those arising from any human relation . . . duty to a moral power higher than the state.
—Chief Justice Hughes, *U.S. v. Macintosh*, 283, U.S. 633, 1931

The proper office of religion is to regulate the heart of men, humanize their conduct, infuse the spirit of temperance, order, and obedience.
—David Hume, *Concerning Natural Religion*, 1779

Religion is the mind and will of God, existing as God exists, objectively outside of men and of peoples, superior to all men, exacting from man the obedience due by the creature to the Creator.
—John Ireland, address, August 11, 1913

Religion, occupying herself with personal destinies and keeping this in contact with the only absolute realities which we know, must necessarily play an eternal part in human history.
—William James, *Varieties of Religious Experience*, 1902

Religion . . . shall mean for us, the feelings, acts, and experiences of individual men in their solitude, so far as they apprehend themselves to stand in relation to whatever they may consider the divine.
—William James, *The Varieties of Religious Experience*, 1902

Religion is not an opiate, for religion does not help people to forget, but to remember. It does not dull people. It does not say *Take*, but *Give*.
—Bede Jarrett, *The Catholic Mother*, 1956

Religion may be defined as the natural belief in a Power or Powers beyond our control, and upon whom we feel ourselves dependent.
—M. Jastrow, *The Study of Religion*, 1911

Reading, reflection and time have convinced me that the interests of society require the observation of those moral precepts only in which all religions agree (for all forbid us to murder, steal, plunder, or bear false witness) and that we should not intermeddle with the particular dogmas in which all religions differ, which are totally unconnected with morality.
—Thomas Jefferson, letter to James Fishback, September 27, 1809

No person can be religious alone, however rich may be the ecstasy or despair of his isolation. Authentic religion . . . is rather a relationship in which one person responds reverently to another person.
—P.E. Johnson, *Personality and Religion*, 1957

Religion is neither a theology nor a theosophy; it is more than that; it is a discipline, a law, a yoke, and indissoluble engagement.
—Joseph Joubert, *Pensées*, 1838

The moral capacity of man is the foundation and interpreter of all religion.
—Immanuel Kant, *Religion Within the Limits of Pure Reason*, 1793

A religion is the organized quest of a people for salvation, for helping those who live by the civilization of that people to achieve their destiny as human beings.
—Mordecai Kaplan, *The Future of the American Jew*, 1948

Whatever else it is—let us be clear about that from the outset—religion is something we belong to, not something which belongs to us; something that has got hold of us, not something we have got hold of.
—Ronald A. Knox, *University and Anglican Sermons*, 1964

A religion which does not tie the soul of man up with some permanent reality beyond the show of sense is no religion.
—J.A. Leighton, *Man and the Cosmos*, 1922

Life, more life, a larger, richer, more satisfying life, is in the last analysis the end of religion.
—James Leuba, in *The Monist*, July 1901

Theoretically, religion wishes to make men serene and inwardly peaceful by reaching a loving and forgiving God. But in practice, there is too much undissolved wrath and punishment in most religions.
—Joshua Loth Liebman, *Peace of Mind*, 1946

The religion that sets men to rebel and fight against their Government, because, as they think, that Government does not sufficiently help some men to eat their bread in the sweat of other men's faces, is not the sort of religion upon which people can get to heaven.
—Abraham Lincoln, *Washington Chronicle*, March 4, 1865

The worst kind of religion is no religion at all.
—James Russell Lowell, in *Review of Reviews*, October 1891

Religion is proposed not as a transcendent revelation of the nature of man and the world, but as a means of weathering the storms of life, or of deepening one's spiritual existence, or of preserving the social order, or of warding off anxiety.
—Leo Lowenthal and N. Guterman, *Prophets of Deceit*, 1949

A religion would not be worth my adherence if I could live up to it perfectly.
—Geddes MacGregor, *The Hemlock and the Cross*, 1963

Religion is about fellowship and community. . . . The task of religion is the maintenance and extension of human community.
—John Macmurray, *The Structure of Religious Experience*, 1936

Religion, like everything great and noble and demanding within us, increases the tension in mankind; and together with the tension, suffering; and with the suffering, spiritual effort; and with the spiritual effort, joy.
—Jacques Maritain, *Ransoming the Time*, 1941

Our religion *had* to mean more to [African Americans]. We had to emote, we had to lose ourselves in it. We had to sing and shout, and after it was all over we had to have a big meal and have something going on Sunday afternoon. Because when Monday came, it was back out into the fields, or back to the janitor's job, or back in Miss Ann's kitchen scrubbing the floor.

—Calvin Marshall, in *Time*, April 6, 1970

What the religious interest strives to do is to preserve intact an infantile image of the ideal father, perfect and "pure" and sinless.

—E.D. Martin, *The Mystery of Religion*, 1924

Religion is the sigh of the oppressed creature, the feeling of a heartless world, just as it is the spirit of unspiritual conditions. It is the opium of the people.

—Karl Marx, *Critique of Hegelian Philosophy*, 1844

It is a technique by which the human being gains more personal value from personal adjustment with responsive cosmic activities.

—Shailer Matthews, *The Growth of the Ideal God*, 1931

Religion, according to the Hindu, is not compounded of dogmas and creeds. Religion is a way of life in consonance with rationality and Truth. Truth is not and cannot be revealed once and for all—it must ever be a progressive revelation.

—Harold F. Mazumdar, Preface, *The Bibles of Mankind*, 1939

There are said to be ten thousand definitions of religion.

—John Morley, *Nineteenth Century*, April 1905

Religion, whatever destinies may be in store for it, is at least for the present hardly any longer an organic power.

—John Viscount Morley, *On Compromise*, 1874

Organized religion is too respectable, too much at home in America, and so too much inclined to abdicate its responsibility as a judge of society.

—Herbert J. Muller, *Religion and Freedom in the Modern World*, 1963

The function of religion is to confront the paradoxes and contradictions and the ultimate mysteries of man and the cosmos; to make sense and reason of what lies beneath the irreducible irrationalities of man's life; to pierce the surrounding darkness with pinpoints of life, or occasionally to rip away for a startling moment the cosmic shroud.
—Lewis Mumford, *The Conduct of Life*, 1951

A religion is not a proposition, but a system; it is a rite, a creed, a philosophy, a rule of duty, all at once.
—John Henry Newman, *A Grammar of Assent*, 1870

Religion, as a mere sentiment, is to me a dream and a mockery.
—John Henry Newman, *Apologia pro Vita Sua*, 1864

Religion—The one perfect definition of religion is *The Life of God in the Soul of Man*.
—Joseph Fort Newton, in *Publishers Weekly*, February 26, 1949

Natural religion . . . finds a God who is majestic, but not majestic enough to threaten human self-esteem.
—Reinhold Niebuhr, *Do the State and Nation Belong to God or Man?*, 1937

Many people are turning to religion as they would to a benign sedative, to soothe their nerves and to settle their minds.
—P. A. O'Boyle, in *McCall's*, June 19, 1955

Religion floods our darkness with a divine light. . . . Religion brings into the focus of attention the two supreme values—God and the human soul.
—John A. O'Brien, *Religion—Does It Matter?*, 1944

The secular world, particularly in political forms, is finding that it cannot maintain its supremacy without some religious sanction, and consequently is busy manufacturing spurious religious faiths to bolster its own inadequacies.
—Whitney J. Oates, *The American School*, Summer 1940

Religion in its true sense emphasizes the insight into our experiences and the consciousness that insists upon learning something from them.
—Carol Ochs, *Women and Spirituality*, 1983

The formulas and instruments of all our inherited religions were shaped in accordance with a world-outlook and a world-order which we have outgrown and to which we can never return.
—Max C. Otto, *Religious Liberals Reply*, 1947

Men hate and despise religion, and fear it may be true.
—Blaise Pascal, *Pensées*, 1670

Religions, as they grow by natural laws out of man's life, are modified by whatever modifies life.
—Walter Pater, *The Renaissance*, 1873

Religion though it begins in a seminal individual inspiration, only comes to great flower in a great church coextensive with a civilization.
—C.S. Peirce, *Collected Papers*, 1931

Religion is nothing else but love of God and man.
—William Penn, *Some Fruits of Solitude*, 1693

Religion is man's sense of the disposition of the universe to himself.
—Ralph Barton Perry, *The Approach to Philosophy*, 1908

Religion is the serious and social attitude of individuals or communities toward the power or powers which they conceive as having ultimate control over their interests and destinies.
—James B. Pratt, *The Religious Consciousness*, 1924

Religion indeed wishes to be useful and beautiful, but it also means to be true.
—James Bissett Pratt, *Can We Keep the Faith?*, 1941

We miss the true spirit of religion if we recommend it on account of its secular advantages.
—Sarvepalli Radhakrishnan, *Eastern Religions and Western Thought*, 1939

Religion can be the greatest of blessings or the greatest of curses. Historically it seems to have been both.
—David Rosenberg, *The Book of J*, 1990

The religion of man . . . has neither temples, nor altars, nor rites, and is confined to the purely internal cult of the supreme God and the eternal obligations of morality.
—Jean Jacques Rousseau, *Social Contract*, 1762

When organized religion is completely accepted by the mass as no more than a pleasing and fashionable facet of culture, then it falls prey to the mass-produced platitude.
—Stanley Rowland, Jr., in *The Nation*, July 28, 1956

[Religion] in its highest historical forms is the interpretation both of the eternal and of the spirit of loyalty through emotion, and through a fitting activity of the imagination.
—Josiah Royce, *The Philosophy of Loyalty*, 1908

Anything which makes religion a second object, makes religion no object. . . . He who makes religion his first object, makes it his whole object.
—John Ruskin, *Lecture on Architecture and Painting*, 1853

In politics, religion is now a name; in art, a hypocrisy or affectation.
—John Ruskin, *Modern Painters*, III, 1856

Most religions are absolutist. Claims to revelation militate against rational argument and compromise. In this sense all religions contain totalitarian possibilities; for totalitarianism, which welds the state into a single body "knit together as one man" is really the religious impulse, the worship of leadership and ideology, the cult of Person or Book, directed towards secular ends.
—Malise Ruthven, *The Divine Supermarket*, 1989

Religion is an intercourse, a conscious and voluntary relation, entered into by a soul in distress with the mysterious power upon which it feels itself to depend, and upon which its fate is contingent.
—Auguste Sabatier, *Esquisse d'une Philosophie de la Religion*, 1891

Religion is human experience interpreted by human imagination.
—George Santayana, *The Sense of Beauty*, 1896

When the American poor turn to religion, as most of them do, they turn not to faith in revolution, but to a more radical revolt against faith in their fellow man.
—Herbert Wallace Schneider, *Religion in the 20th Century*, 1952

Religion is the metaphysics of the masses.
—Arthur Schopenhauer, "A Dialogue," *Essays*, 1851

The great characteristic of our age is not its love of religion, but its love of talking about religion.
—Fulton J. Sheen, *The External Galilean*, 1934

Religion is the supreme art of humanity.
—Abba Hillel Silver, *Where Judaism Differed*, 1957

Religion makes the adventurous leap from the spirit of man to the Universal Spirit it calls God.
—Edmund W. Sinnott, *The Biology of the Spirit*, 1955

One cannot invent a religion.
—Charles P. Snow, *The Two Cultures and the Scientific Revolution*, 1961

People prefer a religion which makes them feel safe and good rather than right and real.
—Ralph W. Sockman, *The Highway of God*, 1941

We are afraid of religion because it interprets rather than just observes. Religion does not confirm that there are hungry people in the world; it interprets the hungry to be our brethren whom we allow to starve.
—Dorothee Soelle, *Death by Bread Alone*, 1978

Religion is the hunger of the soul for the impossible, the unattainable, the inconceivable. . . . This is its essence and this is its glory. This is what religion *means*. Anything which is less than this is not religion.
—W.T. Stace, *Time and Eternity*, 1952

For some reason, too deep to fathom, men contend more furiously over the road to heaven, which they cannot see, than over their visible walks on earth.
—Walter Parker Stacy, in Sam J. Ervin, Jr., *Humor of a Country Lawyer*, 1983

For after all the great religions have been preached and expounded, or have been revealed by brilliant scholars, or have been written in books and embellished in fine language with finer covers, man—all man—is still confronted with the Great Mystery.
—Luther Standing Bear, *Land of the Spotted Eagle*, 1933

By positing God it inhibits man from laying claim to being
God. It prevents his becoming less than man through the ar-
rogance of claiming to be more.
—Milton Steinberg, *A Believing Jew*, 1951

The unity of God, the freedom of man, and the creation of the
world. Upon these three pillars, and upon them alone, rests
and must rest every revealed religion, including the religion
of Christ, if it is to retain the name of revealed religion.
—S.L. Steinheim, *Offenbarungslehre*, 1856

We have just enough religion to make us hate, but not
enough to make us love one another.
—Jonathan Swift, *Thoughts on Various Subjects*, 1706

The theological mould which shaped political theory from the
Middle Ages to the seventeenth century is broken. . . . Religion, ceasing to be the master-interest of mankind, dwindles
into a department of life with boundaries which it is extrava-
gant to overstep.
—R.H. Tawney, *Religion and the Rise of Capitalism*, 1926

The heart of Religion is not an opinion about God, such as
philosophy might reach as the conclusion of an argument; it
is a personal relation with God.
—William Temple, *Nature, Man and God*, 1934

There is a religion of nature written in the hearts of everyone
of us from the first creation; by which all mankind must
judge of the truth of any instituted religion whatever.
—Matthew Tindale, *Christianity as Old as the Creation*, 1730

While the law permits the Americans to do what they please,
religion prevents them from conceiving, and forbids them to
commit, what is rash or unjust.
—Alexis de Tocqueville, *Democracy in America*, 1839

True religion is the establishment by man of such a relation
to the Infinite Life around him, as, while connecting his life
with this Infinitude and directing his conduct, is also in
agreement with his reason and with human knowledge.
—Leo Tolstoy, *What Is Religion?*, 1902

Religion is Man's attempt to get into touch with an absolute
spiritual Reality behind the phenomena of the Universe, and,
having made contact with It, to live in harmony with It.
—A. J. Toynbee, *A Study of History, Reconsiderations*, 1961

Religion does not always make life *better*, but not often does it fail to make life *different*.

—D.E. Trueblood, *The Logic of Belief*, 1942

Religion, like water, may be free, but when they pipe it to you, you've got to help pay for the piping. And the piper!

—Abigail Van Buren, "Dear Abby," newspaper column, April 28, 1974

Realization is real religion; all the rest is only preparation.

—Swami Vivekananda (1863–1902), *Complete Works of*, 1950

The goal of all religions is the same, but the language of the teachers differs. The goal is to kill the false "I" so that the real "I," the Lord, will reign.

—Swami Vivekananda (1863–1902), *The Yoga and Other Works*

Religion is the everlasting dialogue between humanity and God.

—Franz Werfel, *Between Heaven and Earth*, 1944

Religion is a profound humility, a universal charity.

—Benjamin Whichcote (1609–83), *Sermons*

Religion is tending to degenerate into a decent formula wherewith to embellish a comfortable life.

—Alfred North Whitehead, *Science and the Modern World*, 1925

Religion is the vision of something which stands beyond, behind, and within, the passing flux of immediate things; something which is real, and yet waiting to be realized . . . something that gives meaning to all that passes, and yet eludes apprehension.

—Alfred North Whitehead, *Science and the Modern World*, 1925

Religion is what the individual does with his own solitariness.

—Alfred North Whitehead, *Religion in the Making*, 1927

Some religious people abolish hatred because they're religious. Others are fanatical, and they invoke hatred because they are religious. I believe that religion could be a marvelous way of humanizing society. Others believe that religion is here to serve fanatics, to punish, to chastise, to torture, to torment.

—Elie Wiesel, in *USA Today*, August 28, 1990

REPENTANCE

Repentance . . . is recoil, recoil not from the bad act and its painful consequences, but from the principle underlying the act.
—Felix Adler, *An Ethical Philosophy of Life*, 1918

The notion of repentance is so fundamental in the Koran and in the Sunna that any sin, any offense would be completely forgiven once the person repents.
—Abdullahi Ahmed An-Na'im, in *New Perspectives Quarterly*, Spring 1989

O Lord, do not cast aside thy servant;
He is cast unto the mire; take his hand!
The sin which I have sinned, turn to mercy!
The iniquity which I have committed, let the wind carry
    away!
My many transgressions tear off like a garment!
—Babylonian Hymn (c. 6th century B.C.)

In the place where repentant sinners stand perfect saints cannot stand.
—*Berakot, Talmud*, c. 400

Repentance is a sovereign remedy for all sins, a spiritual wing to rear us, a charm for our miseries, a protecting amulet to expel sin's venom, an attractive lodestone to draw God's mercy and graces unto us.
—Robert Burton, *The Anatomy of Melancholy*, III, 1621

He who has committed a sin and has repented, is freed from that sin, but he is purified only by the resolution of ceasing to sin and thinking, "I will do so no more."
—*Code of Manu*, c. 1200–500 B.C.

We need to repent of the sins of others with which we find ourselves identified . . . by sharing in their economic or other advantages, by our loyal self-identification with groups that have sinned.
—Harold De Wolf, *Theology of the Living Church*, 1953

Christ saved one thief at the last gasp, to show that there may be late repentance.
—John Donne, sermon, May 30, 1621

The real God is the relentless One who pursues us and gives us no peace until our religiosity is transformed by repentance.
—A. Roy Eckardt, in *Christian Century*, November 17, 1954

The end of passion is the beginning of repentance.
—Owen Felltham, *Resolves*, c. 1620

Those who are well have no need of a physician, but those who are sick; I came not to call the righteous, but sinners.
—*Holy Bible*, Mark 2:17

Those whom I love, I reprove and chasten; so be zealous and repent.
—*Holy Bible*, Revelation 3:19

This alone will turn a wolf into a sheep, make a publican a preacher, turn a thorn into an olive, make a debauchee a religious fellow.
—St. John Chrysostom, *Hom.* 5, c. 388

He that feels himself alarmed by his conscience, anxious for the attainment of a better state and afflicted by the memory of his past faults, may justly conclude that the great work of repentance has begun.
—Samuel Johnson, in *The Rambler*, April 6, 1751

What is repentance but a kind of leave-taking, looking backward indeed, but yet in such a way as precisely to quicken the steps toward that which lies before.
—Sören Kierkegaard, *Philosophical Fragments*, 1844

Repentance was perhaps best defined by a small girl: "It's to be sorry enough to quit."
—C.H. Kilmer, *The New Illustrator*, 1945

Let not a repentant sinner imagine that he is remote from the estate of the righteous because of the sins and misdeeds that he has done. This is not true, for he is beloved and precious to God as if he had never sinned.
—Maimonides, *Mishneh Torah*, 1170

A sincere repenter of faults is like him who hath committed none.
—Mohammed (7th century), *Sayings of, Wisdom of East Series*

Reason effaces other griefs and sorrows, but engenders those of repentance.
—Michel de Montaigne, *Essays*, 1580

Our repentance is not so much regret for the ill we have done as fear of the ill that may happen to us in consequence.
—La Rochefoucauld, *Maxims*, 1665

Repentance is not self-regarding, but God-regarding. It is not self-loathing, but God-loving.
—Fulton J. Sheen, *Peace of Soul*, 1949

Collective sinning is a dire reality, but collective repentance is usually too diluted to be curative.
—Ralph W. Sockman, *The Highway of God*, 1941

Repentance is . . . not only a realization of failure, not only a burst of contrition for having failed the good, not only a readiness to admit this failure freely . . . but also a determination not to fail the good again.
—Douglas V. Steere, *Door into Life*, 1948

There is in repentance this beautiful mystery—that we may fly fastest home on broken wing.
—William L. Sullivan, *Epigrams and Criticisms in Miniature*, 1936

Repentance, of all things in the world, makes the greatest change; it changes things in heaven and earth; for it changes the whole man from sin to grace.
—Jeremy Taylor, *Holy Living*, 1650

He who says "I will sin and repent, and sin again and repent again" will be given no chance to repent.
—*Yoma, Mishnah*, c. 400

RESPONSIBILITY

Fate is something outside of us. What really plays the dickens with us is something in ourselves. Something that makes us go on doing the same sort of fool things, however many chances we get.
—James M. Barrie, *Dear Brutus*, 1917

So long as men and women believed themselves to be responsible beings, called to choose, and accountable to God for their choices, life might be tragic, but it was not trivial.
—Sydney Cave, *The Christian Way*, 1949

Be assured that if thou failest, none other—not nature, nor man, nor angel, nor Creator—will render the service or bestow the love due from thee.
—Stanton Coit, *Social Worship*, 1913

The peculiar character of an individual human being in distinction from an atom lies in this, that he is the owner of himself and responsible to himself.
—Martin C. D'Arcy, *God and the Supernatural,* 1920

If a man cast the blame of his sloth and inefficiency upon others, he will end by sharing the pride of Satan and murmuring against God.
—Feodor Dostoevsky, *The Brothers Karamazov,* 1880

Naturalistic determinism has not yet found a place for the concept of individual responsibility.
—Ralph H. Gabriel, *The Course of American Democratic Thought,* 1940

Outside the sphere of individual responsibility there is neither goodness or badness. . . . Only where we ourselves are responsible for our own interests and are free to sacrifice them has our decision moral value.
—Friedrich A. Hayek, *The Road to Serfdom,* 1945

One is responsible for one's own life. Passivity provides no protection.
—Madeleine Kunin, in *The Christian Science Monitor,* September 4, 1987

Is there no such thing as moral responsibility and social accountability at all? Is every mean or vicious thing that you or I as ordinary individuals do, not sin, but rather an expression of "illness"? Who would seriously hold that a society could long endure which consistently subscribed to this flaccid doctrine?
—O. Hobart Mowrer, address, Cincinnati, Ohio, September 1959

The nidus of the malady from which our civilization suffers lies in the individual soul and is only to be overcome within the individual soul.
—Wilhelm Roepke, in *Modern Age,* Summer 1959

Action, however far it spreads, comes back to its recorded page, black or white, to the one man that sent it forth, that he must read it to the last syllable in the Presence where there is no deceiving.
—William L. Sullivan, *Under Orders,* 1944

Does any one really believe he can escape from the responsibility for what he has done and thought in secret?
. . . The centre of our whole being is involved in the centre of all being; and the centre of all being rests in the centre of our being.

—Paul Tillich, *The Shaking of the Foundations*, 1949

RESURRECTION

Yet that bodies of all men—both those who have been born and those who shall be born, both those who have died and those who shall die—shall be raised again, no Christian ought to have the shadow of a doubt.

—St. Augustine, *Enchiridion*, 421

Earth to earth, ashes to ashes, dust to dust, in sure and certain hope of the Resurrection unto eternal life.

—*The Book of Common Prayer* (American version), 1876

The life and spirit of all our actions is the resurrection, and a stable apprehension that our ashes shall enjoy the fruits of our pious endeavors; without this, all religion is a fallacy.

—Thomas Browne, *Religio Medici*, 1635

We believe and teach that Christ, in the same flesh in which he died, rose from the dead and ascended to the right hand of God in the highest heaven.

—Henry Bullinger, *The Helvetic Confession*, 1536

One item about the resurrection of Jesus has sometimes been overlooked: he showed himself after death only to those who loved him.

—George A. Buttrick, *Sermons Preached in a University Church*, 1959

Let none of you say that this flesh is not judged and does not rise again . . . for as you were called in the flesh, you shall also come in the flesh.

—St. Clement of Rome, *Second Epistle to the Corinthians*, c. 100

The Incarnation . . . is simply God taking upon the divine self human suffering and humiliation. The resurrection is the divine victory over suffering, the bestowal of freedom to all who are weak and helpless. This and nothing else is the central meaning of the biblical story.

—James H. Cone, *Speaking the Truth*, 1986

The resurrection of Jesus was at once God's endorsement of his work, and the necessarily unique, authoritative event designed to shock us out of the conventional religious grooves so that we become aware that not rationality, mysticism, ritual, nor magic can bring us, unaided, to the most important truth of all: this comes from beyond us and it comes as a gift.
—Douglas A. Fox, *Buddhism, Christianity, and the Future of Man*, 1972

I am the resurrection and the life; he who believes in me, though he die, yet shall he live.
—*Holy Bible*, John 11:25

The entire character of a man's whole life depends on whether he answers "Yes" or "No" to the historic fact of the Resurrection.
—John E. Large, *The Small Needle of Doctor Large*, 1962

What did Resurrection mean but victory over death and therefore victory over sin and therefore the evidence of a new power at work in the world and therefore the opening of the gates of a new life?
—Edwin Lewis, *A Philosophy of the Christian Revelation*, 1940

The risen Christ, when he shows himself to his friends, takes on the countenance of all races and each can hear him in his own tongue.
—Henri de Lubac, *Catholicism*, 1927

The whole history of the Christian life is a series of resurrections. . . . Every time a man finds his heart is troubled, that he is not rejoicing in God, a resurrection must follow; a resurrection out of the night of troubled thought into the gladness of the truth.
—George MacDonald (1824–1905), *Selections from*

It is not belief in some vague intangible essence, but the reestablishment of personal life on the farther side of the grave, the conviction that the total personality, invested by God with a perfect organism, lives on.
—Robert J. McCracken, sermon, March 29, 1964

He who maintains that the resurrection is not a biblical doctrine has no share in the world to come.
—*Mishna: Sanhedrin*, 10.1, c. 200

What reason have atheists for saying that we cannot rise again? Which is the more difficult, to be born, or to rise again? That what has never been, should be, or that what has been, should be again? Is it more difficult to come into being than to return to it?

—Blaise Pascal, *Pensées*, 1670

The Lord's Resurrection is not an isolated fact, it is a fact that concerns the whole of mankind; from Christ it extends to the world; it has a cosmic importance . . . the source of meaning of the human drama, the solution of the problem of evil, the origin of a new form of life, to which we give the name of Christianity.

—Pope Paul VI, Easter sermon, 1964

Zen works miracles by overhauling the whole system of one's inner life and opening up a world hitherto entirely undreamt of. This may be called a resurrection.

—D.T. Suzuki, *Zen Buddhism*, 1956

It is an indication, not of what occurs in the lives of other men, but of what does *not* occur in the lives of other men.

—D.E. Trueblood, *The Logic of Belief*, 1942

Easter means—hope prevails over despair. Jesus reigns as Lord of Lords and King of Kings. Oppression and injustice and suffering can't be the end of the human story. Freedom and justice, peace and reconciliation, are his will for all of us, black and white, in this land and throughout the world. Easter says to us that despite everything to the contrary, his will for us will prevail, love will prevail over hate, justice over injustice and oppression, peace over exploitation and bitterness.

—Bishop Desmond Tutu, *Crying in the Wilderness*, 1982

It is a very mixed blessing to be brought back from the dead.

—Kurt Vonnegut, Jr., in *The New York Times*, April 30, 1980

The dead shall rise, life shall return to the bodies, and they shall breathe again. . . . The whole physical world shall become free from old age and death, from corruption and decay, forever and ever.

—*Zend-Avesta*, 6th century B.C.

REVELATION

All revelation is given, not in the form of directly communicated knowledge, but through events occurring in the historical experience of mankind, events which are apprehended by faith as the "mighty acts" of God.
—John Baillie, *The Idea of Revelation in Recent Thought*, 1956

At best God can only reveal Himself to us in terms of our experience in our historic setting. And the revelation that comes to us is to cooperate with God to bring form and order into the world as it is.
—John Elof Boodin, *God and Creation*, 1934

Sacred literatures (of most religions, though not all) are as a usual rule regarded as in some sense the word of God or the gods, revealed to man. In other words they are . . . regarded as inspired books. The degree of inspiration, or the nature of it, varies among the religions, and within any given faith.
—Charles S. Braden, *The Scriptures of Mankind*, 1952

When one has sought long for the clue to a secret of nature, and is rewarded by grasping some part of the answer, it comes as a blinding flash of revelation. . . . This conviction is of something revealed, and not something imagined.
—Lawrence Bragg, *Science and the Adventure of Living*, 1950

Revelation is such knowledge of the divine will as cannot be found through submersion in myself or in the secret of the world, but . . . an act of personal self-impartation from outside our own range, in which God gives us himself.
—Emil Brunner, *The Word and the World*, 1931

The scientist bridles at the word "revelation," but he could not discover anything, if it were not there already waiting to be found, free gift before it could be discovered.
—George A. Buttrick, *Sermons Preached in a University Church*, 1959

There was plainly wanting a divine revelation to recover mankind out of their universal corruption and degeneracy, and without such a revelation it was not possible that the world should ever be effectually reformed.
—Samuel Clarke, *Discourse Concerning the Unchangeable Obligations of Natural Religion*, 1705

I gradually came to disbelieve in Christianity as a divine revelation . . . and have never since doubted even for a single second that my conclusion was correct.
—Charles Darwin (1809–82), *Autobiography of*

Revealed truths are above our intelligence, and I would not dare submit them to the feebleness of my reason.
—René Descartes, *Discourses*, 1637

Reason and revelation cannot be in conflict because they are on different sides of the gap; revelation is part of that to which we react while reason is part of our reaction.
—Nels F.S. Ferré, *Faith and Reason*, 1946

It is universally acknowledged that revelation itself is to stand or fall by the test of reason.
—Edmund Gibson, *Second Pastoral Letter*, 1780

With the approach of death I care less and less about religion and truth. One hasn't long to wait for revelation and darkness.
—Graham Greene, *A Sort of Life*, 1971

So have no fear of them; for nothing is covered that will not be revealed, or hidden, that will not be known.
—*Holy Bible*, Matthew 10:26

The secret things belong unto the Lord our God; but the things that are revealed belong to us and to our children for ever.
—*Holy Bible*, Deuteronomy 29:29

Any person seasoned with a just sense of the imperfections of natural reason, will fly to revealed truth with the greatest avidity.
—David Hume, *Dialogues Concerning Natural Religion*, 1779

Revelation when genuine is simply the record of the immediate experience of those who are pure enough in heart and poor enough in spirit to be able to see God.
—Aldous Huxley, *The Perennial Philosophy*, 1945

Those who deny Revelation shall not enter Paradise until the camel goes through the eye of a needle.
—*Koran*, c. 625

If reason were able to find out the truth about God, revelation would not be necessary.
—Richard Kroner, *Perspectives on a Troubled Decade*, 1950

A revelation is to be received as coming from God, not because of its internal excellence, or because we judge it to be worthy of God; but because God has declared it to be His in as plain and undeniable a manner as He has declared creation and providence to be His.
—William Law, *The Case of Reason or Natural Religion Fairly and Fully Stated*, 1731

Revelation does not give anything to the human race which human reason, if left to itself, would not attain; but it has given and still gives the most important of these things earlier.
—G.E. Lessing, *Education of the Human Race*, 1780

What education is to the individual, revelation is to the whole human race.
—G.E. Lessing, *Education of the Human Race*, 1780

To talk of meanings, and hence of symbols and signs, is to talk of revelation, and to talk of revelation is to talk of the conveyance of truth.
—Edwin Lewis, *A Philosophy of the Christian Revelation*, 1940

He that takes away reason, to make way for revelation, puts out the light of both.
—John Locke, *Essay on Human Understanding*, 1690

The Rule of Faith once lost, souls wander and perish. The effect of this is that man have come to state, as scientifically certain, that there is no definite doctrine in revelation.
—Henry Edward Manning, *Lectures of*, 1872

If we believe in the revelation, we believe in what is revealed, in all that is revealed, however it may be brought home to us, by reasoning or in any other way.
—John Henry Newman, *Grammar of Assent*, 1870

Revelation means the moment in our history through which we know ourselves to be known from beginning to end, in which we are apprehended by the knower.
—H. Richard Niebuhr, *The Meaning of Revelation*, 1941

Before reaching us, divine revelation has passed through social contexts whose coloring it tended to assume; and to catch its spirit it is often necessary to relive the past and breathe its atmosphere.
—Ferdinand Prat, Preface, *Jesus Christ*, 1951

Revelation is not a series of propositions about God; it is the record of God's acts in time, His often violent intrusions into human history.
—Philip Scharper, in *The Critic*, August-September 1962

He who does not believe that revelation is continuous does not believe in revelation at all.
—George Bernard Shaw, *The Quintessence of Ibsenism*, 1890

The stumbling block of revelation is the belief in God in time, God in history. But this is exactly what theology must affirm: God's revelation is the event of Jesus Christ.
—Roger L. Shinn, *Christianity and the Problems of History*, 1953

Current revelation is equally plain with that of former days in predicting the yet future manifestations of God through His appointed channels. The canon of scripture is still open; many lines, many precepts, are yet to be added.
—James E. Talmage, *Articles of Faith*, 1920

If you say you have a revelation from God, I must have a revelation from God too before I can believe you.
—Benjamin Whichcote, *Aphorisms*, 1753

REVENGE

The precept "Resist not evil," was given to prevent us from taking pleasure in revenge, in which the mind is gratified by the sufferings of others, but not to make us neglect the duty of restraining men from sin.
—St. Augustine, *To Publicola*, 398

A man that studieth revenge keeps his own wound green.
—Francis Bacon, *Essays*, 1597

In taking revenge a man is but even with his enemy; but in passing it over, he is superior.
—Thomas Fuller, *Gnomologia*, 1732

Revenge is the poor delight of little minds.
—Juvenal, *Satires*, 128

When Jesus says that we should turn the other cheek he is telling us that we must not take revenge; he is not saying that we should never defend ourselves or others.
—*The Kairos Document*, rev. 2nd ed., 1986

Ah, God! what trances of torments does that man endure
who is consumed with one unachieved revengeful desire.
—Herman Melville, *Moby Dick*, 1851

Revenge is barren. It feeds on its own dreadful sin.
—J.C.F. von Schiller, *Wilhelm Tell*, 1804

He who wishes to revenge injuries by reciprocated hatred will
live in misery.
—Baruch Spinoza, *Ethics*, 1677

REVERENCE

The Jews would not willingly tread upon the smallest scrap
of paper in their way, but took it up; for possibly, said they,
the name of God may be on it.
—Samuel Taylor Coleridge, *Aids to Reflection*, 1825

The name of God may be written upon that soul thou tread-
est on.
—Samuel Taylor Coleridge, *Aids to Reflection*, 1825

There is much in the world that cannot be explained without
knowing what came before life and what is to come after it,
and of that we know nothing, for faith is not knowledge. All
that we can do is to take refuge, in reverence and submission.
—Edward Grey, in Margot Asquith, *Autobiography*, 1922

Therefore let us be grateful for receiving a kingdom that
cannot be shaken, and thus let us offer to God acceptable
worship, with reverence and awe; for our God is a consuming fire.
—*Holy Bible*, Hebrews 12:28-29

All real joy and power of progress in humanity depend on
finding something to reverence, and all the baseness and
misery of humanity begin in a habit of disdain.
—John Ruskin, *The Crown of Wild Olives*, 1866

A man is ethical only when life, as such, is sacred to him,
that of plants and animals as that of his fellowman, and
when he devotes himself helpfully to all life that is in need
of help.
—Albert Schweitzer, *Out of My Life and Thoughts*, 1933

I should not say that where fear is there is also reverence . . .
but where reverence is, there is fear.
—Socrates, Plato's *Euthyphro*, Vol. III, c. 380 B.C.

Pigs eat acorns, but neither consider the sun that gave
them life, nor the influence of the heavens by which they
were nourished, nor the very root of the tree from whence
they came.
—Thomas Traherne (1634?–1704), *Centuries of Meditation*

REWARD AND PUNISHMENT

When God punishes sinners, He does not inflict His evil on
them, but leaves them to their own evil.
—St. Augustine, *Enarrationes in Psalms*, 10, c. 415

To be gone from the kingdom of God, to be an exile from
God's city, to be cut off from the divine life, to be without the
manifold sweetness of God—is so mighty a punishment that
no torments that we know can be compared with it.
—St. Augustine, *Enchiridion*, 421

This is our highest reward that we should fully enjoy God,
and that all who enjoy Him should enjoy one another in Him.
—St. Augustine, *De Moribus Ecclesiae*, 368

Since it is most certain and undeniable that the happiness of
the blessed shall continue forever without mixture of misery,
so likewise shall the unhappiness of the damned continue
forever without mixture of comfort.
—Robert Bellarmine, *On the Ascent to God*, 1616

Since every reward is sought for the reason that it is held to
be good, who shall say that the man, that possesses goodness, does not receive his reward?
—Boethius, *Consolations of Philosophy*, c. 524

Great is the conduct of a man who lets rewards take care of
themselves—come if they will or fail to come—but goes on his
way, true to the truth simply because it is true, strongly loyal
to the right for its pure righteousness.
—Phillips Brooks, *Perennials*, 1898

Verily God does not reward man for what he does, but for
what he is.
—Chuang-tzu, c. 300 B.C.

The whole world is kept in order by punishment, for a guilt-
less man is hard to find; through fear of punishment the
whole world yields the enjoyments which it owes.
—*Code of Manu*, c. 1200–500 B.C.

And it often happens that a man with fifty murders on his head loses it but once. Where, then, will he pay the penalty for forty-nine of them? You must charge God with lack of justice, if there be not judgment and recompense after this world.

—St. Cyril of Jerusalem, *Catechetical Lectures*, 350

A fundamental, and as many believe, the most essential part of Christianity, is its doctrine of reward and punishment in the world beyond; and a religion which has nothing at all to say about this great enigma we should hardly feel to be a religion at all.

—G. Lowes Dickinson, *The Greek View of Life*, 1896

Man punishes the action, but God the intention.

—Thomas Fuller, *Gnomologia*, 1732

Sin is a suppurating wound; punishment is the surgeon's knife.

—St. John Chrysostom, *Homilies*, c. 388

The sin they do by two and two they must pay for one by one.

—Rudyard Kipling, *Tomlinson*, 1891

If, moreover, God should chastise men according to their deserts, He would not leave even a reptile on the back of the earth!

—*Koran*, c. 625

The object of punishment is prevention from evil; it never can be made impulsive to good.

—Horace Mann, *Lectures on Education*, 1840

All religions promise a reward . . . for excellences of the *will* or heart, but none for excellences of the head or understanding.

—Arthur Schopenhauer, *The World as Will and Idea*, II, 1818

Every person that does any evil, that gratifies any passion, is sufficiently punished by the evil he has committed, by the passion he serves, but chiefly by the fact that he withdraws himself from God, and God withdraws Himself from him.

—John Sergieff of Cronstadt (1829–1908), *My Life in Christ*

Men suffer individually for the deeds they themselves have done.

—*Sutra-Krit-Anga*, between 600 and 200 B.C.

To demand the good of victory without the existence of an antagonist, is to demand something with no meaning.
—William Temple, *Mens Creatrix*, 1917

What reward can there be for one that has passed his whole life, not only without pleasure, but in pain, if there is nothing to be expected after death.
—St. Thomas More, *Utopia*, 1516

RIGHT

Extremity of right is wrong.
—John Clarke, *Paroemiologia Anglo-Latina*, 1639

Better than one who knows what is right is one who is fond of what is right; and better than one who is fond of what is right is one who delights in what is right.
—Confucius, *Analects of*, c. 5th century B.C.

To know what is right and not do it is the worst cowardice.
—Confucius, *Analects*, c. 500 B.C.

I do think that the result of the sense that the world is corrupt and teetering is that everybody harks back to times when things were hopeful, like defeating Hitler and coming home. If you mean by nostalgia to include such things as regularity and hope—that if you do what's right in the world, you will be rewarded—then I think that nostalgia is the right word.
—Roderic Gorney, in *Los Angeles Times*, June 6, 1991

There is a way which seems right to a man, but its end is the way to death.
—*Holy Bible*, Proverbs 14:12

Nature in an absolute manner wills that right should at length obtain the victory.
—Immanuel Kant, *Perpetual Peace*, 1795

Let us have faith that right makes might; and in that faith let us dare to do our duty as we understand it.
—Abraham Lincoln, speech, New York, February 21, 1859

It's not enough to be right. That's too little. It's also important to be strong. The history of the world shows that more often people who were right lost than won.
—Andrzej Milczanowski, in *The New York Times*, January 28, 1989

One truth is clear; whatever is, is right.
—Alexander Pope, *An Essay on Man*, 1732

Right and wrong are the same for all in the same circumstances.
—Richard Price, *The Principal Questions in Morals*, 1758

So far there has been no known human society in which the distinction between right and wrong, and the obligation to do right, have been denied.
—A.J. Toynbee, *A Study of History*, Vol. XII, *Reconsiderations*, 1961

RIGHTEOUSNESS

Beware of the man of complete unquestionable virtue, the upstanding self-righteous citizen, who for all creatures of weakness has one general attitude: "Give them hell."
—David Abrahamsen, *Who Are the Guilty?*, 1958

Nothing will do except righteousness; and no other conception of righteousness will do, except Christ's conception of it.
—Matthew Arnold, *Literature and Dogma*, 1873

The humblest citizen of all the land, when clad in the armor of a righteous cause, is stronger than all the hosts of Error.
—William Jennings Bryan, speech, 1896

The saint is able to suffer for the sins of a man as though they were his own. To live in the life of others, this alone is righteousness.
—Martin Buber, *Jewish Mysticism and the Legends of Baalshem*, 1916

The righteousness of God means the righteousness that God imparts by his word, the acquittal that frees man of his sin.
—Rudolf Bultmann, "The Concept of Revelation," 1929, in *Existence and Faith*

In the kind of world that I see in history there is one sin that locks people up in all their other sins . . . the sin of self-righteousness.
—Herbert Butterfield, *Christianity and History*, 1950

The question is, not how we can be righteous, but how, though unrighteous and unworthy, we can be considered as righteous.
—John Calvin, *Institutes*, II, 1536

Let not the nation count wealth as wealth; let it count righteousness as wealth.
> —Confucius, *Great Learning*, 5th century B.C.

And the effect of righteousness will be peace, and the result
of righteousness, quietness and trust for ever.
> —*Holy Bible*, Isaiah 32:17

In my vain life I have seen everything; there is a righteous
man who perishes in his righteousness, and there is a
wicked man who prolongs his life in his evil-doing.
> —*Holy Bible*, Ecclesiastes 7:15

Righteousness in this: whosoever believeth in God, and the
Last Day, and the angels, and the Book, and the Prophets;
and whosoever, for the love of God, giveth of his wealth unto
his kindred, unto orphans, and the poor, and the wayfayer,
and to the beggar, and for the release of captives . . . and
who are patient in adversity . . . these are the righteous.
> —*Koran*, ii, c. 625

A cold, self-righteous prig who goes regularly to Church, may
be far nearer to hell than a prostitute. But, of course, it is
better to be neither.
> —C.S. Lewis, *Christian Behavior*, 1943

In a region bright with golden lustre—center of light and immortality—the righteous after death shall dwell in bliss.
> —*Mahabharata*, 800 B.C. to A.D. 400

If a grain of wheat, buried naked, sprouts forth in many
robes, how much more so the righteous!
> —Meir. T., *Sanhedrin*, 90b, c. 150

When men look for the victory of righteousness to come without their own bitter sacrifice and the shedding of their own
heart's blood, righteousness is always beaten.
> —W.G. Peck, *The Divine Revolution*, 1927

A good sermon of Mr. Gifford's at our church. . . . He showed,
like a wise man that righteousness is a surer moral way of
being rich, than sin and villainy.
> —Samuel Pepys, diary, August 23, 1668

The angel of righteousness is delicate and meek and gentle.
> —*Shephard of Hermas*, c. 148

I like life, and I also like righteousness. If I cannot keep the two together, I will let life go and choose righteousness.
—*Works of Mencius*, c. 300 B.C.

RISK AND SAFETY

The consciousness of abiding safety in the bosom of the Church is one of the most serious obstacles to an honest confrontation with the Christian faith.
—Peter L. Berger, *The Precarious Vision*, 1961

Historically, risk-takers are people who shatter the illusion of knowledge. They are willing to try something that everyone thinks is outrageous or stupid.
—Daniel J. Boorstin, in *U.S. News & World Report*, January 26, 1987

A man who really thought of nothing but getting safe to heaven would be as bad as a man in a shipwreck who thought of nothing but getting himself safe into a boat.
—Bernard Bosanquet, address, Ethical Society, 1886

We're always attracted to the edges of what we are, out by the edges where it's a little raw and nervy.
—E.L. Doctorow, in *Los Angeles Times*, April 5, 1989

For without risk there is no faith, and the greater the risk, the greater the faith.
—Sören Kierkegaard, postscript, *Philosophical Fragments*, 1846

If the creator had a purpose in equipping us with a neck, he surely meant for us to stick it out.
—Arthur Koestler, *Encounter*, 1970

There is no temper of the soul more antithetic to New Testament religion than that which plays for safety.
—A. Victor Murray, *Personal Experience and the Historic Faith*, 1939

If you take no risks, you will suffer no defeats. But if you take no risks, you win no victories.
—Richard M. Nixon, in *U.S. News & World Report*, March 30, 1987

A man who is good for anything ought not to calculate the chance of living or dying; he ought only to consider whether in doing anything he is doing right or wrong—acting the part of a good man or a bad.
—Plato, "Apology," *Dialogues*, 399 B.C.

All inquiries carry with them some element of risk. There is no guarantee that the universe will conform to our predispositions.

—Carl Sagan, *Broca's Brain*, 1979

Reform implies risks, but risks are better than not doing anything. I prefer the risk of reform to the risk of inactivity.

—Carlos Salinas de Gortari, in *The Washington Post*, May 12, 1988

There is an element of venture or risk in every statement of the truth. Yet we can take this risk in the certainty that this is the only way in which truth can reveal itself to finite and historical beings.

— Paul Tillich, *The Protestant Era*, I, 1948

RITUAL

The foundations and institutes, just as once the new Christian chapels and congregations stood side by side with pagan temples and heathen shrines, may oust their rivals, and assume the monopoly of ritual.

—Louis Berman, *The Glands and Human Personality*, 1921

Ritualism, n. A Dutch Garden of God where He may walk in rectilinear freedom, keeping off the grass.

—Ambrose Bierce, *Devil's Dictionary*, 1906

Ritual may be man-made in the sense that human hands fashioned it. But what inspired those hands to do their work is the Divine Influence.

—Ben Zion Bokser, *Perspectives on a Troubled Decade*, 1950

We ought to do in due order all things which the Lord hath commanded us to perform at appointed times. The offerings and services he has commanded to be performed carefully, and not to be done in a haphazard or disorderly way, but at fixed times and season.

—St. Clement of Rome, *First Epistle to the Corinthians*, c. 100

Difference of rite ought not to involve differences of faith.

—Christopher Dawson, *The Judgment of the Nations*, 1942

Granted that ritual in any realm from courtesy to worship can become formal, empty, and stiff. Nevertheless, with all its dangers it is an absolute necessity. We cannot . . . train children in the spirit of religion if the appropriate activities of worship and devotion are forgotten.

—Harry Emerson Fosdick, *World's Work*, February 1929

The fact, however, that Christian ritual and its accompanying theology is a *living* culture pattern gives it a functional value as a rallying point of the emotions, hopes and fears of mankind through two thousand years of religious experience.

—E.O. James, *Christian Faith and Ritual: A Historical Study*, 1965

The Jewish ritual is the expression of the history of a people that, when faithful to Judaism, sees history as a manifestation of God's will.

—Maurice Samuel, *The Professor and the Fossil*, 1956

Any ritual is an opportunity for transformation. To do ritual, you must be willing to be transformed in some way. That inner willingness is what makes the ritual come alive and have power.

—Starhawk, in *Utne Reader*, November/December 1987

Brahmanism thus sagely resolves the Western dispute as to the necessity or advisability of ritual. It affirms it for those who have not attained the end of all ritual. It lessens and refines ritual as spiritual progress is made upwards; it dispenses with it altogether when there is no longer need for it.

—John Woodroffe, *Sakiti and Sakta*, 1959

acrifice

In so far as man himself, consecrated by God's name and dedicated to God, dies to the world that he may live for God, he is a sacrifice.

—St. Augustine, *The City of God*, X, 426

The sacrifice most acceptable to God is complete renunciation of the body and its passions. This is the only real piety.

—St. Clement of Alexandria, *De Spectaculis*, c. 200

For me not personally to be present at a sacrifice, is as if I did not sacrifice.

—Confucius, *Analects*, 5th century B.C.

You give but little when you give your possessions. It is when you give of yourself that you truly give.

—Kahlil Gibran, *The Prophet*, 1923

Sacrificial love does more than create a defensive middle; it also presents a transformative witness to a world where the pursuit of self-actualization is the highest value, a world where self-asserting violence is the norm.

—Richard B. Hays, "An Emergency Directive,"
The Christian Century, April 22, 1992

For I desire steadfast love and not sacrifice, the knowledge of God rather than burnt offerings.

—*Holy Bible*, Hosea 6:6

It is only through the mystery of self-sacrifice that a man may find himself anew.

—C.G. Jung, *Two Essays on Analytical Psychology*, 1928

Nothing that we consider evil can be offered to God in sacrifice. Therefore, to renounce life in disgust is not sacrifice. . . . One of the chief tasks of Christian asceticism is to make our life and our body valuable enough to be offered to God in sacrifice.

—Thomas Merton, *No Man Is an Island*, 1955

In bringing themselves, worshippers offer the best of sacrifices, the full and truly perfect oblation of noble living.

—Philo, *Special Laws*, c. A.D. 10

Sacrifice signifies neither amputation nor repentance. It is, in essence, an act. It is the gift of oneself to the being of which one forms a part.
—Antoine de Saint-Exupéry, *Flight to Arras*, 1942

He who sacrifices his life to achieve any purpose for an individual or for humanity is practicing life-affirmation.
—Albert Schweitzer, *Indian Thoughts*, 1936

There is no Christian truth so clearly revealed as this, that the spirit of every Christian must be a spirit of sacrifice.
—P.A. Sheehan, *Mary, The Mother of God*, 1902

We must offer the Lord whatever interior sacrifice we are able to give Him, and His Majesty will unite it to that which He offered to the Father upon the Cross, so that it will have the value won for it by our will, even though our actions may be in themselves trivial.
—St. Teresa of Ávila, *The Interior Castle*, 1577

By the waters of Babylon, there we sat down and wept, when we remembered Zion. . . . For there our captors required of us songs, and our tormentors, mirth, saying, "Sing us one of the songs of Zion!"
—*Holy Bible*, Psalms 137:1, 3

For the Lamb in the midst of the throne will be their shepherd, and he will guide them to springs of living water; and God will wipe away every tear from their eyes.
—*Holy Bible*, Revelation 7:17

Sadness lies at the heart of every merely positivistic, agnostic, or naturalistic scheme of philosophy.
—William James, *Varieties of Religious Experience*, 1902

The great enemy of the soul is not trial but sadness, which is the bleeding wound of self-love.
—F.X. Lasance, *Remember-Thoughts*, 1936

So much pleasure, and so little joy; so much learning, and so little wisdom . . . the one divine thing left to us is sadness. . . . Without sadness where were brotherliness?. . . She is the Spartan sauce which gives gusto to the remainder-viands of life, the broken meats of love. . . . All things take on beauty which pass through the hueless flame of *her* aureole.
—Francis Thompson, *Moestitiae Encomium*, 1910

SAINTS AND SINNERS

Fancy believing in sinners and not believing in saints.
—Anisetta, in Aubrey Menen, *The Backward Bride*, 1950

I contemplate the saints more pleasantly when I envisage them as the teeth of the Church cutting off men from their errors and transferring them to her body after their hardness has been softened as if by being bitten and chewed.
—St. Augustine, *On Christian Doctrine*, 397

A minor saint is capable of loving minor sinners. A great saint loves great sinners.
—Rabbi Israel Baal Shem-Tov, (1700–60), *Judaism*

A hero gives the illusion of surpassing humanity. The saint doesn't surpass it, he assumes it, he strives to realize it in the best possible way.
—Georges Bernanos, *Last Essays of*, 1955

There is no man who is not potentially a saint, and sin or sins, even the blackest, are but accidents that in no way alter the substance.
—Leon Bloy, *The Pilgrim of the Absolute*, 1909

In his holy flirtation with the world, God occasionally drops a handkerchief. These handkerchiefs are called saints.
—Frederick Buechner, *Wishful Thinking: A Theological ABC*, 1973

Only God knows how many married saints there have been. Perhaps when and if we get to heaven we may find that some of the brightest jewels in His crown are obscure husbands and wives, fathers and mothers, that nobody paid any attention to here on earth.
—John C. Cort, *The Grail*, August 1957

It is great to live with the saints in Heaven, but it is hell to live with them on earth.
—Richard J. Cushing, speech, Boston, February 1964

The true way to worship the saints is to imitate their virtues.
—Desiderius Erasmus, *Handbook of the Christian Knight*, 1503

The word *saint* means a man called out from among sinners, and in this sense all good men are saints.
—François Fénelon (1651–1715), *Spiritual Letters*

Let the saints say what they will, they have a sly liking for strong sinners.
—Harry Emerson Fosdick, *On Being a Real Person*, 1943

For the Lord loves justice; he will not forsake his saints. The righteous shall be preserved for ever.
—*Holy Bible*, Psalms 37:28

The world is not yet with them, so they often seem in the midst of the world's affairs to be preposterous. Yet they are impregnators of the world, vivifiers and animators of potentialities of goodness which but for them would lie forever dormant.
—William James, *The Varieties of Religious Experience*, 1902

The difference between ordinary people and saints is not that saints fulfill the plain duties which ordinary men neglect. The thing saints do have not usually occurred to ordinary people at all.
—A.D. Lindsay, *Two Moralities*, 1940

The saint . . . is one who succeeds in giving us at least a glimpse of eternity, despite the thick opacity of time.
—Henri de Lubac, *Paradoxes*, 1948

A saint is like a tree. He does not call anyone, neither does he send anyone away. He gives shelter to whoever cares to come, be it a man, woman, child or an animal. If you sit under a tree it will protect you from the weather, from the scorching sun as well as from the pouring rain, and it will give you flowers and fruit. Whether a human being enjoys them or a bird tastes of them matters little to the tree; its produce is there for anyone who comes and takes it.
—Anandamayi Ma, *As the Flower Sheds Its Fragrance*, 1983

The saint . . . wants himself to be simply a window through which God's mercy shines on the world. And for this he strives to be holy . . . in order that the goodness of God may never be obscured by any selfish act of his.
—Thomas Merton, *Life and Holiness*, 1963

If you would in fact have a literature of saints, first of all have a nation of them.
—John Henry Newman, *The Idea of a University*, 1852

To make a saint, it must indeed be by grace; and whoever doubts this does not know what a saint is, or a man.
—Blaise Pascal, *Pensées*, 1670

If, having God, for other goods I faint,
Call me what thing you will—but not a saint.
—Shaikh Saadi, *Gulistan*, c. 1265

The true saint goes in and out amongst the people, eats and sleeps with them, buys and sells in the market, marries and takes part in social intercourse, and never forgets God for a single moment.
—Abu Said (died 1049), in T.W. Arnold and A. Guillaume, *The Legacy of Islam*

The saints in the spiritual world are like rays of the sun in the material world. God is the eternal, life-giving Sun, and the saints are the rays of this wise Sun.
—John Sergieff of Cronstadt (1829–1908), *My Life in Christ*

It is far more dangerous to be a saint than to be a conqueror.
—George Bernard Shaw, Preface, *Saint Joan*, 1923

If the first step on Man's road toward sainthood is the renunciation of Man's traditional role of being his brother's murderer, the second step would be an acceptance of Man's new role of being his brother's keeper.
—A.J. Toynbee, *A Study of History*, Vol. XII, *Reconsiderations*, 1961

The saints are neither special creations nor spiritual freaks, but those who have learned St. Augustine's aspiration: "My life shall be a real life, being wholly full of Thee."
—Evelyn Underhill, *Concerning the Inner Life*, 1926

The saints were like magnifying glasses, bringing to light the subtle loveliness of whatever came along, whether of nature, of grace, or of art. They were God's showmen.
—Hubert Van Zeller, *We Die Standing Up*, 1949

One of the chief functions of the saints is to provide us other Christians with proximate living examples of how Christ would apply His thought and action to the specific circumstances of our own vocations.
—John J. Wright, in *The Way*, October 1962

SALVATION

Salvation is not putting a man into Heaven, but putting Heaven into man.
—Maltbie D. Babcock, *Thoughts for Everyday Living*, 1901

But salvation is not actualized only in the last moment of one's life, or only in eternity. It is anticipated. The human being must enter upon a whole salvation process, a process that begins here on earth and ends in eternity.
—Leonardo and Clodovis Boff, *Salvation and Liberation*, 1984

From all evil and mischief; from sin; from the crafts and assaults of the Devil; from Thy wrath, and from everlasting damnation, Good Lord, deliver us.
—*The Book of Common Prayer*, 1662

Every great religion has some term descriptive of its ultimate goal. In Christianity it is *salvation*, in Hinduism it is *Moksha*. Each religion defines it differently, and employs different methods in its achievement, but in the end the quest in all religions seems to be for supremely enduring satisfaction either in this life or beyond.
—Charles S. Braden, *Man's Quest for Salvation*, 1941

For the greatest and most regal work of God is the salvation of humanity.
—St. Clement of Alexandria, *Paedagogus*, c. 220

I can never believe that a man may not be saved by that religion, which doth but bring him to the true love of God and to heavenly mind and life; nor that God will ever cast a soul into hell that truly loveth Him.
—Samuel Taylor Coleridge, *Aids to Reflection*, 1825

Those of us who were brought up as Christians and have lost our faith have retained the sense of sin without the saving belief in redemption.
—Cyril Connolly, *The Unquiet Grave*, 1944

No one in good faith can ever be lost.
—A.J. Cronin, *The Keys of the Kingdom*, 1941

In the Christian tradition, the history of salvation begins, not with the choosing of Abraham, but with the creation of the world.
—Jean Danielou, *The Lord of History*, 1958

The process of salvation must come from within.
—*Dhammapada*, c. 5th century B.C.

It was, thanks no doubt to heavenly power and aid, that the doctrine of salvation like the rays of the sun, suddenly lighted up the whole world.
—Eusebius, *Ecclesiastical History*, c. 192

Man was meant to realize the divine potential within him. He misses the mark when he fails to do so. He has attained salvation when he achieves his full spiritual potential as a human being, created in the image of God.
—Roland B. Gittelsohn, *The Meaning of Judaism*, 1970

If our assurance of salvation were made to depend upon our knowledge that every word of the Bible was of divine origin, our hopes of eternal life would be altogether obscure.
—Washington Gladden, *Who Wrote the Bible?*, 1891

In returning and rest you shall be saved; in quietness and in trust shall be your strength.
—*Holy Bible*, Isaiah 30:15

No man has the right to abandon the care of his salvation to another.
—Thomas Jefferson, *Notes on Religion*, 1776

God never draws anyone to Himself by force and violence. He wishes all men to be saved, but forces no one.
—St. John Chrysostom, sermon, c. 388

The essence of religion is the human quest for salvation.
—Mordecai Kaplan, *Future of the American Jew*, 1948

The Church's own littleness is the key to its greatness. God wishes to show that man's salvation is His work, and not man's.
—John La Farge, *An American Amen*, 1958

God gives light sufficient for its salvation, to every soul that attains to the use of reason in this life.
—Juan de Lugo (1583–1660), *De Fide*, XIX

He desires that all men should be saved . . . and the fault is in the will which does not receive Him. . . . But why the Majesty does not remove or change this fault of will in every man (for it is not in the power of man to do it), or why He lays this fault to the charge of the will, when man cannot avoid it, it is not lawful to ask.

—Martin Luther, *Bondage of the Will*, 1525

If the degree of enlightenment of a people admits, all truths necessary to the salvation of the human race ultimately can be constructed upon knowledge gained by reason.

—Moses Mendelssohn, *Gegenbetrachtungen*, 1770

In no single act or passion can salvation stand: far hence, beyond Orion and Andromeda, the cosmic process works and shall work forever through unbegotten souls.

—Frederic W.H. Myers, *Human Personality*, 1906

There is no such thing as a single scheme of salvation. Salvation is not the monopoly of any church. All paths lead to the hilltop of one and the same God-consciousness. The different religions are suited to the different aspirants in their various stages of progress.

—Swami Nikhilananda, *Perspectives on a Troubled Decade*, 1950

Let no one then mistake, let no one deceive himself . . . outside the Church, no one is saved; he who leaves it is himself responsible for his own death.

—Origen (185–254), *Hom.* III, no. 5

To save one's soul is not an instantaneous deed, but a life-long adventure. . . . The creation of a type of personality through loyalty to concrete values as these are at issue in everyday experience.

—Max C. Otto, *Things and Ideals*, 1924

The Buddha came to save the world, and his method for the accomplishment of this end is the destruction of ignorance and the dissemination of knowledge as to the true values of life and the wise way to live. The Buddha indeed cannot save us; we must do that for ourselves . . . in large part through the attainment and application of his knowledge or insight.

—J.B. Pratt, *The Pilgrimage of Buddhism*, 1928

True salvation, deliverance from life and suffering, cannot be imagined without complete denial of the will.

—Arthur Schopenhauer, *The World as Will and Idea*, 1819

If mankind, united in sin, faces a need for salvation, then the answer to that need is universal.
—Roger L. Shinn, *Christianity and the Problem of History*, 1953

A child cannot "save his soul" in a vacuum—salvation must be effected in a social environment in which love of God and man must be in constant operation.
—Roland Simonitsch, *Sanctity and Success in Marriage*, 1956

The Church is like an ark of Noah, outside of which nobody can be saved.
—St. Thomas Aquinas (1225–74), *Exposition of the Apostles' Creed*

Pray always for all the learned, the oblique, the delicate. Let them not be quite forgotten at the throne of God when the simple come into their kingdom.
—Evelyn Waugh, in Richard Holloway, *Beyond Belief*, 1981

By salvation I mean . . . a present deliverance from sin, a restoration of the soul to its primitive health, its original purity, a recovery of the divine nature.
—John Wesley (1703–91), *A Further Appeal to Men of Reason and Religion*, in *Works*, XII

SANCTITY

Blessedness is one with divinity.
—Boethius, *Consolations of Philosophy*, c. 523

Sanctity consists in but one thing—fidelity to the order of God.
—J.P. de Caussade, *Abandonment*, 1880

The whole history of religious enthusiasm bears witness that the highest sanctity often runs on the very borderlines of sanity.
—Ronald A. Know, *Miracles*, 1928

Some folk who would be horrified to think themselves saintly live in an almost continuous consciousness of God.
—John W. Lynch, *Hourglass*, 1952

Sanctity of life is not a peculiar benefit which is offered to some and denied to others, but it is the common lot and duty of all.
—Pope Pius XI, *Casti Connubi*, December 31, 1930

SANCTITY

There is sanctity in pure knowledge, as there is in pure beauty, and the disinterested quest of truth is perhaps the greatest purification.

—George Sarton, *History of Science*, 1927

He who thinks himself more blessed because he enjoys the benefits which others do not . . . is ignorant of true blessedness.

—Baruch Spinoza, *Tractatus Theologico-Politicus*, 1670

Blessedness lieth not in much and many, but in one and oneness.

—*Theologica Germanica*, 14th century

SECURITY

It was for the sake of *security* that the people of ancient times turned to the Baals and other idols. Today, our oppressors turn to money and military power and to the so-called security forces. But their security is our insecurity. We experience their security as intimidation and repression, terror, rape and murder. Those who turn to the idols for security demand our insecurity as the price that must be paid.

—Center of Concern, *The Road to Damascus: A Challenge to the Churches of the World*, 1989

Security is a feeling that there is a larger and more enduring life surrounding, appreciating, upholding the individual, and guaranteeing that his efforts and sacrifice will not be in vain.

—Charles H. Cooley, *Social Progress*, 1908

This is the Hartford heresy. Economic, material security, life insurance, endowments, annuities take the place of a providential destiny, so that ultimate values are not built upon a rock whose name is Peter, but upon a rock whose name is Prudential.

—William T. Costello, address, December 1948

The only security that man has ever had has been in the warm enfoldment of the natural and social environment.

—A. Eustace Haydon, *This Is My Faith*, 1956

I lift up my eyes to the hills. From whence does my help come?

—*Holy Bible*, Psalms 121:1

Social security depends on *personal* security. And *personal* security depends on *spiritual* security. Spiritual security is primary, in the sense that every other kind of security stems from it. Without spiritual security, there just can't be any other kind of lasting security.

—John E. Large, *The Small Needle of Doctor Large*, 1962

A recognition of truth and the practice of virtue is the title to security for both the individuals, and the whole of mankind.

—John of Salisbury, *Politcratius*, 1159

An overemphasis on temporal security is a compensation for a loss of the sense of eternal security.

—Fulton J. Sheen, *Peace of Soul*, 1949

Life wants to secure itself against the void that is raging within. The risk of eternal void is to be met by the premium of temporal insurance . . . social security, old age pensions, etc. It springs no less from metaphysical despair than from material misery.

—Franz Werfel, *Between Heaven and Earth*, 1947

SELF

To "lose self" in a Society of some kind is the only means of saving self.

—R.H. Benson, *The Friendship of Christ*, 1912

This [Self] is never born, nor does It die, nor after once having been, does It go into non-being. This [Self] is unborn, eternal, changeless, ancient. It is never destroyed even when the body is destroyed.

—*Bhagavad-Gita*, c. 2nd century B.C.

The Self is to be described as not *this*, not *that*. It is incomprehensible, for it cannot be comprehended.

—*Brhadaranyaka Upanishad*, prior to 400 B.C.

When we come to know that our whole environment and everything that happens is God's hand upon us . . . every detail of life is a means arranged by Him to lead us to Himself; then we find that our great trouble is self.

—John Chapman, *Spiritual Letters of*, 1944

lf the evil is done, by one's self one suffers; by
vil is left undone, by one's self one is purified. The
he impure stand and fall by themselves, *no one*
another.

—*Dhammapada*, c. 5th century B.C.

In our loss of the perception of the Void and our conviction
that particular things are finally real, we come to believe in
the separate, isolated reality of some enduring self within us
for which we plan and hope great things. Alas, we are frustrated in our hoping because all through our lives our hopes
are incompletely attained or, if fulfilled, strangely unsatisfying after all.

—Douglas A. Fox, *Buddhism, Christianity, and the Future of Man*, 1972

Where religion goes wrong it is because, in one form or another, men have made the mistake of trying to turn to God
without turning away from self.

—Aelred Graham, *Christian Thought and Action*, 1951

The Buddha began with the idea of nonself, really a reaction
against His time. But many Buddhists think that nonself . . .
is the basis of all truth. In this, they are considering a means
to be an end, a raft to be the shore, the finger pointing to be
the moon.

—Thich Nhat Hanh, *The Raft Is Not the Shore*, 1975

Soundless, formless, intangible, undying, tasteless, order-
less, eternal, immutable, beyond Nature, is the Self.

—*Katha Upanishad*, prior to 400 B.C.

As the soul ceases to be "self-regarding" in its activities, it
becomes "God-regarding."

—Edward Leen, *Progress Through Mental Prayer*, 1940

Man can become part of God's unity, which is eternal, only
by forgetfulness of self.

—Rabbi Nachman of Bratislava (1772–1811), in *Judaism*

It turns out that our notions of what a "self" is and how it
might feel fulfilled have no more objective status than most
of the rest of reality. It seems we make ourselves up as we go
along.

—Maureen O'Hara, speech, Association for Humanistic Psychology Conference,
August 1, 1992

There must be a place where hopes and dreams are nurtured, and that place is only without ourselves. A place to clean the grime of life, a place that waits for us to stay and look inside that we might see the truth.

—Cliff Roberston, in *The Christian Science Monitor*, June 18, 1987

Thou wilt never escape from thy self until thou slay it. Thy self, which is keeping thee far from God, and saying "So-and-so has treated me ill . . . such a one has done well by me"— all this is polytheism; nothing depends upon the creatures, all upon the Creator.

—Abu Said (died 1049), in R.A. Nicholson,
Translations of Eastern Poetry and Prose

Self-love, in the true sense, is the love of one's real good—of truth, of virtue, of beauty, of God. It is the strongest in those who are most alive in their higher nature. It is the opposite of selfish love.

—John Lancaster Spalding, *Glimpses of Truth*, 1903

Self is the one invincible foe when acting with the four cardinal passions: anger, pride, deceitfulness, and greed.

—*Uttaradhyayana-sutra*, c. 500 B.C.

Self is the only prison that can ever bind the soul.

—Henry Van Dyke (1852–1933), "The Prison and the Angel"

SERENITY

A serene spirit accepts pleasure and pain with an even mind, and is unmoved by either. He alone is worthy of immortality.

—*Bhagavad-Gita*, between 500 and 200 B.C.

There's naught so much the spirit calms as rum and true religion.

—Lord Byron, *Don Juan*, 1819

Seek not to have that everything should as you wish, but wish for everything to happen as it actually does happen, and you will be serene.

—Epictetus, *Enchiridon*, VIII, c. 110

He who discerns all creatures in his Self, and his Self in all creatures, has no disquiet thence. What delusion, what grief can be with him?

—*Isavasya Upanishad*, between 700 and 400 B.C.

Serenity comes not alone by removing the outward causes and occasions of fear, but by the discovery of inward reservoirs to draw upon.
—Rufus M. Jones, *The Testimony of the Soul*, 1936

The final wisdom of life requires not the annulment of incongruity but the achievement of serenity within and above it.
—Reinhold Neibuhr, *The Irony of American History*, 1952

Undisturbed calmness of mind is attained by cultivating friendliness toward the happy, compassion for the unhappy, delight in the virtuous, and indifference toward the wicked.
—Patanjali (2nd century B.C.), *Yoga Aphorisms*

SERMONS

The church bell sometimes does better work than the sermon.
—American proverb

Ministers have learned nice people don't like ugly sermons.
—Waldo Beach, *News and Observer* (Raleigh, North Carolina), July 26, 1959

The making and delivery of an effective sermon is not only the most conspicuous, but the most influential single service the minister is privileged to render in the whole round of the week's activity.
—Charles R. Brown, *The Art of Preaching*, 1922

The best sermon is that preached in such human understanding that a hearer can say: "It was preached for me as though I had been alone."
—George A. Buttrick, *Jesus Come Preaching*, 1931

Every attempt in a sermon to cause emotion, except as the consequence of an impression made on the reason, or the understanding, or the will, I hold to be fanatical and sectarian.
—Samuel Taylor Coleridge, *Table-Talk*, January 7, 1833

The devil's favorite Sunday-morning entertainment is the sermon which does not cause a ripple of disturbance, intellectual, moral or emotional, to man, woman, or beadle.
—A.C. Craig, *Preaching in a Scientific Age*, 1954

A near-hit bolt of lightning can create a lot more Christian thinking than a longwinded sermon.
—Duane Dewel, in *A Little Treasury of Main Street, U.S.A.*, 1952

I'd rather see a sermon than hear one any day; I'd rather one
should walk with me than merely tell the way.
—Edgar A. Guest (1881–1959), "Sermons We See"

If the sermons that ought to be preached were preached, half
the congregations of half the churches would get up and
leave in indignation before half the sermons were over.
—Sydney J. Harris, *Pieces of Eight*, 1982

He that has but one word of God before him, and out of that
word cannot make a sermon, can never be a preacher.
—Martin Luther (1483–1546), *Table-Talk*

The great object of modern sermons is to hazard nothing;
their characteristic is decent debility.
—Sydney Smith, in *Edinburgh Review*, 1802

No sermon lands effectively on the field of a sinful heart unless at some point it opposes the trend of that heart's earthly
desire.
—Ralph W. Sockman, *The Highway of God*, 1941

When the congregation becomes the norm by which sermons
are measured, a minister has put a mortgage on his soul.
—Ralph W. Sockman, *The Highway of God*, 1941

SEXUALITY

What has been encouraged as healthy sexuality is but an expression of the brutal, fiendish rationalism (not reason) that
harries love, and the relationship between man and woman
has become one of the saddest commentaries of our time.
—Ruth Nanda Anshen, *Our Emergent Civilization*, 1947

Sex which is not integrated and transfigured by spirit is always evidence of man's subjugation to the genus.
—Nicholas Berdyaev, *Dream and Reality*, 1939

The sexual act takes on qualitative significance and value
which transcends the other meanings the sexual act can
have, when lovers use the act purposely to become parents.
For now the two lovers express their faith in love itself, in the
possibilities open to their children within the social order
and in this world.
—Peter A. Bertocci, *Sex and Religion Today*, 1953

Married love is a creative enterprise. It is not achieved by accident or instinct. Perfunctory coitus is a confession of lack of intelligence and character. There is a profound beauty and even holiness in the act of fecundation.
—Alexis Carrel, *Reader's Digest*, July 1939

Human sexuality is too noble and beautiful a thing, too profound a form of experience, to turn into a mere technique of physical relief, or a foolish and irrelevant pastime.
—J.V.L. Casserley, *The Bent World*, 1955

The creation of one flesh in the biblical sense involves the joining of two total existences, economically, spiritually, and psychologically, and not just the union of two bodies. To attempt the one without the other is dangerous to the entire relationship.
—William G. Cole, *Sex in Christianity and Psychoanalysis*, 1955

Christianity places the sexual instinct under a spiritual law, and permits its gratification only for the definite purpose of creating a Christian home.
—Father Cuthbert, *Catholic Ideals in Social Life*, 1904

There is a tendency to think of sex as something degrading; it is not, it is magnificent, an enormous privilege, but, because of that, the rules are tremendously strict and severe. . . . It is easy to serve God in most other ways, but it is not so easy here.
—Francis Devas, *The Law of Love*, 1954

It is not true that the relations between the sexes are of the same order with the rest of man's instincts. They have social consequences which place them in a class apart.
—Ernest Dimnet, *What We Live By*, 1932

The fact that God had ordained the sexual act as our only means of procreation must, to some of our Victorian forefathers, have betrayed a singular lack of celestial sensitivity.
—Douglas A. Fox, *Buddhism, Christianity, and the Future of Man*, 1972

There's no question about it. The sex-related issues are going to be the most important issues facing all churches in the foreseeable future. Abortion, AIDS, premarital sex, homosexuality, all those are going to be at the vortex.
—George Gallup, Jr., in *Los Angeles Times*, June 6, 1991

Grandeur and beauty come to the moment of sexual union from the total of what a man and a woman have been able to express in all the rest of their life together. Sexual union will then be the culmination of past love, and the sustenance of love to come.

—Henri Gibert, *Love in Marriage*, 1964

Can all Christian morality about sex be reduced to a sure body of knowledge, with no possibility of increased or refined understanding?

—David Hedendorf, "A Pagan Protests Presbyterian Sex," in *Christian Century*, February 26, 1992

Sexuality is a force to be controlled and transformed; its energy must be channeled and educated.

—Bakole wa Ilunga, *Paths of Liberation*, 1984

Whoever cannot bridle his carnal affections, let him keep them within the bounds of lawful wedlock.

—Lactantius, *The Divine Institutes*, c. 310

There are people who want to keep our sex instinct inflamed in order to make money out of us. Because, of course, a man with an obsession is a man who has very little sales-resistance.

—C.S. Lewis, *Christian Behavior*, 1943

Christian teaching about sex is by no means clear in detail, but what shines with pellucid clarity throughout the Christian tradition is that sex is a very holy subject.

—Geddes MacGregor, *The Hemlock and the Cross*, 1963

We pray that the young men and women of today and tomorrow will grow up with the realization that sex is a beautiful flame they carry in the lantern of their bodies.

—Demetrius Manousos, address, March 14, 1950

The sexual act has no resemblance to any other act: its demands are frenzied and participate in infinity. It is a tidal wave able to cover anything and bear away everything.

—François Mauriac, *What I Believe*, 1962

I believe that the real issue about premarital sex is the risk of producing illegitimate children who from the start are denied the protection every human society has found it necessary to give.

—Margaret Mead, in *Redbook*, October 1962

If the union of man and woman is the fruit of a love that is given in purity, generosity and fidelity, then the body itself is spiritualized in the service of a love that ennobles it, and, with God's blessing, sanctifies.

—Jean Mouroux, *The Meaning of Man*, 1948

In truth all experiences of the Divine Unity and Holiness depend on the union between man and woman, for the ultimate meaning of this act is very lofty.

—Rabbi Nachman of Bratislava (1772–1811), in *Judaism*

Sex is just about the most powerful and explosive force that is built into us. Every instinct and every bit of counseling experience I have had tells me that it is too dangerous a commodity to be handed over to people with no strings attached.

—Norman Vincent Peale, *Man, Morals and Maturity*, 1965

For the very reason that sexual power is so noble and necessary and good, it needs the preserving and defending order of reason.

—Josef Pieper, *Fortitude and Temperance*, 1954

To reduce cohabitation and the conjugal act to a simple organic function for the transmission of seed would be converting the home, the sanctuary of the family, into a mere biological laboratory.

—Pope Pius XII, address to Italian Midwives, October 1946

The beauty of love . . . vanishes if its mere physical expression be consciously sought as a means of sensual gratification, without the spiritual and aesthetic accompaniments that alone give it human value.

—Harry Roberts, letter to the *New Statesman and Nation*, August 29, 1931

Perhaps when we know more we shall be able to say that the best sexual ethic will be quite different in one climate from what it would be in another, different again with one kind of diet than from what it would be with another.

—Bertand Russell, *Marriage and Morals*, 1929

We have two tyrannous physical passions: concupiscence and chastity. We become mad in pursuit of sex: we become equally mad in the persecution of that pursuit. Unless we gratify our desire the race is lost; unless we restrain it we destroy ourselves.

—George Bernard Shaw, Preface, *Androcles and the Lion*, 1914

Creation is the work of omnipotence. But procreation is pro-creation, a kind of deputy creation. So that sex in its essential nature is man's greatest glory in the physical order.
—F.J. Sheed, *Society and Sanity*, 1953

Where there is an ongoing relationship of caring. Where there is a sense of humor. Where there is a sense of mutual mercy. Where there is a sense that God has given sex to you . . . there is nothing livelier. But when it is merchandised as a commodity for instant gratification, there is nothing deadlier than sex.
—William Swing, in *Episcopalian*, March 1986

Nature is to be reverenced, not blushed at. It is lust, not the act itself, that makes sexual union shameful; it is excess, not the [marital] state as such, that is unchaste.
—Tertullian, *De Anima*, c. 209

As long as the sexual act itself corresponds to the rational order, the abundance of pleasure does not conflict with the proper mean of virtue. . . . And even the fact that reason is unable to make a free act of cognition of spiritual things simultaneously with that pleasure does not prove that the sexual act conflicts with virtue.
—St. Thomas Aquinas, *Summa Theologiae*, 1272

I was asked the question, "After Christianity, what?" Sex, in its many permutations, is surely the glue, ambience, and motive force of the new humanism.
—John Updike, in *The New York Times*, April 7, 1068

SHAME

Shame is the mark of a base man, and belongs to a character capable of shameful acts.
—Aristotle, *The Nicomachean Ethics*, c. 340 B.C.

Shame kills faster than disease.
—Buchi Emecheta, *The Rape of Shavi*, 1985

As painful as shame is, it does seem to be the guardian of many of the secret, unexplored aspects of our beings. Repressed shame must be experienced if we are to come to terms with the good, the bad, and the unique of what we are.
—Robert Karen, "Shame," in *The Atlantic*, February 1992

Experiences of shame appear to embody the root meaning of the word—to uncover, to expose, to wound. They are experiences of exposure, exposure of peculiarly sensitive, intimate, vulnerable aspects of self. The exposure may be to others, but whether others are or are not involved, it is always . . . exposure to one's own eyes.

—Helen Merrell Lynd, *On Shame and the Search for Identity*, 1958

Shame is real. It's the hot on the cheek, the dense blood felt along its implacable route up behind the ears and across the forehead. Adrenaline, as in anger, but here it immobilizes. The terrible fact of being "caught."

—Kate Millett, "The Shame Is Over," in *Ms.*, January 1975

I have called shame and embarrassment Quislings of the organism. . . . As the Quislings identify themselves with the enemy and not with their own people, so shame, embarrassment, self-consciousness and fear restrict the individual's expressions. Expressions change into repressions.

—Fritz Perls, *Ego, Hunger, and Aggression*, 1969

In shame there is no comfort, but to be beyond all bounds of shame.

—Philip Sidney, *Arcadia*, 1590

I never wonder to see men wicked, but I often wonder to see them not ashamed.

—Jonathan Swift, *Thoughts on Various Subjects*, 1706

Where there's no shame before men, there's no fear of God.

—Yiddish proverb

SILENCE

Think not silence the wisdom of fools; but, if rightly timed, the honor of wise men, who have not the infirmity, but the virtue of taciturnity.

—Thomas Browne, *Christian Morals*, 1680

As a Christian preacher, what I envy the Buddha more than I can say is his silence, and I envy the Buddhist monks and teachers the way they emulate that silence. I envy them because when you come right down to it, of course, the kinds of things that you talk about in religion are always very difficult and usually quite impossible to put into words.

—Frederick Buechner, *The Hungering Dark*, 1969

How can you expect God to speak in that gentle and inward voice which melts the soul, when you are making so much noise with your rapid reflections? Be silent and God will speak again.
—François Fénelon, (1651–1715), *Spiritual Letters*, no. XXII

Cautious silence is the holy of holies of worldly wisdom.
—Baltasar Gracián, *The Art of Worldly Wisdom*, 1647

Even a fool who keeps silent is considered wise; when he closes his lips, he is deemed intelligent.
—*Holy Bible*, Proverbs 17:28

Among all nations there should be vast temples raised where people might worship Silence and listen to it, for it is the voice of God.
—Jerome K. Jerome, *Diary of a Pilgrimage*, 1891

No sooner are the lips still than the soul awakes, and sets forth on its labors.
—Maurice Maeterlinck, *The Treasure of the Humble*, 1897

That soul is not idle which, holding itself in the presence of God, keeps interior silence. . . . For the will to keep silence is an act of veneration.
—F. Malava (fl. 1671), *A Simple Method*

To admit that it is a world to which God seems not to be speaking is not a renunciation of faith; it is a simple acceptance of an existential religious fact. It should not disconcert anyone who knows . . . that the silences of God are also messages with a definite import of their own.
—Thomas Merton, *Faith and Violence*, "Apologies to an Unbeliever," 1968

Listen or thy tongue will keep thee deaf.
—Native American saying

Silence is needed that man may be whole. If a man has within himself the substance of silence, he need not always be watching the movements of his heart or ordering them by his will.
—Max Picard, *The World of Silence*, 1952

All my days I grew up among the sages, and I have found nothing better for a person than silence.
—*Pirke Aboth, Talmud*, between 2nd and 4th centuries

A man may seem to be silent, but if his heart is condemning others he is babbling ceaselessly. But there may be another who talks from morning till night and yet he is truly silent.
—Abba Poemen, quoted by Henri J. Nouwen, *The Way of the Heart*, 1981

Silence is the fence around wisdom.

—Proverb

The world would be happier if men had the same capacity to be silent that they have to speak.
—Baruch Spinoza, *Ethics*, 1677

The cruelest lies are often told in silence.
—Robert Louis Stevenson, *Virginibus Puerisque*, 1881

The drama of religious history has been to hear the strain of a voice through the silence. Perhaps the core of faith can be defined as the certainty that even in the silence there is a message.
—David J. Wolpe, *In Speech and in Silence: The Jewish Quest for God*, 1992

SIN

Why blame the world? The world is free of sin; the blame is yours and mine.
—Abu'l-Ala-Al-Ma'arri (973–1057), in R.A. Nicholson, *Translation of Eastern Poetry and Prose*

The soul which does not live in God is the author of its own evil; that is why it sins.
—St. Ambrose, *De Isaac et Anima*, c. 387

Sin would be only an evil for him who commits it, were it not a crime towards the weak brethren, whom it corrupts.
—Henri Amiel, *Journal of*, 1882

No matter how many new translations of the Bible come out, the people still sin the same way.
—Anonymous

No one sins by an act he cannot avoid.
—St. Augustine, *De Libero Arbitro*, c. 400

Most newspaper headlines are more effective examples of man's sin writ large than any book on theology can ever hope to be.
—Robert McAfee Brown, *Patterns of Faith in America Today*, 1957

He who separates himself from sinners walks in their guilt.
—Martin Buber, *Jewish Mysticism and the Legends of Baalshem*, 1916

Sin is poison poured into the stream of time.
—George A. Buttrick, *Sermons Preached in a University Church*, 1959

It is one thing to perceive this or that particular deed to be sinful . . . and another thing to feel sin within us independent of particular actions.
—Samuel Taylor Coleridge, *Aids to Reflections*, 1825

Fight thine own sins, not the sins of others.
—Confucius, *Analects of*, c. 5th century B.C.

A private sin is not so prejudicial in this world as a public indecency.
—Miguel de Cervantes, *Don Quixote*, 1605

If a man commits a sin, let him not do it again; let him not delight in it, for the accumulation of evil is painful.
—*Dhammapada*, c. 5th century B.C.

Many sinners would not have been saved if they had not committed some greater sin at last, than before; for the punishment of that sin, hath brought them to a greater remorse of all their other sins formerly neglected.
—John Donne, sermon, LXXXX, 1640

That God by an immediate agency of his own, creates the sinful volitions of mankind, is a doctrine not warranted, in my view, either by Reason, or Revelation.
—Timothy Dwight, *Theology Explained and Defended*, 1818

There are no incorrigible sinners; God has no permanent problem children.
—Nels F.S. Ferré, *The Christian Understanding of God*, 1951

We do not need artificially to conjure up a sense of sin. All we need to do is to open our eyes to facts. Take one swift glance at the social state of the world today. . . . That should be sufficient to indicate that this is no fool-proof universe automatically progressive but that moral evil is still the central problem of mankind.
—Harry Emerson Fosdick, *Christianity and Progress*, 1922

The least trifle of a distraction cannot withdraw your soul
from God, since nothing withdraws us from God but sin.
—St. Francis de Sales (1567–1622), *Consoling Thoughts of*

He that falls into sin is a man; that grieves at it, is a saint;
that boasteth of it, is a devil.
—Thomas Fuller, *The Holy State and the Profane State*, 1642

The greatest of all sins is the philosophizing of sin out of
existence.
—Harold C. Gardiner, *Tenets for Readers and Reviewers*, 1944

The real trouble with our times is not the multiplication of
sinners, it is the disappearance of sin.
—Étienne Gilson, in *Ensign*, March 1952

When thinking of sinners we shall never go wrong to include
ourselves.
—Aelred Graham, *Christian Thought and Action*, 1951

We are not punished for our sins, but by them.
—Leon Harrison, *The Religion of a Modern Liberal*, 1931

Sin is not an offense against God, but against our humanity.
—E.G. Hirsch, *Reform Advocate*, 1894, VII

If we say we have no sin, we deceive ourselves, and the truth
is not in us.
—*Holy Bible*, I John 1:8

One man's sin may be another man's duty and a third man's
bliss. . . . A democratic community cannot recognize the category of sin, legislate against it and punish those for whom
the proscribed action is not sinful.
—Sidney Hook, address, National Institute on Religious Freedom and Public
Affairs, Washington, D.C., in *The New York Times*, November 21, 1962

Its effect on the soul is to be measured neither by the guilt
nor by the temporal punishment inexorably fixed, but by
that deep sense of loneliness it brings with it.
—Bede Jarrett, *Meditations for Layfolk*, 1915

We may not sin in order to prevent another's sinning.
—St. John Chrysostom (347–407), *In 1 Cor. Homil. XIV*

The historical Jesus has a different category of sins from that of the Old Testament or of Paul or of ecclesiastical writers after him. The sins which occupied the attention of Jesus were hypocrisy, worldliness, intolerance, and selfishness. The sins which occupy the principal attention of the Church . . . are impurity, murder, the drinking of alcohol, swearing, the neglect of the Church's services and ordinances.
—Robert Keable, in *Atlantic Monthly*, December 1928

The worst type of sin, in fact the only "mortal sin" which has enslaved man for the greater part of his history, is the institutionalized sin. Under the institution, vice appears to be, or is actually turned into, virtue. Apathy toward evil is thus engendered; recognition of sin becomes totally effaced; sinful institutions become absolutized, almost idolized, and sin becomes absolutely moral.
Laurenti Magesa, in Alfred T. Hennelly, S.J.,
"The Red-Hot Issue: Liberation Theology," in *America*, May 24, 1986

Talk about sin will not be intelligible to one who has no sense of lack, no sense of life's being at cross-purposes, no sense of self-defeat.
—James A. Martin, Jr., *Fact, Fiction and Faith*, 1960

Sin is not exhausted in describing individual acts which aren't very nice. "Sin" is fundamentally a description of our entire situation, one of separation from God, alienation from him, arising out of our rebellion, our refusal to do his will, our insistence upon following our own wills.
—Robert McAfee, *Patterns of Faith in America Today*, 1957

Man is a sinner not because he is finite but because he refuses to admit that he is.
—Reinhold Niebuhr, *Christianity and Power Politics*, 1940

Suffering and taking sin upon himself might have been right for that preacher of small people. But I rejoice in great sin as my great solace.
—Friedrich Nietzsche, *Thus Spake Zarathustra*, 1883

Sin is a tree with a great many branches, but it has only one root, namely, the inordinate love of self.
—Kirby Page, *Living Joyously*, 1950

The impurity of the world is a dark covering before the face of the soul and it preventeth it from discerning spiritual wisdom.
—Palladius of Egypt, *Paradise of the Fathers*, c. 300

Sin is disease, deformity, weakness.

—Plato, *The Republic*, c. 370 B.C.

Sin in his [Buddha's] opinion is essentially irrational conduct; conduct that tends to destroy more values than it creates, either for the actor or other sentient beings whom it affects.

—J.B. Pratt, *The Pilgrimage of Buddhism*, 1928

The heart and the eye are the agents of sin.

—Proverb

Boredom is a vital problem for the moralist, since at least half the sins of mankind are caused by the fear of it.

—Bertrand Russell, *The Conquest of Happiness*, 1930

Most people are angry with the sinner, not with the sin.

—Seneca, *De Ira*, c. A.D. 43

The worst sin towards our fellow-creatures is not to hate them, but to be indifferent to them; that's the essence of inhumanity.

—George Bernard Shaw, *Socialism of*, 1926

Sin repented can still leave a crushing weight upon the soul, even one sin.

—Frank J. Sheed, *Theology and Sanity*, 1946

The sins that we should hate most are not those of our neighbor but our own. These are the only sins over which God has given us immediate power.

—Raphael Simon, *Hammer and Fire*, 1959

Sin is disappointing. Whoever got out of sin half as much pleasure as he expected?

—Ignatius Smith, *Christ Today*, 1932

Tremble before a minor sin, lest it lead you to a major one.

—*Talmud: Derek Eretz*, 1.26, c. 500

Only a fool could deny the fact of sin, though we may choose to call it by another name,

—Gerald Vann, *The Heart of Man*, 1945

The big moment is not when a man sins but when a man surrenders to the direction of his sin.

—Hubert Van Zeller, *We Die Standing Up*, 1949

To sin is to poison the public reservoir.
—Leslie D. Weatherhead, *Psychology, Religion and Healing*, 1951

The evil of sin consists in its being the fully witful rejection of God; it is, as it were, an attempt to annihilate God, and, were this possible, it would do so. . . . It is only in so far as we realize that God is one supreme Reality that we can realize that sin is the one supreme evil.
—Bruno Webb, *Why Does God Permit Evil?*, 1941

The basic formula of all sin is: frustrated or neglected love.
—Franz Werfel, *Between Heaven and Earth*, 1944

It is obvious from faith in Holy Scripture that no one can sin without weakening or disturbing peace with God and in consequence with every creature.
—John Wyclif, *De Officio Regis*, 1378

SINCERITY

Seek much after this, to speak nothing with God, but what is the sense of a single unfeigned heart.
—Samuel Taylor Coleridge, *Aids to Reflection*, 1825

I do not see how a man without sincerity can be good for anything. How can a cart or carriage be made to go without yoke or crossbar?
—Confucius, *Sayings of*, 5th century B.C.

In the visible temple you fall down on the knees of your body, but nothing is accomplished thereby if in the temple of the breast you stand up against God.
—Desiderius Erasmus, *Enchiridion*, 1501

The sincerity which is not charitable proceeds from a charity which is not sincere.
—St. Francis de Sales, in Albert Camus, *The Spirit of St. Francis of Sales*, 1641

Who can tell where sincerity merges into humility, and where it folds itself over and becomes hypocrisy, and where it touches self-righteousness.
—Salvador de Madariaga, *Englishmen, Frenchmen, Spaniards*, 1931

Sincerity is the way to Heaven.
—Mencius, c. 300 B.C.

SKEPTICISM

Religious minds prefer scepticism. The true saint is a profound sceptic; a total disbeliever in human reason, who has more than once joined hands on this ground with some who were at best sinners.
— Henry Adams, *Education of Henry Adams*, 1906

Scepticism means, not intellectual doubt alone, but moral doubt.
— Thomas Carlyle, *Heroes and Hero Worship*, 1840

Once it was the skeptic, the critic of the status quo, who had to make a great effort. Today the skeptic is the status quo. The one who must make the effort is the man who seeks to create a new moral order.
— John W. Gardner, *Self-Renewal*, 1963

Skepticism is less reprehensible in inquiring years, and no crime in juvenile exercitation.
— Joseph Glanville, *The Vanity of Dogmatizing*, 1661

The deepest, the only theme of human history, compared to which all others are of subordinate importance, is the conflict of scepticism with faith.
— J.W. von Goethe (1749–1832), *Wisdom and Experience*

Through his scepticism the modern man is thrown back upon himself; his energies flow towards their source and wash to the surface those psychic contents which are at all times there, but lie hidden in the silt as long as the stream flows smoothly in its course.
— C.G. Jung, *Modern Man in Search of a Soul*, 1932

A sound belief is always accompanied by a sane skepticism. It is only by disbelieving in some things that we can ever believe in other things. Faith does not mean credulity.
— Samuel H. Miller, *The Great Realities*, 1955

If a man have a strong faith he can indulge in the luxury of scepticism.
— Friedrich Nietzsche, *The Twilight of the Idols*, 1889

Scepticism, riddling the faith of yesterday, prepares the way for the faith of tomorrow.
— Romain Rolland, *Jean Christophe*, 1912

It is the tension between creativity and skepticism that has produced the stunning and unexpected findings of science.

—Carl Sagan, *Broca's Brain*, 1979

Sceptical scrutiny is the means, in both science and religion, by which deep thoughts can be winnowed from deep nonsense.

—Carl Sagan, in *Time*, October 20, 1980

Skepticism often makes big calls on our faith.

—Maurice Samuel, *Prince of the Ghetto*, 1948

Scepticism is an exercise, not a life; it is a discipline fit to purify the mind of prejudice and render it all the more apt, when the time comes, to believe and to act wisely.

—George Santayana, *Scepticism and Animal Faith*, 1923

Scepticism is the chastity of the intellect.

—George Santayana, *Scepticism and Animal Faith*, 1923

Skeptic always rhymes with septic; the spirit died of intellectual poisoning.

—Franz Werfel, *Realism and Inwardness*, 1930

SORROW

When the heart weeps for what it has lost, the spirit laughs for what it has found.

—Anonymous

Jewish tears are the heaviest. They have the weight of many centuries.

—Leon Bloy, *Pilgrim of the Absolute*, 1909

You cannot prevent the birds of sorrow from flying over your head, but you can prevent them from building nests in your hair.

—Chinese proverb

There is no greater sorrow than to recall happiness in times of misery.

—Dante, *Inferno*, c. 1320

Heaven knows we need never be ashamed of our tears, for they are rain upon the blinding dust of earth, overlying our hard hearts.

—Charles Dickens, *Hunted Down*, 1867

If sorrow devours me, and I lose what is dearest to me; if I feel no comfort, and no prayer of mine is heard, it can only lead me to Thee; so be welcome, flame and sword!
—Annette von Droste-Hulshoff (1797–1848), *The Spiritual Year*

Let us rather be thankful that our sorrow lives in us as an indestructible force, only changing its form, as forces do, and passing from pain into sympathy—the one poor word which includes all our best insight and our best love.
—George Eliot, *Adam Bede*, 1859

Where sorrow is concerned, not repression but expression is the wholesome discipline.
—Sidney Greenberg, *Treasury of Comfort*, 1954

Sorrow is better than laughter, for by sadness of countenance the heart is made glad.
—*Holy Bible*, Ecclesiastes 7:3

Every man has his secret sorrows which the world knows not; and oftentimes we call a man cold when he is only sad.
—Henry Wadsworth Longfellow, *Hyperion*, 1839

That mortal man who hath more of joy than of sorrow in him, that mortal man cannot be true. . . . The truest of all men was the Man of Sorrows.
—Herman Melville, *Moby Dick*, 1851

The man who has never wept over the sorrows of his people is blind to the taller peaks of life.
—Kirby Page, *Living Creatively*, 1932

Every man has a rainy corner in his life.
—Jean Paul Richter, *Titan*, 1803

Sorrow draws towards great souls as thunder-storms do to mountains, but the storms also break upon them; and they become the clearing point in the skies for plains beneath them.
—Jean Paul Richter, *Death of an Angel and Other Writings*, 1844

Earth has no sorrow that Heaven cannot heal.
—St. Thomas More, *Come, Ye Disconsolate*, 1535

Tears are the silent language of grief.
—Voltaire, *Philosophical Dictionary*, II, 1764

If the world has indeed been built of sorrow, it has been built by the hands of love, because in no other way could the soul of man, for whom the world was made, reach the full stature of its perfection. Pleasure for the beautiful body, but pain for the beautiful soul.

—Oscar Wilde, *De Profundis*, 1905

SOUL

The soul of man is the lamp of God.

—Anonymous

Soul is actuality in the sense in which knowledge is so, for the presence of the soul is compatible both with sleep and with waking, and waking is analogous to the exercise of knowledge . . . the soul is the first actualization of a natural body potentially having life.

—Aristotle (384–322 B.C.), *De Anima*

The rational soul wanders round the whole world and through the encompassing void, and gazes into infinite time, and considers the periodic destructions and rebirths of the universe, and reflects that our posterity will see nothing new, and that our ancestors saw nothing greater than we have seen.

—Marcus Aurelius, *Meditations*, c. 170

The soul is a stranger in this world.

—Bahya ben Joseph ibn Pakuda, *Hobot HaLebabot*, 1040

Spirit unites itself inwardly to soul and transfigures it. The distinction between spirit and soul does not imply their separation.

—Nicholas Berdyaev, *Freedom and the Spirit*, 1935

The soul has aspiration toward a truth in which it can repose.

—Bernard Bosanquet, address, 1903

Everywhere the human soul stands between a hemisphere of light and another of darkness on the confines of two everlasting hostile empires—Necessity and Free Will.

—Thomas Carlyle, *Essays: Goethe's Works*, 1832

The soul is the aspect of ourselves that is specific of our nature and distinguishes man from all other animals. We are not capable of defining this familiar and profoundly mysterious entity.

—Alexis Carrel, *Man, the Unknown*, 1935

527

The feet carry the body as affection carries the soul.
—St. Catherine of Siena, *Dialogo*, cap. xxvi, c. 1378

It [the soul] is truly an image of the infinity of God, and no words can do justice to its grandeur.
—William Ellery Channing (1780–1842), *Works*

When I reflect on the nature of the soul, it seems to me by far more difficult and obscure to determine its character while it is in the body, a strange domicile, than to imagine what it is when it leaves it, and has arrived in the empyreal regions, in its own and proper home.
—Cicero, *Tusculanarum Disputationum*, bk. I, 44 B.C.

The individual soul is a thing created in the fullness of time to have just those characteristics which the time requires if God's purpose is to be fulfilled.
—R.G. Collingwood, *The Idea of History*, 1946

As the least beautiful of our kind is human, and humanity the most beautiful thing in our world, everyone is capable of transfiguration when the comely soul shines through.
—Lane Cooper, *Evolution and Repentance*, 1935

However far back we go in the history of the race, we can never find a time or place where man was not conscious of the soul and of a divine power on which his life depended.
—Christopher Dawson, *Religion and Culture*, 1947

The fact of our being able to form abstract or universal ideas is, in itself, a proof of the immateriality, or, as it is technically called, the spirituality of the soul, a proof that the soul is, in its essence, independent of matter.
—Richard Downey, *Critical and Constructive Essays*, 1934

In its highest sense [the soul is] a vast capacity for God. . . . A chamber with elastic and contractile walls, which can be expanded, with God as its guest, illimitably, but which without God shrinks and shrinks until every vestige of the Divine is gone, and God's image is kept without God's Spirit.
—Henry Drummond, *Natural Law in the Spiritual World*, 1883

I affirm that there is a power in the Soul which is unmoved by time or the flesh: this power floweth from the Spirit, yet abideth therein. Yea, it is all spirit.
—Meister Eckhart (1260–1327?), *Meister Eckhart*

In the mystic sense of the creation around us, in the expression of art, in a yearning towards God, the soul grows upward and finds fulfilment of something implanted in its nature.

—Arthur Eddington, *The Nature of the Physical World*, 1928

The term *souls* or spirits is as improper as the term *gods*. Soul or Spirit signifies Deity and nothing else. There is no finite soul nor spirit. Soul or Spirit means only one Mind, and cannot be rendered in the plural.

—Mary Baker Eddy, *Science and Health*, 1908

We cannot describe the natural history of the soul, but we know that it is divine.

—Ralph Waldo Emerson, *The Method of Nature*, 1840

The soul, mindful of its ethereal nature, presses upward with exceedingly great force, and struggles with its weight. It distrusts things seen. . . . It seeks those things which truly and everlastingly are.

—Desiderius Erasmus, *Enchiridion*, 1501

Whether or not the philosophers care to admit that we have a soul, it seems obvious that we are equipped with something or other which generates dreams and ideals, and which sets up values.

—John Erskine, *On the Meaning of Life*, 1937

When the soul is troubled, lonely and darkened, then it turns easily to the outer comfort and to the empty enjoyment of the world.

—St. Francis of Assisi (1181?–1226), *Little Flowers of*

Only the conviction that it is the darkness within us which makes the darkness without, can restore the lost peace of our souls.

—Friedrich Froebel, *Mottoes and Commentaries of Mother-Play*, 1843

The human soul is no more than a spark of the divine in us, which upon death returns to reunite with God as the original source of its being, than is the body.

—Simon Greenberg, *Patterns of Faith in America Today*, 1957

Soul is the greatest thing in the least continent.

—Elizabeth Grymeston, *Miscellanea—Meditation*, 1604

The soul of man (whose life or motion is perpetual contemplation or thought) is the mistress of two potent rivals, the one reason, the other passion, that are in continual suit.
—James Harrington, *The Commonwealth of Oceana*, 1656

The bounds of the soul thou shalt not find, though you travel every way.
—Heraclitus (535–475 B.C.), *Fragments*

The soul needs a physical body here . . . but when . . . the body is no longer an adequate instrument through which the soul may function, it lays the present body aside and continues to function through a more subtle one.
—Ernest Holmes, *The Science of Mind*, 1938

And I will say to my soul, Soul, you have ample goods laid up for many years; take your ease, eat, drink, and be merry. But God said to him, "Fool! This night your soul is required of you; and the things you have prepared, whose will they be?"
—*Holy Bible*, Luke 12:19-20

Close by the rights of man, side by side with them, are the rights of the soul.
—Victor Hugo, *Les Misérables*, 1862

The whole sum of God that there is on earth, within all men, concentrates itself in a single cry to affirm the soul.
—Victor Hugo, *William Shakespeare*, 1864

There is plenty of evidence for an Original Virtue underlying Original Sin. . . . The knowledge that there is a central chamber of the soul, blazing with the light of divine love and wisdom, has come, in the course of history, to multitudes of human beings.
—Aldous Huxley, *The Devils of Loudon*, 1952

Is there, as the medieval mystics taught, a "spark" at the core of the Soul, which never consents to evil, a Divine nucleus in the heart of the personality, which can take no stain?
—W.R. Inge, *The Philosophy of Plotinus*, 1918

By the word soul, or psyche, I mean the inner consciousness which aspires.
—Richard Jefferies, *The Story of My Heart*, 1883

Our soul is *made* to be God's dwelling-place; and the dwelling-place of the soul is God, which is *unmade*.
—Juliana of Norwich, *Revelations of Divine Love*, 15th century

Deep within us all there is an amazing inner sanctuary of the soul, a holy place, a Divine Center, a speaking Voice. . . . Life from the Center is a life of unhurried peace and power. It is simple. It is serene. It is amazing. It is radiant.
—T.R. Kelly, *A Testament of Devotion*, 1941

No soul shall bear the burden of another.
—*Koran*, c. 265

In the laboratory there can be found no trace of the soul except certain rather undignified phenomena which give rise to the illusion that we have one.
—Joseph Wood Krutch, *The Modern Temper*, 1929

Christianity teaches that the human soul is directly related to God. Such immediacy is the hallmark of the Divinity of the soul and the center of our freedom.
—Helmut Kuhn, *Freedom Forgotten and Remembered*, 1943

The essences of our soul were a breath in God before they became a living soul, they lived in God before they lived in the created soul, and therefore the soul is a partaker of the eternity of God and can never cease to be.
—William Law, *Appeal to All That Doubt*, 1740

There is no emptiness of soul ever for those whose life is devoted to God.
—William Lawson, *For Goodness Sake*, 1951

Every soul is as a world apart, independent of everything else except God.
—G.W. von Leibniz, *Discourse on Metaphysics*, 1685

It was in the recognition that there is in each man a final essence, that is to say an immortal soul, which only God can judge, that a limit was set upon the dominion of men over men.
—Walter Lippmann, *The Good Society*, 1937

On this earth of ours there are but few souls that can withstand the dominion of the soul that has suffered itself to become beautiful.
—Maurice Maeterlinck, *The Treasure of the Humble*, 1895

Our whole being subsists in virtue of the subsistence of the spiritual soul which is in us a principle of creative unity, independence and liberty.
—Jacques Maritain, *The Person and the Common Good*, 1947

Were our heaven never overcast, yet we meet the brightest morning only in escape from recent night; and the atmosphere of our souls, never passing from ebb and flow of love into a motionless constance, must always break the white eternal beams into a colored and tearful glory.
—James Martineau, *Hours of Thought on Sacred Things*, 1879

Our souls are like those orphans whose unwedded mothers die in bearing them: the secret of our paternity lies in their grave, and we must there learn it.
—Herman Melville, *Moby Dick*, 1851

Nothing is more difficult than to realize that every man has a distinct soul, that every one of all the millions who live or have lived, is as whole and independent a being in himself, as if there were no one else in the whole world but he.
—John Henry Newman, *Parochial and Plain Sermons*, 1843

There are souls in all living things, even in those which live in the waters.
—Origen, *De Principus*, c. 254

The soul should not attribute to itself but to God, its toil for virtue.
—Philo, *Allegories*, c. A.D. 10.

Of all things which a man has, next to the gods, his soul is the most divine and most truly his own.
—Plato, *Laws*, bk. IV, 4th century B.C.

It is no use saying that modern scientists have totally given up the use of the word "soul." They may have given up the word. They cannot help making use of the thing.
—John Cowper Powys, *A Philosophy of Solitude*, 1933

The human soul, in so far as science can penetrate, is the last chapter of cosmic history as far as it has been written. It is in the soul that Divinity resides.
—Michael Pupin, in *The American Magazine*, September, 1927

The greater number of men pass through life with souls asleep.
> —Paul Sabatier, *The Life of St. Francis of Assisi*, 1920

A dramatic centre of action and passion . . . utterly unlike what in modern philosophy we call consciousness. The soul causes the body to grow, to assume its ancestral shape, to develop all its ancestral instincts, to wake and to sleep by turns . . . and at the same time determines the responses that the living body shall make to the world.
> —George Santayana, *The Realm of Truth*, 1938

The soul is master of every kind of fortune: itself acts in both ways, being the cause of its own happiness and misery.
> —Seneca, *Epistolae*, 98, c. A.D. 63

The soul in action is nothing but thought transforming itself into works.
> —Antonin Sertillanges, *Recollections*, 1950

My soul is myself; the well-spring or point of consciousness, or center of inner activity . . . the most real thing in the universe to me; the start for all other knowing, the test by which I judge all other data.
> —Upton Sinclair, *What God Means to Me*, 1935

The man who in this world can keep the whiteness of his soul, is not likely to lose it in any other.
> —Alexander Smith, *Dreamthorp*, 1863

Smaller than the hundredth part of a tip of hair, the Soul of the living being is capable of infinity. Male is he not nor female nor neuter, but is joined with whatever body he takes as his own.
> —*Svetasvatara Upanishad*, c. 600 B.C.

In each soul, God loves and partly saves the whole world which that soul sums up in an incommunicable and particular way.
> —Pierre Teilhard de Chardin, *The Divine Milieu*, 1960

Each of us possesses a soul, but we do not prize our souls as creatures made in God's image deserve, and so we do not understand the great secrets which they contain.
> —St. Teresa of Ávila, *The Interior Castle*, 1577

The soul is the primary principle of our nourishment, sensation, movement, and understanding.
—St. Thomas Aquinas, *Summa Theologiae*, 1272

The human soul is a silent harp in God's quire, whose strings need only to be swept by the divine breath to chime in with the harmonies of creation.
—Henry David Thoreau, *Journal*, August 10, 1838

Science's horizon is limited by the bounds of Nature, the ideologies by the bounds of human social life, but the human soul's range cannot be confined within either of these limits.
—A.J. Toynbee, *Study of History*, Vol. XII, *Reconsiderations*, 1961

There is no separation between your soul and the soul of the universe. In the deepest sense you are the great universal soul. Man is God incarnate.
—Ralph Waldo Trine, *What All the World's A-Seeking*, 1896

There is only one such Self, and that one self is you. Standing behind this little nature is what we call the Soul. . . . He is the Soul of your soul. . . . You are one with Him.
—Swami Vivekanada (1862–1902), *The Yoga and Other Works*, 1953

We call "soul" that which animates. Owing to our limited intelligence we know scarcely anything more of the matter. . . . No one has found it, or ever will find it.
—Voltaire, *Philosophical Dictionary*, II, 1764

Every soul is valuable in God's sight, and the story of every soul is the story of self-definition for good or evil, salvation or damnation. Every soul is valuable in God's sight. Or, with the secularization of things we may say: every soul is valuable in man's sight.
—Robert Penn Warren, address, Columbia University, 1954

SPIRITUALITY

The great error of the doctrines on the spirit has been the idea that by isolating the spiritual life from all the rest, by suspending it in space as high as possible above the earth, they were placing it beyond attack, as if they were not thereby simply exposing it to be taken as an effect of mirage!
—Henri Bergson, *Creative Evolution*, 1911

The tragedy of life is not death but in what dies inside a man while he lives—the death of genuine feeling, the death of inspired response, the death of the awareness that makes it possible to feel that pain or the glory of other men in oneself.
—Norman Cousins, in *Saturday Review*, October 2, 1954

The life of a religious might be compared to the building of a cathedral . . . once a firm foundation has been laid, the building rises slowly.
—Margaret Wyvill Ecclesine, *A Touch of Radiance*, 1966

To know that what is impenetrable to us really exists, manifesting itself as the highest wisdom and the most radiant beauty which our dull faculties can only comprehend in their most primitive forms—this knowledge, this feeling is the center of true religiousness.
—Albert Einstein, *Living Philosophies*, 1931

To glorify God is to be engaged in a concrete spirituality that refuses to draw marked distinctions between sacred and secular, contemplation and deed, theology and ethics.
—Douglas John Hall, *Imaging God: Dominion and Stewardship*, 1986

If we should venture to name this deep-set desire which we call religious it might be represented as an ultimate demand for self-preservation; it is man's leap for eternal life in some form, in presence of an awakened fear of fate.
—William E. Hocking, *The Meaning of God in Human Experience*, 1928

Let each one remember that he will make progress in all spiritual things only insofar as he rids himself of self-love, self-will and self-interest.
—St. Ignatius Loyola, *Spiritual Exercises*, 1548

There is in every true woman's heart a spark of heavenly fire, which lies dormant in the broad daylight of prosperity, but which kindles up, and beams and blazes in the dark hour of adversity.
—Washington Irving, *The Sketch Book*, 1819

Women, the early Church wrote and Western society maintains, are less spiritual than men because they are "nearer to
nature." Christian women . . . are beginning to reply, "Yes.
Nearer to nature, less spiritualized and therefore holier." Nature, creation, bodies, blood, death and darkness are all part
of God's plan and men's determination to deny them, escape
from them and exploit them go some way to explaining the
un-godly mess we are all in.
>—Sara Maitland, *A Map of the New Country: Women and Christianity*, 1983

There are two worlds, "the visible and the invisible," as the
Creed speaks—the world we see, and the world we do not
see. And the world which we do not see as really exists as
the world we do see.
>—John Henry Newman, *Parochial and Plain Sermons*, IV, 1843

In the spiritual life there is nothing obligatory. Those who
have spirit in them will live in the spirit, or will suffer horri-
bly in the flesh.
>—George Santayana, *The Realm of Essence*, 1928

If ever you would be Divine, you must admit this principle:
That spiritual things are the greatest, and that spiritual
strength is the most excellent, useful, and delightful.
>—Thomas Traherne (1634–74), *Centuries of Meditation*

To be religious is to have a life that flows with the presence
of the extraordinary.
>—Ann Belford Ulanov, in *Vogue*, December 1985

The spiritual life . . . means the ever more perfect and willing
association of the invisible human spirit with the invisible
Divine Spirit for all purposes; for the glory of God, for the
growth and culture of the praying soul.
>—Evelyn Underhill, *Man and the Supernatural*, 1927

The first step that the soul of the faithful man made, placed
him in the Good-Thought Paradise; the second step . . . in
the Good-Word Paradise; the third step . . . in the Good-Deed
Paradise; the fourth step . . . in the Endless Lights.
>—*Zend-Avesta*, c. 700 B.C.

SUCCESS
Individuals who suffer from success have what I call the four
A's—arrogance, a sense of aloneness, the need to seek ad-
venture, and adultery.
>—Steven Berglas, in *Time*, November 4, 1991

I think there are very broad cultural patterns that are resisting authority—that are resisting inhibitions on everyone living the way they want to live. It's not just that religion is less important. It's the tremendous emphasis that's placed on success, results—which puts more pressure on a certain shaving of the rules in order to achieve success.
> —Derek C. Bok, in *The Christian Science Monitor*, July 27, 1987

Don't confuse fame with success. One is Madonna; the other is Helen Keller.
> —Erma Bombeck, address, Meredith College commencement,
> in *USA Today*, May 20, 1991

The compulsion of success in business has tended to make a man neglectful of his Christian faith. He finds he must somehow try to reconcile what one observer has described as the impersonal imperative of profit and efficiency with the personal imperative of Christian ethics.
> —Marquis W. Childs and Douglass Cater, *Ethics in a Business Society*, 1954

When a man has done all he can do, still there is a mighty, mysterious agency over which he needs influence to secure success. The only way he can reach it is by prayer.
> —Russell H. Conwell, *What You Can Do with Your Will Power*, 1917

In the United States, there's a Puritan ethic and a mythology of success: He who is successful is good. In Latin countries, in Catholic countries, a successful person is a sinner. In Puritan countries, success shows God's benevolence. In Catholic countries, your God loves you only when you've suffered.
> —Umberto Eco, in *The New York Times*, December 13, 1988

While we fight among ourselves about doctrine we are united in the common worship of money and material success.
> —Eric Gill, *Autobiography*, 1941

Among the humble and great alike, those who achieve success do so not because fate and circumstance are especially kind to them. Often the reverse is true. They succeed because they do not whine over their fate but take whatever has been given to them and go on to make the most of their best.
> —Sidney Greenberg, *Say Yes to Life*, 1982

What definition did Jesus give of "success"? He said that true success is to complete one's life. It is to attain to eternal life; all else is failure.
> —Toyohiko Kagawa, *The Religion of Jesus*, 1931

How a man is to fare in this world is something which the gospel (in contrast with novels, romances, lies, and other time-wasting) does not waste its time by considering.
—Sören Kierkegaard (1813–55), *Meditations from*

Succeed we must, at all cost—even if it means being a *dead* millionaire at fifty.
—Louis Kronenberger, "Our Unhappy Happy Endings," in *The Cart Before the Horse*, 1964

Success is somebody else's failure. Success is the American Dream we can keep dreaming because most people in most places, including thirty million of ourselves, live wide awake in the terrible reality of poverty.
—Ursula K. Le Guin, address, Bryn Mawr College commencement, 1986, *Dancing at the Edge of the World*

The secrets of success are a good wife and a steady job. My wife told me.
—Howard Nemerov, in *Writer's Digest*, December 1988

Why should we be in such desperate haste to succeed, and in such desperate enterprises? If a man does not keep pace with his companions, perhaps it is because he hears a different drummer.
—Henry David Thoreau, *Walden*, 1854

Suffering

Whosoever grows wrathful for any reason against his sufferings has therein departed from the way of the just, because he may not doubt that these things have happened to him by divine dispensation.
—Peter Abelard, *The Story of My Misfortunes*, 1135

Suffering was a curse from which man fled, now it becomes a purification of the soul, a sacred trial sent by Eternal Love, a divine dispensation meant to sanctify and ennoble us, an acceptable aid to faith, a strange initiation into happiness.
—Henri Amiel, *Journal*, 1882

The pangs of pain, of failure, in this mortal lot, are the birth-throes of transition to better things.
—John Elof Boodin, *Cosmic Evolution*, 1925

The state of health is a state of nonsensation, even of nonreality. As soon as we cease to suffer, we cease to exist.
—E. M. Cioran, *Drawn and Quartered*, 1971

It is in suffering that we are withdrawn from the bright superficial film of existence, from the sway of time and mere
things, and find ourselves in the presence of a profounder
truth.
—Yves Congar, *God, Man and the Universe*, 1950

Suffering which produces the kind of character we admire
and love is not only not regrettable but precious.
—Martin C. D'Arcy, *Problem of Evil*, 1928

Suffering is the substance of life and the root of personality,
for it is only suffering that makes us persons.
—Miguel de Unamuno, *The Tragic Sense of Life*, 1913

No suffering befalls the man who calls nothing his own.
—*Dhammapada*, c. 5th century B.C.

God's suffering for man was the Nadir, the lowest point in
God's humiliation; man's suffering for God is the Zenith, the
highest point of man's exaltation.
—John Donne, sermon, February 29, 1627

When sufferings come upon him man must utter thanks to
God, for suffering draws man near unto the Holy One,
blessed be He.
—Rabbi Eleazar Ben Jacob, *Talmud*, c. 4th century

No dogma of religion is surer than this: if one would be close
to God hc must suffer.
—Walter Elliott, *The Spiritual Life*, 1914

What thou avoidest suffering thyself seek not to impose on
others.
—Epictetus, *Enchiridion*, c. A.D. 100

Those who accept what they suffer have no suffering of the
will, and thus they are in peace.
—François Fénelon (1651–1715) *Spiritual Letters*

To suffer is almost the only good we can do in this world; for
rarely do we perform any good without mixing up some evil
along with it.
—St. Francis de Sales (1567–1622), *Consoling Thoughts of*

What is the greatest evil of suffering? Not the suffering itself but our rebellion against it, the state of interior revolt which so often accompanies it.
—Jean Grou, *Meditations in the Form of a Retreat*, c. 1795

None knows the weight of another's burden.
—George Herbert, *Outlandish Proverbs*, 1640

The saint's willingness to suffer results in an integrated, balanced personality; it liberates the capacity for love.
—Caryll Houselander, *Guilt*, 1941

Suffering out of love of God is better than working miracles.
—St. John of the Cross, *Steps to Perfection*, c. 1584

There is no remembrance more blessed, and nothing more blessed to remember, than suffering overcome in solidarity with God; this is the mystery of suffering.
—Sören Kierkegaard, *Christian Discourses*, 1847

I do not believe that sheer suffering teaches. If suffering alone taught, all the world would be wise, since everyone suffers. To suffering must be added mourning, understanding, patience, love, openness and the willingness to remain vulnerable.
—Anne Morrow Lindbergh, in *Time*, February 5, 1973

The more Christian a man is, the more evils, sufferings, and deaths he must endure.
—Martin Luther, *Freedom of a Christian*, 1520

Nine-tenths of our suffering is caused by others not thinking so much of us as we think they ought.
—Mary Lyon (1797–1849), in Gamaliel Bradford, *Journal*

Suffering is a test of faith. . . . If God's love calls you in suffering, respond by self-surrender, and you will learn the mystery of love.
—J. Messner, *Man's Suffering and God's Love*, 1941

One of the tendencies of our age is to use children's suffering to discredit the goodness of God. . . . In this popular pity, we mark our gain in sensibility and our loss in vision. If other ages felt less, they saw more.
—Flannery O'Connor, *A Memoir of Mary Ann*, 1962

Neither power nor wealth, neither education nor ability, neither gifts of creativity nor stores of human energy can insure
against the reality that suffering will be our companion at
some time during our journey. It is a presence as inseparable
from the human condition as food and oxygen are from human life. It is part of our legacy.

—Paula Ripple, *Growing Strong at Broken Places*, 1986

It is not easy to accept the premise that one of life's basic
conditions is inescapable suffering, true though this proves
to be.

—Nancy Wilson Ross, *Buddhism: A Way of Life and Thought*, 1980

It is one of the many things in God's dealing with us, that
seems so very mysterious, that He should have made suffering a condition of sanctity.

—P.A. Sheehan, *Mary, the Mother of God*, 1902

The modern view is that suffering has no purpose because
nothing that happens has any purpose. The world is run by
causes, not by purposes.

—W.T. Stace, *Religion and the Modern Mind*, 1952

The value of human life lies in the fact of suffering, for where
there is no suffering, no consciousness of karmic bondage,
there will be no power of attaining spiritual experience and
thereby reaching the field of non-distinction. *Unless we agree
to suffer we cannot be free from suffering.*

—D.T. Suzuki, *Essence of Buddhism*, in Thomas Merton,
Zen and the Birds of Appetite, 1968

Only when men shall roll up the sky like a hide, will there be
an end to misery, unless God has first been known.

—*Svetasvatara Upanishad*, prior to 400 B.C.

God hath ordered it that we may learn to bear one another's
burden; for no one is without fault, no one but hath a burden; no one is sufficient for himself.

—Thomas à Kempis, *Imitation of Christ*, 1441

If thou can be still and suffer awhile thou shalt without
doubt see the help of God come in thy need.

—Thomas à Kempis, *Imitation of Christ*, 1441

Suffering is of the essence of life, because it is the inevitable product of an unresolved tension between a living creature's essential impulse to try to make itself into the centre of the Universe and its essential dependence on the rest of Creation and on the Absolute Reality.
—A.J. Toynbee, *An Historian's Approach to Religion*, 1956

A religious sensibility encourages us to respond to God's identification with our pain and need by empathizing with the pain and needs of others. Through that empathy we rise above the debilitating limits that selfishness places upon us.
—James M. Wall, "The Language of Sacrifice," in *Christian Century*, October 14, 1992

Do not be afraid when you suffer. . . . Forget the vulgar, insultingly patronizing fairy tale that has been hammered into your heads since childhood that the main meaning of life is to be happy. The only true happiness is to share in the sufferings of the unhappy. . . . It is much better to have the screaming sensitivity of the soul uncovered by any protective skin than to have tear-proof rhinoceros skin in combination with the cold fish blood.
—Yevgeny Yevtushenko, address, Juniata College commencement, in *U.S. News & World Report*, May 27, 1991

SUICIDE

Parricide is more wicked than homicide, but suicide is the most wicked of all.
—St. Augustine, *On Patience*, c. 425

God has reserved to Himself the right to determine the end of life, because He alone knows the goal to which it is His will to lead it. It is for Him alone to justify a life or to cast it away.
—Dietrich Bonhoeffer, *Ethics*, 1955

Suicide is man's attempt to give a final human meaning to a life which has become humanly meaningless.
—Dietrich Bonhoeffer, *Ethics*, 1955

He that stabs another can kill his body; but he that stabs himself, kills his own soul.
—Robert Burton, *The Anatomy of Melancholy*, II, 1621

There is only one philosophical problem that is really serious, and that is suicide. To decide whether life is worth living or not is to answer the fundamental question in philosophy.
—Albert Camus, *Le Mythe de Sisyphe*, 1942

I am killing myself to prove my independence and my new terrible freedom.
—Feodor Dostoevsky, *The Possessed*, 1871

It is the suicide who dares to rebel against the plans of an all-wise God, who tries, though in vain, to force his way through to escape what he fears, who is blind to the whisperings of the graces of God in his heart and who is materialistic enough to see only the things of the earth, disregarding the things eternal.
—Adolph Dominic Frenay, *Is Life Worth Living?*, 1933

In Christian thought, the supreme fact in the life of the individual was death. In the life of the Liberal state, the climactic experience was suicide.
—John Emmet Hughes, *The Church and the Liberal Society*, 1944

Hurry, my children, hurry. They will start parachuting out of the air. They'll torture our children. Lay down your life with dignity. Let's get gone. Let's get gone.
—Jim Jones, People's Temple, Guyana, 1978

Suicide is not abominable because God forbids it; God forbids it because it is abominable.
—Immanuel Kant, *Lecture at Königsberg*, 1775

It is very certain that, as to all persons who have killed themselves, the Devil put the cord round their necks, or the knife to their throats.
—Martin Luther (1483–1546), *Table-Talk*

Some of the destruction that curses the earth is *self-destruction*; the extraordinary propensity of the human being to join hands with external forces in an attack upon his own existence is one of the most remarkable of biological phenomena.
—Karl Menninger, *Man Against Himself*, 1938

Suicide thwarts the attainment of the highest moral aim by the fact that, for a real release from this world of misery, it substitutes one that is merely apparent.
—Arthur Schopenhauer, *Studies in Pessimism*, 1851

Those who commit suicide are powerless souls, and allow themselves to be conquered by external causes repugnant to their nature.
—Baruch Spinoza, *Ethics*, 1677

Only He who gave the soul may take it back!
—Hanina B. Teradion, *Talmud: Aboda Zara*, c. 500

Everything naturally loves itself, the result being that every-thing naturally keeps itself in *being*, and resists corruption as far as it can. Wherefore suicide is contrary to the inclina-tion of nature, and to charity whereby every man should love himself.
—St. Thomas Aquinas, *Summa Theologiae*, 1272

There is no refuge from confession but suicide; and suicide is confession.
—Daniel Webster, argument at trial of Captain White for murder, April 6, 1830

SUPERNATURAL

The constants in all religion are the mystery of the universe, the nostalgia of the human spirit for an order beyond the show and flux of things to which it believes itself akin, and the belief that it has evidence of such an order.
—Gaius Glenn Atkins, *Religion Today*, 1933

To the successive abandonment of the Supernatural we have added the rebellion against humanity.
—John D. Fee, *Secularism*, 1947

Nature expresses the law in process, the supernatural the end to which it tends.
—David Hume, *Dialogues Concerning Natural Religion*, 1779

There are few among our ecclesiastics and theologians who would spend five minutes in investigating alleged supernat-ural occurrences in our own time. It would be assumed that if true it must be ascribed to some obscure natural cause.
—W.R. Inge, *Outspoken Essays*, 1919

Nothing is more irritating to the modern than this dogma of the supernatural, a dogma that cannot . . . be demonstrated by human reason; it requires God's revelation to bring to our knowledge this fact that man is supernaturalized.
—William J. McGucken, *The Philosophy of Catholic Education*, 1951

There is nothing impossible in the existence of the supernat-ural. Its existence seems to me decidedly probable.
—George Santayana, *The Genteel Tradition at Bay*, 1931

Every human creature is the object of some particular Providence that enables it to receive the supernatural. How, where, and when, is the mystery of God.

—Anscar Vonier, *The Human Soul,* 1913

SUPERSTITION

It were better to have no opinion of God at all, than such an opinion as is unworthy of him: for the one is unbelief, the other is contumely: and certainly superstition is the reproach of the Diety.

—Francis Bacon, *On Superstition,* 1597

Superstition may easily creep into the religion of Christians if that religion be allowed to express itself solely by exercises and ceremonies without regard to the inner worship of the spirit, which is faith, hope, and charity.

—R.L. Bruckberger, *Toward the Summit,* 1956

Superstition is the religion of feeble minds.

—Edmund Burke, *Reflections on the Revolution in France,* 1790

Religion is not removed by removing superstition.

—Cicero, *De Divinatione,* c. 78 B.C.

Because we can commit ourselves only to such truth as is capable of verification by approved methods . . . we are therefore under necessity of regarding Christianity, at least in certain alleged factual and conceptual features of it, as a quite . . . indefensible superstition.

—John Dewey, *A Common Faith,* 1934

Religions are born and may die, but superstition is immortal.

—Will Durant, *The Age of Reason Begins,* 1961

There are none more silly, or nearer their wits end, than those who are too superstitiously religious.

—Desiderius Erasmus, *The Praise of Folly,* 1511

Superstition is the serpent that crawls and hisses in every Eden and fastens its poisonous fangs in the hearts of men.

—Robert Ingersoll (1833–99), *The Truth*

Superstition obeys pride as a father.

—Michel de Montaigne, *Essays,* bk. 2, ch. 12, 1580

How blest would our age be if it could witness a religion freed from all the trammels of superstition!
—Baruch Spinoza, *Theologico-Political Treatise*, 1670

On the grave of faith there blooms the flower of superstition.
—Gustave Thibon, *Christianity and Freedom*, 1952

Superstition may be defined as constructive religion which has grown incongruous with intelligence.
—John Tyndall, *Fragments of Science*, II, 1896

Superstition is to religion what astrology is to astronomy— the mad daughter of a wise mother.
—Voltaire, *Essay on Toleration*, 1766

Conscience without judgment is superstition.
—Benjamin Whichcote, *Moral and Religious Aphorisms*, 1753

Even Christians who in practice dislike superstition as much as I do still often treat it as a minor aberration to be hushed up rather than a radical perversion to be denounced.
—John Wren-Lewis, *They Became Anglicans*, 1959

SYMBOLS

Whoever has the symbol has thereby the beginning of the spiritual idea; symbol and reality together furnish the whole.
—Odo Casel, *Mysterium*, 1926

One of the most malignant aspects of the [sixties] was the extent to which everyone began to deal exclusively in symbols. . . . Marijuana was a symbol; long hair was a symbol, of course, and so was short hair; natural food was a symbol— rice seeds, raw milk. Now, this was all very interesting. To be present at a moment when an entire society was so starved for meaning it made totems out of quite meaningless choices.
—Joan Didion, in *The Christian Science Monitor*, June 18, 1987

Most mistakes in philosophy and logic occur because the human mind is apt to take the symbol for the reality.
—Albert Einstein, *Cosmic Religion*, 1931

Symbols are deeper than words; speak when words become silent; gain where words lose in meaning; and so in hours of holiest worship the Church teaches, by symbols, truth language may not utter.
—A.M. Fairbairn, *Catholicism, Roman and Anglican*, 1899

What it accomplishes is to reduce beliefs to make-believes, observance to ceremony, prophecy to literature, theology to esthetics.

—Abraham Joshua Heschel, *Religious Symbolism*, 1955

Symbolism is not sober judgment; it is a simplification and subordination of the concrete complexity in order to point a moral.

—Ralph Barton Perry, *Puritanism and Democracy*, 1944

The thoughtless, conventional use of religious symbols may be not only dishonest but deadening.

—James Bissett Pratt, *Can We Keep the Faith?*

Symbols are the primary mode of our becoming aware of things. They are the way we register meanings in our depths.

—Gail C. Richardson, *Religious Symbolism*, 1955

Man's ultimate concern must be expressed symbolically, because symbolic language alone is able to express the ultimate.

—Paul Tillich, *The Dynamics of Faith*, 1957

Tao

Before Heaven and Earth existed, from the beginning Tao was there. It is Tao that gave ghosts their holy power, that gave holy power to Dead Kings. It gave life to Heaven, gave life to Earth. . . . It . . . has no duration; its age is greater than that of the Longest Age, yet it does not grow old.

—Chuang-tzu (4th century B.C.),
Three Ways of Thought in Ancient China

Tao though possessed of feeling and power of expression is passive and formless. It can be transmitted yet not received, apprehended yet not seen. Its root is in itself, having continued from of old before heaven and earth existed.

—Chuang-tzu (4th century B.C.), *Texts of Taoism*

What there was before the universe, was Tao; Tao makes things what they are, but is not itself a thing. Nothing can produce Tao; yet everything has Tao within it, and continues to produce it without end.

—Chuang-tzu (4th century B.C.), *Texts of Taoism*

The perfecting of self implies virtue; the perfecting of others, wisdom. These two, virtue and wisdom, are the moral qualities of the *hsing*, or nature, embodying the Tao, or Right Way.

—Confucius, *Doctrine of the Mean*, 5th century B.C.

That which Heaven has conferred is called the Nature; accordance with this nature is called the Tao (Way or Path), the regulation of this way is called Instruction.

—Confucius, *Doctrine of the Mean*, 5th century B.C.

He who attains Tao is everlasting. Though his body may decay he never perishes.

—Lao-tzu, *Tao Te Ching*, c. 5th century B.C.

There was something undefined and coming into existence before Heaven and Earth. How still it was and formless, standing alone and undergoing no change; reaching everywhere and in no danger of being exhausted! I do not know its name, and I give it the designation of the Tao. It may be regarded as the Mother of all things! . . . Man takes his law from Earth, the Earth takes its law from Heaven; Heaven takes its law from Tao. The law of the Tao is its being what it is.

—Lao-tzu, *Tao Te Ching*, c. 5th century B.C.

The way is like an empty vessel, that yet may be drawn from without even needing to be filled. It is bottomless; the very progenitor of all things in the world. In it all sharpness is blunted, all tangles untied, all glare tempered, all dust smoothed. It is like a deep pool that never dies.

—Lao-tzu, *Tao Te Ching*, c. 5th century B.C.

The perfect Way [Tao] is without difficulty
Save that it avoids picking and choosing.
Only when you stop liking and disliking.
Will all be clearly understood.

—Seng-Ts'an, *Hsin-hsin Ming*, c. 593

TECHNOLOGY

Man, desiring no longer to be the image of God, becomes the image of the machine.

—Nicholas Berdyaev, *The Fate of Man in the Modern World*, 1935

It is. . . a clear sign of modern man's profound degradation that the idea of annihilating his precious machines, his adored machines, is so shocking to him, whereas he considers with such coldness the massacre of millions of people by the same machines.

—Georges Bernanos, *Last Essays of*, 1955

Ours is a world of nuclear giants and ethical infants.

—Omar Bradley, address, Armistice Day, 1948

If the Day of Judgment came tomorrow, and God asked us what we had made of His revelation, of His grace and our freedom . . . we would be hard put to it to explain the advantages of a machine civilization whose highest efficiency is used for murder and slavery.

—R.L. Bruckberger, *Our Sky to Share*, 1952

Uncontrolled technology can certainly bring down disaster, perhaps irreparable, on our race. The only protection against it is a growth in man's spiritual and moral maturity proportionate to his growth in technical skill and power.

—W. Norris Clarke, in *America*, September 26, 1959

To worship the Machine, to worship the Thing it produces, is to worship a Fetish. . . . The Machine-believer proudly flaunts the fact that he has rid himself of God.

—John Cournos, *Autobiography*, 1935

A little "splitting" of the rays of religion and a little "releasing of the energy" of the Bible seems in order. If we would only spend sums like the two billion dollars spent on our atomic bombs to harness the forces of God's teachings, what a blessing it would be for the human race.
　　　　　　　　　　　—Richard J. Cushing, *Permanent Industrial Peace*, 1946

The danger of the cult of technological progress lies in its tendency to restrict and confine mankind within the adoring contemplation of his own creative power.
　　　　　　　　　　　—Jean Danielou, *The Lord of History*, 1958

The hope that technology will save us or will miraculously effect our moral improvement is a kind of modern idolatry.
　　　　　　　　　　　—Rudolf Diesel, *Theory and Construction of a Rational Heatmotor*, 1894

Technology has wiped out the frontiers that formerly separated men, countries and peoples. Man has become a citizen of the world. Thus, modern man finds himself in an environment without spiritual unity or religious homogeneity.
　　　　　　　　　　　—Albert Dondeyne, *Faith and the World*, 1962

The effect of technology on the entire world has been to impel mankind toward a single, all-embracing civilization, a civilization characterized largely by the domination of machines over men, but even more by the domination of standardization over spontaneity and of means over ends.
　　　　　　　　　　　—James W. Douglass, *The Non-Violent Cross*, 1966

Most of the dangerous aspects of technological civilization arise, not from its complexities, but from the fact that modern man has become more interested in the machines and industrial goods themselves than in their use to human ends.
　　　　　　　　　　　—René Dubos, *A God Within*, 1972

Only technology has permitted us to put a city to the sword without quite realizing what we are doing.
　　　　　　　　　　　—Joseph Wood Krutch, "If You Don't Mind My Saying So,"
　　　　　　　　　　　in *The American Scholar*, Summer, 1967

Technology is not in itself opposed to spirituality and to religion. But it presents a great temptation.
　　　　　　　　　　　—Thomas Merton, *Conjectures of a Guilty Bystander*, 1968

If anything could testify to the magical powers of the priesthood of science and their technical acolytes, or declare unto mankind the supreme qualifications for absolute rulership held by the Divine Computer, this new invention alone should suffice. So the final purpose of life in terms of the megamachine at last becomes clear: it is to furnish and process an endless quantity of data, in order to expand the role and ensure the domination of the power system.
—Lewis Mumford, "The Myth of the Machine," in *The Pentagon of Power*, 1970

I have stood within nine miles, not of our biggest, but one of our sizeable nuclear explosions. I stood riveted, dumbfounded, awe-stricken. I had a feeling that I was looking into eternity.
—Thomas E. Murray, address, December 4, 1951

No scientific development has ever brought man face to face with the problem of good and evil more starkly than the achievement whereby he summoned atomic energy forth from the deep recesses of the universe.
—Thomas E. Murray, *Nuclear Policy for War and Peace*, 1960

The great tragedy of our time is that mechanization can no longer be prevented; we become more mechanical as the machine eats into our lives.
—Robert Payne, in *Saturday Review*, April 15, 1950

Modern technology unfolds before contemporary man a vision so vast as to be confused by many with the infinite itself. As a consequence, one attributes to it an impossible autonomy, which in turn is transformed in the minds of some into an erroneous conception of life and of the world.
—Pope Pius XII, *Allocution*, December 24, 1953

The technological society has relegated religion, the arts and all other elements of high culture to a limbo from which they may still return to revenge themselves.
—Philip Rieff, at an international symposium on the technological society, North American Newspaper Alliance, June 1966

In an age in which mankind's collective power has suddenly been increased, for good or evil, a thousandfold through the tapping of atomic energy, the standard of conduct demanded from ordinary human beings can be no lower than the standard attained in times past by rare saints.
—A.J. Toynbee, *A Study of History*, Vol. XII, *Reconsiderations*, 1961

The machine is one of the most compelling rational of human discoveries. The madness is in those who would use a rational thing to further the irrational ends of exploitation and domination.

—Gregory Vlastos, *Christian Faith and Democracy*, 1939

Ethics alone will decide whether atomic energy will be an earthly blessing or the source of mankind's utter destruction.

—Werner Von Braun, in *This Week*, January 24, 1960

The real cause for dread is not a machine turned human, but a human turned machine.

—Franz E. Winkler, *Man: The Bridge Between Two Worlds*, 1960

TEMPTATION

An expert seaman is tried in a tempest, a runner in a race, a captain in a battle, a valiant man in adversity, a Christian in temptation and misery.

—St. Basil (330–379), *Homilies* 8

Some day, in years to come, you will be wrestling with the great temptation, or trembling under the great sorrow of your life. But the real struggle is here, now in these quiet weeks.

—Phillips Brooks (1835–93), *Perennials from*

He who knows that his body is life froth, and as unsubstantial as a mirage, will break the flower-tipped arrow of the Great Tempter and never see the King of Death.

—*Dhammapada*, c. 5th century B.C.

Every temptation, every tribulation is not deadly. But their multiplicity disorders us, discomposes us, unsettles us, and so hazards us.

—John Donne, sermon, Spring 1618

The last temptation is the greatest treason: To do the right deed for the wrong reason.

—T.S. Eliot, *Murder in the Cathedral*, 1935

There is no attack of the enemy so violent, that is, no temptation so formidable, that an eager study of the Scriptures will not easily beat off.

—Desiderius Erasmus, *Enchiridion*, 1501

All the temptations of hell cannot sully a soul which is displeased with them.

—St. Francis de Sales (1567–1622), *Consoling Thoughts of*

But the serpent said to the woman, You will not die. For God knows that when you eat of it your eyes will be opened, and you will be like God, knowing good and evil.

—*Holy Bible*, Genesis 3:4-5

Temptation is not an effect of original sin; it made its appearance in the earthly paradise. But since then it has gained in power.

—Charles Journet, *The Meaning of Evil*, 1961

No virtue is ever so strong that it is beyond temptation.

—Immanuel Kant, *Lecture at Königsberg*, 1775

God delights in our temptations, and yet hates them; He delights in them when they drive us to prayer; He hates them when they drive us to despair.

—Martin Luther (1483–1546), *Table-Talk*

The evil inclination is to be compared to a conjurer who runs around among people with a closed hand daring them to guess what is in it. . . . Everyone therefore runs after him. Once the conjurer stops for a moment and opens his hand, it becomes clear to everyone that it is completely empty.

—Moses Luzzato (1707–47), *Mesillat Yesharim*

He that can apprehend and consider vice with all her baits and seeming pleasures, and yet abstain, and yet distinguish, and yet prefer that which is truly better, he is the true warfaring Christian.

—John Milton, *Aeropagitica*, 1644

And let us fence us in with faith and comfort us with hope and smite the devil in the face with the firebrand of charity. . . . That fire of charity, thrown in his face, striketh the devil suddenly so blind that he cannot see where to fasten a stroke on us.

—St. Thomas More, *Dialogue of Comfort*, 1535

As we go up the scale of spiritual excellence, temptation follows us all the way, becoming more refined as our lives are more refined, more subtle as our spiritual sensitiveness is keener.

—A. Victor Murray, *Personal Experience and the Historic Faith*, 1939

God is better served in resisting a Temptation to Evil, than in many formal Prayers.

—William Penn, *Some Fruits of Solitude*, 1718

When we resist temptation it is usually because temptation is weak, not because we are strong.
—La Rochefoucauld, *Maxims*, 1665

The cunning livery of hell.
—William Shakespeare, *Measure for Measure*, c. 1604

In the hour of grievous temptation reason is a slender reed on which to lean. As Adam found to his sorrow, eating of the tree of the *knowledge* of good and evil by no means guarantees that one will choose the good.
—Edmund W. Sinnott, *The Biology of the Spirit*, 1955

The whole effort—the object—of temptation is to induce us to substitute something else for God. To obscure God.
—R.H.J. Stewart, *Spiritual Conferences of*, 1952

What augments our spiritual forces?—a temptation which has become overcome.
—Alexander Yelchaninov (1881–1934), *Fragments of a Diary*

THEOLOGY

Sacred theology is superior to philosophy, both theoretically and practically; theoretically, because it is more perfect knowledge of God and His creatures; practically, because moral philosophy is insufficient to direct man to God as his last end.
—Mortimer Adler, *Vital Speeches*, December 1949

Theology itself is coming to confess that ours is a time in which God is dead.
—Thomas J. Altizer, in *Christian Century*, July 7, 1965

Dogmatic theology is an attempt at both literary and scientific criticism of the highest order; and the age which developed dogma had neither the resources nor the faculty for such a criticism.
—Matthew Arnold, *Literature and Dogma*, 1873

Health is the state about which medicine has nothing to say: Sanctity is the state about which theology has nothing to say.
—W.H. Auden, in *Atlantic Monthly*, May 1970

The theologian who has no joy in his work is not a theologian at all. Sulky faces, morose thoughts and boring ways of speaking are intolerable in this science.
—Karl Barth, obituary, in *The New York Times*, December 11, 1968

Theology, or something that goes under that name, is still kept alive by the faithful, but only by artificial respiration.
—Carl L. Becker, *Heavenly City of the 18th Century Philosophers*, 1932

Theology itself, that is not based on the profoundest morality, is an empty cloud that sails through the summer air, leaving as much drought as it found.
—Henry Ward Beecher, address, May 8, 1883

A theology—any theology—not based on a spiritual experience is mere panting—religious breathlessness.
—Leonardo and Clodovis Boff, *Salvation and Liberation*, 1984

The theology of liberation can be understood only by two groupings of persons: the poor, and those who struggle for justice at their side—only by those who hunger for bread, and by those who hunger for justice in solidarity with those hungering for bread. Conversely, liberation theology is not understood, nor can it be understood, by the satiated and satisfied—by those comfortable with the status quo.
—Leonardo Boff and Clodovis Boff, *Liberation Theology: From Dialogue to Confrontation*, 1986

Thinking is not worship, but if it is initiated by a wrench of sorrow which banishes the half-gods of our superficial existence, God may appear.
—Richard C. Cabot, *What Men Live By*, 1914

Any theology which attempts to speak to an age in its own language runs the danger of compromising the eternal message of the Gospel with the temporarily plausible conviction of the time.
—Kenneth Cauthen, *The Impact of American Religious Liberalism*, 1962

The theological conviction that the God of the Bible is the liberator of the poor and the downtrodden has been and is the important distinction between black and white religion. White Christianity may refer to liberation in limited times and places as shown by the abolitionists, the social gospel preachers, and the recent appearance of political and liberation theologians in Europe and America. But liberation is not and has never been the dominant theme in white church songs, prayers, and sermons. The reason is obvious: white people live in and identify with a social, economic, and political situation which blinds them to the biblical truth of liberation.
—James H. Cone, *Speaking the Truth*, 1986

Theology is unapologetically *pre*scriptive. It does not claim to be value-free or neutral. Theologians draw upon the beliefs of a particular tradition to suggest a course of action, an appropriate response, a way of life commensurate with what the faith teaches. Theology can be wrong; it cannot be noncommittal.

—Harvey Cox, *Religion in the Secular City*, 1984

Natural Theology says not only look up and look out—it also says look down and look in, and you will find the proofs of the reality of God in the depth of your own nature.

—Christopher Dawson, *Religion and Culture*, 1947

It illuminates our spirit with a transforming fire, and brings it into contact with those spirits who verily serve the Lord.

—Diodicus, *Spiritual Perfection*, 5th century

I consider theology to be the rhetoric of morals.

—Ralph Waldo Emerson, in *North American Review*, April 1866

Where there is no theology, there is no religion.

—Henry Fairlie, in *Chicago Tribune*, May 3, 1987

Theology is nothing else than anthropology. . . . The knowledge of God is nothing else than a knowledge of man.

—Ludwig Feuerbach, *The Essence of Christianity*, 1841

The fact that astronomies change while the stars abide is a true analogy of every realm of human life and thought, religion not least of all. No existent theology can be a final formulation of spiritual truth.

—Harry Emerson Fosdick, *The Living of These Days*, 1956

Theology must be man's critical reflection on himself, on his own basic principles. Only with this approach will theology be a serious discourse, aware of itself, in full possession of its conceptual elements.

—Gustavo Gutierrez, *A Theology of Liberation*, 1973

We cannot have an authentic theology in our time without dialogue with contemporary men.

—Bernard Haring, *The Johannine Council*, 1963

In no circumstances can the study of theology or the mind's assent to theological propositions take the place of what William Law calls "the birth of God within."

—Aldous Huxley, *The Perennial Philosophy*, 1945

A professorship of theology should have no place in our institution.
> —Thomas Jefferson, letter to Thomas Cooper, 1814,
> referring to the University of Virginia

The divine test of a man's worth is not his theology but his life.
> —Morris Joseph, *Judaism as Creed and Life*, 1903

Now I maintain that all attempts of reason to establish a theology by the aid of speculation alone are fruitless, that the principles of reason as applied to nature do not conduct us to any theological truths, and consequently, that a rational theology can have no existence, unless founded upon the laws of morality.
> —Immanuel Kant, *Critique of Pure Reason*, 1781

So significant you are, so universally relevant. But how, and by what right? Beware of asking; that way lies theology.
> —Ronald A. Knox, *Stimuli*, 1951

Theology does not receive her first principles from any other science, but immediately from God by revelation.
> —Pope Leo XIII, *Holy Scripture*, 1893

Theologies are judged, in the long run, not by their symmetry or elaborateness, but by their contribution to the solution of human problems.
> —Eugene W. Lyman, *Theology and Human Problems*, 1910

We have had our last chance. . . . The problem is basically theological. It must be of the spirit if we are to save the flesh.
> —Douglas MacArthur, when the Japanese surrendered at Tokyo, 1945

The churches would do well to shore up their resources of constructive theology. They will have to be ready to take a stand, to speak for truth or to deny that there is such a thing!
> —Martin E. Marty, *The New Shape of American Religion*, 1958

To be still searching what we know not, by what we know, still closing up truth to truth as we find it, this is the golden rule in *Theology* as well as in *Arithmetic*, and makes up the best harmony in a Church.
> —John Milton, *Areopagitica*, 1644

Theology is the fundamental and regulating principle of the whole Church system.

—John Henry Newman, *Via Media*, 1837

University education without theology is simply unphilosophical. Theology has at least as good a right to claim a place there as astronomy.

—John Henry Newman, *On the Scope and Nature of University Education*, 1852

As a common core of religious affirmation, the "fatherhood of God and the brotherhood of man" reduces theology to triviality.

—James Hastings Nichols, *Religion in America*, 1958

What is known and knowable in theology is God in relation to self and to neighbor, and self and neighbor in relation to God. This complex of related beings is the object of theology.

—H. Richard Niebuhr, *The Purpose of the Church and Its Ministry*, 1956

Theology is reflection upon the reality of worship and explication of it. As such it is a rational affair . . . faith seeking to understand

—Albert C. Outler, in *Christian Century*, February 3, 1960

More often than not, attacks upon theology come from uncritical use on the part of theologians themselves of *devotional* language in a context where *theological* language is called for.

—John E. Smith, *Reason and God*, 1961

Theology is not eternal. Only God is eternal, and no human mind or concept will ever capture that eternal reality.

—John Shelby Spong, *Into the Whirlwind*, 1983

The term "theo-logy" implies, as such, a mediation, namely, between the mystery, which is *theos*, and the understanding, which is *logos*.

—Paul Tillich, *The Protestant Era*, 1948

The chief aim of this science is to impart a knowledge of God, not only as existing in Himself, but also as the origin and end of all things, and especially of rational creatures.

—St. Thomas Aquinas, *Prologue Summa Theologiae*, 1272

Theology is an incubus that a humanist can never shake off. He may seek refuge from theism in atheism or from animism in materialism. But after each desperate twist and turn he will find himself committed to some theological position or other. Theology is inescapable, and it is dynamite.
— A.J. Toynbee, *A Study of History*, Vol. XII, *Reconsiderations*, 1961

It is difficult to see how a Christian theologian, especially if he be a sociologist and an historian to boot, could find rest in anything but in an ecumenically oriented theology.
— Joachim Wach, *Church, Denomination and Sect*, 1946

THOUGHTS

Everything proves the solidarity of individuals, and no one can think at all except by means of the general store of thought, accumulated and refined by centuries of cultivation and experience.
— Henri Amiel, *Journal*, 1882

There are no dangerous thoughts; thinking itself is dangerous.
— Hannah Arendt, in *The New Yorker*, December 5, 1977

Thought pure and simple is as near to God as we can get; it is through that we are linked with God.
— Samuel Butler, *Notebooks of*, 1912

Thinking *plus* agonized questioning of the scheme of things which has rolled me in the dust, has not the confident appeal of the believer to his God; but if it is serious it will probably come to that.
— Richard C. Cabot, *What Men Live By*, 1914

Beautiful it is to understand that a Thought did never die; that as thou, the originator thereof, hast gathered and created it from the whole Past, so thou wilt transmit it to the whole Future.
— Thomas Carlyle, *Sartor Resartus*, 1836

In truth we should be aware above all that our thoughts have three possible sources—God, the devil and ourselves.
— John Cassian, *Conferences*, I, ch. 19, c. 420

The Dean of Humanities spoke with awe "of an approaching scientific ability to control man's thoughts with precision."—I shall be very content to be dead before that happens.
— Winston S. Churchill, address, Massachusetts Institute of Technology, March 30, 1949

The highest possible stage in moral culture is when we recognise that we ought to control our thoughts.
—Charles Darwin, *The Descent of Man*, 1871

If you would live a high life, you must begin by encouraging the growth of high thoughts. If you would voyage Godward, you must see to it that the rudder of thought is right.
—W.J. Dawson, *The Making of Manhood*, 1895

Thinking is another attribute of the soul; and here I discover what properly belongs to myself. This alone is certain; but how often? as often as I think.
—René Descartes, *Meditations*, 1641

All that we are is the result of what we have thought.
—*Dhammapada*, c. 5th century B.C.

A vivid thought brings the power to paint it; and in proportion to the depth of its source is the force of its projection.
—Ralph Waldo Emerson, address, May 5, 1879

God intends even our thoughts to set forward the sanctification of our souls, and it rests with ourselves whether they do so or not.
—François Fénelon (1651–1715), *Spiritual Letters of*

The rise of thought beyond the world of sense, its passage from the finite to the infinite, the leap into the super-sensible which it takes when it snaps asunder the links of the chain of sense, all this transition is thought and nothing but thought.
—G.W.F. Hegel, *Logic*, 1816

Thoughts invite us, more than words and deeds, to continue in sin, for thoughts can be concealed, while words and deeds cannot.
—Sören Kierkegaard (1813–55), *Meditations from*

All thinking is not prayer. But thinking can be prayer, just as walking and talking and washing the floor can be prayer.
—Vincent McNabb, *The Craft of Prayer*, 1951

Man is but a reed, the most feeble thing in nature; but he is a thinking reed. . . . All our dignity consists, then, in thought.
—Blaise Pascal, *Pensées*, 1670

He whose heart has been set on the love of learning and true wisdom, and has exercised this part of himself, *that* man *must* without fail have thoughts that are immortal and divine, if *he lay hold on truth.*

—Plato, "Timaeus," 90, *Dialogues*, c. 370 B.C.

Human thought, like God, makes the world in its own image.

—Adam Clayton Powell, Jr., *Keep the Faith Baby!* 1967

Carry thy thoughts forward through eternity toward that universal sun; thou shalt not arrive at darkness nor emptiness; what is empty dwells only between the worlds, not around the world.

—Jean Paul Richter, *Reminiscences*, 1841

They are never alone that are accompanied with noble thoughts.

—Philip Sidney, *Arcadia*, 1590

TIME

What then is time? If no one asks me, I know; if I want to explain it to a questioner, I do not know.

—St. Augustine, *Confessions of*, XI, 397

Time is the author of authors.

—Francis Bacon, *The Advancement of Learning*, 1605

Time exists because there is activity. . . . Time is the product of *changing* realities, beings, existences.

—Nicholas Berdyaev, *Solitude and Society*, 1947

Time is a file that wears and makes no noise.

—H.C. Bohn, *Handbook of Proverbs*, 1855

My mission is to kill time, and time's to kill me in its turn. How comfortable one is among murderers.

—E. M. Cioran, *Drawn and Quartered*, 1971

Time is precious, but truth is more precious than time.

—Benjamin Disraeli, speech, September 21, 1865

The here-and-now is no mere filling of time, but a filling of time with God.

—John Foster, *Requiem for a Parish*, 1962

Let time flow by, with which we flow on to be transformed into the glory of the children of God.
—St. Francis de Sales (1567–1622), *Consoling Thoughts of*

All that really belongs to us is time; even he who has nothing else has that.
—Baltasar Gracián, *The Art of Worldly Wisdom*, 1647

The past is not dead; it is not even past. People live on inner time; the moment in which a decisive thought or feeling takes place can be at any time. Timeless feelings are common to all of us.
—Martha Graham, in *Dance Magazine*, May 1989

Time is the herald of Truth.
—Elizabeth Grymeston, *Miscellanea—Meditations*, 1604

The watch upon the horizon is the waiting in darkness for uncreated light. And within the luminous night, you learn to see that the end of time undulates like aurora curtains at the boundary of the soul.
—Suzanne Guthrie, "Praying the Apocalypse," in *The Christian Century*, November 4, 1992

Time is the rider that breaks youth.
—George Herbert, *Jacula Prudentum*, 1640

To understand the teaching of the Bible, one must accept its premise that time has a meaning which is at least equal to that of space; that time has a significance and sovereignty of its own.
—Abraham Joshua Heschel, *The Sabbath*, 1951

That which is, has been; that which is to be, already has been; and God seeks what has been driven away.
—*Holy Bible*, Ecclesiastes 3:15

Time, whose tooth gnaws away everything else, is powerless against truth.
—Thomas Henry Huxley, *Administrative Nihilism*, 1871

He that hopes hereafter to look back with satisfaction upon past years, must learn to know the present value of single minutes.
—Samuel Johnson (1696–1772), *The Rambler*

Ask what Time is, it is nothing else but something of eternal duration become finite, measurable and transitory.
—William Law, *Appeal to All that Doubt*, 1740

Time, although the philosophers declare it to be completely distinct from eternity, is certainly an available instrument for reaching the Eternal.
—John W. Lynch, *Hourglass*, 1952

Terrible and sublime thought, that every moment is supreme for some man or woman, every hour the apotheosis of some passion.
—William McFee, *Casuals of the Sea*, 1916

I'm convinced that time has no existence in the mind at all. We partition time out of necessity, so that if I say I will be somewhere at 1 o'clock, we agree on what 1 o'clock is. Civilization couldn't function otherwise. But our minds are a swirling mass of images and recollections that are connected, and it's the connections that count.
—Arthur Miller, in *U.S. News & World Report*, January 11, 1988

Time cures sorrows and squabbles because we all change and are no longer the same persons. Neither the offender nor the offended is the same.
—Blaise Pascal, *Pensées*, 1670

Time is the chariot of all ages to carry men away.
—Francesco Petrarch, *View of Human Life*, c. 1346

The moving image of eternity.
—Plato, "Timeaus," *Dialogues*, c. 380 B.C.

Pythagoras, when he was asked what time was, answered that it was the soul of this world.
—Plutarch, *Platonic Questions*, c. A.D. 66

As is well known, the Devil is the Prince of Time, and God is the King of Eternity. Time without end, that is Hell. Perfect presence, that is Eternity.
—Denis de Rougemont, *Endymion*, 1880

The slow, the silent power of time.
—J.C.F. von Schiller, *Wallenstein's Death*, 1799

Time is that which in all things passes away; it is the form under which the will to live has revealed to it that its efforts are in vain; it is the agent by which at every moment all things in our hands become as nothing, and lose all value.
—Arthur Schopenhauer, *The Vanity of Existence*, 1851

The conception of time as an objective blank in which particular events . . . succeed one after another has completely been discarded. The Buddha . . . knows no time-continuity; the past and the future are both rolled up in this present moment of illumination.
—D.T. Suzuki, *Essays in Zen Buddhism*, 1970

Time, a maniac scattering dust.
—Alfred Tennyson, *In Memoriam*, 1850

As if you could kill time without injuring eternity.
—Henry David Thoreau, *Walden*, 1854

TOLERANCE

The full circle of spiritual truth will be completed only when we realize that, but for a destiny not fully understood, we might actually have been born in the other person's faith.
—Marcus Bach, in *Rotarian Magazine*, December 1962

God is the only being in the universe who has a right to be intolerant. In fact, if He were tolerant He would not be God.
—Donald Grey Barnhouse, *Words Fitly Spoken*, 1969

Tolerance in the sense of moderation or superior knowledge or scepticism is actually the worst form of intolerance.
—Karl Barth, *Church Dogmatics*, 1940

Toleration is good for all, or it is good for none.
—Edmund Burke, speech, House of Commons, 1773

Is there any religion whose followers can be pointed to as distinctly more amiable and trustworthy than those of any other?
—Samuel Butler, *Notebooks*, 1912

More and more people care about religious tolerance as fewer and fewer care about religion.
—Alexander Chase, *Perspectives*, 1966

Tolerance implies a respect for another person, not because he is wrong or even because he is right, but because he is human.
> —John Cogley, in *Commonweal*, April 24, 1959

Tolerance means that we shall give our enemies a chance.
> —Morris R. Cohen, *The Faith of a Liberal*, 1946

Human diversity makes tolerance more than a virtue; it makes it a requirement for survival.
> —René Dubos, *Celebrations of Life*, 1981

Tolerance grows only when faith loses certainty; certainty is murderous.
> —Will Durant, *The Age of Faith*, 1950

I would no more quarrel with a man because of his religion than I would because of his art.
> —Mary Baker Eddy (1821–1910), *Miscellany*, 1914

Apocalyptic religion has its merits, but tolerance is not one of them.
> —W.R. Forrester, *Christian Vocation*, 1951

When will the churches learn that intolerance, personal or ecclesiastical, is an evidence of weakness: The confident can afford to be calm and kindly; only the fearful must defame and exclude.
> —Harry Emerson Fosdick, *Adventurous Religion*, 1926

All religions must be tolerated, and the sole concern of the authorities should be to see that one does not molest another, for here every man must be saved in his own way.
> —Frederick the Great, order, June 22, 1740

Tolerance . . . is the lowest form of human cooperation. It is the drab, uncomfortable, halfway house between hate and charity.
> —Robert I. Gannon, address, Boston, April 23, 1942

America, settled by peoples of many regions, races, religions, colors, creeds, and cultures, should, by moral example, lead the way in helping "to make the world safe for differences." . . . Understanding religious differences makes for a better understanding of other differences and for an appreciation of the sacredness of human personality as basic to human freedom.
—Frank P. Graham, *Christian Leadership and Today's World*, 1940

The tolerance of the skeptic . . . accepts the most diverse and indeed the most contradictory opinions, and keeps all his suspicions for the "dogmatist."
—Jean Guitton, *Difficultés de croire*, 1948

It is well that the stately synagog should lift its walls by the side of the aspiring cathedral, a perpetual reminder that there are many mansions of the Father's earthly house as well as in the heavenly one; that civilized humanity . . . is mightier than any one institution.
—Oliver Wendell Holmes, *Over the Teacups*, 1891

Judge not, and you will not be judged; condemn not, and you will not be condemned; forgive, and you will be forgiven.
—*Holy Bible*, Luke 6:37

Since each virtue shines by its own proper light, the merit of tolerance is resplendent with a very special glory.
—John of Salisbury, *Policraticus*, 1159

Do not despise others because, as it seems to you, they do not possess the virtues you thought they had; they may be pleasing to God for other reasons which you cannot discover.
—St. John of the Cross (1542–91), *The Living Flame of Love*

The modern theory that you should always treat the religious convictions of other people with profound respect finds no support in the Gospels. Mutual tolerance of religious views is the product not of faith, but of doubt.
—Arnold Lunn, *Now I See*, 1937

Tolerance is a better guarantee of freedom than brotherly love; for a man may love his brother so much that he feels himself thereby appointed his brother's keeper.
—Everett Dean Martin, *Liberty*, 1930

Toleration . . . is not true liberty when it is only a gracious concession by the state to the individual. Gracious concessions are incompatible with liberty of religion which is not something that a state, or an absolutist church offers, but that which the citizen claims and the law protects.
—Cecil Northcott, *Religious Liberty*, 1948

Toleration is not the *opposite* of Intolerance, but is the *counterfeit* of it. Both are despotisms. The one assumes itself the right of withholding liberty of conscience, and the other of granting it.
—Thomas Paine, *Rights of Man*, 1792

Our attitude to other religions should be defined in the spirit of that great saying in a play of Sophocles, where Antigone says, "I was not born to share men's hatred, but their love."
—Sarvepalli Radhakrishnan, *The Philosophy of*, 1952

Now that there is and can be no longer an exclusive national religion, tolerance should be given to all religions that tolerate others, so long as their dogmas contain nothing contrary to the duties of citizenship.
—Jean Jacques Rousseau, *The Social Contract*, 1762

Religious toleration, to a certain extent, has been won because people have ceased to consider religion so important as it was once thought to be.
—Bertrand Russell, *Free Thought and Official Propaganda*, lecture, March 24, 1922

Like the bee gathering honey from different flowers, the wise man accepts the essence of different Scriptures and sees only the good in all religions.
—*Srimad Bhagavatam*, between 1200 and 500 B.C.

It [toleration] implies a confession that there are insoluble problems upon which even revelation throws but little light.
—Frederic Temple, *Essays and Reviews*, 1860

What is toleration? It is the appurtenance of humanity. We are all full of weakness and errors; let us mutually pardon each other our follies—it is the first law of nature.
—Voltaire, "Toleration," in *Philosophical Dictionary*, 1764

The longer I live, the larger allowances I make for human infirmities.
—John Wesley, letter to Samuel Furley, February 21, 1756

TRADITION

We have some articles of faith from the Holy Scriptures and others we have received by the tradition of the Apostles, which the Apostles preached and the Fathers believed, and the Martyrs confirmed with their blood.
—St. Basil, *Treatise on the Holy Ghost*, II, c. 375

Every attempt of a given tradition in Protestantism to be faithful to its own best insights and to submit them to fresh scrutiny in the light of the gospel will finally draw us the [Church] closer together.
—Robert McAfee Brown, in *Commonweal*, September 24, 1965

Like a man turned into a brute . . . as were the victims of Circe—he who repudiates the ecclesiastical traditions embraces the human heresies, ceases to be a man of God and becomes unfaithful to the Lord.
—St. Clement of Alexandria, *Stromata*, lib. vii, cap. xvl, c. 193

People are always talking about tradition, but they forget we have a tradition of a few hundred years of nonsense and stupidity, that there is a tradition of idiocy, incompetence, and crudity.
—Hugo Demartini, *Contemporary Artists*, 1977

Tradition is the witness of the Spirit; the Spirit's unceasing revelation and preaching of good tidings. . . . It is, primarily, the principle of growth and regeneration.
—Georges Florovsky, *The Church of God*, 1934

By "Tradition" I mean that body of revealed truths, received by the Apostles from the lips of Christ Himself or told them by the Holy Ghost, that has come down to us, delivered as it were by hand, and preserved in the Catholic Church by unbroken succession.
—Pietro Gasparri, *The Catholic Catechism for Adults*, 1932

You are the sons of the prophets and of the covenant which God gave to your fathers, saying to Abraham, "And in your posterity shall all the families of the earth be blessed."
—*Holy Bible*, Acts 3:25

Tradition means that instinctive mind of the Church, that inspired sense of hers, which enables her to handle the Word of God.
—R. Kehoe, in *Eastern Churches Quarterly*, October 1946

Tradition is everywhere the mother of religion; it precedes and engenders sacred books, as language precedes and engenders scripture; its existence is rendered immovable in the sacred books, as the existence of the Word is rendered immovable in Scripture.

—Jean Baptiste Lacordaire, *Conferences of*, c. 1850

The liberties we talk about defending today were established by men who took their conception of man from the great religious tradition of Western civilization, and the liberties we inherit can almost certainly not survive the abandonment of that tradition.

—Walter Lippmann, in the New York *Herald Tribune*, December 16, 1938

Human traditions, instituted to propitiate God, to merit grace, and to make satisfaction for sins, are opposed to the Gospel and the doctrine of faith.

—Philip Melanchthon, *Augsburg Confession*, 1530

I believe in the virtue of traditions, and I recall having often spoken this phrase: "Memory is revolutionary." If one has the ambition of preparing the century to come, breaking with the past or being ignorant of it amounts to cutting one's own roots and drying up on the spot.

—François Mitterrand, in *The New York Times*, January 19, 1988

I have left you two things and you will not stray as long as you hold them fast. The one is the book of God [the Koran], and the other the Tradition of His Prophet.

—Mohammed (7th century), *Dictionary of Islam* , 1885

We know tradition as a living social process constantly changing, constantly in need of criticism, but constant also as the continuing memory, value system and habit structure of a society.

—H. Richard Niebuhr, *The Purpose of the Church and Its Ministry*, 1956

Tradition should be deabsolutized, but not scrapped. We're in a two thousand year continuity, and that which expresses continuity is valuable. In a state of flux on doctrine, continuity of tradition has even more value.

—James A. Pike, interviewed by Christopher S. Wren, *Look*, February 22, 1966

For how can anything come into use, if it has not first been handed down?

—Tertullian, *On the Soldier's Crown*, c. 211

Tradition is not only kept by the Church—it lives in the Church, it is the life of the Holy Spirit in the Church.
—Timothy Ware, *The Orthodox Church*, 1963

Large strata and movements in the western world are outside the church. But the religious tradition operates in them still in an indirect and disguised way. The river has gone underground; it has not ceased to flow.
—Amos Wilder, *Modern Poetry and the Christian Tradition*, 1952

TRINITY

We worship one God in Trinity, and Trinity in Unity, neither confounding the Persons, nor dividing the substance, for there is one Person of the Father, another of the Son, and another of the Holy Ghost; but the godhead of the Father, of the Son, and of the Holy Ghost is one, the glory equal, the majesty co-eternal.
—*Athanasian Creed*, c. 500

The operations of the Trinity are indivisible, even as the essence of the Trinity is indivisible.
—St. Augustine, *De. Trin.*, c. 397

The Persons themselves are nothing else than one God, one divine Substance, one divine Nature, one divine and supreme Majesty.
—St. Bernard, *De Consideratione*, c. 1150

The existence in Three Persons of the one Godhead is the foundation of the supernatural order; that is, of the communication by God to His free and intelligent creatures of His own life and happiness.
—Valentin-M. Breton, *The Blessed Trinity*, 1934

Theoretically it [the Trinity] is the affirmation of a full rich life in God as distinct from all abstract and barren conceptions of his being. Practically, it is the affirmation that the true nature of God must be learned from his historic revelation in Christ, and from the experience which Christ creates.
—William Adams Brown, *Christian Theology in Outline*, 1906

In the liturgical life of [Russian] Orthodoxy . . . the name of the Holy Trinity predominates over the name of Jesus, which shows that the knowledge of Christ is inseparably connected with that of the Holy Trinity.
—Sergius Bulgakov, *The Orthodox Church*, 1935

Although the Son and the Holy Ghost are in a certain sense derived from the Father, so that only the Father is without any source, they are in no wise created by Him, but are co-eternal and coessential with Him.

—Johannes Scotus Erigena, *The Division of Nature*, 867

It affirms that the mystery of God is to be defined by means of the character of Jesus Christ. . . . It asserts that the love which we see is Jesus Christ, and experience in the Holy Spirit, is one with the eternal power and being of Almighty God.

—Langdon Gilkey, *Maker of Heaven and Earth*, 1959

God is recognized as *Spirit* only when known as the Triune. This new principle is the axis on which the History of the World turns. "When the fullness of the time was come, God sent his Son," is the statement of the Bible. This means nothing else than that *self-consciousness* has reached the phase of development whose resultant constitutes the Idea of Spirit.

—G.W.F. Hegel (1770–1831), *The Philosophy of History*

Go therefore and make disciples of all nations, baptizing them in the name of the Father and of the Son and of the Holy Spirit.

—*Holy Bible*, Matthew 28:19

For we recognize one God, but only in the attributes of Fatherhood, Sonship, and Procession, both in respect of cause and effect and perfection of subsistence, that is, manner of existence, do we perceive difference.

—St. John of Damascus (675–749), *Exposition of the Orthodox Faith*

The three persons in the Godhead are three in one sense and one in another. We cannot tell how—and that is the mystery.

—Samuel Johnson, in *Boswell's Life of*, August 22, 1773

The Church is accustomed most fittingly to attribute to the Father those works of the divinity in which power excels, to the Son those in which wisdom excels, and those in which love excels to the Holy Ghost.

—Pope Leo XIII, *The Holy Spirit*, 1904

Between the Trinity and Hell there lies no other choice.

—V. Lossky, *The Mystical Theology of the Eastern Church*, 1957

The doctrine of the Trinity . . . is more satisfactory than all the ancient and modern pantheons wherein we ascend beyond the many gods or values to someone who is limited by them.
—H. Richard Niebuhr, *The Meaning of Revelation*, 1941

If there be three distinct and separate Persons, then three distinct and separate Substances. . . . And since the Father is God, the Son is God, and the Spirit is God . . . then unless the Father, Son and Spirit are three distinct Nothings, they must be three distinct Substances, and consequently three distinct Gods.
—William Penn, *Sandy Foundation Shaken*, 1667

The Trinity is not necessary. . . . Our Lord never heard of it. The apostles knew nothing of it.
—James A. Pike, sermon, New York, August 30, 1964

Why do you complain that the proposition God is three in one is obscure and mystical and yet acquiesce meekly in the physicist's fundamental formula "two P minus PQ equals IH over Pi where I equals the square root of minus I" when you know quite well that the square root of I is paradoxical and Pi is incalculable?
—Dorothy L. Sayers, *Current Religious Thought*, 1947

All those who believe in a Trinity in the essence of God are tritheists . . . true atheists.
—Michael Servetus, *De Trinitatis Erroribus*, 1531

What doth it profit thee to discuss the deep mystery of the Trinity, if thou art lacking in humility and so displeasing to the Trinity. . . . I would rather choose to feel compunction than to know its definition.
—Thomas à Kempis, *Imitation of Christ*, 1441

In the mystery of the Trinity . . . lies the chief infraction against the faith of Israel, which rests on the certainty of a free and direct communication between Creator and Creation.
—Franz Werfel, *Between Heaven and Earth*, 1944

TRUST

The more miserable we know ourselves to be, the more occasion we have to confide in God, since we have nothing in ourselves in which to confide.
—St. Francis de Sales (1561–1622), *Consoling Thoughts of*

Every relationship of trust between two men has its roots in a faith which extends far beyond their relation to one another, the faith that there exists an obligation valid for all subjects, all places and all times.
—Karl Heim, *The Certitudes of Faith*, 1923

Can anyone think of believing in God without trusting Him? Is it possible to trust in God for the big things like forgiveness and eternal life, and then refuse to trust Him for the little things like clothing and food?
—Oswald C.J. Hoffmann, *Life Crucified*, 1959

When we grow afraid of life and death, let us have the sense of the trustworthiness of the universe, of its encompassing embrace and its sustaining care.
—Joshua Loth Liebman, *Peace of Mind*, 1946

A man who should act, for one day, on the supposition that all the people about him were influenced by the religion which they professed, would find himself ruined before night.
—Thomas Babington Macaulay, in *Edinburgh Review*, January 1831

Things infinite and divine . . . are given not so much for definition as for trust; are less the objects we think of than the very tone and color of our thought, the tension of our love, the unappeasable thirst of grief and reverence.
—James Martineau, *Hours of Thought on Sacred Things*, 1879

Sin arises out of mistrust. Man is afraid to trust the divine destiny and to accept his limits. The rebellion that follows is a decisive act of repudiation, a trusting of self over against God.
—James I. McCord, *The Nature of Man*, 1962

Delay not the health of thy soul through trust in friends or in neighbors; for men will forget sooner than thou thinkest; it is better to make provision betimes and send before thee some good than to trust in other men's help.
—Thomas à Kempis, *Imitation of Christ*, 1441

TRUTH

There can be no conflict between philosophical and theological truths, although theologians may correct the errors of philosophers who try to answer questions beyond the competence of natural reason, just as philosophers can correct the errors of theologians who violate the autonomy of reason.
—Mortimer Adler, *Vital Speeches*, December 1949

To hate truth as truth . . . is the same as to hate goodness
for its own sake.
—Ethan Allen, *Reason the Only Oracle of Man*, 1794

So long as we are able to distinguish any space whatever between the truth and us we remain outside it.
—Henri Amiel, *Journal of*, 1882

Never to have seen the truth is better than to have seen it
and not to have acted upon it.
—Anonymous

Rightness perceptible to the mind alone. . . . Rightness dis-
tinguishes it from every other thing which is called rightness.
. . . Truth and rightness and justice define each other.
—St. Anselm, *Dialogue on Truth*, c. 1080

The high-minded man must care more for the truth than for
what people think.
—Aristotle, *Nicmachean Ethics*, c. 240 B.C.

Turn not to the outside world! Into thine own self go back! In
the inner man alone resides truth.
—St. Augustine, *On True Religion*, 390

Truth is indeed one name for Nature, the first cause of all
things true.
—Marcus Aurelius, *Meditations*, c. 170

Truth, which only doth judge itself, teacheth, that the inquiry of Truth, which is the love-making, or wooing of it; the
knowledge of Truth, which is the presence of it; and the belief of Truth, which is the enjoyment of it; is the sovereign
good of human nature.
—Francis Bacon, *Essays*, 1597

Truths are first clouds; then rain, then harvest and food.
—Henry Ward Beecher, *Life Thoughts*, 1858

Truth is meant to save you first, and the comfort comes
afterwards.
—Georges Bernanos, *The Diary of a Country Priest*, 1937

Speak the truth and shame the devil.
—Miguel de Cervantes, *Don Quixote*, 1605

A thing is not truth until it is so strongly believed in that the believer is convinced that its existence does not depend on him.

—John Jay Chapman, *Essays*, 1910

Those who know the truth are not equal to those who love it.

—Confucius, *Analects*, c. 500 B.C.

Truth lies over the city like mist over rainy streets. Men are enveloped by it and pass through it. Some pause and are transformed. There is in every vital truth an element of contemplation.

—James W. Douglass, *The Non-Violent Cross*, 1966

He that speaks the truth executes no private function of an individual will, but the world utters a sound by his lips.

—Ralph Waldo Emerson, "Character," in *Essays* (2nd series), 1844

One of the supreme hours of human experience arrives when a man gets his eye on something concerning which he is persuaded that it is the eternal truth.

—Harry Emerson Fosdick, *A Great Time to Be Alive*, 1944

At the core of everything I write is the feeling that the denial of the truth imprisons us even further in ourselves. Of course, there's no one "truth." The great things, the insights that happen to you, come to you in some internal way.

—Paula Fox, in *Publishers Weekly*, April 6, 1990

Although it may not be always advisable to say all that is true, yet it is never allowable to speak against truth.

—St. Francis de Sales, *Introduction to the Devout Life*, 1609

Truth makes the Devil blush.

—Thomas Fuller (1608-61), *Gnomologia*, 1732

I say that as concerns the truth, of which mathematical demonstrations gives us the knowledge, it is the same as that which the Divine Wisdom knows.

—Galileo, *Dialogue on the Great World Systems*, 1632

I believe in the message of truth delivered by all the religious teachers of the world.

—Mohandas K. Gandhi (1869–1948), *The Essential Gandhi*

He who dies for the truth finds holy ground everywhere for his grave.

> —German proverb

It is not always needful for truth to take a definite shape: it is enough if it hovers about us like a spirit and produces harmony: it is wafted through the air like the sound of a bell, grave and kindly.

> —J.W. von Geothe (1749–1832), *Maxims and Reflections*

Truth is not for or against anything; truth simply is.

> —Aelred Graham, *Christian Thought and Action*, 1951

Truth is more ancient than error, for error is nothing else but deviation and swerving from truth.

> —John Hales (1584–1666), *Private Judgment in Religion*

The best test of truth is the power of the thought to get itself accepted in the competition of the market.

> —Justice Oliver Wendell Holmes, *Abrams v. U.S.*, dissenting opinion, 1919

Truthful lips endure for ever, but a lying tongue is but for a moment.

> —*Holy Bible*, Proverbs 12:19

It is the customary fate of new truths to begin as heresies and to end as superstitions.

> —Thomas Henry Huxley, *The Coming of Age of "The Origin of Species,"* 1893

Let each of us look for truth where it is most accessible and where it speaks the language he best understands.

> —L.P. Jacks, *Religious Perplexities*, 1922

Truth is essentially a relation between two things, an idea, on the one hand, and a reality outside of the idea, on the other.

> —William James, *The Meaning of Truth*, 1907

The truth may be one, final, determined, but my apprehension of it can never be anything of the kind; it is changing continuously.

> —Bede Jarrett, *Meditations for Layfolk*, 1915

Since there is no complete truth, our movement toward it is itself the only form in which truth can achieve completion in existence, here and now.
—Karl Jaspers, *Tragedy Is Not Enough*, 1952

The very notion of truth is a culturally given direction, a part of the pervasive nostalgia for an earlier certainty.
—Julian Jaynes, *The Origin of Consciousness in the Breakdown of the Bicameral Mind*, 1976

In the rise of intellectuals, truth has become a prime casualty. They think that there is only Truth with a capital T, which they feel that they have found and must deliver to others.
—Paul Johnson, in *U.S. News & World Report*, March 27, 1989

To comprehend the truth rationality itself must conform to all the laws of the spiritual world . . . and be related to all the vital and moral forces of the spirit.
—Aleksei Khonyskov, *Satchineniya*, 1911

Truth as it exists in God's mind has a royalty of its own; banish it from the earth if you will, by police measures, but it will still reign a monarch in exile.
—Ronald A. Knox, *Stimuli*, 1951

The quiet voice of sober truth wins out in the long run against the strident noise of passion, provided it does not hesitate to appeal to the deepest foundations of our existence, to the work of God Himself.
—John La Farge, *An American Amen*, 1958

We believe that there is no body of philosophers however wrong, no individual however stupid, who has not had at least a glimpse of the truth.
—Lactantius, *Inst. Div.*, VII, c. 310

When all treasures are tried . . . truth is the fairest.
—William Langland, *Piers Plowman*, c. 1400

No one draws closer to a knowledge of the truth than he who has advanced far in the knowledge of divine things, and yet knows that something always remains for him to seek.
—St. Leo (390?–461), *Sermon in Nativitate Domini*, IX

For tho' every Truth is One, yet our Sight is so feeble, that we cannot (always) come to it Directly, but by many Inferences, and laying of things together.
—Charles Leslie, *Certainty of the Christian Religion*, 1719

Veracity is a plant of paradise and its seeds have never flourished beyond the walls.
—Niccolò Machiavelli, in George Eliot, *Romola*, 1863

Be not content to know the Truth; rouse your heart to love it.
—B.W. Maturin, *Self-Knowledge and Self-Discipline*, 1905

The key of the world is given into our hands when we throw ourselves unreservedly into the service of the highest truth we know.
—G.S. Merriam, *The Chief End of Man*, 1897

Truth is a quality belonging primarily to judgments, and whatever our views as to its ultimate nature, I think we might all agree that a judgment is true when and only when it states a fact.
—William Pepperell Montague, *Ways of Knowing*, 1940

There is no ultimate test of truth besides the testimony borne to truth by the mind itself.
—John Henry Newman, *A Grammar of Assent*, IX, 1870

It is neither possible for man to know the truth fully nor to avoid the error of pretending that he does.
—Reinhold Niebuhr, *Human Destiny*, 1943

A spiritual truth is valid only when it does not contradict universal reason, one's inner experience, and the experience of other seers of truth.
—Swami Nikhilananda, *Perspectives on a Troubled Decade*

Such is the irresistible nature of truth that all it asks, and all it wants, is the liberty of appearing. The sun needs no inscription to distinguish him from darkness.
—Thomas Paine, *The Rights of Man*, 1791

He who does not bellow the truth when he knows the truth makes himself the accomplice of liars and forgers.
—Charles Péguy, *Basic Verities*, 1943

Truth often suffers more by the heat of its defenders, than from the arguments of its opposers.
—William Penn, *Fruits of Solitude*, 1693

To be absolutely sure of the truth of matters concerning which there are many opinions is an attribute of God not given to man.
—Plato, *Laws*, c. 360 B.C.

Man passes away; generations are but shadows; there is nothing stable but truth.
—Josiah Quincy, speech, September 17, 1830

If we could grasp the whole truth at a glance, as the Logos does, we should see what now is dark to us.
—Josiah Royce, *The Spirit of Modern Philosophy*, 1889

The simplest and most necessary truths are always the last believed.
—John Ruskin, *Modern Painters*, 1856

Eternal truths . . . are . . . tenets which the remotest ancestors of man are reputed to have held, and which his remotest descendants are forbidden to abandon.
—George Santayana, *The Realm of Truth*, 1938

He who sets out in search of Truth must leave Superstition forever and wander down into the land of Absolute Negation and Denial. He must then go . . . where the mountains of Stern Reality will rise before him. *Beyond* them lies Truth.
—Olive Schreiner, *Story of an African Farm*, 1883

Truth is a kingdom which belongs to those who give themselves to it, lead where it may, cost what it will, use or not use.
—Ralph W. Sockman, *The Highway of God*, 1941

Ethical truth is as exact and peremptory as physical truth.
—Herbert Spencer, *Social Statics*, 1851

Truth is the aristocracy of language.
—Synesius of Cyrene (died 414), *Essays and Hymns of*

Truth is the system of propositions which have unconditional claim to be recognized as valid.
—A.E. Taylor, *Philosophical Review*, XIV, 1908

Truths and roses have thorns about them.

—Henry David Thoreau, *Walden*, 1854

Man discovers truth by reason only, not by faith.

—Leo Tolstoy, *On Life*, 1887

It is one thing to wish to have truth on our side, and another to wish sincerely to be on the side of truth.

—Richard Whateley, *On the Love of Truth*, 1825

The truths which are not translated into lives are dead truths, and not living truths.

—Woodrow Wilson, address, October 1904

nity

Nobody can, even for the sake of unity, do violence to his conscience and to truth itself. Whoever in conscience feels obliged to understand the Word of God in a certain way cannot and may not declare he understands it otherwise.

—Bernard Alfrink, address to Interfederal Assembly of Pax Romana, Washington, D.C., July 1964

It is impossible to keep men together in one religious denomination, whether true or false, except they be united by means of visible signs or sacraments.

—St. Augustine, *Contra Faust*, xix, c. 400

In increasingly wide circles men are striving for unity. Lying at the centre of all and providing the only enduring cement is religious unity.

—H.N. Bate, *Faith and Order World Conference*, 1928

The mystic, the authoritarian, the sacramentarian, the radical individualist, these—to mention only a few of the more outstanding types—must be reckoned with in any comprehensive program for Christian unity.

—William Adam Brown, *Christian Unity: Its Principles and Possibilities*, 1921

Whatever task God is calling us to, if it is yours it is mine, and if it is mine it is yours. We must do it together—or be cast aside together.

—Howard Hewlett Clark, *Anglicans*, 1904

We live in succession, in division, in part, in particles. Meantime within man is the soul of the whole; the wise silence; the universal beauty, to which every part and particle is equally related; the eternal ONE.

—Ralph Waldo Emerson, "The Over-Soul," in *Essays*, 1841

One world, waiting surely, for who shall carry to it and place in its empty hands one Faith—the only thing that can ever truly and fundamentally unite it.

—W.H.T. Gairdner, *Echoes from Edinburgh*, 1910

And though a man might prevail against one who is alone, two will withstand him. A threefold cord is not quickly broken.

—*Holy Bible*, Ecclesiastes 4:12

Behold, how good and pleasant it is when brothers dwell in unity!
—*Holy Bible*, Psalms 133:1

When we turn *to* each other, and not *on* each other, that's victory. When we build each other and not destroy each other, that's victory. Red, yellow, brown, black and white—we're all precious in God's sight. Everybody is somebody.
—Jesse L. Jackson, in the *Los Angeles Times*, April 2, 1988

But our appeal for unity is intended to be, above all, an echo of the prayer which Our Savior addressed to His Divine Father at the Last Supper: "That all may be one, even as Thou, Father, in Me and I in Thee; that they may be one in Us."
—Pope John XXIII, *Encyclical*, November 11, 1961

As man increases his knowledge of the heavens, why should he fear the unknown on earth? As man draws nearer to the stars, why should he not also draw nearer to his neighbor?
—Lyndon B. Johnson, news conference, Johnson City, Texas, August 29, 1965

The contribution of religion to the unity of all human beings is made, not in the intellectual but in the spiritual realm.
—Edward J. Jurji, *The Christian Interpretation of Religion*, 1932

The whole notion of Christian solidarity grows out of, and is centered in, the common participation of a common table.
—Ronald A. Knox, *The Window in the Wall*, 1956

If in the past Christianity, Judaism, or Islam placed itself at the center of the search for truth and unity, there is now a shift away from this kind of tribal centricity to the notion that it is God who is at the center and all the religious traditions of the world must inevitably intersect at this center. One can no longer speak about one's faith outside the ambience of the plurality of religious traditions.
—Madonna Kolbenschlag, *Lost in the Land of Oz*, 1988

A divided world is seen more and more to call for a united Church if the hurt of that world is to be healed.
—Edwin Lewis, *A Philosophy of the Christian Revelation*, 1940

We are bound together by a more primitive and fundamental unity than any unity of thought and doctrine; we all have the same human nature and, considered in their extra-mental reality, the same primordial tendencies.
—Jacques Maritain, *Ransoming the Time*, 1944

The world's inability to achieve a unity of thought and to end spiritual divisions is the real reason society is so deeply unhappy, so poor in ideas and enthusiasm, and so lacking in shared spiritual concepts which are its own inner joy, nobility and strength.

—Barrett McGurn, *A Reporter Looks at the Vatican*, 1962

Unto the true unity of the Church it is sufficient to agree concerning the doctrine of the Gospel and the administration of the Sacraments: nor is it necessary that human traditions, rites, or ceremonies instituted by men should be alike everywhere.

—Philip Melanchthon, *Augsburg Confession*, 1530

In order to be united we must love one another; in order to love one another we must know one another, in order to know one another we must meet one another.

—Désiré Joseph Mercier (1851–1926), in *The Monitor* (of San Francisco Roman Catholic Archdiocese), December 1960

Ultimately, the churches themselves must decide what the one great Church is to be, and, in conversation with each other, seek to achieve it. Councils, so long as they last, are always means and never ends.

—Lewis S. Mudge, Jr., *Unity in Mid-Career*, 1963

The desire to come together as brothers must not lead to a watering down or subtracting from the truth. Our dialogue must not weaken our attachment to our faith.

—Pope Paul VI, *Ecclesiam Suam*, August 1964

The Humble, Meek, Merciful, Just, Pious, and Devout Souls, are everywhere of one religion; and when Death has taken off the Mask, they will know one another, tho' the divers Liveries they wear here make them Strangers.

—William Penn, *Some Fruits of Solitude*, 1693

The true Church government is to leave the conscience to its full liberty . . . and to seek unity in the Light and in the Spirit, walking sweetly and harmoniously together in the midst of different practices.

—Isaac Pennington (1616–79), *Works*, Pt. I

Only one thing can give unity in the Church on the human level: the love which allows another to be different even when it does not understand him.

—Karl Rahner, quoted in Herder Correspondence Feature Service, July 1965

We don't reach Christian unity by riding roughshod over sincere convictions and trying to create, with all possible speed, a superchurch to confront the Goliaths of the modern world.
—David H. Read, *Sons of Anak*, 1964

The legacy from the best prophets of the past is a conception of a united world. The coming order is a world order. And any religion that hesitates to proclaim this gospel is neither an heir of the prophets of the past nor the parent of the achievement of the future.
—Curtis W. Reese, "The Content of Religious Liberalism," in *Religious Humanism*, 1991

We are all one, united in our eternal image which is the image of God, and the source in us all of our life and our coming into existence.
—John Ruysbroeck (1293–1381), *The Mirror of Eternal Salvation*

Every quest for unity among men implies first of all that a man who is engaged in it is careful to see that he has this unity in his own person.
—Roger Schutz, *Unity: Man's Tomorrow*, 1963

Any religion that is going to unite men . . . must have room for mystics, prophets, and for priests, and it must be a religion of such a character as will prevent the priests from stoning the prophets.
—George Bernard Shaw, in *The New Commonwealth*, January 2, 1920

We desire unity of religion but not when purchased at the cost of the unity of truth.
—Fulton J. Sheen, *Communism and the Conscience of the West*, 1948

All creatures seek after unity; all multiplicity struggles toward it—the universal aim of all life is always this unity. All that flows outward is to flow backward into its source—God.
—Johann Tauler (1290–1361), *Life and Sermons*

If there cannot be immediate unity of faith, there must be unity of love, expressing itself in common effort in social, economic and political relations.
—John J. Wright, address, Maynooth, Ireland, 1961

UNIVERSE

Cease not to think of the Universe as one living Being, possessed of a single Substance and a single soul.
—Marcus Aurelius, *Meditations*, c. 170

We are impelled by a hidden instinct to reunion with the parts of the larger heart of the universe.

—John Elof Boodin, *Cosmic Evolution*, 1925

Man and Mind are a part and outcome of the universe, and any explanation which left them out would miss one of its greatest wonders.

—Borden P. Bowne, *Theism*, 1902

When we once understand that the universe is a great smelting-pot, and the Creator a great founder, where can we go that will not be right?

—Chuang-tzu, (4th century B.C.), *Texts of Taoism*

Since we preconceive by an indubitable notion that He [God] is a living being and . . . that there is nothing in all nature superior to Him, I do not see that anything can be more consistent . . . than to attribute life and divinity to the universe.

—Cicero, *De Natura Deorum*, II, 5, 44 B.C.

So long as we see the universe in the relation of use to ourselves, it remains cold, indifferent, meaningless to us; but when we see it in relation to God, sharing the life which is God, but sharing it even more imperfectly than ourselves, then the process of nature is no longer a meaningless intimidating mechanism, but pathetic and forgivable to us even as we are to ourselves.

—A. Clutton-Brock, *The Spirit*, 1919

It is not impossible that to some infinitely superior being the whole universe may be as one plain, the distance between planet and planet being only as the pores in a grain of sand, and the spaces between system and system no greater than the intervals between one grain and the grain adjacent.

—Samuel Taylor Coleridge, *Omniana*, 1812

How could anyone observe the mighty order with which our God governs the universe without feeling himself inclined . . . to the practice of all virtues, and to the beholding of the Creator Himself, the source of all goodness, in all things and before all things?

—Nicolaus Copernicus, Preface, *De Recolutionibus Orbium Coelestium*, 1543

The whole universe is but the footprint of the divine goodness.

—Dante, *Of Monarchy*, c. 1300

It could be that God has not absconded but spread, as our vision and understanding of the universe have spread, to a fabric of spirit and sense so grand and subtle, so powerful in a new way, that we can only feel blindly of its hem.
—Annie Dillard, *Pilgrim at Tinker Creek*, 1974

The beginning seems to present insuperable difficulties unless we agree to look on it as frankly supernatural.
—A.S. Eddington, *The Expanding Universe*, 1933

There is a soul at the center of nature, and over the will of every man, so that none of us can wrong the universe.
—Ralph Waldo Emerson, "Spiritual Laws," in *Essays* (1st series), 1841

Paley's simile of the watch is no longer applicable to such a world as this. It must be replaced by the simile of the flower. The universe is not a machine, but an organism, with an indwelling principle of life. It was not made, but it has grown.
—John Fiske, *Idea of God*, 1887

Did the atoms take counsel together and devise a common plan and work it out? That hypothesis is unspeakably absurd, yet it is rational in comparison with the notion that these atoms combined by mere chance, or by chance produced such a universe as that in which we live.
—Robert Flint, *Theism*, 1876

In ultimate analysis, the universe can be nothing less than the progressive manifestation of God.
—J.B.S. Haldane, interview, in *The British Weekly*, March 3, 1932

Faith in God is synonymous with the brave hope that the universe is friendly to the ideals of man.
—A.E. Haydon, in *Journal of Religion*, March 1927

The Cosmos (Nature, Universe) is the highest unity that we know. . . . The Cosmos . . . is creative. This does not mean making something from nothing, but rather making the new out of the old. . . . Since the Cosmos is the highest known unity and is creative, we call it God. God and the Cosmos are one.
—John H. Hershey, in *Unity*, May-June 1955

And God said, "Let there be light; and there was light. . . .
And God called the light Day, and the darkness he called
Night. And there was evening and there was morning, one
day. And God said, "Let there be a firmament in the midst of
the waters, and let it separate the waters from the waters".
. . . And God called the firmament Heaven.

—*Holy Bible*, Genesis 1:3, 5-6, 8

I find no difficulty in imagining that, at some former period,
this universe was not in existence, and that it made its appearance in consequence of the volition of some pre-existing
Being.

—Thomas Henry Huxley, *Life of Darwin*, 1883

If the universe is running down like a clock, the clock must
have been wound up at a date which we could name if we
knew it. The world, if it is to have an end in time, must have
had a beginning in time.

—W.R. Inge, *God and the Astronomers*, 1933

Everything points with overwhelming force to a definite
event, or series of events, of creation at some time or times,
not infinitely remote. The universe cannot have originated by
chance out of its present ingredients, and neither can it have
been always the same as now.

—James H. Jeans, *Eos, or the Wider Aspects of Cosmogony*, 1928

The infinite expanse of the universe, its growth through im-
measurable periods of time, the boundless range of its
changes, and the rational order that pervades it all, seems to
demand an infinite intelligence behind its manifestations.

—David Starr Jordan, *The Relation of Evolution to Religion*, 1926

If causality has broken down and events are not rigidly governed by the pushes and pressures of the past, may they not
be influenced in some manner by the "pull" of the future—
which is a manner of saying that "purpose" may be a concrete physical factor in the evolution of the universe.

—Arthur Koestler, *The Sleepwalkers*, 1959

If the universe is so bad, or even half so bad, how on earth
did human beings ever come to attribute it to the activity of a
wise and good Creator?

—C.S. Lewis, *The Problem of Pain*, 1944

This wonderful ordering of the sun, the planets and the comets cannot but be the work of an intelligent, all-powerful Being.
—Issac Newton, *Scholium of Principia*, 1687

The road from discrete scientific observations to large-scale explanations of the origin and destiny of the universe always passes through political, social, religious, and cultural precincts.
—Mark Noll, "Theology, Science, Politics: What Darwin Meant,"
in *Christian Century*, August 26/September 2, 1992

The plots of God are perfect. The Universe is a plot of God.
—Edgar Allan Poe, in *Democratic Review*, November 1844

The entire universe, as I see it, is the outward manifestation of Mind Energy, of spirit, or to use the older and better word, of God.
—Milton Steinberg, *A Believing Jew*, 1951

This vast universe is a wheel. Upon it are all creatures that are subject to birth, death, and rebirth. Round and round it turns, and never stops. It is the wheel of Brahman.
—*Svetasvatara Upanishad*, before 400 B.C.

The universe is a collector and conservator, not of mechanical energy, as we supposed, but of persons. All round us, one by one, like a continual exhalation, "souls" break away, carrying upwards their incommunicable load of consciousness.
—Pierre Teilhard de Chardin, *The Phenomenon of Man*, 1955

The universe shows us nothing save an immense and unbroken chain of cause and effect.
—Paul Henri Thiry, Baron d'Holbach, *The System of Nature*, 1770

The whole universe together participates in the divine goodness more perfectly, and represents it better than any single creature whatever.
—St. Thomas Aquinas, *Summa Theologiae*, 1272

We of the modern West are the only people in the whole history of the world who have refused to find an explanation of the universe in a divine mind and will.
—Gerald Vann, *The Heart of Man*, 1945

Just as light is diffused from a fire which is confined to one spot, so is this whole universe the diffused energy of the supreme Brahman.

—Vishnu, *Puranas*, c. 500 B.C.

The universe construed solely in terms of efficient causation of purely physical interconnections, presents a sheer, insoluble contradiction.

—Alfred North Whitehead, *The Function of Reason*, 1929

Values

I can see no hope for our unhappy world save that which lies in the renewal of the moral and spiritual values which our common ideal of faith has created.

—Sholem Asch, *Spirit in Man*, 1941

Man-made values are not only unsatisfying but they are groundless. God alone can give fixity and permanence to values and hence is to be defined as "The Supreme Value of the Universe."

—E.S. Brightman, *Religious Values*, 1925

The Christian mind clings to a hierarchy of values. No sane man would ascribe equal value to his brain and his feet, his eye and his fingernail. In the pursuit of knowledge, the Christian intellectual observes a comparable scale of values.

—F.X. Canfield, *The Catholic Bookman's Guide*, 1962

There no longer exists any articulate public consensus in the West on the ultimate values which once formed the living soul of its culture.

—Norris Clark, in *America*, March 31, 1962

The ultimate test of religious values is nothing psychological, nothing definable in terms of *how it happens*, but something ethical, definable only in terms of *what is attained*.

—George A. Coe, *The Spiritual Life*, 1900

Things have in fact just that value which God sees in them, and no other. To Him, the All Holy and All Wise, the pomps and successes of men and what are sometimes called the "substantial rewards of life" are simply of no worth whatever.

—Edward F. Garesche, *The Things Immortal*, 1919

Spiritual values have meaning only in human relations and are as much a part of the evolutionary process as the physical structure of man.

—A. Eustace Haydon, *The Quest of the Ages*, 1929

Values, human values, can survive only if, reaching out toward a metaphysical condition which their dream shapes foreshadow, they *find* it.

—William E. Hocking, *Human Nature and Its Remaking*, 1918

All Faith consists essentially in the recognition of a world of spiritual values behind, yet not apart from, the world of natural phenomena.
—W.R. Inge, *Faith and Its Psychology*, 1910

Religious life is not threatened merely by vexing restrictions. It can also be threatened by the spread of false values—such as hedonism, power-seeking, greed—which are making headway in various countries and which in practice stifle the spiritual aspirations of large numbers of people.
—Pope John Paul II, speech, Helsinki, Finland, in the *Los Angeles Times*, June 6, 1989

It is precisely because the Church does not desire to entrust the question of values to irreligious hands that Catholic institutions of higher learning exist.
—Howard Mumford Jones, *General Education*, 1934

If we are to have values of the intrinsic and eternal type, we must take by faith as real the kind of world in which they can live.
—Rufus M. Jones, *Spirit in Man*, 1941

The faith we have to build is a faith in the values of this world, not in the values of another.
—Harold J. Laski, *Reflections on the Revolution of Our Time*, 1943

Man's chief purpose . . . is the creation and preservation of value; that is what gives meaning to our civilization, and the participation in this is what gives significance, ultimately to the individual and human life.
—Lewis Mumford, *Faith for Living*, 1950

Since no way can be found for deciding a difference in values, the conclusion is forced upon us that the difference is one of tastes, not one as to any objective truth.
—Bertrand Russell, *Religion and Science*, 1935

VANITY

One ought not to be furnished out more elaborately than need requires, nor to be more solicitous for the body than is good for the soul.
—St. Basil the Great, *Address to Young Men on the Reading of Greek Literature*, c. 370

Nothing can exceed the vanity of our existence but the folly of our pursuits.
—Oliver Goldsmith, *The Good Natr'd Man*, 1768

For the fate of the sons of men and the fate of beasts is the same; as one dies, so dies the other. They all have the same breath, and man has no advantage over the beasts; for all is vanity.

—*Holy Bible*, Ecclesiastes 3:19

The ugliest vanity is the vanity of one who boasts of his humility.

—Jacob Klatzkin, *In Praise of Wisdom*, 1943

What greater vanity can there be, than to go about by our proportions and conjectures to guess at God? And to govern both him, and the world according to our capacity and laws?

—Michel de Montaigne, *Essays*, bk. 2, ch. 12, 1580

Vanity is the polite mask of pride.

—Friedrich Nietzsche, *Human, All Too Human*, 1878

What renders the vanity of others insupportable is that it wounds our own.

—La Rochefoucauld, *Maxims*, 1665

Nothing makes one so vain as being told that one is a sinner.

—Oscar Wilde, *The Picture of Dorian Gray*, 1891

VICE

There is no vice so completely contrary to our nature that it obliterates all trace of nature.

—St. Augustine, *City of God*, XIX, 426

The same vices that are gross and insupportable in others we do not notice in ourselves.

—Jean de la Bruyère, *Caractères*, 1688

Search others for their virtues, thyself for thy vices.

—Benjamin Franklin, *Poor Richard's Almanac*, 1758

Vice makes Virtue shine.

—Thomas Fuller, *Gnomolgia*, 1732

It is not possible to form any other notion of the origin of vice than as the absence of virtue.

—St. Gregory of Nyssa (c. 335–c. 395), *The Great Catechism*

Whatever was passion in the contemplation of man, being brought forth by his will into action, is vice and the bondage of sin.
—James Harrington, *The Commonwealth of Oceana*, 1656

If he does really think there is no distinction between virtue and vice, why, sir, when he leaves our houses let us count our spoons.
—Samuel Johnson, in *Boswell's Life of*, 1772

If vices are diseases, they cease to be vices, and theology in sending the drunkard or the gambler to the physician, relinquishes its last connection with reality: the ethical task.
—Fritz Kunkel, *In Search of Maturity*, 1943

Sensuality is the vice of young men and of old nations.
—W.E.H. Lecky, *History of European Morals*, 1869

When our vices quit us we flatter ourselves with the belief that it is we who quit them.
—La Rochefoucauld, *Maxims*, 1665

No man is discerned to be vicious as soon as he is so, and vices have their infancy and their childhood, and it cannot be expected that in a child's age should be the vice of a man.
—Jeremy Taylor, *Sermons*, 1651

VIRTUE

Reverence for superiors, respect for equals, regard for inferiors—these form the supreme trinity of virtues.
—F. Adler, *Creed and Deed*, 1877

Virtue, like art, constantly deals with what is hard to do, and the harder the task the better success.
—Aristotle, *The Nicomachean Ethics*, c. 340 B.C.

As to virtue leading us to a happy life, I hold virtue to be nothing else than perfect love of God.
—St. Augustine, *The Morals of the Catholic Church*, 388

Virtue is like a rich stone—best plain set.
—Francis Bacon, *Essays*, 1597

A man's virtue is in his behavior in the face of his destiny.
—Lyman Bryson, *Perspectives on a Troubled Decade*, 1950

No beauty leaves such an impression, strikes so deep, or links the souls of men closer than virtue.
—Robert Burton, *Anatomy of Melancholy*, II, 1621

Virtue ennobles the blood.
—Miguel de Cervantes, *Don Quixote*, 1605

In nothing is the uniformity of human nature more conspicuous than in its respect for virtue.
—Cicero, *The Laws*, 52 B.C.

We do not say as the Stoics do impiously that virtue in man and in God is the same.
—St. Clement of Alexandria, *Miscellanies*, c. 200

The determined scholar and the man of virtue will not seek to live at the expense of injuring their virtue. They will even sacrifice their lives to preserve their virtue complete.
—Confucius, *Analects of*, c. 5th century

Sweeter than the perfume of sandalwood or of the lotus-flower is the perfume of virtue.
—*Dhammapada*, c. 5th century B.C.

There are virtues which become crimes by exaggeration.
—Alexandre Dumas, *The Count of Monte Cristo*, 1844

True virtue . . . is that consent, propensity, and union of heart to being in general, which is immediately exercised in a general good-will.
—Jonathan Edwards, *The Nature of True Virtue*, 1758

The less a man thinks or knows about his virtue the better we like him.
—Ralph Waldo Emerson, "Spiritual Laws," in *Essays* (1st series), 1841

To be proud of virtue is to poison yourself with the antidote.
—Benjamin Franklin, *Poor Richard's Almanac*, 1758

Moderation is the silken-string running through the pearl-chain of all virtues.
—Thomas Fuller, *The Holy State and the Profane State*, 1642

The first step to Virtue, is to love Virtue in another man.
—Thomas Fuller, *Gnomologia*, 1732

He who will warrant his virtue in every possible situation is
either an impostor or a fool.
—C.A. Helvetius, *De l'Esprit*, 1758

For growth in virtue the important thing is to be silent
and work.
—St. John of the Cross (1542–91), *Maxims*, 295

To bring forth and preserve, to produce without possessing,
to act without hope of reward, and to expand without waste,
this is the supreme virtue.
—Lao-tzu, *Tao Te Ching*, c. 500 B.C.

The highest proof of virtue is to possess boundless power
without using it.
—Thomas Babington Macaulay, *Review of Aitkin's Life of Addison*, 1843

There are no national virtues. We are alone, each one of us.
If we are good, the virtues of others will not make us better.
We cannot borrow morals.
—Aubrey Menen, *Dead Man in the Silver Market*, 1953

I cannot praise a fugitive and cloistered virtue, unexercised
and unbreathed, that never sallies out and sees her adversary.
—John Milton, *Areopagitica*, 1644

If everyone were clothed with integrity, if every heart were
just, frank, kindly, the other virtues would be well-nigh useless, since their chief purpose is to make us bear with patience the injustice of our fellows.
—Molière, *Misanthrope*, 1666

Now of all the benefits of virtue, the contempt of death is
the chiefest.
—Michel de Montaigne, *Essays*, 1580

There is a strange tendency in men and women to lay claim
to the more exalted Christian virtues without having acquired the basic ones.
—John Middleton Murry, *Not as the Scribes*, 1959

The power of a man's virtue should not be measured by his
special efforts, but by his ordinary doing.
—Blaise Pascal, *Pensées*, 1670

Virtue is the art of the whole life.
—Philo, *Allegorical Interpretation*, c. A.D. 10

Virtue is a kind of health, beauty and habit of the soul.
—Plato, *The Republic*, 270 B.C.

He who dies for virtue's sake does not perish.
—Plautus, *Caetivi*, 200 B.C.

Where there is no temptation, there can be little claim to virtue.
—William H. Prescott, *The Conquest of Peru*, 1847

As virtue is the business of all men, the first principles of it are written in their hearts in characters so legible that no man can pretend ignorance of them.
—Thomas Reid, *The Works of*, 1863

Only virtue can compel Heaven, and there is no distance to which it cannot reach.
—*Shu Ching*, c. 490 B.C.

Those are far astray from a true estimate of virtue who expect for their virtue, as if it were the greatest slavery, that God will adorn them with the greatest rewards.
—Baruch Spinoza, *Ethics*, II, 1677

A slight failing in one virtue is enough to put all the others to sleep.
—St. Teresa of Avila, in *Life*, 1565

All that unites with the universal is virtue. All that separates is sin.
—Swami Vivekananda (1863–1902), *Works of*

A man who is virtuous and a coward has no marketable virtue about him.
—Woodrow Wilson, address, October 1914

VISION

But is it with man's Soul as it is with Nature; the beginning of Creation is—Light. Till the eye have vision, the whole members are in bonds.
—Thomas Carlyle, *Sartor Resartus*, 1836

Some may be color-blind, but others see the bright hues of sunrise. Some may have no religious sense, but others live and move and have their being in the transcendent glory of god.
—William Cecil Dampier, *A History of Science*, 1942

Behind every civilization there is a vision.
—Christopher Dawson, *Dynamics of World History*, 1957

The astonishing thing about the human being is not so much his intellect and bodily structure, profoundly mysterious as they are. The astonishing and least comprehensible thing about him is his range of vision; his gaze into the infinite distance; his lonely passion for ideas and ideals.
—W. MacNeile Dixon, *The Human Situation*, 1937

The high, contemplative, all-commanding vision, the sense of Right and Wrong, is alike in all. Its attributes are self-existence, eternity, intuition and command. It is the mind of the mind.
—Ralph Waldo Emerson, in *North American Review*, April 1866

Progress will be carried forward by a series of dazzling visions.
—Victor Hugo, *William Shakespeare*, 1864

The vision splendid of immortality which uplifted and transfigured the first Christians . . . has grown sadly intermittent in our grey secularized lives.
—D.G.M. Jackson, in *Advocate* (Melbourne, Australia), November 3, 1949

Methinks we have hugely mistaken this matter of Life and Death. Methinks that what they call my shadow here on earth is my true substance. Methinks that in looking at things spiritual, we are too much like oysters observing the sun through the water, and thinking that thick water the thinnest of air.
—Herman Melville, *Moby Dick*, 1851

A vision is to be esteemed the more noble the more intellectual it is, the more it is stripped of all image and approaches the state of pure contemplation.
—Henry Suso (c. 1295–1365), *Leben*. cap. liv.

Vision looks inward and becomes duty. Vision looks outward and becomes aspiration. Vision looks upward and becomes faith.
—Stephen S. Wise (1847–1949), *Sermons and Addresses*

War

A great war always creates more scoundrels than it kills.

—Anonymous

Peace should be the object of your desire; war should be waged only as a necessity, and waged only that God may by it deliver men from the necessity and preserve them in peace.

—St. Augustine, *To Publicola*, 398

The point was that there were people who could destroy mankind and that they were foolish and arrogant, crazy, and must be begged not to do it. Let the enemies of life step down. Let each man now examine his heart. Without a great change of heart, I would not trust myself in a position of authority. Do I love mankind? Enough to spare it, if I should be in a position to blow it to hell? Now let us all dress in our shrouds and walk on Washington and Moscow. Let us lie down, men, women, and children, and cry, "Let life continue —we may not deserve it, but let it continue."

—Saul Bellow, *Herzog*, 1964

Always look out, my young friend, when the theologians start talking about a just war. It is such a comprehensive and reasonable phrase that it really ought to be prohibited.

—Heinrich Böll, *Letter to a Young Catholic*, 1958

We believe that the cause for which our country is standing in this war is directly related to those great truths for which the Church stands.

—Arthur Judson Brown, quoted in *President Wilson and the Moral Aims of the War*, 1917

What millions died—that Caesar might be great.

—Thomas Campbell, *The Pleasures of Hope*, 1799

Under the sky is no uglier spectacle than two men with clenched teeth, and hellfire eyes, hacking one another's flesh; converting precious living bodies, and priceless living souls, into nameless masses of putrescence, useful only for turnip-manure.

—Thomas Carlyle, *Past and Present*, 1843

If war is the collective sin they say it is, let us then collectively quit participating in the sin.
—Christian Century, January 31, 1924

We often hear it said: "If God existed there would be no wars." But it would be truer to say: If God's laws were observed there would be no wars.
—Yves Congar, *God, Man and the Universe*, 1950

The source of peace is within us; so also the source of war. And the real enemy is within us, and not outside. The source of war is not the existence of nuclear weapons or other arms. It is the minds of human beings who decide to push the button and to use those arms out of hatred, anger or greed.
—Dalai Lama, speech, Costa Rica, in *The Wall Street Journal*, June 17, 1989

We must be at war with evil, but at peace with men.
—J.E.E. Dalberg-Acton, (Lord Acton), address, 1877

If we will not be peaceable, let us then at least be honest, and acknowledge that we continue to slaughter one another, not because Christianity permits it, but because we reject her laws.
—Jonathan Daymond, *Essay on War*, 1823

The occasions to which the concept of the just war can be rightly applied have become highly restricted. A war to "defend the victims of wanton aggression" where the demands of justice join the demands of order, is today the clearer case of a just war. . . . The concept of a just war does not provide moral justification for initiating a war of incalculable consequences to end such oppression.
—Angus Dun and Reinhold Niebuhr, in *Christianity and Crisis*, June 13, 1955

The real moral line between what may be done and what may not be done by the Christian lies not in the realm of distinction between weapons but in the realm of the motives for using and the consequences of using all kinds of weapons.
—Dun Commission, in *Christianity and Crisis*, December 11, 1950

The ancient theory of the just war breaks down when victory is impossible, when the weapons are so undiscriminating as to destroy both sides.
—Editorial, in *Christian Century*, August 3, 1960

Might not the human and environmental damage, and the assaults to the spirit each and every war trails in its wake, blight any peace? The ends may be justified—restitutive response to aggression—but the means, the *jus in bello*, may be unjust or unjustifiable, even if pains are taken to avoid direct targeting of civilians.
—Jean Bethke Elshtain, "Just War and American Politics," in *Christian Century*, January 15, 1992

War is so cruel a business that it befits beasts and not men . . . so pestilential that it brings with it general blight upon morals, so iniquitous that it is usually conducted by the worst bandits, so impious that it has no accord with Christ.
—Desiderius Erasmus, *The Praise of Folly*, 1511

We shall better overcome the Turks by the piety of our lives than by arms; the empire of Christianity will thus be defended by the same means by which it was originally established.
—Desiderius Erasmus, *Education of a Christian Prince*, 1516

The blood of a nation ought never to be shed except for its own preservation in the utmost extremity.
—François Fénelon, *Telemachus*, 1699

Every war of the future will be a war of religion, for no country will go to war till it can give its cause the color of a Crusade and so secure for its maintenance absolute loyalty of a heroic quality in the whole population.
—W.R. Forrester, *Christian Vocation*, 1951

War is the greatest of all the awful and complex moral situations of the world—second only to the final judgment day. . . . It is a moral pestilence. It is wrong on both sides.
—P.T. Forsyth, *The Christian Ethic of War*, 1916

There never was a good war or a bad peace.
—Benjamin Franklin, letter to Josiah Quincy, September 11, 1773

A soldier is a man whose business it is to kill those who never offended him, and who are the innocent martyrs of other men's iniquities. Whatever may become of the abstract question of the justifiableness of war, it seems impossible that the soldier should not be a depraved and unnatural thing.
—William Godwin, *The Enquirer*, 1797

We shall never stop war, whatever machinery we may devise, until we have learned to think always, with a sort of desperate urgency and an utter self-identification, of single human beings.
—Victor Gollancz, *From Darkness to Light*, 1956

We have one foot in genesis and the other in apocalypse, and annihilation is always one immediate option.
—Michael Harrington, *Toward a Democratic Left*, 1968

Proclaim this among the nations: Prepare war, stir up the mighty men. Let all the men of war draw near, let them come up. Beat your plowshares into swords, and your pruning hooks into spears; let the weak say, "I am a warrior."
—*Holy Bible*, Joel 3:9-10

What we need to discover in the social realm is the moral equivalent of war: something heroic that will speak to men as universally as war does, and yet will be compatible with their spiritual selves as war has proved itself to be incompatible.
—William James, *The Varieties of Religious Experience*, 1902

War should belong to the tragic past, to history; it should find no place on humanity's agenda for the future.
—Pope John Paul II, homily at Coventry Cathedral, 1982

Fight for the cause of God against those that fight against you: but commit not the injustice of attacking them first. . . . Kill them whenever ye shall find them and eject them from whatever place they have ejected you.
—*Koran*, c. 625

Where armies have been quartered brambles and thorns grow. . . . He who takes delight in the slaughter of men cannot have his will done in the world.
—Lao-tzu, *Tao Te Ching*, 5th century

What a cruel thing is war: to separate and destroy families and friends; and mar the purest joys and happiness God has granted us in this world: to fill our hearts with hatred instead of love for our neighbors, and to devastate the fair face of this beautiful world.
—Robert E. Lee, letter to his wife, December 25, 1862

Who can reflect on the sacredness of human life in view of its eternal destinies, without coming to the conclusion that war, with its attendants, hatred, destruction and slaughter, is incompatible with the high dictates of religion.
—L. Levi, *International Law*, 1888

War is the greatest plague that can afflict humanity; it destroys religion, it destroys states, it destroys families. Any scourge is preferable.
—Martin Luther (1483–1546), *Table-Talk*

If the opposing sides are Christian, they share the sin of caricaturing their Faith; if the one side is Christian, and the other not, Christians sin gravely if they are the aggressors.
—C.C. Martindale, *The Catholic Bedside Book*, 1953

The one thing a belligerent state can never lawfully do is this: it may not directly intend to kill the innocent.
—Lawerence L. McReavy, in *Clergy Review*, February 1941

War can be justified only on the ground that it is a necessary means for keeping the peace.
—Désiré Joseph Mercier, *Voix de la Guerre*, 1937

The verbal Christian belief in the sanctity of life has not been affected by the impersonal barbarism of twentieth century war.
—C. Wright Mills, *The Causes of World War III*, 1958

Lo, Allah loveth those who battle for His cause . . . swear by Allah . . . that marching about, morning and evening, to fight for religion is better than the world and everything in it; and verily the standing of one of you in the line of battle is better than superrogatory prayers performed in your house for sixty years.
—Mohammed (570–632), in S. Lane-Poole, *Speeches and Table-Talk of Mohammed*

War is the collapse of the divine order which God is striving with man's co-operation to establish in the world.
—Charles Clayton Morrison, *The Christian and the War*, 1942

The world continues to sow wars and reap wretchedness. When wars threaten or come, we complain bitterly. But we live and think things that breed discontent, distrust and fear. . . . We violate, with abandon, many, if not all, of the laws of the Creator, and then call on the atomic bomb to save us from our own folly.
—Thomas E. Murray, address, December 4, 1956

The man who has renounced war has renounced a grand life.
—Friedrich Nietzsche, *The Twilight of the Idols*, 1889

In so far as we conquer the demons who stir up war and disturb peace, we perform better service for our ruler than they who bear the sword.
—Origen, *Against Celsus*, VIII, 246

It is true that if we can win the war by use of one means which will incidentally and without intending it mean the death of 100,000 civilians or of another which in the same way will kill one million civilians then we may not use the second and larger since the excess of evil is not required for the defense of our right.
—Wilfred Parsons, *Ethics of Atomic War*, 1947

Can anything be more ridiculous than that a man has a right to kill men because he dwells on the other side of the water, and because his prince has a quarrel with mine, although I have none with him?
—Blaise Pascal, *Pensées*, 1670

Peace cannot be limited to a mere absence of war, the result of an ever precarious balance of forces. No, peace is something built up day after day, in the pursuit of an order intended by God, which implies a more perfect form of justice among men and women.
—Pope Paul VI, *The Development of Peoples*, 1966

The powers of this world, founded upon force and forging ever more perfect weapons of death, will always dismiss Him as impossible.
—W.G. Peck, *The Divine Revolution*, 1927

How could you . . . not grieve at war and delight in peace, being children of one and the same Father?
—Philo, *Confusion of Languages*, c. A.D. 10

The theory of war as an apt and proportionate means of solving international conflicts is now out of date.
—Pope Pius XII, Christmas message, 1948

He that preaches war is the devil's chaplain.
—Proverb

When war begins, the Devil makes Hell bigger.
—Proverb

To be finally justified there should be some reasonable expectation that a war can produce more good than evil, or at least achieve a lesser evil than not resorting to arms would lead to.
—Paul Ramsey, *War and the Christian Conscience*, 1961

What red-blooded American could oppose so shining a concept as victory? It would be like standing up for sin against virtue.
—Matthew B. Ridgway, *The Korean War*, 1967

The wars of mankind are like children's fights—all meaningless, pitiless and contemptible.
—Jallaludin Rumi (1207–73), *Masnavi*

The first reason for all wars, and for the necessity of nation defense, is that the majority of persons, high and low, in all European nations, are Thieves, and, in their hearts, greedy of their neighbors's goods, lands, and fame.
—John Ruskin, *Fors Clavigera*, 1871

O war! thou son of Hell!
—William Shakespeare, *Henry VI, Part II*, c. 1591

I am tired and sick of war. Its glory is all moonshine. It is only those who have neither fired a shot nor heard the shrieks and groans of the wounded who cry aloud for blood, more vengeance, more desolation. War is hell.
—William T. Sherman, address, June 19, 1879, according to letter in *The National Tribune*, Washington, D.C., November 26, 1914

The arms race is based on an optimistic view of technology and a pessimistic view of man. It assumes there is no limit to the ingenuity of science and no limit to the deviltry of human beings.
—I.F. Stone, "Nixon and the Arms Race," in *The New York Review of Books*, March 27, 1969

There are two ways of avoiding war: one is to satisfy everyone's desire, the other, to content oneself with the good. The
former is not possible due to the limitations of the world and
therefore there remains this second alternative of contentment.
—Unto Tahtinen, *Non-Violence as an Ethical Principle*, 1964

An evil so atrocious, and so universal, a course so straight to
the abyss of nothingness, cannot be borne with unless it be
erected into an absolute in hearts poisoned with hatred.
—Gustave Thibon, *Études; Carmelitaines*, 1939

War and Christianity are incompatible; you cannot conquer
war by war; cast out Satan by Satan; or do the enormous evil
of war that good may come of it.
—Norman Thomas, letter, January 31, 1937

The grandeur of war lies in the utter annihilation of puny
man in the great conception of the State, and it brings out
the full magnificence of the sacrifice of fellow-countrymen for
one another.
—Heinrich von Treitschke, *Politics*, 1890

War is a continuation of policy by the use of different means.
—Karl Von Clausewitz, *Vom Krieg*, 1833

Eternal peace is a dream, and not even a beautiful one. War
is a part of God's world order. In it are developed the noblest
virtues of man: courage and abnegation, dutifulness and self-
sacrifice. Without war the world would sink into materialism.
—Helmuth Von Moltke, letter to J.K. Bluntschli, December 1880

The horrors of modern warfare, though ghastly beyond all
previous tragedies, are not the worst alternatives now confronting Christendom and Democracy.
—Edmund A. Walsh, address, July 27, 1952

Woe to us human beings of the 20th century, that we have
seen innocent children pay the price for the mistakes of
adults.
—Elie Wiesel, in *The New York Times*, May 22, 1987

War is only a sort of dramatic representation, a sort of dramatic symbol of a thousand forms of duty.
—Woodrow Wilson, speech, May 11, 1914

WEALTH

How great a judgment, O rich man, do you draw down upon yourself! The people go hungry, and you close your granaries; the people weep, and you turn your finger-ring about. Unhappy man, who has the power but not the will to save so many souls from death.

—St. Ambrose, *De Nabuthe*, 395

The character which results from wealth is that of a prosperous fool.

—Aristotle, *Rhetoric*, c. 322 B.C.

The people who believe most that our greatness and welfare are proved by our being very rich, and who must give their lives and thoughts to becoming rich, are just the very people whom we call Philistines.

—Matthew Arnold, *Culture and Anarchy*, 1869

As to worldly riches, if you do not possess them, let them not be sought after on earth by doing evil; and if you possess them, let them by good works be paid up in heaven.

—St. Augustine, *To Publicola*, 398

In this world it is not what we take up, but what we give up, that makes us rich.

—Henry Ward Beecher, *Life Thoughts*, 1858

Not a single outstanding teacher of moral wisdom has failed to warn that riches tend to isolate their owners, make them petty, vulnerable, a little ridiculous.

—Bernard Iddings Bell, *A Man Can Live*, 1947

However, if thou shouldst happen to possess such earthly riches, use them not according to thy pleasure, but according to the necessities of the time: in this way thou shalt use them as if using them not.

—St. Bernard, *De Consideratione*, 1150

The man who dies rich dies disgraced.

—Andrew Carnegie, 1889, in Dwight MacDonald, *The Ford Foundation*

Can you rise superior to your riches? Say so, and Christ does not draw you away from the possession of them.

—St. Clement of Alexandria (died c. 215), *The Rich Man's Salvation*

He does not see, poor wretch, that his life is but a gilded torture, that he is bound fast by his wealth, and that his money owns him rather than he owns it.
—St. Cyprian of Carthage, *The World and Its Vanities*, c. 250

Mammon is a serpent which twineth herself around the world. She devoureth him at last who waiteth upon her.
—Amar Das (c. 1565), in M.A. Macauliffe, *The Sikh Religion*

The great fault of modern democracy—a fault that is common to the capitalist and the socialist—is that it accepts economic wealth as the end of society and the standard of personal happiness.
—Christopher Dawson, *The Modern Dilemma*, 1932

Faith is wealth! Obedience is wealth! Modesty also is wealth! Hearing is wealth, and so is Charity! Wisdom is sevenfold riches.
—*Dhammapada*, c. 5th century B.C.

From the patristic period to the present, the Church has affirmed that misuse of the world's resources or appropriation of them by a minority of the world's population betrays the gift of creation since "whatever belongs to God belongs to all."
Economic Justice for All, Catholic Social Teaching and the U.S. Economy, Bishops' Pastoral Letter, 1986

But perhaps you are deceived by the fact that many who know not God possess wealth in abundance, are full of honors, and enjoy great authority. These unhappy men are uplifted the higher, that their fall may be greater.
—Marcus Minucius Felix, *Octavius*, 3rd century

It is not a crime to be rich, nor a virtue to be poor. . . . The sin lies in hoarding wealth and keeping it from circulating freely to all who need it.
—Charles Fillmore, *Prosperity*, 1940

If your riches are yours, why don't you take them with you to t'other world.
—Benjamin Franklin, *Poor Richard's Almanac*, 1758

Moderate Riches will carry you; if you have more, you must carry them.
—Thomas Fuller, *Gnomologia*, 1732

If our society continues at its present rate to become less livable as it becomes more affluent, we promise all to end up in sumptuous misery.

—John W. Gardner, *No Easy Victories*, 1968

It is impossible for the truly religious man to become rich if what constitutes wealth must in any sense be subtracted from others.

—Christian Gauss, *A Primer for Tomorrow*, 1934

Superior want of conscience . . . is often the determining quality which makes a millionaire out of one who otherwise might have been a poor man.

—Henry George, *Progress and Poverty*, 1879

He who has enough to satisfy his wants, and nevertheless ceaselessly labors to acquire riches, either in order to obtain a higher social position, or that subsequently he may have enough to live without labor, or that his sons may become men of wealth and importance—all such are incited by a damnable avarice, sensuality and pride.

—Henry of Langenstein (1325–97), *Tractutus Bipartibus de Contractibus*

How can true happiness proceed from wealth, which in its acquisition causes pain; in loss, affliction; in abundance, folly.

—*Hitopadesa*, 13th century

But those who desire to be rich fall into temptation, into a snare, into many senseless and hurtful desires that plunge men to ruin and destruction. For the love of money is the root of all evils.

—*Holy Bible*, I Timothy 6:9-10

It is easier for a camel to go through the eye of a needle than for a rich man to enter the kingdom of God.

—*Holy Bible*, Matthew 19:24

The gods only laugh when men pray to them for wealth.

—Japanese proverb

It is not a sin to have riches, but it is a sin to fix our hearts upon them.

—St. John Baptist de la Salle, *Les devoirs du chrétien*, 1710

The rich man is not one who is in possession of much, but one who gives much.
—St. John Chrysostom, *Homilies*, c. 388

The excessive hoarding of riches by some deprives the majority. . . . Thus, the very wealth that is accumulated generates poverty.
—Pope John Paul II, speech, Durango, Mexico, May 9, 1990

All the riches of the world and the glory of creation, compared with the wealth of god, are extreme and abject poverty.
—St. John of the Cross (1542–91), *The Ascent of Mount Carmel*

Riches ennoble a man's circumstances, but not himself.
—Immanuel Kant, *Lecture at Königsberg*, 1775

The hereafter never rises before the eyes of the careless child, deluded by the delusion of wealth. "This is the world," he thinks, "there is no other"—thus he falls again and again under my sway.
—*Katha Upanishad*, prior to 400 B.C., Death Speaking

We need to realize that money is not the ultimate power of the world. It is not money itself, but the *love* of money that is the root of all evil. If you let this love blot out courage, work, art, romance—then you are closing yourself into a narrower and narrower cage.
—Lewis Lapham, in *Publishers Weekly*, February 5, 1988

If wealth is to be valued because it gives leisure, clearly it would be a mistake to sacrifice leisure in the struggle for wealth.
—John Lubbock, *The Pleasures of Life*, 1887

Where wealth is, there are also all manner of sins; for through wealth comes pride, through pride dissension, through dissension wars, through wars, poverty, through poverty, great distress and misery. Therefore, they that are rich, must yield a strict and great account; for to whom much is given, of him will much be required.
—Martin Luther, (1483–1546) *Table-Talk*

The heart which haunts the treasure-house where the moth and rust corrupt, will be exposed to the same ravages as the treasure.
—George MacDonald, *Unspoken Sermons* (1st series), 1869

Riches are not from an abundance of worldly goods, but from a contented mind. It is difficult for a man laden with riches to climb the steep path that leadeth to bliss.

—Mohammed (7th century), *Sayings of,* Wisdom of the East Series

Wealth tends to corrupt the mind and to nourish its love of power, and to stimulate its oppression.

—Gouverneur Morris, speech, July 1788

There are two kinds of rich men: firstly, rich atheists, who, being rich, understand nothing of religion . . . secondly, the pious rich men, who, being rich, understand nothing of Christianism. So they profess it.

—Charles Péguy, *Basic Verities,* 1943

Wealth, which is constantly being augmented by social and economic progress, must be so distributed among the various individuals and classes of society that the common good of all . . . be thereby promoted.

—Pope Pius XI, *Quadragesimo Anno,* 1931

When you are young and impecunious, society conditions you to exchange time for money, and this is quite as it should be. Very few people are hurt by having to work for a living. But as you become more affluent, it somehow is very, very difficult to reverse that process and begin trading money for time.

—William H. Rehnquist, in *Time,* June 13, 1988

We need greater virtues to sustain good than evil fortune.

—La Rochefoucauld, *Maxims,* 1665

It is impossible to conclude, of any given mass of acquired wealth, merely by the fact of its existence, whether it signifies good or evil to the nation in the midst of which it exists.

—John Ruskin, *Unto This Last,* 1860

Rich and poor alike
Are bondsmen of the clay;
And they who most possess
Have most from Heaven to pray.

—Shaikh Saadi, *Gulistan,* c. 1265

Man is the only animal which esteems itself rich in proportion to the number and voracity of its parasites.

—George Bernard Shaw, *The Socialism of,* 1926

No one has the right to despise the rich until, like Our Lord, he has proven himself free from the passion to possess . . . and then he will not wish to despise any one.
—Fulton J. Sheen, *Way to Happiness*, 1953

Genuine Christianity teaches men not so much how to make and save riches as to how to get rid of them with the greatest possible advantage to their eternal salvation.
—Ignatius Smith, *Christ Today*, 1932

The wealthy don't go to church anymore; they go to a museum on Sunday afternoon. That's why we have magnificent museums being built instead of magnificent churches.
—John Hall Snower, quoted in Paul Wilkes, "The Episcopalians: A Church in Search of Itself," *The New York Times*, September 1, 1985

If Heaven had looked upon riches to be a valuable thing, it would not have given them to such a scoundrel.
—Jonathan Swift, *Letter to Miss Vanhomrigh*, August 12, 1720

Better is a beggar who is in the hand of God, than the rich who are safely housed in a comfortable dwelling.
—*The Teaching of Amen*, c. 1000 B.C.

No one goes to Hades with all his immense wealth.
—Theognis, *Maxims*, 6th century B.C.

Man ought to possess external things not as his own but as common, so that he is ready to communicate them to others in their need.
—St. Thomas Aquinas, *Summa Theologiae*, 1272

A man is rich in proportion to the number of things he can afford to let alone.
—Henry David Thoreau, *Walden*, 1854

Every degree of luxury hath some connection with evil.
—John Woolman, *Journal*, 1774

Wealth desired for its own sake obstructs the increase of virtue, and large possessions in the hands of selfish men have a bad tendency.
—John Woolman, *A Word of Remembrance and Caution to the Rich*, 1793

There are people it is necessary to consider as rich—one is he who is perfect in wisdom; the second whose body is healthy, and he lives fearlessly; the third, who is content with that which has come; the fourth, he whose destiny is a helper in virtue; the fifth, who is well-famed in the eyes of the sacred things; and by the tongues of the good; the sixth, whose trust is on this one pure, good religion of the Mazda-worshippers; and the seventh, whose wealth is from honesty.
—*Zend-Avesta*, c. 700 B.C.

WILL

No inferior thing depraves the will, but the will depraves itself by following inferior things inordinately.
—St. Augustine, *City of God*, XI.6, 426

It is astonishing how the act of placing our own will as far as possible in unison with the Will of God restores our tranquility.
—Arthur Christopher Benson, *From a College Window*, 1906

I know not in what wicked, yet wonderful way, the will, when turned towards evil by sin, imposes a constraint on itself; so that on the one hand such constraint, since it is voluntary, cannot avail to excuse the will, and, on the other hand, the will, being drawn away and allured, is unable to resist the constraint.
—St. Bernard of Clairvaux (1010–1153), *Serm. in Cant.*

The will, being inseparable from the nature of man, is not annihilated; but it is fettered by depraved and inordinate desires, so that it cannot aspire after anything that is good.
—John Calvin, *Institues*, I, 1536

No man is a creature of will. According to what his will is in this world, so will he be when he has departed this life.
—*Chandogya Upanishad*, prior to 400 B.C.

All things in the world appear plainly to be the most arbitrary that can be imagined . . . and plainly the product, not of necessity but will.
—Samuel Clarke, *Demonstrations*, 1706

As we had no part of our will on our entrance into this life, we should not presume to any on our leaving it, but soberly learn to will which He wills.
—William Drummond, *The Cypress Grove*, 1673

The will is that by which the mind chooses anything.
—Jonathan Edwards, *The Freedom of the Will*, 1754

Out of disbelief [in God] we have impudently assumed that all of life is now subject to our own will. And the disasters that have come from willing what cannot be willed have not at all brought us to some modesty about our presumptions.
—Leslie Farber, in Melvin Maddocks, "Can Therapists Be Running Out of Talk?" in *The Christian Science Monitor*, May 14, 1986

In this world will alone, as it lies concealed from mortal eyes in the secret obscurities of the soul, is the first link in a chain of consequences that stretches through the whole invisible realm of spirit.
—J.G. Fichte (1762–1814), *The Vocation of Man*

Our wills are the slaves of the accumulated influence of our interior companionships. What we can do is to get new mental images.
—Harry Emerson Fosdick, *The Hope of the World*, 1933

The doctrine that the will alone is the way to power is a most woe-begone theory for the relief to the morally sick.
—J.A. Hadfield, *The Psychology of Power*, 1923

The will of the world is never the will of God.
—William Hamilton, *Interpretation*, October 1957

The will is a faculty to choose *that only* which reason independent of inclination recognizes as practically necessary, i.e. as good . . . a faculty of determining oneself to action *in accordance with the conception of certain laws.*
—Immanuel Kant, *Metaphysics of Ethics*, 1785

Dante said "In God's will lies our peace," but we better first make sure that it is God's will we are obeying, and not that of a frail human being, his whim or prejudice, or our own fear.
—George Lawton, *Aging Successfully*, 1946

Will signifies nothing but the power, or ability, to prefer or choose.
—John Locke, *Essay Concerning Human Understanding*, 1690

The human will is like a beast of burden. If God mounts it, it wishes and goes as God wills; if Satan mounts it, it wishes and goes as Satan wills. Nor can it choose its rider. . . . The riders contend for its possession.
—Martin Luther, *De Servo Arbitrio*, 1525

Our wills are not ours to be crushed and broken; they are ours to be trained and strengthened.
—Hamilton Wright Mabie, *The Life of the Spirit*, 1898

Man's will hath some liberty to work a civil righteousness, and to choose such things as reason can reach into; but it hath no power to work the righteousness of God.
—Philip Melanchthon, *Augsburg Confession*, 1530

Will is the child of desire, and passes out of the dominion of its parent only to come under that of habit.
—John Stuart Mill, *Utilitarianism*, 1863

By *will*, or rational appetite in general, we mean the faculty of inclining towards or striving after some object defined simply as the *capacity of self-determination*.
—John A. O'Brien, *Is the Will Free?*, 1946

Will is one of the principal organs of belief, not that it forms belief, but because things are true or false according to the side on which we look at them.
—Blaise Pascal, *Pensées*, 1670

The determinations of what we call the will are, in fact, nothing more than a particular case of the general doctrine of association of ideas, and therefore a perfectly mechanical thing.
—Joseph Priestley, *The Doctrine of Philosophical Necessity*, 1778

In the power of willing . . . nothing is to be found but acts which are purely spiritual and wholly inexplicable by the laws of mechanism.
—Jean Jacques Rousseau, *Discourse on Inequality*, 1755

The will is the only permanent and unchangeable element in the mind . . . it is the will which . . . gives unity to consciousness and holds together all its ideas and thoughts, accompanying them like a continuous harmony.
—Arthur Schopenhauer, *The World as Will and Idea*, II, 1818

A simple homogeneous mental state, forming the link between feeling and action, and not admitting of subdivisions.
—Herbert Spencer, *Essays: Political, Scientific, and Speculative*, 1858–74

As his will cannot be determined but by a motive which is
not in his own power, it follows that he is never the master of
the determination of his own peculiar will.
—Paul Henri Thiry, Baron d'Holbach, *The System of Nature*, 1770

WISDOM

Wisdom consists in the highest use of the intellect for the
discernment of the largest moral interest of humanity. It is
the most perfect willingness to do the right combined with
the utmost attainable knowledge of what is right. . . . Wisdom consists in working for the better from the love of
the best.
—Felix Adler, *Life and Destiny*, 1913

The greatest good is wisdom.
—St. Augustine, *Soliloquies*, 387

Wisdom is the tears of experience, the bridge of experience
and imagination over time. It is the listening heart, the
melancholy sigh, the distillation of despair to provide a realistic, if often despondent, view of the world.
—Daniel Bell, address, Brandeis University commencement,
in *The New York Times*, May 27, 1991

Wisdom is the highest virtue, and it has in it four other
virtues; of which one is prudence, another temperance, the
third fortitude, the fourth justice.
—Boethius, *Consolations of Philosophy*, c. 523

Should it be said that the Greeks discovered philosophy by
human wisdom. I reply that I find the Scriptures declare all
wisdom to be a divine gift.
—St. Clement of Rome, *Stromateis*, 200

The fear of God is not the beginning of wisdom. The fear of
God is the death of wisdom. Skepticism and doubt lead to
study and investigation, and investigation is the beginning of
wisdom.
—Clarence Darrow, speech, Columbus, Ohio, 1929

By thoughtfulness, by restraint and self-control, the wise man may make for himself an island which no flood can overwhelm.

—*Dhammapada*, c. 5th century B.C.

All wisdom may be reduced to two words—wait and hope.

—Alexandre Dumas, *The Count of Monte Cristo*, 1844

When God lights the soul with wisdom, it floods the faculties, and that man knows more than ever could be taught him.

—Meister Eckhart (1260?–1327?), R.B. Blakney, in *Meister Eckhart*

Wisdom rises upon the Ruins of Folly.

—Thomas Fuller, *Gnomologia*, 1732

I heartily scorn that kind of wisdom that is attained only through cooling off or lassitude.

—André Gide, *Journal*, January 25, 1931

Wisdom is that olive that springeth from the heart, bloometh on the tongue, and beareth fruit in the actions.

—Elizabeth Grymestom, *Miscellanea—Meditations*, 1604

A man of truest wisdom will resign his wealth, and e'en his life in a good cause.

—*Hitopadesa*, 13th century

No mention shall be made of coral or of crystal; the price of wisdom is above pearls.

—*Holy Bible*, Job 28:18

The tents of robbers are at peace, and those who provoke God are secure, who bring their God in their hand. But ask now the beasts, and they will teach you; the birds of the air, and they will tell you; or the plants of the earth, and they will teach you; and the fish of the sea will declare to you.

—*Holy Bible*, Job 12:6-8

[Wisdom is] pursuing the best ends by the best means.

—Francis Hutcheson, *Inquiry Concerning the Origin of Our Ideas of Beauty and Virtue*, 1725

All the wisdom in the world and all human cleverness compared with the infinite wisdom of God is sheer and extreme ignorance.

—St. John of the Cross (1542–91), *The Ascent of Mount Carmel*

Tragedy is a tool for the living to gain wisdom, not a guide by which to live.

—Robert F. Kennedy, speech, March 18, 1968

[Wisdom is] the science of happiness or of the means of attaining the lasting contentment which consists in the continual achievement of a greater perfection or at least in variations of the same degree of perfection.

—G.W. von Leibniz, *Discourses on Metaphysics and Monadology*, 1714

All the wisdom of the world is childish foolishness in comparison with the acknowledgment of Jesus Christ.

—Martin Luther (1483–1546), *Table-Talk*

The foundation and pillar of wisdom is to recognize that there is an original Being . . . and that all . . . exist only through the reality of His being.

—Maimonides, *Yad: Yesode HaTorah*, 1180

We maintain that human wisdom is a means of education for the soul, divine wisdom being the ultimate end.

—Origen, *Contra Celsus*, c. 230

Watch this only, brethren, that no one of you be found only not speaking or meditating wisdom, but even hating and opposing those who pursue study of wisdom.

—Origen (185–254), *Homilies on Psalm XXVI*

The virtue of wisdom more than anything else contains a divine element which always remains.

—Plato, *The Republic*, c. 370 B.C.

Wisdom without fear of God is despicable.

—*Talmud: Tosefa Derek Eretz*, c. 500

Of all human pursuits the pursuit of wisdom is the most perfect, the most sublime, the most profitable, the most delightful.

—St. Thomas Aquinas, *Summa contra Gentiles*, c.1260

A person without wisdom mistakes what is false for what is true, and what is true for what is false, while a wise person knows what is true and what is false and is not confused about such things.

—Tripitaka Master Hua, "Contemplating the Oneness of Everything," in *Vajra Bodhi Sea*, March 1992

Pure wisdom always directs itself towards God; the purest wisdom is knowledge of God.

—Lew Wallace, *Ben Hur*, 1880

When a man is on the point of drowning, all he cares for is his life. But as soon as he gets ashore, he asks "Where is my umbrella?" Wisdom, in life, consists in not asking for the umbrella.

—John Wu, *Beyond East and West*, 1951

WONDER

Men go forth to wonder at the height of mountains, the huge waves of the sea, the broad flow of rivers, the extent of the ocean, the course of the stars—and forget to wonder at themselves.

—St. Augustine, *Confessions*, X15, 397

We carry within us the wonders we seek without us.

—Thomas Browne, *Religio Medici*, 1635

The man who cannot wonder, who does not habitually wonder (and worship), were he President of the innumerable Royal Societies . . . is but a Pair of Spectacles behind which there is no Eye.

—Thomas Carlyle, *Sartor Resartus*, 1836

In wonder all philosophy began; in wonder it ends; and admiration fills up the interspace. But the first wonder is the offspring of ignorance: the last is the parent of adoration.

—Samuel Taylor Coleridge, *Aids to Reflection*, 1825

Wonder is the attitude of reverence for the infinite values and meaning over God's purpose and patience in it all.

—George Walter Fiske, *The Recovery of Worship*, 1931

The material world, indeed, is infinitely more wonderful than any human contrivance, but wonder is not religion, or we should be worshipping railroads.

—John Henry Newman, *Parochial and Plain Sermons*, 1843

WORK

All action must be done in a more and more Godward and finally a God-possessed consciousness; our work must be a sacrifice to the Divine.

—Aurobindo, *Synthesis of Yoga*, 1950

Though the rich have no outward want to urge them, they have as great a necessity to obey God. . . . God has strictly commanded work to all.
—Richard Baxter, *Christian Directory*, I, ch. X, 1673

And first of all, whatever good work you begin to do, beg of Him with most earnest prayer to perfect it.
—St. Benedict, *Rule of*, c. 530

He who labors as he prays lifts his heart to God with his hands.
—St. Bernard of Clairvaux, *Ad Sororem*, c. 1130

When you have learned to believe in God's purpose for you as an individual, you are immediately lifted out of the mass and become significant and meaningful in the eyes of God and of man.
—John Sutherland Bonnell, *What Are You Living For?*, 1950

If you do your work with complete faithfulness . . . you are making as genuine a contribution to the substance of the universal good as is the most brilliant worker whom the world contains.
—Phillips Brooks, *Perennials*, 1898

The Author of our nature has written it strongly in that nature, and has promulgated the same law in His written word; that man shall eat his bread by his labor; and I am persuaded that no man, and no combination of men, can, without great impiety, undertake to say that he *shall not* do so—that they have no sort of right either to prevent the labor or to withhold the bread.
—Edmund Burke, *Second Letter to Gentlemen in Bristol*, 1777

The modern world is so out of sympathy with the language and atmosphere of religion that it is hard for most people to recognize religion in work.
—Richard C. Cabot, *What Men Live By*, 1914

Each individual has his own kind of living assigned to him by the Lord as a sort of sentry post so that he may not heedlessly wander throughout life.
—John Calvin, *Institutes*, III, 1536

We should accustom ourselves to think of our position and work as sacred and well-pleasing to God, not on account of the position and work, but on account of the word faith from which the obedience and work flow.

—John Calvin, *Institutes*, III, 1536

There is dignity in work only when it is work freely accepted.

—Albert Camus, *Notebooks*, 1935–42

Blessed is he who has found his work; let him ask no other blessedness. He has a work, a life purpose.

—Thomas Carlyle, *Past and Present*, 1843

The Buddhist point of view takes the function of work to be at least three-fold: to give a man a chance to utilise and develop his faculties; to enable him to overcome his ego-centredness by joining with other people in a common task; and to bring forth the goods and services needed for a becoming existence.

—John Carmody, *Holistic Spirituality*, 1983

Each of us has his gift. Let us not imagine that we are disinherited by our heavenly Father, any one of us. Let us be ourselves, as God made us, then we shall be something good and useful.

—James Freeman Clarke, *Self-Culture*, 1881

All societies in history have evolved some form of division of labor. I doubt that any future society can or should avoid such division entirely. But in our society specialization is running amok. The sickness it induces—mastery of the minutiae and neglect of the momentous—now imperils the existence of our species.

—Harvey Cox, *The Seduction of the Spirit*, 1973

The inner ear of each man's soul hears the voice of Life, "Find your work, and do it!" Only by obedience to this command can he find peace.

—Frank Crane, *The Looking Glass*, 1917

Within this thin wafer of bread is caught up symbolically the labor of plow and of sowing, of harvest and threshing, of milling, of packing, of transportation, of financing, of selling and packaging. Man's industrial life is all there.

—Wilford O. Cross, *Prologue to Ethics*, 1963

Labor we all earnestly in the wages of some lawful calling,
that we may have our portion of this world by good means.
—John Donne, *Sermons*, 1640

The sum of wisdom is, that the time is never lost that is devoted to work.
—Ralph Waldo Emerson, *Success*, 1844

There is nothing in the whole world so dangerous as a sense
of vocation without a belief in God.
—W.R. Forrester, *Christian Vocation*, 1951

Labor, as well as fasting, serves to mortify and subdue the
flesh. Provided the labor you undertake contributes to the
glory of God and your own welfare, I would prefer that you
should suffer the pain of labor rather than that of fasting.
—St. Francis de Sales, *Introduction to the Devout Life*, 1609

The merits of each one depends not directly on what sort of
soil God has given him to cultivate, but on what use he
makes of what God has given.
—Edward F. Garesche, *Ever Timely Thoughts*, 1925

There is no kind of serviceable labor to increase human hap-
piness and human welfare which may not rightly be called a
Christian vocation.
—Georgia Harkness, *The Modern Rival of Christian Faith*, 1953

Sweet is the sleep of a laborer, whether he eat little or much;
but the surfeit of the rich will not let him sleep.
—*Holy Bible*, Ecclesiastes 5:12

Six days shall work be done, but on the seventh day you
shall have a holy Sabbath of solemn rest to the Lord; whoever does any work on it shall be put to death.
—*Holy Bible*, Exodus 35:2

What does man gain by all the toil at which he toils under
the sun? A generation goes, and a generation comes, but the
earth remains for ever.
—*Holy Bible*, Ecclesiastes 1:3-4

Those who labor on the earth are the chosen people of God, if ever he had a chosen people, whose breasts he has made his peculiar deposit for substantial and genuine virtue. It is the focus in which he keeps alive that sacred fire, which otherwise might escape from the face of the earth.
—Thomas Jefferson (1743–1826), *Works*, Washington ed., VIII, 405

If Christians are also joined in mind and heart with the most Holy Redeemer, when they apply themselves to temporal affairs, their work in a way is a continuation of the labor of Jesus Christ himself, drawing from it strength and redemptive power.
—Pope John XXIII, *Matter et Magistra*, May 15, 1961

Do without attachment the work you have to do; for a man who does his work without attachment attains the Supreme Goal verily. By action alone men like Janaka attained perfection.
—Sri Krishna, in the *Bhagavad-Gita*, c. 200 B.C.

Thank God every morning when you get up that you have something to do that day which must be done, whether you like it or not.
—James Russell Lowell (1819–91), *Letters*

The only work of which we are absolute masters and over which we have sovereign power, the only one that we can dominate, encompass in a glance, and organize, concerns our own heart.
—François Mauriac, *Cain, Where Is Your Brother?*, 1962

Does God work? This is a crucial question, for the denigration of work and the degradation of the worker in both antiquity and modernity are supported by the view that the gods do not have to work. That is what makes them gods.
—M. Douglas Meeks, *God the Economist*, 1989

Whatsoever kind the works may be: eating, drinking, working with the hand, teaching, I add that even they are plainly sins.
—Philip Melanchton, *Common Topics*, 1521

When God foreclosed on Eden, he condemned Adam and Eve to go to work. Work has never recovered from that humiliation.
—Lance Morrow, "What Is the Point of Working?" in *Fishing in the Tiber*, 1988

Without a personal sense of vocation gained in the solitary struggles of the soul with its Maker and Redeemer the minister will always be deficient.
—H. Richard Niebuhr, *The Purpose of the Church and Its Ministry*, 1956

Manual labor is a blessing and a dignity. . . . If it be glorious as the world fancies to repel a human foe, how much more is he to be honored who stands up when Want comes upon us, like an armed man, and puts him to rout!
—Theodore Parker, *Thoughts on Labor*, 1841

Any legitimate and beneficial State intervention in the field of work must be such as to preserve and respect its personal character, both in principle and within the limits of possibility, as regards execution.
—Pope Pius XII, broadcast, June 1, 1941

One who works conscientiously, not expecting any reward other than virtue, seems to work far more virtuously and more ingenuously than he who expects some reward beyond virtue.
—Pietro Pomponazzi, *On the Immortality of the Soul*, 1516

Every vocation is ultimately founded on the salutary selfishness by which an individual, despite the whole world, seeks to save his own immortal soul.
— M. Raymonds, *The Man Who Got Even With God*, 1941

A vocation necessarily creates a tension, a crisis, a tug-of-war in the soul. . . . "Fearful lest having Him, one might have naught else besides." He who takes us by the finger may seize the hand.
—Fulton J. Sheen, in *Our Sunday Visitor*, March 11, 1962

Unlike the prodigal son, people today do not purposely seek out strange and alien places where, devoid of ties and relationships, they tend the swine of others. It is the structures of violence that force them to do it. The alienation that the Bible calls death is built into life at the most important point—at our work.
—Dorothee Soelle, *Death by Bread Alone*, 1978

The Great Governour of the world hath appointed to every man his proper post and province, and let him be never so active out of his sphere, he will be at a great loss, if he do not keep his own vineyard and mind his own business.
—Richard Steele, *The Tradesman's Calling*, 1684

No man can complain that his calling takes him off from religion; his calling itself, and his very worldly employment in honest trades and offices, is a serving of God.
—Jeremy Taylor, *Holy Living*, 1650

Where our work is, there let our joy be.
—Tertullian, *Women's Dress*, c. 220

Be not proud of good work; for God's judgments are thiswise and man's otherwise; for ofttimes what pleaseth man displeaseth God.
—Thomas à Kempis, *Imitation of Christ*, 1441

If you would avoid uncleanness, and all the sins, work earnestly, though it be at cleaning a stable.
—Henry David Thoreau, *Walden*, 1854

The spiritual driving force transmitted from religion to work has gathered such momentum . . . that work has eventually become an end in itself instead of continuing to be . . . an incidental means of spiritual edification.
—A.J. Toynbee, *Man at Work in God's World*, 1955

The basic sense of vocation which once gave meaning and direction to all walks of life has been the casualty of collectivism, existentialism and sexualism, three of the moods induced by widespread practical atheism.
—John J. Wright, address, Rome, March 11, 1962

WORLD

Beware of this world with all its wariness; for it is like to a snake, smooth to the touch, but its venom is deadly.
—Al-Hasan Al-Basri (died 728), in *Sufism*

All the great religions of the world supply, for those who can subscribe to their arguments and affirmations, a world-conception that has logical simplicity and serene majesty.
—Gordon W. Allport, *The Individual and His Religion*, 1950

The standing miracle of this visible world is little thought of, because always before us, yet, when we arouse ourselves to contemplate it, it is a greater miracle than the rarest and most unheard-of marvels.
—St. Augustine, *The City of God*, 426

The world will not perish just because we cannot do everything. God still has things under control.
—Hans Urs von Balthasar, *Prayer*, 1962

The World is a kingdom whereof God is the King . . . and absolute monarchy . . . by the title of Creation . . . God is the end as well as the beginning of the divine monarchy of the world.
—Richard Baxter, *A Holy Commonweatlh*, 1659

Our natural world is apparcntly in thc victorious grip of the inane for it is dominated by corruptibility and death, animosity and hatred, egoism and discord. Man is overwhelmed by the meaningless evil of the whole of life.
—Nicholas Berdyaev, *Freedom and Spirit*, 1944

This universe of things is a ladder whereby we may ascend to God, since among these things are God's footprints, some God's image, some corporeal, some spiritual, some temporal, some eternal.
—St. Bonaventure, *Journey of the Mind to God*, 1259

All is not right with the world, but with the grace of God we can in a measure recreate the world into something nobler and more beautiful.
—John Elof Boodin, *God and Creation*, 1934

God calls on us to become creators, to make the world new and in that sense to bring something into being which was not there before.
—John Elof Boodin, *God and Creation*, 1934

The created world is but a small parenthesis in eternity.
—Thomas Browne, *Christian Morals*, 1680

The world is not an inn, but a hospital, and a place, not to live, but to die in.
—Thomas Browne, *Religio Medici*, 1635

God has not made it necessary that the great majority of mankind should be heretics or infidels in order to take care of the earth, and leave us believers free to devote ourselves solely to ascetic exercises and the salvation of our souls.
—Orestes Brownson, in *Brownson's Quarterly*, July 1863

If heaven is our country, what is the earth but a place of exile? If the departure out of the world is but an entrance into life, what is the world but a sepulchre? What is a continuance in it but an absorption in death?
—John Calvin, *Institutes*, III, 1536

. . . as you get older, you realize that it is an absolute miracle that anything works at all in the world. Instead of seeing it, as you do when you are young, as a place which is basically rational with small areas of insanity, you see it quite the other way around; the whole place is a complete madhouse.
—John Cleese, in *Films & Filming*, October 1988

Come, look at this world, glittering like a royal chariot; the foolish are immersed in it, but the wise do not touch it.
—*Dhammapada*, c. 5th century B.C.

He who has gotten the whole world plus God has gotten no more than God by himself.
—Meister Eckhart (1260?–1327?), *Meister Eckhart*

There is consolation in the assurance that whatever becomes of this husk of a planet, the inner meaning of it, hope itself, God, man's ideal, continually progresses and develops.
—William Faulkner, speech accepting Nobel Prize, January 1951

A feeble compromise between God and world will satisfy neither. God will reject you, and the world will drag you falling into its snares.
—François Fénelon (1651–1715), *Spiritual Letters*

The partition of the world into a natural order overlaid by a supernatural order which keeps breaking through is to a well-instructed mind impossible.
—Harry Emerson Fosdick, *As I See Religion*, 1932

You fear to quit the medleys of the world, where vanity reigns, where avarice tarnishes the most beautiful virtues, whcrc infidelity holds dominion with the sway of a despot, where virtue is trampled under foot and vice carries off the prize of honor.
—St. Francis de Sales (1567–1622), *Consoling Thoughts of*

If we could look steadily at the world and see it as it is in the eyes of God many of our estimates would be amazingly changed.
—Edward F. Garesche, *The Things Immortal*, 1919

In the great body of the world the divine murmur finds as many veins whereby it may come at us as there are creatures over which the very divinity rules.
—St. Gregory the Great, *Book of Morals*, V, 584

If the church doesn't listen to the world, then the world will never listen to the church.
—Bernard Haring, in *The New York Times*, June 14, 1964

By equating God and the universe, we give back to the world what long ago was taken away. The world we live in, with our thoughts, passions, delights, and whatever stirs the mortal frame, must surely take on a deeper meaning. Songs are more than longitudinal sound vibrations, sunsets more than transverse electromagnetic oscillations, inspirations more than the discharge of neurons, all touched with a mystery that deepens, the more we contemplate and seek to understand.
—Edward Harrison, in *The Christian Science Monitor*, August 31, 1988

The world is what I share with others.
—Martin Heidegger, *Sein und Zeit*, 1927

The world would be consistent without God; it would also be consistent with God; whichever hypothesis a man adopts will fit experience equally well.
—W.E. Hocking, *The Meaning of God in Human Experience*, 1912

And God said, Let the waters under the heaven be gathered together unto one place, and let the dry land appear: and it was so. And God called the dry land Earth; and the gathering together of the waters called he Seas: and God saw that it was good.
—*Holy Bible*, Genesis 1:9-10

God, it is obvious, if He is to be an object worthy of our adoration must be kept unspotted from the World that adores Him.
—C.E.M. Joad, *Philosophical Aspects of Modern Science*, 1932

The world that is knowable and describable has taken on a greater interest and importance than the realm that is entered by faith and spiritual vision.
—Rufus M. Jones, *A Call to What Is Vital*, 1949

The world is a sum of appearance, and must have some
transcendent ground.

—Immanuel Kant, *Critique of Pure Reason*, 1781

The notion of the world's being a great machine, going on
without the interposition of God . . . is the notion of material
and fate . . . to exclude providence and God's government in
reality out of the world.

—G.W. von Leibniz, *A Collection of Papers Which Passed Between the late learned
Dr. Leibniz and Dr. Clarke*, 1717

Our roots are in the dark; the earth is our country. Why did
we look up for blessing—instead of around, and down? What
hope we have lies there. Not in the sky full of orbiting spy-
eyes and weaponry, but in the earth we have looked down
upon. Not from above, but from below. Not in the light that
blinds, but in the dark that nourishes, where human beings
grow human souls.

—Ursula K. Le Guin, "A Left-Handed Commencement Address,"
Dancing at the Edge of the World, 1983

What a glorious world Almighty God has given us! How
thankless and ungrateful we are, and how we labor to mar
His gifts.

—Robert E. Lee, letter to his wife, August 4, 1861

Authentic religion has always enabled man to see that the
power by which he can endure the world requires him to
change the world.

—Paul L. Lehman, *Religion and Culture*, 1959

The world is a league of rogues against the true people, of
the vile against the generous.

—Giacomo Leopardi, *Pensieri*, 1838

Perhaps the world *may* suddenly have burst into being one
fine day; but if so, it is a world which just as logically might
not have been, and it is in that sense a colossal accident,
with no necessity of reason behind it.

—A.O. Lovejoy, *The Great Chain of Being*, 1933

The world is not only the devil's but the devil himself.

—Martin Luther, letter, January 10, 1539

The world?—It is a territory under a curse, where even its pleasures carry with them their thorns and their bitterness. . . . A place where hope, regarded as a passion so sweet, renders everybody unhappy; where those who have nothing to hope for, think themselves still more miserable, where all that pleases, pleases never for long; and where *ennui* is almost the sweetest destiny and the most supportable that one can expect in it.

> —Jean Baptiste Massillon (1663–1742), *Sermons*

We mortals are on board a fast-sailing never-sinking world-frigate, of which God was the ship-wright; and she is but one craft in a Milky-Way fleet, of which God is the Lord High Admiral. The port we sail from is forever astern.

> —Herman Melville, *White Jacket*, 1850

This world is a most holy Temple, into which man is brought there to behold Statues and Images, not wrought by mortal hands, but such as by the secret thought of God hath made sensible, as intelligible unto us.

> —Michel de Montaigne, *Essays*, Bk. 2, ch. 12, 1580

The attitude of the Christian in regard to the world is not simple. He cannot follow his tendencies without restraint, but neither can he reject and destroy everything. His attachment should be considered and should be accompanied by constant purifications.

> —Yves Montcheuil, *For Men of Action*, 1951

To apply the laws of the spirit to the activities of this earth is at once a desecration and denial of religion, and a bewildering and unsettling of the social order.

> —Paul Elmer More, *Shelburne Essays*, 1904

Just as a hand held before the eyes conceals the greatest mountain, so does petty earthly life conceal from view the vast lights and mysteries of which the world is full.

> —Rabbi Nachman of Bratislava (1772–1811), in Martin Buber,
> *Die Chassidischen Bucher*

The world is sweet to the lips, but bitter to the taste. It pleasures us at first, but not at last. It looks gay on the outside, but evil and misery lie within.

> —John Henry Newman, *Parochial and Plain Sermons*, 1843

It is better that the world shall be feared than that it be embraced with a good conscience.
—Reinhold Niebuhr, in *Christian Century*, April 22, 1926

All this visible world is but an imperceptible point in the ample bosom of nature.
—Blaise Pascal, *Pensées*, 1670

The world is certainly a great and stately Volume of natural Things; and may be not improperly styled the Hieroglyphics of a better.
—William Penn, *Some Fruits of Solitude*, 1718

The world is the fairest of creations, and the Creator the best of Causes.
—Plato, *The Republic*, c. 370 B.C.

In the world as it is, the richness of the outer stirs us all to the wonder of the inner whose greatness is displayed in acts so splendid.
—Plotinus (203–262), *The Enneads*

The world and all that it contains can exist, but it need not necessarily; only God must exist as He creates all the worlds ex nihilo.
—Rabbi Nachman of Bratislava (1772–1811), in *Judaism*

The future is hidden from us, but the past warns us that the world in the end belongs to the unworldly.
—Sarvepalli Radhakrishnan, *Eastern Religions and Western Thought*, 1939

The world is not an illusion; it is not nothingness, for it is willed by God and therefore is real. . . . The reality of the world is not in itself but it is in the thought and being of the Creator. It is what God thought and willed it to be before it was.
—Sarvepalli Radhakrishnan, *Philosophy of*, 1952

Truly understood the entire world is one great symbol, imparting in a sacramental manner, by outward and visible signature, an inward and spiritual essence.
—Kathleen Raine, *The Land Unknown*, 1975

The Church must either condemn the world and seek to change it, or tolerate it and conform to it. In the latter case it surrenders its holiness and its mission.
—Walter Rauschenbusch, *Christianity and the Social Crisis*, 1907

The great need of the Church today is a flaming conviction of the activity of God in the world.
—R. Roberts, *The Contemporary Christ*, 1938

The good world is not innocent. It does not ignore evil; it possesses and still conquers evil.
—Josiah Royce, *Spirit of Modern Philosophy*, 1892

So lies the sick world in the arms of God, who not for an instant leaves it alone, without whom we should not live.
A. Maude Royden, *Federal Council Bulletin*, January 1931

If in our world there are vales of tears, there are hillsides also of joy and laughter and peaks of splendor shining in the sun.
—H. Samuel, *Belief and Action*, 1937

The world is just a scaffolding up which souls climb to the kingdom of Heaven.
—Fulton J. Sheen, *The Life of All Living*, 1929

A good man finds every place he treads upon holy ground; to him the world is God's temple.
—John Smith (1618–52), *The Excellence and Nobleness of True Religion*

If consciousness means what it claims to mean, not everything of worth in the World is traceable to an origin with Man, reference to Man, or application to Man's use.
—M.C. Swabey, *The Judgment of History*, 1954

The wonder is not that there should be obstacles and sufferings in this world, but that there should be law and order, beauty and joy, goodness and love.
—Rabindranath Tagore, *Sadhana*, 1913

The whole world is sustained by God's charity.
—*Talmud, Berakot*, c. 500

Your enjoyment of the world is never right, till every morning you awake in Heaven; see yourself in your Father's Palace; and look upon the skies, the earth, and the air as Celestial Joys; having such a reverend esteem of all, as if you were among the Angels.
—Thomas Traherne (1634–1704), *Centuries of Meditation*

To be truly wise is to have learnt to see God, but to see God is also to see and love and labor for the world he has made.
—Gerald Vann, *Eve and the Gryphon*, 1946

The world does not stand or fall with discoveries or inventions, nor with the trample of armed hosts and the thunder of bombing planes. The world stands or falls with the laws of life which Heaven has written in the human conscience.
—Pierre Van Paasen, *Days of Our Years*, 1940

Unless the city of God pre-exists in heaven it cannot descend to earth. Therefore those who deny that Divine city cannot build on earth the city of their dreams.
—E.I. Watkins, *Men and Tendencies*, 1937

God is the binding element in the world. The consciousness which is individual in us is universal in him: the love which is partial in us is all-embracing in him.
—Alfred North Whitehead, *Religion in the Making*, 1927

WORLDLINESS

The world with all its goods cannot content the heart of man; for he was created not for them, but for God alone; hence God alone can make him happy and content.
—St. Alphonsus de Liguori, *Preface for Death*, c. 1760

It is quite impossible for the Church, for any Church, to mix itself up . . . in the secular controversies of the day without losing more for itself than it can gain for the community.
—A.J. Balfour, *The Mind of*, ed. by W.F. Short, 1918

The world and that infinite variety of pleasing objects in it, do so allure and enamour us, that we cannot so much as look towards God, seek him, or think on him as we should.
—Robert Burton, *The Anatomy of Melancholy*, III, 1621

Among men there is no nation so savage and ferocious as to deny the necessity of worshipping God, however ignorant it may be respecting the nature of his attributes.
—Cicero, *The Laws*, 52 B.C.

I do not struggle against the world, I struggle against a greater force, against my *weariness* of the world.
—E.M. Cioran, *Drawn and Quartered*, 1971

If a man be weighed down with worldliness, he shall sink like an overladen boat in the world's ocean.
—Amar Das, c. 1565, in M.A. Maculiffe, *The Sikh Religion*

Worldliness is not, in the last analysis, love of possessions, or the habit of courting great personages. It is simply the weakness of fibre which makes us take our standards from the society round us.

—Ronald A. Knox, *Stimuli*, 1951

Death is not more certainly a separation of our souls from our bodies than the Christian life is a separation of our souls from worldly tempers, vain indulgences, and unnecessary cares.

—William Law, *Christian Perfection*, 1726

If a man of this world is attracted by things of this world and is estranged from his Creator, he is corrupted and he can corrupt the entire world along with him.

—Moses Luzzato (1707–47), *Mesillat Yesharim*

To put the temporal in the place of God, when done with full deliberation, is the sin of pride in all its gravity.

—Jean Mouroux, *The Meaning of Man*, 1948

We are sometimes in danger of looking on the temporal as something profane, as if God were only active in the spiritual. The temporal is not foreign to God.

—Anders Nygren, in *Ecumenical Review*, I, 3, 1949

There is no more mistaken path to happiness than worldliness, revelry, high life.

—Arthur Schopenhauer, *Essays*, 1841

Behold heavenly goods and thou shalt see that all these temporal goods be as none but that they shall be full uncertain, and more grieving than easing; for they are never had without business and dread.

—Thomas à Kempis, *Imitation of Christ*, 1441

It is lawful to desire temporal blessings, not putting them in the first place, as though setting up our rest in them, but regarding them as aids to blessedness, inasmuch as they support our corporal life and serve as instruments for acts of virtue.

—St. Thomas Aquinas, *Summa Theologiae*, 1272

Like many or all of those who have placed their heaven in this earth, I have found in it not merely the beauty of heaven, but the horror of hell also.

—Oscar Wilde, *De Profundis*, 1896

WORSHIP

O my Lord if I worship thee from fear of Hell, burn me in Hell, and if I worship thee from hope of Paradise, exclude me thence; but if I worship thee for Thine own sake, then withhold not from me Thine Eternal Beauty.
—Rabia Al-Adawiyya (8th century), *Readings from the Mystics of Islam*, 1950

God is to be worshipped by faith, hope, and love.
—St. Augustine, *On Faith, Hope and Charity*, c. 421

All true and acceptable worship to God is offered in the inward and immediate moving and drawing of His own Spirit, which is neither limited to places, times, or persons.
—Robert Barclay, *Apology for the Quakers*, 1678

The mind of Man is so made that, at first sight, an attitude of neutrality in the matter of the worship of God is felt to be more violently shocking than the worship of false gods.
—Pierre Bayle, *Dictionary*, 1697

Religious worship is only as it were a postern by the side of the great portals of beauty and nobility and truth. One whose heart is filled with a yearning mystery at the sight of the starry heavens, who can adore the splendor of noble actions, courageous deeds, patient affections, who can see and love the beauty so abundantly shed abroad in the world . . . he can at all these moments draw near to God, and open his soul to the influx of the Divine Spirit.
—Arthur Christopher Benson, *From a College Window*, 1906

It is a man listening through a tornado for the Still Small Voice . . . a soul standing in awe before the mystery of the Universe . . . a hungry heart seeking for love . . . Time flowing into Eternity. . . . It is a man climbing the altar stairs to God.
—Dwight Bradley, in *The Congregationalist*, October 1928

Is the minister or priest or elder really in charge of the worship service? I find the opposite. I am strongly subordinated by the liturgy itself, and thus by the congregation.
—Jim Burklo, "Coffee Hour: America's True Religion," in *Co-Evolution Quarterly*, Spring 1984

Whenever beauty overwhelms us, whenever wonder silences our chattering hopes and worries, we are close to worship.
—Richard C. Cabot, *What Men Live By*, 1915

Our mind cannot conceive of God without ascribing some worship to Him.
—John Calvin, *Institutes*, I, 1536

Wonder is the basis of Worship.
—Thomas Carlyle, *Sartor Resartus*, 1836

In my view it is true to say that we can worship Nature or Humanity or Art, or God. I believe that all of these are the same activity, but that they differ in quality.
—Howard E. Collier, *The Place of Worship in Modern Medicine*, 1944

The new doctrine [of positivism] will institute the Worship of Women, publicly and privately, in a far more perfect way than has ever been possible. It is the first permanent step toward the worship of Humanity.
—Auguste Comte, *Positive Polity*, 1820

In the act of worship itself, the experience of liberation becomes a constituent of the community's being. . . . It is the power of God's Spirit invading the lives of the people, "buildin' them up where they are torn down and proppin' them up on every leanin' side."
—James H. Cone, *Speaking the Truth*, 1986

Man is made to adore and obey; but . . . if you give him nothing to worship, he will fashion his own divinities and find a chieftain in his own passions.
—Benjamin Disraeli, *Coningsby*, 1844

Who worships God as God, God hears. But he who worships God for worldly goods, worships not God; he worships what he worships God for and employs God as his servant.
—Meister Eckhart (1260?–1327?), *Meister Eckhart*

The simplest person, who in his integrity worships God, becomes God.
—Ralph Waldo Emerson, "The Over-Soul," *Essays* (1st series), 1841

The language of worship seems far, and yet lies very nigh; for what better note can our frail tongues lisp than the voice of wind and sea, river and stream, those grateful servants giving all and asking nothing, the soft whisper of snow and rain eager to replenish, or the thunder proclaiming a majesty too great for utterance.
—Michael Fairless, *The Roadmender*, 1895

The worship of God is as natural to men, as is neighing to horses or barking to dogs.
—Marsilio Ficino, *Theologica Platonica*, 1474

Worship is a way of living, a way of seeing the world in the light of God. To worship is to rise to a higher level of existence, to see the world from the point of view of God.
—Abraham Joshua Heschel, *Man's Quest for God*, 1954

As long as man is man, so long will religion endure, and, with it, the obligation of worship.
—F. Hettinger, *Natural Religion*, 1898

True worship is not a petition to God: it is a sermon to ourselves.
—E.G. Hirsch, *Reform Advocate*, III, 1892

Worship, or prayer, is the especial sphere of the will in religion.
—William E. Hocking, *The Meaning of God in Human Experience*, 1912

O come, let us worship and bow down: let us kneel before the Lord our maker.
—*Holy Bible*, Psalms 95:6-7

Worship arises as spontaneously in the heart of the religious devotee, as love arises in the heart of the youth who has found in the maiden beauty, inspiration, and understanding.
—Charles C. Jasey, in *Journal of Religion*, XV, October, 1935

Follow and worship God in the exercise of virtue, for this way of worshipping God is the most holy.
—Flavius Josephus, *Against Apion*, c. A.D. 93

Much of what we do in our Church services has lost its relevance to the poor and the oppressed. Our services and the sacraments have been appropriated to serve the need of the individual for comfort and security.
—*The Kairos Document*, rev. 2nd ed., 1986

The liturgy, like the feast, exists not to educate but to seduce people into participating in common activity of the highest order, where one is freed to learn things which cannot be taught.
—Aidan Kavanagh, *Elements of Rite*, 1966

There is something in us which demands, and finds satisfaction in, the act or at least the attitude of worship. But, since there is nothing in the visible creation which has a dignity corresponding to that attitude, we may be very sure that there is more in existence than our visible creation contains.
—Ronald A. Know, *Broadcast Minds*, 1932

Surely religion is the worship of the true, superstition of the false. And what makes all the difference is what you worship, not how you worship.
—Lactantius, *Divine Institutes*, c. 310

Wisdom precedes, religion follows; for the knowledge of God comes first, His worship is the result of knowledge.
—Lactantius, *Divine Institutes*, c. 310

Worship is the free offering of ourselves to God; ever renewed, because ever imperfect. It expresses the consciousness that we are His by right, yet we have not duly passed into His hand.
—James Martineau, *Hours of Thought*, Vol. II, 1879

Worshipers in spirit and truth are to be found in all confession and all Churches, and they are recognizable by a sign, and they love one another, in a manner of speaking, not in spite of what separates them but in some way or other because of what separates them.
—François Mauriac, *What I Believe*, 1962

This solitary response to reality is the deepest religious experience one can have. It is turning from the periphery of life to the core of existence. In this solitary moment it is as if one entered into the scheme of things.
—Bernard E. Meland, *Modern Man's Worship*, 1934

Whatever each man worships inwardly is his God, whether he knows it or not. He who has a ruling passion worships one God, good or evil. He who is carried at random by impulses has many gods; perhaps as shiftless, as shapeless, as unworthy, as any heathen divinities.
—F.W. Newman, *Theism*, 1858

To know whom you worship, let me see you in your shop, let me hear you in your trade, let me know how you rent your houses, how you get your money, how you kept it and how you spent it.
—Theodore Parker, *Sermon of Conventional and Natural Sacraments*, 1849

Whether the worship of a God is a good thing or not depends on how God is conceived.
—Ralph Barton Perry, *The Humanity of Man*, 1956

When someone says "Oh, I can worship God anywhere," the answer is, "Do you?"
—James A. Pike, *Beyond Anxiety*, 1953

You say there is but one way to worship and serve the Great Spirit. If there is but one religion, why do you white people differ so much about it? Why not all agreed, as you can all read the book?
—Red Jacket, Seneca Indian Chief, to delegate from Evangelical Mission Society of Massachusetts, 1805

The act of worshipping is itself the process by which we first define God.
—Willard L. Sperry, *Reality and Worship*, 1925

Ecstatic worship which is devoid of charity is for all practical purposes heathen.
—William Temple, *Christian Faith and the Common Life*, 1938

People don't come to church for preachments, of course, but to daydream about God.
—Kurt Vonnegut, Jr., in *The New York Times*, April 30, 1980

The worship of God is not a rule of safety—it is an adventure of the spirit, a flight after the unattainable. The death of religion comes with the repression of the high hope of adventure.
—Alfred North Whitehead, *Science and the Modern World*, 1925

The first step in the act of worship is to relax and to become aware of that upon which we are dependent, that which sustains us in every breath we breathe.
—Henry N. Wieman, *Methods of Private Religious Living*, 1929

The reality of Christian worship cannot be restored by injection of saccharine. Paul Claudel pillories the procedure: "If the salt hath lost its savour, wherewith shall it be salted?" *With Sugar!*
—Amos N. Wilder, *Theology and Modern Literature*, 1958

Youth

Young men have a passion for regarding their elders as senile.

—Henry Adams, *The Education of Henry Adams*, 1906

Like a rustic at a fair, we are full of amazement and rapture, and have no thought of going home, or that it will soon be night.

—William Hazlitt, *On the Feeling of Immortality in Youth*, 1807

There is a feeling of Eternity in Youth, which makes us amends for everything. To be young is to be as one of the Immortal Gods.

—William Hazlitt, *On the Feeling of Immortality in Youth*, 1807

The young are looking for living models whom they can imitate and who are capable of rousing their enthusiasm and drawing them to a deeper kind of life. More than anything else, the young need sure guides to go with them on the paths of liberation that God maps out for them.

—Bakole wa Ilunga, *Paths of Liberation*, 1984

The universe is not altogether as God meant it to be. We are here partly to change it. One of his mercies is that as men grow older and used to things, he takes them away and puts the universe in the hands of young, fresh men.

—Cleland B. McAfee, *Near to the Heart of God*, 1954

There's always a hunger, when you're young, to go from peak to peak and avoid the valleys. I had a pretty hilariously gloomy few years in the '70s. But today I'm quite at home wandering those valleys and occasionally climbing a peak.

—Peter O'Toole, in *Time*, February 6, 1989

Of all the curable illnesses that afflict mankind, the hardest to cure, and the one most likely to leave its victim a chronic invalid, is adolescence.

—Bonaro W. Overstreet, *Understanding Fear*, 1951

The deepest definition of youth is, life as yet untouched by tragedy.

—Alfred North Whitehead, *Adventures of Ideas*, 1933

eal

Zeal is a great ease to a malicious man, by making him believe he does God service, whilst he is gratifying the bent of a perverse revengeful temper.

—Joseph Addison, *The Spectator*, 1714

Zeal is fit only for wise men, but is found mostly in fools.

—Thomas Fuller, *Gnomologia*, 1732

Zealotry is often, it seems to me—and fundamentalism is just one form of it—an escape from anxiety. If you're really scared, then the simple answer is going to be better than the complicated answer.

—Roger Heyns, in *The Christian Science Monitor*, June 30, 1989

If we have learned anything at all in the two thousand years of Christian history, we should have learned that few things are more dangerous than zeal without knowledge.

—Charles Kegley, *Religion in Modern Life*, 1957

Zeal, not rightly directed, is pernicious; for as it makes a good cause better, so it makes a bad cause worse.

—*Old Farmer's Almanac*, 1860

Violent zeal for truth hath an hundred to one odds to be either petulancy, ambition, or pride.

—Jonathan Swift, *Thoughts on Religion*, 1728

Nothing spoils human Nature more than false Zeal. The *Good-nature* of an heathen is more God-like than the furious *Zeal* of a Christian.

—Benjamin Whichcote, *Moral and Religious Aphorisms*, 1753